Morpheme-internal Recursion in Phonology

Studies in Generative Grammar

Editors
Norbert Corver
Harry van der Hulst

Founding editors
Jan Koster
Henk van Riemsdijk

Volume 140

Morpheme-internal Recursion in Phonology

Edited by
Kuniya Nasukawa

DE GRUYTER
MOUTON

ISBN 978-1-5015-2697-8
e-ISBN (PDF) 978-1-5015-1258-2
e-ISBN (EPUB) 978-1-5015-1241-4
ISSN 0167-4331

Library of Congress Control Number: 2019957104

Bibliographic information published by the Deutsche Nationalbibliothek
The Deutsche Nationalbibliothek lists this publication in the Deutsche Nationalbibliografie;
detailed bibliographic data are available on the Internet at http://dnb.dnb.de.

© 2021 Walter de Gruyter, Inc., Berlin/Boston
This volume is text- and page-identical with the hardback published in 2020.
Typesetting: Integra Software Services Pvt. Ltd.
Printing and binding: CPI books GmbH, Leck

www.degruyter.com

Contents

List of Contributors —— VII

Kuniya Nasukawa
Introduction —— 1

Phillip Backley and Kuniya Nasukawa
Recursion in melodic-prosodic structure —— 11

Edoardo Cavirani and Marc van Oostendorp
A theory of the theory of vowels —— 37

Marcel den Dikken and Harry van der Hulst
On some deep structural analogies between syntax and phonology —— 57

Chihkai Lin
Decomposition and recursive structure: Glide formation and vowel lowering in East Asian languages —— 117

Xiaoxi Liu and Nancy C. Kula
Multi-layered recursive representations for depressors —— 143

Filiz Mutlu
Embedding of the same type in phonology —— 181

Hitomi Onuma and Kuniya Nasukawa
Velar softening without precedence relations —— 207

Markus Pöchtrager
Recursion and GP 2.0 —— 237

Clemens Poppe
Head, dependent, or both: Dependency relations in vowels —— 267

Geoffrey Schwartz
Defining recursive entities in phonology: The Onset Prominence framework —— 307

Ali Tifrit
Obstruent liquid clusters: Locality, projections and percolation —— 329

Hisao Tokizaki
Recursive strong assignment from phonology to syntax —— 383

Language Index —— 409

Subject Index —— 411

List of Contributors

Phillip Backley is Professor of English Linguistics at Tohoku Gakuin University, Japan. He gained a PhD in phonology from the University of London (UCL) in 1998, and has published on a range of topics in theoretical phonology, language acquisition and the history of English. He is actively involved in the development of an element-based (cf. feature-based) approach to segmental representation, and is the author of *An Introduction to Element Theory* (EUP, 2011) and co-editor (with Kuniya Nasukawa) of *Strength Relations in Phonology* (Mouton 2009).

Edoardo Cavirani is a FWO Marie Skłodowska-Curie Actions—Seal of Excellence postdoctoral researcher at the Center for Research in Syntax, Semantics and Phonology of KU Leuven. He holds a MA in Historical and Comparative Linguistics from the University of Pisa and a PhD (Doctor Europaeus) from the University of Pisa and the University of Leiden.

Marcel den Dikken is Senior Researcher at the Theoretical Linguistics Department of the Research Institute for Linguistics) of the Hungarian Academy of Sciences, Budapest, and Research Professor at the School of English and American Studies of Eötvös Loránd University (ELTE). He is series editor (with Liliane Haegeman, Joan Maling and Maria Polinsky) of *Studies in Natural Language and Linguistic Theory* (Springer, Dordrecht), editor of *The Cambridge Handbook of Generative Syntax* (CUP 2013), author of *Particles: On the Syntax of Verb-particle, Triadic, and Causative Constructions* (OUP 1995), *The Structure of the Noun Phrase in Rotuman* (LINCOM Europa 2003), *Relators and Linkers: The Syntax of Predication, Predicate Inversion, and Copulas* (MIT Press 2006) and *Dependency and Directionality* (CUP 2018), and co-author (with Hans Broekhuis) of *Syntax of Dutch. Nouns and Noun Phrases, Vol. 2* (Amsterdam University Press 2012).

Harry van der Hulst is Professor, Linguistics at University of Connecticut. His research interests cover various aspects of phonology, with a focus on word and phrasal stress, syllabic structure, features and segmental structure, sign language, language change and evolution, the interplay between phonetics and phonology, and linguistic analysis of graphic narratives. He has published over 170 articles and 29 edited volumes in these areas. Recent work includes *Asymmetries in Vowel Harmony: A Representational Approach* (2018, Oxford University Press) and *Radical CV Phonology: A Theory of Segmental and Syllabic Structure* (2020, Edinburgh University Press). Van der Hulst is Editor-in-Chief of *The Linguistic Review* and co-editor of the series 'Studies in generative grammar' (both with De Gruyter Mouton).

Nancy C. Kula is Professor of linguistics in the Department of Language and Linguistics at the University of Essex. She has worked on a range of issues in phonology including segmental representations, tone and prosody and phonological interfaces with morphology and syntax. Her empirical focus mainly centers on Bantu languages. She is co-editor (with Bert Botma and Kuniya Nasukawa) of the *Bloomsbury Companion to Phonology* and has published in a wide range of journals.

Chihkai Lin received his M.A. degree from the Graduate Institute of Linguistics at National Taiwan University (2008) and his Ph.D. degree from the Department of East Asian Languages and Literatures at the University of Hawai'i at Mānoa (2015), where he studied under

Dr. Alexander Vovin. Currently, he is a project assistant professor in the Department of Applied Foreign Languages at Tatung University (Taiwan). He specializes in phonology and historical linguistics focusing on East Asian languages. His research interests include historical changes in Chinese dialects, Japanese and Korean based on philological data, and synchronic phonology in Austronesian languages, Chinese, Japanese and Korean.

Xiaoxi Liu is a final year PhD student in the Department of Language and Linguistics at the University of Essex, working on Element Theory representations with focus on depressor effects and broader consonant-tone interaction. Her thesis investigates the similarities and differences between depressors in Bantu languages and Chinese dialects with the goal of proposing a unified analysis that exploits multi-layered element representations.

Filiz Mutlu is a graduate student of linguistics at the University of Ljubljana. She started developing a theory of phonological representations in 2015 at Boğaziçi University for her MA thesis, with the central idea that asymmetry is the building principle of phonology as well as other components of language. Currently she is working on her doctoral thesis, where she develops her theory (Spatial Phonology) further and claims that linguistic structures are geometric objects of up to three dimensions. These objects are roughly translatable to trees, but crucially they have underpinnings in the representation of space and magnitude in vertebrates structures grow to the right, upwards and to the front.

Kuniya Nasukawa is Professor of English Linguistics at Tohoku Gakuin University, Japan. He has a Ph.D. in Linguistics from University College London (UCL), and his research interests include prosody-melody interaction and precedence-free phonology. He has written many articles covering a wide range of topics in phonological theory. He is author of *A Unified Approach to Nasality and Voicing* (Mouton 2005), co-editor (with Phillip Backley) of *Strength Relations in Phonology* (Mouton 2009), co-editor (with Nancy C. Kula and Bert Botma) of *The Bloomsbury Companion to Phonology* (Bloomsbury 2013), and co-editor (with Henk van Riemsdijk) of *Identity Relations in Grammar* (Mouton 2014).

Hitomi Onuma is a full-time lecturer at Iwate Medical University, Japan. She received her Ph.D. in Literature from Tohoku Gakuin University in 2015. Her research interests and publications include various aspects of segmental and prosodic phonology, particularly concerning the status and behaviour of empty nuclei. Currently she has worked in the framework of precedence-free phonology.

Marc van Oostendorp is Senior Researcher at the Department of Variationist Linguistics at the Meertens Institute of the Royal Netherlands Academy of Arts and Sciences. He holds an MA in Computational Linguistics and a PhD from Tilburg University. He is co-editor (with Colin J. Ewen, Elizabeth V. Hume and Keren Rice) of *The Blackwell Companion to Phonology* (Wiley-Blackwell 2011).

Markus Pöchtrager received his Ph.D. in General Linguistics at the University of Vienna in 2006. From 2008 to 2017 he was a faculty member at the department of linguistics at Boğaziçi University (İstanbul), and from 2017 onwards at the University of Vienna. His research focuses on phonology, phonological metatheory, phonology-morphology interaction, linguistics as a cognitive science, Finno-Ugric and Scandinavian languages as well as Altaic and Caucasian languages.

Clemens Poppe is an Assistant Professor of Linguistics at Waseda University, Japan. He holds a Ph.D. in Linguistics from the University of Tokyo, and previously worked as a postdoctoral researcher at the National Institute for Japanese and Linguistics in Tokyo under the auspices of the Japan Society for the Promotion of Science. His fields of interest include phonology, morphology, and dialectal variation.

Geoff Schwartz is Associate Professor in the Faculty of English at Adam Mickiewicz University (UAM), Poznań, Poland. He received his Ph.D. in Slavic Linguistics from the University of Washington (Seattle) in 2000. He has been employed at UAM since 2002, where his teaching has concentrated on acoustic phonetics and L2 speech acquisition, and was awarded a post-doctoral degree (Polish habilitacja) in 2010. In recent years, he has been working in phonological theory, developing the Onset Prominence representational framework, and continuing his work on L2 phonological acquisition. His articles have appeared in numerous journals, including *Journal of Linguistics*, and he is a regular participant at important phonology and L2 acquisition conferences.

Ali Tifrit is Associate Professor of Linguistics at the University of Nantes, France. He is member of the Laboratoire de Linguistique (LLing UMR6310 CNRS—University of Nantes). His research interests are focusing on formalisms and on the definition of phonological primitives (features and elements) and their relation to phonological activity. He has a particular interest in the synchrony and diachrony of French and Romance languages. He published works on the hierarchical organisation of segments in a unary perspective and on phonological processes (palatalization, spirantization, epenthesis) in a Government Phonology framework.

Hisao Tokizaki is Professor of English Linguistics at Sapporo University, Japan. He has a Ph.D. in Linguistics from University of Tsukuba, and his research interests include the syntax-phonology interface and linguistic typology. He has written many articles covering a wide range of topics in the theory of interface. He is the author of *Syntactic Structure and Silence: A Minimalist Theory of Syntax-Phonology Interface* (Hitsuji syobo), co-editor (with Yoshihito Dobashi) of a special issue of *Linguistic Analysis* 38(3/4), *Universal Syntax and Parametric Phonology* (2013).

Kuniya Nasukawa
Introduction

Motivation

For the Generative Grammar approach to the study of language, recursion is a key concept not only in the debate on how structure is organised within the language faculty but also on the origins of language itself. Researchers with an interest in the evolution of language (Reuland 2009, Chomsky 2010) have argued that natural language in its present form developed from single-word expressions through the use of a recursive merge device.

The phonology literature also often refers to recursive structure in the analysis of recurrent phenomena such as stress and intonation patterns, which rely on (morpho-)syntactic structures generated by syntactic computation. As such, this recursive structure is in fact (morpho-)syntactic rather than phonological (Scheer 2011, Nasukawa 2015).

To establish whether recursive structure exists in phonology or not, we must investigate recursion in morpheme-internal phonological structure, since this cannot be accessed by (morpho-)syntax. There are two opposing views about recursion in phonology.

One view maintains that phonology is recursion-free (no recursive structure-building). Instead, it assumes that phonological structure within a morpheme consists of a set of linearly ordered segments (a string-based flat structure) in the lexicon, and that phonology is not responsible for building lexical phonological structure (Pinker and Jackendoff 2005; Neeleman and van de Koot 2006; Samuels 2009; Scheer 2008, 2011).

According to the opposing view, morpheme-internal phonological structure refers not to precedence properties but to a set of features which are concatenated hierarchically. In this approach, syntax is responsible for merging not only lexical items such as morphemes and words, but also phonological categories (primitives) to build the phonological structure of morphemes in the lexicon (Nasukawa 2014, 2015, 2016; Nasukawa and Backley 2015).

This volume will provide the first platform for debate on the place of recursive structure in phonology and on the formal status of phonology in the language faculty. It has its origins in the workshop entitled 'Recursion in Phonology' held at Tohoku Gakuin University, Sendai, Japan on 1–2 September 2016, where six of the papers included here were first presented (Chihkai Lin, Kuniya Nasukawa, Hitomi

Onuma, Clemens Poppe, Geoffrey Schwartz and Hisao Tokizaki). The remaining papers are by other prominent scholars in the field. It is encouraging that the issue of recursion in phonology has also attracted interest and support from those leading the research project 'Evolinguistics: Integrative Studies of Language Evolution for Co-creative Communication' (funded by MEXT/JSPS KAKENHI Grant-in-Aid for Scientific Research on Innovative Areas #4903, Grant Number JP18H05081).

Clearly, a volume of this size cannot do justice to a topic as broad as that of recursion in morpheme-internal phonology. Nevertheless, we hope that these papers will convey something of the scope and influence that recursive hierarchical structure appears to have on the analysis of apparently unrelated phenomena across different languages and different domains of linguistic study.

Abstracts

Phillip Backley and Kuniya Nasukawa
Recursion in melodic-prosodic structure

Backley and Nasukawa argue that Phonological information comes in two kinds: melodic information describes the qualitative properties of sounds while prosodic information describes how sounds are organised into larger structures such as syllables and feet. Traditionally, each is represented as an independent domain and described using a unique set of structural units. But there are advantages in integrating the two domains into one unified structure. In this paper, melody-prosody integration succeeds by allowing elements, the units of melody, to also function as prosodic constituents, thereby eliminating the need for labels such as *nucleus*, *syllable* and *foot*. The smallest prosodic domain ('nucleus') is represented by an element from the set {|A|, |I|, |U|}, chosen by parameter to reflect the quality of the default vowel in a language, e.g. English has |A| as its structural head to reflect its default [ə]. Contrastive vowels are then expressed by allowing the head to support dependent structure – constructed via the recursive concatenation of elements functioning as units of melody. Reversing established assumptions, dependents are the main contributors of linguistic (contrastive) information while heads take on a largely structural role. This brings phonology more into line with syntax, where dependents rather than heads are informationally rich.

Edoardo Cavirani and Marc van Oostendorp
A theory of the theory of vowels

Cavirani and van Oostendorp represent the most common vowel contrasts in a theory that allows only (recursive) embedding of treelets. Such a theory needs neither features nor elements. We show that from such a theory we can actually derive some common properties of the element set |A, I, U|: why are there only three of them? And why does |A| behave differently from the other two? Furthermore, the theory also gives a natural place to both schwa and the completely empty nucleus. We also show how this theory is related to some earlier proposals in the literature.

Marcel den Dikken and Harry van der Hulst
On some deep structural analogies between syntax and phonology

The principal aim of **den Dikken and van der Hulst's** chapter is to bring phonology and syntax together with an outlook on linguistic analysis that uses the same representational system in morphosyntax and all levels of phonological analysis, including phonological structure above the syllable, the internal organization of the syllable, and the structure of segments. The central tenet of the approach is the generalization of complementation, specification, adjunction and conjunction relations from syntax to phonological structure. Recursive X-bar-theoretic structures are employed in phonology in the representation of geometrical relations of all kinds (both segmental and suprasegmental). A special role in the phonosyntax of the syllable/foot is played by the phonological counterpart to the 'light v' of syntactic structures. The chapter closes by offering an explanation for the fact that recursion in phonology is less pervasive than it is in syntax.

Chihkai Lin
Decomposition and recursive structure: Glide formation and vowel lowering in East Asian languages

Lin argues that a sequence of Sino-Japanese vowels [e] and [u] undergoes glide formation and vowel lowering ([eu] → [jo]). A similar sequence is attested in Tsou, but only glide formation occurs ([eu] → [ju] or [eu] → [ew]).

In Sino-Korean, a sequence of vowels [o] and [i] also undergoes glide formation and vowel lowering ([oi] → [we]). The objective of this study is to investigate glide formation and vowel lowering in the three languages from an element-based approach, paying specific attention to the necessity of decomposition and the application of recursive structure. It is shown that Sino-Japanese mid vowel [e] is decomposed into two elements |I A| and Sino-Korean mid vowel [o] into elements |U A|. The decomposed element |I| or |U| undergoes glide formation. In addition, if the decomposed element |A| interacts with the following high vowel, the high vowel is lowered. In Tsou, vowel lowering is not attested. To differentiate the changes in Sino-Japanese and Sino-Korean from the processes in Tsou, Lin suggests that recursive structure is an inevitable mechanism for the changes, [eu] → [jo] in Sino-Japanese and [oi] → [we] in Sino-Korean. In Tsou, recursive structure is necessary for the process, [eu] → [ew].

Xiaoxi Liu and Nancy C. Kula
Multi-layered recursive representations for depressors

Liu and Kula investigate depressor consonant effects as an example of the interaction between segmental and prosodic structure, in particular consonantal structure and tone. Contrary to expectation it is shown that the whole spectrum of laryngeal specifications can trigger depressor effects viz. voicing, breathiness, (voiceless) aspiration and plain voiceless, within the range of predominantly southern Bantu languages investigated. This distribution is accounted for by proposing a multi-layered recursive element geometry that allows the element |L| – central to the representation to depressor effects – to be represented recursively on different levels in a hierarchical representation with the flexibility of |L| appearing in different dominance relations that then allow the different laryngeal specifications to act as depressors. The connection between element |L| and depression follows from the tripartite identity of |L| in Element Theory as representing voicing, low tone, and nasality. The proposed recursive structure captures the complex depressor effects and at the same time manages to account for the asymmetry between, on the one hand, attested low tone – voicing interaction and, on the other hand, unattested low tone – nasality interactions.

Filiz Mutlu
Embedding of the same type in phonology

Mutlu models consonant clusters and affricates as recursive structures within a novel theory. The view of phonological structure offered here is basically identical to syntactic structure. That is, consonants are represented as consonantal phrases in which other consonantal phrases can be embedded. The depth of embedding is restricted by the notion of *strength difference*: The *matrix consonantal phrase* must be stronger (roughly, more obstruent) than the embedded one. Languages have a limit on how small a strength difference can exist between the matrix and the embedded consonantal phrase in morphologically simplex words. Such modelling correctly predicts a number of phenomena, including the phonotactic strength of affricates and the existence of emergent stops in the correct environments, e.g. *el(t)se, Alham(b)ra*.

Hitomi Onuma and Kuniya Nasukawa
Velar softening without precedence relations

It is generally assumed that phonological analyses, and especially segmental analyses, must refer to precedence relations between segments in order to successfully capture edge effects across boundaries and the directionality of assimilation. However, **Onuma and Nasukawa** challenge this established tradition and offer an alternative analysis of segmental phenomena without referring to precedence relations in phonological representation. As a case study, we analyse velar softening, a well-known phonological regularity in English, within the framework of Precedence-free Phonology (Nasukawa 2014, 2015, 2016; Nasukawa and Backley 2017). We propose that the process in question be analysed as an agreement effect involving the |A|-headed [|A||I|] set, which may be expressed without referring to precedence relations.

Markus Pöchtrager
Recursion and GP 2.0

Phonology is usually assumed to lack recursion. However, any such claim rests on a particular view of the workings of phonology, one that (i) countenances only a limited set of constituents that a phonological string can be broken down into and (ii) assumes that the labels of those constituents are adequate (or even relevant in the discussion).

In this article **Pöchtrager** argues, based on evidence from English vowel length, the internal structure of Putonghua vowels, Québec French vowel laxing as well as vowel reduction in general that there is reason to believe that such a view of phonology is mistaken. Work in Government Phonology (Kaye, Lowenstamm and Vergnaud 1985, 1990) has shown that mainstream concepts of constituency are often inadequate and thus questionable. By going over various such mainstream assumptions, Pöchtrager shows that in a non-arbitrary theory of phonology, recursive structures are not just convenient, but actually necessary in order to express various asymmetries we find in phonology. This is reflected in a more recent version of the theory, Government Phonology 2.0 (Pöchtrager 2006).

Clemens Poppe
Head, dependent, or both: Dependency relations in vowels

Poppe argues in favor of an element-based approach to vowel structure in which dependency between elements is defined structurally. Building on earlier work in dependency-based phonology, he proposes that the vocalic place node dominates a head place node and an optional dependent place node. Because both nodes may contain the same element, in this approach it is possible to have a three-way contrast: at the underlying level, the same element(s) may have head status, dependent status, or both. Poppe presents support for this approach to vowel structure from the vowel systems of (RP) English and Middle Korean, showing that, apart from the presence vs. absence of an element, for both languages we need to distinguish between two types of contrast: one between head and dependent elements, and one between vowels with and without identical elements. His paper concludes with a discussion of alternative dependency-based approaches, showing that, in contrast to the proposed structural approach to headedness, in these approaches it is not possible to constrain the number of identical elements in the same vowel to two.

Geoffrey Schwartz
Defining recursive entities in phonology: The Onset Prominence framework

Although it is commonly assumed that phonology is not recursive in the same way that syntax is, it is impossible to evaluate this assumption without first establishing clear definitions of the entities that are claimed not to recur. In the

Onset Prominence framework, both segments and larger prosodic constituents are derivative units that evolve from a primitive stop-vowel CV sequence. Under this view, **Schwartz** argues that each 'segment' is a recursion of the representational hierarchy built from the CV. Further, a recursive submersion mechanism is parametrically available, forming a range of constituents, from syllables with 'coda' consonants, to prosodic words and phrases. Unrestricted submersion produces configurations conducive to prosodic features traditionally associated with 'stress-timed' rhythm, including phonetically robust lexical stress and vowel reduction.

Ali Tifrit
Obstruent liquid clusters: Locality, projections and percolation

Tifrit aims to characterize the structure and the behavior of liquids in a slightly modified Government Phonology 2.0 framework (Pöchtrager 2006, Zivanovic and Pöchtrager 2010). He investigates the case of /Obstruent+Liquid/ (OL) clusters and proposes a representation of liquids explaining their behavior. These groups suffered misconception: the obstruent and the liquid are clearly unequally structured. The former can project while the latter cannot and, by consequence, must find a host. Tifrit discusses cases of lenition in a CV framework (Lowenstamm 1996, Scheer 2004) and illustrates the questions arising with OL clusters acting sometimes as a single element and sometimes as two distinct objects. The author underlines the theoretical issues that are related to the flatness of the CV model: *Locality* and *Infrasegmental Government*. Tifrit then reconsiders the internal content and structure of liquids. He proposes new analyses of cases of lenition, surface changes, compensatory lengthening and metatheses by formalizing them in GP2.0. Given the structures he proposes, most of the properties and behaviour of OL clusters are now expected. The main consequence of this proposal is that the problem of Locality does not arise anymore and *Infrasegmental Government* is no longer necessary.

Hisao Tokizaki
Recursive strong assignment from phonology to syntax

Tokizaki argues that stress is assigned to a constituent according to the labels assigned by the rule Set Strong. Set Strong assigns the label Strong to a set and Weak to a terminal when they are Merged. Set Strong recursively applies to syllables, words, phrases and sentences as the derivation proceeds. It is argued that stress location in derivational words is explained by Stem Stress, which is ascribed to Set Stress. In a morpheme in languages with weight-sensitive stress system, Set Stress assigns Strong to a heavy syllable, which is analyzed as a set of syllables. In a morpheme in languages with fixed stress location, Set Stress assigns Strong to a syllable that is a singleton set, which may Flip the linear order of syllables at Externalization. This analysis shows that a phonological rule Set Strong together with morphosyntactic Merge recursively applies to a set and a terminal within morphemes as well as in words and phrases, building a hierarchical prosodic structure.

Acknowledgements: I am grateful to all the contributors, not only for providing their own papers, but also for agreeing to review several other papers in the volume. In addition, the following people kindly acted as reviewers: Eugeniusz Cyran, Björn Köhnlein, Andrew Nevins, Bridget Samuels, Hidetoshi Shiraishi, Péter Szigetvári, Shanti Ulfsbjorninn, Jeroen van de Weijer. Without their valuable efforts, this volume could not have been completed. Furthermore, I thank Phillip Backley for his comments and advice on earlier versions.

This work was supported by the following MEXT/JSPS KAKENHI grants: Grant-in-Aid for Scientific Research on Innovative Areas #4903 (Evolinguistics) Grant Number JP18H05081, Grant-in-Aid for Scientific Research (S) Grant Number JP19H05589, Grant-in-Aid for Scientific Research (B) Grant Numbers JP26284067 and JP15H03213, and Grant-in-Aid for Scientific Research (C) Grant Number JP15K02611.

Kuniya Nasukawa
Vienna, June 2019

References

Chomsky, Noam. 2010. Some simple evo devo theses: how true might they be for language? In Richard Larson, Viviane Deprez and Hiroko Yamakido (eds.), *The Evolution of Human Language: Biolinguistic Perspectives*, 45–62. Cambridge: Cambridge University Press.

Hauser, Marc D., Noam Chomsky and W. Tecumseh Fitch. 2002. The faculty of language: what is it, who has it, and how did it evolve? *Science* 298, 1569–1579.

Kaye, Jonathan, Jean Lowenstamm and Jean-Roger Vergnaud. 1985. The internal structure of phonological elements: a theory of charm and government. *Phonology Yearbook* 2, 303–328.

Kaye, Jonathan, Jean Lowenstamm and Jean-Roger Vergnaud. 1990. Constituent structure and government in phonology. *Phonology* 7(2),193–231.

Kula, Nancy C. 2002. *The Phonology of Verbal Derivation in Bemba*. LOT Dissertation series 65. Utrecht: Holland Academic Graphics.

Kula, Nancy C. 2012. On the representation of tone in Element Theory. In Eugeniusz Cyran, Henryk Kardela and Bogdan Szymanek (eds.), *Sound Structure and Sense: Studies in Memory of Edmund Gussmann*, 353–370. Lublin: Wydawnictwo KUL.

Lowenstamm, Jean. 1996. CV as the only syllable type. In Jacques Durand and Bernard Laks (eds.), *Current trends in Phonology: Models and Methods*, 419–44. CNRS, Université Paris X and University of Salford: University of Salford Publications.

Nasukawa, Kuniya. 2014. Features and recursive structure. *Nordlyd* 41(1),1–19. *Special Issue on Features* edited by Martin Krämer, Sandra-Iulia Ronai and Peter Svenonius.

Nasukawa, Kuniya. 2015. Recursion in the lexical structure of morphemes. In Marc van Oostendorp and Henk van Riemsdijk (eds.), *Representing Structure in Phonology and Syntax*, 211–238. Berlin/Boston: Mouton de Gruyter.

Nasukawa, Kuniya. 2016. A precedence-free approach to (de-)palatalisation in Japanese. *Glossa: A Journal of General Linguistics* 1(1).9,1–21, DOI: http://dx.doi.org/10.5334/gjgl.26

Nasukawa, Kuniya and Phillip Backley. 2017. Representing moraicity in Precedence-free Phonology. *Phonological Studies* 20, 55–62.

Nespor, Marina and Irene Vogel. 1986. *Prosodic Phonology*. Dordrecht: Foris.

Pinker, Steven and Ray Jakendoff. 2005. The faculty of language: What's special about it? *Cognition* 95, 201–236.

Pöchtrager, Markus A. 2006. The structure of length. Ph.D. dissertation. University of Vienna.

Reuland, Eric. 2009. Language: symbolization and beyond. In Rudolf Botha and Chris Knight (eds.), *The Prehistory of Language*, 201–224. Oxford: Oxford University Press.

Samuels, Bridget. 2009. The third factor in phonology. *Biolinguistics* 3.2, 355–382.

Scheer, Tobias. 2004. *A Lateral Theory of Phonology: What Is CVCV, and Why Should It Be?* Berlin and New York: Mouton de Gruyter.

Scheer, Tobias. 2008. Why the prosodic hierarchy is a diacritic and why the interface must be direct. In Jutta M. Hartmann, Veronika Hegedüs and Henk van Riemsdijk (eds.), *Sounds of Silence: Empty Elements in Syntax and Phonology*, 145–192. Oxford: Elsevier.

Scheer, Tobias. 2011. *A Guide to Morphosyntax-phonology Interface Theories: How Extra-phonological Information Is Treated in Phonology since Trubetzkoy's Grenzsignale*. Berlin and New York: Mouton de Gruyter.

Živanovič, Sašo and Markus A. Pöchtrager. 2010. GP 2, and Putonghua, too. *Acta Linguistica Hungarica* 57(4), 357–380.

Phillip Backley and Kuniya Nasukawa
Recursion in melodic-prosodic structure

1 Introduction

There is a longstanding tradition in phonology of distinguishing between two kinds of phonological information, melodic (segmental) and prosodic (organisational). Melodic information describes individual segments, while prosodic information is concerned with the way segments are organised into larger constituents such as syllables and words. To capture this distinction between melodic and prosodic information, it is generally assumed that phonological representations consist of two independent modules, melodic structure and prosodic structure. On the one hand, melodic structure uses melodic units (e.g. features, elements) to express phonological categories and/or the phonetic characteristics of speech sounds. Meanwhile, prosodic structure uses prosodic units (e.g. nuclei, rhymes, syllables, feet, words) to specify the domains within which we find melodic units showing regular patterns. For example, sonority differences between segments are usually relevant only within the syllable domain or between adjacent syllables (Selkirk 1984, Clements 1990, Duanmu 2009), while weakening effects such as vowel reduction and consonant lenition tend to operate within the foot or word domain.

Apparently, then, there are good grounds for making a formal distinction between melodic and prosodic structure: each one employs a unique set of units, and each one encodes its own unique type of phonological information. Moreover, there is ample evidence that each one can be targeted by phonological processes independently of the other. For example, most segmental processes bring about a change in melodic structure while leaving prosodic structure (e.g. vowel/consonant length) unaffected. Conversely, vowel-glide alternations such as *i~j* and *u~w* involve a change in prosodic organisation (*i/u* being linked to a syllable nucleus, *j/w* to a syllable onset) while melodic properties remain constant.

In this paper, however, we challenge this view in which melody and prosody are kept distinct in phonological representations; instead, we propose that the two belong in a single integrated structure. A unified melodic-prosodic structure is possible, we argue, if it can be shown that the same units are able to represent both melodic (segmental) and prosodic (organising) properties. Below we demonstrate how phonological elements (Harris and Lindsey 1995, Backley 2011), which are conventionally used to represent only melodic properties, may also take on an organising role and be used in place of standard prosodic constituents. Furthermore, we show how the use of recursive structure is integral to the well-formedness of the unified (melody-prosody) model being proposed.

2 Melody-prosody integration

2.1 Motivation

Although most scholars still adhere to the mainstream view that melody and prosody should be separated in representations, there are also arguments for *not* representing melody and prosody as independent entities. This is the position we defend here, our motivation resting on two factors which suggest the need for a unified melodic-prosodic structure.

First, melody and prosody should be integrated because the two regularly interact. Clearly, interaction is possible even between autonomous parts of a representation, but if these different parts refer to different structural units, then we are forced to conclude that any such interaction is based on random relations. For example, in languages such as English and Swedish, aspirated stops are usually restricted to syllable onsets. That is, the melodic unit which represents stop aspiration – the element |H| (or alternatively, the feature [constricted glottis]) – invariably appears in a syllable onset rather than a nucleus or a coda. However, it is not obvious how a formal link between the melodic unit |H| and the prosodic unit 'onset' can be expressed. These two units belong to different vocabularies, making the relation between them no more than a stipulation. But if melody and prosody are unified into a single structure and represented in terms of the same units, then it may be possible to explain – rather than merely describe – why a given melodic property tends to be associated with a given prosodic property.

A second reason for rejecting the traditional division between melody and prosody is linked to the idea of empty structure. Government Phonology (e.g. Harris 1990; Kaye, Lowenstamm and Vergnaud 1990; Cyran 2010; Charette 1991) and its offshoots (e.g. van der Hulst 2003, Scheer 2004) employ representations in which a prosodic unit can be pronounced even if it has no melodic units associated with it. The typical case is a melodically unspecified or 'empty' nucleus, which may be phonetically realised as a default vowel such as [ə] or [ɨ] if the required prosodic conditions are met. In a standard feature-based approach to segmental structure, this would be considered an anomaly because, if features are responsible for defining a segment's phonetic qualities, then the absence of features should equate to silence.

But in a Government Phonology approach, where segments are represented by elements rather than by features, the same outcome is legitimate. This is because elements encode marked phonological properties rather than phonetic qualities. So, the absence of elements merely expresses the absence of marked properties – which means that the empty nucleus can still be realised as an unmarked or default vowel. In this way, an audible segment can be pronounced in a position which contains no melodic units. This has the effect of blurring the division between melody and prosody. In traditional terms, melodic structure represents segmental information while prosodic structure represents relational or organising information; but in the Government Phonology approach just described, this distinction breaks down as we find segments being associated with prosodic rather than melodic structure. This provides a further reason for rejecting the standard melody-prosody distinction, and instead, for combining the two into a unified representation.

If melodic and prosodic information are to be integrated into a single structure, then it makes sense for both to be 'speaking the same language' by using the same structural units. Following the Precedence-free Phonology approach described in Nasukawa and Backley (2015), we propose to eliminate from representations the conventional labels for prosodic constituents (e.g. onset, nucleus, syllable, foot, word) and replace them with elements – the units which, until now, have been associated only with melodic structure. In employing the same units at all levels of representation, we move closer towards our goal of unifying melodic and prosodic structure by avoiding the need to refer to units which specify only one kind of information (i.e. melodic or prosodic). Our claim, therefore, is that phonological representations refer only to elements: the elements in melodic structure have an interpretive function and provide information about segmental properties, while the elements in prosodic structure take on an organising function and provide information about relational or organizing properties. After all, phonological representations are primarily concerned with segmental expressions and how these are organized in morphemes. And because morphemes are identified by their melodic properties, it follows that they should be represented using only the units of melodic structure, i.e. elements.[1]

---

[1] Alternative approaches, in which all melodic properties are represented in terms of structural (organising) properties, are discussed elsewhere in this volume. In particular, the reader is referred to the contributions by Edoardo Cavirani and Marc van Oostendorp, Markus Pöchtrager, Geoff Schwartz, and Marcel den Dikken and Harry G. van der Hulst.

Below we show how elements are phonetically interpreted at the melodic level, while at the prosodic level they enter into head-dependency relations with one another. We argue that these head-dependency relations account for the phonotactic and distributional patterns which we observe in morphemes and which are traditionally expressed in terms of prosodic structure.

2.2 Rethinking hierarchical structure

To reiterate the main point, we propose that elements function not only as melodic units but also as prosodic constituents. However, it emerges that not all elements behave this way – it is chiefly the resonance elements |A|, |I| and |U| that have this dual function. This is not surprising, given that these elements are primarily associated with nuclei, and that it is nuclei which function as the building blocks of prosodic structure (cf. onsets, which are mostly irrelevant to higher-level prosodic relations). In traditional descriptions of hierarchical prosodic structure, a nucleus first projects to a rhyme node, then to a syllable, then to a foot, and so on. The question, then, is how this familiar representation of the prosodic hierarchy will change if we pursue an approach in which melody and prosody are unified into a single structure.

If there is no division between melodic structure and prosodic structure, then logically, there is no interface between the two. This state-of-affairs marks a clear departure from the traditional approach to phonological structure, in which it is assumed (i) that the lowest level of the prosodic hierarchy consists of terminal units – either syllabic constituents such as nuclei or bare timing slots such as skeletal positions – and (ii) that these terminal units interface with units of melodic structure such as features or elements. But by pursuing the idea being proposed here, that melody and prosody form a single structure, we are forced to abandon the assumption that prosodic structure terminates at the point where it meets the melodic (segmental) level. Instead, prosody and melody may be viewed as contiguous parts of one continuous hierarchy.

In a hierarchical model, a structural head has scope over everything it dominates. For example, in a standard view of prosodic structure the head of a foot 'contains' all the material associated with the nuclei immediately below it. Putting this another way, the foot node is the instantiation of its constituent properties – that is, it embodies the properties specified in its dependent syllables. And a similar relation holds between all adjacent levels on the hierarchy. In the case of a nucleus, which is usually regarded as a terminal node on the prosodic hierarchy, it may instead be viewed as the instantiation of all the vocalic properties that are associated with it. These properties may be expressed by features such as [±high] and [±back] or, following the Element Theory approach we employ here, by the resonance elements |I|, |U| and |A|. In other words, the unit conventionally labelled 'nucleus' is nothing more than the embodiment of its constituent elements. We argue that these melodic elements are associated directly with nuclei, so there is no need to posit any intervening level of structure (e.g. timing slots) or to refer to any interface between melody and prosody.

The details of this unified melodic-prosodic hierarchy will be described in section 4. This is preceded by an overview of element representations. We describe how elements differ from standard features in some fundamental ways, making them ideally suited to the recursion-based hierarchical model being developed here.

3 Element-based vowel representations

3.1 Elements

Like features, elements are units of melodic structure which represent phonological categories. Unlike features, however, they are associated with acoustic patterns in the speech signal rather than with properties of articulation (Harris and Lindsey 1995, Nasukawa and Backley 2008, Backley 2011, Nasukawa 2017). The relevant acoustic patterns are those that are thought to be linguistically significant – that is, they carry linguistic information about the identity of morphemes. For example, the element |H| represents the pattern of aperiodic noise energy that is observed in fricatives and in the release phase of stops, while the element |U| represents a formant pattern in which sound energy is concentrated at the lower end of the spectrum, as is found in labials, velars and rounded vowels (Nasukawa and Backley 2008, Backley and Nasukawa 2009, Backley 2011).

Although Element Theory exists in several forms (Backley 2012), standard versions use the six elements shown in (1). Each element is associated with its own unique acoustic pattern (Harris and Lindsey 1995; Nasukawa and Backley 2008, 2011; Backley and Nasukawa 2009, 2010).

(1) Elements and their acoustic patterns
   a. Vowel (resonance) elements
      |I| 'dip'   low F1 with high spectral peak – convergence of F2 and F3
      |U| 'rump' low spectral peak – lowering of all formants
      |A| 'mass' central spectral energy mass – convergence of F1 and F2

b. Consonant (laryngeal) elements
   |ʔ| 'edge'   abrupt and sustained drop in amplitude
   |H| 'noise'   aperiodicity, noise
   |L| 'murmur'   periodicity, nasal murmur

As shown here, the elements naturally divide into two subsets. The resonance elements |A|, |I| and |U| are associated with patterns which relate to formant structure, so they are primarily associated with vowels. Meanwhile, the laryngeal elements |H|, |L| and |ʔ| refer to other properties of the speech signal such as noise energy and amplitude, so they appear mainly in the representation of consonants.

Elements do not just refer to aspects of the physical speech signal, however. They are also linked to the abstract phonological categories that are present in mental representations. These representations are used by native speakers to identify individual morphemes and words. Furthermore, each of the acoustic cues described in (1) is directly associated with a particular phonological category. Note that these linguistic categories do not always respect the traditional division between vowels and consonants. For example, the formant cues associated with the 'vowel' elements |I|, |U| and |A| describe vowel quality; but in addition, they distinguish consonant place properties too. So, at an abstract level the 'vowel' elements contribute to the representation of both vowels and consonants. Similarly, the 'consonant' elements |ʔ|, |H| and |L| capture the characteristics of consonants such as the presence of noise energy and rapid changes in amplitude; but they also refer to vowel properties which are contrastive in some vowel systems, such as nasality and lexical tone. The following table illustrates how each element contributes to nuclear and non-nuclear expressions.

(2) Elements and their phonological properties
   a. Vowel (resonance) elements

	nuclear	non-nuclear
|I|	front vowels	coronal: dental, palatal POA
|U|	rounded vowels	dorsal: labial, velar POA
|A|	non-high vowels	guttural: uvular, pharyngeal POA

   b. Consonant (laryngeal) elements

	non-nuclear	nuclear
|ʔ|	oral/glottal occlusion	creaky voice (laryngeal vowels)
|H|	aspiration, voicelessness	high tone
|L|	nasality, obstruent voicing	nasality, low tone

Whereas orthodox distinctive features are bivalent (i.e. they have a plus and a minus value), elements are monovalent or single-valued. This means that lexical contrasts are expressed in terms of an element's presence/absence rather than in terms of its plus/minus value. Another characteristic of elements is their 'autonomous interpretation', which allows an element to be phonetically interpreted by itself since it has its own 'autonomous phonetic signature' (Harris and Lindsey 1995: 34). Having said that, expressions usually involve a combination of elements. In standard Element Theory (Harris 1994, Backley 2011), for example, the elements |I| and |A| are realised individually as [i] and [ɑ] respectively. But they can also combine to form a complex expression |I A|, which is pronounced as a front mid vowel such as [e] or [ɛ]. Consonants are also represented by complex expressions. For example, |U| (labiality), |ʔ| (occlusion) and |H| (noise) are realised individually as [w], [ʔ] and [h] respectively, whereas in combination they are pronounced as [p] – the realisation of the complex expression |U ʔ H|.

3.2 |I|, |U|, |A| as prosodic constituents

In phonological representation, prosodic structure is normally based on relations between rhymes/nuclei – onsets are rarely involved in prosodic patterning. And this is reflected in the Precedence-free Phonology model of representation that we employ here, in which it is exclusively the vowel elements |I|, |U| and |A| – the units that encode the contrastive properties of nuclei – which have a prosodic function. We argue that |I|, |U| and |A| not only carry lexical information about the identity of vowel segments, they also project beyond the melodic structure to higher prosodic levels, where they form head-dependent relations with one another. As these asymmetric relations progress upwards through the prosodic hierarchy, they mark out a series of successively wider prosodic domains which correspond to traditional units such as rhyme, syllable, foot and word. Because this can be achieved by referring only to |I|, |U| and |A|, there is no need to introduce the constituent labels 'rhyme', 'syllable', 'foot' and 'word' into the structure. The result is a representation which integrates melodic and prosodic information into a unified melody-prosody structure, but one which minimizes the number of different structural units it uses. Even 'nucleus' is not recognised as a formal constituent, since a nucleus is nothing more than an instantiation of the melodic units (i.e. |I|, |U| and |A|) associated with it. (Note that, for convenience, we will continue to use the term 'nucleus' as an informal label for the prosodic domain associated with a vowel. Strictly speaking, however, there is no prosodic constituent called 'nucleus' in the representations proposed here.)

Like all constituents in this integrated melodic-prosodic structure, a nucleus contains units (elements) that are combined via head-dependent relations. The head of a nucleus must be one of the vowel elements |I|, |U| or |A|, the choice being language-specific and determined by parameter. In English, for example, the head of a nucleus is |A|. This head element can either stand alone, or it can support a dependent element also from the |I|/|U|/|A| set. If a head element stands alone, it is pronounced as a weak or default vowel, as in (3a) (the representation of weak vowels will be discussed in section 3.3). But if it takes a dependent, then the whole expression is realized phonetically as a full or lexically contrastive vowel, as in (3bc) (the representation of full vowels will be discussed in section 3.4). Below it will be shown how the quality of a full vowel derives largely from the properties of its dependent element(s), rather than from those of its head.

(3) |I|, |U|, |A| as prosodic constituents
   a. [ə]   b. [i]   c. [e]

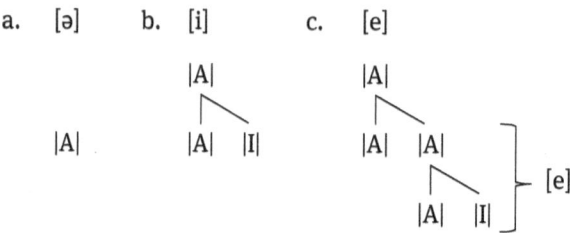

In this model, phonological structure is assumed to be recursive. That is, a dependent element can have a dependent of its own, which will occupy a lower (i.e. more deeply embedded) position in the structure. For example, the mid vowel in (3c) requires one more level of embedding than the high vowel in (3b). In principle, there is no restriction on the amount of complexity (embedding) that a structure may have. But on the other hand, representations are never more complex than they need to be – they must be complex enough to express the set of contrasts in a language, but that is all. So, the complexity of a language's vowel system will always dictate the number of levels of embedding required in representations for a given language. In all cases, vowel structure involves chains of binary head-dependency relations holding between tokens of the vowel elements |I|, |U| and |A|.

In addition to supporting dependent structure, the head of a nucleus also projects upwards in its role as a prosodic head. And depending on the prosodic level in question, the head element can function as the head of a syllable-sized domain, a foot-sized domain, or a word-sized domain. This is illustrated in (4), where consonants are shown as whole segments since consonant structure is not relevant to the issue of head projection.

(4) ['betə] 'better'

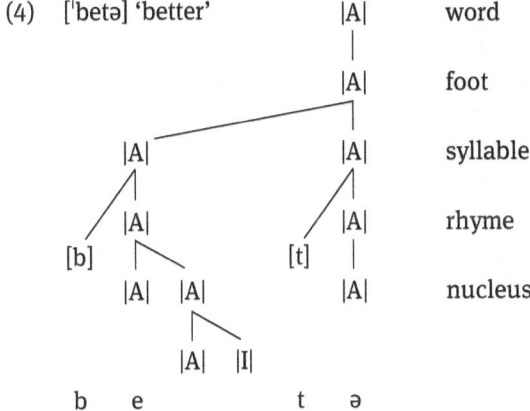

The structure of consonants will be described in more detail in section 4. For the moment, it may be noted that (4) departs from the conventions of Dependency Phonology (Anderson and Ewen 1987) and Government Phonology (Harris and Kaye 1990, Harris 1994) by representing trochaic words as right-headed structures. This follows Nasukawa and Backley (2015: 68), where it is claimed that constituent heads are important structurally but have a low informational load, while dependents are less important for structure-building but are rich in terms of information. For an overview of the Precedence-free Phonology approach, and a detailed discussion of the relation between phonological structure and phonetic realisation, see Nasukawa (2017).

If elements can function as prosodic units in this way, then phonological structures need only refer to elements and to the head-dependency relations holding between them – traditional prosodic labelling ('rhyme', 'syllable', etc.) becomes superfluous. As (4) shows, the head element projects upwards to every level of the prosodic hierarchy, defining successively wider prosodic domains as it does so. In this way, it is still possible to identify prosodic domains for the purposes of describing phonological patterns, but it can be done without referring to the usual constituent labels.

There are at least two advantages of adopting this approach. First, we avoid having to use constituents that are specific to just one level of structure – for example, 'syllable' only refers to the syllable level; and at the same time, we minimize the inventory of structural units employed in representations. Second, we make it easier to understand how and why melody and prosody interact – that is, why melodic (segmental) patterns are often sensitive to their prosodic context. For example, vowel reduction in English occurs in the weak part of a foot, but when this pattern is described in traditional terms it needs to be stipulated, as the relation between the prosodic label 'foot' and the melodic units |I|/|U|/|A| appears to be arbitrary. On the other hand, if the same units are used to describe both melodic and prosodic structure, then melody-prosody interaction begins to 'make sense' as a potential or even expected way for languages to behave.

So, the Precedence-free Phonology model being described here reinforces the idea of a unified representation in which elements are used to represent phonological information at every level of melodic and prosodic structure. These elements fulfil their familiar role as interpretable units of melody, but they also have an organising function by concatenating recursively via head-dependency relations to create successively larger prosodic domains – and thus, to generate successively larger phonological strings.

3.3 Empty nuclei and default vowels

The motivation for allowing only |I|, |U| and |A| to function as prosodic heads comes from the way that so-called 'empty' nuclei are phonetically realized. In the previous section we argued for a unified representation in which the traditional split between melodic structure and prosodic structure is obscured. And this view is supported within the government/licensing approach to representation (Charette 1991, 2003; Harris 1997; Kaye 2000; Cyran 2010; Scheer 2004), in which the distinction between melody and prosody has always been somewhat blurred. For example, a nucleus may be pronounced even when it is empty – that is, when it has no elements associated with it. In other words, it is possible for prosodic structure to be phonetically realized even in the absence of lexical melodic structure.

An empty nucleus typically functions as a default vowel and is pronounced with a central or non-peripheral quality somewhere within the range [ə]~[ɨ]~[ɯ]. Default vowels often appear in loanwords, when the native phonology requires a nucleus to be pronounced and there is no lexical vowel in the original borrowed form. For example, English has a schwa-like vowel between consonants that cannot form a complex onset, e.g. [gəˈdænsk] *Gdansk*, [kəˈnjuːt] *Cnut* (or *Canute*). In Japanese the quality of a default vowel is closer to a high back [ɯ], which breaks up consonant sequences in loanwords such as [takɯɕiː] *taxi*, [akɯseɾɯ] *accel(erator)*. Because the precise quality of a default vowel varies from one language to another, it is usually treated in terms of a language-specific parameter.

Vowel qualities such as [ə]~[ɨ]~[ɯ] make ideal default vowels because they are usually non-contrastive in vowel systems; after all, the purpose of a default vowel is to fill a nucleus without introducing any new linguistic (contrastive) information. In languages showing vowel reduction effects, such as English, these are also the vowel qualities that occupy weak prosodic positions. Because default vowels ([ə]~[ɨ]~[ɯ]) are associated with weak syllables, and because their distribution (in weak syllables) is complementary to that of full vowels (in strong syllables), we will claim that [ə], [ɨ] and [ɯ] are the weak realizations of the three full vowels that are phonetically closest to them – namely, [a], [i] and [u] respectively (Nasukawa 2014). Furthermore, because the full vowels [a], [i] and [u] are represented by the resonance elements |A|, |I| and |U|, we will assume that the same elements |A|, |I| and |U| are also latently present in their weak counterparts [ə], [ɨ] and [ɯ] – that is, in so-called 'empty' nuclei. The structures for [ə], [ɨ] and [ɯ] are given in (5). Note that these vowels are represented by 'minimal' structures: when a lone |A|, |I| or |U| stands as a single-element expression with no dependent structure, it is realised as a central vowel [ə], [ɨ] or [ɯ].

(5) |I|, |U|, |A| as default vowels

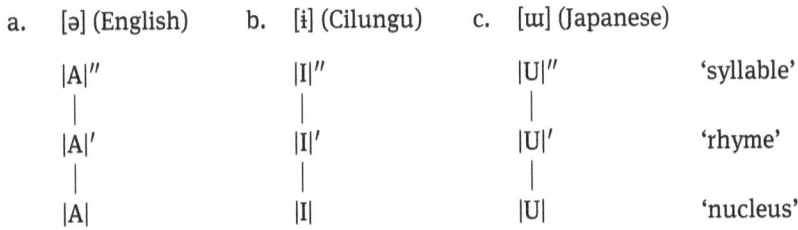

a. [ə] (English)   b. [ɨ] (Cilungu)   c. [ɯ] (Japanese)

|A|″ |I|″ |U|″   'syllable'
 | | |
|A|′ |I|′ |U|′   'rhyme'
 | | |
|A| |I| |U| 'nucleus'

These structures represent vowels in their most basic form: they are weak, non-peripheral vowels because they contain just a single element. And because they have no dependent structure, they carry no contrastive/lexical information. In this sense, the element that is present in each expression has a purely structural role: it functions as a prosodic constituent (i.e. a nucleus) and it can also be phonetically interpreted as a default (i.e. non-lexical) vowel. We observe a typological split between languages based on the quality of their default vowel. As shown in (5), languages with |A| as their head element have a schwa-like default vowel (e.g. English), those with |I| have a high central [ɨ] (e.g. Cilungu), and those with [U] have a back [ɯ] as their default vowel (e.g. Japanese). In acoustic terms, a latent element provides the phonetic baseline onto which other elements' acoustic patterns are superimposed. However, if no other elements are present (i.e. in an empty nucleus) then this baseline resonance is exposed and the head element becomes audible.

Support for the representations in (5) comes from physical evidence relating to the acoustic properties of the vowels in question. Unlike distinctive features, which mostly refer to properties of articulation (e.g. tongue position in [high] and [back], lip shape in [round]), elements are associated with acoustic patterns in the speech signal. We should therefore expect to find a similar acoustic shape in vowels that contain the same element. Specifically, the vowels in each of the weak-strong pairs [ə]-[a], [ɨ]-[i] and [ɯ]-[u] ought to have spectral patterns that are, at least to some extent, alike (Nasukawa 2014).

(6) Default vowels and full vowels compared
  a. |A| as [ə] |I| as [ɨ] |U| as [ɯ]
  b. |A| as [a] |I| as [i] |U| as [u]

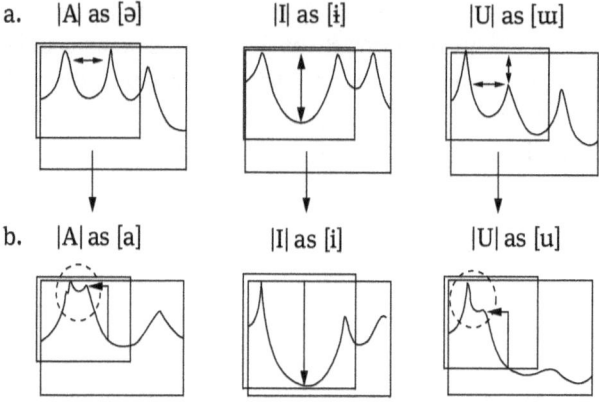

Consider first the spectral shape of [a] in (6b), which appears to be an exaggerated version of the equivalent shape for the corresponding weak vowel [ə]. The 'mass' pattern (see figure (1) above) associated with the element |A| is characterised by F1-F2 convergence, and this pattern is more prominent in [a] than in [ə] since the F1 and F2 energy peaks are closer together (i.e. they fully converge). Turning to strong [i] versus weak [ɨ], the difference again comes down to the prominence or salience of the relevant acoustic pattern. The 'dip' pattern associated with |I| is marked by a high F2 peak, which creates a trough or dip between F1 and F2. The trough in [i] is visibly deeper and more prominent than in [ɨ], and for this reason it may be understood as an exaggerated form of 'dip'. Finally, [u] and [ɯ] both display the 'rump' pattern associated with |U|, in which acoustic energy is concentrated at low frequencies. This produces a falling spectral shape which is sharper and more exaggerated in strong [u] than in weak [ɯ].

The acoustic similarities shown in (6) lend support to the idea that a so-called 'empty' nucleus is in fact not empty, because it contains a latent element which is realized as baseline resonance. And this relates to the point made earlier concerning the labelling of prosodic units: if an 'empty' or unspecified nucleus contains a default element, then this default element is enough to represent the nucleus in question – there is no need for an additional constituent label 'nucleus' because the nucleus is already defined by a default |I|, |U| or |A|. The same applies to constituents at higher prosodic levels too. As illustrated by the structure in (4), the element which serves as the head of a nucleus is projected to successively higher levels and becomes the head of successively larger prosodic domains. At each level this head element defines the prosodic domain in question, so there is no advantage in renaming these domains using arbitrary labels such as 'syllable', 'foot' and 'word'.

3.4 Contrastive vowels

The minimal structures in (5) are pronounced as weak vowels rather than as full vowels because a lone head element produces only baseline or default resonance. That is, a minimal structure can express only a minimal amount of phonological information: it signals the presence of a nucleus, but one which has no lexical/contrastive properties. By contrast, a full vowel has a more complex structure containing dependent elements, and it is this additional structure which expresses contrastive properties. As shown in (7b) and (7c), an endocentric head-dependency relation between elements increases structural complexity, which in turn allows an expression to carry lexical information.

(7)   Endocentric head-dependency
   a.   [ə]   b.   [a]   c.   [i]

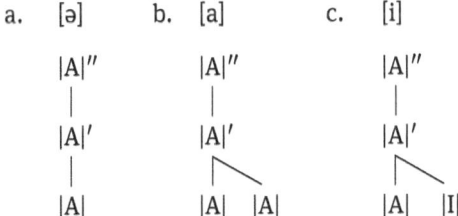

In (7a), repeated from (5), the lone head element |A| is pronounced as a schwa-like vowel; this is the realization of (non-contrastive) baseline resonance. But in (7b) this head |A| takes another token of |A| as a dependent, and the 'mass' (high F1) acoustic pattern of this dependent |A| is superimposed onto the schwa-type baseline. In effect, the acoustic pattern associated with the dependent element masks the baseline resonance and listeners perceive a low 'mass' vowel [a]. In (7c) too, the baseline resonance is inaudible because it is overridden by the properties of a dependent element; the dependent |I| means that the expression is realised as [i].

Using the simple structures in (7) it is possible to represent three contrastive vowels: [i] (dependent |I|), [u] (dependent |U|) and [a] (dependent |A|). But clearly, this is not enough for describing the vowel systems of most languages. To express additional vowel contrasts we need to allow for further element combinations, which means introducing more levels of embedding into the structure. Note that, although element embedding is a characteristic of the approach being developed here, it follows the conventions of element-based phonology by requiring elements to combine asymmetrically. In standard versions of Element Theory (Harris 1994, Cyran 1997, Backley 2011), as well as in Dependency Phonology (Anderson and Jones 1974, Anderson and Ewen 1987) and Particle Phonology (Schane 1984, 1995), mid vowels are represented by element compounds in which the relative salience of heads and dependents affects phonetic realization. For example, the expressions |I̲ A| and |I A̲| contain the same elements but the difference in their headedness makes them phonetically distinct: the |I̲|-headed structure |I̲ A| is realized as [e] while |A̲|-headed |I A̲| is pronounced as a more open [æ].

The recursive model of melodic representation being developed here also requires an asymmetry between elements, but it expresses this relation structurally rather than by using a diacritic (i.e. an underline). This is illustrated by the structures in (8).

(8) Vowels with complex structures
    a. [a]   b. [e]   c. [æ]

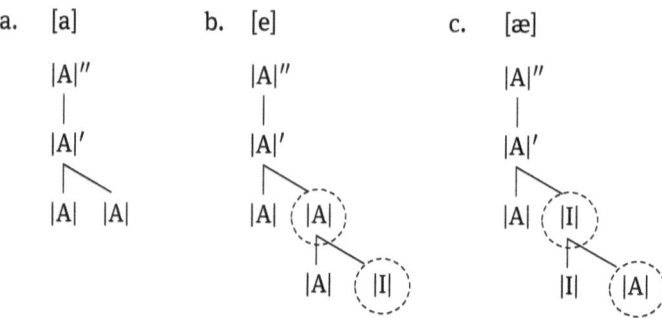

It is the most deeply embedded part of the structure – that is, the 'lowest' dependent – which makes the biggest contribution to the phonetic interpretation of an expression. In (8a) dependent |A| is the only unit in the structure which carries contrastive information, so the expression is realized as a low vowel [a]. (8b) contains an additional level of embedding and therefore two dependent elements (circled). Here the palatal resonance associated with dependent |I| predominates over its local head element |A| to produce a high mid [e].

In (8c) this asymmetric relation between |A| and |I| is reversed, with |A| in the most embedded part of the structure; since the 'mass' properties of this dependent |A| are more prominent than the 'dip' properties of its local head element |I|, the result is a more open [æ]. In all cases, then, phonetic interpretation depends not only on which elements are present, but also on the position of each element in the hierarchy of head-dependent relations.

In principle, there is no limit to the number of levels of embedding that a structure may have. But at the same time, representations are never more complex than they need to be. The grammar of a language must generate a set of melodic structures which is big enough to capture all the lexical contrasts in that language, but no more. And in most languages (i.e. those with more than three contrastive vowels) this will require element concatenation. Every instance of element concatenation introduces a new head-dependency relation, and therefore, an additional level of embedding. In a typical triangular vowel system comprising [a i u e o], only the structures in (8a) (for [a i u]) and (8b) (for [e o]) are needed. Compare this with a language such as Turkish, which requires an extra level of embedding to accommodate additional vowels such as [ü] and [ö], as in (9bc). Note that the structural head in Turkish is |I| rather than |A|, which is reflected in the [ɨ] quality of its baseline resonance – see (5) above.

(9) Vowel structures in Turkish
    a. [ɨ]   b. [ü]   c. [ö]

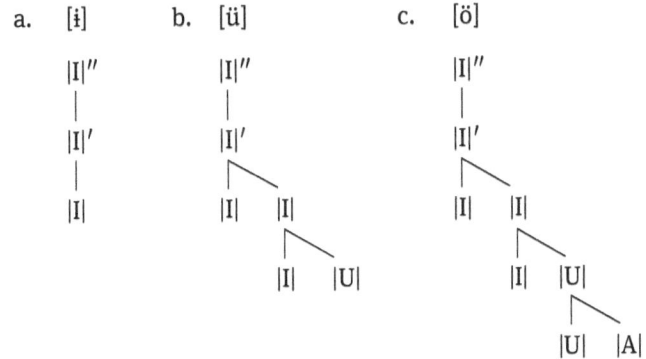

As these examples demonstrate, successive levels of embedding are introduced in a recursive fashion until all the required vowel contrasts are uniquely represented. Note that there is a direct relation between the complexity of an expression and the complexity of the resulting speech signal when that expression is pronounced, since each dependent element produces a unique modulation of the carrier signal away from its baseline pattern (Harris 2005, 2009).

What emerges from this discussion is that, in the Precedence-free Phonology approach, heads and dependents have quite different roles in phonological structure (Nasukawa and Backley 2015). Head elements are important for structure-building because (i) they support dependent elements and (ii) they project to higher prosodic levels. On the other hand, they are not important for phonetic realization: in full vowels the head element is masked by the acoustic properties of its dependent(s); it is only in the absence of dependent structure that the head element is heard – and even then it is realized as baseline resonance, which carries no melodic information (Nasukawa 2014, 2016, 2017; Nasukawa and Backley 2005). Meanwhile, the opposite is true for dependents: they are unimportant for structure-building because they are merely added to existing structure and do not project to higher prosodic levels; but they do make an important contribution to phonetic interpretation because they represent the most salient melodic properties in a complex expression.

3.5 Vowel weakening

Models of vowel representation must express the lexical contrasts and natural classes that are observed across languages. They should also capture aspects of dynamic behaviour such as vowel weakening and other dynamic phonological effects. Crosswhite (2000) and others describe two kinds of vowel weakening motivated by two different forces: centrifugal systems are driven by contrast enhancement, which neutralizes contrasts in favour of the peripheral vowels [a], [i] and [u], while centripetal systems aim for prominence reduction and produce reduced vowels with a central quality such as [ə] or [ɨ]. Harris (2005), on the other hand, develops a unified approach in which all instances of vowel weakening derive from the same mechanism – namely, the suppression of dependent element structure in weak positions. We adopt Harris's approach here and apply it to the hierarchical element structures described above.

In Element Theory it is assumed that after part of an element expression is suppressed, speakers can still pronounce any remaining parts of the structure. In some cases, this reduced structure will still be complex, i.e. its head element will have at least one dependent, as in (10ab). In other cases, it will lose all its dependents to leave a minimal structure consisting of just a bare head element, as in (10c).

(10) Element suppression

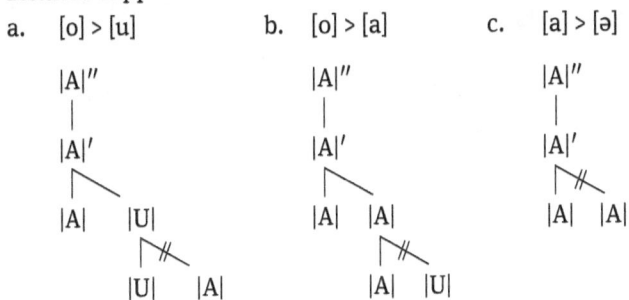

The vowel reduction pattern in (10a) is found in Bulgarian, where stressed [e o] alternate with [i u] in unstressed syllables, e.g. r[ó]guf 'of horn', r[u]gát 'horned' (Petterson and Wood 1987). This change involves suppressing the element that is lowest in the structure, namely, dependent |A|. When this happens, the |U| immediately above dependent |A| remains intact; and because this |U| is also a dependent (of the ultimate head |A|), it contributes to phonetic interpretation. By itself, dependent |U| is realized as [u]. Meanwhile, the weakening effect in (10b) is observed in Russian (Crosswhite 2000: 110); and again, the most deeply embedded element (dependent |U|) is suppressed, leaving behind its local head (the |A| above it). Because this |A| is also a dependent (again, of the ultimate head |A|), it is pronounced. On its own, dependent |A| is realized as [a].[2] In (10c) too, the lowest element in the structure is targeted. In this case, however, it leaves behind only the head element. Recall from (7a) that the ultimate head of an expression functions as a default vowel and is phonetically realized as baseline resonance (here, a weak [ə]).

This approach to vowel weakening makes two assumptions (Backley and Nasukawa 2018). First, it assumes that vowel reduction operates blindly and uniformly – the process always targets the most deeply embedded layer(s) of a vowel's structure. Second, reduction is a structure-depleting process, meaning that an expression which undergoes weakening always loses some of its structural complexity. And these two assumptions lead to some interesting observations about the abstractness of element-based representations – and indeed, about the abstractness of phonetic symbols. Consider, for example, the following patterns of mid vowel reduction (neutralisation) in Italian and Slovene.

---

[2] There is no anomaly in the fact that the dependency relation between |U| and |A| is different in Bulgarian [o] (10a) and Russian [o] (10b). Element structures are primarily a reflection of phonological rather than phonetic properties, and consequently, phonetically similar sounds can have non-identical representations if they function differently in different languages.

(11) Vowel reduction in Italian
   a. Italian (Krämer 2009: 100)

	stressed	unstressed
[ɛ] > [e]	[orto'pɛdiko] 'orthopaedist'	[ortope'diːa] 'orthopaedics'
[ɔ] > [o]	['lɔdʒika] 'logics'	[lodʒika'mente] 'logically'

   b.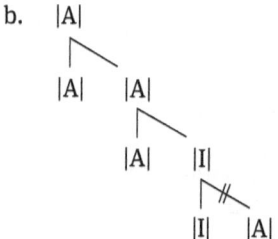

(12) Vowel reduction in Slovene
   a. Slovene (Bidwell 1969, Crosswhite 2001: 31)

	stressed	unstressed
[e] > [ɛ]	['reːtʃ] 'word' nom. sg.	[rɛ'tʃiː] 'word' gen. sg.
[o] > [ɔ]	['moʒ] 'man' nom. sg.	['mɔ'ʒjeː] 'men' nom. pl.

   b.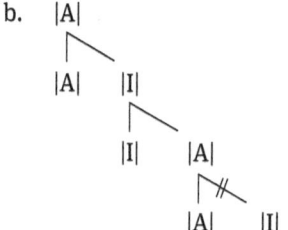

The four mid vowels [e ɛ o ɔ] are present in Italian and Slovene, pronounced with similar phonetic qualities in both languages. However, vowel weakening reveals that these vowels have different phonological identities in the two systems. The alternations in (11a) suggest that in Italian [e o] must be structurally less complex than [ɛ ɔ], since vowel reduction is a structure-depleting process and it is [e o] which appear in weak (unstressed) positions. But in Slovene the opposite is true – in (12a) [e o] weaken to [ɛ ɔ], so [ɛ ɔ] must be less complex than their tense counterparts [e o]. This difference does not derive from the vowel reduction process itself, which operates uniformly by suppressing the lowest element(s) in any target structure. Rather, it must result from the way elements are organised in the target structures concerned, as can be seen by comparing (11b) with (12b): in Italian the full vowel [ɛ] in (11b) weakens to [e] when its lowest dependent |A| is suppressed, while in Slovene the full vowel [e] in (12b) reduces to [ɛ] by losing dependent |I|.

This difference suggests that the relation between phonological structure and phonetic realisation is an indirect one – something that Element Theory has always maintained. Since element expressions are mental objects, there is no precise or consistent correspondence between elements and the physical (e.g. articulatory) properties of spoken language. So, to determine a vowel's element structure we focus primarily on its phonological behaviour rather than on its phonetic properties. This point is highlighted in the above examples, which illustrate how processes such as vowel weakening can shed light on phonological representations, regardless of their precise phonetic qualities. If weakening operates blindly on any target vowel, then the typological differences we find – between Italian 'tensing' in (11) and Slovene 'laxing' in (12), for instance, and between centrifugal and centripetal vowel reduction systems – cannot be accounted for by assuming that different structure-changing mechanisms are at work. Instead, they must stem from differences in the way individual vowels are represented in terms of their hierarchical element structures.

4 Recursion in consonant structure

It was mentioned above that, although elements can have a prosodic function in addition to their melodic function, this only applies to the resonance elements |I|, |U|, |A|. The remaining elements – the non-resonance elements |H|, |L|, |ʔ| – serve a more conventional role: they represent segmental categories in consonants. In this section we show how element structure in consonants, like that in vowels, is recursive; that is, element concatenation again makes use of successive layers of element embedding.

In all languages, C and V combine to form a basic prosodic unit in which the two constituents have unequal status: C is dependent on V. This is captured in syllable structure terms by saying that a rhyme (containing V) takes an onset (containing C) as its dependent. And although the representational approach described in section 3 rejects conventional notions of syllable structure, it can still express the same asymmetric relation. It does this by positioning consonant expressions below vowel expressions on a single hierarchical element structure. A syllable-sized CV unit such as [bi] or [zi] (an obstruent followed by a high front vowel) is thus represented as in (13).[3]

---

[3] As the name implies, Precedence-free Phonology uses representations in which no reference is made to any precedence relations between sounds. In terms of linearity, therefore, there is no difference between right-branching and left-branching (Nasukawa 2011).

(13) A syllable-sized unit (Precedence-free Phonology model)

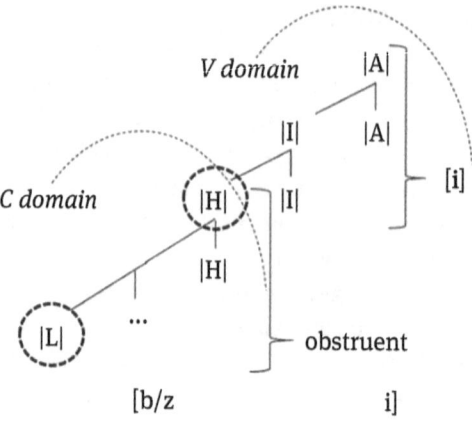

[b/z   i]

The V-domain in the upper part of (13) contains the element structure for the vowel [i]. It has |A| as its structural head, which takes |I| as a dependent. And since dependents make a bigger contribution to phonetic realization than heads, the entire V-domain is pronounced as [i] (see (7c) above). Then the C-domain, as a dependent of the V-domain, is embedded within it. The head of the C-domain is |H|, which is a dependent of the lowest element in the V-domain, namely |I|. The appearance of the noise element |H| indicates that the structure from this point downwards has the characteristics of a consonant. Consonant structure is built up in the same way as vowel structure, with additional elements being concatenated by introducing further levels of embedding. This will be illustrated in (14) below.

Representing a V-domain and a C-domain as a unified structure reflects the fact that, in phonological terms, the two behave as a single, syllable-sized prosodic unit. Nevertheless, in phonetic terms each domain is distinct – we perceive a consonant sound followed by a vowel sound. This derives from the fact that the upper and lower parts of the unified CV structure have incompatible phonetic (physiological) properties: the upper domain is vocalic while the lower domain is consonantal. And as such, they cannot be realised simultaneously;[4] for speakers, the only option is to pronounce them in sequence. The question, however, is how language users determine the order of C and V sounds in a sequence, if this information is not encoded explicitly in representations. Using the CV structure in (14) we illustrate how the linear ordering of

---

4 Languages do not have, for example, obstruent vowels or vocalic obstruents (Ladefoged and Maddieson 1996).

individual sounds falls out from the network of head-dependent relations in an expression (Nasukawa, Backley, Yasugi and Koizumi 2019).

(14) Recursive structure in vowels and consonants: the CV unit [kʰi]

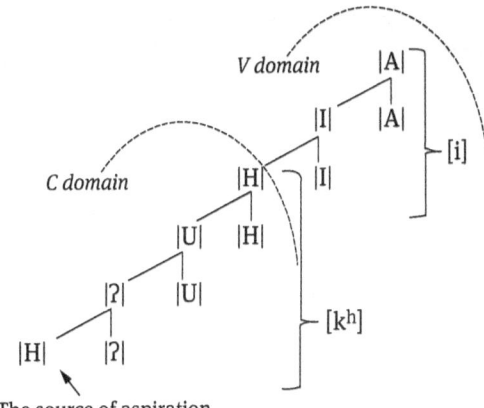

In (14) the ultimate head of the CV-sized structure is the highest |A|. It will be recalled from section 3.3 that a head |A| is pronounced as [ə] (i.e. the acoustic baseline) if no dependent elements are present. But in this case the head element |A| has a dependent |I|, and the acoustic signature of this dependent |I| overrides that of its head. As a result, the |A|-headed expression |A I| is realised as [i]. (For an explanation of how other vocalic expressions are realized, see Nasukawa 2016.)

Moving one structural level down, this |I| element now functions as a domain head and takes |H| as its dependent. The noise element |H| represents a range of obstruent-type properties including voicelessness and aspiration (see (2) above), indicating that everything below it in the structure refers to a consonant. As already noted, this consonantal domain (headed by |H|) cannot be realised simultaneously with the vocalic domain above it (headed by |A|) because the two domains involve articulatory gestures that are incompatible. At the next level of embedding the element |H| takes |U| as a dependent, where single |U| is realised as velar resonance (Nasukawa 2016, cf. Backley and Nasukawa 2009). Thus, the consonant is identified as a velar obstruent of some kind. This |U| then becomes a head, taking the edge element |ʔ| (defining occlusion) as its dependent. The consonant structure up to this point (i.e. [[ʔ U]ᵤ H]ₕ) may be phonetically realised as a velar stop [k].

Finally, the lowest part of the structure contains a second token of |H|. As a dependent of |ʔ|, this |H| occupies the most deeply embedded part of the structure, which maximises its ability to carry linguistic information – recall that dependents are structurally unimportant but informationally rich. This means that this lower |H| is realised in its exaggerated (prominent) form, namely, as aspiration. Thus, the |H|-headed domain is interpreted as an aspirated velar plosive [k^h]. Together with the vocalic structure above it, the entire expression in (14) is realised as the CV-sized unit [k^{h}i]. This outcome is determined by the principle of phonetic interpretation in (15) (Nasukawa, Backley, Yasugi and Koizumi 2019).

(15) Type A (CV) precedence:
   A domain located at a lower level (C domain) is phonetically realised before a domain located at a higher level (V domain).

This general principle, dubbed Type A, is observed in the vast majority of languages, including English. In (15) it is formulated in terms of a domain's position in the hierarchical element structure. But it may also be expressed by referring to the extent of the carrier signal's modulation: a domain associated with a bigger modulation (typically an obstruent consonant) precedes a domain with a smaller modulation (typically a vowel). This alternative way of interpreting (15) is based on the idea that domains located at the lower end of the hierarchy contain more linguistic information than those higher up, and it assumes that consonants tend to be richer in linguistic information than vowels (i.e. consonant representations employ a larger set of contrastive properties).

In the small number of languages which do not observe the Type A principle, we find a mechanism of phonetic realisation that is exactly the reverse of the one described in (15). The Mayan language Kaqchikel is one such system, in which the structure in (14) is predicted to have a VC realisation rather than CV. Following Nasukawa, Backley, Yasugi and Koizumi (2019), we assume that Kaqchikel adheres to the alternative principle of realisation in (16).

(16) Type B (VC) precedence:
   A domain located at a higher level (V domain) is phonetically realised before a domain located at a lower level (C domain).

Expressed in terms of carrier signal modulations, Kaqchikel should display a pattern that is the opposite of the Type A pattern. That is, in the Type B pattern a domain associated with a bigger carrier signal modulation (typically an obstruent consonant) will be phonetically realised after a domain with a smaller modulation (typically a vowel).

The parametric difference between Type A precedence and Type B precedence (Nasukawa 2016) rests on the following two assumptions. First, all languages use the same hierarchical melodic structure, which is defined only by head-dependency relations between elements. And second, cross-linguistic variation is limited to whether a language uses a V-final or a V-initial precedence relation when phonological structure is phonetically realised. This typological variation is formalised as a parametric choice between (15) and (16). An explanation for why (15) is far more widespread than (16) may involve a discussion of physiological and psychological factors as well as purely linguistic factors. For the moment we leave this question open; further research will be needed to fully understand the general preference for the CV pattern over the VC pattern.

5 Summary

We have outlined a unified model of phonological structure which represents both melody and prosody by referring only to elements. In addition to performing their usual melodic functions, elements are projected upwards through the prosodic hierarchy to define successively wider prosodic domains. These domains replicate the standard prosodic units labelled 'nucleus', 'syllable', 'foot' and 'word'. The motivation for rejecting these traditional labels is that they are specific to just one part of structure, namely prosody. And this presents a problem, such that if melody and prosody are described using different sets of units, we fail to capture any non-arbitrary relation between them. We have also argued that a minimal 'syllable' contains just a bare head element, either |A|, |I| or |U|, selected by parameter. The choice of head element reflects the way a given language interprets empty nuclei.

References

Anderson, John and Colin J. Ewen. 1987. *Principles of Dependency Phonology*. Cambridge: Cambridge University Press.
Anderson, John and Charles Jones. 1974. Three theses concerning phonological representations. *Journal of Linguistics* 10, 1–26.
Backley, Phillip. 2011. *An Introduction to Element Theory*. Edinburgh: Edinburgh University Press.
Backley, Phillip. 2012. Variation in Element Theory. *Linguistic Variation* 12(1), 57–102.
Backley, Phillip and Kuniya Nasukawa. 2009. Representing labials and velars: A single 'dark' element. *Phonological Studies* 12, 3–10.
Backley, Phillip and Kuniya Nasukawa. 2010. Consonant-vowel unity in Element Theory. *Phonological Studies* 13, 21–28.

Backley, Phillip and Kuniya Nasukawa. 2018. Segment-internal structure: Evidence from vowel reduction. Paper presented at the 15th Old World Conference in Phonology (OCP15), University College London, University of London (12–14 January 2018).

Bidwell, Charles E. 1969. *Outline of Slovenian Morphology*. Pittsburgh: University Center for International Studies, University of Pittsburgh.

Cavirani, Edoardo and Marc van Oostendorp. This volume. A theory of the theory of vowels.

Charette, Monik. 1991. *Conditions on Phonological Government*. Cambridge: Cambridge University Press.

Charette, Monik. 2003. Empty and pseudo-empty categories. In Stefan Ploch (ed.), *Living on the Edge: 28 Papers in Honour of Jonathan Kaye*, 465–479. Berlin and New York: Mouton de Gruyter.

Clements, George N. 1990. The role of the sonority cycle in core syllabification. In John Kingston and Mary E. Beckman (eds.), *Papers in Laboratory Phonology I: Between the Grammar and Physics of Speech*, 283–325. Cambridge: Cambridge University Press.

Crosswhite, Katherine M. 2000. Vowel reduction in Russian: A unified account of standard, dialectal, and 'dissimilative' patterns. In Katherine M. Crosswhite and Joyce McDonough (eds.), *University of Rochester Working Papers in the Language Sciences*, Vol. Spring 2000, no.1, 107–171.

Crosswhite, Katherine M. 2001. *Vowel Reduction in Optimality Theory*. New York and London: Routledge.

Cyran, Eugeniusz. 1997. *Resonance Elements in Phonology: A Study in Munster Irish*. Lublin: Folium.

Cyran, Eugeniusz. 2010. *Complexity Scales and Licensing in Phonology*. Berlin: Mouton de Gruyter.

Dikken, Marcel den and Harry G. van der Hulst. This volume. On some deep structural analogies between syntax and phonology.

Duanmu, San. 2009. *Syllable Structure: The Limits of Variation*. Oxford: Oxford University Press.

Harris, John. 1990. Phonological Government. *Phonology* 7, 255–300.

Harris, John. 1994. *English Sound Structure*. Oxford: Blackwell.

Harris, John. 1997. Licensing inheritance: An integrated theory of neutralisation. *Phonology* 14, 315–370.

Harris, John. 2005. Vowel reduction as information loss. In Philip Carr, Jacques Durand and Colin J. Ewen (eds.), *Headhood, Elements, Specification and Contrastivity*, 119–132. Amsterdam: John Benjamins.

Harris, John. 2009. Why final obstruent devoicing is weakening. In Kuniya Nasukawa and Phillip Backley (eds.), *Strength Relations in Phonology*, 9–45. Berlin and New York: Mouton de Gruyter.

Harris, John and Geoff Lindsey. 1995. The elements of phonological representation. In Jacques Durand and Francis Katamba (eds.), *Frontiers of Phonology: Atoms, Structures, Derivations*, 34–79. Harlow, Essex: Longman.

Harris, John and Jonathan D. Kaye. 1990. A tale of two cities: London glotalling and New York City tapping. *The Linguistic Review* 7, 251–274.

Hulst, Harry G. van der. 2003. Dutch syllable structure meets Government Phonology. In Takeru Honma, Masao Okazaki, Toshiyuki Tabata and Shin-ichi Tanaka (eds.), *A New Century of Phonology and Phonological Theory: A Festschrift for Prof. Shosuke Haraguchi on the Occasion of His Sixtieth Birthday*, 313–343. Tokyo: Kaitakusha.

Kaye, Jonathan. 2000. A users' guide to Government Phonology. Ms., University of Ulster.
Kaye, Jonathan, Jean Lowenstamm and Jean-Roger Vergnaud. 1990. Constituent structure and government in Phonology. *Phonology* 7, 193–231.
Krämer, Martin. 2009. *The Phonology of Italian*. Oxford: Oxford University Press.
Ladefoged, Peter and Ian Maddieson. 1996. *The Sounds of the World's Languages*. Oxford and Cambridge, MA: Blackwell.
Nasukawa, Kuniya. 2011. Representing phonology without precedence relations. *English Linguistics* 28, 278–300.
Nasukawa, Kuniya. 2014. Features and recursive structure. *Nordlyd* 41(1),1–19. *Special Issue on Features* edited by Martin Krämer, Sandra-Iulia Ronai and Peter Svenonius.
Naukawa, Kuniya. 2016. A precedence-free approach to (de-)palatalisation in Japanese. *Glossa: A Journal of General Linguistics* 1(1), 9. DOI: http://dx.doi.org/10.5334/gjgl.26.
Nasukawa, Kuniya. 2017. The phonetic salience of phonological head-dependent structure in a modulated-carrier model of speech. In Bridget Samuels (ed.), *Beyond Markedness in Formal Phonology* (Linguistik Aktuell 241), 121–152. Amsterdam: John Benjamins.
Nasukawa, Kuniya and Phillip Backley. 2005. Dependency relations in Element Theory: Markedness and complexity. In Nancy Chongo Kula and Jeroen van de Weijer (eds.), *Proceedings of the Government Phonology Workshop. Special issue of Leiden Papers in Linguistics* 2.4., ULCL, Leiden University, 77–93.
Nasukawa, Kuniya and Phillip Backley. 2008. Affrication as a performance device. *Phonological Studies* 11, 35–46.
Nasukawa, Kuniya and Phillip Backley. 2011. The internal structure of 'r' in Japanese. *Phonological Studies* 14, 27–34.
Nasukawa, Kuniya and Phillip Backley. 2015. Heads and complements in phonology: A case of role reversal? *Phonological Studies* 18, 67–74.
Nasukawa, Kuniya, Phillip Backley, Yoshiho Yasugi and Masatoshi Koizumi. 2019. Challenging cross-linguistic typology: Right-edge consonantal prominence in Kaqchikel. *Journal of Linguistics* 55(3), 611–641.
Petterson, Thore and Sidney Wood. 1987. Vowel reduction in Bulgarian and its implications for theories of vowel production: A review of the problem. *Folia Linguistica* 2(4), 261–79.
Pöchtrager, Markus A. This volume. Recursion and GP 2.0.
Schane, Stanford A. 1984. The fundamentals of Particle Phonology. *Phonology Yearbook* 1, 129–156.
Schane, Stanford A. 1995. Diphthongization in particle phonology. In John A. Goldsmith (ed.), *The Handbook of Phonological Theory*, 586–608. Oxford: Blackwell.
Scheer, Tobias. 2004. *A Lateral Theory of Phonology: What Is CVCV and Why Should It Be?* Berlin: Mouton de Gruyter.
Schwartz, Geoffrey. This volume. Defining recursive entities in phonology: The Onset Prominence framework.
Selkirk, Elisabeth O. 1984. On the major class features and syllable theory. In Mark Aronoff and Richard T. Oerhle (eds.), *Language Sound Structure: Studies in Phonology Dedicated to Morris Halle by His Teacher and Students*, 107–113. Cambridge, MA: MIT Press.

Edoardo Cavirani and Marc van Oostendorp
A theory of the theory of vowels

1 Introduction

One line of research in theories of phonological primitives, such as features or elements, is to reduce the number of such primitives. Feature geometry theories can be seen as a way to do this: a segment is a tree that consists of a treelet (a subtree) of place features, a treelet of aperture features, etc. Especially within Element Theory, there has been a tendency to reduce the number of representational primitives also in other ways. A radical example of this is so-called Radical CV Phonology by van der Hulst (1988, 1994, 1996, 2015), which claims that there are only two such primitives, called C and V, which can be interpreted differently in different parts of the tree.

Would it be possible to reduce the number of primitives even further? And what would the ultimate reduction be? Would there be a possibility of giving a representation for segments that would not include *any* elements? We know that graph theory, in particular the theory of trees, that already plays such an important role in grammatical theory, is a rather strong mathematical tool – could we not build a theory of vowels on it? This would imply that we have a theory in which the original elements |A, I, U| themselves have internal structure, and such structure would only be treelets. We think we can, and the following can be seen as a complete definition of vowel representations in natural language motivated by the *desiderata* above.

It is the purpose of this paper to sketch what such a theory would look like. By doing so, we are basically building a metatheory of Element Theory. Our 'data' are most vocalic systems that can be successfully derived from the elements |A, U, I| and combinations thereof. We try to derive such systems making no use of elements. The resulting theory would therefore have the same consequences as 'normal' element theories, but it would give an answer to questions such as why there are three elements and why these elements each have their own special properties.

2 Vowels without features of elements: A proposal

We first define the vowel recursively, assuming that we have treelets, i.e. structures that consist of a mother node and one or two daughters, where the daughters can themselves be further treelets:

(1) a. The empty node (also written as Ø) is a vowel, i.e. a treelet.
b. If σ, τ are treelets, the structure in which σ dominates τ is also a treelet.
c. If σ, τ, υ are treelets, and {τ, υ} are balanced, the structure in which σ dominates
τ and υ is also a treelet.

The definition in (1c) relies on a definition of 'balance' that is familiar from search algorithms, and to which we will return below (we will ignore it for now). The definition in (1) gives us in principle an infinite number of treelets, of which the following are some simple examples:

(2) a. Ø   (1a)

  b.   Ø
       | (1b)
       Ø

  ci. Ø
      /\   (1c, with σ, τ and υ empty)
      Ø Ø

  cii. Ø
       /\   (1c, with σ, τ empty and υ = 2b)
       Ø |
         Ø

  ciii. Ø
        /\   (1c, with σ empty and τ, υ = 2b)
        | |
        Ø Ø

The Ø signs in these treelets are *not* labels, and in fact have no special status. We put them here purely for reasons of clarity; leaving them out would give the same mathematical structures. Also, linear order is irrelevant, so that (cii) could also be represented as:

(3) Ø
     /\
     | Ø
     Ø

Further treelets can be formed by replacing daughter treelets in any of these representations by another treelet. For instance, we can take (2ciii) and replace one of its daughters by (2ci); this is because the definition in (1) is recursive:

(4)   ∅   ∅   ∅
     /\   +   /\   > /\
     | | ∅ ∅ | /\
     ∅ ∅   ∅ ∅ ∅

In principle, since the original definitions in (1) are recursive, we can go on doing this forever and generate an infinite number of potential vowels. The treelets in (2) have a special status: they are as it were the most primitive structures that exist in the theory, as they are the only ones which can be formed by applying the definitions in (1) at most once. The result of the operation in (4) is more complicated.

There are thus 5 'primitive' treelets. We propose that each of these represents one of the primitives of Element Theory:

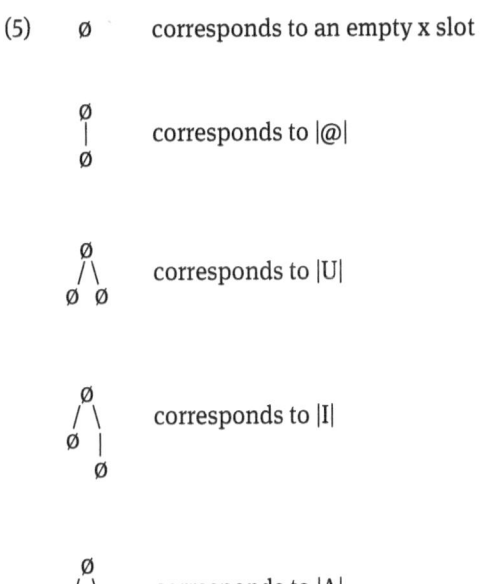

(5)   ∅   corresponds to an empty x slot

      ∅
      | corresponds to |@|
      ∅

      ∅
     /\   corresponds to |U|
     ∅ ∅

      ∅
     /\   corresponds to |I|
     ∅ |
        ∅

      ∅
     /\   corresponds to |A|
     | |
     ∅ ∅

Logic teaches us that, since linear order is irrelevant, there can be only three binary treelets, corresponding exactly to the typical number of 'normal' elements, and one unary treelet for the schwa interpretation (in section 2.2, we will go into the question why we think each individual treelet has the interpretation we have provided here).

By assuming that elements are primitive treelets, we have thus derived their number, and by assuming that treelets are recursive, we have also derived another property of Element Theory, viz. that there is no substantive difference between and an element and a combination of elements: they are all (pronounceable) vowels. In other words, when we combine treelets (per 1ciii), the resulting tree is again a representation of a vowel, with an interpretation that is familiar from Element Theory, or to be more precise, of Particle Phonology (Schane 1984), because there is no headedness in our representations, and the same treelet can occur more than once. This is true in particular for the |A| treelet. E.g. in (4) above we see |A| combined with |U|, so that the resulting tree is a representation for /o/, and the following would be a representation for /ɔ/:

(6)
```
    Ø           Ø              Ø
   / \    +    / \      >     / \
  |  |        | / \          | / \
  Ø  Ø        Ø Ø Ø          Ø | / \
                               Ø Ø Ø

   |a|         /o/            /ɔ/
```

One does not have to have the 'derivational history' of a treelet (as in 7b) to understand its phonetics; by reading a tree one layer (of 7a) at a time, one also gets the desired interpretation:

(7) a.
```
         Ø
        / \
       | / \
       Ø | / \
         Ø Ø Ø
```
     b.
```
              |A|
           @  |A|
           @  |U|
```

The top layer is a binary treelet with two non-empty daughters; this is interpreted as an |A| element. The second layer consists of a unary set (a schwa) plus another binary treelet with two non-empty daughters, so this is again an |A| element, of which again one of the daughters is a schwa; the other is a treelet with two empty daughters, which is an |U|. This representation can thus be interpreted as the element combination |A|.@.|A|.@.|U|, or, given that @ is an element that does not add any specific value (other than background noise; Harris 1994) as |A|.|A|.|U|, which is an /ɔ/ in Particle Phonology.

2.1 Balance and the limits of recursion

The |A| treelet allows for recursion in this way – limited, we propose, only by extralinguistic factors such as the ability of humans to distinguish vowel heights from each other articulatorily or acoustically. Note that the |U| treelet does not allow any kind of further embedding, because each of its daughters should be empty by definition (if they are not, the treelet is simply not interpreted as |U|). |I| does allow for embedding of |U|, giving us /y/:

(8) a.   Ø
         / \
        Ø / \
           Ø Ø
     b. |I|
          |U|

All front rounded vowels will have this treelet as part of their representation. Other types embeddings are universally not allowed, because of what we call the 'balance property' of phonological representations, which we have hitherto not discussed. This property is easily defined informally:

(9) The number of embeddings N(T) in a treelet T, is the number of steps it takes to go from the root of T to the most deeply embedded leaf.

(10) A binary tree {A, B} is **balanced**, if N(A) – N(B) ≤ |1| (Adelson-Velsky and Landis 1962)

In other words, the two daughters of a node should have a similar amount of structure: one can be at most one level deeper than the other. If we embed something else than a |@| treelet or a |U| treelet into an |I| treelet, we get a tree that is not balanced. This for instance would be the result of putting an |I| inside another |I|:

(11) a.   Ø
         / \
        Ø / \
           Ø |
              Ø
     b. |I|
         |I|
         @

The first daughter of the top node has a number of embedding of 0 (because it is an empty set), the second daughter (the embedded |I|) has a number of embedding of 2, so the difference between the two nodes becomes too big, and there is no balance. The embedding of |U| in |I| is balanced, however (see 8): the first daughter of |I| still has an embedding of 0, but the second one (the |U|) has an embedding of 1. This difference is within the limits put forward by (10).

Note that this implies that |A| can embed twice into itself, because each daughter is non-empty, and has therefore a number of embedding of at least 1. The representation of /ɔ/ above (7) is therefore balanced. We cannot embed three |A|'s into each other in this way, however, as then the 'simple' daughter of the top node (@) becomes too simple (note that this also derives the (nearly absolute; Crothers 1978) maximal 4-degrees height of vowel systems). We can do more embedding, but in that case, each of the daughters needs more internal structure.

Note that we have tacitly assumed so far that schwa formation is not recursive: we cannot embed a single treelet into another single treelet. The following are not feasible representations:

(12) a. Ø
         |
         Ø
         |
         Ø

     b. Ø
         |
         Ø
         |
         Ø
         |
         Ø

We assume that the reason for this is that such structure is redundant: a schwa embedded in a schwa would still be phonetically interpreted as a schwa. The second structure in (12) would still be interpreted as @.@.@=@ For this reason, schwa embedding is also not allowed to 'balance' treelets that would otherwise be unbalanced, i.e. we cannot 'save' a recursive |A| by making one arm into a 'big' schwa along the lines of (12).

2.2 Some examples of vowel sets

For the sake of saving space on the page or on your computer screen, we will from now on write our treelets in a kind constituent notation, so that schwa is {Ø}, |U| is [Ø,Ø], etc. Using the kinds of representations just outlined, we can now define a number of well-known vowel sets. For instance, a three-vowel set [u i a] has the following elements:

(13) a. [Ø,Ø]   (|U|=[u])
     b. [Ø,[Ø]]   (|I|=[i])
     c. [[Ø],[Ø]] (|A|=[a])

We can call (13a) the |U| treelet, (13b) the |I| treelet and (13c) the |A| treelet. The language does not have schwa, hence no unary treelets. Such a vowel inventory can be described in the following way:

(14) a. All vowels are binary treelets.
     b. The treelets that are daughters of vowels are at most unary.

Taken together, (1) and (14) give a precise definition of the language. We assume that (1) is universal: it just defines what it means to be a vowel. (14b) filters out those treelets that are universally available, but not as vowels in this language. (14) is therefore what needs to be acquired by a language learner. This could be a matter of parameter setting. In a four vowel language that also includes schwa, the requirement in (14a) is replaced by (14a)':

(14) a'. All vowels are monovalent or binary treelts.

If we instead cancel (14b) and add the assumption (14b') instead, we get a six vowel set (assuming that an |A| set that dominates another |A| set is still also an [a] because of redundancy):

(14) b.' Vowel sets have an embedding depth of at most 2.

(15) [Ø,Ø]   (|U|=[u])
     [Ø,[Ø]]   (|I|=[i])
     [[Ø],[Ø]]   (|A|=[a])
     [Ø, [Ø, Ø]]   (|I.U|=[y])
     [[Ø],[Ø,Ø]]   (|A.U|=[o])
     [[Ø],[Ø,[Ø]]]   (|A.I|=[e])
     [[Ø],[[Ø],[Ø]]]   (|A.A|=[a])

Disallowing the front rounded vowels involves adding an extra requirement:

(16) Binary nodes cannot be sisters to empty nodes.

Extending the embedding depth to level 3 instead of level 2, we of course also extend the vowel set even further, viz. to a 5-vowel set:

(17) [Ø,Ø]   (|U|=[u])
    [Ø,[Ø]]   (|I|=[i])
    [[Ø],[Ø]]   (|A|=[a])
    [[Ø],[Ø,Ø]]   (|A.U|=[o])
    [[Ø],[Ø,[Ø]]]   (|A.I|=[e])
    [[Ø],[[Ø],[Ø]]]   (|A.A|=[a])
    [[Ø],[[Ø],[Ø,Ø]]]   (|A.A.U|=[ɔ])
    [[Ø],[[Ø],[Ø,[Ø]]]]   (|A.A.I|=[ɛ])
    [[Ø],[[Ø],[[Ø],[Ø]]]]   (|A.A.A|=[a])

We can understand lowering processes by embedding an |A| vowel in another vowel. In other words, the calculus for at least the most common vowel inventory types can be described with a small set of possible restrictions on sets. Notice that the view on vowel structure which we thus get is not incompatible with autosegmental views of frontness or roundness harmony: these sets can behave as autosegmental elements and spread. Height harmony would need to have a different representation, on the other hand, but the theory is not different in this respect from element theory, as expected.

2.3 Extensions to larger segmental inventories

Obviously, segmental inventories do not just consist of vowels – and even within vocalic phonology there are many distinctions we have not made yet – we will need representations for nasality, for tone, and many other distinctions. Space does not permit to go into these details, but note that we can make use of the kinds of ideas developed in other Element-based frameworks (such as RcvP; see below) in which the same elements can have different phonetic interpretations, depending on their position in the tree. Making segmental trees bigger (having ever more recursion) will expand our space of possibilities.

3 Substance reduction and set theory: Some precedents

3.1 Early precursors

Ours is not the first proposal for reducing the number of representational primitives. Several proposals have been put forward with a similar aim. Since our work represents a rather extreme move along this line of research, we think it is important to recapitulate the most relevant stages of this research line. More importantly, this will also give us the room to stress the differences and similarities between our proposal and the preceding ones.

One of the first of this type of measures to reduce the number of representational primitives is Feature Geometry (Clements 1985), which (implicitly and informally) applies the notion of set to the unordered bundles of features of Chomsky and Halle (1968). As a result, segments become sets of subsets of features, which are formally conceived of as organized in 'groups' headed by nodes in a (segmental) tree.[1] Crucially, the geometric restructuring of the featural content of segments allows for generalizations which target subsets, i.e. representational nodes.[2] As a matter of fact, this framework reduces the computational components of phonology (e.g. both the structural description and the structural change of a given rule can now just refer to the relevant parent node), rather than the representational one. Even if representations are still as rich as they were before, though, with Feature Geometry, trees enter the subsegmental scene.

As a matter of fact, trees have already been on the marketplace for phonological theories since a few years (see section 3.5 below). Indeed, assuming the Structural Analogy Hypothesis, whereby both morphosyntactic and phonological structures are represented as dependency relations holding between representational primitives, Anderson and Jones (1974) developed Dependency Phonology (henceforth DP; see also Anderson 1985, 1992; Anderson and Ewen 1987; van der Hulst 2006, 2011). Within such a model, the organization of features essentially parallels the one proposed by Clements (1985), with major nodes corresponding to laryngeal, manner and place categories. Differently from Feature Geometry, the representational primitives co-occurring under the relevant nodes are arranged according to a variable head-dependent schema: given two features α and β, the relationship they enter into can be either α- or β-headed, each corresponding to a (potentially contrastive) phonological expression. As a matter of fact, dependency

---

[1] According to Clements (1985: 230), this embodies the view according to which "the varying degrees of independence among phonetic features can be expressed by a hierarchical grouping such that higher-branching categories tend to be more independent than low-branching categories. More exactly, the relative independence of any two features of feature classes is correlated with the number of nodes that separate them".

[2] More recently, Bale et al. (submitted: 1) resort to set theory in a more explicit fashion: "taking [...] feature bundles to be sets [and natural classes sets of sets] allows us to apply ideas from set theory to phonology". This allows them to propose the reconceptualization of a fully underspecified segment as empty set, which, in turn, "can be used to define a natural class over all segments".

relations are suggested to hold also between nodes and sub-nodes. However, no restrictive theory constraining the various combinatorial possibilities has been developed, resulting in overgeneration; see van der Hulst (2006, 2011) for a brief discussion.

One difference between Feature Geometry and DP concerns the representational primitives, which are binary in the former case and unary in the latter. Furthermore, the primitives proposed by DP are "(in an Aristotelian sense) 'substances' in themselves rather than properties of substances'. Whereas mainstream binary features are arguably properties of segments, DP-primes are segments themselves. Indeed, such primes can occur independently as fully pronounceable phonological segments" (van der Hulst 2006: 455). Traditionally, these primes have been referred to as components, their primary phonetic interpretation being acoustic (e.g. "|V|, a component which can be defined as 'relatively periodic', and |C|, a component of 'periodic energy reduction'"; Anderson and Ewen 1987: 151).

Many DP proposals were further elaborated within e.g. Radical CV Phonology (henceforth RcvP: van der Hulst 1988, 1994, 1996, 2015) and Government Phonology (henceforth GP: Kaye *et al* 1990; Charette 1991; Lowenstamm 1996 and Scheer 2004). Both RcvP and GP maintain a similar conception of primes, which are unary, 'substantial' and combinable in head-dependent structures. RcvP and GP, though, attempt to solve the overgeneration problem DP suffered due to the lack of a constrained theory of primes (and their combinatorial possibilities). These frameworks proposed two different solutions, which are briefly described in what follows.

3.2 RcvP

In order to limit the generative power of the system developed within DP, RcvP capitalizes on a suggestion already present in Anderson and Ewen (1987), according to which a given component can occur under different nodes of the segmental tree. This is the case, for instance, for the |i| and |u| components, which are interpreted as high and low tone, respectively, when occurring under the tonological node (Anderson and Ewen 1987: 273).[3] The possibility for the same component to occur in various structural positions, in turn, allows for the formalization of similarities (same component) and differences (different structural position) among

---

[3] Interestingly, Anderson and Ewan (1987: 215) argues for the identity of |a| and |V|. As we will see below, this alleged identity is in line with our proposal, as well as with those proposed e.g. by Rennison (1998) within the GP camp.

(the phonetic interpretation of) segments. Together with the head-dependent asymmetry DP shares with Feature Geometry, this possibility allows for a further reduction of the number of components: a contrast previously formalized by e.g. two features can now be conveyed by one and the same component occurring in a head or dependent guise, or in different structural positions. For instance, the |V| component can translate [sonorant] and [voice] depending on its head vs dependent status, or it can identify sonorants, vowels, [low] and [open place] depending on its structural position.

RcvP exploits these possibilities to their maximal extent by constraining the typology of structures to head-dependent configurations of just two primes: |C| and |V| (against the |C|, |V|, |O| |G|, |K|, |i|, |u|, |a|, |@|, |A|, |l|, |t|, |d|, |r|, |L| and |n| of DP), which are organized in an arboreal structure such as the one in (18), where '|CxV|' means that |C| and |V| can combine, '|C   V|' that they cannot, and DP gestural labeled nodes (on the left; Clements 1985) are "defined in purely structural terms" (on the right), 'p.c.' and 's.c.' indicating the primary and secondary component, respectively; van der Hulst 2017):

(18) RcvP translation of DP segmental tree

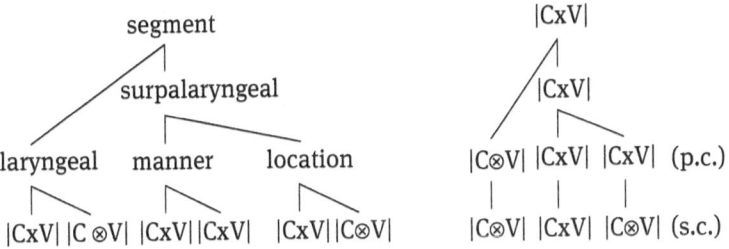

Notice that, even though RcvP, as DP, assumes that components have a default (acoustic) phonetic interpretation, |C| and |V| are assigned specific interpretations depending on their a) syllabic position (onset head vs onset dependent vs rhyme head vs rhyme dependent), b) class (manner vs location vs laryngeal), c) component status (primary vs secondary) and d) element status (head vs dependent). RcvP therefore comes as close to completely reducing the role of differences between elements as one can get without really abandoning the whole concept of elements completely. It does not seem to make sense, for instance, to develop a model with only *one* primitive. One can then only differentiate different structures by counting; and the same can be obtained by having no primitives at all.

3.3 GP and GP 2.0

As mentioned above, DP-style representational primitives are kept in both RcvP and GP, inasmuch as they all resort to unary primes which are acoustically grounded and combinable in head-dependent structure. In the GP literature, these primes are known as elements. Clearly rooted in DP (and Particle Phonology; Schane 1984), elements are introduced by Kaye et al (1985) and further developed along various directions, which differ in the element number and/or in the way elements can combine (see Backley 2012 for an overview and a brief discussion of the variants on the market).

In its standard form (Backley 2011), there are six elements, which are extensionally equivalent to the objects defined within RcvP by means of elements and (unlabeled) gestural nodes:

(19) GP vs. RcvP (van der Hulst 2017)

GP elements			
|?|		|A|	
|I|		|U|	
|H|		|L|	

RcvP elements			
Aperture		C	V
Location		C	V
Laryngeal (Phonation/Tone)		C	V

As discussed in the preceding section, the resort to an arboreal structure enriched with gestural nodes allows RcvP to shrink the number of elements to a binary set. Notice, however, that the gestural nodes constitute a sort of representational primitives themselves, even if of a different nature than components/elements. As a consequence, GP and RcvP display the same number of elements, the difference between the two theories consisting mostly in the presence *vs* absence, within the representational toolbox, of the gestural nodes. In other words, GP and RcvP differ in the relative balance between structure and substance: whereas GP decides to minimize structure and maximize substance (*viz* many elements on small trees), RcvP gets rid of most substance by maximally exploiting the structural dimension (*viz* a few elements on bigger trees).

Among the directions GP evolved into, variants can be found that try to reduce substance in a similar fashion.[4] One of the targets of Occam's razor is the |A| element, which is repeatedly shown to behave differently from other vocalic/resonance elements such as |I| and |U|. For instance, |A| is argued to be more syllabic than |I| and |U|, thereby showing a preference for occupying the head position of nuclei while avoiding the nuclear dependent position.[5] Furthermore, |A| is shown to interact with nasalization and length.[6]

As discussed above, the price to pay for substance reduction is structure enrichment. As a consequence, |A| is replaced by structure. For instance, in order to formalize the preference for |A| syllabicity, Rennison (1998) proposes to associate the phonetic counterpart previously related to |A| (i.e. a centrally converging F1–F2 acoustic pattern) with the presence of a nuclear position lacking any elemental specification (whose unmarked status is thus representationally encoded; see Cavirani and van Oostendorp 2017 for a similar proposal).

An even more extreme development of GP towards substance reduction is represented by what came to be known as GP 2.0 (Pöchtrager 2006; Živanović and Pöchtrager 2010; Kaye and Pöchtrager 2013; Schwartz 2010), which eliminates |H|, |ʔ| and |A| by resorting to structures and mechanisms inspired by syntactic analogues, such as control,[7] m-command[8] and head-adjunction. Let's focus now on |A| (referring the reader to Kaye and Pöchtrager 2013 for |H| and |ʔ|).

---

[4] While discussing the variants which resort to more elaborate arboreal structure to get rid of elements, Backley (2012: 75) warns that the standard theory "manages to strike a useful balance between the two, providing a restrictive model of phonological knowledge in which elements are abstract enough to function as cognitive units of linguistic structure yet concrete enough to be realized phonetically without the need for explicit rules of phonetic interpretation".

[5] As discussed in Backley (2012), this could be the reason why, for instance, diphthongs such as [ai] and [au] are typologically less marked than [ia] and [ua], which is in turn possibly related to the fact that only the latter diphthongs are reinterpreted as glide-vowel sequences. This shows that, whereas |I| and |U| may be (re)interpreted as belonging to the onset preceding the |A| nucleus, the same does not hold for |A|, which keep on projecting to its nuclear node.

[6] For instance, in French, where only |A| nuclei can be lengthened and nasalized (Ploch 1995).

[7] In Pöchtrager (2006:77) control is described as, "[an] unannotated x in a non-maximal onset projection must be controlled by its xO [*viz* the onset head]." In GP2.0 control is generalised to structures occurring in nuclear projections. Its general effect is that of making the controlled point inaccessible.

[8] Živanović and Pöchtrager (2010) define m-command as a sort of licensing necessary for phonetic interpretation, whereby terminals, i.e. elements or empty structural position, can be interpreted only if m-commanded. In the case of an empty structural position, m-command has the same effect of spreading, the commanded receiving the same phonetic interpretation of the commander.

As just mentioned, |A| is argued to display a special interaction with length: "more specifically, |A| seemed to make bigger structure possible" (Pöchtrager 2015: 261). As a matter of fact, what is traditionally referred to as |A| is formalized as pure structure, where the extra structure is guaranteed via head adjunction: "in the case of head adjunction, the head xN projects to another level but remains the same type, i.e. an xN" (Pöchtrager 2015: 261). This is shown in (20), where the arrow between xN and its sister (in [a]) represents control:

(20) GP 2.0 vocalic elements

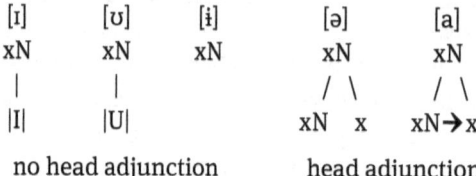

As shown in (20), both [ə] and [a] are represented as pure structure. The only difference is the presence in the latter of control, which is thus deemed the responsible for the [a]-interpretation of such an empty structure, otherwise sounding [ə]. Note that "the control relationship also expresses that within [a] both positions are used up, while in [ə] there is one position (the non-head) available. In some sense, [ə] takes up less room than [a]. This neatly capture Lowenstamm's (1996) observation that [ə] is the shorter version of [a][9]" (Pöchtrager 2015: 261). Furthermore, the lack of control in [ə] is considered to be the reason why it can be coloured by adjacent melody: the absence of control leaves "one position [...] available", which can thus host elements spreading from adjacent structures (e.g. in the analysis of Putonghua proposed in Živanovič and Pöchtrager 2010).

3.4 Comparison

As shown in the preceding sections, a research line can be identified within the DP-inspired tradition which aims at reducing substance by exploiting structure. This is particularly evident in the case of RcvP, which attempts at minimizing

---

[9] Note, also, that control is somehow analogous to standard GP headedness, whereby controllers head controlees. See Cavirani and van Oostendorp (2017) for a slightly different proposal on the structural relatedness of [a], [ə] and empty nuclei.

substance (only |C| and |V| are left) by enriching the structural dimension, whereas GP minimizes structure and maximizes substance (|ʔ|, |H|, |L|, |A|, |I| and |U|). Even within the latter, though, variants have been proposed that prefer to pay a little structural price to get rid of elements (which reduce to |I|, |U| and |L|).

Focusing on the vocalic half of the phonological world, we try to go even further by eliminating all the substantial content. More precisely, following the path initiated by DP and RcvP, we exploit the possibility for a given primitive to occur in different structural positions, the difference laying in the fact that, instead of components, we replace ("Aristotelian") substance with pure structure, namely with treelets which are recursively nested under other treelets.

This move echoes the attempts we mentioned above to reduce e.g. |a| to |V| (Anderson and Ewan 1987: 215) or |A| to empty nuclear positions (Rennison 1998). In a similar fashion, we propose a representational account of markedness whereby, differently from Rennison (1998), [ə] is represented as single-branched treelet hosting an empty node.

Furthermore, assuming that, as proposed e.g. by Lowenstamm (1996), Pöchtrager (2006) and Živanovič and Pöchtrager (2010), [ə] is the shorter version of [a] and that "|A| seemed to make bigger structure possible" (Pöchtrager 2015: 261), we represent [a] as a binary treelet containing two nodes that, in turn, host an empty node each. In prose, this means that [a] is tantamount to two schwas. This allow us to get rid of the control mechanism introduced by Pöchtrager (2006; 2015) and Živanovič and Pöchtrager (2010) to account for the difference between two sounds—[a] and [ə]—that are otherwise represented in an identical fashion. Note that we keep something similar to head-adjunction, even if, as a matter of fact, we do not need to make any head-dependent distinction.

Together with control, we can also get rid of the c-command solution proposed by Pöchtrager (2015) to solve the problems raised by the Complexity Condition[10] (Harris 1990). In a nutshell, the concerns of Harris (1990) and Pöchtrager (2015) relate to the preference for complex elemental structures to occupy the head position of diphthongs, thus for diphthongs' heads to contain |A|.

According to Pöchtrager (2015), the "problems [of Harris (1990) account] stem from a failure to take into account the individual nature of elements, their individual character". As a consequence, Pöchtrager (2015) proposes the

---

10 "a. Let α and β be segments occupying the positions A and B respectively. Then, if A governs B, β must not be more complex than α; b. The complexity value of a segment is simply calculated by determining the number of elements of which it is composed" (Harris 1990: 274).

structures in (20) as well as c-control, a mechanism evidently (though 'unfaithfully'[11]) borrowed from syntactic theory. In the present paper, rather than introducing c-command, we derive the same effect from the structural properties of 'elements', namely from their "individual nature": complex structures preferably contain [a] because its representation consists of two nodes that can be further expanded by adjoining additional vocalic structures (with the limitations discussed in section 1.2 above).

Similarly, the representations we propose for |I| and |U|, whereby only the former present expandable nodes (see (6)), might account for their asymmetrical behavior. This asymmetry is also discussed in Pöchtrager (2015: 258), who claims that "the English vowel system never allows combinations of |I| and |U| within some phonological expression. [This] is true for monophthongs [and] diphthongs".[12] As in the case of |A|, we encode this asymmetry in the representations we propose for |I| and |U|, rather than resorting to c-command, whereby "I can bind U, but U must not bind I", where "α binds β iff α c-commands β" (Pöchtrager 2015: 263).

With respect to standard element theory (Backley 2011), a crucial difference concerns phonetic interpretation. As we mentioned above, the standard theory provides "a restrictive model of phonological knowledge in which elements are abstract enough to function as cognitive units of linguistic structure yet concrete enough to be realized phonetically without the need for explicit rules of phonetic interpretation". Note that the more elements/substance we replace by structure, the more complex the phonetic interpretation procedure. Assuming strict modularity, though, whereby phonology and phonetics are two different realms and the former is translated into the latter in a lexical access fashion (Scheer 2014), this problem is perhaps not that dangerous. If anything, there would be an issue of learnability, which is arguably much simpler assuming that primes are at the same time cognitive *and* concrete units, as per the element standard theory.

---

11 As recognized by Pöchtrager (2015: 270) himself, "syntactic binding is about co-reference, while phonological bounding [is about] distributional restrictions on melody". There seem to be other problems with binding and c-command as well, as c-command (alone) is not enough, for it needs an extra mechanism to constrain its application domain (for this reason, c-command has been 'expanded' into the c++command in Živanovič and Pöchtrager 2010). However, "the locality of binding cannot be captured by this alone, but also by no other command relationship I can envision. How this boundedness is formally captured is another question" (Pöchtrager 2015: fn 11).

12 Other asymmetries listed by Pöchtrager (2015), which can be accounted for by our representational proposal, are the fact that Turkish has a) two /e/'s but only one /o/ and b) a |U|-harmony that is more restricted than |I|-harmony.

4 Conclusion: Substance as structure

From one fairly simple definition in (1), we can derive a theory that seems to mimic the results of known Element Theories. However, this theory has two properties that are seemingly disadvantageous. First, it does not seem to add a lot of new empirical coverage to what we know from Element Theory, also because the latter is fairly successful. Secondly, although the theory we present is extremely simple, it leads to representations of even simple vowels like /ɔ/ that are rather difficult to read (such as those in (17)).

In other words, our graph theoretic definition gives a notational variant of existing theories in an obtuse notation. So why would it be helpful to consider this? We believe that in most practical analyses it will be more useful to write vowels in terms of familiar |I|, |A|, |U| representations, but the set theoretic definition gives us insight into the internal structure of these elements: why there are three of them, why only one of them can fully embed, whereas the other two are heavily deficient in this respect and, possibly, why we have at most 4 degrees of vowel height. We thus get a deeper insight into the reason why elements function a certain way that would not be available if we treat them as completely primitive, atomic elements. At the same time, for studying e.g. the vowel set of a particular language, we may not always need to know why elements function in some way. This is of course familiar from most kinds of (linguistic) analysis. For instance, for the analysis of stress, we typically do not need to give the full internal structure of all vowels involved: we use the 'higher-order' representation of IPA symbols with the understanding that these stand for combinations of elements. On the other hand, sometimes certain features may be relevant for the assignment of stress (like height features, or tone).

Our theory is similarly a theory of vocalic elements; it aims to explain the properties of these elements, but in the everyday business of phonological analysis, it may not be necessary to refer to them all the time.

Notice that, since our system has definite properties, it is not compatible with all the possible interpretations of element theory. For instance, it is impossible to introduce a notion like 'headedness' into the system without making crucial changes to it. The kind of asymmetry that headedness applies can only come about by an extra theoretical device that is not available in the current theory.

References

Adelson-Velsky, Georgy and Evgenii Landis. 1962. An algorithm for the organization of information. *Proceedings of the USSR Academy of Sciences* (in Russian) 146, 263–266. [English translation by Myron J. Ricci in Soviet Math. Doklady 3,1259–1263].
Anderson, John and Charles Jones. 1974. Three theses concerning phonological representations. *Journal of Linguistics* 10, 1–26.
Anderson, John and Colin J. Ewen. 1987. *Principles of Dependency Phonology*. Cambridge: Cambridge University Press.
Anderson, Stephen. 1985. *Phonology in the Twentieth Century: Theories of Rules and Theories of Representations*. Chicago, IL: The University of Chicago Press.
Backley Phillip. 2011. *An Introduction to Element Theory*. Edinburgh: Edinburgh University Press.
Backley Phillip. 2012. Variation in Element Theory. *Linguistic Variation* 12(1),57–102.
Bale, Alan, Charles Reiss and David Ta-Chun Shen. Submitted. Sets, rules and natural classes: { } vs. [ ].
Botma, Bert and Marc van Oostendorp. 2012. A propos of the Dutch vowel system 21 years on, 22 years on. In Bert Botma and Roland Noske (eds.), *Phonological Explorations: Empirical, Theoretical and Diachronic Issues*. Berlin: Mouton de Gruyter.
Cavirani, Edoardo and Marc van Oostendorp. 2017. The markedness of silence. In Bridget Samuels (ed.), *Beyond Markedness in Formal Phonology*. Amsterdam: John Benjamins, 101–120.
Charette, Monik. 1991. *Conditions on phonological government*. Cambridge: Cambridge University Press.
Chomsky, Noam and Morris Halle. 1968. *The Sound Pattern of English*. New York: Harper and Row.
Clements, George. N. 1985. The geometry of phonological features. *Phonology Yearbook* 2, 225–252.
Crothers, John. 1978. Typology and universals of vowel systems in phonology. In Joseph H. Greenberg, Charles A. Ferguson and Edith A. Moravcsik (eds.), *Universals of Human Language: Phonology, Vol. 2*. Stanford: Stanford University Press, 95–152.
Harris, John. 1990. Segmental complexity and phonological government. *Phonology* 7, 255–300.
Harris, John and Geoff Lindsey. 2000. Vowel patterns in mind and sound. In Noel Burton-Roberts, Philip Carr and Gerry Docherty (eds), *Phonological Knowledge: Conceptual and Empirical Issues*. Oxford: Oxford University Press, 185–205.
Hulst, Harry G. van der. 1988. The geometry of vocalic features. In Harry G. van der Hulst and Noval Smith (eds.), *Features, Segmental Structure and Harmony Processes*. Dordrecht: Foris, 77–126
Hulst, Harry G. van der. 1994. An introduction to Radical CV Phonology. In Susanna Shore and Maria Vilkuna (eds.), *SKY 1994: Yearbook of the Linguistic Association of Finland*. Helsinki, 23–56.
Hulst, Harry G. van der. 1996. Radical CV Phonology: the segment – syllable connection. In Jacques Durand and Bernard Laks (eds.). *Current Trends in Phonology: Models and Methods, Vol 1*, 333–363. CNRS/ESRI Paris X.
Hulst, Harry G. van der. 2006. Dependency Phonology. In Keith Brown (ed.), *The Encyclopedia of Language and Linguistics, 2nd edition, Volume 3*, 451–458. Oxford: Elsevier.

Hulst, Harry G. van der. 2011. Dependency-based phonologies. In John A. Goldsmith, Jason Riggle and Alan Yu (eds.), *The Handbook of Phonological Theory*, 2nd edition, 533–570. Malden, MA: Wiley-Blackwell.

Hulst, Harry G. van der. 2015. The opponent principle in RcvP: binarity in a unary system. In Eric Raimy and Charles Cairns (eds.), *The Segment in Phonetics and Phonology*, 149–179. Chichester: Wiley-Blackwell.

Hulst, Harry G. van der. 2017. The integration of segmental and syllabic structure in Radical CV Phonology. Paper presented at the workshop The Interface Within. What relations hold between prosody and melody?, Meertens Institute, Amsterdam, The Netherlands (13 March 2017).

Kaye, Jonathan D., Jean Lowenstamm and Jean-Roger Vergnaud. 1985. The internal structure of phonological representations: a theory of charm and government. *Phonology Yearbook* 2, 305–328.

Kaye, Jonathan D., Jean Lowenstamm and Jean-Roger Vergnaud. 1990. Constituent structure and government in phonology. *Phonology* 7, 193–231.

Kaye Jonathan D. and Markus Pöchtrager. 2009. *GP 2.0*. Paper presented at the Government Phonolog Round Table 2009, Piliscsaba, Hungary.

Kaye, Jonathan D. and Markus Pöchtrager. 2013. GP 2.0. *SOAS Working Papers in Linguistics* 16, 51–64.

Lowenstamm, Jean. 1996. CV as the only syllable type. In Jacques Durand and Bernard Laks (eds.), *Current Trends in Phonology: Models and Methods*, 419–442. Salford: European Studies Research Institute, University of Salford Publications.

Nasukawa, Kuniya. 2015. Recursion in the lexical structure of morphemes. In Marc van Oostendorp and Henk van Riemsdijk (eds.), *Representing Structure in Phonology and Syntax*, 211–238. Berlin and Boston: Mouton de Gruyter.

Ploch, Stefan. 1995. French nasal vowels: a first approach. *SOAS Working Papers in Linguistics* 5, 91–106.

Pöchtrager, Markus A. 2006. The structure of length. Ph.D. dissertation, University of Vienna.

Pöchtrager, Markus A. 2010. Does Turkish diss harmony? *Acta Linguistica Hungarica* 57(4), 458–473.

Pöchtrager, Markus A. 2012. Deconstructing A. Paper presented at the MFM Fringe Meeting on Segmental Architecture, Manchester, U.K.

Pöchtrager, Markus A. 2015. Binding in phonology. Marc van Oostendorp and Henk van Riemsdijk (eds.), *Representing Structure in Phonology and Syntax*, 255–275. Berlin and Boston: Mouton de Gruyter.

Reiss, Charles. 2017. Substance Free Phonology. In S. J. Hannahs and Anna R. K. Bosch (eds.), *Handbook of Phonological Theory*, 425–452. London: Routledge.

Rennison, John R. 1998. Contour segments without subsegmental structures. In Eugeniusz Cyran (ed.), *Structure and Interpretation: Studies in Phonology*, 227–245. Lublin: Folium.

Schane, Sanford A. 1984. The fundamentals of Particle Phonology. *Phonology Yearbook* 1, 129–155.

Scheer, Tobias. 2004. *A Lateral Theory of Phonology: What is CVCV, and Why Should It Be?* Berlin and New York: Mouton de Gruyter.

Scheer, Tobias. 2012. *Melody-free syntax and two phonologies*. Paper presented at the Annual Conference of the Réseau Français de Phonologie (RFP), Paris (25–27 June 2012).

Scheer, Tobias. 2014. Spell-out, post-phonological. In Eugeniusz Cyran and Jolanta Szpyra-Kozlowska (eds.), *Crossing Phonetics-Phonology Lines*, 255–275. Newcastle upon Tyne: Cambridge Scholars Publishing.

Schwartz, Geoff (2010). Auditory representations and the structures of GP 2.0. *Acta Linguistica Hungarica* 57(4), 381–397.

Živanović, Sašo and Markus A. Pöchtrager. 2010. GP 2, and Putonghua too. *Acta Linguistica Hungarica* 57(4), 357–380.

Marcel den Dikken and Harry van der Hulst
On some deep structural analogies between syntax and phonology

1 Introduction

A commonly held view in theoretical linguistics is that the formal organization of phonology is fundamentally different from that of syntax. Claims to that effect in the literature concern either representational aspects or derivational ones (cf. Halle and Bromberger 1989: phonology has extrinsic rule ordering, syntax does not). In the representational domain, it is customary to state that whereas recursion is a fundamental property of syntax, phonological structure is non-recursive:

> Recursion consists of embedding a constituent in a constituent of the same type, for example a relative clause inside a relative clause (.....). This does not exist in phonological structure: a syllable, for instance, cannot be embedded in another syllable. (Pinker and Jackendoff 2005: 10)

> syntax has recursive structures, whereas phonology does not. (Neeleman and van de Koot 2006: 1524)

> syllabic structure is devoid of anything resembling recursion. (Bickerton 2000)

Neeleman and van de Koot (2006: 1524), as well as Scheer (2013), even reject the idea that phonological organization appeals to any notion of constituency; see also Carr (2006) for skepticism regarding syntax/phonology parallelism.

Contrary to these views, it has been remarked more than once that there is an 'obvious' parallelism between the structure of syllables (with an onset/rhyme division, and a division between nucleus and coda in the latter) and the structure of a 'simple' sentence (Kurylowicz 1948, Pike and Pike 1947, Fudge 1987):

(1) a. 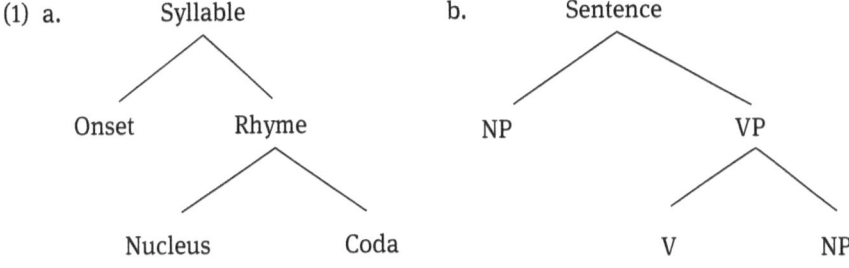   b.

Carstairs-McCarthy (1999) speculates that the structure of syllables may have served as a model for syntax in the course of language evolution, a view that is criticized in Tallerman (2006), who also doubts that the parallelism is real, let alone that syntax copied phonology; Bickerton (2000), in his review of Carstairs-McCarthy (1999), shares this latter view. Despite these objections, various phonologists have pursued the parallelism in (1), and more specifically a parallelism between (1a) and canonical X-bar structure (see (2), below).[1] Völtz (1999) proposes an X-bar model for syllable structure that explicitly proposes that both the Onset and the Coda can form maximal projections, as in (3) (where 'O' stands for 'Onset', 'P' for 'Peak' (i.e. Nucleus), and 'C' for 'Coda'):

(2)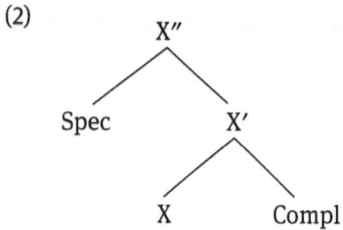

(3) Universal structure of the syllable

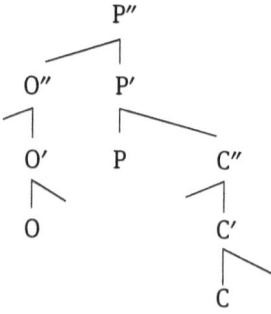

---

[1] Levin (1985) pursues this idea, although in her conception of phonological X-bar structure, the head nucleus can itself be a branching unit (Levin 1985: 105ff.), which runs counter to standard X-bar theory. We also note that she admits various levels of adjunction (leading to an iteration of the maximal N″ level; see p. 163) to deal with word-final consonant clusters. We will appeal to adjunction in this work as well.

It may be useful to point out at this early stage in the paper that our adoption of standard X-bar theory in what follows does not put us into conflict with current minimalist syntax. X-bar theory is still a staple of generative syntactic theory today, notwithstanding Chomsky's (1994, 1995: 4) 'bare phrase structure', which aimed to make the bar levels and possibly also the labels redundant: in current minimalist theorizing, both head/phrase distinctions and node labels continue to play a central role (see Chomsky 2013). X-bar theory is such a useful representational vehicle because it regularises recursion in a particularly simple and transparent way, directly codifying the fundamental phrase structure properties of *endocentricity* and *projection*.

Whatever the merit of these parallels, no mention is made of a potential further parallelism that would involve **recursion**. To avoid miscommunication and controversy, it will be important to be clear on what is meant by 'recursion'. By 'recursion' is understood the containment/embedding of a complex structure inside a larger complex structure of the same type (see e.g. van der Hulst 2010a). Thus [$_A$ B [$_C$ D [$_E$ F G]]] instantiates recursion: the complex structure labelled 'A' contains another complex structure of the same type, labelled 'C', which in turn embeds another complex structure of the same type, labelled 'E'. Nodes A, C and E are representationally constituted in the same way: we are dealing with the 'Russian doll' structure characteristic of recursion. Note that when it comes to the question of whether nodes A, C and E are of the same type, what matters is their *geometrical properties* – NOT their label. It is certainly imaginable that A, C and E have the same label (in which case we are dealing with 'self-embedding' recursion). But even if A, C and E do not have the same label, the structure [$_A$ B [$_C$ D [$_E$ F G]]] is still recursive. In what follows, 'recursion' is understood in its most inclusive sense.

Most writers, while acknowledging that phonotactic structure is constituency-based (and making reference to X-bar(ish) organization of syllables), propose that phonological (often called 'prosodic') constituency is 'strictly layered', which means that no constituent contains a constituent of the same type. This explicitly bars (self-embedding) recursion. With reference to 'higher' phonological/prosodic structure, recursion *has* been recognized, but here it is then said to reflect the recursive structure of syntax, at least to some extent (Ladd 1996 [2008], Wagner 2005, van der Hulst 2010b, Hunyadi 2010).[2] Limiting recursion in phonology to units that have morpho-syntactic structure is tantamount to saying that no recursion will be found *within* morphemes (or simplex words), where whatever structure exists cannot be a mapping from morpho-syntactic structure.

However, some phonologists – whose proposals differ in several ways that will not concern us here – have argued that syllable structure can display recursion (Smith 1999, 2003; Garcia-Bellido 2005; van de Weijer and Zhang 2008; van der Hulst 2010b). Following van der Hulst's (2010b) cue, the present chapter will support the idea that syllable structure shares non-trivial properties with syntactic structure (parallels that cannot have been inherited from syntactic phrasing), including, crucially, recursion. We will resolve certain problems that arise for van der Hulst's original proposal, which will lead us to introduce structural properties in syllable structure that mirror aspects of more current versions of syntactic

---

[2] In section 6 we briefly discuss the question as to what limits phonological recursivity in morpho-syntactically structured expressions.

structure, specifically proposing a parallel to the so-called 'light *v*' of current 'minimalist' syntactic inquiry.

Our principal conclusion is that there is only one syntactic (or 'computational') system which underlies both phonological structure and morpho-syntactic structure (as well as operations). Whatever differences are found between the two systems are primarily due to the fact that both modules differ in their basic alphabet. Thus, we support what John Anderson calls 'The Structural Analogy Assumption' (SAA: Anderson 1987):

(4) The Structural Analogy Assumption
The same structural properties are to be associated with different levels of representation except for differences which can be attributed to the different character of the alphabet involved (as in the case of planes) or to the relationship between the two levels (as may be the case with any pair of levels), including their domains.

Here 'planes' refers to syntax and phonology. Structural analogy holding between levels within planes will not be our concern here. Anderson pursues the SAA within a dependency framework. Van der Hulst (2005, in prep.) develops Anderson's dependency approach in his Radical CV Phonology model. While Anderson works within a dependency model (which, crucially, does not recognize constituency), we examine parallels between syntax and phonology from a headed constituency perspective. We will not dwell on this issue here. Our main thesis ('there is only one syntactic system') can be worked out in different ways depending on the precise syntactic and phonological structures that we compare. In both domains, there has always been, and will continue to be, development, which, at times, may suggest that there are no analogies at all, or that resemblances are trivial or coincidental. As a consequence, the recovery of pervasive analogies may require presenting structure in one domain or the other in perhaps novel ways, which may lead to new perspectives on the representation in either domain. In this chapter, we take a particular proposal for syntactic structure as our point of departure, showing that parallel structures may shed new light on phonological phenomena.

Though in this chapter our focus will be on syllable structure, we will also address segmental structure, including the potential interweaving of both levels. In this context, we will discuss the applicability of X-bar structure within phonological segments, as in (4b) (van der Hulst 2005):

(5) a.

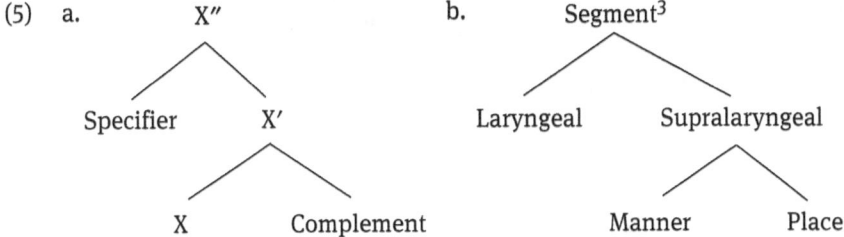

The chapter is organized as follows. In section 2 we will begin with outlining a proposal made in van der Hulst (2010b). Section 3 then develops this idea in more depth, leading to a proposal to import 'light v' structures into the representation of syllables and feet. In Section 4, we show how the model accounts for different types of 'foot structure' (trochaic, iambic, coordinate). Section 5 discusses segment-*internal* X-bar structure (cf. (5)). Here we also address the issue of 'segmental integrity', i.e. whether segmental structure and syllable structure are strictly separated or rather, as we will argue, integrated. In section 6 we offer an explanation for the fact that recursion in phonology is less pervasive than in syntax. Section 7 offers our main conclusions.

2 Van der Hulst (2010)

The central point of van der Hulst (2010) lies in a particular construal of the idea that so-called 'Codas' can be entire syllables. Adopting his 'C/V notation',[4] van der Hulst (2010b) proposes the structure in (6b) rather than the more traditional (6a) for a 'monosyllabic' word like Dutch *kan* 'can'. In approaches such as Government Phonology, especially those versions that adhere to a strict CV principle, such a monosyllabic word would be a sequence of two 'syllables' (or Onset/Rhyme 'packages'), which could then be taken to form a structure or lateral relation comparable to a 'trochaic foot':

---

3 This structure follows the original proposal in Clements (1985). van der Hulst (2005) argues that the later idea to abandon a manner node (attaching manner features directly to the root node) should not be followed.

4 Note that we are not claiming in this paper that all of language is built up from Cs and Vs. This is a specific proposal for phonology. It may be that phonology and syntax could ultimately be tackled with the help of the same two primitives in both domains (and that the labels for these primitives should be different from 'C' and/or 'V'), but this is not under discussion here. This chapter is about representation, not substance.

(6) a.

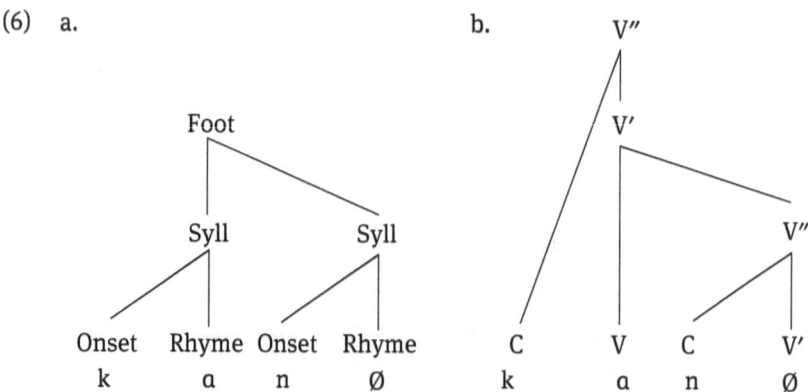

b.

In the notation in (5b) the labels 'C' and 'V' are analogous to the labels 'N' and 'V' in syntax; they are phonological categories to which segmental units can be associated. Taking the V unit to be the head of a syllable (which therefore, as a whole, belongs to the category V as well), Codas are complements, which are thus expected to be maximal projections (cf. (2)). The crucial point in (6b) is that the complement of the V-head is a maximal V-projection (in short, a complete syllable).

The next step in van der Hulst's proposal is to adopt the same kind of structure for more obviously disyllabic strings such as Dutch *káno* 'canoe', as in (7). This establishes a perfect isomorphism between a 'closed syllable' and a branching foot, which, from a metrical point of view, behave as units of stress in languages, such as Dutch, in which 'closed syllables' are heavy for stress. This equivalence is widely acknowledged, yet does not find a formal basis in any other model, although so-called moraic models capture the equivalence by referring to the fact that a closed syllables contain two morae, on a par with a sequence of two light syllables.[5]

---

[5] A different proposal for the structural equivalence between CVC 'heavy syllables' and CVCV (feet) can be found in Ulfsbjorninn (2015) within the 'strict CV' Government Phonology model.

(7) a.   b.

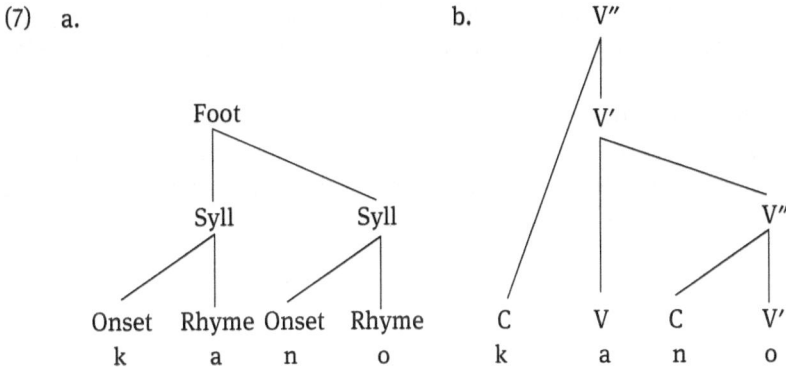

The embedding of syllables inside syllables does not have to stop here. A full structure of a so-called ternary foot, sometimes referred to as a 'superfoot' (as in English *vanity*), displays degree-2 embedding.

(8)

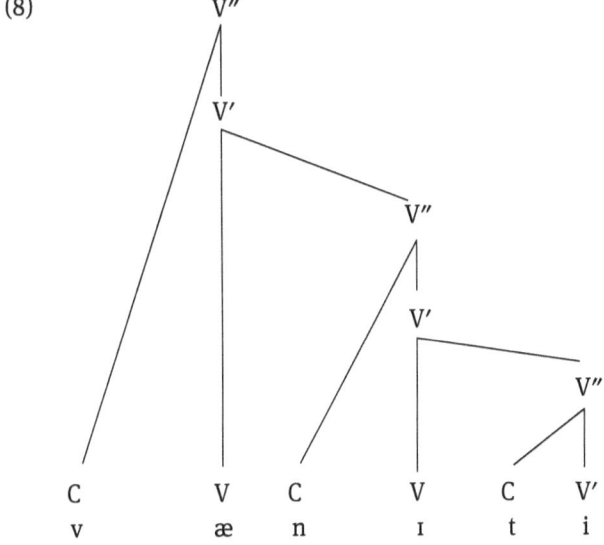

This structure is a perfectly legitimate object also in, for example, English *Winnepesaukee*, *hippopotamus*. An interesting consequence of this proposal is that it is now immediately clear why in poetic rhyming the initial Onset can be ignored, but not the second (or indeed the third, in forms like *sanity* ~ *vanity*). The initial consonant of such structures is external to the whole sequence that forms the rhyming unit. The structure in (8) formally captures the rhyming unit as well as the special position of the initial Onset (which can or must be different), as opposed to the other more deeply embedded Onsets (which must be identical).

The preceding proposal faces one problem: a matrix syllable can itself be a 'closed syllable' (as in *banjo*; in (9) we represent the Dutch pronunciation), which would seem to leave no room for the closing /n/ consonant, given that the 'Coda' position in (9b) is taken by the syllable /jo/:

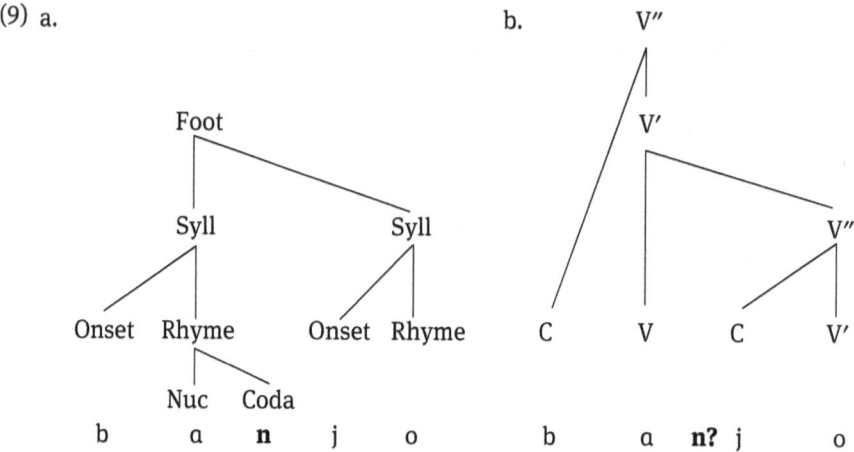

Three apparent 'solutions' present themselves, which we will briefly discuss (and dismiss) in the ensuing paragraphs.

Firstly, one might consider adjoining to /n/ to the syllable head, thus forming a branching 'Nucleus'. But this would destroy the X-bar analogy since the head of an X-bar projection must be 'atomic'; it cannot itself contain a full X-bar-theoretic internal structure (there are no phrases within heads).[6]

A second possibility would be to embrace a proposal by Botma, Ewen, and van der Torre (2008), where an analysis is given for a range of facts clustering around postvocalic liquid+stop sequences in English. One of the more striking properties of such sequences is that when they occur after a long tense vowel or diphthong, the stop must be coronal (see (10a)). For postvocalic liquid+stop sequences that occur after a short vowel, no such coronality restriction applies, as (10b) shows.

---

[6] We ignore at this juncture the segment-internal complexity of the nuclear vowel itself; we return to this issue in section 5.

(10) a. wield   /wi:ld/   colt   /kəʊlt/
     *wielk */wi:lk/ *colp */kəʊlp/
  b. silt   /sɪlt/   Celt   /kɛlt/
     silk   /sɪlk/   kelp   /kɛlp/

The well-known generalization that lies behind these data is that tense vowels are equivalent to lax vowel + one consonant. As such both 'exhaust' the bipositional rhyme. Word-finally, bipositional rhymes can be followed by one 'extra' consonant (as in *team* or *film*, where the extra consonant is /m/ in both cases) and 'extra' coronal consonants (traditionally referred to as the 'appendix'; see Fudge 1987), raising the question how these 'extras' are structurally represented.

Botma et al. (2008) argue that in *wield* the 'extra' liquid and the 'appendix' /d/ can form an onset to a (silent-headed) second syllable, with the liquid being an 'Onset Specifier'. The two consonants are said to end up in a *Specifier-Head agreement* relation, which is taken to account for the fact that the stop (the head of the Onset) and the liquid (the Onset Specifier) will share their place specification:

(11)   (= Botma et al.'s (26))

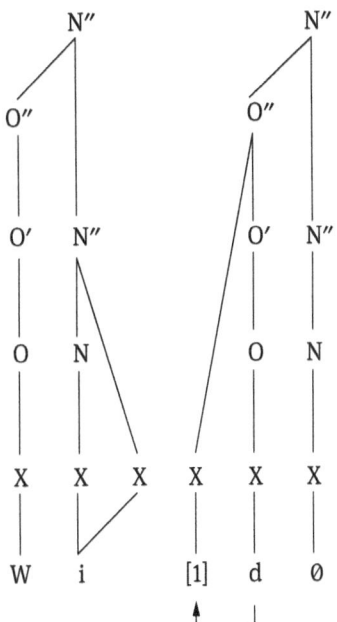

Applied to the case at hand, one might consider extending this idea to the structure of *banjo* as follows:[7]

(12) a.

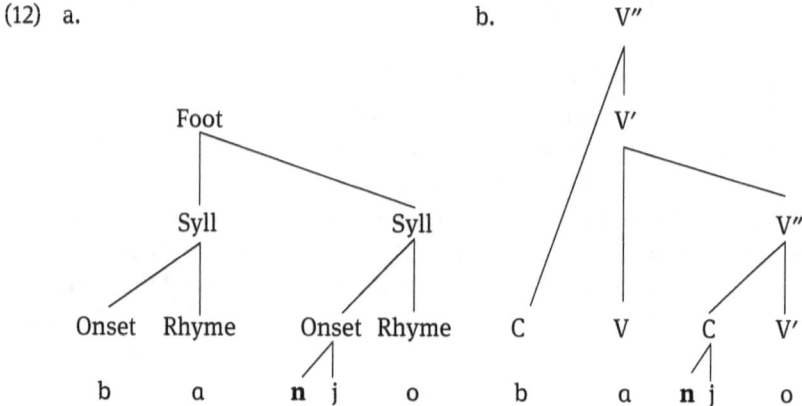

A problem with this idea is that sequences such as /ld/ and /nj/ systematically fail to serve as Onsets of word-initial syllables in English and Dutch (i.e., there are no words beginning with *ld* or *nj*). While differences between word-initial and medial onsets do exist, it is then usually the case that word-initial onsets display more options, not fewer; e.g. in Dutch /kn/ is possible word-initially, but not word-medially; see Trommelen (1983) and van der Hulst (1984). Also, the appeal made by Botma et al. to Specifier-Head agreement to force the stop to be coronal seems to us to be a misapplication of a syntactic notion to phonological analysis. To the extent that relations of Specifier-Head agreement arise in syntax, they are found only in *functional* structures (the head I usually agrees with SpecIP, C sometimes agrees with SpecCP), not in lexical ones ('object agreement' is by no means rare cross-linguistically, but arguably implicates a functional head outside the lexical core); and phonology arguably lacks anything corresponding to functional structure in syntax (see the opening paragraph of section 3.2, below).[8]

---

[7] They do not consider, nor will we here, postulating an 'empty nucleus' between the /n/ and /j/, arriving at a 'trisyllabic' structure, as would, or could, be adopted in a (strict CV) government approach; but see fn.8.

[8] A third issue that arises in connection with Botma et al.'s (2008) proposal is that these authors explicitly do not exclude a representation for *wield* in which the liquid (now realized as a 'dark' [ɫ]) is mapped by itself into the Coda position of the second syllable in a trisyllabic sequence, with the stop as the Onset of the third syllable; see their (27). Apart from the fact that this creates structural ambiguity, it would seem that there is now nothing about the structure

A third approach would be to give embedded syllables a 'complementizer' position, which could contain the 'Coda' consonant. But this would again entail an introduction into phonological structure of functional layers, which seems to us unwarranted. We return to this lack of analogy between syntax and phonology in the next section, where we propose to 'enlighten' phonology with the introduction of a parallel to the syntactic notion of 'light *v*'.

3 Enlightened phonology: The benefits of 'light *v*' in phonology

3.1 'Light *v*' in syntax: A brief historical perspective

In syntax, the external argument of the verb is different in a number of fundamental ways from the verb's internal argument(s). Thus, the internal argument(s) can influence the aspectual (*Aktionsart*) properties of the sentence but the external argument never does; and the verb can form an idiomatic expression together with its internal argument(s) but not with its external argument. Such pervasive asymmetries led Kratzer (1996) to hypothesize that the external argument is *radically* external to the 'minimal VP': it is introduced in the specifier of an extension of the core verbal phrase.[9] Kratzer called this extension 'VoiceP', based on the insight that the external argument is syntactically projected only in certain voices (the active, perhaps the passive, but certainly not the middle voice or *vox media*). Chomsky (1995) bought into the idea that the external argument is severed from the core verbal phrase, and called the extension of VP in whose specifier the external argument is introduced '*v*P', where '*v*' is a 'light verb' merged immediately with VP. This *v* is a lexical head in the sense that it plays a key role in the syntactic deployment of the argument structure of the verb. In this respect, it is fundamentally different from purely functional categories such as I(nfl) or C(omp).

---

in which the liquid and the stop are mapped into different syllables that could be held responsible for the shared coronality of the liquid and the following stop: the two are not in a Spec-Head agreement relation here.

9 We note on the side that the external argument is often externalized further, to SpecIP. But relying on such externalization cannot suffice to ensure across the board that the external argument is different from the internal argument(s) in ways that involve argument and event structure: even when the external argument is not raised to SpecIP (as e.g. in transitive expletive constructions such as Dutch *Er at iemand een appel* '(lit.) there ate someone an apple, someone was eating an apple'), it still behaves differently from the internal argument(s) in these ways.

Severing the external argument from V gives the VP more space to accommodate internal arguments, along the lines of Larson's (1988) original proposal for the syntax of ditransitive constructions: with the specifier position of V no longer needed for the introduction of the external argument, it can be used for one of the internal arguments of the verb. Larson (1988) and Hale and Keyser (1993) converge on the conclusion that the SpecVP position, when filled by an argument at D-structure, is reserved for the Theme argument (the argument of which a (change of) state or position is predicated, as in *John broke the vase* and *The vase broke*: in both sentences, *the vase* is introduced in SpecVP; in the second example, it is raised from there to SpecIP). In keeping with the Uniformity of Theta Assignment Hypothesis (UTAH; Baker 1988), which says that identical thematic relations between items are represented by identical structural relations between those items at the level of D-structure, there is a tight connection between base-generation of an argument in SpecVP and the Theme role. The complement-of-V position is used for non-Theme material: an argument projected in this position can be a Patient (as in *John hit Bill*) or a propositional argument (as in *Bob saw [that John hit Bill]*); non-arguments (including secondary predicates, such as the *to*-PP in prepositional dative constructions, and on Larson's assumptions even certain adverbial modifiers) can also be merged in the complement-of-V position. Apparently V is rather flexible regarding the relations between itself and its complement.[10] The UTAH has always been most successful with respect to predicate–argument relations involving specifier positions: SpecVP is tied one-to-one to the Theme role, Spec*v*P is usually (and, depending on one's approach to sentences such as *John fears snakes*, with an Experiencer subject, perhaps exclusively) tied to the Agent role. The link between the complement-of relation and thematic roles is much more obscure. Until more is known about the thematic properties of the complement-of relation, it will be sensible to confine the scope of the UTAH to specifiers:

(13) **Uniformity of Theta Assignment Hypothesis (UTAH)** (specifier-only version)
Specifier positions in the lexical core[11] are associated with unique thematic content in underlying representations.

---

10 We see this flexibility also in our discussion of the structure of the phonological *v*-VP: the complement-of-V position in phonology can be filled by a variety of different consonant types, and by 'propositional arguments' (i.e. dependent syllables in trochaic feet).
11 By 'the lexical core' in syntactic structures, we mean minimally the root-VP, perhaps plus its 'light' extension *v*P but excluding functional projections higher up the tree. It should be

Interestingly, as soon as the complement-of-V position is taken, an additional argu-ment of the verb that is not its external argument must be projected in SpecVP, and will, in keeping with (13), necessarily be construed as a Theme. This explains straightforwardly that *John hit Bill* and *John hit Bill unconscious* are minimally different with respect to the thematic role of *Bill*: in the former sentence, where *Bill* is in the complement-of-V position, *Bill* is the Patient; in the latter, with the secondary predicate *unconscious* now occupying the complement-of-V position, *Bill* must be mapped into the SpecVP position, and is interpreted as the Theme.

To summarize, the projection of the 'light verb' v in syntax is an extension of the lexical VP and harbors the external argument (Agent) of the verb, freeing up the SpecVP position for the projection of the Theme, and the complement-of-V position for the introduction of non-Theme dependents of the verb. The range of possible verb phrases with an external argument that the 'light verb' hypothesis gives rise to can be summarized as follows:[12]

(14) a. [$_{vP}$ DP$_{Agent}$ [$_{v'}$ v [$_{VP}$ [$_{V'}$ V]]]]   *John laughed*
     b. [$_{vP}$ DP$_{Agent}$ [$_{v'}$ v [$_{VP}$ [$_{V'}$ V DP$_{Patient}$]]]]   *John hit Bill*
     c. [$_{vP}$ DP$_{Agent}$ [$_{v'}$ v [$_{VP}$ DP$_{Theme}$ [$_{V'}$ V]]]]   *John killed Bill*
     d. [$_{vP}$ DP$_{Agent}$ [$_{v'}$ v [$_{VP}$ DP$_{Theme}$ [$_{V'}$ V Pred]]]]   *John hit Bill unconscious*
                                                                                      John hit Bill into the hospital
                                                                                      John gave a book to Bill
     e. [$_{vP}$ DP$_{Agent}$ [$_{v'}$ v [$_{VP}$ [$_{V'}$ V CP]]]]   *Bob saw that John hit Bill*
     f. [$_{vP}$ DP$_{Agent}$ [$_{v'}$ v [$_{VP}$ [$_{V'}$ V [$_{SC}$ DP Pred]]]]]   *Bob saw John hit Bill*

---

noted that the most successful applications of UTAH have always been focused on the relation between SpecVP and the Theme role, which does indeed seem to be very strict: any argument externally merged in SpecVP is a Theme. For the external argument, things are less clear cut: much depends on how microscopic one's view of the structure of the lexical core outside VP is. Observationally, external arguments of verbal constructs can be Agents (as in *John hit Bill*) or Cause(r)s (as in *The earthquake destroyed the village* or *John accidentally broke the vase*) or Experiencers (as in *John fears snakes*). Different flavors of v can be introduced to differentiate between Agents and Cause(r)s, and Experiencers could possibly be introduced as internal arguments and externalized via raising (cf. *Snakes frighten John*). Our focus here, as in the discussion of syllable structure, will be on the restrictions imposed on SpecVP.

12 In all of these structures, 'DP' stands for 'Determiner Phrase' (the 'noun phrase' including any and all of its functional attributes), and the subscript on DP references the thematic role borne by the argument in question. In (14f), 'SC' stands for 'small clause'. In addition to these verb phrase types, there may also be the possibility of not projecting v and, as a consequence, not having an external argument. This may be what characterizes the syntax of unaccusative/ergative constructions. We will not need to concern ourselves with these here.

The *v*-VP structure forms an integral part of syntactic structures. The 'light verb' extension of the lexical VP is a key ingredient in our understanding of thematic relations as well as event structure and aspect. To this *v*-VP structure, adverbial material can be adjoined, and outside it functional projections can be introduced, such as IP and CP, whose role it is to regulate properties of syntactic constructs that are not the purview of the argument-structural core, such as inflection, negation, mood and modality, question formation, and variation in linearization.

3.2 'Light *v*' in phonology: Preliminary remarks

Throughout this work, we explore the possibility that phonology projects X-bar structures entirely analogous to those recognized in syntax. To be sure, phonological and syntactic structures are not fully on a par: arguably, phonology entirely lacks the kinds of *functional* projections to which we alluded at the end of the previous paragraph. Phonological structures employ the basic 'argument-structural' layers and their complement and specifier positions, and they may also make fruitful use of the adjunction operation to bring in additional material that cannot be accommodated in the complement and specifier positions in the *v*-VP structure.[13] But there is no obvious role to play in phonology for functional projections such as IP and CP, whose specifier positions are usually not filled by base-generation but get occupied as a result of movement operations that externalize material from the argument-structural core of the structure. Phonology provides no plausible cases of such externalization: melodic material is always associated with positions internal to the core. The kinds of long-distance dependencies seen in raising and operator movement constructions in syntax, for which an appeal to specifier positions of functional projections is called for, are entirely absent from phonology, as are candidates for exponence of the heads of such functional projections (i.e. phonology has no plausible counterparts to such staples of syntactic constructs as determiners or complementizers). Like complex morphological constructs, phonological structures arguably lack functional structure altogether; functional structure is the province of the kinds of dependencies that syntax specializes in. In part, functional categories are licensers of properties which cannot be satisfied in the position of External Merge (such as

---

13 In our discussion of foot structures in section 4 and segmental structure in section 5, we will make an appeal to adjunction in phonological X-bar structures. Our focus until then will be on specification and complementation.

case and agreement, or [+wh]). For the remaining part, functional categories are present in order for syntax to get a handle on variation in linear order involving information-structural properties (topicalization, focalization, extraposition, etc.). Neither of these considerations comes into the picture in phonology. This is why functional structure has no place in phonology.

But though phonology arguably does not deal in functional categories projecting outside the core, one of our major claims in this chapter is that it does recognize the same kind of complex representation of the core that syntax has been argued to feature: on top of the projection of V (which in phonology represents the *vowel*, not the *verb*) we will have occasion to postulate a projection of a 'light *v*'. In syllabic structure, it is the specifier position of *v*P that harbors the Onset, which is the analogue of the external argument in syntax. Inside VP, the structure of the syllable accommodates a variety of different material, often but not invariably associated with the traditional Coda constituent. We will discover that there are interesting regularities regarding the association of melodic material with the SpecVP position in the structure of the syllable – regularities that are reminiscent of those discovered for syntax under the rubric of UTAH. Thus, we announce the birth of a phonological cousin for UTAH, which we will name UMAH:

(15) **Uniformity of Melody Assignment Hypothesis (UMAH)**
Specifier positions[14] in the syllabic core[15] are associated with unique melodic content in underlying representations.

---

[14] The formulation here refers to position*s*, but in the present work its application is only rigorous for SpecVP, which is tied to sonorant. Since this position is flanked by little *v* and V (which are both vowel positions and thus sonorant), one might argue that this is why SpecVP, sandwiched between two sonorant elements, must also be sonorant. We note, however, that the SpecVP position can also become associated with non-sonorant melodic content, via Internal Merge: see the discussion in section 3.4. Just as in syntax (see (13)), association of content with core specifier positions is restricted only in underlying representations (i.e. for cases of External Merge).

[15] As in the case of 'the lexical core' in our syntactic discussion, by 'the syllabic core' in phonological structures we mean minimally the root-VP, perhaps plus its 'light' extension *v*P. And once again our focus will be on SpecVP, which seems privileged to accept only sonorant material under External Merge. The complement-of-V position is clearly tolerant of a wide range of different constituents (consonantal as well as 'propositional': entire syllables can be embedded in the complement-of-V position, as we will see). The specifier position of *v*P is reserved for consonantal material, but its melodic specification seems much more variable than the melodic specification of SpecVP. Here again there is a parallel with syntax (recall from fn. 2 the range of theta-roles that external arguments can have).

One UMAH subgeneralization that will emerge from the discussion to follow is that whenever the syllabic SpecVP position is underlyingly associated with melodic content, this content must be *sonorant*: non-sonorant material cannot be mapped into SpecVP in underlying representations. This corresponds, as we will see, to the observed tendency for Coda consonants to be (restricted to) sonorant consonants, with SpecVP corresponding to one of the structural positions that can be mapped into the traditional Coda.

Obviously, and superficially, coda consonants in many languages can be non-sonorant, but in such cases, as we argue below, these obstruents are merged in the complement-of-V position, which, unlike SpecVP, is not limited to sonorants.

Another interesting property of SpecVP in phonology which we will discover is that the presence of this position is required when we are dealing with a lax vowel, which is spelled out in *v* (i.e. is a 'lax vowel'): what this suggests is that lax vowels are like 'affecting verbs' (verbs that always take a Theme argument, projected in SpecVP).

With these remarks as background, let us now develop the *v*-VP structure of the syllable and the roles played by the 'light *v*', and highlight some of the salient benefits of this structure.

3.3 Chinese prenuclear glides in the v-VP structure of the syllable

Van de Weijer and Zhang (2008) tackle Chinese prenuclear glides with the help of a syntax-inspired 'X-bar structure' with multiple specifiers, such that the glide is in the inner specifier position and the onset in the outer specifier:

(16) (= van de Weijer and Zhang's (18))

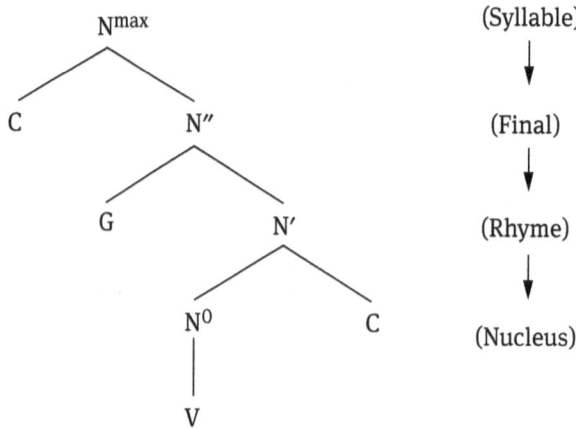

The main point of this structure is that it allows the authors to express the fact (which they demonstrate in detail) that Chinese prenuclear glides belong neither to the Onset nor to the traditional Rhyme.

Note, however, that to say that (16) is an X-bar-theoretic approach to Chinese pre-nuclear glides presupposes a major modification of traditional X-bar theory: multiple specifiers are not available in X-bar theory proper; in fact, it is only when one abolishes traditional X-bar theory (as in Chomsky's 1994, 1995: Ch. 4 'bare phrase structure') that multiple specifiers become available.[16] Also, accommodating Chinese prenuclear glides with the aid of a structure of the type in (16) does little to alleviate the Chinese-specific nature of the analysis: multiple specifier structures of the type in (16) do not seem to have any demonstrated or apparent use outside the realm of prenuclear glides in Chinese. Let us therefore explore a different approach, one which eschews multiple specifiers, and exploits X-bar structures familiar from current syntactic analysis.

In developing our analysis of Chinese prenuclear glides, we take optimal advantage of the hypothesis that the V-projection in phonology (for the vowel) can be associated with a structural extension projected by a 'light v', just as the V-projection in syntax (for the verb) can have a 'light v' on top of it:

(17)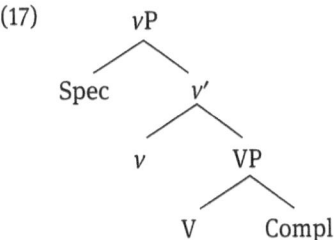

The specifier position of the v-projection is the position for the 'traditional' Onset; the complement position of V is the standard position for the traditional

---

16 Note that the simplified X-bar-theoretic structures of Kayne (1994), which do away with the X'/XP distinction, do not allow for multiple specifiers any more than traditional X-X'-XP structures do. It is really only the complete abolition of traditional X-bar labels that makes multiple specifier structures legitimate. The usefulness of such structures in syntactic analysis has always remained a controversial matter. Thus, for multiple nominative constructions in Japanese (which served as the typical illustration of a TP with multiple specifiers) analyses are available which do not require any particular functional head to accommodate more than a single specifier. Chomsky's (1994, 1995: Ch. 4) introduction of multiple specifier structures was born out of the desire to allow v to both introduce the external argument in a specifier position and check accusative Case against the object in a specifier position. In more recent approaches, Case is checked under Agree, and 'object shift' no longer targets SpecvP.

Coda, although, as we will see in the ensuing subsections, the option of a SpecVP position (which is not shown in (17)) can accommodate melodic material that falls under the traditional notion of Coda; this would be the site for sonorant consonants mentioned above. When *v* and V are spelled out together, and realized ('spelled out') at *v*,[17] the *v*′ represents the traditional Rhyme; when spell-out of *v*-V is at V, it is VP that corresponds to the Rhyme. On the basis of the structure in (17), then, the Rhyme is defined as the minimal structural constituent containing the spell-out position of the syllable Nucleus and its complement (if any).

We propose that Chinese syllables containing a prenuclear glide are characterized by the fact that the glide spells out the *v*-position in the structure in (16), and the Nucleus is spelled out at V – in other words, *v* and V get discrete lexicalizations; we are dealing with a 'serial vowel construction', parallel to 'serial verb constructions' in syntax (for which at least a subset is plausibly analyzed as *v*-V sequences in which *v* and V are spelled out separately; see e.g. den Dikken and Sybesma 1998). When *v* is spelled out as a glide and the syllable nucleus is spelled out at V, the Rhyme corresponds to VP (because V is spelled out); and the Onset of course remains the constituent in Spec*v*P. The prenuclear glide sits right in between the Onset and the Rhyme, and does not strictly belong to either – though, to be sure, it is the head of a structural extension (the *v*P 'shell') of the nucleus.[18]

---

17 Let us clarify what we mean by 'spell(ing) out'. In all cases in which *v* does *not* have melodic content different from that of V (thus unlike what we saw in the Chinese case), the *v* and V positions enter into a chain (cf. 'head movement' in syntax). This chain, which has its melodic content contributed by V, needs to be spelled out in one of the two positions tied together by the chain. In the default case, spell-out of melodic content is at V; but as we will see in our discussion of the tense/lax distinction in section 3.4, spell-out at *v* is what characterizes lax vowels.

18 Note that this is not tantamount to claiming that the prenuclear glide, by itself, is the head of the syllable. The head of the syllable is the *v*-V complex. In Chinese words featuring a prenuclear glide, the two parts of this complex each have their own surface exponent: the glide spells out *v*, and the vowel is the exponent of V. (For the English diphthong /ɪə/ in words like *weird*, it also seems plausible to say that *v* and V have discrete exponents, /ɪ/ and /ə/, resp.; again, the head of the syllable is the *v*-V complex as a whole. See the discussion of (34b) in section 3.5.)

As a logical alternative, the Mandarin prenuclear glide could in principle be accommodated in SpecVP, with the Rhyme then confined to the V′ node. But because we are dealing, in the Mandarin cases, with a glide that is transparently vocalic in origin, it seems to us more attractive to place this glide in a vocalic position: *v* in the structure in the main text. Moreover, on our approach, the Rhyme can be defined as a maximal projection: VP. In virtue of the fact that both *v* and V have melodic content, a Mandarin syllable with a prenuclear glide is – on the representation in the main text – a kind of sesquisyllable (i.e. a syllable and a half).

(18)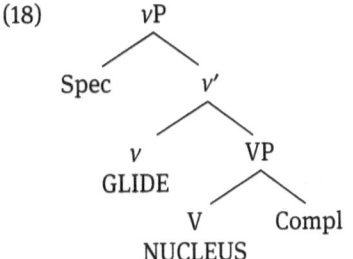

From this perspective, the parameter that distinguishes Chinese from, say, English when it comes to prenuclear glides is that whereas in English they are an integral part of the Onset (which can have its own X-bar structure, thus allowing for multiple consonants; see (19)), in Chinese these glides are lexicalizations of *v* (in between the Onset and the spell-out site of the Nucleus, i.e. V) – a possibility afforded by the license to spell out *v* and V by discrete elements. This kind of parametric difference between languages resembles the parametric difference in syntax between serializing and non-serializing languages: languages that have 'serial verb constructions' allow *v* and V to be spelled out by different elements whereas languages that do not will lack such constructions. (In point of fact, it turns out that Chinese not only has 'serial *vowel* constructions' (i.e. prenuclear glides) but also 'serial *verb* constructions' – but this is probably an accident rather than something 'deep': we see no particular reason to expect that the 'serialization parameter' will be set the same way for vowelsand verbs within individual languages.)

The proposal in (18) embodies what we present as the universal structure of the syllable, encapsulated in (19), which replaces Völtz's (1999) structure in (3):

(19)   Universal structure of the syllable

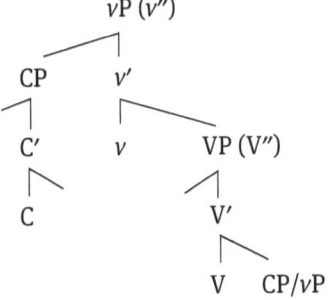

As shown, the complement of V can either be a 'consonant phrase' or, indeed, a full syllable (which is how we incorporate van der Hulst's proposal that syllables can contain syllables, which we will return to below).

3.4 The tense/lax distinction in the v-VP structure of the syllable

The benefits of the *v*-VP structure of the syllable also come to the fore in the representation of the difference between long vowels and diphthongs, on the one hand, and short vowels, on the other, and in distinguishing tense and lax vowels. In this section, we will talk about the latter.

Our central hypothesis regarding the difference between tense and lax vowels is (20):[19]

(20) a. lax vowels are spelled out at *v*
 b. tense vowels are spelled out at V

We will use this hypothesis in an analysis of the Dutch vowel system and syllable structure.

Dutch systematically distinguishes in its phonology between two types of vowels, often differentiated by the labels *tense* and *lax*. Of these, the former are often phonetically 'long', but extra duration is not the unifying property of tense vowels – not all tense vowels are phonetically long (in particular high tense vowels are quite short), and open syllables with a tense vowel count as light (not heavy) in terms of stress (see van der Hulst 1984), which supports the claim that they are not phonologically long.[20] The lax vowels are marked; in concert with this, Dutch has fewer lax vowels than tense vowels. Lax vowels must be followed by a consonant; tense vowels do not have to be, but when they are (largely only in word-final position), they deliver so-called 'superheavy' syllables. Word-internally, tense vowels tend not to be followed by a tautosyllabic consonant (while lax vowels must be followed by a consonant, arguably tautosyllabic; see the discussion of *kop* 'cup' and *kom* 'bowl' later in this section). Word-finally, where extra consonantal

---

[19] This hypothesis was ultimately inspired by Polgárdi's (2008) approach to the tense/lax distinction in Dutch, although the two outlooks differ fundamentally. Polgárdi's idea that Dutch lax vowels *must* properly govern a silent Nucleus strikes us as an anomaly: proper government is always a privilege, never an obligation.

[20] If they were phonologically long, given that stress is Dutch is weight-sensitive, these vowels would be expected to attract stress, but they do not.

material is possible (see below), tense vowels can be followed by one consonant less than lax vowels. These are the main explananda. In the following paragraphs, we will show that the *v*-V system provides insightful explanations for them, and establishes interesting parallels with the structure of the syntactic verb phrase.

For the contrast between /tɛmpo/ *tempo* 'id.' and */tempo/, the central hypothesis in (20) gives us an immediate account, in conjunction with our previous hypothesis that sonorant consonants can be mapped into SpecVP: see (21) (where the arrows point to the spell-out position for the Nucleus). With the tense vowel spelled out at V, the b-structure in (21) cannot yield */tempo/.[21] What we see here is that the complement of V can not only be CP but also *v*P (recall (19), above). This testifies to the 'flexibility' of the complement-of-V position, and captures the van der Hulst proposal for syllable embedding, but it avoids the problem discussed in section 2 because the presence of an embedded syllable does not come in the place of a closing sonorant consonant for the first syllable, which occurs in Spec of VP (while it is still true that the embedded syllable *v*P and CP are in complementary distribution as options for the complement of V.

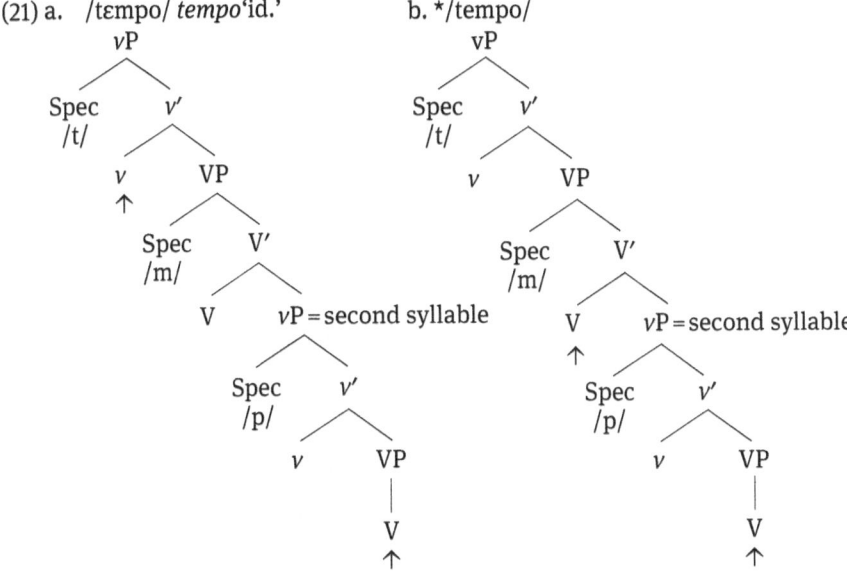

---

21 Spelling the b-structure in (21) out as is would deliver the ungrammatical */tmepo/, which is bad because /tm/ does not occur tautosyllabically in prevocalic position. Dutch proper onsets (as occurring word-internally) cannot have a nasal in second position. In the text discussion above (27), we argue that a tense vowel, spelled out at V, cannot have SpecVP filled with independent melodic content – and we link this to a kind of 'doubly-filled Comp effect'.

The lax vowel /ɛ/ is legitimate as the head of the stressed initial syllable in (21a) thanks to the fact that there is a Coda consonant present in SpecVP: the nasal /m/, a sonorant that is eligible for insertion in SpecVP. We will explain below what happens when a stressed lax vowel is followed by a non-sonorant consonant. But let us first discuss what goes awry when a lax vowel heads a stressed *open* syllable, as in (22a), to be contrasted with (22b).

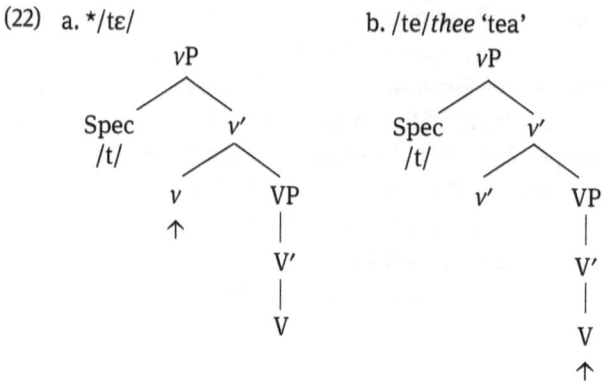

Without any segmental material in SpecVP, the distinction between *v* and V as the spell-out site for the Nucleus cannot be made: shifting the arrow from V to *v* would be a vacuous operation. Universally, the default spell-out position for the Nucleus is V. Because shifting the spell-out site of the vowel over to *v* is vacuous in the absence of an occupant of SpecVP, it follows that without any segmental material in SpecVP, (22) can only be realized as /te/, with the vowel spelled out at V; (22a) cannot survive.

In a tense/lax system, in which spelling the Nucleus out at *v* or V is contrastive, a vowel can only be spelled out in *v* (i.e. 'be lax') if SpecVP is projected and occupied. This, we believe, is the quintessence of the markedness of lax vowels in languages such as Dutch: (i) the universal default is for the Nucleus to be spelled out at V (so tense vowels are inherently less marked than lax ones); and (ii) spelling the Nucleus out at *v* is allowed only if the *v* and V positions are separated by some non-vocalic melodic material associated with SpecVP, which is precisely what a lax vowel requires. Lax vowels are, in a sense, 'obligatorily transitive' (see Anderson 2011), like 'affecting verbs' – that is, they require a 'theme argument'.

This simple approach to the distinction between tense and lax vowels, hinging on a difference in spell-out site (V versus *v*, resp.) which is afforded by the *v*-V approach, also gives us an account for the contrast between *sofa* (with tense 'o') and *koffie* 'coffee' (with lax 'o') (both with initial stress), the latter featuring what van der Hulst (1984, 1985, 2006) has called a 'virtual geminate'. Let us start with the representation of *sofa*, which features a tense vowel in the first syllable. A tense vowel in Dutch is happy to occur in an 'open' syllable. In our terms, this translates into the statement that a tense vowel does not require filling of the Spec of VP – in fact, it cannot have SpecVP occupied. So the V-head of the first syllable is welcome to take as its complement the substring *fa*, represented as the second syllable in a trochaic foot[22] – i.e. a vP in the complement of the tense vowel, spelled out at V:[23]

(23) /sofa/*sofa* 'id.'

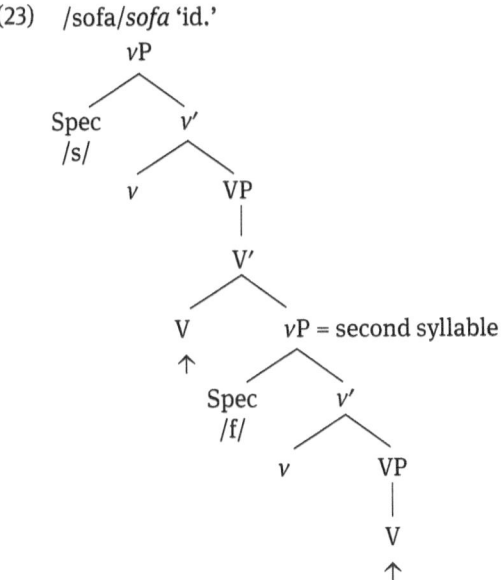

Now what happens when we are dealing with a lax vowel in the first syllable, as in *koffie* 'coffee'? One thing that will change is the spell-out locus for the Nucleus: lax vowels are spelled out at v. But shifting the upward-pointing arrow from V to v in (23) brings about no substantive change: v and V are string-adjacent, so shifting the arrow from V to v is a vacuous operation when SpecVP is not projected (as in (23)). So in the representation of *koffie* 'coffee', SpecVP must be projected (as required by the 'transitivity' of the lax vowel), and it must in addition be associated with non-vocalic melodic content. The

---

[22] Indeed, our proposal that syllables can be embedded in syllables represents feet as such, rather than as sequences of syllables; see section 4 for further discussion.
[23] We will see below that both a tense vowel and a stressed lax vowel plus following consonant (see *tempo*) can take vP as a complement.

SpecVP position can be occupied via base-generation ('External Merge' in current syntactic terminology) only by insertion of a sonorant (as in *tempo*). But there is no sonorant consonant in *koffie*, which means that the specifier position of VP is unoccupied in the base. If the SpecVP position remained unoccupied, the first syllable of this trochee could not contain a lax vowel. So SpecVP must get filled, but it cannot be filled here via External Merge. Thankfully, there is a way out of the dilemma: positions that are not filled via External Merge can be occupied in the course of the derivation via Internal Merge, i.e. the 'recycling' of material externally merged into the structure. So the dilemma posed by *koffie* is solved by 'moving' the /f/ into the SpecVP position, and making it simultaneously the Onset of the second syllable and part of the Coda of the first. 'Movement' should, of course, not be taken literally: the /f/ is not moving around the structure of the word; 'movement' is a metaphor. The way in which this metaphor has customarily been formally expressed in phonology is via *spreading*, or *multiple association*: the melodic material represented by /f/ is associated both with the Onset position of the second syllable and with the SpecVP position of the first:

(24) /kɔfi/*koffie* 'coffee'

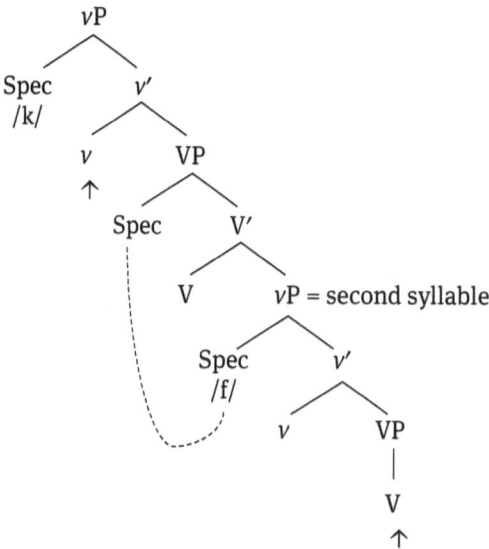

In languages in which the doubly linked melodic material can be spelled out in both positions, this results in gemination. (Phrased in terms current in syntactic analysis, what we would say is that both copies in the chain are realized.) In Dutch (which does not have surface geminate consonants), the melodic material is spelled out just once, in the Onset position of the second syllable.[24] But importantly, this material is *also* associated with the SpecVP position in the first syllable, which licenses the spell-out of the Nucleus at v thanks to the fact that the SpecVP position is projected and associated with melodic material (albeit covertly).[25]

At this point, it may be worth commenting in some more detail on the ways in which SpecVP can be used in the structure of the syllable, and drawing a useful parallel with syntax. In the preceding discussion, we had initially restricted SpecVP to *sonorant* consonants. But in the analysis of Dutch *koffie*, we allowed non-sonorant melodic material to 'spread' to SpecVP in a structure in

---

[24] In *koffie*, the non-sonorant melodic material for the intervocalic consonant is externally merged in the Onset position (Spec*v*P) of the second syllable. It is spelled out there rather than in the SpecVP position of the first syllable, to which it spreads. A reviewer points out that in syntax, when a constituent externally merged in some relatively low structural position links up via Internal Merge to a position higher up the tree, it is usually the higher position that serves as the spell-out site. This is because this higher position is typically one in which some property important to the interface between syntax and semantics/information structure is satisfied. On the syntax/semantics side of the grammar, this is usually a cogent reason to spell the multiply associated element out in the position of Internal Merge. On the phonology side, other considerations play a role to adjudicate the locus of spell-out. Onset Maximization is one important such consideration. We submit that it is for this purpose that the multiply associated /f/ in (24) receives its surface exponent in the Spec*v*P position of the second syllable, not in the SpecVP of the first.

Note that Dutch orthography actually spells the 'f' twice. This convention is also used in the writing of words such as /kɔma/ *komma* 'comma' (cf. tense /koma/ *coma* 'id.') and /fɛlʉm/ *vellum* 'id.' (cf. tense /felʉm/ *velum* 'id.'). For cases such as *komma* and *vellum*, in which the stressed lax vowel is followed by a sonorant consonant, it is sufficient for the licensing of vowel spell-out at v to have the sonorant associated just with SpecVP, where the sonorant is legitimately merged: spreading the melodic content of the sonorant down to the Onset position of the second syllable is not required for this purpose. If the sonorant in *komma* and *vellum* is externally merged in the first vowel's SpecVP (see the main text below for an alternative), spreading nonetheless does take place, with an eye toward satisfaction of Onset Maximization, which causes the intervocalic sonorant to be spelled out as the Onset of the second syllable. So in the representation *komma* and *vellum*, too, we postulate a link between the first syllable's SpecVP position and the second syllable's Spec*v*P. (Note that phrased in syntactic terms, spreading from the SpecVP of the first vowel to the Spec*v*P of the second vowel is a case of 'downward movement', customarily thought to be prohibited in syntactic structures because the 'trace' left by such movement cannot be licensed. The adoption of the 'copy theory of movement' has made the apparent ban on downward movement much less obvious. This is an area where we hope that phonology can inform syntax. We plan to return to this in future research.)

[25] Schwa is not restricted to occur only in a structural environment in which SpecVP is occupied. We assume that schwa is not the reflex of melodic content that is underlyingly present under v or V but instead is the surface realization of a Nucleus that is phonologically empty (i.e. not associated with melodic content).

which this position is projected but not filled via External Merge. Why doesn't the association of non-sonorant material with SpecVP violate the restriction on filling SpecVP exclusively with sonorant material? Larson's (1988) analysis of the double object construction suggests an answer to this question from a syntactic perspective. For Larson, the SpecVP position is 'ordinarily' the position into which the Theme argument is merged (as in *John gave a book to Mary*); but in the syntax of the double object construction (*John gave Mary a book*), Larson takes SpecVP to be occupied by the indirect object (i.e., the Goal, not the Theme; the latter is 'demoted' to adjunct status). The strongest possible interpretation of the Uniformity of Theta Assignment Hypothesis (UTAH: Baker 1988) would take it to establish biunique relations between particular thematic roles (here, the Theme) and structural positions (here, SpecVP), which would lead one to expect that the SpecVP position ought to be uniquely and exclusively associated with the Theme role. But Larson is aware that Baker himself formulated the UTAH less strictly, in a way that leaves open precisely the kind of exploitation of SpecVP that Larson advocates. Baker's UTAH says that identical thematic relations between items should be represented by identical structural relations between those items at D-structure. For SpecVP in syntax, this means that whenever it is filled by an argument through External Merge (i.e. at D-structure), this argument will be a Theme; but if for whatever reason SpecVP is *not* filled via External Merge (e.g. because V is dethematized, as in Larson's analysis of the dative shift alternation), it will be free to be occupied by a non-Theme via Internal Merge. When we now return to SpecVP in our phonological representations, we see that it is subject to a restriction on External Merge that says that only sonorant consonants can be inserted there; but when SpecVP is structurally projected *without* being associated with melodic content through External Merge, it is free to be associated with non-sonorant melodic material via Internal Merge. The parallel with Larsonian syntactic structures is perfect. (By this, of course we do not mean to suggest that Larsonian syntactic structures *themselves* are perfect: we will not commit ourselves to any particular analysis of ditransitive sentences here.)

We have now derived an analysis of Dutch *koffie* and similar such disyllabic words with a lax vowel in the first syllable and a single non-sonorant consonant in intervocalic position which gives a particularly precise expression to van der Hulst's (1984, 1985) insight that the intervocalic consonant in such words is a 'virtual geminate'. The intervocalic /f/ in *koffie* is Externally Merged as the onset of the second syllable, but is also associated, via Internal Merge, with the SpecVP position of the first syllable. It is thanks to this association of /f/ to SpecVP that spelling out the Nucleus of the first syllable at v (i.e. realizing it as a lax vowel) is legitimate. When the intervocalic consonant *is* a sonorant (as in *komma* 'comma', two logical possibilities present themselves: either the sonorant is externally merged in the Onset of the second syllable and internally merged to SpecVP (like the /f/ of *koffie*), or the inverse takes place (cf. fn. 24). In the latter case the Internal Merge is driven by the requirement that syllables prefer Onsets. However, we know of no argument to represent *koffie* as different from *komma*.

Next, let us consider how to analyze monosyllabic *kop* 'cup' and *kom* 'bowl', featuring a lax vowel followed in the first case by an obstruent and in the second by a sonorant. Here again, we need a license to spell the Nucleus out at *v*. Such spell-out is legitimate only if SpecVP is projected and associated with melodic material. For *kom*, this is easy to achieve:

(25) /kɔm/*kom* 'bowl'

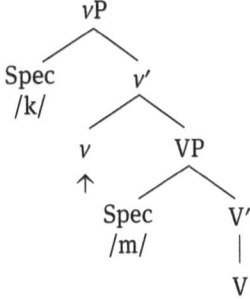

In (25), the nasal is Externally Merged in SpecVP, and the complement-of-V position is not used. This structure is well-formed as is: projection of SpecVP is not contingent on projection of a complement for V. The parallel with syntax is once again informative: in *There arrived a plane*, the notional subject is a Theme, which by Larson's (1988) and Hale and Keyser's (1993) application of UTAH must be base-merged in SpecVP; but the verb (*arrive*) here has no complement (unlike in *There arrived a plane at the airport*), so there is nothing sitting in the complement-of-V position.[26] In neither *There arrived a plane (at the airport)* nor *kom* 'bowl' is the V position radically empty: it is in a chain with *v*,

---

26 In *He fell*, the Theme is base-merged in SpecVP but then raises to SpecIP for licensing purposes. In phonology, there is no movement into the specifier position of a functional projection, so the element base-generated in SpecVP stays put. This is precisely what happens in syntax in *There arrived a plane*, which is why we included this sentence in the main text.

which is where the head of the *v*-VP structure (the verb *arrive* or the lax vowel /ɔ/) is spelled out.[27]

Without the nasal in SpecVP, the structure in (25), with the arrow pointing to *v* as the spell-out site of the Nucleus, falls apart. Recall that with SpecVP unprojected, the distinction between *v* and V as the spell-out site for the Nucleus cannot be made. Shifting the arrow from V to *v* would be a vacuous operation; spell-out in v requires a consonant (via External or Internal merge) in SpecVP. It follows that without the nasal in SpecVP, (25) can only be realized as /ko/ (as in *Ko*, a proper name; with a tense /o/), not as */kɔ/. Put differently (but equivalently), when SpecVP is empty, the arrow can only point to V; and an arrow pointing to V delivers a tense vowel, in languages (such as Dutch, with its tense/lax distinction) in which the locus of vocalic spell-out is distinctive.

For *kop*, with a /p/ instead of a sonorant following the lax vowel /ɔ/, we cannot resort to External Merge in SpecVP: after all, /p/ is not a sonorant, so base-insertion of this consonant in SpecVP violates the phonological equivalent of UTAH (i.e. UMAH). But we *can* in principle insert /p/ in the complement-of-V position, and then associate its melodic content with the SpecVP position via 'spreading' (or 'Internal Merge'), as in (26). This creates a virtual geminate of sorts.[28] The fact that *kom* and *kop* end up with different structures finds some justification in Dutch, based on the allomorphy of the diminutive suffix: while *kom* 'bowl' forces schwa insertion (*kommetje* 'little bowl'), *kop* 'cup' does not (its diminutive is *kopje*, not *koppetje*[29]).

---

27 Here we are assuming that an unaccusative construction such as *There arrived a plane (at the airport)* contains a projection of *v*, despite the absence of an Agent. In approaches that tie the distribution of v to predication (such as den Dikken 2006), the presence of a projection of *v* in the structure of *There arrived a plane (at the airport)* can be straightforwardly ensured on the plausible hypothesis that *there* (the so-called 'expletive') is in a predication relation with the VP. We will not dwell on this matter further here.
28 In this case, Dutch spelling does not use double consonants. A language like Swedish, where the situation may be similar phonologically, does use double spelling word-finally.
29 We note that *koppetje* is not non-existent: it occurs as the diminutive of *kop* in its meaning of 'head'. For *pop* 'puppet, doll', the diminutive with schwa insertion (*poppetje*) also occurs alongside *popje*; see van der Hulst (2008) for detailed discussion of the Dutch diminutive.

(26) /kɔp/ *kop* 'cup'

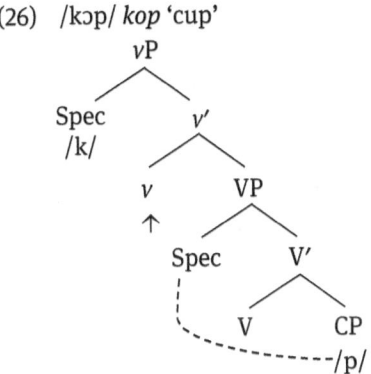

Note that in this analysis of the Dutch tense/lax distinction, no recourse needs to be had to a polysyllabic representation of an ostensibly monosyllabic word such as *kop* 'cup': the final /p/ in (26) occupies the Coda position of the single syllable constituted by *kop*; no second syllable with an empty Nucleus is necessary, unlike in Government Phonology approaches (Kaye, Lowenstamm and Vergnaud 1990).[30] In van der Hulst (2010b), given that pairs like *sofa* /sofa/ and *sof* /sɔf/ 'bummer' are on a par in metrical terms, *sof* is represented disyllabically. In the current analysis, the equivalence is that a heavy syllable such as *sof* will initiate a 'foot' structure and be a 'foot' on its own, and *sofa* likewise constitutes a single foot, with /fa/ as the embedded syllable.[31]

---

[30] In Government Phonology's 'strict CV' model, Vs (and Cs) govern and license other Cs and Vs, but they are not joined in tree structures. Takahashi (1993) argues that positing both structures and government relations introduces a redundancy. But in syntax at least, government relations (now called Agree relations) are *defined* in terms of structure: c-command is a prerequisite for government/Agree, and c-command is a relation between nodes in a tree. The c-command relation is indispensable in the account of non-local dependencies. If all dependencies in linguistic structures were spec-head and head-complement relations, relations would be superfluous. But both in syntax and in phonology, dependencies/relations seem to be able to reach beyond the spec-head and head-complement configurations. It may be possible to recast apparently non-local relations in a local way; but that is not something this chapter can meaningfully address. Unless and until this recasting is successful, it seems to us that relations (in particular, c-command/Agree) remain necessary; and structures certainly are, too.

[31] If it should turn out, after all, to be essential for metrical reasons to represent *kop* and *sof* as disyllables, this can be achieved in our proposal by drawing yet another parallel with syntax, this time in the realm of 'object shift' and 'exceptional Case-marking (ECM)'. In Bošković (1997, 2002), it is argued for English that 'object shift', which we can represent as movement of a DP to SpecVP, is merely optional for direct objects of verbs (as in *John admires Bill*) but obligatory in the case of overt subjects of non-finite (small) clausal complements (as in *John considers Bill (to be) a genius*). Bošković's proposal thus makes a distinction with respect to association with SpecVP between the complement of the verb, on the one hand, and the specifier of the

The active ingredient in the analysis throughout is the distinction between spell-out at *v* (for lax vowels) and spell-out at V (for tense vowels), in conjunction with a particular hypothesis regarding the licensing of 'Nuclear' spell-out at *v*. In this theory, the difference between lax /kɔt/ *kot* 'cot' and tense (but not long) /kot/ *koot* 'talus' is made very straightforwardly with reference to the locus of spell-out of the Nucleus: a lax Nucleus is spelled out at *v*, and requires SpecVP to be projected and associated with melodic material; a tense Nucleus is spelled out at V (the default spell-out site for syllable Nuclei), and cannot have SpecVP projected (see (27) for the structures with tense vowels). We can think of the inverse correlation between occupancy of SpecVP and occupancy of V as a kind of 'doubly-filled Comp effect' familiar from syntax (cf. esp. Sportiche's 1996 'doubly-filled Voice filter'): when the Nucleus is spelled out at V, its specifier cannot occupied by an element with independent melodic content.

(27)   /kot/*koot* 'talus'

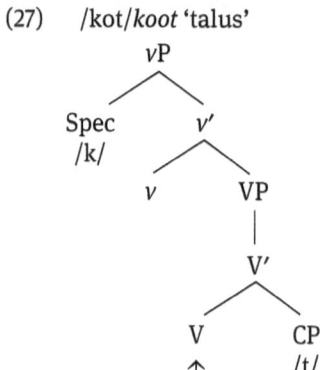

---

complement of the verb, on the other. Suppose that we carry this distinction over to syllabic structure, and differentiate with respect to asso¬ciat¬ion with SpecVP between the complement of the V-head, on the one hand, and the Onset of the syllable in the complement of the V-head of the first syllable, on the other. (Note that the subject of the non-finite clausal complement of a verb is in a geometrical relation with the matrix verb that is entirely on a par with the geometrical relation between the Onset of the second syllable of a trochee and the V-head of the first syllable: in both cases, the relation between the matrix V and the specifier is a 'niecehood' relationship.) If in addition we strengthen the distinction into a genuine dichotomy, we arrive at the result that association of a postnuclear non-sonorant consonant with the *specifier* of VP is possible only if it is mapped into the Onset (i.e. *the specifier*) position of a second syllable, in a trochaic foot whose second Nucleus remains unpronounced because it is properly governed (in the sense of Government Phonology) by the V-head of the first syllable. It is thanks to its occupancy of the *specifier* position of the second (silent-headed) syllable that /p/ has the license to 'spread' to the *specifier* position of the VP in the first syllable. On this approach, *kop* 'cup' is like *koffie* 'coffee' with respect to the structural position of the obstruent, with the difference between the two being that there is no overt second verb 'at the bottom' in the former.

The syllable in (27) is called a 'superheavy syllable'. Such a syllable can end in an obstruent or in a sonorant (see (28c)). Superheavy syllables can either have tense vowels followed by a tautosylalbic consonant, as in (27) and (28c), or lax vowels followed by two tautosyllabic consonants, as in (28d). In (28) we compare the structures of heavy and super-heavy syllables. What structurally distinguishes the heavy syllables in (28a) and (28b) from the superheavy ones in (28c) and (28d) is that in the latter, two positions in VP are associated with melodic content via External Merge: in (28c) both SpecVP and the complement-of-V position are occupied, and in (28d) melodic content is base-generated in the V and the complement-of-V positions; by contrast, in (28a) and (28b) only one position in the VP (SpecVP in the former, and the complement-of-V position in the latter) is filled via External Merge.

(28) a. /ram/*ram* 'ram' (cf. (25))   b. /rap/*rap* 'fast' (cf. (26))

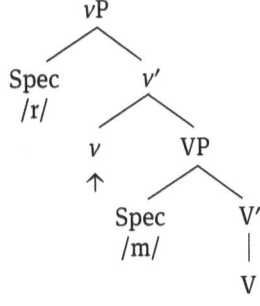
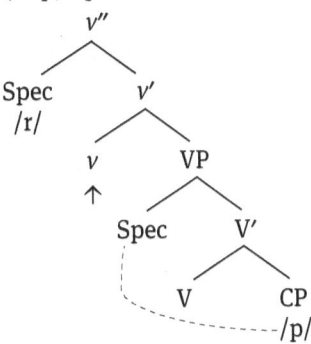

c. /ram/*raam* 'window' (cf. (27))[32]   d. /ramp/*ramp* 'disaster'

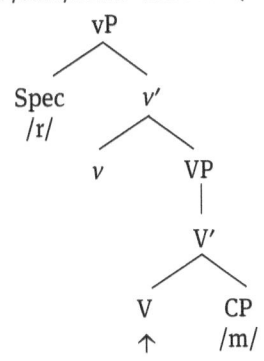
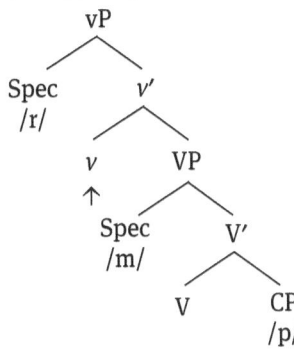

---

32 Phonetically, as Gussenhoven (2008) has shown, the tense vowel in *raam* is truly long. We do not represent this structurally: the /a/ occupies just a single V-position in the structure. As the text discussion above (28) shows, the fact that *raam*, like *koot* (where the /o/ is not phonetically long), is superheavy follows without the /a/ being assigned two spots in the structure.

The structure for *ramp* differs from the ones for *ram* and *rap* in being 'ditransitive': both dependent positions in the Rhyme are occupied via External Merge, one (SpecVP) by the nasal and the other (the complement-of-V position) by the stop. Both *ram* and *rap* are 'mono-transitive', but, as we have seen, in different ways: External Merge here targets only one dependent position in the Rhyme, but in *ram* the dependent is in SpecVP whereas in *rap* the dependent is externally merged in the complement-of-V position, and 'spreads' to SpecVP via Internal Merge.[33] The External Merge sites of the closing consonants in *ram* and *rap* are different, but what unites the two cases and distinguishes them as a pair from *ramp* is that they both have just a single consonant in the Rhyme. 'Ditransitive' *ramp*, by contrast, has both SpecVP and the complement-of-V position occupied via External Merge, making it 'superheavy'.

3.5 A note on Coda clusters

In Dutch /ram/ *raam* 'window', with the tense vowel /a/ spelled out in V and SpecVP being unfillable when V is occupied, the complement-of-V position is the *only* position in which /m/ can be inserted when it follows a tense vowel.[34] This leads us to predict that it should not be possible to fill the complement-of-V position with some other consonant *in addition to* the sonorant. Likewise, a

---

[33] Along these lines, our structures make the distinction between a monomoraic syllable (cf. the structure in (22b), for *thee* 'tea'), a bimoraic one (*kop*, *kom*), and a trimoraic one (*ramp*) in terms of the vowel (one mora) plus the number of internal 'arguments' (with each adding a mora).

[34] Note that the sonorant consonant in *raam* 'window' is inserted not in SpecVP but in the complement-of-V position, and that it does not get associated with SpecVP at all because the tenseness of the vowel allows the SpecVP position to remain entirely unprojected. Does this contradict what we had said previously about the locus of sonorants? It does not: the relation between specific melodic content and specific structural positions is not biunique. What UMAH in (15) says, for SpecVP, is that it can uniquely be base-filled by sonorants – put differently, sonorants are the only segments that can be base-inserted in that position. This is crucially not the same as saying that sonorants can only be inserted in SpecVP. Sonorants can show up in *any* position in the syllabic template (recall also the brief discussion of *komma*), even including the Nucleus position (in the case of syllabic nasals and liquids): they are truly *factotum* elements. So there is no problem with the fact that /m/ is in the complement-of-V position in (28c): the complement-of-V position is a perfectly legitimate position for sonorant.

syllable like *ramp* can also not be augmented with another consonant. This prediction is borne out by the fact that */ramp/ *raamp and */rɑmpk/ *rampk are impossible.

However, it would appear that superheavy syllables can be augmented, but only if the extra consonant is a coronal:[35] /mant/ *maand* 'month' is grammatical alongside /man/ *maan* 'moon', /start/ *staart* 'tail' is grammatical alongside /star/ *staar* 'cataract', and /falt/ *vaalt* 'dung heap' occurs alongside /fal/ *vaal* 'faint, pale'; all these words have the same tense /a/. Likewise, /rɑmpt/ is a possible sequence, although, as it happens, only as an inflected form, as in the 3rd person singular of the verb *kampen* 'struggle': *het bedrijf kampt met grote verliezen* 'the company is struggling with large deficits'.

To accommodate these cases, we exploit internal complexity inside the Coda constituent:

(29) /part/*paard* 'horse'

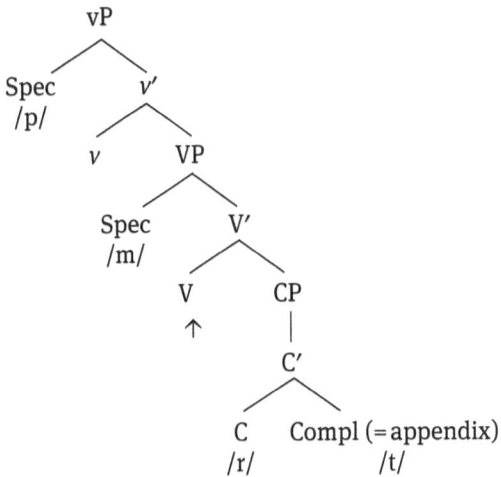

---

[35] From a synchronic point of view, there is no obvious explanation for this restriction to coronal 'augments' other than an appeal to the widely acknowledged 'unmarked' status of coronal place. See also section 5.5 for relevant discussion.

(30) /kɑmpt/ *kampt* 'is struggling'

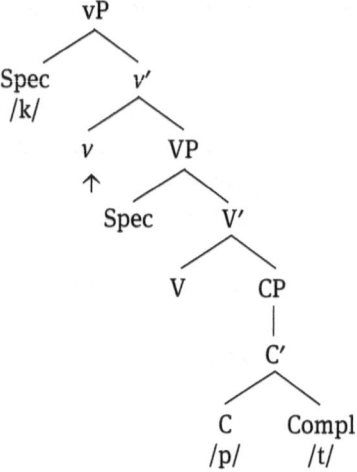

The Coda cluster can actually be made even more complex by adding a /s/ after the /t/, as in the second syllable of *voorwaarts* 'forward', transcribed as /ʋarts/. We can accommodate /t+s/ in the complement of the liquid.

(31) /ʋarts/ (*voor*)*waarts* '(for)ward'

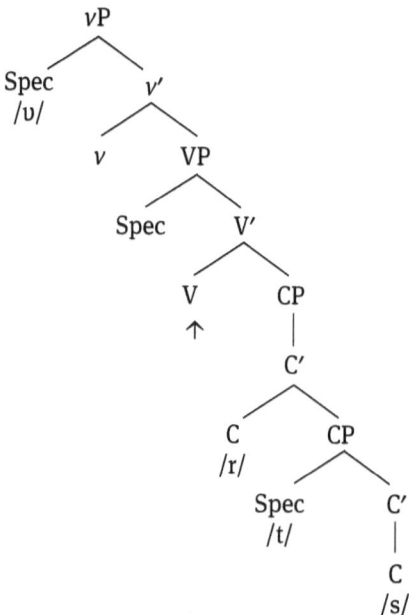

The restriction that a superheavy syllable in Dutch can be followed by a consonant cluster only if the extra consonant(s) is/are coronal has an interesting companion in English. There, when the syllable Nucleus is a tense vowel, a sonorant consonant that follows it can, in turn, be followed by another consonant only if this is a coronal (thus, *wield* but not **wielk*, and (Glenn) *Gould* but not **goulp*); by contrast, a lax vowel + sonorant sequence can readily be followed by a non-coronal consonant (so that alongside *silt* we also find *silk*). The proposal for Dutch straightforwardly extends to these English cases.

Following a short/lax vowel that is spelled out in *v*, a postvocalic sonorant +stop sequence can be accommodated in the structure of the syllable by mapping the sonorant into SpecVP (recall that sonorants have the unique license to be base-generated in SpecVP), so that the stop following it can occupy the complement-of-V position all by itself, as in (32) – the representation of English *silt* and *silk*.

(32)

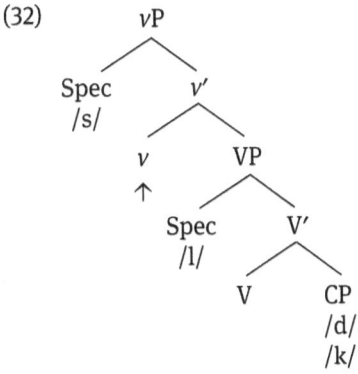

But a tense vowel, spelled out in V, precludes occupancy of SpecVP. The postvocalic sonorant must be mapped into the complement-of-V position. If followed by a stop that is also mapped into the Coda, the sonorant must form a cluster with the stop in the complement-of-V position. Thus, for English *wield*, we arrive at (33) as the structure of the syllable.

(33)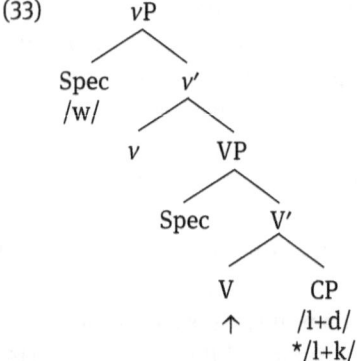

Since the sonorant in SpecVP in (32) does not form a consonant cluster together with the stop in the complement-of-V position, the two can be specified for place information entirely independently of one another, and there is no requirement that the stop be coronal. This freedom is absent in the presence of a tense vowel because, with the vowel spelled out in V, SpecVP is unavailable for External Merge of the sonorant; this consonant must hence be mapped into the complement-of-V position and form a consonant cluster with the following stop, and (in English just as in Dutch) such a cluster is well-formed only if the stop is coronal.

The restriction on liquid+stop sequences also applies in the case of long lax vowels and diphthongs (e.g. *mold* but not *molk). We can understand this when we examine the representation of these Nuclei in English. Following Szigetvári (2016), we represent English long lax vowels such as /ɔː/ and /ɑː/ as in (34a), with /h/ as a glottal glide occupying SpecVP;. This representation carries over to the diphthongs /aj/, /aw/ and /ow/ as well. And (34b) is a natural representation in our system for the diphthong /ɪə/ in *weird*.

(34)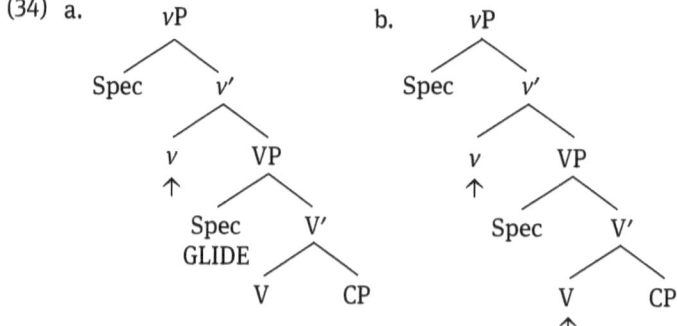

In both (34a) and (34b), the SpecVP position is unavailable for a consonant that is not part of the long vowel or diphthong – in (34a) because the position is occupied, and in (34b), just as in the case of tense vowels, because the V-head is filled (which precludes occupancy of SpecVP).³⁶ So here again, although sonorant consonants can in principle be merged in SpecVP, this opportunity is blocked. The postvocalic sonorant must therefore be mapped into the complement-of-V position, just as in (33).³⁷

4 Foot structure in X-bar phonology

In section 2 we discussed how the notion of embedding one syllable inside another entails a different perspective on foot structure: a bisyllabic (trochaic) foot is replaced by a structure (which can as such form a foot, given that foot structure is independently needed; see below) in which one syllable is embedded in another (recall (6)). In the present section, we would like to make some tentative proposals for how feet might be (re)analyzable in a theory that acknowledges syllable embedding. Looking at the question from a general, *a priori* perspective in the context of our 'phonology is syntax' program, there is a first division to be made between *(a)* foot structures in which one syllable is embedded within another in such a way that it occupies a structural position made available in the *v*-V structure of the syllable, and *(b)* foot structures in which there is no such embedding. For examples of type *(a)*, in sections 2 and 3 we have already come across the plausible case of a subordination approach to trochaic feet, with the subordinate syllable in *complement* position. Depending on one's theory of foot structure, this is where the reanalysis of foot structure in terms of recursive syllable structure could stop. Various students of stress have argued *against* any other foot type, including iambic feet, either only when weight-sensitive (Hayes 1995, Kager 1993) or more generally (cf. van de Vijver 1998 and van der Hulst 1997). Whatever the merit of these proposals, we will here explore what kind of structures might be entertained to capture prosodic 'WS' units.

---

36 Moreover, filling SpecVP with consonantal material in (34b) would cause the exponents of *v* and V to become discontinuous, hence unpronounceable as a diphthong.
37 A reviewer asks what our account of the Rhyme of *excerpt* is. In the rhotic pronunciation of this word, a short schwa (spelled out in *v*) is followed by /r/ in SpecVP, and a legitimate /pt/ Coda cluster (cf. *apt*, which has the same gross structure). Here we are not dealing with a tense vowel, long lax vowel or diphthong followed by a sonorant plus obstruent cluster. We regard the non-rhotic version of *excerpt* as a phonetic variant of the rhotic one.

Formally speaking, bearing in mind syntactic analogues, reanalyses of foot structure, as well as of 'higher' prosodic units, could involve embedding, adjunction or coordination. In the following subsections, we will first repeat our proposal for capturing trochaic feet in terms of embedding 'syllables inside syllables', adding that an apparent trochaic unit might also result from adjunction. We will then turn to iambic patterns, proposing to analyze these as 'derived structures'. Finally, we consider the issue of prosodic (or phonological words), which we propose to analyze in terms of coordination.

4.1 Trochees

In the discussion in section 3, we discovered that a syllable (i.e. vP) can occur as the complement of the V-head of the preceding syllable. When this occurs, the structure that is derived captures the idea of a trochaic foot: the second syllable is structurally subordinate to the first one, and located on the recursive side in a right-branching structure, with the Nucleus of the first syllable as the head of the structure. To illustrate, let us repeat the structure assigned to Dutch *sofa* in section 3.4 as in (35). Since the Nucleus of the first syllable is the head, it attracts the stress, resulting in the strong-weak pattern defining the trochee.

(35) /sofa/ sofa 'id.'

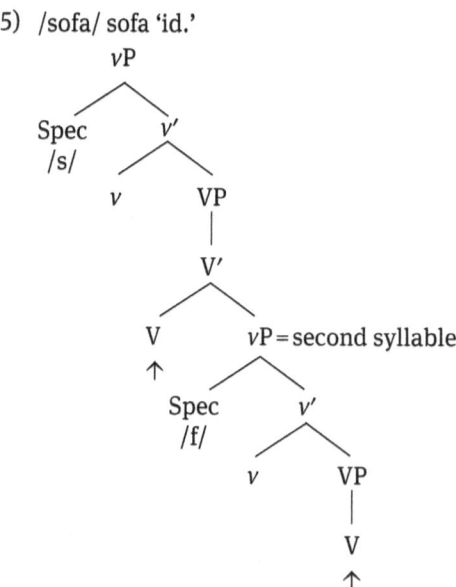

For dactyls (i.e., feet with the stress pattern σ̱σσ, where the underscore marks stress, such as *rickety* and *vanity*), for which traditional metrical phonology requires a ternary foot, the syllable subordination approach that we are advocating for trochees makes a simple extension available involving two levels of embedding, as in the structure in (39).[38] Van der Hulst (2012) draws attention to the fact that the structures in (35) and (36) provide a structural basis for poetic rhyming patterns that involve these entire structures minus the highest onset. Traditional foot structure provides no such account.

(36) /rɪkɪti/ *rickety*

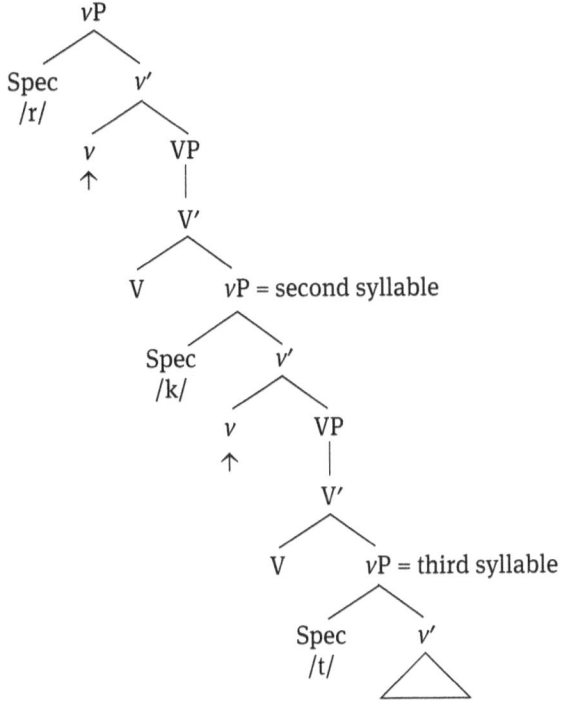

An obvious objection to this proposal is that, in principle, we could represent more complicated structures with additional degrees of embedding. But the

---

38 In the structure in (36), we suppressed the multiple association of the stops /k/ and /t/ with the SpecVP positions above them. Recall the discussion in section 3.4 of the fact that a tense/lax distinction can be made only in structures in which v and V are separated by melodic material that is not associated with v or V (or, more simply put, in structures in which SpecVP is projected). For the discussion of foot structure in this section, this detail is immaterial.

naked fact that infinite embedding is a formal-theoretical option does not imply that natural languages impose no limits on such embedding. In syntactic structures, processing considerations curtail multiple embedding (van der Hulst 2010a). Likewise, processing considerations of a different kind limit recursion in phonology. In section 6 we discuss briefly which 'forces' are at work in phonology to make structures that go beyond two degrees of embedding unlikely.

It is generally the case, in syntax, that recursive structures can either result from complementation or from adjunction. There is no *a priori* reason to reject the same two options in phonology. The trochaic structure is recursive because the complement (i.e. dependent) of a head is identical to the maximal projection of the head. This is the kind of recursion that is illustrated in (36). The dependent, which causes recursion, is a complement to the head. But a V-headed structure (a syllable) should in principle also be embeddable inside a larger V-headed structure as an adjunct. Adjunction of a syllable to a trochaic foot would deliver a 'superfoot', which has been the usual account of dactylic patterns. However, if indeed such SWW patterns are structurally ambiguous (resulting from embedding or adjunction), it behooves us to ask whether the occurrence of one or the other can be positively identified. Presumably, as a general rule of thumb, adjunction is resorted to as a last resort: the structure-building engine's first resort will always be to exploit complementation and specification. We see this in syntax, too. What this could mean in phonology is that the adjunction structures result from syllables that remain unparsed, especially in weight-sensitive systems, because they are simply too small (too light) to form a foot by themselves.

4.2 Toward a representation for iambic feet

Moving on to iambs (WS patterns), consider first the structural option of having the specifier position of the vP occupied by an entire syllable – i.e. by another vP, as in (37):

(37)

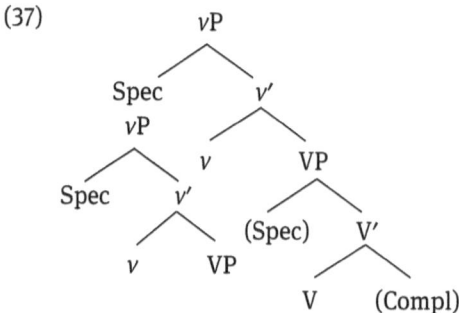

At best, (37) could only represent iambic feet whose stressed syllable lacks an Onset: after all, the first, unaccented syllable occupies the specifier position of the stressed syllable; the specifier position of vP is ordinarily the position for Onsets. To the extent that iambic feet exist in which the accented syllable is (necessarily) Onsetless, they might be candidates for the structure in (37). But no iambic foot whose second syllable has a true Onset could ever be represented in these terms.

While this problem suffices to reject (37) as a structural option for iambs on phonological grounds, there is a further general consideration – emerging from our research program to establish structural analogies between phonology and syntax – which could potentially explain why there are no iambic feet structured as in (37). From syntax, we are familiar, from a variety of different contexts, with the apparent fact that 'bare' propositions (small clauses and complementizerless tensed clauses) very strongly tend not to occur as subjects of predication. As an illustration, consider the following. The sentences *I saw John leave*, *I saw it happen*, and *It happened that John left* are all fine. But 'squeezing' the first two sentences into one by replacing *it* with [*John leave*], which would be semantically perfectly coherent, delivers an ill-formed result: **I saw John leave happen*. By contrast, the *it* of *I saw it happen* can readily be associated with a proposition in 'extraposed' position (as in the third sentence), yielding *I saw it happen that John left*. The ungrammaticality of **I saw John leave happen* is directly germane to the question of whether (37) could represent a well-formed (iambic) foot. In **I saw [[John leave] happen]*, we have one verbal small clause (vP) embedded in another, as its subject/specifier. The result is woeful (regardless, in fact, of the category of the small clauses: **I consider [[John smart] obvious]* is also impossible). As a general rule, 'bare' propositions (subject-predicate structures) cannot be embedded as specifiers inside larger propositional structures. A variety of attempts have been made in the syntax literature to understand this ban. But since we are not aware of an explanatory proposal that covers the entire range of cases, we will content ourselves here with stating what appears to be an empirical generalization: in syntax, 'bare' propositions (subject-predicate structures) cannot be embedded as specifiers of propositions.

Of course it could be that the root of this generalization lies in the semantics – the fact that we have phrased it in terms of propositions (a semantic notion) may be indicative of this. If so, this generalization may not tell us anything about whether (37) is or is not legitimate in metrical phonology. But we actually suspect that we are dealing here with a deeply structural restriction on specification structures, and will henceforth consider (37) not to be grammatical.

If, then, the structure in (37) is not an option for iambic feet, what to do with such feet, if they truly exist? One intuitively highly plausible way to model the structure of iambic feet in line with the syntax-inspired X-bar-theoretic approach is to treat the first syllable of an iambic foot, on the analogy of syntax, as a *TOPIC* (as in *Mary, I really like*) rather than as a subject:

(38)

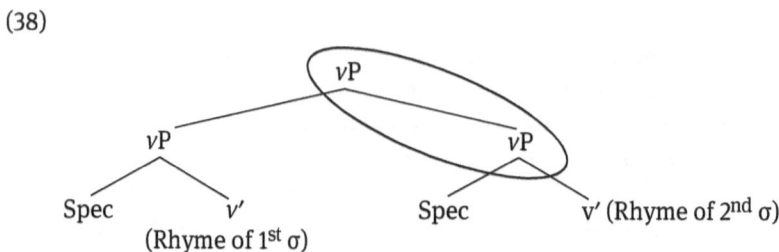

In the structure in (38), the ellipse highlights the 'host' structure. Repetition of the *v*P level of the host is indicative of adjunction, as distinct from specification.[39] This structurally marks the initial unstressed syllable of an iambic foot as *extraprosodic*, in the same way that the initial topic of a topicalization construction in syntax is structurally marked as *extrasentential* (and usually not pitch-accented).

The unaccented syllable of an iambic foot is welcome to have both an Onset and a Coda, as is the stressed syllable: their internal structures are in fact entirely independent of one another. We thus never expect Codas to 'shift' over to Onset positions, nor is ambisyllabicity expected in iambic feet. This is all as it should be.[40]

---

39 A reviewer finds that such adjunction has no analogue in syntax. We disagree. The existence of 'scrambling' phenomena is indicative of the existence of topicalization at the level of the 'bare' predication, *v*P (see also the cartography literature (e.g. Belletti 2004) on low topic positions – customarily represented there with the aid of designated functional projections; we reject functional projections for phonology, and consider there to be underwhelming support for TopP-structures in syntax). Admittedly, '*Mad Magazine* sentences' (*Me wear a tie?!*), which may be the closest thing in syntax to a *v*P occurring by itself as the root, do not allow topicalization (*A tie, I would never wear* vs. **A tie, me wear?!*), but this likely has to do with the speech act involved (cf. rhetorical yes/no-questions, which likewise resist topicalization: **A tie, would I ever wear?!*).

40 The initial syllable of an iambic foot, occupying a position outside the X-bar structural core (a topic or left-dislocated position), is not in a properly governed position: we know this from syntax, where we can point to the impossibility of complementizer omission as an indication to this effect (cf. *Every sane person knows (that) Trump is a buffoon* vs. **(That) Trump is a buffoon, every sane person knows*). So the nucleus of the unstressed initial syllable of an iamb

The syntax literature contains many examples of topicalization phenomena featuring so-called 'connectivity effects' – effects which suggest that the topic binds a copy in clause-internal position that remains either entirely silent (as in the case of 'ordinary' topicalization: *Mary, I don't like*) or partially silent (as in analyses of certain left-dislocation phenomena; cf. German *Maria, ich mag die nicht*, where *die* is a resumptive pronoun in clause-internal position). We could now imagine that iambic feet of the type in (38) would also have the *v*P-adjoined syllable in initial position bind a (partially) silent copy in the complement of the V-head of the accented syllable, and could show 'connectivity effects' (harmony) via this copy. On an analysis of this sort, such iambs really are not underlying feet at all: what underlies them is a trochee whose second syllable is silenced (in part or in full). Along this path, we get a novel and productive purchase on van de Vijver's (1998) conclusion that only trochees exist and that iambs should be represented in trochaic terms.

Given that iambic feet are always weight-sensitive (Hayes 1995), consisting of a heavy, 'bimoraic' stressed syllable that is preceded by a light unstressed syllable, we propose that the structure in (38) results from adjoining a syllable to a structure that is itself a (monosyllabic) *trochaic* foot. As per a proposal in van der Hulst and Ritter (1998), who provide an analysis of so-called minor syllables in Kammu, the resulting structure could, in fact, be called 'prosodic word'.[41] Adjunction of a weak syllable to a following trochaic foot is independently required for initial unstressed syllables in languages like English (as in *balloon* or *rebellion*; the second example, where the weak syllable is adjoined to a 'bisyllabic' trochee produces an amphibrachic (WSW) structure).[42]

---

is not licensed to remain silent. This probably explains the English pronunciation of *Cnute*, with its intrusive schwa: in the iambic foot with /kV/ as the adjoined initial syllable, the Nucleus cannot remain silent because it is not properly governed; a schwa obligatorily spells out the Nucleus. The fact that the other Germanic languages pronounce this name with an initial /kn/ sequence indicates that in these languages this sequence can be represented as a legitimate Onset cluster whereas in English it cannot be. In indigenous words which historically have /kn/ Onset clusters, such as *knee*, English has 'solved' the problem not by constructing an iambic foot with an intrusive schwa as the Nucleus of the adjoined initial syllable, but by cluster reduction (via deletion of the /k/).

41 As suggested in van der Hulst (1997: 120), it is possible that a language with a prosodic 'colon' unit (Hayes 1995: 217) also displays multiple right-strong prosodic words within the domain of (long) morphosyntactic words.

42 We refer to Martínez-Paricio (2013) for a general theory of 'layered (recursive) feet', which, in our approach, all involve adjunction.

4.3 Coordination

While we expect that adjoined syllables are weak, unstressed (or even lacking an overt vowel, as do minor syllables in Kammu),[43] forming units that are usually called (weight-sensitive) iambic feet, colon or even prosodic words, we need to also address the question how full-fledged feet combine into prosodic words that account for primary stress, i.e. represent which foot is the head foot of the word.

We here assume that the subordinate, embedded constituent in the structure of a foot is by definition the weak member and as such intrinsically light (just like adjoined syllables). A heavy syllable thus cannot be embedded. So in a SW Dutch word like *súltan*, *sul* and *tan* (both heavy) will have to form a structure different from any of the ones considered so far in this section: complementation and adjunction (which can only accommodate light dependent syllables) are both unsuitable.[44]

In syntax, there is one more relationship, besides complementation, specification and adjunction, which two constituents can be engaged in: the coordination relation, seen in conjunction and disjunction constructions (*John and/or Bill*). Coordination used to be represented in terms of ternary (or n-ary) branching, with the con/disjunction particle and the con/disjuncts grouped together into a flat structure. But more recent work in syntax has discovered that coordination obeys the binary branching hypothesis. One argument for this is the fact that *Every man and his wife came to the party* allows for a bound-variable interpretation of *his*, whereas *His wife and every man came to the party* does not – something that follows if the first conjunct asymmetrically c-commands the second: the first example is then a garden-variety case of bound-variable pronoun binding, and the second can be assimilated to the 'weak crossover' effect seen in *His wife loves every man*, which likewise makes no bound reading for *his* available. Facts of this sort favor an analysis of coordination in which the first conjunct serves as the specifier of a phrase that contains the conjunction and the second conjunct:

---

[43] This may be a modality effect with no counterpart in syntax: phonological recursion in our view encodes rhythmic structure (see section 6, where we make this explicit). Thus, if a closed syllable is always heavy, it will initiate (i.e., be modeled as) a matrix syllable..

[44] The conclusion that sultan does not have a recursive foot structure is supported by the fact that the diminutive of Dutch *sultan* is *sultannetje*, with schwa insertion, and not **sultantje*: the second syllable (tan) behaves like a stressed syllable despite being less prominent than *sul*. There are some cases like this for which some speakers accept the short form of the diminutive; for such cases one might want to postulate a metrical representation involving complementation (as a true trochee), with the second syllable 'reduced' in some way; see van der Hulst (2008).

(39)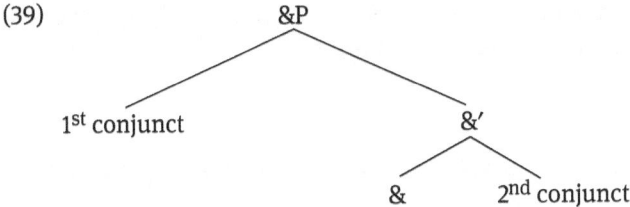

This facilitates an analysis of feet of the *sultan* type, where each of the two constituent syllables is closed and heavy, and the relationship between the two must be such that neither is linked to the other as a dependent, via complementation or adjunction.[45]

The head '&' usually has an overt lexicalization in simple two-way coordinations in languages such as English: *John and/or Bill*. So-called asyndetic coordination (with a silent '&') is possible cross-linguistically for such simple coordination constructions; and in coordination constructions with more than two con/disjuncts, one often finds that all but the last &-head remain silent (*Tom, Dick and Harry*).[46] The fact that in syntactic coordination the deepest conjunct pair behaves differently from preceding conjuncts (in being more likely to take a non-silent conjunction) may have an interesting parallel in phonology. It has been shown that the deepest pair of feet, in a right-branching structure, may behave differently from higher structure, as captured in the occurrence of a SW relationship for the deepest foot pair. See van der Hulst (1984) for an analysis of Dutch stress which states that in the phonological word the right conjunct is labelled strong if and only if it branches.

In conclusion, we propose that 'feet' are combined into the phonological word via conjunction.[47] If the rightmost, structurally deepest foot carries

---

[45] In coordination structures in syntax (at least in Germanic), prosodically the most prominent member of the structure is usually the last one (cf. *Tom, Dick and HARry*). In sultan, for which the main text suggests a coordination approach, primary stress falls on *sul*, the first conjunct. This is not necessarily a contradiction: stress rules work differently at different levels. But this is certainly a matter that should be looked into further if the coordination approach to words like sultan is to be successfully pursued.

[46] The circumstances under which the &-head can or must remain silent need not concern us here: what matters is that a silent allomorph of & exists.

[47] Of course, we also need to look at the alternative of invoking adjunction. It has been argued in van der Hulst (1996, 2012) that the assignment of primary stress take priority over secondary, rhythmic stress. This means that the foot that expresses primary stress is assigned first. The subordinate status of other feet can then follow from recursively adjoining feet to the primary stress foot.

primary stress this means that the word tree has a right-branching structure, which branching nodes being labelled as 'strong'.

5 X-bar structure inside segments and segmental integrity

In this section, we extend the X-bar-theoretic approach to phonological structure to the internal structure of segments, representing the segment as an X-bar projection of a manner component, with laryngeal and place specifications accommodated in the specifier and complement positions, resp., of this X-bar structure. That is, we now delve into a development of the structure in (4b), repeated here, in pursuit of the hypothesis that the fact that segments have an X-bar-theoretic organization of the type in (4b) prevents them from taking additional complements or specifiers outside this structure. We will examine what kinds of consequences this has for the relationship between segmental and suprasegmental phonology.[48]

(4) a.

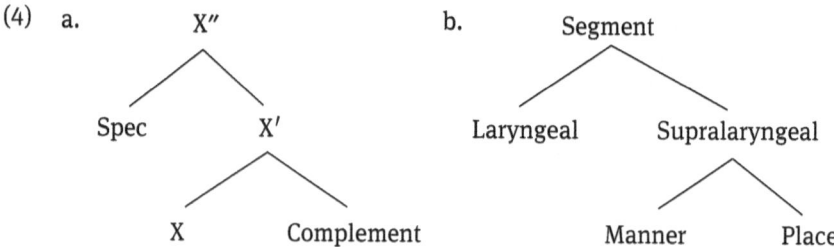

---

[48] In Mutlu (2017), very intelligent use is made of X-bar structure 'below the head', in the representation of the internal structure of segments and also in the representation of the structures resulting from the combination of segments (syllables). Throughout her work, Mutlu exploits the complement-of and specifier-of relations to great effect. It seems to us, however, that she goes too far in this exercise, by allowing constructs that themselves already have a specifier and/or a complement to in turn take a specifier and/or a complement higher up the tree. The most restrictive X-bar-theoretic hypothesis is to say that the fact that segments have an X-bar-theoretic organization of the type in (4b) *prevents them from taking additional complements or specifiers* outside this structure. This is the premise of the discussion to follow.

5.1 Vowels as syllable heads

One immediate implication of pursuing X-bar-theoretic approaches to both the segment and the syllable lies in the delimitation of the candidate set for the function of syllable Nucleus. It is of course perfectly well known that Nuclei are usually vowels, though syllabic consonants also exist. It is not as well known, perhaps, that what unites the kinds of consonants that can be used as syllable Nuclei with the set of vowels is the fact that these are all lack a contrastive specification for laryngeal properties (voicing, in particular[49]). Vowels are voiced by default (though voiceless vowels have been reported to exist, e.g. in Japanese, here voicing is not contrastive); and syllabic consonants are typically sonorants (liquids, nasals), for which voicing is also not distinctive: liquids and nasals can be devoiced, but this is usually an effect of their environment, such as the devoicing of liquids following stops in the Onset position of a stressed syllable in English; syllabically used sonorants are never contrastive for laryngeal properties. Why should there be this correlation between being usable as a syllable Nucleus and lacking a distinctive specification for laryngeal properties?

The answer to this question is straightforward, given our X-bar-theoretic outlook on the structure of the segment and the structure of the syllable. Syllables are *v*Ps, with the Onset as the specifier and the Coda (if present) in the VP (either in SpecVP or in the complement-of-V position). Syllables typically, perhaps invariably, have an Onset (with /ʔ/ as the Onset of apparently Onsetless syllables). Their Spec*v*P position is occupied by this Onset. Laryngeal information, whenever distinctive, is also projected as a specifier: recall (4b). If, as standard X-bar theory has it, there is exactly one specifier per head, it follows that the nucleus, whose Spec*v*P position is occupied by the Onset, cannot also have a laryngeal specifier, hence cannot be contrastively specified for laryngeal information.

5.2 Onset clusters

In the syntax of phonology, clusters of segments are represented with the aid of specification and complementation, with the choice between the two being

---

[49] If phonation types (breathy voice, creaky voice) represent laryngeal properties and can be phonologically contrastive in Nuclei, then two possibilities present themselves. In syllables without Onsets, phonation can be mapped into Spec*v*P. In syllables that do have an Onset (and whose Spec*v*P is hence taken), phonation can be represented as a secondary articulation, with the aid of adjunction.

contextually determined. In observance of sonority sequencing, an /sk/ cluster in Coda position has a structure representing /s/ as the head and that of /k/ in its complement (as in (40)), whereas /sk/ in onset position has the structure for /s/ in the specifier position of the structure for /k/ (as shown in (41)).

(40)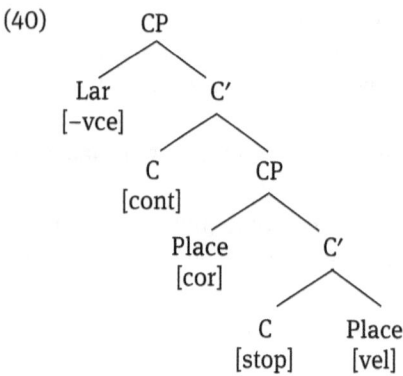

(41)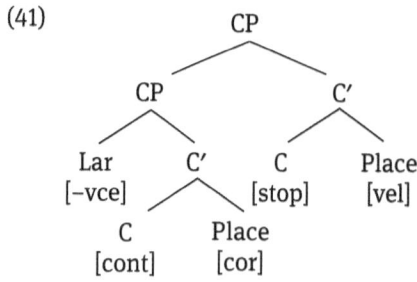

Note that in (41) the /s/ is represented as the specifier of the plosive. Because laryngeal information for /k/ is ordinarily represented in the plosive's specifier position, in /sk/ Onset clusters it is impossible to specify the fricative and the plosive separately for laryngeal information: the laryngeal specification for the /sk/ onset cluster is housed in the specifier position of the fricative. This derives the fact that in English /sk/-onsets, the /k/, even when immediately preceding the nucleus of a stressed syllable, is not aspirated: aspiration is not a feature for which fricatives are specifiable in English; since the fricative is the host of the laryngeal features for the entire /sk/ onset cluster, it follows that /k/ cannot be aspirated in this environment.

In the Coda cluster structure in (40), the plosive is again not specified for laryngeal information of its own, this time because the specifier position of the plosive is occupied by the place specification for the fricative. Even though it is no longer a sister of the manner-head of the fricative, the place specification [cor] is still uniquely associated with the fricative: only the fricative manner-head (C[cont]) c-commands this place specification, so only this manner-head can establish an Agree relation with this place feature. Place specification in phonological structures obtains under closest c-command, not under sisterhood. A close syntactic parallel here is with accusative Case assignment, which often seems to take place under sisterhood, but the only generalization that fits the entire bill is one that says that accusative Case is assigned under Agree (i.e., closest c-command). Thus, compare *I considered this proposal*, in which *this proposal* is the verb's sister, with *I considered this proposal interesting*, where the same noun phrase is now the verb's niece (i.e. a daughter of verb's sister), on the plausible assumption that *consider* in the latter example takes a small clause [*this proposal interesting*] as its complement. In the same way in which this *proposal* is 'shifted downward' into a niecehood relation with the verb ('exceptional Case-marking') under the addition of the secondary predicate *interesting*, so also the place specification for the fricative /s/ (which is 'ordinarily' its complement) is 'shifted downward' into a niecehood relation with the fricative's manner-head (C[cont]) ('exceptional Place-marking'). The 'integrity of the segment' can thus be broken, under the influence of the placement of a full X-bar structure in the complement of a head.

In both (40) and (41), there is room for but a single laryngeal specification, harbored by the specifier of the fricative in both cases. The stop does not have space for a laryngeal specification of its own: its specifier position is occupied, in (40) by the place specification of the fricative, and in (41) by the entire structure of the fricative. The fact that the stop cannot itself be specified for laryngeal properties accounts directly for voicing assimilation in clusters of the fricative+stop. A clear connection presents itself here with the work of Kehrein and Golston (2004), and also Golston and van der Hulst (1999) and van der Hulst (in prep.), where it is argued that syllabic units (Onsets, Nuclei and Codas) can have only one laryngeal and place specification.

So far in this discussion of consonant clustering we have confined ourselves to clusters with an initial fricative and a following stop. Such clusters obey the sonority sequencing principle in Coda position (which is what gives rise to the head–complement structure in (40)) but apparently violate it in Onset position. A sonority scale violation is averted, however, by placing the fricative in the specifier position of the plosive in /sk/ onset clusters, as in (41). With this in mind, let us see what the system should say about /ks/ clusters. These obey the sonority scale in onset position but apparently violate it in coda position. Structurally this means that a /ks/ cluster serving as a syllable onset will have the more sonorous element (i.e., /s/) as the complement of the less sonorous element (/k/), whereas a /ks/ cluster in coda position will have the /k/ as the specifier of /s/.

Entirely parallel remarks apply to stop+liquid clusters. So, in an English /kl/ cluster in Onset position, /k/ takes the liquid as its complement. This entails that the laryngeal specification for the cluster is in the specifier position of the structure for /k/. The liquid hosts the place information for the plosive in its specifier, and hence cannot itself be specified for laryngeal properties. The /kl/ Onset cluster has just a single laryngeal specification – the one in the specifier position of /k/, which is the element for [–voice]. This laryngeal specification scopes over the entire cluster. This derives the fact that in stop+liquid onset clusters in English, the liquid is devoiced. For Dutch, which has no aspiration of voiceless plosives in onsets of stressed syllables, the /l/ in /kl/ onset clusters will be voiced by *default*; the voicing of /l/ in this context is not explicitly represented in the structure. More generally, the prediction that this analysis of stop+C sequences in Onset position makes is that the second element should never be *contrastively* specifiable for laryngeal properties, which seems correct: only liquids, nasals and voice-assimilating fricatives occur in second position in such Onset clusters.

5.3 Codas and the place properties of the Nucleus

The complement position of the manner-head is the locus for the specification of place of articulation. The place feature does not necessarily have to be the complement of the manner-head; but it does have to be in a 'closest c-command' relation with the manner-head (recall the discussion of (40), above). In syllables whose complement-of-V position is occupied by a (non-sonorant) Coda, this leads to the prediction that the distinctive place-of-articulation properties of the syllable Nucleus will be 'shifted downward' into the specifier position of the Coda consonant in the complement-of-V position. In light of the fact that this specifier position is 'ordinarily' the locus of the laryngeal specification of this consonant, this leads to the expectation that a Coda consonant in the complement-of-V position which has to harbor the place specification for the Nucleus cannot be contrastively specified for laryngeal properties.

This delivers a simple perspective on 'final devoicing' in languages such as Dutch or German. When a non-sonorant consonant serves as the Coda of a closed syllable, this consonant is necessarily deprived of voicing, and surfaces voiceless. This follows since, sitting in the complement-of-V position, this consonant must harbor the place feature of the Nucleus, and can itself only have the unmarked value for voicing, which in Dutch and German is [–vce].

For languages (such as English) which do not have final devoicing, the most straight-forward interpretation of the facts, from the perspective of our proposal, would be that their non-sonorant Codas are only *apparent* Codas: structurally, they are mapped into the Onset position of a following syllable (with a silent Nucleus).

5.4 Adjunction: Nasality, tone, secondary articulation

Beyond the head, specifier, and complement positions, additional distinctions can be made with the aid of another mechanism familiar from phrase-structure syntax: *adjunction*. Adjunction is a useful tool for making the oral/nasal distinction. When nasality is strictly confined to an individual segment (for instance, only to the vowel nucleus), adjunction takes place directly at the level of the head. But the nasality marker can also be adjoined higher up the tree. By exploiting the level of adjunction, we can account for the 'reach' of the nasal property (thus, Golston and van der Hulst (1999: 156) point out that nasality can associate to the entire syllable).

For tone, an approach in terms of adjunction also suggests itself, especially for 'spreading' tonal autosegments: adjuncts can have scope over a large portion of the structure; the higher they are adjoined, the wider their scope. Secondary articulations are naturally expressed in the structure with the help of adjunction as well. We will see this at work in the following subsection, where we revisit the place-of-articulation restriction on Coda clusters consisting of a sonorant and a stop, brought up previously in section 3.5, to fill in the details.

5.5 Coda clusters and place of articulation

We have come across a few situations in which both a sonorant and a stop had to be accommodated in the complement-of-V position (as in English *wield*), and we have seen that such situations impose severe place-of-articulation restrictions on the Coda cluster. To under-stand these properly, we need to consider carefully what the resulting consonant cluster looks like – and for this, an understanding of the internal structure of consonants, along the lines of (4b), is highly revealing.

In sonorant+stop sequences which are mapped into the complement-of-V position, the stop is in the complement position of the sonorant. This, in conjunction with the fact that the complement position of a consonant is where its place of articulation is specified, entails that the sonorant of a Coda cluster cannot be specified *by itself* for place. The structure in (42), for a cluster such as /lt/, makes this immediately clear:[50]

(42)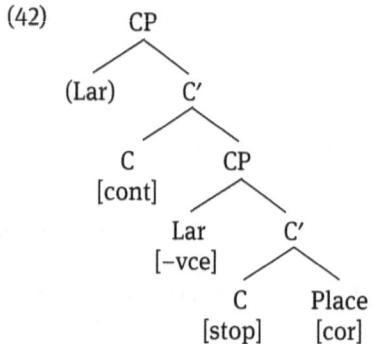

In this structure, the liquid+stop sequence has but a single specification for place: that of the stop, with which the sonorant agrees. This specification must be coronal: otherwise, the liquid, whose C-head c-commands the place specification in the complement of the stop, would be unpronounceable. This is how we derive the fact that the liquid+stop sequence following a long vowel or diphthong in English must be coronal (*wield* vs. **wielk*).

For nasal+stop sequences in Coda position, Botma et al. (2008: sect. 7) find a picture similar to the one documented for liquid+stop sequences in this position. Again, when the preceding Nucleus is a long vowel or a diphthong, nasal+stop Coda clusters can only be coronal (at least in monomorphemic words[51]): the only allowable such sequences are coronal (*fiend*, *find* and *wont* 'inclined', but not **liemp*, contrasting with *limp*, with a short vowel). English

---

50 We placed 'Lar' in the highest specifier position in parentheses because laryngeal information is non-contrastive in the case of liquids, hence arguably phonologically represented only when marked.

51 We added this parenthesis because, as is well known, long vowels and diphthongs can perfectly well be followed by a sequence of a non-coronal nasal and /d/ when this /d/ represents the past-tense or past-participial morpheme: *seemed*, *claimed* and *rhymed* are cases in point. For such sequences, morpheme-to-syllable homomorphism may lead to a structure in which there are two syllables present, the second one representing the inflectional morpheme. The nasal is mapped into the Onset position of the second syllable, and the stop /d/ forms its Coda, occupying the complement-of-V position by itself. (The Nucleus of the second syllable is silent in the examples quoted above; but under the right circumstances, which we will not attempt to characterize, this Nucleus is spelled out as schwa or /ɪ/, as in *learnéd society*.)

We note for full disclosure that Dutch does allow tautomorphemic sequences of a non-coronal nasal and a coronal stop following a long tense vowel: /freːmt/ *vreemd* 'strange'.

nasals ordinarily have a variety of different places of articulation. Why can't these all be shared equally by the two C's in the cluster in (42)? To see this, we need to understand place specification in a bit more detail.

For simplicity of initial illustration, we had used the features [cont], [vce], [stop] and [cor] in our structure in (42). But we believe that the entire *SPE*-based system of distinctive features can and should be replaced with a system in which, throughout the entire range of contrasts, only two unary features or 'elements' are used: |V| for 'open', and |C| for 'closed'. The interpretation of these features depends on the location of these features in the hierarchical structure. For consonants, in the manner of articulation domain (the head of the structure in (4b)) |V| 'open' translates as 'continuant' and |C| as 'stop'; and in the place system (the complement position), |V| means 'low and back', and |C| as 'high and front'. To represent a coronal consonant in this system, a |C| in complement position, marking 'high and front', is sufficient all by itself. But a velar consonant cannot just be marked for place by |V|, which means 'low and back': the 'back' component is certainly appropriate, but to ensure a velar output, the feature |C| must be added as a modifier of |V|, to raise the place articulation up to the velum. For labial consonants, too, a representation involving adjunction is needed: labial(ization) is a secondary articulatory gesture, marked once again as |C| (closing of the lips) in an adjoined position, this time to the element |C|. The details regarding the representation of velar and labial consonants need not concern us. What is important for our purposes is that while plain coronal consonants such as /t/ have their place of articulation specified by a bare element |C| in complement position, velar /k/ and labial /p/ require the presence of a *modifier* in an *adjunction* position to the basic place element.

Let us now return to the structure in (42). Sonorant+stop sequences in the complement-of-V position force the sonorant and the stop into sharing a single place specification in the complement of the stop, under Agree (or c-command). For coronals, this is straightforward: the C-head representing the liquid can engage in a 'long-distance agreement' relation with the place feature |C| in the stop's complement. Now consider velar and labial nasal+stop sequences. Here, the Agree relation between the nasal and the place specification of the stop in (42) fails to fully specify the nasal for the same place of articulation as the stop, which is complex, involving an adjunction structure. This causes the result to crash. In the case of a *coronal* nasal+stop sequence, by contrast, Agree specifies the nasal in just the right way: both nasal and stop are specified as 'plain' |C|, interpreted as 'high and front' (i.e. [coronal]). This explains why tautomorphemic nasal+stop sequences in Coda position following a long vowel or diphthong, where these sequences must be mapped into the complement-of-V position, can only be coronal.

6 Reflections on why recursion is more pervasive in syntax than in phonology

The central thesis of this chapter is that phonology and syntax have recourse to the same computational system, i.e. that both modules are maximally analogous. This thesis goes beyond the claim that both phonology and syntax build hierarchical structures. This claim is commonly made (though not supported by all linguists) with the proviso that the nature of the hierarchical organization is fundamentally different with phonology adhering to 'strict layering', while syntax displays recursive structure. Accepting that recursion is available to phonology does not entail that phonology will display the same amount of recursive structure as morphosyntax. The kinds of structures that are employed in both modules do not exist in a vacuum, but rather are formed to accommodate the substances that these structures are grounded in.

We have already pointed out that syntax displays more syntactic structure than phonology due to the lack of a parallel to morphosyntactic functional categories in the latter. However, there is an additional reason for why recursion in phonology is less pervasive. If we accept the fact that semantic, conceptual structure (Anderson would say 'conceptual *substance*') is inherently recursive, we expect morphosyntax be isomorphic to this semantic, conceptual structure as much as is possible. Certain factors that cause syntactic displacements of various kinds entail a lack of isomorphism, creating a mismatch between morphosyntactic structure and semantic-conceptual structure, which testifies to the relative autonomy of the two modules. Phonological structure accommodates phonetic-perceptual substance, which arguably is not inherently recursive. Rather, as the result of motoric actions, it is essentially sequential.

This may lead to a view that phonology is 'flat' (see Scheer 2013), perhaps only displaying recursion when expressions are morphosyntactically structured. But recursion in phonology is limited even in this case because there is a 'flattening force' that causes disrhythmic structures that contain lapses (sequences of weak units, 'SWWW ... ') to flatten by breaking up in smaller rhythmic units (i.e. SW SW), as shown in Giegerich (1985). This in itself shows that phonological structure is not entirely flat. After all, if there is rhythmic structure this means that the units (syllables, words, etc.) display a structure in which certain units are 'subordinated' to others. Standard metrical phonology has chosen to formally represent this 'subordination' by grouping units into binary, headed constituents. The crucial point of van der Hulst's (2010b) proposal was that subordination can also be encoded in terms of embedding, which then establishes a perfect formal parallel with recursion in syntax.

But the same flattening forces that limit phonological recursion in morphosyntactically structure expressions also prevent level-3 embedding in monomorphemic units. A sequence of four syllables is therefore not structured as a quaternary 'foot'.

(43)
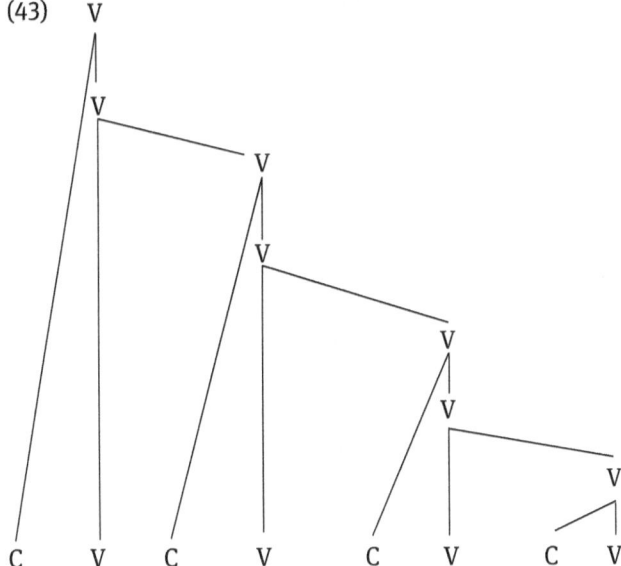

Although formally perfectly correct, (43) creates a dysrhythmic sequence SWWW that does not match the rhythmic structure of a quadrisyllabic sequence. Indeed, a string of four CV units is likely to display an alternating rhythmic structure (SWSW), which suggests the presence in the structure of two consecutive units, each with level embedding:

(44)
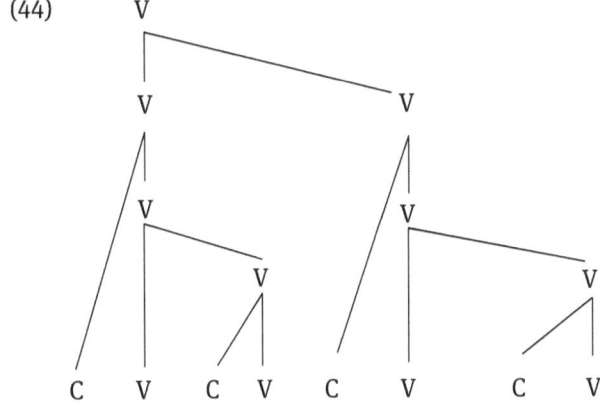

(44) is 'flatter' than (43) and this, we suggest (merely making explicit what most phonologists would take for granted), is a consequence of the rhythmic nature of the 'phonetic substance' that phonotactic structure represents. Beyond the 'magic number' 3, unbounded recursion gives in to rhythm.

7 Conclusion

In this chapter, we have explored a 'radical' approach to the structural analogy assumption. Rather than making suggestions for parallelism based on a 'naïve' version of syntactic theory, we have investigated in detail potential uses in both phonology and syntax of mechanisms that are standardly thought of as being exclusively syntactic, such as recursion, X-bar structure, and, more specifically, the 'light v' structure of multi-argument constructs. We have seen that assigning subordination structures to phonology – not just at the level of the foot but also within the syllable and even in the representation of segments – opens up explanatory perspectives on many a persistent question.

One question that this leaves us with is why, if recursion in phonology is curtailed to a depth of embedding that does not go beyond a structure that is dactylic, phonology could not be limited to adjunction (rather than subordination). If the computational system that is available to phonology and syntax makes both subordination and adjunction available to accommodate apparently recursive effects, why would phonology not limit itself to adjunction? This question boils down to asking whether subordination or adjunction is the default option. If recursion is, as Chomsky now argues, 'The Basic Property' of language, we would be inclined to take subordination as the default mechanism. The usefulness of subordination in phonology reveals itself at many different levels, as we have shown. None of the more microscopic predictions (including but not restricted to those made in connection with 'segment integrity') would be made by a model confining itself to adjunction as the combinatory mechanism in phonology. Recursion in phonology is real, and its results are revealing.

References

Anderson, John. 1987. The tradition of structural analogy. In Ross Steele and Terry Threadgold (eds.), *Language Topics: Essays in Honour of Michael Halliday*, 33–43. Amsterdam: John Benjamins.

Anderson, John. 2011. *The Substance of Language, Volume III: Phonology-Syntax Analogies.* Oxford: Oxford University Press.
Baker, Mark. 1988. *Incorporation: A Theory of Grammatical Function Changing.* Chicago: Uni-versity of Chicago Press.
Belletti, Adriana. 2004. Aspects of the low IP area. In Luigi Rizzi (ed.), *The Structure of CP and IP. The Cartography of Syntactic Structures, Vol.2*, 16–51. Oxford: Oxford University Press.
Bickerton, Derek. 2000. Calls aren't words, syllables aren't syntax: review of Carstairs-McCarthy on language-origins. *Psycoloquy* 11(114).
Bošković, Željko. 1997. *The syntax of Non-finite Complementation.* Cambridge, MA: MIT Press.
Botma, Bert, Colin Ewen and Erik Jan van der Torre. 2008. The syllabic affiliation of postvocalic liquids: an onset-specifier approach. *Lingua* 118, 1250–1270.
Bromberger, Sylvain and Morris Halle. 1989. Why phonology is different. *Linguistic Inquiry* 20 (1), 51–70.
Carr, Philip. 2006. Universal grammar and syntax/phonology parallelisms. *Lingua* 116, 634–656.
Carstairs-McCarthy, Andrew. 1999. *The Origins of Complex Language: An Inquiry into the Evolutionary Beginnings of Sentences, Syllables and Truth.* Oxford: Oxford University Press.
Chomsky, Noam. 1994. Bare phrase structure. *MIT Occasional Papers in Linguistics.* Cambridge, MA: MIT Department of Linguistics and Philosophy, MITWPL.
Chomsky, Noam. 1995. *The Minimalist Program.* Cambridge, MA: MIT Press.
Chomsky, Noam. 2013. Problems of projection. *Lingua* 130, 33–49.
Clements, George N. 1985. The geometry of phonological features. *Phonology Yearbook* 2, 225–252.
Dikken, Marcel den. 2006. *Relators and Linkers.* Cambridge, MA: MIT Press.
Dikken, Marcel den and Rint Sybesma. 1998. Take-serials light up the middle. Paper presented at GLOW Tilburg. Ms., CUNY Graduate Center and University of Leiden.
Fudge, Eric. 1987. Branching Structure within the Syllable. *Journal of Linguistics* 23(2), 359–377.
Garcia-Bellido, Paloma. 2005. The morphosyntax and syntax of Phonology: the svarabhakti construction in Spanish. *Estudios de Lingüística del Español* 22.
Giegerich, Heinz J. 1985. *Metrical Phonology and Phonological Structure.* Cambridge: Cambridge University Press.
Golston, Chris and Harry van der Hulst. 1999. Stricture is structure. In Ben Hermans and Marc van Oostendorp (eds.), *The derivational residue in phonological Optimality Theory*, 153–174. Amsterdam: John Benjamins.
Gordon, Mantthew. 1998. The phonetics and phonology of non-modal vowels: a crosslinguistic perspective, *Berkeley Linguistic Society* 24, 93–105.
Gussenhoven, Carlos. 2008. Vowel duration, syllable quantity, and stress in Dutch. In Kristin Hanson and Sharon Inkelas (eds.), *The Nature of the Word*, 181–198. Cambridge, MA: MIT Press.
Hale, Kenneth and Samuel Jay Keyser. 1993. On argument structure and the lexical expression of syntactic relations. In Kenneth Hale and Samuel Jay Keyser (eds.), *The View from Building 20*, 53–104. Cambridge, MA: MIT Press.
Hayes, Bruce. 1995. *Metrical Stress Theory: Principles and Case Studies.* Chicago: University of Chicago Press.
Hulst, Harry van der. 1984. *Syllable Structure and Stress in Dutch.* Dordrecht: Foris.

Hulst, Harry van der. 1985. Ambisyllabicity in Dutch. In Hans Bennis and Frits Beukema (eds.), *Linguistics in the Netherlands 1985*, 57–67. Dordrecht: Foris.
Hulst Harry van der. 1996. Separating primary accent and secondary accent. In Rob Goedemans, Harry van der Hulst and Ellis Visch (eds.), *Stress Patterns of the World Part I. HIL Publications 2*, 1–26. The Hague: Holland Academic Graphics.
Hulst, Harry van der. 1997. Primary accent is non-metrical. *Rivista di Linguistica* 9/1, 99–127.
Hulst, Harry van der. 2005. The molecular structure of phonological segments. In Philip Carr, Jacques Durand and Colin J. Ewen (eds.), *Headhood, Elements, Specification and Contrastivity*, 193–234. Amsterdam: John Benjamins.
Hulst, Harry van der. 2008. The Dutch diminutive. In Colin J. Ewen, Harry van der Hulst and Nancy C. Kula (eds.), *Trends in prosodic phonology*. *Lingua* 118(9),1288–1306.
Hulst, Harry van der. 2010a. Re Recursion. In Harry van der Hulst (ed.), *Recursion and Human Language*, xv–liii. Berlin: Mouton de Gruyter.
Hulst, Harry van der. 2010b. A note on recursion in phonology. In Harry van der Hulst (ed.). *Recursion and Human Language*, 301–342. Berlin: Mouton de Gruyter.
Hulst, Harry van der. in prep. Principles of Radical CV Phonology.
Hulst, Harry van der. 2012. Deconstructing stress. *Lingua* 122, 1494–1521.
Hulst, Harry van der and Nancy Ritter. 1998. Kammu minor syllables in Head-driven Phonology. In Eugeniusz Cyran (ed.), *Structure and Interpretation: Studies in Phonology*. Lublin: Folium, 163–182.
Hunyadi, László. 2010. Cognitive grouping and recursion in prosody. In Harry van der Hulst (ed.), *Recursion and Human Language*, 343–370. Berlin: Mouton de Gruyter.
Kager, René. 1993. Alternatives to the iambic-trochaic law. *Natural Language and Linguistic Theory* 11, 381–432.
Kaye, Jonathan, Jean Lowenstamm and Jean-Roger Vergnaud. 1990. Constituent structure and government in phonology. *Phonology* 7, 193–231.
Kayne, Richard. 1994. *The Antisymmetry of Syntax*. Cambridge, MA: MIT Press.
Kehrein, Wolfgang and Chris Golston. 2004. A prosodic theory of phonation contrasts. *Phonology* 21, 1–33.
Kratzer, Angelika. 1996. Severing the external argument from its verb. In Johan Rooryck and Laurie Zaring (eds.), *Phrase Structure and the Lexicon*, 109–137. Dordrecht: Kluwer.
Kurylowicz, J. 1948. Contribution a la theorie de la syllabe. *BPTJ* 8, 80–114.
Ladd, D. Robert. 1996. *Intonational Phonology*, 2nd edition 2008. Cambridge: Cambridge University Press.
Larson, Richard. 1988. On the double object construction. *Linguistic Inquiry* 19, 335–391.
Levin, Juliette. (1985). A metrical theory of syllabicity. Ph.D. dissertation, Massachusetts Institute of Technology.
Martínez-Paricio, Violeta. 2013. An exploration of minimal and maximal metrical feet. PhD dissertation, CASTL, University of Tromsø.
Mutlu, Filiz. 2017. Valence and saturation in phonology. M.A. Thesis, Boğaziçi University.
Neeleman, Ad, and Hans van der Koot. 2006. On syntactic and phonological representations. *Lingua* 116(10),1524–1552.
Pike, Kenneth L. and Eunice V. Pike. 1947. Immediate constituents of Mazateco syllables. *International Journal of American Linguistics* 13(2),78–91.
Pinker, Steven and Ray Jackendoff. 2005. The faculty of language: what's special about it? *Cognition* 95, 201–236.

Polgárdi, Krisztina. 2008. The representation of lax vowels in Dutch: a loose CV approach. *Lingua* 118, 1375–1392.
Rowicka, Grazyna. 1999. On trochaic Proper Government. In John Rennison and Klaus Kühnhammer (eds.), *Phonologica 1996: Syllables!?*, 273–288. The Hague: Holland Academic Graphics.
Scheer, Tobias. 2013. Why phonology is flat: the role of concatenation and linearity. Paper presented at the 11th Rencontres du Réseau Phonologique Français, Nantes (1–3 July 2013).
Smith, Norval S. H. 1999. A preliminary account of some aspects of Leurbost Gaelic Syllable structure. In Harry van der Hulst and Nancy Ritter (eds.), *The Syllable: Views and Facts*, 557–630. Berlin: Mouton de Gruyter.
Smith, Norval S. H. 2003. Evidence for recursive syllable structures in Aluku and Sranan. In Dany Adone (eds.), *Recent Development in Creole Studies*, 31–52. Tübingen: Niemeyer.
Sportiche, Dominique. 1996. Clitic constructions. In Johan Rooryck and Laurie Zaring (eds.), *Phrase structure and the lexicon*, 213–276. Dordrecht: Kluwer.
Szigetvári, Péter. 2016. No diphthong, no problem. In Jolanta Szpyra-Kozłowska and Eugeniusz Cyran (eds.), *Phonology: Its Faces and Interfaces*, 123–141. Frankfurt am Main: Peter Lang.
Takahashi, Toyomi. 1993. A farewell to constituency. *UCL Working Papers in Linguistics* 5, 375–410.
Tallerman, Maggie. 2006. Challenging the syllabic model of 'syntax-as-it-is'. *Lingua* 116, 689–709.
Trommelen, Mieke. 1983. *The Syllable in Dutch: With Special Reference to Diminutive Formation*. Dordrecht: Foris.
Ulfsbjorninn, Shanti. 2015. A field theory of stress. Ph.D. Dissertation, School of Oriental and African Studies, University of London.
Vijver, Ruben van de. 1998. The Iambic Issue: iambs as a result of constraint interaction Ph. D. dissertation,. Vrije Universiteit Amsterdam.
Völtz, Michael. 1999. The syntax of syllables: why syllables are not different. In: John Rennison and Klaus Kühnhammer (eds.), Phonologica 1996. The Hague: Holland Academic Graphics, 315–321.
Wagner, Michael. 2005. Prosody and recursion Ph.D. dissertation, . Massachusetts Institute of Technology.
Weijer, Jeroen van de and Jisheng Zhang. 2008. An X-bar approach to the syllable structure of Mandarin. *Lingua* 118, 1416–1428.

Chihkai Lin
Decomposition and recursive structure: Glide formation and vowel lowering in East Asian languages

1 Introduction

Three languages in East Asia, Japanese, Korean and Tsou,[1] all exhibit what appears to be instances of glide formation and vowel lowering, as in (1).

(1) a. Sino-Japanese ʲeu → joː kʲeu → kjoː 'cooperate' 協 Lin (2008)
 b. Sino-Korean oi → we koiŋ → kweŋ 'explode' 轟 Lin (2008)
 c. Tsou e → j tueu → tuju 'three' Chen (2002)
 d. Tsou u → w uveu → úvew 'eighteen' Chen (2002)

In Sino-Japanese (1a), the interaction of vowels [e] and [u] is a diachronic change. Within a morpheme, mid vowel [e] with prevocalic glide interacts with the following high vowel [u].[2] The mid vowel [e] turns into glide [j], and the high vowel [u] is lowered to [o]. A parallel development is observed in Sino-Korean (1b), also as a diachronic change. The mid vowel [o] becomes glide [w], and the high vowel [i] is lowered to [e]. In Tsou, the sequence of vowels [e] and [u] involves two synchronic processes of glide formation. In (1c), mid vowel [e] shifts to glide [j]; in (1d), high vowel [u] turns into glide [w].

The examples in (1) can be accounted for in Element Theory (Backley 2011; Nasukawa 2014, 2015ab, 2016). The changes/processes in the three languages all involve decomposing a mid vowel into elements and then rearranging the elements with other elements within a morpheme. The mid vowel [e] in Sino-Japanese is initially decomposed into elements |I| and |A|. The decomposed elements undergo separate changes. The element |I| independently receives its phonological status as a prevocalic glide [j]. The element |A| interacts with the following high vowel [u] (element |U|) and lowers the high vowel to mid vowel ([u] → [o]). A similar change is also observed in Sino-Korean. The mid vowel [o]

---

[1] Tsou is a Formosan language spoken in Central Taiwan. In the examples of Tsou, stress is marked by the diacritic on vowel as in *úvew* where vowel *u* is stressed.
[2] According to Frellesvig (2010: 321), there is prevocalic glide *-j-* in Sino-Japanese [je.u], but it is only phonetically pronounced in Early Middle Japanese. The prevocalic glide is phonologically recognized later in Late Middle Japanese ([ʲeu] > [jeu]).

is decomposed into elements |U| and |A|. The element |U| becomes glide [w], and the element |A| interacts with the following vowel [i]. Likewise, the interaction leads to mid vowel [e]. In Tsou, only glide formation takes place, vowel [e] turning into glide [j] or vowel [u] into [w].

The above analyses bring out two unexplored issues in Element Theory (Backley 2011; Nasukawa 2014, 2015a, 2015b, 2016). Vowels are represented by three basic elements: |I|, |A| and |U|, phonetically realized as vowels [i], [a] and [u]. Mid vowels are originally composed of two elements, |A I| for vowel [e] and |A U| for vowel [o], as observed in Maga Rukai, a Formosan language, *i-k-caki:* (negative) → *i-k-cke:* (positive) 'excrement' and in Sino-Japanese, [au] → [oː] 'cherry three' (Backley 2011: 29–30). Although composing mid vowel [e] or [o] by using the three basic elements is accounted for in Element Theory, two issues are left unclarified as to whether the reversed change of decomposing mid vowels into elements is a possible direction and as to whether recursive structure can differentiate the phonological changes/processes in the three languages. As the issue concerned with decomposition needs to be explored in detail, I would like to discuss whether decomposing mid vowels leads to corresponding elements as they appear in compounds, |A I| for vowel [e] and |A U| for vowel [o]. As suggested by the examples in (1a) and (1b), mid vowels interact with other vowels and undergo phonological changes, such as glide formation and vowel lowering. If the changes in (1a) and (1b) can be captured in decomposition, I suggest that elements are realized not only in a unidirectional method (high vowel + low vowel → mid vowel) but also in a bidirectional mechanism (high vowel + low vowel → mid vowel; mid vowel → high vowel + low vowel).

The examples in Tsou (1c) and (1d) are concerned with the second issue, that is, the internal structure of a segment, recursive structure in particular. As suggested by the interaction of the element from the decomposed elements with the following vowel in Sino-Japanese and Sino-Korean, the mid vowel turns into glide, and the interaction lowers the high vowel ([e.u] → [jo], [o.i] → [we]). The Tsou example in (1c) shows a simpler process without interaction of the decomposed elements with the following vowel ([e.u] → [ju]). If indeed there is decomposition as in [e] → |A I|, element |A| in Tsou example disappears. Only element |I| retains and shifts to prevocalic glide. In this study, I aim to seek the differences between the changes in Sino-Japanese/Sino-Korean and the processes in Tsou by probing into whether recursion is applicable and whether it makes the distinction. I suggest that recursive structure is a crucial factor not only in differentiating Sino-Japanese in (1a) from Tsou in (1c) in the changes ([eu] → [jo] vs. [eu] → [ju]) but also in distinguishing the two changes in (1c) and (1d) in Tsou.

To investigate the two issues, I introduce the theoretical representation of elements in section 2. More examples of glide formation and vowel lowering in Sino-Japanese, Sino-Korean, and Tsou are provided in section 3 with the decomposing changes and the interaction of the decomposed elements with the following vowels. How Sino-Japanese and Tsou differ in the interaction of the decomposed elements with the following vowel is discussed in section 4. To account for the discrepancy in the changes between Sino-Japanese and Tsou, recursive structure (Nasukawa 2014, 2015ab, 2016) is adopted to show the differences. Section 5 provides a conclusion.

2 Interaction in the three languages: An element-based approach

In this section, I sketch Element Theory and the representations of vowels in the three languages in terms of elements.[3]

2.1 A sketch of Element Theory

Element Theory is a phonological theory utilizing elements to present segments. In most versions of this theory (Backley 2011), there are six basic elements: |I|, |A|, |U|, |ʔ|, |H| and |L|. The first three elements, |I|, |A|, |U|, are the three key elements for vowels. Different combinations of the three elements render different vowels.[4] Single use of the elements |I|, |A|, |U| represents vowels [i], [a] and [u], respectively. To express other vowels, such as mid vowels [e] and

---

3 There are three related phonological theories to Element Theory: Particle Theory (Schane 1984ab, 1995, 2005), Dependency Phonology (Anderson and Jones 1974, 1977; Durand 1986, 1990; Anderson 1987; Anderson and Ewen 1987; den Dikken and van der Hulst 1988; van der Hulst 1989, 2006, 2011; Ewen 1995), and Government Phonology (Harris 1990; Kaye, Lowenstamm and Vergnaud 1990; Charette 1991; Harris and Lindsey 1995).

4 As discussed in great detail about the phonetic foundation for the three basic elements, Harris and Lindsey (1995) and Backley (2011) use dIp pattern for |I| element, rUmp pattern for |U| element and mAss pattern for |A| element. Besides, the three basic elements |I|, |U|, |A| are classified according to position of peak(s) and position of trough(s), as shown below (Backley 2011: 24).

	|I|	|U|	|A|
position of peak(s):	low, high	low	central
position of trough(s):	central	central, high	low, high

[o], the three basic elements have to be combined. Mid vowel [e] comes from compounding elements |I| and |A|, and mid vowel [o] from |U| and |A|. Backley (2011) provides phonological evidence for the compound of elements |I| and |A| for vowel [e] and that of elements |U| and |A| for vowel [o].[5] For example, diphthongs [ai] ~ [æi] in Middle English underwent monophthongization and turned into [ɛː] and [ɔː], as in [aiçt] 'eight' and [lau] 'law' (Backley 2011: 27). Backley (2011) also discusses similar changes in Japanese and Maga Rukai. In Japanese, monophthongization is a common change as in the alternation of [itai] ~ [iteː] 'painful' in native Japanese and vowel coalescence in [kjau] → [kjoː] 'capital' in Sino-Japanese. Merger of low vowel [a] and high vowel [i] or [u] is also observed in Maga Rukai. This change is triggered by deleting vowel [a], as in the negative form [i-k-valuː] 'bee', whose corresponding positive form is [vloː]. When vowel [a] in the negative form is deleted, the element |A| merges into |U|, leading to vowel [o].

The emergence of mid vowels due to the merger of high and low vowels is commonly attested among languages. In Element Theory, it is assumed that combining elements |I| and |A| (or |U| and |A|) forms mid vowel [e] (or mid vowel [o]) in a direction (high vowel + low vowel → mid vowel). However, what is left unknown is whether the mid vowels can be parsed into the elements in a reversed direction as well (high vowel + low vowel → mid vowel; mid vowel → high vowel + low vowel). In this study, I argue that decomposing mid vowels into a sequence of high and low vowels represented by elements is a valid operation. The decomposed elements function at different levels to reach different goals, glide formation for instance.

First, according to Lee (1998: 16), there are two ways of decomposing a segment, portrayed in (2).

(2)   a.   b.   c.

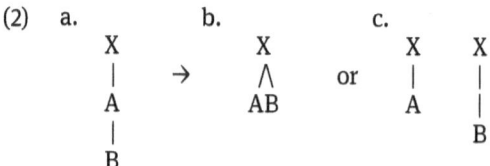

Suppose segment X is composed of elements A and B (2a). If decomposition must take place, there are possible two outputs. In (2b), the two elements are attached under the same skeleton X. In (2c), the elements A and B are detached

---

5 Backley (2011) has provided phonetic evidence for the compounds of |I A| and |U A|. Thus, I omit the phonetic evidence.

and placed under different skeletons so that there are two segments in the output. The decomposition in (2b) is observed in Sino-Japanese and Sino-Korean, and I will discuss them in section 3.1. The change in Tsou, which is similar to (2c), is discussed separately in section 3.2.

Before I proceed to discuss the decomposition in the three languages, it should be briefly discussed here about the notion of dependency relationship of head and dependent in Dependency Phonology. As Backley (2011: 44) points out, head-dependency comes from the asymmetry of two objects when they are linked in a structure, and there are two ways of presenting the head-dependency. For example, both vowels [e] and [ɛ] are represented by the same compound of elements |I A| in Tunica (Backley 2011: 42). A distinction can be made by treating the element |I| as the head in vowel [e] and the element |A| as the head in vowel [ɛ]. Thus, the structure of vowel [e] is |I̲ A| and that of vowel [ɛ] is |I A̲|. It is also possible that the difference between vowels [e] and [ɛ] is that the former contains a head ([e] = |I̲ A|) and the latter has no head ([ɛ] = |I A|). The three elements can also be combined for vowels. In Backley (2012: 87), vowel [ø] corresponds to |U A I̲| and vowel [œ] to |I U A̲|.

The vowels in the three languages in terms of elements are shown in Table 1. In a consistent fashion, the head in each vowel is underlined.

Table 1: Elements for vowels in Japanese, Korean and Tsou.

Japanese	[a] = |A̲|	[i] = |I̲|	[ɯ] = |U|	[e] = |I̲ A|	[o] = |U̲ A|	
Korean	[a] = |A̲|	[i] = |I̲|	[u] = |U̲|	[e] = |I̲ A|	[o] = |U̲ A|	[ɨ] = | |
	[ə] = |A|			[ɛ] = |I A̲|		
Tsou	[a] = |A̲|	[i] = |I̲|	[u] = |U̲|	[e] = |I̲ A|	[o] = |U̲ A|	[ʉ] = |U̲ I|

Modern Japanese has five vowels: [a], [i], [ɯ], [e], and [o].[6] Vowels [a] and [i] bear headedness in elements |A̲| and |I̲|. Mid vowels [e] and [o] contain two elements |I A| and |U A|, in which elements |I| and |U| are headed, respectively. As for vowel [ɯ], Backley and Nasukawa (2016: 276) suggest that vowel [ɯ] should be treated as non-headed |U| and vowel [u] as headed |U̲|. In this study, I follow their suggestion.

---

6 In the history of the Japanese language, the back high vowel is rounded [u]. No modern Japanese dialect distinguishes [u] from [ɯ].

In Korean, I adopt a vocalic system with eight vowels: [a], [ɛ], [o], [ə], [e], [i], [u] and [ɨ] (Park 1996; Lee 1998; Rhee 2002).[7] According to Lee (1998), Rhee (2002), and Heo (2013), Korean vowels [a], [i], [u] and [ə] are represented by one element |A|, |I| and |U|. Vowels [a], [i] and [u] are headed ([a] = |A̲|, [i] = |I̲|, [u] = |U̲|), while vowel [ə] is not ([ə] = |A|). Korean has three mid vowels [e], [ɛ] and [o]. The three vowels present headedness as in |I̲ A| for vowel [e], |I A̲| for vowel [ɛ] and |U̲ A| for vowel [o]. Korean vowel [ɨ] is treated as empty. Given that Korean has a stark contrast between vowel [a], vowel [ə] and vowel [ɨ], the vowel [a] is headed (|A̲|) and vowel [ə] is non-headed (|A|). Vowel [ɨ], therefore, cannot be represented by element |A|. As suggested by Backley (2011: 33), in a language that distinguishes vowels [ə] and [ɨ], one vowel contains element and the other is empty. The fact that element |A| is given to vowel [ə] causes vowel [ɨ] to be empty (| |).

There are six vowels in Tsou: [a], [i], [u], [e], [o] and [ʉ] (Chen 2002: 45).[8] Following the convention of how elements are assigned to Japanese and Korean vowels, vowels [a], [i] and [u] are represented by headed elements |A̲|, |I̲| and |U̲|, respectively. Compounding elements are used with headed element |I̲ A| for vowel [e] and |U̲ A| for vowel [o]. With respect to vowel [ʉ], I follow Backley's (2012: 87) representation for combining elements. I treat vowel [ʉ] as |U̲ I| headed on element |U|.

3 Phonological changes in Sino-Japanese and Sino-Korean and processes in Tsou

Three languages spoken in East Asia are the targets in this section. I focus on Sino-Japanese and Sino-Korean in section 3.1 and Tsou in section 3.2. Section 3.3 discusses two problems in sections 3.1 and 3.2.

---

[7] The exact number of vowels in Korean is controversial. According to Lee (1998: 28), there are other systems with nine vowels or ten vowels depending on how diphthongs [ui] and [oi] are interpreted. A ten-vowel system treats the two diphthongs as monophthongs, [ui] = [ü] and [oi] = [ö]. In a nine-vowel system, [ui] is a diphthong, but [oi] is a monophthong (= [ö]). Shin, Kiaer, and Cha (2013: 102), based on phonetic measurement, propose a seven-vowel system, [i, ɛ, a, ʌ, ɯ, o, u], in which there is no distinction between vowels [e] and [ɛ]. The mid front vowels can be a pair of [e] and [ɛ] (Lee 1998, Rhee 2002) or a pair of [e] and [æ] (Park 1996).
[8] Similar vocalic system for [i, ʉ, u, e, a, o] is also proposed by Tung (1964), Zeitoun (2000), and Chang and Pan (2016). In Ho (1976), Wright and Ladefoged (1997) and Chang and Pan (2016), the six vowels are [i, ɨ, u, e, a, o]. Although there are different interpretations of the high central vowel, this study adopts [ʉ].

3.1 Phonological changes in Sino-Japanese and Sino-Korean

The phonological changes of glide formation and vowel lowering in Sino-Japanese (3.1.1) and Sino-Korean (3.1.2) are discussed in this section. The examples show two changes in mid vowels [e] and [o], which not only reduce to glides but also interact with the following high vowels and lower the high vowels.

3.1.1 Changes in Sino-Japanese

Japanese has at least three lexical strata: native Japanese, Sino-Japanese, that is, loans from Chinese, and foreign loans. The target in this study is Sino-Japanese, a group of morphemes from Chinese divisions III and IV[9] of *Xiánshè* 咸攝 '*Xián* category',[10] which illustrates the interaction of mid vowel [e] and back vowel [u].[11] More examples are provided in (3).[12]

---

[9] As morphemes in Sino-Japanese are loans from Middle Chinese, the analysis of Sino-Japanese phonology always follows the convention of traditional Chinese phonology. According to Tung (2005: 161), division, also used as grade in traditional Chinese phonology, refers to the position of a low vowel as a nucleus. There are four divisions. Division I refers to low back vowel and division II to front low vowel. Division III includes glide [j] and division IV contains high front vowel [i]. Phonemically, the four divisions are /ɑ/ (division I), /a/ (division II), /ja/ (division III) and /ia/ (division IV), phonetically corresponding to [ɑ] (division I), [a] (division II), [jɛ] (division III) and [ie] (division IV).
[10] As for *Xiánshè* 咸攝 '*Xián* category', it is one of the sixteen categories of rhymes (*shè*) in traditional Chinese phonology. In this category, the rhyme consists of a low vowel and a bilabial nasal coda -*m* or a bilabial stop coda -*p*. In this study, the interaction of mid vowel [e] and high vowel [u] occurs in a group of morphemes ending in bilabial stop. When the Chinese are borrowed into Japanese, the Chinese CVP (consonant + vowel + bilabial stop) syllables have to be repaired by inserting a high vowel [u], CVP > CVPU. For example, the morpheme 蝶 'butterfly' from division IV is reconstructed as *thiɛp in Middle Chinese (Tung 2005). When this morpheme is borrowed into Japanese, the Japanese phonotactic constraint amends this morpheme by inserting a high back vowel -*u* (*thiɛp > tepu [tje.pu]).
[11] In modern standard Japanese, the back high vowel is unrounded [ɯ]. In the history of Japanese, the back high vowel is rounded [u]. As this study discusses the historical development, the back high vowel is treated as rounded.
[12] According to Tung (2005), the Middle Chinese of the six examples is *njæp for 鑷 'tweezers', *zjæp for 涉 'wade', *kjep for 劫 'disaster', *jæp for 葉 'leaves', *thiɛp for 蝶 'butterfly', and *ɣiɛp for 協 'cooperate'. The six examples are from two different divisions, and the Middle Chinese is reconstructed with three vowels -æp, -ep and -ɛp. When those words are borrowed into Japanese, they turn into mid front vowel -ep (< -jæp, -jep, -iɛp).

(3) Divisions Phonological changes   Meaning   Kanji
    III   de.pu → de.u [dʲe.u] → zjo: 'tweezers' 鑷
              se.pu → se.u [sʲe.u] → sjo: 'wade'   涉
              ke.pu → ke.u [kʲe.u] → kjo: 'disaster' 劫
              e.pu → e.u [ʲe.u] → jo: 'leaves'   葉
    IV   te.pu → te.u [tʲe.u] → tjo: 'butterfly' 蝶
              pu   → ke.u [kʲe.u] → kjo: 'cooperate' 協

First, Japanese consonant [p] underwent complex phonological changes: intervocalic lenition /-p-/ → /-w-/ and fricativization /p/ → /f/ → /h/ (Frellesvig 2010). The intervocalic [p] continues to lenite and finally reaches full deletion.[13] Meanwhile, the mid vowel [e] is phonetically palatalized, but not yet phonologically recognized (Numoto 1986: 252, Frellesvig 2010: 321). After the lenition of intervocalic -p- is complete, the mid vowel [e] starts to interact with the high back vowel [u], following the pattern in (4) exemplified by the change of 協 [kje.u] 'cooperate'.[14]

(4) a. [kje.u]   b. [kjo]   c. [kjo:]
       O   N   N   O   N   O   N
       | | | ⌐\ | ⌐\   ⌐\
       X   X   X   X X   X   X   X   X   X   X
       | | | | | | | | | |
       | |A| | | | |A| | | |A|→ |
       | ←|I|←|U| | |I| |U| | |I| |U|→ |
       k   e. u   →   k j   o   →   k   j   o:

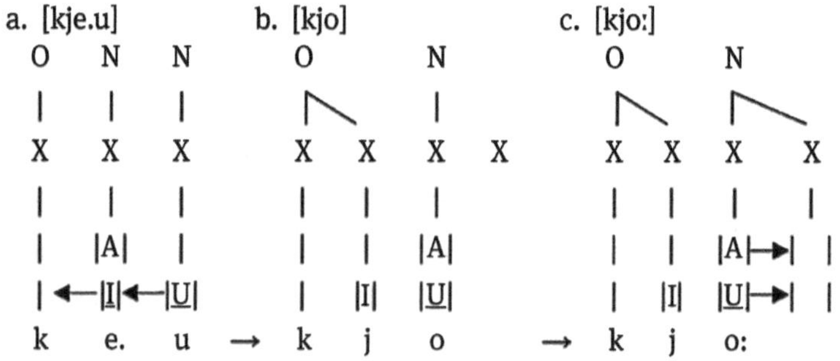

13 The consonant [p] in word-initial position also underwent lenition, but it became glottal fricative h-.
14 The structures in (4) and those for Sino-Korean and Tsou in this section follow Government Theory in which branching is only allowed to be from left to right, as shown below.

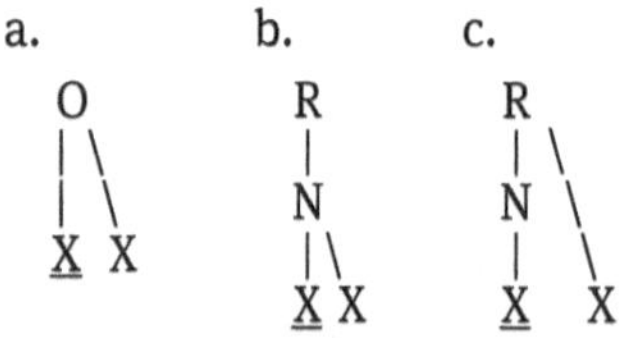

a.   b.   c.
   O   R   R
   |\ | |\
   | \   N   N \
   X X |\ | \
                   X X   X   X

The three structures are called constituent government. This view assumes the relation to be head-initial. For example, in a consonant cluster like /tr/, /t/ governs /r/, or in a diphthong /ai/, /a/ governs /i/.

In (4), the example 協 [kʲe.u] 'cooperate' has two separate syllables. When the mid vowel [e] interacts with the high back vowel [u], elements |I| and |U| move forward. The movement causes the prevocalic glide [j] to be phonologically recognized, and back vowel [o] appears (4a → 4b). After the change, one skeleton in the second syllable is left unassociated (4b). As Japanese has long vowels, compensatory lengthening takes place to guarantee that the unassociated skeleton is connected again with syllable [kjo]. The whole syllable is lengthened [kjo:] (4b → 4c).[15]

3.1.2 Changes in Sino-Korean

Like Japanese, Korean also has at least three lexical strata: native Korean and Sino-Korean, a stratum borrowed from Chinese, and foreign loans. To illustrate the interaction of mid vowel [o] and high vowel [i], the target in this study is Sino-Korean, a group of morphemes from Chinese division II of *Gěngshè* 梗攝 '*Gěng category*'[16] with *Hékǒu* 合口 'roundedness'.[17] More examples are shown in (5).[18]

(5) Divisions Phonological changes   Meaning   Hanza
    II   hoik → hwek ~ høk   'divide'   劃
               hoik → hwek ~ høk   'receive'   獲
               koik → kwek ~ køk   'a family name' 虢
               hoiŋ → hweŋ ~ høŋ   'horizontal'   橫
               koiŋ → kweŋ ~ køŋ   'explode'   轟
               koiŋ → kweŋ ~ køŋ   'wide'   宏

---

15 According to Frellesvig (2010: 321), there are four types of interaction in Sino-Japanese: /iu/, /ʲeu/, /au/ and /ʷou/. The changes of the four types are [iu] > [ju:], [ʲeu] > [jo:], [au] > [wɔ:] > [o:] and [ʷou] > [wo:] > [o:]. The changes suggest a merger of [ɔ:] and [o:] in the historical changes of Sino-Japanese (Numoto 1986: 253).
16 *Gěngshè* 梗攝 is another category of the sixteen rhymes in traditional Chinese phonology. In this category, a syllable ends in velar coda -ŋ or -k.
17 *Hékǒu* 合口 refers to labial glide [w] in traditional Chinese phonology.
18 According to Tung (2005), the Middle Chinese of the six examples is *xuæk for 劃 'divide', *ɣuæk for 獲 'receive', *kuɐk for 虢 'a family name', *ɣuɐŋ for 橫 'horizontal', *xuæŋ for 轟 'explode', and *ɣuæŋ for 宏 'wide'. When the Middle Chinese is borrowed into Korean, the labial glide [w] and low vowel merged as mid vowel [o]. In this category, the high vowel [i] is inserted when it is in front of a velar consonant, due to the transition from vowel [o] to velar coda. Take 轟 'explode' as an example. Its Middle Chinese is *xuæŋ, which undergoes low vowel coalescence ([uæŋ] → [oŋ]) and high vowel insertion ([oŋ] → [oiŋ]). Thus, the form is [koiŋ].

When mid vowel [o] interacts with high vowel [i], the output is [we]. Mid vowel [o] turns into labial glide [w], and high vowel [i] is lowered to [e] (Lee and Ramsey 2000).[19] In modern Korean, the sequence [we] can also be optionally monophthongized as [ø] (Sohn 1999; Lee and Ramsey 2000; Kang 2003; Martin 2006; Lee and Ramsey 2011).[20] The interaction of mid vowel [o] and high vowel [i] is illustrated by 轟 'explode' in (6).

(6) a. [koiŋ]   [kweŋ]   b. [koiŋ]   [køŋ]

```
     O N     O       O   N  O         O  N      O         O  N   O
     | ∧     |       |   ∧  |         |  ∧      |         |  |   |
     X X  X  X       X X X  X         X  X X    X         X  X   X
     | |  |  |       | | |  |         |  | |    |         |  |   |
     | |A| |  |      | | |A| |        |  |A| |   |        |  |A| |
     |←|U|←|I| |     |  |U| |I|       |  |U| |I| |        |  |U| |
     |  |  |  |      |  |  |  |       |  |  |  |  |       |  |I| |
     k  o  i  ŋ  → k  w  e  ŋ        k  o  i  ŋ  →  k  ø  ŋ
```

In (6), in the interaction of vowels [o] and [i], glide formation and vowel lowering can be observed in the change in (6a), *koiŋ* > *kweŋ*. Elements |U| and |I| moves forward. Hence, glide [w] appears, and vowel [i] is lowered. If monophthongization occurs, the output becomes a rounded vowel [ø] in (6b), *koiŋ* > *køŋ*. In this case, element |I| mergers into elements |A| and |U|, and the three elements lead to vowel [ø]. As vowel length is not distinctive in modern Korean, the output is monomoraic after vowel change.[21]

3.1.3 Decomposition of mid vowels in Sino-Japanese and Sino-Korean

The morphemes from Chinese divisions III and IV of *Xiánshè* 咸攝 'Xián category' in Sino-Japanese and those from Chinese division II of *Gĕngshè* 梗攝

---

[19] In the historical development of Korean, *oi* is still [oi] in the 18th century (Park 2008: 172).
[20] According to Lee and Ramsey (2011: 294), if there is no consonant in word-initial position, *we* is still pronounced as [we] without undergoing monophthongization.
[21] As Martin (2006) suggests, [oi], which could alternatively be long [øː], should be associated with two moras in history.

'Gěng category' with Hékǒu 合口 'roundedness' in Sino-Korean undergo similar changes, involving glide formation and vowel lowering, as shown in (7).[22]

(7)   Sino–Japanese | Sino–Korean

a. Glide formation

```
        N       N       O    |   N               O
        |       |       |    |   /\              |
        X       X       X    |  X  X             X   X   X
        |       |       |    |  |  |             |   |   |
       |A|     |U|    |I| |A|,|U||A||I|        |U| |A|,|I|
       |I|                    |  |U|
        e   +   u   →   j    |   o   +   i   →   w
```

b. Vowel lowering

```
        N       N       N    |   N                   N
        |       |       |    |   /\                  |
        X       X       X    |  X  X             X   X
        |       |       |    |  |  |             |   |
       |A|     |U|    |I|   |A| |A| |I|        |U| |A|
       |I|                   |U| |U|                |I|
        e   +   u   →   o    |   o   +   i   →   e
```

The examples in (7) have suggested that a sequence of vowels [eu] ([oi]) become [jo] ([we]), respectively. The mid vowel [e] in Sino-Japanese is decomposed into |I A|. The element |I| independently turns into glide [j]. The other decomposed element |A| interacts with the following vowel [u] (= |U|).[23] The interaction of element |A| with element |U| lowers the high vowel [u] to mid vowel [o]. Sino-Korean shows similar changes, vowel [o] being decomposed

---

22 The two changes in (7) are not in an ordering. Glide formation does not feed vowel lowering. Instead, the two changes occur simultaneously. In addition, the back vowel should be [u] instead of [ɯ] in historical Japanese phonology. Thus, the change in (7) for Sino-Japanese is represented by vowel [u] with a headed element |U|.
23 Backley (2011: 65) suggests that vowels [i] and [u] share the similar elements with the corresponding glides [j] and [w].

into |U A|. Element |U| shifts to glide [w] and element |A| interacts with the following vowel [i] (= |I|). The output is [we]. The full change is shown in (8) (N = Nucleus, O = Onset).

(8) Sino-Japanese   Sino-Korean

```
      N      N          O    N      N               O    N
      |      |          |    |      ⌐¯¯¯¯¯¯¬        |    |
      X      X          X    X      X      X        X    X
      |      |          |    |      |      |        |    |
     |A|    |U|        |I|  |A|    |A|    |I|      |U|  |A|
     |I|                     |U|    |U|                  |I|
      e  +   u    →     j    o      o  +   i   →    w    e
```

The changes in (8) illustrate the decomposition of vowels [e] and [o] into elements |I A| and |U A|, and the decomposed elements undergo glide formation and interact with the following vowel. The change in Sino-Japanese ceases when the output is [jo]. However, as the data in (6) show, the change in Sino-Korean can continue even if the output is [we]. The output [we] in Sino-Korean may undergo monophthongization [we] → [ø]. When this change takes place, the elements are combined into a complex compound |I U A| for vowel [ø] with the head on element |I| (Backley 2012: 87).[24]

3.2 Phonological processes in Tsou

In Tsou, a sequence of vowels [e] and [u] does not interact. The vowel independently turns into glide. Chen (2002) reports that palatal glide [j] can alternate with vowel [e] in a sequence of vowels [e] and [u].[25] In addition to the example

---

[24] In |I U A| for vowel [ø], the three elements are interpreted as that the elements |I U| are closer to each other than to the |A| element. However, Lee (1998: 29) suggests two licensing constraints in Korean: (a) |I| and |U| cannot be combined and (b) |U| does not license operators. The two constraints eliminate vowel ö (= [ø]), which is |A I U| in Lee's notation, from the vowel inventory (cf. Backley's (2012: 87) notation for vowel [ø] = |U A I|). Although Lee (1998) and Backley (2012) hold different views on how vowel [ø] is combined, I do not intend to argue against any of them, since vowel [ø] is not the target in this study.
[25] Chen (2002) argues that underlyingly there are no palatal and labial glides. They are vowels /e/ and /u/ as the underlying forms. The surface forms are interpreted as [j] and [w].

in (1c), whose underlying form is [tu.eu], two more examples, *júso* and *vóju*, are provided in (9) (Chen 2002: 35).²⁶ In (9), the process is illustrated by the word 'three'.²⁷

(9) a. /tueu/ ⟶ [tú.ju] 'three'

```
        N   N   N           N   O   N
        |   |   |           |   |   |
        X   X   X           X   X   X
        |   |   |           |   |   |
       |U| |A| |U|         |U| |I| |U|
           |I|
        t   u  e  u    →    t   u   j   u
```

b. /euso/ → [jú.so] 'two'
c. /voeu/ → [vó.ju] 'eight'

According to Chen (2002: 35–36), the underlying forms of the three examples in (9) include mid vowel [e]. In their surface forms, the mid vowel [e] reduces to palatal glide [j] when it is in word-initial or intervocalic position. In the three Tsou examples, although the mid vowel [e] is followed by high vowel [u], the two vowels do not interact. Instead, only glide formation takes place. This single process in Tsou significantly differs from those in Sino-Japanese and Sino-Korean in the interaction where two adjacent vowels undergo monophthongization.

The second process in Tsou, as shown in (1d), is that the mid vowel [u] in the sequence of vowels [e] and [u] reduces to glide [w]. This change is attested when the two vowels appear in word-final position, and the mid vowel [e] does not appear intervocalically. More examples are listed in (10) (Chen 2002: 35). I also show the process of the word 'eighteen' in (10).

---

26 According to Blust and Trussel's online Austronesian Comparative dictionary (http://www.trussel2.com/acd/), the Proto-Austronesian of the three examples is *duSa for two, *tulu for three and *walu for eight. The proto forms suggest that the mid vowel [e] should stem from alveolar consonant [d] or [l].
27 In Chen (2002), *y* is used for palatal glide. In this study, Tsou *y* is replaced by *j*. Chen (2002) also provides prosodic feature with a stress marker for each example. In this study, the prosodic features are retained.

(10) a. /uveu/ → [úvew] 'eighteen'

```
      N        N   N        N        N
      |        |   |        |        ⋀
      X        X   X        X        X   X
      |        |   |        |        |   |
     |U|      |A| |U|      |U|      |A| |U|
              |I|                    |I|
      u    v   e   u    →    u   v   e   w
```

b. /mehaveu/ → [mehavew] 'eight bars of X'
c. /mehateu/ → [mehatew] 'three bars of X'

Although the examples in (9) and (10) are attested in the same sequence, they differ in the phonological environment. The mid vowel [e] in either word-initial or intervocalic position reduces to glide [j]. On the other hand, the high vowel [u] in word-final position reduces to bilabial glide [w]. For example, the word *uveu* 'eighteen' in (10) has two vowels [e] and [u] after consonant [v]. In word-final position (as well as non-intervocalic for mid vowel [e]), the high vowel [u] reduces to glide [w].

The decomposition in Tsou differs from that in Sino-Japanese and Sino-Korean. The sequence of vowels [e] and [u] in non-final or intervocalic position does not generate a new vowel. Instead, the contact of the two vowels only renders prevocalic glide ([eu] → [ju]), as shown in (11).

(11)
```
     N        N       O   N           O   N
     |        |       |   |           |   |
     X        X       X   X           X   X
     |        |       |   |           |   |
    |A|      |U|     |I| |U|  |A|  → |I| |U|
    |I|
     e    +   u   →   j   u           j   u
```

The mid vowel [e] is decomposed into |I A|, and the element |I| shifts to glide [j]. Nevertheless, the element |A| does not interact with the following vowel [u], and it is left unassociated. The stranded element |A| in (11) needs to be removed from the structure. In certain vowel weakening processes, such as [e] → [i] (|A I| → |A I|) and [o] → [u] (|A U| → |A U|) (element suppression as shaded in the examples), Backley

(2011: 35) suggests that suppressing element |A| in mid vowels for vowel weakening would lead to vowel raising. It might be argued that the glide formation from mid vowel [e] in Tsou also involves two steps: vowel weakening ([e] → [i]) and glide formation [i] → [j]. This argument is not completely excluded in this study, but a simpler process is proposed by appealing to recursive structure. I will discuss this issue in section 4.

Besides the prevocalic glide formation, high vowel [u] in Tsou reduces to glide [w] when it appears in word-final position (/eu/ → [ew]). This change does not involve decomposing the mid vowel. It is simply recognized as reinterpreting the high vowel [u]. According to Backley (2011: 65), the pairs of vowel and glide are represented by the same element, |U| for [u] and [w] and |I| for [i] and [j]. The difference between vowel and glide is their distribution. Vowel is part of rhyme, assigned to nucleus. Glide, on the other hand, belongs to non-nucleus position (Backley 2011: 65). Glide formation in the change [eu] → [ew] in Tsou is portrayed in (12) by changing the status from nucleus of element |U| to other position.

(12)
```
     N           N           N
     |           |          ╱╲
     X           X          X   X
     |           |          |   |
    |A|         |U|        |A| |U|
    |I|                    |I|
     e     +     u    →     e   w
```

3.3 Problems in sections 3.1 and 3.2

Thus far, I have discussed the decomposition in Sino-Japanese, Sino-Korean, and Tsou. It is apparent that mid vowel [e] in Sino-Japanese and mid vowel [o] in Sino-Korean can be parsed into the corresponding elements |I A| and |U A|. The data and analyses in sections 3.1 and 3.2 support the hypothesis that mid vowels can be decomposed into the elements identical to the basic three elements. From the three elements, there are compounds |I A| for the vowel [e] and |U A| for the vowel [o]. In addition to decomposition, I also have discussed the glide formation from back vowel ([u] → [w]) in Tsou. The process is simply a change of position of the element from nucleus to other position.

There are two problems in sections 3.1 and 3.2. The decomposition in (8) follows the standard view of government-based approach. A question is concerned with the status of prevocalic glide. In (8), the prevocalic glide belongs to the onset. Nevertheless, Lawrence (2004: 24) argues that the prevocalic glide in Sino-Japanese is part of the nucleus, not part of the onset. Similar argument is also proposed by Lee (1998: 45) for Korean. It is apparent that the government-based approach and the status of the prevocalic glide are contradictory. The other problem is the stranded element |A| in Tsou in (11). To obtain a faithful output, it is necessary to erase the element |A| from the structure.

To avoid the misinterpretation of prevocalic glide in Sino-Japanese and Sino-Korean, and the procedure of erasing the stranded elements, I argue that if recursive structure is incorporated, the two problems can be avoided. To show how recursive structure solves the two problems, I adopt Nasukawa's recursive structure (2014, 2015ab, 2016) and discuss in section 4 below.

4 Recursive structure in the changes in Sino-Japanese/Sino-Korean and process in Tsou

The structures in section 3 account for glide formation and vowel lowering in Sino-Japanese and Sino-Korean without recognizing the possibility of recursive structure. The Tsou examples, however, present a completely different process. In section 3, I have shown that high vowel [u] in Tsou independently becomes glide [w] without interacting with the preceding mid vowel [e]. The phonological environment in Tsou is similar to the one in Sino-Japanese. Both of them are in a sequence of vowels [e] and [u] and in word-final position. In Sino-Japanese, the sequence of vowels [e] and [u] not only involves glide formation [j] but also generates a new vowel [o], whereas in Tsou only glide formation is observed in the output.

In section 3, I have discussed one possible way of analyzing the sequence of vowels [e] and [o] with two steps: (a) raising mid vowel to high vowel, e.g. [e] → [i] and (b) changing the position of the element from nucleus to non-nucleus position, [i] → [j]. Although the two steps specify the change of glide formation, I argue that this issue can also be solved in terms of recursive structure. There are two ways of presenting the internal hierarchy.[28] The structure in (13) follows the basic tree diagram in X-bar approach with three basic notions: the head, the Spec (= specifier) and the Comp (= complement) (Nasukawa 2014, 2015b).

---

[28] More details concerning recursive structure are discussed by van der Hulst (2010ab).

(13)

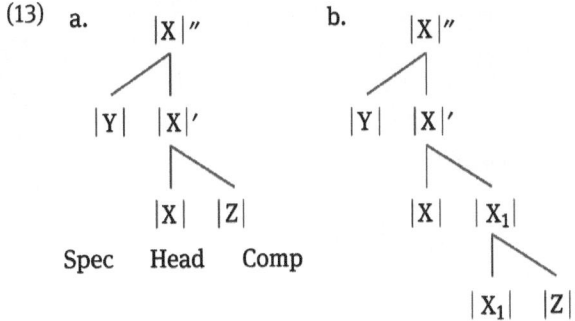

    Spec Head Comp

In (13a), |Y| occupies the Spec, which is higher than the other constituents. In this position, the segment is interpreted as a consonant. If element |I| appears in the Spec, it is glide [j]; if element |U| appears in this position, it is glide [w]. |X| is the head in the structure, followed by the Comp (= |Z| in 13a), which is the dependent (Dep) of the head. When the head is taken by element |A| and the Comp by element |U|, the phonetic realization is [au]. Together with the Spec, element |I| for instance, there is [jau]. A more complex tree is (13b) in which the Spec corresponds to |Y|, the head to |X|, and the Comp to |X1|, which also functions as the head for |Z|. Structure (13b) can represent mid vowel [e] or [o] by adding the adjunct to structure (13a). More details are provided in (15) below.

According to Nasukawa (2014, 2016), there are three heads (baseline resonance): |A|-type (ə), |I|-type (i) and |u|-type (ɯ). The fundamental structure of Japanese vowel is shown in (14) (Nasukawa 2014).

(14)   a. ɯ   b. a   c. i   d. ɯ

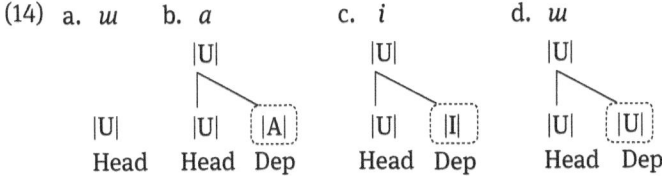

In building the structure for Japanese vowels, the head is taken by element |U| (= vowel [ɯ]) in (14a). When the dependent appears, the phonetic realization varies. In (14b), when the dependent is taken by element |A|, the phonetic realization is vowel [a]. When the dependent is element |I|, the phonetic realization is vowel [i] (14c). As for vowel [ɯ], the dependent is element |U|. With regard to vowels [e] and [o], they are represented in a more complex structure, as in (15).

(15) a. *e*   b. *o*

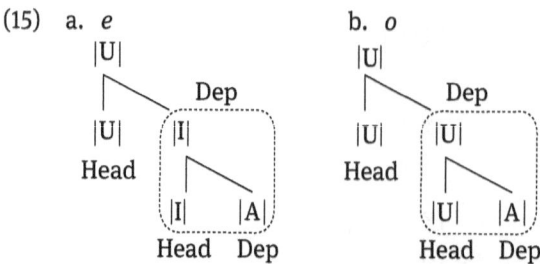

In (15a), at the higher level, the head is |U| and the dependent is |I|, which also functions as the head for the dependent |A| at the lower level. Similar structure is also applicable to mid vowel [o].

If there is prevocalic glide, the structure requires the Spec. Take English as an example. When element |I| takes the Spec, the output is glide [j]. If element |A| takes the head, the vowel is [ə]. In (16a), the output is [jə]. When other element appears in the Comp, the output is [ji] (= |I|), [ju] (= |U|), or [ja] (= |A|), shown in (16b), (16c) and (16d) below.

(16) a. *jə*   b. *ji*   c. *ju*   d. *ja*

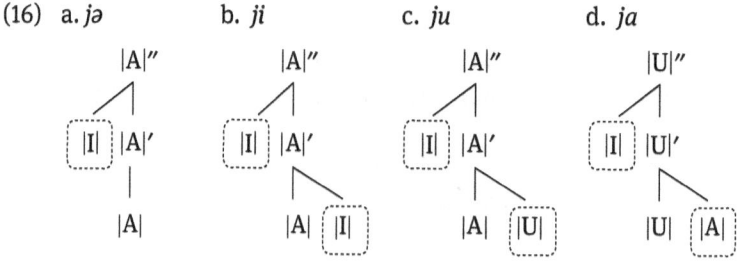

The structure in (17) expresses recursive structure for [je] and [jɛ]. When the Spec is taken by element |I|, the head by |A|, and the Comp also by |A| with a dependent |I|, the output is [je]. When the head is taken by |A| and the Comp by |I| with a dependent |A|, the output is [jɛ].

(17) a. *je*   b. *jɛ*

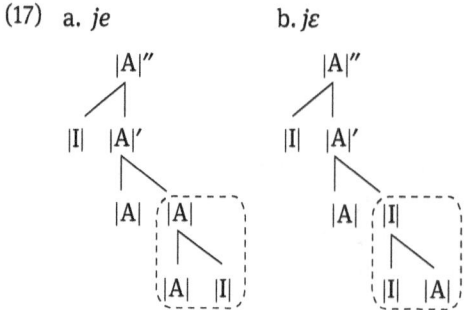

The structure in (18) is a simplified version without giving a status to the Spec. The structure is shown merely by the head and the dependent, as in (18) for Japanese [ɯ], [e] and [ja] (Nasukawa 2016).

(18) a. ɯ   b. e   c. ja

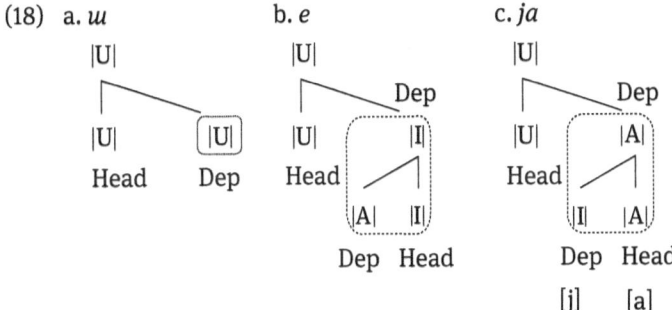

For Japanese vowel [ɯ], the structure in (18a) includes the head taken by element |U| with the dependent |U|. For vowel [e], an embedded structure is a necessity. The structure (18b) for vowel [e] includes compounding elements at different levels. The higher level consists of the head |U| and the dependent |I|, which also functions as the head for the dependent |A| at the lower level. The structure (18c) for [ja] resembles (18b) for mid vowel [e] in terms of hierarchy, but they are different in the dependent at the higher level. The dependent at the higher level in (18c) is taken by element |A|. At the lower level, element |A| functions as the head, and the dependent is element |I|, which is interpreted as glide [j].

This study uses the representation in (18) to analyze glide formation and vowel lowering in Sino-Japanese and Tsou as cases of recursive structure. The recursive structure of the changes of [ⁱeu] → [joː] in Sino-Japanese is given in (19).²⁹

---

29 According to Nasukawa (2014), the head plays a role that is acoustically weak. In Japanese, the head is |U| (Backley and Nasukawa 2016; Nasukawa 2016).

(19) je + u → jo

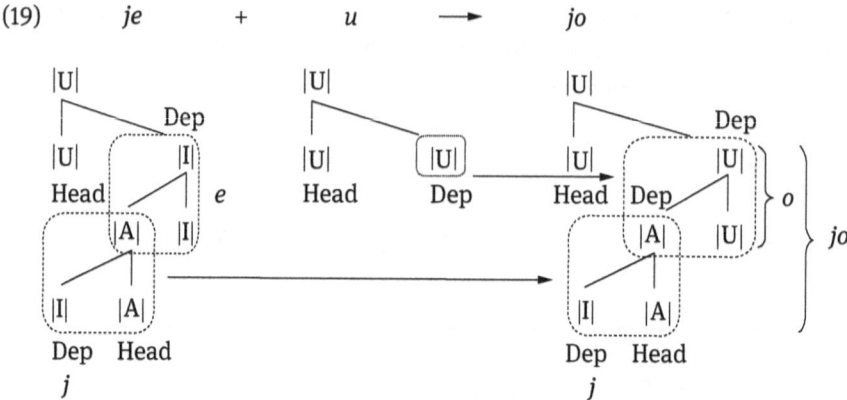

In (19), mid vowel [je] is represented by a compound of two elements |I| and |A| with two levels. At the higher level, elements |A| and |I| represent vowel [e]: at the lower level, element |I| represents prevocalic glide. As for vowel [u], it is represented by a single element |U|.[30] The interaction mainly takes place at the high level by replacing the element |I| in vowel [e] with the element |U| in vowel [u]. The replacement of element |I| leads to a similar structure to [ja] (=18c) at the lowest level. Meanwhile, element |A|, also as the dependent at the higher level, interacts with element |U|. The interaction renders a structure phonetically corresponding to vowel [o].[31] Consequently, the output is [jo] with three levels.[32]

The glide formation in Tsou is shown in (20), in which the head in the structure is taken by element |A|.[33]

---

[30] Due to the fact that the prevocalic glide is only realized at the phonetic level [C^{j}eu] in Early Middle Japanese, I do not specifically mark the glide in (19).

[31] As Nasukawa (2015ab) contends, the dependent is phonetically prominent. In (19), element |A| mainly functions at the higher level as the dependent for vowel [o]. At the lowest level, element |A| is simply for building the structure.

[32] In (4), I have suggested that mora is preserved in Japanese by lengthening the vowel. As Element Theory does not specifically deal with compensatory lengthening, I omit the prosodic change in (19).

[33] This assumption is based on alternation [e] ~ [ə]. According to Chen (2002: 44), vowel [e] reduces to vowel [ə] when it is unstressed, [əmóo] 'house' for example. The weak vowel [ə] is not an underlying vowel for two reasons. First, vowel [ə] is limited to word-initial position. Second, in reduplication like [eemóo] 'build a house', there is no reduction. Thus, I assume Tsou to be a |A|-type language.

(20)

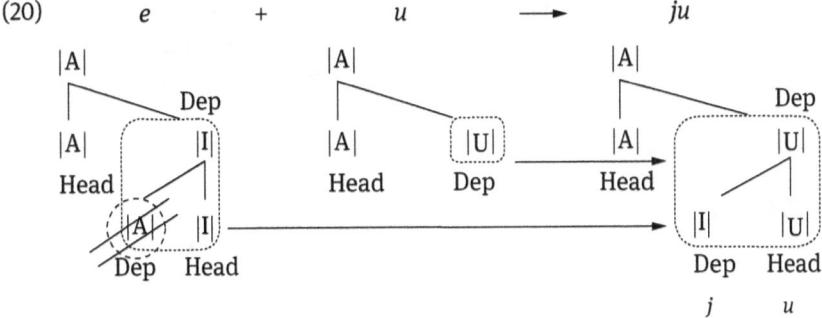

The process in (20) is simpler than that in (19). The structure of high vowel [u] is faithfully preserved in the output. The structure of mid vowel [e], nevertheless, is reconstructed by suppressing element |A| in the output. In other words, the dependent element |A| is removed. Then, the element |I| is combined with high vowel [u]. As element |I| is attached to the lower level as the dependent, the output is [ju].

In addition to the change in (19) and the process in (20), the interaction of vowels [o] and [i] in Sino-Korean is shown in (21).

(21)

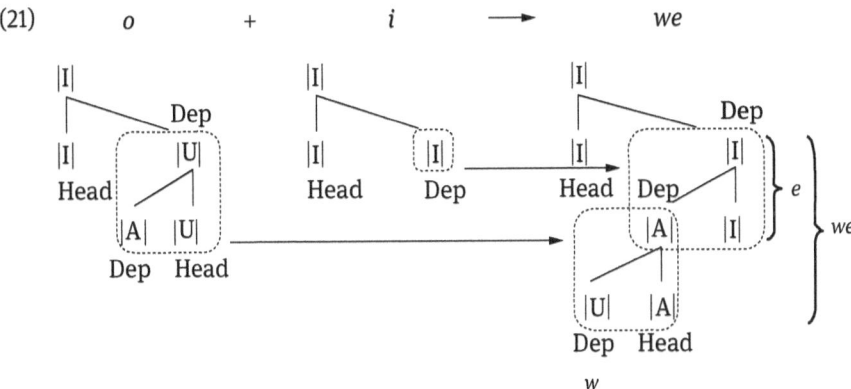

First, I assume Korean to be an |I|-type language.[34] In (21), there is no prevocalic glide before vowel [o]. In the interaction of vowels [o] and [i], the structure of

---

34 It is not easy to determine the head for building structure in Korean. According to Kim-Renaud (2009: 25), the weak vowel in Korean is [ɨ], but it lacks any head, as discussed in Table 1. This weak vowel is regarded as a variant of three default epenthetic vowels [ə], [i], and [ɯ] (Nasukawa 2014: 11). A phonetic analysis by Shin, Kiaer and Cha (2013: 103–104) has shown that vowel [ɨ] is closer to vowel [i] for male native speakers, but it locates in the middle

high vowel [i] is preserved, and mid vowel [o] is added to high vowel [i]. To guarantee that prevocalic glide appears in the right position and that the vowel [e] has a dependent element |A| at the higher level, elements |A| and |U| from vowel [o] need to reverse. The element |U| becomes the dependent at the lowest level, phonetically corresponding to glide [w]. The dependent |A| becomes the head at the higher level and interacts with element |I|. Consequently, the output is [we].

Before closing this section, I would also like to discuss the phonological change in (10), [eu] → [ew], postvocalic glide formation in Tsou. The change also stems from the contact in a sequence of vowels [e] and [u], but it is restricted in word-final position, shown in (22).

(22)

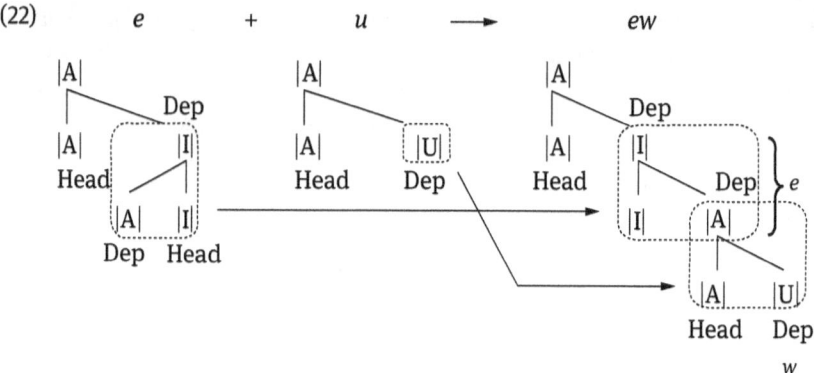

The process in (22) preserves the structure of mid vowel [e]. High vowel [u] is added to mid vowel [e]. Element |A| remains as the head in the output. As the dependent, element |U| is no longer used for high vowel, but for labial glide [w] in the output. A comparison of the processes in (20) and (22) supports recursive structure. The processes have the same sequence of vowels [e] and [u], but the outputs are represented by different structures. When element |A| from the decomposed mid vowel [e] is suppressed in the output, two levels are sufficient for the structure. When the element |A| is preserved in the output, it is necessary to have an extra level for the labial glide [w].

Thus far, I have discussed different changes/processes in the three East Asian languages by using recursive structure. Unlike the structures in (8), (11) and (12), postulating recursive structure within a morpheme crucially avoids the ambiguous status of prevocalic glide in the structure. In the recursive structure, the prevocalic glide in Sino-Japanese and Sino-Korean is grouped with the main

---

of vowels [i] and [u] for female native speakers. To facilitate an effective discussion, I propose that the baseline for Korean is |I|.

vowel. This position conforms to the analysis of prevocalic glide by Lawrence (2004) for Japanese and Lee (1998) for Korean. The prevocalic glide is part of the rhyme.

As the changes/processes in this study involve glide formation in prevocalic and postvocalic positions, the recursive structure can show the changes/processes with different levels. A structure with two levels shows the process simply for prevocalic glide formation in Tsou. On the other hand, a structure with three levels accounts for the complex changes of glide formation and vowel lowering in Sino-Japanese and Sino-Korean.

Beyond the structural motivations for complex changes, the analyses are also used to highlight the positional differences in Tsou. The prevocalic glide formation ([e.u] > [ju]) demands one level, whereas the postvocalic glide formation ([e.u] > [ew]) cannot be fully expressed without providing another level for the offglide. Given that glide formation in different positions requires different levels of representations in Tsou, the recursive structure is a crucial mechanism to show the positional constraints.

5 Conclusion

In this study, I am concerned with glide formation and vowel lowering in Sino-Japanese and Sino-Korean from a diachronic perspective and glide formation in Tsou from a synchronic viewpoint. The two phonological changes are analyzed by an element-based approach, seeking the possibility of decomposing mid vowels and the application of recursive structure. The data in Sino-Japanese and Sino-Korean have revealed two phonological changes with regard to the contact of two vowels [eu] or [oi]. The mid vowels [e] and [o] become glide, and the high vowels [u] and [i] are lowered, [eu] → [jo] and [oi] → [we]. The changes are analyzed as decomposition from mid vowel to two elements [e] → |I A| or [o] → |U A|, and then as an interaction of the element |A| from the mid vowel with the element from the following high vowel. The data in Tsou for a sequence of vowels [e] and [u] involve an independent change of glide formation. When it appears in non-final position, the vowel [e] becomes palatal glide [j] without interacting with the following vowel [u], or when it appears in word-final position, the vowel [u] turns into labial glide [w]. The data in the three languages present two patterns of decomposing mid vowels, and more importantly provide strong evidence for a reversed change, [e] → |I A| and [o] → |U A|, as contrast to the composition change, |I A| → [e] and |U A| → [o]. It is concluded that elements and vowels can be operated bidirectionally (cf. Backley 2011).

To differentiate the change [e.u] → [jo] in Sino-Japanese from that [e.u] → [ju] in Tsou, I have used recursive structure to analyze the data. The glide formation in Sino-Japanese and Tsou illustrates recursive structure and elements preservation at different levels to distinguish simple and complex expressions. Particularly, whether or not element |A| is suppressed in the output determines the structure. A simple expression like [e.u] → [ju] in Tsou is represented by a simpler structure with two levels, and element |A| is suppressed in the output. On the other hand, a complex expression like [e.u] → [jo] in Sino-Japanese is represented by recursive structure with three levels, and element |A| with multiple functions is fully preserved in the output. The change [e.u] → [e.w] in Tsou also supports recursive structure with a representation of labial glide [w] at the lowest level.

Everything taken together, the analyses based on decomposition and recursive structure for Sino-Japanese, Sino-Korean and Tsou have successfully provided a cross-linguistic mechanism for glide formation and vowel lowering within a morpheme. More data from different languages are, of course, needed for further research to obtain a complete typological understanding of this issue.

References

Anderson, John. 1987. Sructural analogy and Dependency Phonology. In John Anderson and Jacques Durand (eds.), *Explorations in Dependency Phonology*, 15–48. Dordrecht: Foris.

Anderson, John and Charles Jones. 1974. Three theses concerning phonological representations. *Journal of Linguiatics* 10, 1–26.

Anderson, John and Charles Jones. 1977. *Phonological Structure and the History of English*. Amsterdam: North-Holland Publishing Campany.

Anderson, John and Colin J. Ewen. 1987. *Principles of Dependency Phonology*. Cambridge: Cambridge University Press.

Backley, Phillip. 2011. *An Introduction to Element Theory*. Edinburgh: Edinburgh University Press.

Backley, Phillip. 2012. Variation in Element Theory. *Language Variation* 12(1), 57–102.

Backley, Phillip and Kuniya Nasukawa. 2016. The origins of Japanese *h* from an element-based perspective. *Studies in Historical Phonology* 1, 269–284.

Blust, Robert and Stephen Trussel. *The Austronesian Comparative Dictionary* (Web edition). http://www.trussel2.com/acd/

Chang, Yungli and Chia-Jung Pan. 2016. *Tsouyu Yufa Gailun* [An Introduction to Tsou Grammar]. Taipei: Council of Indigenous People.

Charette, Monik. 1991. *Conditions on Phonological Government*. Cambridge: Cambridge University Press.

Chen, Yin-Ling. 2002. Tsou phonology: a study of its phonemes, syllable structure and loanwords. MA thesis, National Tsing Hua University, Hsinchu.

Dikken, Marcel den and Harry G. van der Hulst. 1988. Segmental hierarchitecture. In Harry G. van der Hulst and Norval Smith (eds.), *Features, Segmental Structure and Harmony Changes*, 1–59. Dordrecht: Foris.
Durand, Jacques. 1986. French liason, floating segments and other matters in a dependency framework. In Jacques Durand (ed.), *Dependency and Non-linear Phonology*, 161–201. London: Croom Helm.
Durand, Jacques. 1990. *Generative and Non-linear Phonology*. London: Longman.
Ewen, Colin J. 1995. Dependency relations in phonology. In John A. Goldsmith (ed.), *The Handbook of Phonological Theory*, 570–584. Oxford: Blackwell.
Frellesvig, Bjarke. 2010. *A History of the Japanese Language*. Cambridge: Cambridge University Press.
Harris, John. 1990. Segmental complexity and phonological government. *Phonology* 7, 255–300.
Harris, John and Geoff Lindsey. 1995. The elements of phonological representation. In Jacques Durand and Francis Katamba (eds.), *Frontiers of Phonology: Atoms, Structures and Derivations*, 34–79. Harlow: Longman.
Heo, Yong. 2013. An analysis and interpretation of Korean vowel systems. *Acta Koreana* 16(1), 23–43.
Ho, Da-An. 1976. Tsou phonology. *Bulletin of the Institute of History and Philology, Academia Sinica* 47(2), 245–274.
Hulst, Harry G. van der. 1989. Atoms of segmental structure: components, gestures and dependency. *Phonology* 6, 253–284.
Hulst, Harry G. van der. 2006. Dependency Phonology. In Keith Brown (ed.), *The Encyclopedia of Language and Linguistics*, 2nd edition, 451–458. Oxford: Elsevier.
Hulst, Harry van der. 2010a. A note on recursion on phonology. In Harry G. van der Hulst (ed.) *Recursion and Human Language*, 301–342. Berlin and New York: Mouton de Gruyter.
Hulst, Harry van der. 2010b. Recursion. In Harry G. van der Hulst (ed.), *Recursion and Human Language*, i–xv. Berlin and New York: Mouton de Gruyter.
Hulst, Harry G. van der. 2011. Dependency-based phonology. In John A. Goldsmith, Jason Riggle and Alan Yu (eds.), *The Handbook of Phonological Theory*, 2nd edition, 533–570. Malden, MA: Welly-Blackwell.
Kang, Ok-Mi. 2003. *Hangukeo Eumunron* [Korean phonology]. Seoul: Thaehaksa.
Kaye, Jonathan, Jean Lowenstamm and Jean-Roger Vergnaud. 1990. Constituent structure and government in phonology. *Phonology* 7, 193–231.
Kim-Renaud, Young-Key. 2009. *Korean: An Essential Grammar*. New York: Routledge.
Lawrence, Wayne. 2004. High vowels, glides, and Japanese phonology. *Gengo Kenkyu* 125, 1–30.
Lee, Duck-Young. 1998. *Korean Phonology: A Principle-based Approach*. München: Lincom Europa.
Lee, Ik-Sop and Robert Ramsey. 2000. *The Korean Language*. Albany: State University of New York Press.
Lee, Ki-Moon and Robert Ramsey. 2011. *A History of the Korean Language*. Cambridge: Cambridge University Press.
Lin, Chihkai. 2008. Phonological changes of entering tone in Sino-Xenic languages: an Optimality-Theoretic approach. MA Thesis, National Taiwan University, Taipei.
Martin, Samuel. 2006. *Reference Grammar of Korean: A Complete Guide to the Grammar and History of the Korean Language*. Clarendon: Tuttle Publishing.
Nasukawa, Kuniya. 2014. Features and recursive structure. *Nordlyd* 41(1), 1–19. Special issue on Features edited by Martin Krämer, Sandra-Iulia Ronai and Peter Svenonius.

Nasukawa, Kuniya. 2015a. Why the palatal glide is not a consonantal segment in Japanese: an analysis in a dependency-based model of phonological primes. In Eric Raimy and Charles E. Cairns (eds.), *The Segment in Phonetics and Phonology*, 180–198. Malden, MA: Wiley-Blackwell.

Nasukawa, Kuniya. 2015b. Recursion in the lexical structure of morphemes. In Marc van Oostendorp and Henk C. van Riemsdijk (eds.), *Representing Structure in Phonology and Syntax*, 211–238. Berlin and New York: Mouton de Gruyter.

Nasukawa, Kuniya. 2016. A precedence-free approach to (de-)palatalisation in Japanese. *Glossa: A Journal of General Linguistics* 1(1), 9. DOI: http://dx.doi.org/10.5334/gjgl.26.

A precedence-free approach to (de-)palatalisation in Japanese. *Glossa* 1 (1), 9. DOI: http://dx.doi.org/10.5334/gjgl.26.

Numoto, Katsuaki. 1986. *Nihon Kanjion no Rekishi* [A History of Sino-Japanese]. Tokyo, Tokyodou.

Park, Hee-Heon. 1996. *Government Relations in Korean Phonology*. Seoul: Hankuk Publisher.

Park, Chong-Teok. 2008. *Gukgo Eumunron Ui Haeseok* [Explaining Korean Phonology]. Seoul: Kyeongjin Munhwa.

Rhee, Sand-Jik. 2002. Empty nuclei in Korean. Ph.D. dissertation, Leiden University.

Schane, Sanford. 1984a. The fundamentals of particle phonology. *Phonology Yearbook* 1, 129–155.

Schane, Sanford. 1984b. Two English vowel movements: a particle analysis. In Mark Aronoff, Richard Oehrle, Frances Kelly and Bonnie Stephens (eds.), *Language Sound Structure*, 32–51. Cambridge, MA: MIT Press.

Schane, Sanford. 1995. Diphthongization in Particle Phonology. In John A. Goldsmith (ed.), *The Handbook of Phonological Theory*, 586–608. Oxford: Blackwell.

Schane, Sanford. 2005. The aperture particle |a|: Its role and functions. In Philip Carr, Jacques Durand and Colin J. Ewen (eds.), *Headhood, Elements, Specification and Contrastivity*, 586–608. Amsterdam: John Benjamins.

Shin, Ji-Young, Jieun Kiaer and Jaeeun Cha. 2013. *The Sounds of Korean*. Cambridge: Cambridge University Press.

Sohn, Ho-Min. 1999. *The Korean language*. Cambridge: Cambridge University Press.

Tung, T'ung-Ho. 1964. *A Descriptive Study of the Tsou Language, Formosa*. Taipei: Academia Sinica.

Tung, T'ung-Ho. 2005. *Hanyu Yinyunxue* [Chinese Phonology]. Taipei: Wenshizhe.

Wright, Richard and Peter Ladefoged. 1997. A phonetic study of Tsou. *Bulletin of the Institute of History and Philology, Academia Sinica* 68(4), 987–1028.

Zeitoun, Elizabeth. 2000. *Zouyu Cankao Yufa* [A reference grammar of Tsou]. Taipei: Yuan-Liou Publishing.

Xiaoxi Liu and Nancy C. Kula
Multi-layered recursive representations for depressors

1 Introduction

Although there have been ambient theories in the literature on the geometric representations of segments, specific discussions on how such geometric architecture explains tone-segment interactions are rather limited. Depressor effects in tonal languages provide an example of tone-consonant interactions. This paper aims to explore how consonants interact with tone to result in depressor effects restricted to syllables with a specific laryngeal specification of the consonants. We propose a multi-layered recursive element geometry, with particular emphasis on the structural arrangements of tone and phonation, which in Element Theory crucially involve the same primes in their representations.

The organisation of this paper is as follows. Section 2 discusses types of depressors, based on a selection of five languages from Bantu, and one from Khoisan, and summarises the two central issues observed from depressor effects. Section 3 reviews three geometry models: Feature Geometry (Clements 1985), RCVP geometry and some offshoots couched in standard elements (van der Hulst 1989, 2005, 2015, 2017, Kula 2002), and element-based dependency (Botma 2004). These form the background against which the current multi-layered recursive element geometry is proposed in section 4. The proposed geometry will then be applied to some phonological processes to illustrate its wider scope and explore ways in which it can be generalised in section 5. Section 6 offers some concluding remarks.

2 Depressor effects in Bantu and Khoisan

Depressor consonants refer to a set of consonants that have the effect of lowering the tone of the following vowel. This makes syllables that would otherwise surface with a high tone, instead surface with a low tone. Depressor consonants are prevalent in Southern Bantu languages (Rycroft 1976, 1980; Lanham 1960; Bradshow 1999; Mathangwane 1996, etc.) but can also be found in Khoisan languages. Non-African tone languages are also reported to show similar effects such as in Chinese Wu (Ren 1987, Cao 1987, Cao and Maddieson 1992, Shi 1983,

Chen 2015, etc.). Studies on this phenomenon were reported as early as in Beach's (1924) discussions of Xhosa and Chao's (1928) analyses of Wu, where both authors noticed a similar correlation between the voicing of initials and low tone or lower tone registers. The term 'depressor' was not coined until the publication of Lanham's (1958) work on Zulu, where he describes depressor consonants as having "a lowering effect on all, except low level tones". In general, phonetic studies on depressors are more prevalent than phonological analyses, though there have been conflicting claims within both approaches. For phonetic measurements and descriptions of depressors see works by Lanham (1958, 1960, 1969), Rycroft (1976, 1980), Traill, Khumalo and Fridjhon (1987), Ladefoged and Maddieson (1996), Maddieson (2003), Downing and Gick (2005), Jessen and Roux (2002), Chen (2015), Cao and Maddieson (1992), Ren (1987, 1988, 2006), among others. For feature or other phonological analyses of depressors see e.g. Rycroft (1980), Khumalo (1987), Mathangwane (1996, 1998), Bradshaw (1999, 2003), Downing (2009), Chen and Downing (2011), Strazny (2003) and Lee (2008, 2015).

We examine the typology of depressors in six African languages – Zulu, Xhosa, SiSwati, Ikalanga, Tsonga and Tsua, all of which belong to Southern Bantu languages apart from Tsua, which is a language of Central Khoisan. The findings show that there are many different types of depressors that vary from the most unmarked voiced and breathy consonants, to the least expected consonants such as voiceless aspirates. The following sub-sections showcase the different types of depressors attested.

2.1 Unmarked depressors

We categorise depressors into unmarked and marked types, where voicing and breathiness are unmarked and voicelessness and aspiration are marked.[1] Within the unmarked type, voicing is attested as the most common unmarked depressor, followed to a lesser extent by breathy sounds.

---

[1] The common laryngeal setting for voicing and breathiness is that the vocal folds (the full length of the vocal folds for voicing and the front two-thirds for breathiness) loosely vibrate, which results in a relatively low frequency. Thus voicing and breathiness correlate with low tone. By comparison, in voiceless and aspirated sounds, the glottis opens with relatively higher abduction and longitudinal tension, which correlates with higher frequency. Therefore, it is less likely to see voiceless and aspirated sounds interacting with low tone as is seen in depression, hence our treatment of voicing and breathiness as unmarked for depression.

Voiced stops, fricatives, affricates, clicks and their relevant labialised or palatalised forms are recorded as depressors in all six languages. (1) lists the voiced depressors of the six languages in detail.

(1) Unmarked depressors: voicing (DEP = depressors)

Ikalanga	Xhosa	SiSwati	Zulu	Tsonga	Tsua
b, b͡g, b͡z, d, ɖ, d͡z, d͡ʒ, d͡ʒʷ, gʷ, v, z, zʷ, ʒ	b, d, g, dy, v, z, ɣ, h, dl, dz, d͡ʒ, gl, g!, gǁ, mb, nd, ng, mv, nz, nd͡ʒ, ndl	b, d, dl, dv, dz, g, gl, fi, d͡ʒ, mb, ŋgl, v, z, ŋ (ŋg)	bh, d, g, gl, g!, gǁ, v, z, dl, fi	⁽ᵐ⁾b, ⁽ⁿ⁾d, ⁽ⁿ⁾g, dl, bv, dɮ, dz, d͡ʒ,	b, d, dz, ɟ, g, G, gl, gǂ, gǁ, lG, ǁG

In languages that have breathy sounds, non-depressors, such as nasals in Zulu and Xhosa, become depressors once they gain the breathy quality. Hence, in Xhosa, for example, plain nasals [n] and [m] are non-depressors whereas their breathy counterparts [n̤] and [m̤] are depressors. Ikalanga, Xhosa, Zulu and Tsonga in (2) are said to have breathy depressors.

(2) Unmarked depressors: breathiness (DEP=depressors)

Breathy	Ikalanga	Xhosa/Zulu	Tsonga
nonDEP		m, n, ɲ, ŋl, ŋǁ, ŋ!	⁽ᵐ⁾b, ⁽ⁿ⁾d, ⁽ⁿ⁾g, m, n, ɲ, ŋ, l, r, w, j
DEP	ɦ	m̤, n̤, ɲ̈, ŋ̈l, ŋ̈ǁ, ŋ̈!	⁽ᵐ⁾b̤, ⁽ⁿ⁾d̤, ⁽ⁿ⁾g̈, m̤, n̤, ɲ̈, by, dẓ, dʒ̣, ɦ, l̤, r, w, j̈

2.2 Marked depressors

Apart from the unmarked depressors, i.e. those segments associated with voicing, it has been observed that in some languages voiceless aspirates and unaspirated obstruents also act as depressors. This poses an interesting question with respect to the trigger of depression since it has been shown in a number of phonetic studies that the F0 contours for voiceless and aspirated obstruents normally display a rising pitch pattern (Gandour 1974, Jun 1998).

2.2.1 Voiceless aspirates

The first language we discuss with voiceless aspirates as depressors is Tsonga, which is classified as a sub-branch of Nguni (a group within Southern Bantu), in Baumbach (1987), or, as a parallel branch of Nguni according to Doke (1967).

(3) below gives the consonant inventory of Tsonga drawn from Baumbach (1987) and Lee (2009). In this system Lee (2009) reports that all voiceless aspirates (excluding implosives) are depressors, which also function as blockers of High Tone Spreading (HTS), as illustrated in (4).

(3) Tsonga consonant inventory

	Bilabial	(Labio) Dental	Alveolar	alveolar -lateral	Palatal	velar	Glottal
Stops	p ⁽ᵐ⁾b		t ⁽ⁿ⁾d	tl dl		k ⁽ⁿ⁾g	
	pʰ		tʰ	tlʰ dl̤		kʰ	
Implosives		ɓ gɓ					
		ɓʰ					
Prenasals	⁽ᵐ⁾b̤		⁽ⁿ⁾d̤			⁽ⁿ⁾g̈	
Nasals	m		n		ɲ	ŋ	
	m̤		n̤			ŋ̈	
Apprx	w		r	l	j		
	w̤		r̤	l̤	j̤		
Fric	ɸ β	f v	s z		ʃ ʒ	x	ɦ
		ɣ					
Affr		pf bv	ts dz		dʒ tʃ dʒ		
		pfʰ	tsʰ		tʃʰ		
		bɣ	dẓ		dʒ̈		

In Tsonga, there is a process of HTS that spreads a prefix High tone to its following bi-syllabic root except the final syllable. Thus in (4a) the High tone on the prefix /í-/ (marked by an acute accent) spreads to the first syllable /ri/ of the root. By contrast, this HTS is blocked in (4b) due to the root-initial aspirated consonant acting as a depressor. Data and analysis come from Lee (2009). However, in more recent work, Lee (2015) shows that the HTS blocking rule is more complex in that it requires *both* an initial depressor and a H tone in the root. Thus examples in (4c) with a depressor but no H tone in the root show no HTS blocking. Despite this complexity, we can see that depressors play a role in HTS blocking in Tsonga.

(4) Tsonga depressors and HTS
a. **nonDEPs** **Root** **Prefix+Root** **Gloss**
   r   rìbyè   í ríbyè   'it is a stone'
   p   púláⁿgì   í ꜝpúláⁿgì   'it is a plank'
   l   léró   fìí ꜝléró   'it is that one'

b. **DEPs Root Prefix+Root Gloss**
DEPs	Root	Prefix+Root		Gloss
tsʰ	tsʰùrí	í tsʰùrí	*í tsʰûrí	'it is a mortar'
tlʰ	ntlʰàmú	í ntlʰàmú	*í ntlʰâmú	'it is a trap'
tʃʰ	tʃʰìpá	í tʃʰìpá	*í tʃʰîpá	'it is a pensioner'
tʰ	tʰònsí	í tʰònsí	*í tʰônsí	'it is a drop'
kʰ	kʰòswá	í kʰòswá	*í kʰôswá	'it is a half portion'

c. **DEPs Root Prefix+Root Gloss**
DEPs	Root	Prefix+Root	Gloss
b	baku	í báku	'cave'
r̯	r̯ole	í r̯óle	'calf'

A second language with aspirated depressors is Ikalanga from northern Botswana (Mathanwange 1996, 1998). Ikalanga falls within a sub-group of the Shona group of languages, with Shona itself a part of Nguni. The consonant inventory of Ikalanga is given in (5). Unlike Tsonga, Mathanwange (1998) argues that Ikalanga has two groups of voiceless aspirates as listed in (6), with the first group being non-depressor aspirates and the second being aspirated depressors.[2] As further shown in (7), Ikalnaga has a similar blocking effect of HTS induced by aspirated depressors.

(5)   Ikalanga consonant inventory

	Bilabial		(Labio) Dental		Alveolar		Palatal		velar		Glottal
Stops	p	b	t̪, d̪		d, dʷ?				k, kʷ	g, gʷ	
	pʰ		t̪ʰ		tʰ				kʰ, kʰʷ,		
	pʱ				Tʰ				pkʰ, Kʷʰ		
Nasals	m				n, ɲ				ŋ, ŋʷ		
Pre-nas	mb				nd, ndʒ				ŋg, ŋgʷ		
Liquids					l, r						
Fric.		β	f	v	s, sʷ	z, zʷ	ʃ, ʃʷ	3			ɦ
Apprx	ʋ	w, ẇ					j				
Affr	ps	bz			ts	dz, dzʷ	tʃ	dʒ	pk		
					tsʰʷ				bg		
					tsʰ,		Tʃʰ				
					TSʰ						

---

2 As shown in (6), Mathangwane (1998) notationally distinguishes the two types of voiceless aspirates by representing the depressor voiceless aspirates with an uppercase letter.

(6) Two groups of Ikalanga aspirates
Group I: plain and labialised aspirates {p^h, t^h, $\underline{t}^h$, k^h, ts^h k^{hw}}
Group II: aspirated depressors {P^h, T^h, K^{wh}, TS^h, TS^h, ($ɦ$)}

(7) HTS and blocking in Ikalanga
   a. Non-depressors
      ku-ʃímá pʰílé   ku-ʃímá pʰílé 'to hate a bad singer'
   b. Depressors
      ku-ʃímá pʰílé   ku-ʃ ímá Pʰílé 'to hate a steenbuck'

As seen also in Tsonga, HTS applies in the context of non-depressors in Ikalanga (7a), but is blocked when a depressor starts the target syllable (7b) in an otherwise identical context. These two examples contrast the two types of voiceless aspirates given in (6).

A final example language with aspirated depressors is Tsua (Mathes 2015), a Kalahari Khoe East language of Central Khoisan, spoken mainly in Eastern Botswana.³ Being a Khoisan language, Tsua is very distinctive in having a large inventory of click sounds, which can also be depressors, adding another dimension to our understanding of depressors. In Tsua, the aspirated depressors are {p^h, t^h, ts^h, c^h, k^h, q^h, $|^h$, $ǂ^h$, $||^h$, $|q^h$, $ǂq^h$, $||q^h$, h}, according to Mathes (2015). In terms of tonal inventory, Tsua also differs from Bantu in having a wider range of tones with 6 bimoraic tones: H-level, HM-falling, HL-falling, Mid-double-rise (M level), MH-rising and ML-falling.⁴ In addition, there are two extra depressor-induced tones called DH-L (Depressed High Low) and DH-M (Depressed High Mid). The tones that are depressed are marked by a subscript symbol "+" beneath the vowels. Examples of DH-L and DH-M words can be seen in (8), drawn directly from Mathes (2015). The F0 tracings of the eight tones are given in (9).

(8) DH-L and DH-M words in Tsua
    DH-L   DH-M
    gǫ́ò 'aardvark'   khǫ̣́ē 'to stab'
    g|ǫ̣́à 'Silver tree' tshǫ̣́ā 'water'
    tshǫ́è 'person'   gǫ́ā tsúrī 'much later'
    ǂǫ́à 'ash'   g|ǫ̣́ā 'to put in smoothly'

---

3 The classification, and in particular the internal classification, of Khoisan remains under investigation, and therefore the label given here can only be tentative.
4 By contrast, in most Bantu languages there is simply a High vs. Low contrast which phonologically is generally treated as H vs. ∅. There are some Grassfields Bantu languages (northwest of the Bantu area) that have mid-tones, see e.g. Bamileke-Dschang (Hyman 1985, Hyman and Tadadjeu 1976) and Basaa (Hyman 2003), among others.

(9) Eight Tsua tones and their F0 tracings (Mathes 2015: 116)

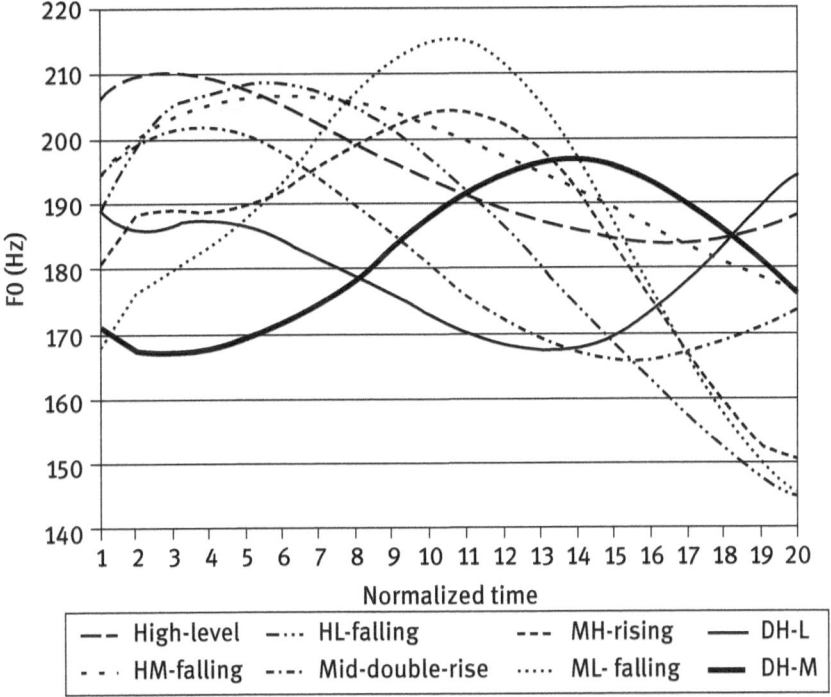

Thus, counter to expectation, there are cases where voiceless aspirates can act as depressors. What about voiceless unaspirates? We explore this in the next sub-section.

2.2.2 Voiceless unaspirates

Based on a number of detailed phonetic studies (e.g. Traill, Khumalo and Fridjhon 1987, Cao 1987, Cao and Maddieson 1992, Shi 1983, Shen, Wooters and Wang 1987, Ren 2006), there is a consensus in the literature that the sounds orthographically associated with the symbols 'b, d, g' in depressor languages such as Zulu, Xhosa and Swati are not truly voiced, but are rather voiceless. These voiceless non-aspirated stops also trigger depressor effects in these languages. Some voiceless fricatives are also argued to be depressors in languages such as Nambya (e.g. Downing and Gick 2005). (10) to (12) provide the consonant inventories of Zulu, Xhosa and Swati. Data are drawn from Doke (1926), Lanham (1960) and Khumalo (1981: 87) for Zulu; McLaren (1936) and Lanham

(1958: 60) for Xhosa; and Rycroft (1976), Bradshaw (1999) and Lanham (1960) for SiSwati.

(10) Zulu consonant inventory

	Bilabial	(Labio) Dental	Alveolar	alveolar -lateral	Palatal	velar	Glottal
Stops/ implos	p(') b		t(') d			k(') g	
	pʰ ɓ		tʰ			kʰ	
Nasals	m		n		ɲ	ŋ	
	m̥		n̥		ɲ̊	ŋ̊	
Approx.	w		l		j		
	w̥				j̊		
Fricatives		f v	s z	ɬ, ɮ	ʃ		h ɦ
Affricates					tʃ	dʒ	
Clicks		| g| ŋ|		ǁ gǁ ŋǁ		! g! ŋ!	
		|ʰ ŋ|ʰ̃		ǁʰ ŋǁ̃		!ʰ ŋ!̃	

(11) Xhosa consonant inventory⁵

	Bilabial	(Labio) Dental	Alveolar		alveolar -lateral	Palatal	velar	Glottal
Stops/ Implosive	p(') b		t(') , tʲ	d, dʲ			k(') g	
	pʰ ɓ		tʰ, tʲʰ				kʰ	
Nasals	m		n			ɲ	ŋ	
	m̥		n̥			ɲ̊	ŋ̊	
Prenas	mb		nd				ŋg	
Apprx	w		r		l	j		
	w̥		ɾ		l̥	j̊		
Fricatives		f v	s	z	ɬ, ɮ	ʃ	ɣ	h ɦ
Affricates			ts	dz		tʃ dʒ	kx	
			tsʰ			tʃʰ		
Clicks		| g| ŋ|			ǁ gǁ ŋǁ		! g! ŋ!	
		|ʰ ŋ|ʰ̃			ǁʰ ŋǁ̃		!ʰ ŋ!̃	

(12) SiSwati consonant inventory

	Bilabial	(Labio) Dental	Alveolar	alveolar- lateral	Palatal	velar	Glottal
Stops/ Implosives	p(') b		t(') dl			k(') g	
	pʰ ɓ		tʰ			kʰ	
Nasals	m		n		ɲ	ŋ	
Prenasals	mp mb̥	mf mv̥				ŋg̈	
Approx.	w		l		j	kl	
Fricatives		f v	s z		ʃ		h hl ɦ
Affricates	dv			dz	tʃ dʒ		
Clicks		| g| ŋ|					
		|ʰ ŋ|ʰ ŋ̈| ŋg̈|					

---

5 McLaren (1936) and Lanham (1958) use /gr/ and /kr/ for [ɣ] and [kx], respectively.

From these three language inventories, and the preceding data from Tsonga, Ikalanga and Tsua, we now summarise depressors in the six languages in the following table in (13). ("+" stands for depressors; "-" for non-depressors, and NA for the non-existence of the phonation type indicated.)

(13) Depressor patterns in the 6 languages

Depressors / Languages	Unmarked		Marked		Nasals	
	voiced	breathy	voiceless aspirates	voiceless unaspirates	nasals	prenasals
Ikalanga	+	NA	+	-	-	-
Tsonga	+	+	+	-	-	-
Zulu	+	+	-	+	-	-
Xhosa	+	+	-	+	-	-
Swati	+	NA	-	+	-	-
Tsua	+	NA	+	-	-	NA

(13) shows a picture where all laryngeal/phonation types shown can act as depressors, i.e. voicing, breathiness, voiceless and aspiration all contribute to depressor effects. By contrast, nasals and prenasalised consonants do not act as depressors unless they are breathy voiced. Thus, spontaneous voicing does not trigger depressor effects, as also seen by the fact that in none of the languages are sonorants depressors. In all languages that have a voicing-breathy contrast, if the voiced sounds are depressors then the breathy ones are too. Voiceless aspirates and voiceless unaspirates are equally split between the 6 languages, but in no language do both act as triggers at the same time. Voiced and breathy sounds thus are the most unmarked triggers while, at least based on these languages, voiceless segments as depressor triggers are more marked whether they are aspirated or not.

However, there is also evidence of voiceless sounds acting as triggers of depression in a completely different language type that attests tone – Chinese. In some dialects of Chinese, e.g. Chinese Wu (Shanghai) and Xiang (e.g. in Shaoyang), voiceless segments can act as depressor triggers. However, as also seen above, this is much less common than voiced or breathy sounds (e.g. Ren 1987, Cao 1987, Cao and Maddieson 1992, Shi 1983, Zhong and Chen 2012). Similar to the cases discussed above, aspiration also contributes to depressor effects in the voiceless cases in Chinese.

The central question that these data raise is what the central feature in depressor effects is? If it is [voice] then it is difficult to see how this same trigger can be found in voiceless sounds. There is furthermore the issue of how, whatever feature is settled on, interacts with tone in order to phonologically trigger tone depression, i.e. how can this consonant-tone interaction best be represented and explained? We pursue these questions following an Element Theory perspective in the next section, developing the idea that only an element-based approach allows us the required flexibility since element interpretation can be manipulated in a way that a feature like [voice] cannot.

3 Feature representations and depressors

We start with the assumption that voiced consonants are the unmarked depressors as the data above show, and therefore that voicing must have some affinity with low tone, rather than high tone which it repels in order to result in a depressor effect. This is particularly aptly captured in element theory where the element |L| represents both voicing and low tone. We use the reduced set of elements as in (14), assuming the central acoustic characteristics as given in Botma, Kula and Nasukawa (2011) as below.[6]

(14) Element   Typical acoustic correlate
      |A| central spectral energy mass (convergence of F1 and F2)
      |I| low F1 with high spectral peak (convergence of F2 and F3)
      |U| low spectral peak (convergence of F1 and F2)
      |ʔ| abrupt and sustained drop in overall amplitude
      |L| periodicity, lowered F0, low pitch
      |H| aperiodicity, raised F0, high pitch

A straightforward analysis would then be one where the triggering voiced consonant imposes its voice element |L| on the following vowel which clashes with the |H| tone of the vowel, with the latter failing to be realised in those languages without complex tones. We return to the details of the analysis and representation in section 4.

A question that arises in any theory that uses a small set of primes as in (14) in Element Theory is: How is such a small set of primitives able to capture the many sounds of the world's languages? The immediate advantage is of course the small and perhaps more realistic number of segments that such a minimalist approach predicts, even under the assumption that all the elements can combine in all possible ways. The usual solution adopted is to assume that

---

[6] There are a number of useful introductory texts on Element Theory that can be consulted for further details, amongst which: Kaye, Lowenstamm and Vergnaud (1985), Harris and Lindsey (1995) and for some recent work see Backley (2011), among others.

within complex representations, where more than one element is present, elements may contribute unequally to the overall representation, i.e. that one may be head and contribute more of its characteristic. In some contemporary analyses, headedness has been used simply as a way of increasing oppositions, with the head versus the non-head counterparts of an element contributing specific distinct characteristics, see e.g. Backley and Nasukawa (2009). One element for which this multiple characteristic approach has been discussed is |L|. The main argument has been for treating voicing and nasality as represented by the same element, as supported by a number of phonological processes (e.g. Nasukawa 1998, 2005; Kula 1999, 2002; Ploch 1999; Botma 2004). A third characteristic of |L| that is assumed, but which is never brought into play much (though see Kula 2012), is that |L| also represents low tone, in the same way that it is assumed that |H| also represents high tone in addition to aspiration and frication. This then leads to an interesting question in terms of representation when |L| is associated with three characteristics viz. voicing, low tone, and nasality. In this case, using only headedness would not allow us to capture the three-way opposition. In the depression cases under discussion, this is crucial as the languages involved reflect this 3-way opposition.[7]

Furthermore, there is an unexpected asymmetry between voicing and nasality in relation to their ability to trigger depression. As the preceding data summary in (13) shows, voicing triggers depression but nasality does not. Therefore, just reliance on the presence of |L| to trigger depression is not sufficient to account for the data. We will aim to resolve this conundrum by proposing more enriched representations for elements, in the spirit of feature geometry, building on earlier work proposing element geometries.

We will also desist from the temptation of creating new features to accommodate the different types of depressors as in Traill, Khumalo and Fridihon (1987), Khumalo (1987), Strazny (2003), for example, and rather show that the enriched representation we propose will both capture the voicing-nasality asymmetry with respect to depression, and also allow for both unmarked and

---

[7] A reviewer points out that this problem may be spurious since only two-way oppositions are ever needed: nasality and voicing for consonants and tone and nasality for vowels that can be captured with headedness. We think the central problem is that headedness would not generate enough oppositions to account for the four attested triggers of depression. In any permutation, it will never be possible to distinguish breathy depressors from voiceless depressors. Consider e.g. voicing: L, nasality: L, plain voiceless: H, voiceless aspiration: H, breathiness: LH, voiceless depressor: HL, aspirated depressor: HL. This is precisely the central puzzle that the paper aims to resolve.

marked depressors to be adequately represented as triggers of depressor effects.

In the next subsections we provide a snapshot of three previous geometry theories, which lay the foundation for our proposed multi-layered recursive element geometry in Section 4.

3.1 Feature geometry

Feature and element geometries are two of the mainstream approaches to sub-segmental representations. Previous studies on the design of feature geometries are found in works by Clements (1985), Sagey (1986) McCarthy (1988), Ladefoged and Halle (1988), Avery and Rice (1989), Clements and Hume (1995), among others. Proposals for element geometries can be found in van der Hulst (1989), Harris (1994), Brockhaus (1995), Kula (2002), Botma (2004), Nasukawa and Backley (2005), Pochtrager and Kaye (2013), Nasukawa (2014), for example.

Clements' (1985) seminal work transforms the classical two-dimensional feature matrices into a multi-tiered hierarchical feature representation for segments. In his model, binary features are non-decomposable terminals that are grouped and organised under three superordinate Class Nodes, viz. Manner, Place and Laryngeal. Manner and Place constitute an intermediate tier called Supralaryngeal. Laryngeal and Supralaryngeal nodes are directly dominated by the Root Node on a higher level, which in turn is connected to the CV tier.

(15) is the well-known representation of Clements' feature geometry. Such a constrained structure is motivated largely by the fact that groups of features tend to act as a set in phonological processes, such as assimilation and dissimilation, without affecting other features. Within this geometry, it is the terminal binary features that are crucially responsible for giving interpretations to segments, whereas the groupings of features into class nodes and the hierarchical structures above the terminal features are predictable from the distinctive features. For example, in (16), the representation for [s] consists of 9 terminal features. From these 9 features, we can work out that it is the sound [s] without involving the structures that dominate these features. As we will see shortly, this aspect of geometric representation in Clements is crucially different from element-based geometries, mainly because of the non-decomposable nature of their primitive 'features'. For the Laryngeal node, the features employed in Clements correspond to those in Halle and Steven (1971) except the [±voiced]. Tone features are assumed to be distinct from Laryngeal features, though the exact features for tones are not included in the geometry.

(15) Clements' (1985) feature geometry (P=primary; S=secondary)

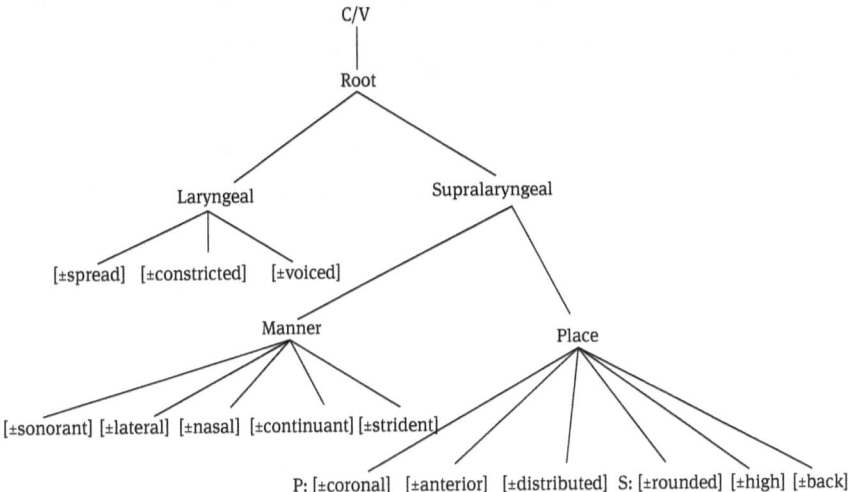

(16) Feature Geometry representation of [s]

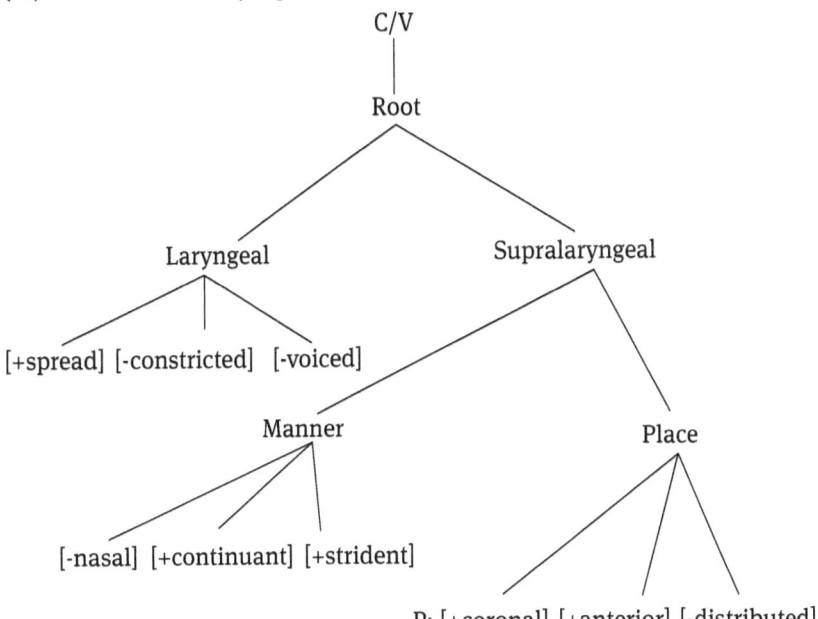

3.2 RCVP

Radical CV Phonology (RCVP) is a proposal in van der Hulst (1989, 1995) that aims to radically reduce segmental features to simply two – C and V – which must then rely on enriched representations to capture segmental contrasts, in addition to different combinations of C and V in differing dependency relations. The proposed representation in (17) divides a segment into a Categorial gesture and a Locational gesture. The Categorial gesture further splits into a head sub-gesture called Stricture, and two dependents – Tone and Phonation sub-gestures. The Locational gesture contains a bipartition of a Primary head sub-gesture and a Secondary dependent sub-gesture. The phonetic interpretations of C and V are such that C denotes an articulatory event of a relatively high degree of closure, stricture or contraction, and their acoustic correlates. V denotes the opposite effects of C, such as high sonorancy. C and V can combine into a head-dependent combination e.g. Cv or Vc, with the head being capitalised. Each sub-gesture allows four simplex element options – {C, Cv, Vc, V} – excluding combinations of identical elements {Cc & Vv}. The limited element combinations are complemented by the head-dependent structures above the Cs and Vs in order to generate the desired number of contrasts. This means that the hierarchical structures play an indispensable role in giving interpretations to segments rather than just the elements themselves. Thus, in contrast to the Clements geometry, it is a combination of both elements and their locations that provides segmental identity. For example, the C in Stricture gives rise to a stop quality whereas the same C in Tone is interpreted as a high tone. Clements' feature geometry and RCVP thus illustrate two extremes in representing sub-segmental structure, in that feature geometry employs a large number of features with minimal involvement of hierarchical structures for segmental interpretations, whereas RCVP uses a minimal number of features but more significantly incorporates geometric structures. What the latter allows is for the same element, e.g. {Cv}, to get a different interpretation depending on its location in the geometry.

(17) RCVP representation of segments

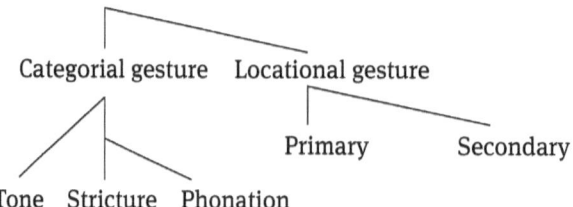

All structures in Phonation and their corresponding interpretations are given in (18), including the 4 complex elements (18b), and the 4 simplex ones (18a), as explained above. Complex structures involve dependency relations between the 4 simplex elements.[8]

(18) Simplex and complex elements in Phonation (van der Hulst 1995)
   a. Simplex:
      C: constricted glottis   Vc: nasal (voice)
      Cv: spread glottis (aspiration)   V: (oral) voice
   b. Complex:
      V⇒C: creaky voice   Vc⇒C: glottalised nasal
      V⇒Cv: breathy voice   Vc⇒Cv: aspirated nasal

In more recent work van der Hulst (2005, 2015) alters the representation in (17), and more closely resembles standard feature geometry in adopting the three central nodes Laryngeal, Manner and Location as Class nodes. All structures are binary branching into head-dependent relations, with vertical lines indicating heads and slant lines dependents. Each Class further branches into a H (ead) and a D(ependent), each of which contain at most two elements (or gestures). The elements are restricted to C and V and they can freely combine only in the head positions of Manner and Place.[9]

In the expression |CxV|, the non-underlined 'x' indicates that C and V can combine; whereas the underlined 'x' means that C and V cannot combine.

---

[8] Dependency relations are marked by ⇒. With the 4 simplex elements {C, Cv, Vc, V}, 8 dependency relations can be derived. Four that are V headed: V⇒C, Vc⇒C, V⇒Cv, Vc⇒Cv and four that are C headed: C⇒V, C⇒Vc, Cv⇒V, Cv⇒Vc. Within phonation C headed structures are prohibited and there is also a possibility that no dependency relation may hold between two elements, which we do not discuss here. See van der Hulst (1995) for details.

[9] These are the assumed representations in van der Hulst (2015). In a recent talk (van der Hulst 2017), it is proposed that both head and dependent elements in Manner can freely combine for onsets. Head elements in Laryngeal can also combine when Laryngeal expresses tone. The Laryngeal for tone in rimes is 'raised' a level up to show its autosegmental status. This is not shown in (19).

(19) Revised RCVP representation of segments

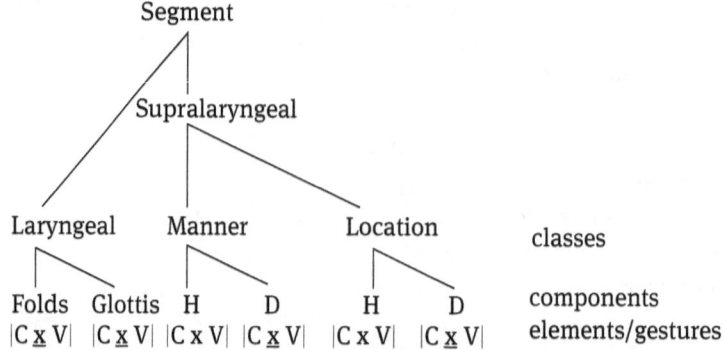

In terms of Laryngeal, van der Hulst (2015) proposes that minimally three articulatory dimensions are required for phonation distinctions, that is, [voice], [constricted], and [spread]. An extra [fortis] is selected as the opposite counterpart of [voice]. The articulatory descriptions of the four features are provided in (20a). Hence the four terminal positions of the Laryngeal node are interpreted as fortis, voiced, constricted and spread, respectively, in (20b). The articulatory descriptions of these four 'features' and the six phonation types generated by Laryngeal are outlined in (20c).

(20) a. Articulatory descriptions of [voice], [fortis], [constricted] and [spread].
[voice]: reduced stretching (elongation) of the vocal folds
[fortis]: increased stretching (elongation) of the vocal folds
[constricted]: in/outward rotation of arytenoid cartilages (medial compression)
[spread]: adduction and abduction of the arytenoid cartilages
b. Structure for the Laryngeal node
Laryngeal

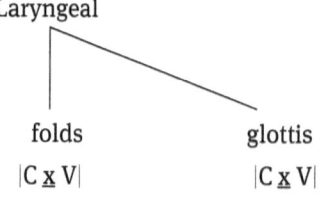

fortis   voiced   constricted   spread
c. Six phonation types
(i) voicing: voiced (V)
(ii) breathiness: voiced, spread (VV)
(iii) creakiness: voiced, constricted (VC)
(iv) aspiration: fortis, spread (CV)

(v) glottalisation: fortis, constricted (CC)
(vi) voiceless: fortis (C)

The representation thus captures the wide range of laryngeal specifications that would aid us in our quest to account for the different depressor triggering consonants, but with the very restricted number of basic primes, there is the complication that dependency relations are held both at the basic element level and also within the overarching structure, meaning that elemental effects and interactions, as seen in depression, will be captured in a less transparent way. It is based on this reasoning that Kula (2002) while adopting the RCVP geometry (17), opts for the use of standard elements within element theory, to avoid added complexity at the elemental level. An articulated version of an element based geometry is developed in Botma (2004), which we discuss briefly below.

3.3 Element-based dependency geometry

Botma's (2004) element-based dependency geometry extends basic geometric representations with closest affinity to Humbert's (1995) structure where Manner dominates Place and Phonation. A representation of this structure is given in (21) below, with phonation re-positioned as a direct dependent of O(nset)/N(ucleus)/C(oda). Botma follows Kehrein (2002) and Kehrein and Golston (2004) in assuming that Phonation is licensed by the prosodic level only, at which level it can be minimally contrastive. The element-based dependency geometry treats both Manner and Phonation as prosodic (because they are both directly linked to O/N), rather than as segmental units (cf. Laryngeal and Location in the most recent version of RCVP). In our proposal in section 4, we will also treat Phonation as prosodic but retain Manner and Place as segmental units.

(21) Element-dependency geometry (Botma 2004)

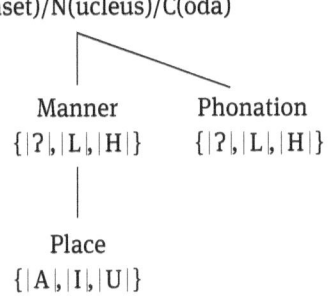

As in dependency phonology vertical dependency differs from branching dependency. In this structure Manner and Place have a vertical dominancy relation but branching with Phonation. Manner and Phonation share the same elements {|ʔ|, |H|, |L|}, among which our element of concern |L| represents voicing or nasalisation in Phonation, and sonorancy in Manner. Specifically, |L| in Phonation is interpreted as nasalisation if another |L| exists in Manner; otherwise |L| in Phonation is expressed as voicing. The dual role of |L| in Phonation is motivated by the complementary relation between nasalisation and voicing, where sonorants can have nasalisation but not voicing contrasts, and obstruents can have voicing but not nasalisation contrasts. Consider the representations of nasals, nasalised vowels and voiced stops in (22).

(22) Representations of plain nasals, nasal vowels and voicing

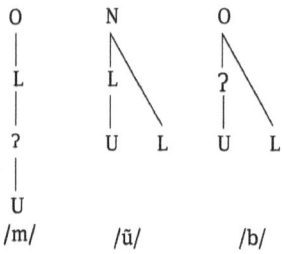

As noted, Phonation is specified with the three elements {|ʔ|, |L|, |H|}. |ʔ| has four variable realisations – glottalisation, ejection, implosive, and creaky voice. |L| is interpreted as either true voicing or nasalisation. |H| is realised as aspiration, breathiness or voiceless. Similar to RCVP, this geometry complements elements with structures to give segment interpretations. A central difference with the RCVP geometry is the leanness of the structure by reliance on elements that remain independently interpretable. Within this representation, nasality and voicing, which are both directly linked to a prosodic constituent (O or N), can be expected to equally interact with tone to trigger depressor effects. But as the data have shown voicing and breathiness trigger depression where plain nasals do not, saying nothing of aspirates and plain voiceless consonants.

We have reviewed three geometry theories which provide insights into segmental representation that we will build on, in our proposed multi-layered recursive element geometry in the next section. A common trait of these geometries is the general tri-partition of Laryngeal (or Phonation), Manner and Place (or Location), although the organisation of these three components and their sub-structures may differ between approaches. An important aspect that element geometries bring, and that we fully endorse, is the integration of elements and hierarchical structures in the phonetic interpretation of segments, so that both the identity and the position of an element in a representation matters for its eventual phonetic output.

4 Multi-layered element geometry

The structure of the multi-layered recursive element geometry we propose is given in (23) in a two-dimensional longitudinal representation, with the three dimensional view in (24). The element geometry is designed to include structures at both the subsegmental level and the prosodic (tonal) tier. The latter will be crucial in explaining the tone-melody interactions in depressor effects. Assumed elemental characteristics are given on the right hand side and will be further explained in the ensuing discussion.[10]

(23) Longitudinal section of the element geometry

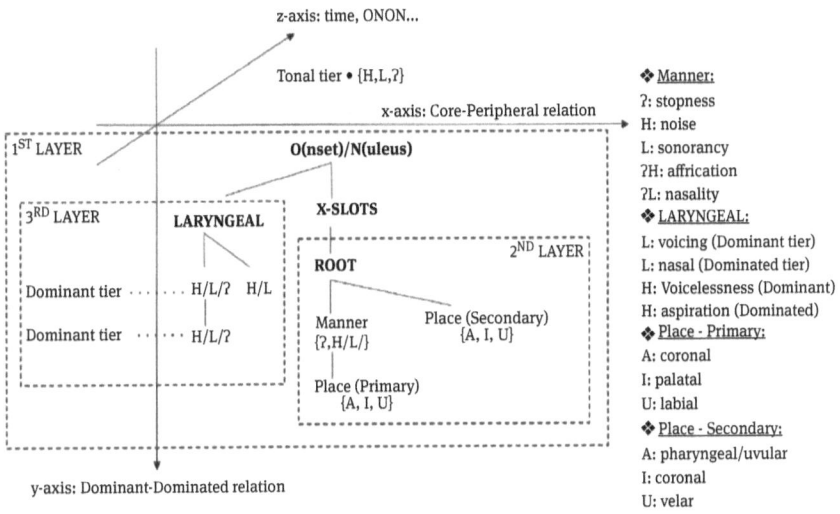

---

[10] At the moment spontaneous voicing is represented with L in Manner and is therefore always present in sonorants and vowels. Voiceless vowels would still have L but with an H in LARYNGEAL.

(24) 3D representation of the element geometry

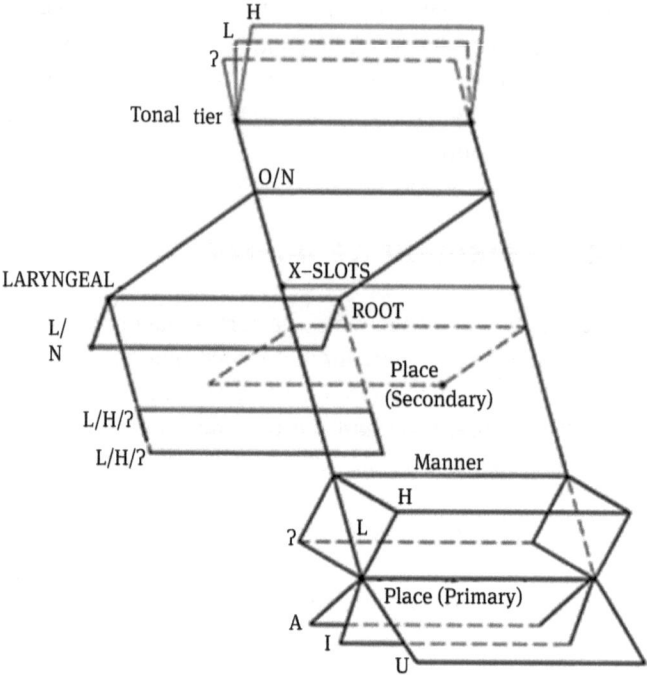

In this model, we propose that the central building block of sub-syllabic structures is the basic template CLASS NODE as illustrated in (25). This is composed of three COMPONENTS – a Dominant and a Dominated tier that constitute the "Core" structure (indicated by vertical lines), and a Peripheral tier (indicated by slanting lines). The presence of a Dominated tier implies the presence of a Dominant tier, but not vice versa.

(25) Basic template CLASS NODE and its three components

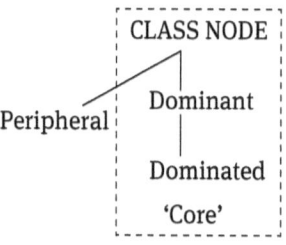

The sub-syllabic structure is built up recursively into three layers (indicated by the dotted boxes in 23). The first layer CLASS NODE O(nset)/N(ucleus) is the overarching outer layer, whose ultimate components ROOT and LARYNGEAL can be expanded further and repeat the basic templatic structure into the 2nd and 3rd layers. In this representation, recursivity of the templatic structure is not unlimited in that only ultimate CLASS NODES (e.g. LARYNGEAL and ROOT) are large enough to be expandable and to hold recursive structures further down. Non-ultimate CLASS NODES are non-expandable. Each layer is a full manifestation of the basic template CLASS NODE that contains Dominant, Dominated and Peripheral tiers, but differs with respect to the content assigned to each of the three components. The x-axis in (23) represents a lateral Core-Peripheral relation; the y-axis reflects a vertical Dominant-Dominated relation; the z-axis symbolises the time.

(26) Three LAYERS of the element geometry

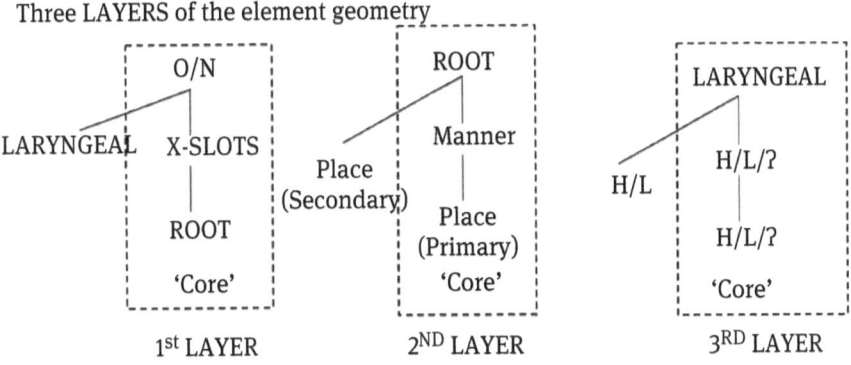

(26) summarises and compares the specific content for Dominant, Dominated and Peripheral tiers across the three layers. It should be noted that the type of tier nodes allowed in a layer accommodate to the level of the CLASS NODE of that layer. For example, for the optional Peripheral LARYNGEAL CLASS NODE, its three components, Dominant, Dominated and Peripheral tiers are composed of the most fundamental and non-decomposable units, here the elements. By comparison, the three components of CLASS NODE ROOT allow larger articulatory units, Manner and Place, which are sets of elements. The larger articulatory units fall in between elements and CLASS NODES. The overarching CLASS NODE O/N, being the top level of the three layers, is compatible with the most complex and largest structures, namely, CLASS NODES. These in turn result in recursive structures at the ultimate Dominated ROOT tier and Peripheral LARYNGEAL tier. The above pattern is in line with the lateral Core-Peripheral

and vertical Dominant-Dominated asymmetric relations in that O/N and ROOT are the Core and thus are expected to hold more complex structures. By contrast, being in a Peripheral position, LARYNGEAL is only able to deal with the least complex elements. In addition, the 'Peripheral' property of LARYNGEAL is also reflected in its Dominant tier which is only capable of licensing the same element on the Dominated tier, in contrast to the Dominant Manner in ROOT being able to license the Dominated Place.

Notice that in the 1st layer CLASS NODE O/N, all three components Dominant, Dominated and Peripheral tiers are expected to accommodate the most complex structure, that is, a recursive structure that further repeats the basic template CLASS NODE at lower levels. Although CLASS NODE ROOT and LARYNGEAL O/N do hold recursive structure, respectively, this is not the case for the Dominant X-SLOTS tier which is non-recursive. We attribute the non-recursiveness of X-SLOTS to the fact that they have a fundamental functional difference compared to ROOT and LARYNGEAL, in that the X-SLOTS are simply place holders that function as a transitional tier indicating the end of sub-segmental and the start of prosodic tiers. In addition, they are non-expandable as they are not ultimate CLASS NODES. Another feature of XSLOTS is that they denote time and precedency along the z-axis. In contrast, viewing from the plane formed by the x and y-axis in (23), no order is assumed for the sub-segmental unit ROOT and the prosodic unit LARYNGEAL. For example, the Core-Peripheral relation between Manner and Place entails no ordered relation, although the two-dimensional geometry looks as if Manner precedes Place.

Interpretations of each element in the element geometry are given on the right side of (23) in four categories – LARYNGEAL, Manner, Place (Primary) and Place (Secondary). Below we will explain each of the three CLASS NODES O/N, ROOT, and LARYNGEAL before we return to how the overall structure explains depressor effects, the asymmetry between nasality and voicing in depression, and the marked and unmarked triggers.

4.1 Onset/Nucleus CLASS NODE

We adopt the idea from Kehrein (2002) and Kehrein and Golston (2004) that LARYNGEAL is directly dominated by the prosodic unit O/N, but differ from Botma (2004) and the revised RCVP (van der Hulst 2015) on the degree of prosody-melody interactions. In Botma (2004), both Phonation and Manner are visible to prosodic structures but we do not see the need for Manner to be visible to prosody as we know of no phonological processes that demonstrate a manner-prosody interaction.[11] Indeed our depressor data suggest that plain nasals, which would contain the triggering |L| in Manner in fact show no depressor effects. Allowing prosody to have access to Manner opens up the expectation that such interactions should occur, both when there is one element in Manner (simplex manner), or when there is a complex Manner, like in affricates.

Instead, we assume that only LARYNGEAL and O/N (or, say tiers above the transitional X-SLOTS tier) are visible to prosody whereas all structures below X-SLOTS are segmental and inaccessible. This guarantees a straightforward and clear-cut laryngeal-tone interaction in depression at the prosodic level without the involvement of segmental units.

4.2 ROOT

We treat Manner as the Core of the CLASS NODE ROOT in line with Botma (2004) and van der Hulst (2015).[12] The central idea is that there always exists at least one Manner element in segments, regardless of whether they are consonants or vowels. We assume that the |L| in Manner refers to sonorancy (spontaneous voicing), which is present in all sonorants (including vowels, approximants and plain nasals).

The sub-structural organisation of Manner is as follows. Since |H| (for noise) and |L| (for sonorancy) do not co-occur in Manner, we assign these two elements on the same tier, indicating that either |H| or |L| exists in one representation. As a result, the Manner |?| and |H|/|L| diverge into two planes before converging back at the Dominated Place (Primary) tier as is shown in (24). This means that Manner tiers |?| and |H|/|L| reside on the same level without a hierarchical relation, contrasting with Botma's complex Manners. The reason for this arrangement is that this simple paralleled tier representation for Manner is

---

[11] The current geometry focuses on laryngeal-tone interactions and excludes the possibility of manner-prosody interactions. We leave the question of manner-prosody interactions open for future research and tentatively propose that if the geometry enables Manner to talk to prosody in minimal steps, then manner-prosody interactions would be possible. However, in our current model, it takes more steps for Manner to interact with tone compared with laryngeal-tone interactions and thus no manner-prosody interactions are assumed.

[12] There are possible counter-arguments to Manner being core as may be evidenced in lenition trajectories, where Manner is always the most unstable property, changing stops to fricatives before Place properties are lost. One response to this is that lenition trajectories are simply idealisations of potentially varying and complex processes of how sounds become less complex, with the possibility that languages may vary in what path they take with stop to debuccalisation processes also possible.

enough to express contrasts; further hierarchies within Manner bring redundancy to the geometry.

4.3 LARYNGEAL

We suggest that there are three elements |H|, |L|, and |?| that can freely occur in either the Core or the Peripheral positions of the CLASS NODE LARYNGEAL. However, LARYNGEAL is subject to certain constraints that restrict the number of oppositions generated. First of all, elements on the Dominant and Dominated tiers in LARYNGEAL must be consistent. This means that if |H| is on the Dominant tier and there is also an element on the Dominated tier, that element must be the same, i.e. |H|. This follows naturally from the Core-Peripheral relation of the overarching structure which says that LARYNGEAL, being the peripheral of the 1st layer O/N, is much more restricted in terms of selecting elements for its Dominant-Dominated tier. By contrast, within the 2nd layer ROOT, because this layer sits in the core position of the O/N layer, higher than LARYNGEAL, ROOT encompasses a greater degree of flexibility in choosing different elements for its Dominant and Dominated tiers. In addition, the dominating relation requires that if the Dominated tier is filled, the Dominant tier must also be filled, but not vice versa. Since voicelessness H is the default state for consonants, and the number of languages that involve ? is less than those with H & L,[13] we will assume that ? occurs restrictively in the core position only, whereas H & L can occur in all three positions of LARYNGEAL. ? and L do not co-exist in LARYNGEAL. Similar to the arguments from RCVP, we treat the addition of the same element in the Peripheral position as redundant, thus $X^x = X$ and $XX^x = XX$ (X could be any one of the three laryngeal elements; normal font size indicates element(s) in the Core and superscripts represent the Peripheral element). In this case, we generate exactly 12 oppositions as is shown in (27).

(27) 12 oppositions generated by LARYNGEAL

L	voicing (dep)	L^L	L^H	breathiness (dep)	$L^?$
LL	nasal (dep)	LL^L	LL^H	breathy nassal (dep)	$LL^?$
H	voiceless (non-dep)	H^H	H^L	voiceless (dep)	$H^?$

---

[13] Although this is a restricted sample, 47.9% of the UPSID languages have ?, which is less than the percentage of languages that have voiced and voiceless consonants (e.g. 63.6% for [b] and 89.4% for [k]).

HH	aspiration (non-dep)	~~HH^H~~	HH^L	aspiration (dep)	~~HH^ʔ~~
ʔ	glottal	ʔ^ʔ	ʔ^H	fortis stop	ʔ^ʟ
ʔʔ	implosive	ʔʔ^ʔ	ʔʔ^H	ejective	ʔʔ^ʟ

Table (27) exhausts all the possible phonation distinctions, which have a descriptor in the following column. Strikethrough representations are ruled out by the constraints discussed above. More discussion on this table, in particular with respect to how this relates to depressor triggers, will be offered in the next section.

4.4 Depressor effects in element geometry

With this multi-layered element geometry proposal, we are now in a position to account for the attested depressor effects. We suggest the following structural distinctions between depressors and their non-depressor counterparts as illustrated in (28). (28a-d) are representations for depressors while (28e-f) are for non-depressors. As already discussed we assume that voicing is represented by |L| on the Dominant tier in LARYNGEAL as in (28a). We maintain the idea that |L| is central to triggering depressor effects and therefore must be present in such segments. Breathiness has a complex structure |LH|, with |L| on the dominant tier and |H| in a peripheral branching location. Note that for ease of writing, elements in the Core of LARYNGEAL (whether on the Dominant or Dominated tiers) are written in normal font size whereas superscripts represent elements in the Peripheral throughout this paper. By comparison, voiceless depressors are a mirror image of the structure of breathiness, where its dominating property voicelessness dwells in the Core, with |L| in the branching peripheral position as in (28c). Aspirated depressors which are the least expected depressors are represented as |HHL|, having an |H| on both the Dominant and Dominated tiers, with |L| as a branching dependent. This representation implies that any aspirated segment that causes depression must contain |L|, which is the source of depression. By contrast, segments which show no depressor effects rightly contain no |L|, as is the case with plain voiceless aspirates represented as |HH| and plain voiceless stops as |H|. This analysis commits us to having two representations of plain voiceless, on the one hand, and voiceless aspirates, on the other, as shown in (28). There is sufficient variation in phonetic analyses and descriptions to suggest that it is probable that these representations can be supported by phonetic facts, although we do not pursue this here. We note though that some phonetic studies, for example, show that voiceless depressors are always accompanied by a certain degree of breathiness or longer durations of noise in higher frequencies (e.g. Downing and Gick 2005, Cao 1992, Chen 2015). It however remains contentious whether breathiness is invariably present in voiceless depressors, with other studies e.g. Traill, Khumalo and Fridjhon (1987), Jessen and Roux (2002), arguing that breathiness is inconsistent in voiceless depressors. We take this surface phonetic variation as clear indication that there is more to the phonological representation than would be achieved by a single representation for plain and aspirated voiceless segments, and the evidence for which are the depressor facts. The |L| in LARYNGEAL in this case accounts for the depressor effects that connects the seemingly unrelated triggers of depression, such as voicing and aspiration, with one shared phonological structure. The increasing complexity of the structures in (28a-d) also reflects the increasing markedness of the four types of depressors.

(28) Depressors vs. non-depressors representations (a-d: depression triggers; e-f: non-depression counterparts)

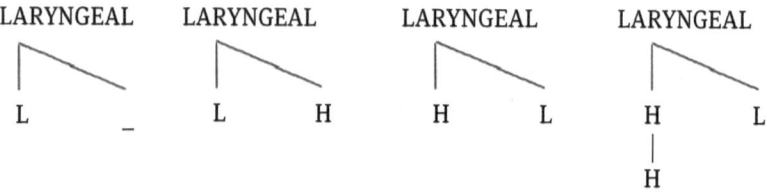

a. Voicing |L| b. Breathiness |L^H| c. Voicelessness |H^L| d. Aspiration |HH^L|

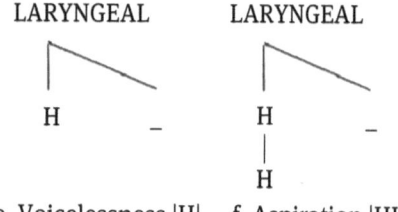

e. Voicelessness |H| f. Aspiration |HH|

Therefore, take the bilabial place of articulation as an example, the structure of the four triggers of depression is schematised in (29).

(29) The representations of four triggers of depression

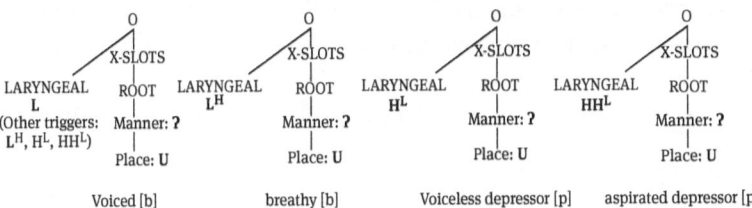

Voiced [b]   breathy [b]   Voiceless depressor [p]   aspirated depressor [pʰ]

For the actual representation of the depressor effect, we follow Kula (2012) in assuming that the Tonal tier functions as a mediator, where the most dominant element of depressors in LARYNGEAL, viz. |L|, is always projected onto this tier (indicated by the leftmost dotted line in 30), and thereby receives the prosodic interpretation of low tone. This projected |L| on the Tonal tier associates to the nearest host – the LARYNGEAL of the following nucleus – and thus any High tone of that vowel is produced as low, resulting in the depressor effect. Consider the illustration of this in (30)

(30) Depressor-tone interaction

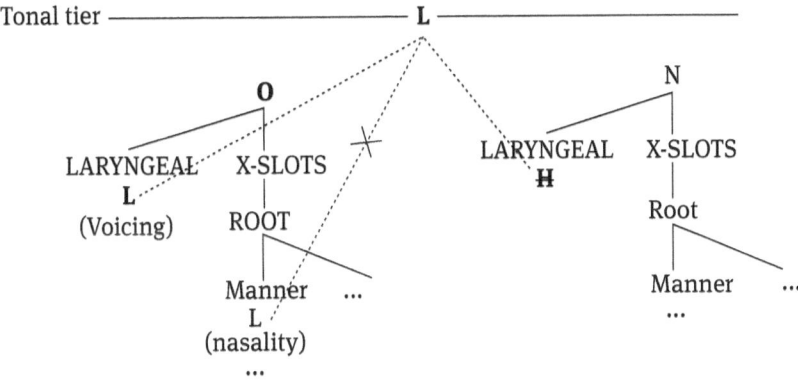

With regard to the asymmetry between voicing and nasality, representations for a true voicing depressor [b], and a non-depressor nasal [m], are displayed in (31a-b) for comparison. In this case, nasality is interpreted by the |L| in Manner. The voicing-nasality asymmetry in depression can be explained by the fact that the embedded |L| in Manner, for non-depressor nasals, is invisible to the Tonal tier (shaded in grey). This means that melody-tone interaction is unlikely to be triggered by plain nasals. On the contrary, the |L| for voicing in [b], from the prosodic unit LARYNGEAL, can easily access the Tonal tier which is also prosodic. This model also predicts the possibility of depressor (breathy) nasals, where the extra breathiness quality |LH| is specified in LARYNGEAL, apart from the |L| in Manner for nasality. This then also highlights that it is not just any |L| that triggers depression, but |L| within LARYNGEAL. Compare the structures for non-depressor and depressor nasals in (31). The structures also capture the fact that depressor nasals are much more marked than non-depressor nasals, i.e. predicting that language systems only have breathy nasals in addition to plain nasals.

(31) Depressor [b], non-depressor vs. depressor (breathy) nasal [m]

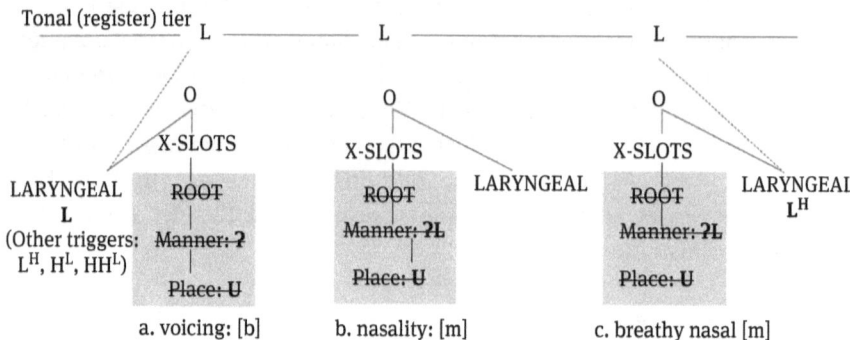

a. voicing: [b]   b. nasality: [m]   c. breathy nasal [m]

The foregoing has shown how the proposed multi-layered recursive segmental representation is able to account for the variation attested in depressor types. The analysis shows that these can all be unified by |L| in LARYNGEAL as the trigger. Our focus has been centrally on the LARYNGEAL Class Node, since our empirical focus was on depressor patterns. In the next section we briefly provide some supporting evidence for the general approach we adopt in the structure of the CLASS NODE, and the role that the proposed structure can be seen to play in explaining other phonological phenomena.

5 Peripherals and derived environment effects (DEE)

This section examines the role of Peripherals of CLASS NODE Onset/Nucleus and ROOT in explaining phonologically derived environment effects (DEE).

DEEs refer to a scenario where the application of a particular phonological process is confined only to a derived environment, but not to the counterpart non-derived environment. The classical presentation of this opacity is given in Kiparsky (1973). Kula's (2008) proposal treats DEEs as reflecting different melodic structures for derived vs. non-derived segments. This is, for example, proposed for the representation of palatals where (32a) is the representation of a derived palatal while (32b) is a lexical one. These representations express the voiceless palatal affricate with the same elements |H ? I|, but crucially in different configurations, where one exploits a peripheral structure and the other does not. What the different configurations capture is the fact that an element in a peripheral position as in (32a) is able to delink and spread element |I| without leaving a trace (element-hopping), while an element in the core part of a structure (32b) must leave a trace when it spreads element |I|. Not leaving a trace is to be understood as equivalent to element delinking. Delinking of elements (element-hopping) is in this way positionally restricted so that it is only possible from a peripheral position. Spreading of elements occurs in core positions only.

(32) Derived (a) vs. non-derived palatal (b) representations

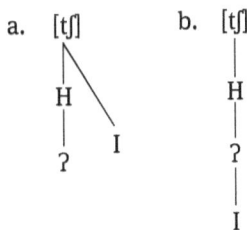

Under the proposed multi-layered element geometry the analysis fits nicely into a fully-fledged subsegmental representation that assigns symmetric roles to the two recursive Peripherals LARYNGEAL and Place (Secondary) in DEE. Below we will discuss DEE under CLASS NODE ROOT first and then the CLASS NODE O/N. In the element geometry proposal, the adjoined-|I| in Kula (2008) resides under the Peripheral Place (Secondary) tier which is directly dominated by the CLASS NODE ROOT. We consider three cases of DEE and the import of the proposed structure below.

5.1 DEE under CLASS NODE ROOT

We consider the representation of secondary place in a peripheral position as providing explanation to opacity effects involving palatalisations in Kinyamwezi and Polish, for example.

Kinyamwezi (Bantu, Tanzania) has a process of palatalisation of root final consonants to create causatives. Palatalisation, for example, affects final /s, k, n/ to produce their palatal counterparts as shown in (33a). This palatalisation process can spread beyond the root final consonant to following consonants of additional suffixes as seen in (33b), where the causative is followed by a perfective suffix whose lexical form is -*ile*, but which surfaces with an intervocalic palatal glide /j/ following palatalisation.[14] However, note that the preceding palatals derived in (33a) are no longer palatal in (33b), i.e. they have undergone depalatalisation. See Maganga and Schadeberg (1992) for further details on Nyamwezi palatalisation.

(33) a. Causative palatalisation
        stem   gloss   causative (derived palatals)
        bis-a   'hide'   biʃ-a   'cause to hide'
        bak-a   'light'   batʃ-a   'cause to light'
        bon-a   'see'   boɲ-a   'cause to see'
   b. Depalatalisation in multiple suffixes
        stem   causative   causative + perfective
        bis-a   biʃ-a   biʃ-ile → bis-ije 'has caused to hide'
        bak-a   batʃ-a   batʃ-ile → bak-ije 'has caused to light'
        bon-a   boɲ-a   boɲ-ile → bon-ije 'has caused to see'
   c. Non-derived palatals – no depalatalisation
        stem   causative + perfective
        buutʃ-a 'carry'   buutʃ-ile → buutʃ-ije 'has caused to carry'
        liiʃ-a   'kill'   liiʃ-ile → liiʃ-ije 'has caused to kill'
        ʃook-a 'go back' ʃook-i-a → ʃooʃ-a 'has caused to go back'

The opacity effect is seen in (33c). Root-final consonants in (33c) are lexical palatals, which by contrast do not undergo depalatalisation when a perfective suffix, which itself undergoes palatalisation, is added. In this case we get a surface sequence of palatals in C_2 (the second consonant) and C_3 (the third consonant) position.

In the element geometry representations, the Peripheral Place (Secondary) of the CLASS NODE ROOT is active, hosting |I| in derived palatals. Since the Peripheral tier can exhibit a greater degree of mobility, this is the target of depalatalisation, as in (34a), while lexical palatals are part of the core structure, as in (34b).

---

[14] Bantu verbs generally have the structure consisting of a CVC- root followed by a final vowel -*a*. Suffixation processes always target the CVC- root (or CVC-VC- derived stem) after which the final vowel -*a* is added, unless the suffix is aspectual in which case the vowel may be something different. In this case the perfective suffix is -*ile* and so the neutral final -*a* does not surface.

(34) Element geometry representations of derived v. non-derived [tʃ]

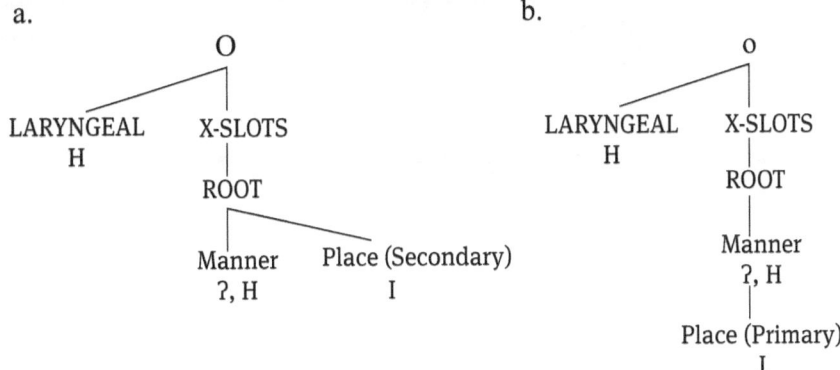

This analysis captures the intuition that derived palatals involve a different structural configuration than lexical ones do. The representation of the derived palatal is one that lends itself to being delinked because it is not part of the core structure. This same analysis is also applicable to Polish spirantisation, which similarly exhibits a phonological DEE. In this case spirantisation targets derived palatals (when they are voiced), the output of first velar palatalisation, as in (35a), but does not apply to lexical palatals in (35b), irrespective of their identical phonetic realisations.

(35) First velar palatalisation and spirantisation

First velar palatalisation[15]   **spirantisation (voiced)**
a. derived palatals
   krok-i-c → kroč-y-ć   ø   'to step'
   wag-i-c → waǰ-i-ć   waž-y-ć 'to weigh'
   strax-i-c → straš-y-ć   ø   'to frighten'

First velar palatalisation   **no spirantisation**
b. non-derived palatals
   bryǰ-ik-ɨ → bryǰ-ek-ɨ   –   'bridge'
   banǰ-o → banǰ-o   –   'banjo'
   ǰem-ɨ → ǰem-ɨ   –   'jam'

---

15 Data in (35) are drawn from Łubowicz (2002), with Rubach (1984) as the first-hand source. We are aware that opinions and analyses of Polish First Velar Palatalisation vary widely and for the case at hand adopt the approach of these two authors, and therefore do not contribute to the ongoing debate in this exposition.

In this case too, it is only those palatals that result from first velar palatalisation, creating palatals with |I| as a secondary place element, that then undergo spirantisation. In this instance the peripheral structure provides a host for an additional element resulting in spirantisation.

5.2 DEE under CLASS NODE O/N

In the previous section, DEEs are explained by the active Peripheral of the CLASS NODE ROOT. However, the proposed recursive structure predicts that the symmetrical Peripheral tier of the CLASS NODE O/N should also induce DEE at a higher level. DEE at the CLASS NODE O/N higher level is illustrated by post-nasal voicing in Puyo-Pongo Quechua (data from Botma 2004).

In this language, post-nasal voicing is morpheme-boundary sensitive, where stem-final nasals always voice the following voiceless initial stops at morpheme boundaries, as in (36b). In mono-morphemic words as in (36a), post-nasal stops can be contrastive in voicing.

(36) Morpheme sensitive nasals in Puyo-Pongo Quechua[16]
    a. Morpheme-internal
        pampaljina 'skirt'   hambi 'poison'
        ʃinki   'soot'   tʃunga 'ten'
        tʃuntina   'to stir the fire' indi   'sun'
    b. Morpheme boundary
        wasi-ta 'the others-OBJ' wakin-da 'the house-OBJ'
        sinik-pa 'porcupine-GEN' kam-ba 'you-GEN'
        satʃa-pi 'jungle-LOC'   hatum-bi 'big one-LOC'

This implies that although morpheme-internal and morpheme-boundary nasals are indistinguishable on the surface, they involve different internal phonological melodic structures which explain their contrasting behaviour. Morpheme-internal nasals are represented with |L| for nasality residing in Manner under the CLASS NODE ROOT, as in (37a). Morpheme-boundary nasals have an extra

---

[16] An anonymous reviewer suggests an alternative coda-mirror (Segeral and Scheer 2001) analysis in which in internal RT sequences, as in (36a), the stops would be in a strong position whereas in (36b) they would be in weak positions, assuming no initial empty CV in this language. We leave a more detailed investigation of this alternative approach to a future occasion.

active Peripheral |L| specified in the Dominant tier of LARYNGEAL as in b) below.[17]

(37) Contrasting nasals structures in Puyo-Pongo Quechua

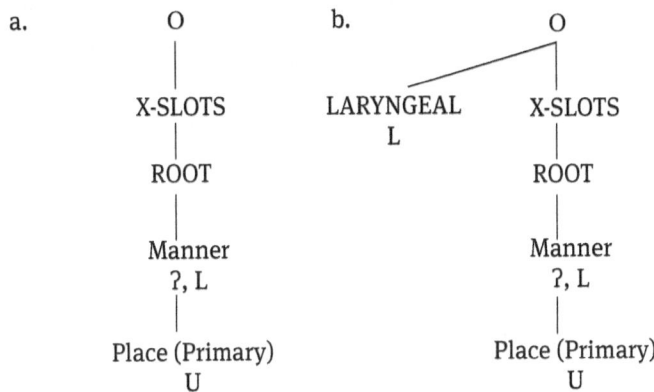

In (37b), postnasal voicing is realised by copying the complete CLASS NODE LARYNGEAL of the nasal to its immediately following voiceless stop. This process is illustrated in (38) where the arrow from /m/ to /p/ represents full LARYNGEAL copying.

(38) Post-nasal voicing as peripheral element copying

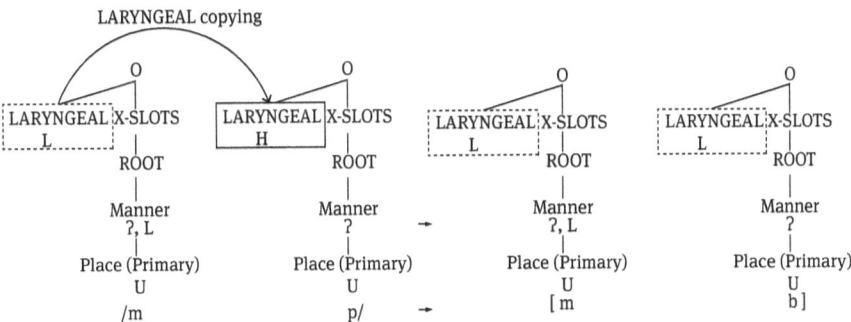

The foregoing discussion thus provides further support for the recursive CLASS NODE structure. We have shown the need and applications of three different

---

[17] Whether derived versus non-derived nasals is the correct terminology/conceptualisation here we leave to further thought and analysis. What is more crucial is that these data provide evidence supporting a language opting to utilize available structures in contrastive ways as evidenced by phonological patterning.

layers from varying phonological processes that utilise the peripheral structures at the different layers. For Layer 1, we have evidence for this from the palatalisation processes. For Layer 2, the depressor effects show how this structure is specifically utilised. And for Layer 3, we see how nasals can be variably represented using peripheral LARYNGEAL to host |L|. Thus, apart from the depressor facts, other phonological processes also support the multi-layered approach adopted here.

6 Conclusion

In this chapter, we were centrally concerned with explaining the attested variation in the triggers of depressors, as mainly seen in Southern Bantu languages, with the broader goal of explaining how tone-consonant interactions can be explained. Since the most unmarked triggers of depression are voiced segments, we used the parallelism that Element Theory offers between the representation of voicing and low tone, as captured by the element |L|, as a central piece in our analysis. The fact that |L| is also used to represent nasals, but plain nasals are themselves never triggers of depressor effects, led us to adopt a representation where |L| appears in multiple positions in a feature geometry. The proposed geometry involves a core template that is replicated recursively in three layers. Each of the three layers organise elements in dominance relations, but also involve a peripheral structure that allows elements to be more loosely associated to the core structure. This representation allows us to explain why nasals with |L| in the core structure show no depressor effects, while voiced sounds with |L| in a peripheral position show depressor effects. The analysis, logically followed, implies that although phonetic studies may give variable results on whether depressor voiceless aspirates or plain voiceless sounds contain some breathiness or not, the phonological representation must contain an |L| somewhere within the representation of these sounds. The more embedded the |L| is in Layer 2, the more marked the structure, and hence the more marked the depressor type. In this sense, the proposed analysis captures the relative markedness of the attested depressor types.

To demonstrate the viability of the proposed multi-layered recursive element geometry, we discussed some examples that provided support for the assumed recursive structures, showing that peripheral structures in all three layers show symmetry in being more loosely attached to the rest of the structure, and therefore the source of disparate phonological patterning in otherwise phonetically identical segments.

References

Avery, Peter and Keren Rice. 1989. Segment structure and coronal underspecification. *Phonology* 6, 179–200.
Backley, Phillip. 2011. *An Introduction to Element Theory*. Edinburgh: Edinburgh University Press.
Backley, Phillip and Kuniya Nasukawa. 2009. Representing labials and velars: a single 'dark' element. *Phonological Studies* 12, 3–10.
Baumbach, Erdmann Johannes Martin. 1987. *Analytical Tsonga Grammar*. Pretoria: University of South Africa.
Beach, Douglas M. 1924. The science of tonetics and its application to Bantu languages. *Bantu Studies* 2, 75–106.
Botma, Bert. 2004. *Phonological Aspects of Nasality: An Element-based Dependency Approach*. LOT Dissertation series 90. Utrecht: Holland Academic Graphics.
Botma, Bert, Nancy C. Kula and Kuniya Nasukawa. 2011. Features. In Nancy C. Kula, Bert Botma and Kuniya Nasuawa (eds.), *The Continuum Companion to Phonology*, 33–63. London: Continuum.
Bradshaw, Mary M. 1999. A crosslinguistic study of consonant–tone interaction. Ph.D. Dissertation, Ohio State University.
Bradshaw, Mary M. 2003. Consonant–tone interaction in Siswati. *Studies in Phonetics, Phonology and Morphology* 9(2), 277–294.
Brockhaus, Wiebke. 1995. *Final Devoicing in the Phonology of German*. Tübingen: Niemeyer.
Cao, Jianfen (曹剑芬). 1987. Lun Gingzhuo Yudaiyinbudaiyin Deguanxi (论清浊与带音不带音的关系). [On voicing and voicelessness], 中国语文 [Chinese] 197, 101–109.
Cao, Jianfen and Ian Maddieson, I. 1992. An exploration of phonation types in Wu Dialects of Chinese. *Journal of Phonetics* 20, 79–92.
Chao, Yuen Ren (赵元任). 1928. *Xiandai Wuyu Yanjiu* (现代吴语研究) [Studies of the modern Wu dialects] (Tsing Hua College Research Institute Monographs 4). Beijing: Tsing Hua College.
Chen, Zhongmin. 2015. Breathy voice and low tone. *Journal of Chinese Linguistics* 43(1), 90–117. Chinese University Press.
Chen, Yiya and Laura J. Downing. 2011. All depressors are not alike: a comparison of Shanghai Chinese and Zulu. In Sónia Frota, Gorka Elordieta and Pilar Prieto (eds.), *Prosodic Categories: Production, Perception and Comprehension, Studies in Natural Language and Linguistic Theory* 82, 243–266. Dordrecht: Springer.
Clements, George N. 1985. The geometry of phonological features. *Phonology Yearbook* 2, 225–252.
Clements, George N. and Elizabeth V. Hume. 1995. The internal organization of speech sounds. In John A. Goldsmith (ed.), *The Handbook of Phonological Theory*, 245–306. Oxford: Blackwell.
Doke, Clement M. (1926). *The Phonetics of the Zulu Language*, 1st edition. Johannesburg: Witwatersrand University Press.
Doke, Clement M. (1967). *The Southern Bantu languages*. London: International African Institute.
Downing, Laura J. 2009. On pitch lowering not linked to voicing: Nguni and Shonagroup depressors. *Languages Sciences* 31, 179–198.
Downing, Laura J. and Bryan Gick. 2001. Voiceless tone depressors in Nambya and Botswana Kalang'a'. *Proceedings of the Annual Meeting, Berkeley Linguistics Society* 27, 65–80.

Downing, Laura, J. and Bryan Gick. 2005. Voiceless tone depressors in Nambya and Botswana Kalanga. *BLS* 27: 65–80.

Gandour, Jack. 1974. Consonants types and tones in Siamese. *Journal of Phonetics* 2(4), 337–350.

Halle, Morris and Kenneth N. Stevens. 1971. A note on laryngeal features. *Quarterly Progress Report* 101, 198–213. Cambridge, MA: Research Laboratory of Electronics, MIT.

Harris, John. 1994. *English Sound Structure*. Oxford: Blackwell.

Harris, John and Geoff Lindsey. 1995. The elements of phonological representation. In Jacques Durand and Francis Katamba (eds.), *Frontiers of Phonology: Atoms, Structures, Derivations*, 34–79. Harlow, Essex: Longman.

Hulst, Harry G.van der . 1989. Atoms of segmental structure: components, gestures and dependency. *Phonology* 6(2), 253–284

Hulst, Harry G. van der. 1995. Radical CV Phonology: The categorical gesture. In Jacques Durand and Francis Katamba (eds.), *Frontiers of Phonology: Atoms, Structures, Derivations*, 80–116. Harlow, Essex: Longman.

Hulst, Harry G.van der . 2005. The molecular structure of phonological segments. In Philip Carr, Jacques Durand and Collin Ewen (eds.), *Headhood, elements, specification and contrastivity*, 193–234. Amsterdam: John Benjamins.

Hulst, Harry G. van der. 2015. The laryngeal class in RcvP and voice phenomena in Dutch. In Johanneke Caspers, Yija Chen, Willemijn Heeren, Jos Pacilly, Niels Schiller and Ellen van Zanten (eds.), *Above and Beyond the Segments*, 323–349. Amsterdam: John Benjamins.

Hulst, Harry G. van der. 2017. The integration of segmental and syllabic structure in Radical CV Phonology. Paper presented at the workshop The Interface Within. What relations hold between prosody and melody?, Meertens Institute, Amsterdam, The Netherlands (13 March 2017).

Humbert, Helga. 1995. Phonological segments: their structure and behaviour. Ph. D. dissertation, University of Amsterdam.

Hyman, Larry M. 1985. Word domains and downstep in Bamileke-Dschang. *Phonology Yearbook* 2, 47–83.

Hyman, Larry M. 2003. Basaa (A43). In Derek Nurse and Gérard Philippson (eds.), *The Bantu Languages*, 257–282. London: Routledge.

Hyman, Larry M. and Maurice Tadadjeu. 1976. Floating tones in Mbam-Nkam. In Larry M. Hyman (ed.), *Studies in Bantu tonology (Southern California Occasional Papers in Linguistics* 3), 57–111. Los Angeles, CA: Department of Linguistics, University of Southern California.

Jessen, Michael and Justus C. Roux. 2002. Voice quality differences associated with stops and clicks in Xhosa. *Journal of Phonetics* 30, 1–52.

Jun, Sun-Ah. 1998. The Accentual Phrase in the Korean prosodic hierarchy. *Phonology* 15, 189–226.

Kaye, Jonathan, Jean Lowenstamm, Jean-Roger Vergnaud. 1985. The internal structure of phonological representations: A theory of charm and government. *Phonology Yearbook* 2, 305–328.

Kehrein, Wolfgang. 2002. Phonological representation and phonetic phasing: affricates and laryngeals. Ph.D. dissertation, University of Marburg.

Kehrein, Wolfgang and Chris Goslton. 2004. A prosodic theory of laryngeal contrasts. *Phonology* 21, 325–257.

Khumalo, J. S. M. 1981. Zulu tonology, Part 1. *African Studies* 40, 53–130.

Khumalo, J. S. M. 1987. An autosegmental account of Zulu phonology. Ph.D. dissertation, University of the Witwatersrand, Johannesburg.
Kiparsky, Paul. 1973. Phonological representations. In Osamu Fujimura (ed.), *Three Dimensions of Linguistic Theory*, 1–135. Tokyo: TEC.
Kula, Nancy C. 1999. On the representation of NC clusters in Bemba. In Renée van Bezooijen and René Kager (eds.), *Linguistics in The Netherlands 1999*, 135–148. Amsterdam: Benjamins.
Kula, Nancy C. 2002. *The Phonology of Verbal Derivation in Bemba*. LOT Dissertation series 65. Utrecht: Holland Academic Graphics.
Kula, Nancy C. 2008. Derived environment effects: a representational approach. *Lingua* 118 (9), 1328–43.
Kula, Nancy C. 2012. On the representation of tone in Element Theory. In Eugeniusz Cyran, Henryk Kardela and Bogdan Szymanek (eds.), *Sound Structure and Sense: Studies in Memory of Edmund Gussmann*, 353–370. Lublin: Wydawnictwo KUL.
Ladefoged, Peter and Morris Halle. 1988. Some Major Features of the International Phonetic Alphabet. *Language* 64(3), 577–582.
Ladefoged, Peter and Ian Maddieson. 1996. *The Sounds of the World's Languages*. Oxford: Blackwell.
Lanham, L.W. 1958. The tonemes of Xhosa. *African Studies* 17, 65–81.
Lanham, L.W. 1960. The comparative phonology of Nguni. Ph.D. dissertation, University of the Witwatersrand, Johannesburg.
Lanham, L. W. 1969. Generative phonology and the analysis of Nguni consonants. *Lingua* 24, 155–162.
Lee, Seunghun J. 2008. Consonant-tone interaction in Optimality Theory. Ph.D dissertation, Rutgers University.
Lee, Seunghun J. 2009. H tone, depressors and downstep in Tsonga. In Masangu Matondo, Fiona McLaughlin and Eric Potsdam (eds.), *Selected Proceedings of the 38th Annual Conference on African Linguistics*, 26–38. Somerville: Cascadilla Press.
Lee, Seunghun J. 2015. Cumulative effects in Xitsonga: High-tone spreading and depressor consonants. *Southern African Linguistics and Applied Language Studies* 33(3), 273–290.
Łubowicz, Anna. 2002. Derived environment effects in OT. *Lingua* 112, 243–280.
Maddieson, Ian. 2003. The sounds of Bantu languages. In Derek Nurse and Gérard Philippson (eds.), *The Bantu Languages*, 15–41. London: Routledge.
Maganga, Clement and Thilo C. Schadeberg. 1992. *Nyamwezi: Grammar, Vocabulary and Texts*. Köln: Rüdiger Köppe Verlag.
Mathangwane, Joyce T. 1996. Phonetics and phonology of Ikalanga: A diachronic and synchronic study. Ph.D. dissertation, University of California, Berkeley.
Mathangwane, Joyce T. 1998. Aspirates: Their development and depression in Ikalanga. *Journal of African Languages and Linguistics* 19, 113–136.
Mathes, Timothy K. 2015. Consonant-tone interaction in the Khoisan language Tsua. Ph.D. Dissertation, New York University.
McCarthy, John J. 1988. Feature geometry and dependency: a review. *Phonetica* 38, 84–108.
McLaren, James. 1936. *A Concise Xhosa-English dictionary*. London, New York and Toronto: Longmans, Green and Co.
Nasukawa, Kuniya. 1998. An integrated approach to nasality and voicing. In Eugeniusz Cyran (ed.) *Structure and Interpretation: Studies in Phonology*, 205–225. Lublin: Folium.
Nasukawa, Kuniya. 2005. *A Unified Approach to Nasality and Voicing*. Berlin and New York: Mouton de Gruyter.

Nasukawa, Kuniya and Phillip Backley. 2005. Dependency relations in Element Theory: markedness and complexity. In Nancy C. Kula and Jeroen van de Weijer (eds.), *Proceedings of the Government Phonology Workshop. Special issue of Leiden Papers in Linguistics* 2(4), 77–93. Leiden: ULCL, Leiden University.

Nasukawa, Kuniya. 2014. Features and recursive structure. *Nordlyd* 41(1), 1–19. Special issue on Features edited by Martin Krämer, Sandra-Iulia Ronai and Peter Svenonius.

Ploch, Stefan. 1999. Nasals on my mind: the phonetic and the cognitive approach to the phonology of nasality. Ph.D. dissertation, School of Oriental and African Studies, University of London.

Pöchtrager, Markus A. and Jonathan Kaye. 2013. GP 2.0. *SOAS Working Papers in Linguistics* 16, 51–64.

Ren, Nianqi (任念麒). 1987. An acoustic study of Shanghai stops (上海话塞音的声学研究). Ms., University of Connecticut, Storrs.

Ren, Nianqi (任念麒). 1988. A fiberoptic and transillumination study of Shanghai stops (上海话塞音的喉部纤维光透照研究). Paper presented at International conference on Wu Dialects, Hong Kong.

Ren, Nianqi (任念麒). 2006. *Shanghainhua fayinleixing he fuyin de qubietezheng* (上海话发音类型和塞辅音的区别特征) [Phonation of Shanghainese and the distinctive features of stops]. Shanghai: Shanghai Lexicographical Publishing House.

Rubach, Jerzy. 1984. *Cyclic and Lexical Phonology: The Structure of Polish*. Dordrecht: Foris.

Rycroft, David K. 1976. *Say It in Siswati*. London: SOAS.

Rycroft, David K. 1980a. Ndebele and Zulu: some phonetic and tonal comparisons. *Zambezia* VIII(ii), 109–128.

Rycroft, David K. 1980b. The 'depression' feature in Nguni languages and its interaction with tone. Paper presented at the International Conference on Linguistics in Central and Southern Africa, Department of African Languages, Rhodes University, Grahamstown, the Republic of South Africa.

Sagey, Elizabeth. 1986. The representation of features and relations in nonlinear phonology. Ph.D. dissertation, Massachusetts Institute of Technology.

Ségéral, Philippe and Tobias Scheer. 2001. La coda-miroir. *Bulletin de la Société de Linguistique de Paris* 96, 107–152. (Older English version: The coda mirror, version 3.1 November 99).

Shen, Zhongwei(沈钟伟), Chuck Wooters and William Shi-Yuan Wang (王士元). 1987. Closure duration in the classification of stops: a statistical analysis (闭塞时长在塞音分类上的作用：统计分析). *The Ohio State University Working Papers in Linguisitcs* 35, 197–209.

Shi, Feng (石峰). 1983. Suzhouhua Zhuoseyin de shengxuefenxi. (苏州话浊塞音的声学分析) [Acoustic analyses of voiced stops in Suzhou]. *Linguistics Study* (语言研究) 1.

Strazny, Philipp. 2003. Depression in Zulu: Tonal effects of segmental features. In Jeroen Maarten van de Weijer, Vincent van Heuven and Harry G. van der Hulst (eds.), *The phonological spectrum: Volume 1, segmental structure*, 223–239. Amsterdam: John Benjamins.

Traill, Anthony, J.S. Mzilikazi Khumalo and Peter Fridjhon. 1987. Depressing facts about Zulu. *African Studies* 46, 255–274.

Zhong, Jianghua (钟江华) and Lizhong Chen (陈立中). 2012. xiandai xiangyu he wuyu zhuoyinshengmu fayintezhengdebijia. (现代湘语和吴语浊音声母发音特征的比较). [Comparisons of voiced onsets between modern Xiang and Wu]. *Journal of Hubei University for Nationalites* (湖北民族学院学报) 30 (4).

Filiz Mutlu
Embedding of the same type in phonology

1 Introduction

Recursion has been sought in phonology at the level of the syllable, and argued to be non-existent (cf. Carr 2006 and works cited therein). Contra this position, an argument for the existence of recursion in GP 2.0 can be found in Pöchtrager (this volume). In GP 2.0, consonants (onset phrases) are embedded in vowels (nuclear phrases). Note that this is not recursion of the same-type such as embedding a CP in another CP in syntax, but it is recursion nevertheless. In this paper, I will posit a novel theory which is set up in such a way that recursion of the same type is a natural property of the system, similar to syntax. This means that phonology is not more restricted in the type of embedding it allows.

In existing partially structural models such as GP 2.0 (Pöchtrager 2006), Aperture Theory (Steriade 1993), Onset Prominence (Schwartz 2016) and Radical CV (van der Hulst 2015 and works cited therein), structural positions host melody (elements, components, etc). This is dissimilar to syntax, where dependent positions host other phrases, yielding recursion. The model proposed here is completely substance-free, hence the only thing positions can host are other phrases. Basically, I propose that a consonant can be embedded in another to yield consonant clusters and affricates. Embedding is naturally restricted by the available positions in the matrix consonantal phrase (spec (ifier), comp(lement), both or none) and the asymmetrical properties of spec vs comp. This means that the structure of consonants automatically yields their combining possibilities, making it unnecessary to stipulate any further mechanisms (more on this in 1.2). In Government Phonology terms, this means reducing both substantive and formal government to the same mechanism. The advantage of modelling consonant clusters as recursion of the same type, however, is not merely a minimalist representation but that it makes more accurate predictions. A case in point is *emergent stops* such as found in *dance*, *else* and in lexicalised forms like *Alhambra*, *thunder* (cf. Ohala 2005, Recasens 2011). This phenomenon makes phonetic sense but it is not accurately predicted by existing models of phonology from the representation of consonants themselves. In this model, there is no embedding possibility which can directly bring together sequences like [ns, ls, nr, mr]. Such sequences can only exist if there is a silent plosive head between them, whose realisation yields [nts, lts, ndr, mbr], etc.

https://doi.org/10.1515/9781501512582-007

In this section, I discuss the motivation behind the need for reconsidering the nature of the primes of phonology (elements, features, and a combination of these with hierarchical structure). In section 2, I discuss what phonotactic strength means and what constitutes a consonant cluster. In Section 3, I introduce a substance-free model of phonology. In section 4, I model consonant clusters and affricates as recursive structures and discuss the advantages of doing so. Section 5 gives a brief sketch of higher level structure which brings consonants and vowels together, as well as an outline of the structure of place properties. Section 6 concludes.

1.1 Phonological primes

A system has small pieces (primes) and principles that determine how primes are brought together to yield complexity. For instance, in feature theory, stopness is expressed with the feature [-cont] and in element theory with the element |ʔ|. There are also partially structural models where manner properties such as stopness are expressed with structure (more on this presently). I will discuss a particular problem concerning the representation of phonological properties, including stopness, in existing models. In brief, it is well-observed that there is a link between manner and phonotactic strength (for instance, where a consonant sits in a consonant cluster.) I will offer a formal definition of phonotactic strength in section 2. Ideally, phonotactic strength should be directly encoded in phonological representation. I will argue that this is not the case with feature-based, element-based or partially structural models. For instance, nasals assimilate to following obstruents but not to preceding ones: *in+possible > impossible* but acne does not become a[kŋ]e. There are at least two observations to be made here. Firstly, both nasals and plosives are stops, but nasal stops are restricted in their place of articulation by a following plosive while the reverse is not the case. For plosives to exert such influence, they must be stronger. In feature theories, the difference between the two is that of the values [±nas] and [±son]. There is no logical reason why a plus value for nasality (sonorancy) should make the same object weaker, or why this particular weakness should result in assimilation. (Assimilation that optionally occurs across words is outside of the scope of this discussion.)

There is also an asymmetry of strength between nasal stops and fricatives. Fricatives are stronger than nasals, since nasals may assimilate to fricatives but not vice versa. In some versions of Element Theory, a nasal stop has the nasality/voicing element |L| and a place property. Fricatives, on the other hand have the noise element |h| and a place property. The only difference between a nasal and fricative is the choice of |L| and |h| respectively. There is nothing in the representation of |L| and |h| that yields this strength difference. The problem only gets worse if nasals also have |ʔ| that makes the governee more complex and therefore stronger than the governor. Harris (1997) takes nasals in clusters to lack a place property, acquiring it from the following plosive. There is nothing in the representation of | L| and |h| which says that an expression with the former should acquire its place property in this way, but the latter should not and cannot. To illustrate, [s] in [sp]# never assimilates in place to [p]: *[fp]. In feature theories, such strength asymmetries are explained by sonority and possibly by arranging features into feature-geometric nodes (Clements 1985). Such arrangement does not follow from the features themselves. As a result, the exact arrangement of features is a matter of discussion (cf. Botma 2004, Harris and Lindsey 1995 and works cited therein). See Harris (2006) for a criticism of sonority. In element theories, the notions of charm (Kaye et al. 1990) and complexity (Harris 1994) amongst others, have been offered to explain asymmetries. For example, charm is the property of an element which determines its combining power and strength. An element can have a negative, positive or neutral charm; elements with the same charm do not combine. The conceptual problem is that there is no principled reason why elements should have the particular charm they have, or have a property like charm at all. Likewise, there is no principle which yields all and only the elements that exist, along with their properties. (This also holds for features). |I| and |U| both have positive charm. One of the empirical problems is that |I| and |U| do in fact combine to yield [y], for instance in French. Complexity means that the more elements an object has, the more phonotactic strength it has. As illustrated in the discussion of |L| vs |h|, it is not necessarily the quantity but the quality of elements that yield different results. I will not go into a detailed criticism of either theory or any of these notions (cf. Pöchtrager 2006, 2012 on charm and complexity). The crucial problem is why stipulations should be necessary at all to explain the behaviour of phonological primes, instead of their behaviour falling right out of the primes themselves.

Secondly, there is a constraint on the direction of assimilation, which is explained, for example, by reference to constituency structure (Harris 1994). This requires additional stipulations on the link between melodic primes and such constituent structure (see Jensen 1994).

A novel theory in a field rich with different theories and their various flavours must earn its keep by bringing clear, self-consistent solutions to longstanding problems. Another such problem, besides the combinatory restrictions and strength- relevant effects of phonological primes, is the emergence of stops in consonant clusters like [ns, nr], yielding [nts, ndr]. A phonetic explanation is possible for emergent stops but no phonological theory derives them in the correct environments from the representation of consonants themselves (cf. Recasens 2011, Ohala 2005).

The representation of affricates is also a matter of discussion. Weijer (2014) notes affricates are not identical to plosives but does not point out their similarity to nasals: neither can be the second consonant in a configuration $C_1C_2\#$ where C_1 is a fricative but both can be C_2 if C_1 is a sonorant: e.g. *pi*[ntʃ] and Swedish *na*[mn] 'name' are fine but *[le[ftʃ], *[le[fn] are not. Transcriptions may have sequences like [zm] as in prism. However, there is a schwa between [z, m] (cf. Algeo 1978, Kenyon 1956). This is not the case with *Thames*. This is not predicted if affricates are regular plosives (Backley 2011, Kehrein 2002 among others) or a contour segment with the same complexity as a plosive (Harris 1990, 1994). Szigetvari (1997) notes affricates do not occur before plosives but concludes it is a property of coronal plosives, hence not relevant to the structure of affricates: *[tp, tsp]#. However, neither do non-coronal affricates occur in this position: German *[pft]# does not exist in morphologically simplex words though [pt]# is fine, e.g. *Konzept* 'concept'. This is a brief selection of the kinds of problems the model will tackle. In particular, emergent stops and the phonotactic strength of affricates are directly related to their recursive structure.

1.2 Partially structural models: Stopness and nasality

In this section I look at some models which partially share the goal of representing phonological properties as positions in a structure.

Steriade (1993) builds Aperture Theory on phonetic insight: She takes segments to be "represented in the phonology as positions defined in terms of degrees of oral aperture". Stops (plosives, affricates, nasals) have two positions: closure and release. In contrast, continuants have only one position, release. While both fricatives and approximants have only a release point, the former has aperture-cum-friction (A_f) and the latter has maximal aperture (A_{max}). Closure is absence of airflow, designated as (A_0). These positions are like autosegmental nodes in the sense they host segmental properties such as place and phonation.

(1) Manner properties, taken from Steriade (1993)

$$
\begin{array}{cccc}
A_0\ A_{max} & A_0\ A_f & A_{max} & A_f \\
| & \vee & | & | \\
\text{place} & \text{place} & \text{place} & \text{place}
\end{array}
$$

The leftmost figure shows a plain plosive, where place is associated with closure only. The following figure shows an affricate, where place is associated with both the closure and release. The next figure is the representation of a glide and the rightmost one is the representation of a fricative.

(2) Stops and nasality, taken from Steriade (1993)

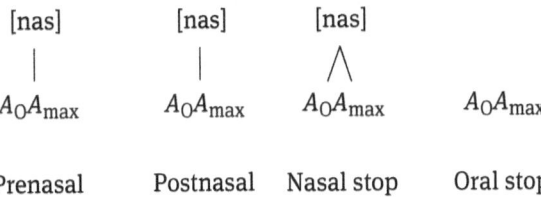

One or both of the positions in a stop can hold nasality, as illustrated in (2): closure (yielding prenasalised stops), release (yielding postnasalised stops) and both closure and release (yielding plain nasals), neither position (yielding oral stops).

There is a fundamental problem with the representation of nasal stops and plosives: Their structure is the same yet their phonotactic strength is not (as discussed in section 1.2 and to be further discussed in section 2). This means that phonotactic strength can vary within the same manner (or that manner cannot be derived through a single mechanism, viz. structure). Then, strength must be derived from an additional mechanism, as it is derived from sonority in feature theory and complexity in element theory. Note that the same problem also holds for affricates: The association of place with the release position and as well as closure yields an affricate, but as discussed in 1.1, affricates are not equal in strength to plosives either.

Interestingly, Pöchtrager (2006) develops a very similar distinction in the representation of stops vs non-stops in the framework of Government Phonology, offering a major revision of said framework: GP 2.0. The motivation is the behaviour of consonants rather than phonetics, and builds on Jensen's (1994) work who argues stops must have an extra position compared to non-stops. Stops (plosives, nasals, and laterals on the basis that they pattern with stops in some languages) have a head position and two dependent positions, in analogy to syntax. In contrast, fricatives have a head position and only one dependent position, and approximants have only a head position. Affricates and other kinds of stops (clicks, ejectives, implosives, etc.) are not modelled.

(3) Nasal stops vs plosives in GP 2.0, taken from Pöchtrager (2006)

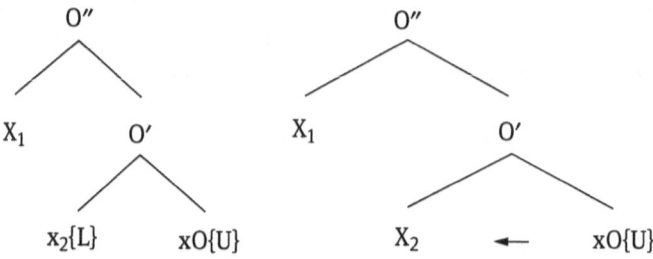

The figure on the left represents [m] and the one on the right represents a lenis [b], as in English *boy*. x_O stands for the onset head, which projects twice to yield a stop. The arrow between the head and the complement of [p] represents a special relationship called *control* which is not relevant to our discussion. Both [m] and [p] have two layers of structure and same number of nodes, and the element |U| (notation in curly brackets) to stand for labiality. [m] also has the nasality element |L|.

The crucial point is that, nasal stops and plosives have exactly the same number of positions, just as in Aperture Theory, and the difference between nasal stops and plosives is that nasal stops have the nasality element |L| hosted in one of these positions. The representation of plosives vs nasal stops runs into the same problem with Aperture Theory, the addition of [nasality] to a structure has no logical link to loss of strength.

Schwartz (2016) offers a new model, Onset Prominence, where a nasal stop has the position (closure) and plosives have more positions (both *closure* and *noise*). Fricatives, like nasal stops, have only one position but these are different in nature: fricatives have only noise.

(4) [p, m, f] respectively, taken from Schwartz (2016)

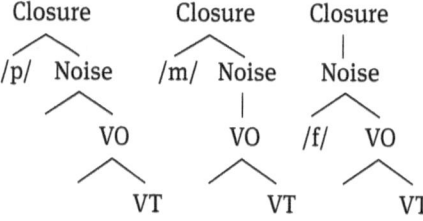

The leftmost figure represents [p], followed by [m] and [f]. In terms of the number of positions it has, [p] is more complex than both [m] and [f]. Regarding the representation of stopness vs friction, this is the most similar model to the one proposed here. However, the same problem concerning the relative strength of nasal stops and fricatives holds in Onset Prominence just as it did with the elements |L| vs |h|: There is no principled reason why one of these positions, noise, must yield more phonotactic strength than the other, closure. (In fact, Schwartz (p.c.) takes stopness to have more strength than friction because it is higher in the structure, in the absence of further mechanisms like submersion or promotion. A discussion of strength, of course, requires a definition of strength, which is found in section 2.) These positions hold melodic primes, such as a place property, similar to both Aperture Theory and GP 2.0.

The model proposed in this paper does not have any melodic primes whatsoever. The representation of phonological manner is basically identical to the representation of syntactic phrases. The representation of phonological place is basically identical to the representation of syntactic heads, both simplex ones such as *rabbit* and compounds such as *killer rabbit*. The representation of phonation and nasality is similar to the representation of syntactic case. Crucially, positions host other segments just as dependent positions in a phrases host other phrases in syntax. The obvious difference is that, if positions host complete segments rather than melodic primes, there are strong predictions on how consonants can come together.

Lastly, structure has a prominent role in dependency-based models such as Radical CV Phonology (van der Hulst 2015 and works cited therein) or the element-based dependency model (Botma 2004). However, in these models the nodes themselves do not take on the job of primes. It is the position of the primes (components/elements) within the larger structure that yields a phonological property. In spirit, the model I propose is similar to Radical CV Phonology in that the behaviour of the system is derived from asymmetry. However, the current model differs crucially in its complete lack of melodic primes and in that structural positions within a segment host other segments rather than melodic primes, both points leading to predictions not captured otherwise such as the clustering possibilities of consonants, which will be discussed in sections 4, 5 and 6.

2 Strength relations

In this section I look at cluster phonotactics in morphologically simplex words to isolate the strength of manner and place properties. I claim that once the relative strength of two objects has been established, that difference is universal, e.g. If [t] is stronger than [n] in a language, it is stronger than [n] in every language. I take *cluster* to mean a phonological relationship between consonants based on one criterion:

(5) If there is a structural relation between A and B, it must hold independently of the vowel context. This means that the sequence is found both at the right edge of a word and within it, e.g. *lamp, lampoon*. ABC is a cluster iff AB, BC are clusters: [str] is a cluster iff [st, tr] are.

The precise nature of said relation between A and B and the resulting configuration is posited in section 4. For now, all I seek is to find out is which sequences fulfill this condition distribution-wise. Using this criterion, I set out to (re)discover the strength relation between A and B. One clear piece of evidence for strength asymmetry in action, or *domination* as I shall call it, is that nasals assimilate in place to obstruents but not vice versa: English *in+elegant* but *im+possible*. For this, domination must be leftwards, a direction common to vowel-dependent affrication, palatalisation, pre-vocalisation (Operstein 2010) and the nasalisation, rhotacisation and lowering of vowels in closed syllables. While some of these processes may also be reversed, no process from a segment to its neighbour occurs only to the right. To illustrate, [i] affricates and palatalises a preceding [t] in Japanese (cf. Yoshida 2001), as in many languages. However, no language has [i] triggering such a process only in a plosive following it. Interestingly, this holds true for syntactic movement as well; for theories assuming movement, it is not debated that leftward movement occurs, but the existence of rightward movement is a matter of debate (cf. Kayne 1994, Rochemont and Culicover 1997). For both interaction between neighbouring segments in phonology and for movement in syntax, rightward implies leftward. I conclude left is the default direction for processes between neighbouring segments including domination, and for AB#, B *dominates* A. The strength of a consonant is measured by the set of objects it dominates, as we will see in (6).

If both #AB and #BA are attested in the same position, such as [rt, tr]# in French (Charette 1990), one of the pairs implies the existence of the other. Though French has [rt, tr]#, unrelated languages have only [rt]# or #[tr] in these positions and no language has only [tr]#. In light of this implicational relation, I take [rt]# to be the default order for that position, and to determine the domination relation, viz. [t] dominates [r]. The reversed string, [tr]#, is also prone to simplification (Charette 1991) and is acquired later than #TR clusters (Demuth and Kehoe 2006).

The table (6) shows domination relations based on data from English, German (Fox 2005), Italian (Kramer 2009), Swedish (Holmes and Hinchliffe 2003, Schadler 2006), Dutch (Booij 1999) and Djapu (Morphy 1983). Read from left to right as BA, B dominates A: The topmost row shows what a plosive can dominate, and under what conditions, e.g. A plosive dominates another plosive iff the dominant plosive is coronal.

(6) Domination relations (plosive: T, fricative: F, affricate: TF, nasal: N, liquid: R, sibilant: S)

dominates	T	F	TF	N	[l]	[r]
T		iff coronal	iff coronal or F is S	✓	✓	✓
F			iff coronal	✓	✓	✓
TF				✓	✓	✓
N				iff coronal	✓	✓
[l]						✓
[r]						

Measured by the set of objects B dominates, there is a stronger than relation between manners such that plosive > fricative > affricate ≈ nasal stop > [l] > [r]. Interestingly, nasals and affricates dominate the same set of objects which is not predicted or noted before: Swedish na[mn] 'name' and German da[mpf] 'steam' are fine while [fn, sm, spf, fts]# are not. However, nasals are dominated by all but liquids while affricates are *indominable*: [mn, ns, nt]# but not *[pft]#. This means strength and dominability are not always in an inverse relation with one another. The details of the phonotactics of affricates and their composition is discussed in 4.

Place adds to strength. Coronality makes B dominant for AB# of the same manner: [mn, pt]#. Interestingly, FT#, as one representative of AB#, has more restrictions: If B is not coronal, A is a sibilant (S) (Kristoffersen 2000): [sp, sk]# but not *[θp, θk]#. Labiality also affects strength. German has #[fl] as in Flug 'flight' but not #[xl]. No language has only [xl] but not [fl] even though it has both [f, x]. English [f] resisted lenition to zero but [x] disappeared. There is no similar evidence for palatality. Hence coronal > labial > dorsal within the manner. Place does not make B dominate above its manner: [nf, rm]# are fine but *[fn, mr]# are not. This means that manner is a more prominent property than place.

3 Valence

I posit a unique and universal structure for each consonant based on its strength as deduced in (6). I claim that the composition of syntactic phrases and consonants is basically identical. Both are built on dependencies: a head may have a comp(lement), a spec(ifier), both or none. I use the terms *spec* and *comp* to express the asymmetry between an external and internal argument respectively and I do not fully subscribe to any particular theory of syntax. The sum total of dependencies equals phonotactic strength. That means, a head with both a spec and comp is stronger than one with only one of the two or neither. Plosives are the strongest dominants so they must have both spec and comp (7b). Approximants are the weakest so they must have neither (7d). I assume that strength decreases as the distance from the head increases and therefore comp is stronger than spec. This asymmetry is also relevant for the remaining two manners: Fricatives (stronger) must have comp (7) and nasals (weaker) spec (7a).

The linear order of dependents is universally unidirectional as will be argued in section 4.2. (also cf. Kayne 1994). The spec is always on the left and the comp on the right. I assume that a consonant is an onset head O^0 that, together with its projections and dependents, forms an onset phrase OP (but onset not meant in the traditional sense). That OP can potentially merge with a nuclear phrase NP (a vowel), but nothing requires the NP to be present; this issue will not be pursued further here. The head of a projection can be empty, like an empty head in syntax, e.g. the empty C head in *I know that/0 you did it*. (In fact, the head itself has internal structure which expresses place properties, to be briefly discussed in section 5).

(7) Projections of the empty onset head O^0

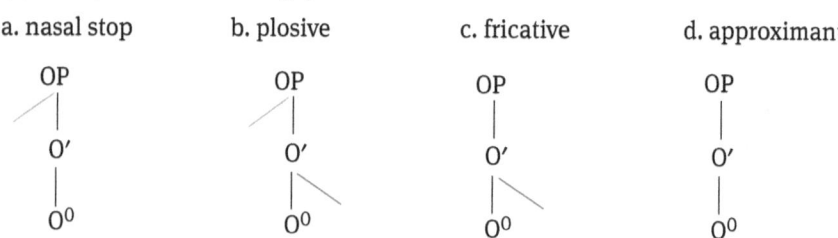

a. nasal stop b. plosive c. fricative d. approximant

Note that the above diagram only gives the bare structures without the relationships holding between the head O^0 and its comp and spec, respectively. (In brief, an operation on a head-spec configuration yields true voicing/nasality and an operation on a head-comp configuration yields aspiration/fortisness.) There are four possible configurations for a phrase, such as an OP, and four phonologically relevant simplex manners (barring contour segments). Phonetically, there are other degrees of constriction such as the difference in turbulence between [f] and [ɸ]. This difference, however, phonologically remains a minor distinction, stridency, between fricatives rather than a major one such as between *fricative* and *approximant*. The number of manners correctly follows from the hypothesis.

4 Saturation

4.1 Direct domination

In section 3 we saw that an onset head O^0 has a certain valence, i.e. it can combine with the argument positions spec and/or comp or none and that each possible combination yields a phonological manner. An argument position can host another phrase, in which case it is *saturated* (filled) by that phrase. Saturation in phonology yields consonant clusters: The weaker OP (the dominee) saturates an argument position of the stronger OP (the dominant). For instance, embedding [n] at the spec of [t] yields [nt] and embedding [r] at the comp of [t] yields [tr]. If A is embedded at an argument position of B, B *directly dominates* B.

(8) Saturation

    a. matrix T and an   b. matrix T and an
        embedded OP   embedded N

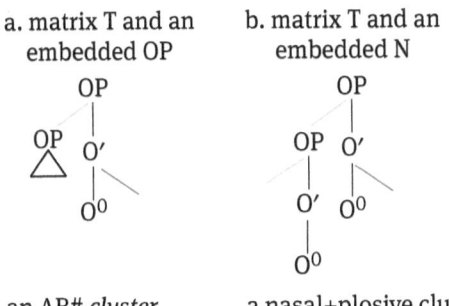

      an AB# *cluster*   a nasal+plosive cluster

(8a) shows a matrix OP with both spec and comp (plosive). It has an embedded OP in the spec yielding an AB# cluster of the type [mp, nt, sp, pt], etc. (8b) illustrates the internal structure of one possible dominee, a nasal stop (only spec), yielding a nasal+plosive cluster. Note that empty-headed OPs are used for illustration purposes only and the head can be filled (see section 5).

(9) All and only the possible direct domination relations

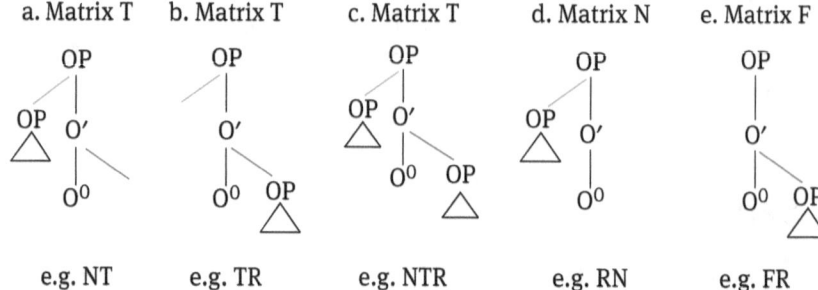

a. Matrix T	b. Matrix T	c. Matrix T	d. Matrix N	e. Matrix F
e.g. NT	e.g. TR	e.g. NTR	e.g. RN	e.g. FR

Plosives have two argument positions, spec and comp. This means that they can host an embedded OP (a dominee) in either position, or in both. (9a) shows a matrix plosive T and a dominee in the spec of T. As the the dominee sits to the left of the matrix head, this yields an AB# configuration, eg: [nt, rt, lt, xt, ft, st, kt, pt, mp, rp, lp, sp, ŋk, rk, lk, sk]#. (9b) shows a matrix T and the dominee sits in the comp on the right, yielding the configuration #BA, eg: #[tr, pl, pr, kl, kr, pn, kn, ps, ks]. (9c) is a matrix T with dominees in both spec and comp, yielding a cluster ABC where B is stronger than both A and C, eg: [ltr, ntr, mpr, mpl, ŋkr, ŋkl, skr, (skl), spr, spl, ptr, ktr].

Nasal stops have only spec therefore they can have a dominee in the spec only, yielding RN# (9d): [rŋ, lŋ, rm, lm, rn, ln, ŋn, mn]. Fricatives have only comp therefore they can have a dominee in the comp only, yielding #FR (9e): #[xr, xl, xn, fr, fl, fn, sr, sl, sn, sm, sf, sx, (sθ)].

This means that the reverse of these, eg: [nr, ls], cannot stand in an immediate domination relation as there is no position to plug in the dominee. The structure of #NR and RF# clusters is explored in section 4.2. In brief, [nr, ls] are really part of the larger structures [n(d)r, l(t)s] respectively (9c). The matrix plosive head is empty and therefore possibly silent. It is realised iff it shares the head (place property) of a dominee. This predicts the existence of *emergent stops* in the correct environments.

Out of the possible configurations in (9), a language chooses subsets in a principled way. I claim that if a language has domination relations, it will have the strongest dominant T and the weakest dominees R, N. (In section 4.2. we will see that even further restrictions can be at play.) This is because the strength of the dominee is subtracted from that of the dominant, and each language has a minimum strength difference requirement (henceforth MSD). In other words, a smaller strength difference implies a larger one, eg: [st]# with a small difference implies [rt]# with a bigger difference.

Even different lexical categories in a language may have different MSD. To illustrate, Turkish verbal roots have only RT# clusters, e.g. *kalk* 'get up', *yırt* 'rip', but Turkish nominals have NT#, ST#, PT# and further possibilities: *bant* 'cellotape', *üst* 'top', *zapt* 'seizure' etc. (9d), with the dominant N, is the next possible configuration, again with its MSD requirement. To continue with the example of Turkish, it has only *film* 'film' and *form* 'form' for RN#. The rhotic varieties of English have RN#, e.g. *arm*, *elm*, *horn*, *kiln* but not MN#. Swedish has both RN# and MN#, e.g. *namn* 'name', *vagn* 'wagon'. Note that a fricative dominant (9e) yields an *onset cluster*. The special properties of onset clusters is to be discussed presently. In sum, the language picks the dominant T and optionally less strong ones, setting an MSD limit for *each* dominant.

The asymmetry of the argument positions spec and comp means that the OPs embedded in them function asymmetrically. This effect is observed in syntax in the different theta roles John has in *John kissed Paul* (agent) and *Paul kissed John* (theme). In phonology, an argument sitting at the weaker spec is relatively weaker and the same argument sitting in the comp is relatively stronger. (The relative strength of these positions is argued for in 3. Briefly, as distance from the head increases, strength decreases.) There is therefore a greater difference of strength between [r, t] in RT# (with [r] in the spec) than in #TR (with [r] in the comp). Let us label the change in the strength of a consonant, based on where it sits in a matrix OP, with a value (x). In the configuration AB# (9a), the strength difference is B − (A − x), and in #AB (9b), A − (B + x). Since the discussion of the actual mathematical expressions of the structures in this model requires a separate paper, let us assign numbers to A, B and x for the purpose of providing an example only. If [t] is 19, [r] is 3, and x is 1, [rt] has a strength difference of 17 and [tr] has a difference of 15.

The difference in the strength of the dominee based on its position within the matrix T means that, for an MSD for T and its dominee(s), T can host stronger dominees in the spec than in the comp. For instance, in rhotic varieties of English, [p] can host R, N, S in the spec: *carp*, *help*, *lamp*, *lisp*. In contrast, it can host only the weakest manner, R, in the comp: *pray*, *play*. This is the only model of phonology that predicts the need for a *steeper slope* in onset clusters from the representation of consonants only. In onset clusters, the set of possible dominees is reduced to coronal sonorants and sibilant fricatives. This further restriction of the dominee to coronality/sibilancy is the subject of a separate paper (cf. Mutlu 2017b).

In (9c), given an MSD between B and its dominees (A+C), the dominees have to share a finite amount of strength between them. To illustrate, English has #[sp, pl, spl, sk, kl,] e.g. *speak*, *play*, *split*, *sky*, *clean* but not *#[skl] (except in the medical terms *sclerosis*, *sclera*). In section 2, we saw that labials are stronger than the velars of the same manner and [l] is stronger than [r]. The weakest plosive [k] can dominate both [s] and [r], e.g. *screen*. But if [r] is replaced by [l], the strength difference grows too small. However, if the dominant is stronger, as with [p], the dominee in the comp can be stronger too: *split, splendid, splice, splay, splurge*, etc.

4.2 Identical iteration

An affricate has different phonotactics than a plosive (cf. Weijer 2014). For instance, while English has *le*[ft], *be*[st], *ap*[t], it does not have *[ftʃ, stʃ, ptʃ]#. German has [ʃp]*ucken* 'spit' but not *[spf] and *Konze*[pt] 'concept' but not morphologically simplex *[pf]*t*. Turkish has *giri*[ft] 'intricate', *ra*[st] 'right', *za*[pt] 'seizure' but not *[ftʃ, stʃ, ptʃ]#. As analysed in section 2, the strongest dominee an affricate can have is a nasal stop: German *da*[mpf] 'steam', *pri*[nts] 'prince', Turkish *hınç* 'anger', English *hinge*. Though there are a few German words with [xts, fts]#, it is a restricted group; only onomatopoeic verbs, e.g. *seufz(en)* 'to sigh'.

An affricate has a plosive and a fricative portion but, as discussed above, it dominates the same set of objects a nasal stop does: approximants and nasal stops. To my knowledge, this is a parallel not noted before. An affricate looks big but behaves as if small as a dominant. Moreover, though an affricate is weak, it is *indominable* even by the strongest dominant [t]: German does not have *[pft]# in morphologically simplex words and [tst]# is attested in three words: *Arzt* 'doctor', *jetzt* 'now', *letzt* 'last'.

(10) The composition of affricates (x is a variable that stands for a place property)

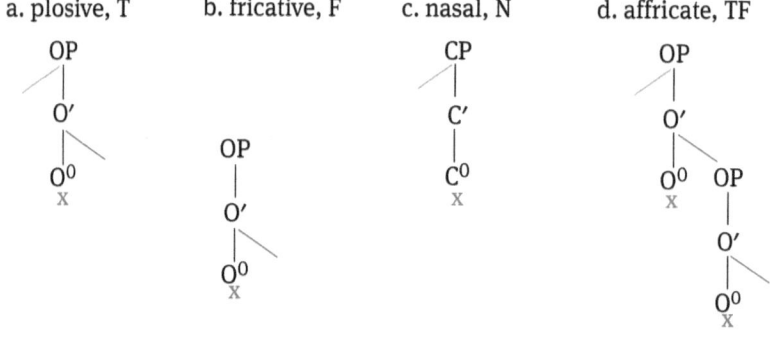

a. plosive, T	b. fricative, F	c. nasal, N	d. affricate, TF
the first part of an affricate.	the second part of an affricate.	Two strong objects T and F combine to yield **strength** equal to that of the weak N. (but **NOT** the actual object N).	The strength of the **comp** of the dominee (F) is subtracted from the strength of the matrix (T), hence the loss of strength.

A plosive has both comp and spec (10a), and a fricative has comp (10b). An affricate has both a plosive and fricative part, but (approximately) the strength of a nasal stop, which only has spec (10c). In section 4.1. we saw that each domination relation yields a strength difference (dominant – dominee) and that languages have a minimum strength difference (MSD) requirement. My hypothesis is that an affricate is a plosive dominating a fricative (10d) and that is why the strength of the comp of the fricative is subtracted from that of the plosive. Roughly, (spec+comp) – (comp) = spec. As the greater part of the strength of the plosive comes from comp, once it has been subtracted from the total, the remaining strength is not enough to dominate another OP with comp, viz., an obstruent. Note that this is a simplified calculation of strength, but sufficient for the purpose of the current discussion. To my knowledge, this is the only model of affricates that derives their strength directly through their composition.

The configuration (10d) also predicts that an affricate must be *indominable*: it is the biggest/strongest object (plosive) PLUS the second strongest OP object (fricative) embedded in it; [p[f]]. Therefore, it is too big to fit into even the strongest dominant [t]. The strength difference is *plosive–plosive–fricative* hence a negative number. German data support this: *[pft] (11b) is not attested and [tst] is attested in just three words: *Arzt* 'doctor', *jetzt* 'now', *letzt* 'last'.

(11) Heavy configurations (x at the head stands for a place variable, such as labiality)

   a. *[spf, sts, fts, xts, stʃ, ftʃ]   b. *[pft, tst, tʃt]

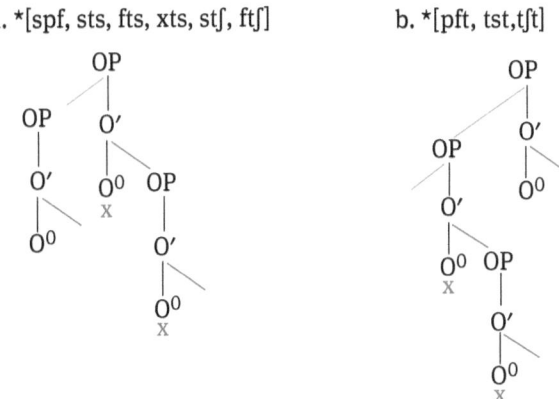

(11a) is a matrix T with two embedded OPs (dominees). The dominee in the comp shares the same head, indicated by x, as the matrix: It is the fricative portion of an affricate. The OP embedded in the spec is also a fricative. The resulting string would be *[spf, xts, fts, sts, stʃ, ftʃ]. (11b) shows embedding at a depth of two: The highest matrix T has another T embedded in its spec. The embedded T, in turn, has a fricative embedded in its comp (yielding an affricate). The resulting structure would be *[pft, tst, tʃt]#. In section 4.1, we saw that structures at the limit of MSD are marginally attested, as in the medical terms *sclerosis, sclera* in English. The weight of these structures is the reason why they are not systematically attested but found in a very restricted set of words in one language, German, e.g. onomatopoeic *seufz(en)* 'to sigh'. Onomatopoeic words can have a lower limit of strength difference, as in English *oink* which is a *superheavy syllable* with a non-coronal cluster. Otherwise all such syllables with a long vowel or diphthong and a final cluster always end in coronals: *paint, *paink* (cf. Fudge 1969).

This model of affricates makes a third prediction about the order of the plosive and fricative components. Stops are homorganic to a plosive if they are embedded in the stopness component of it (spec, left), fricatives when they are embedded in the friction component of it (comp, right).

(12) Direction of homorganicity

    a. Homorganicity of nasals   b. Homorganicity of affricates

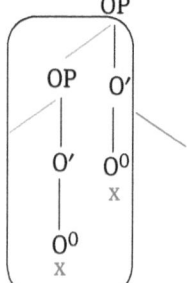 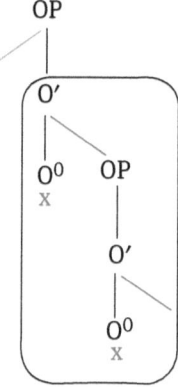

(12) shows two matrix plosives. (12a) has an embedded OP in the spec. The embedded OP has only spec. (12b) has an embedded OP in the comp. The embedded OP has only comp. In both trees, the heads of the matrix and the embedded OP are identical, which means they have the same place property. The blue box in (12a) contains two specs, no comp, and the identical head x. The blue box in (12b) contains two comps, no spec, and the identical head x. Let us call this kind of configuration *identical iteration*. These configurations are homorganic, that is, just as stopness and friction repeats twice in the same direction of that component within a plosive (stopness to the left and friction to the right), the head also repeats.

(13) The homorganicity principle: Identical iteration of the projectional position (spec or comp) entails the identical iteration of the head as well. As a result, nasals are homorganic to the left of a plosive, and fricatives to the right.

The homorganicity principle (13) scopes over the weaker dominee N crosslinguistically. It can also scope over the stronger dominee F, in which case a language cannot have *[px, tx, tf, kf, pθ, kθ]. To my knowledge, there is in fact no language where such clusters are systematically attested to fulfill the cluster criterion (5), i.e. a cluster must be found both word-medially and at the edge in a morphologically simplex domain. Note that [ps, ks] are attested even though they are not homorganic. Sibilants can remain outside of the scope of (13) because their internal structure *itself* has identical iteration; what makes it a fricative and what makes it a sibilant are identical configurations within the projection and within the head, respectively (cf. Mutlu 2017b).

There are languages (Prince languages) where the only type of cluster found is an NT# cluster (Prince 1984). This restriction on cluster phonotactics can be expressed as follows: Only identical iteration is possible, and only in the weak spec (12a), which creates maximal strength difference as discussed in 3. Existing models need to stipulate this restriction. For instance Harris (1997) stipulates that only the nasality element |L| is licensed in a cluster in these languages. This does not follow from the structure of |L| itself since it does not have any structure. In contrast, identical iteration is a phenomenon that emerges from the internal structure of consonants in this model. This is parallel to the case of languages which lack onset clusters but have affricates such as Turkish, e.g. [tʃ]*an* 'bell' Again, these languages have a dominee in the comp because it is an example of identical iteration. In upcoming work on place properties, sibilancy and laterality we will see further examples of the importance of recurring structures in the system.

Lastly, clusters displaying identical iteration behave like a unit, especially if the dominee sits in the position closest to the head, comp (an affricate). This is because identical iteration creates a strong and stable bond between two objects. Further examples of such a bond is discussed in Author (2017): for example, sibilants are objects which have an identically iterating internal structure and hence they can occupy positions which other fricatives cannot, e.g. *straight* but not *#[ftr]. Likewise, [m] has an identically iterating internal structure which makes it possible for it to occur in positions where other nasals do not, e.g. German *Amt* 'office' but not *[np]#. For the same reason, [m] is the most likely nasal stop to appear with a liquid: Turkish has *film* 'film' but not *[ln]. Malayalam has *mleec^{h}am* 'copper' (Cyran 2001) but not #[nl]. The gap for [tl, dl] in English among other languages also has to do with identical iteration and the internal structure of [l], which is the subject of a separate paper.

4.3 Indirect domination

Nasals have only spec and fricatives only comp, therefore they can have an embedded OP in those respective positions only: [rn, sl], i.e. [[r]n] and [s[l]]. This means that their reverse, [nr, ls], cannot form an immediate domination relation as there is no position to plug in the dominee. [nr, ls] are really part of the larger structures [n(d)r, l(t)s] respectively. The matrix plosive head is empty and therefore possibly silent. It is realised iff it shares the head (place property) of an embedded OP. Interestingly, *dense* and *else* can be produced as [dɛnts] and [ɛlts] respectively (cf. Berrey 1940, Ohala 2005, Clements 1987, Warner 2002, inter alia). Likewise, in English, *thumle* turned into *thimble* and *thunre* turned into *thunder*. Even across words, an emergent stop can appear as in *Tam Lin/Tamblin* (a traditional ballad's name).

Before we enter the discussion of silent onset heads, it is necessary to refer to the interpretation of an empty head as a place property. We saw in section 2 that velar (or more generally dorsal) is the weakest place property: for instance, German has [fl]*ug* 'flight' but not *#[xl] where the fricative dominates [l]. I take velarity to be the expression of an empty head. This is based on the strength it adds to a consonant, viz. none. See also Huber (2003) and works cited therein, including Kaye et. al. (1990), Harris and Lindsey (1995) for an analysis of velars as phonologically placeless/empty-headed objects. Below, a velar plosive is represented by [k], though it can have other laryngeal properties.

There is a c-command relation between the argument positions spec and comp (cf. Reinhart 1976). This allows for a domination relation to be formed between the OPs embedded in these positions. Let us call this *indirect domination*, since no consonant is embedded in the other, but rather both of them are embedded in a silent matrix OP.

(14) Domination in ABC where C is a fricative and C is stronger than A

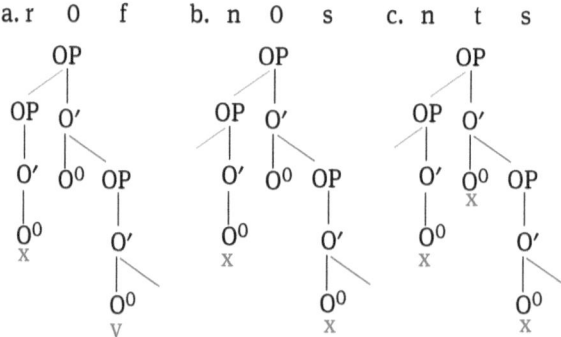

x and y at the head stand for different place properties. (14a) has an empty-headed matrix with, for instance, [r] in the spec and [f] in the comp. [f] indirectly dominates [r] and the matrix head is silent. (14b) has the same matrix, with, for instance, [n] in the spec and [s] in the comp. Both embedded OPs have the same head. The two heads enter into a relation across an empty one. This can result in copying the place property onto the empty head as well. Hence, in (14c), the matrix head is no longer empty and is realised as [t], yielding [nts].

I claim that domination has the following two restrictions: (i) A dominee can be dominated only once, even though a dominant can dominate more than once (as discussed in 4), e.g. in [nts] (14c), [t] dominates [n, s] and therefore [s] cannot indirectly dominate [n]; (ii) A realised head dominates any OPs embedded in it, therefore when there is indirect domination, the matrix is silenced, as in [nOs] (10b). Furthermore, if one of the embedded OPs shares it head (place property) with the silent matrix, then the matrix head is no longer empty and becomes realised, thereby dominating both embedded OPs, e.g. [nts] (14c). (Just as a particular language uses a particular subset of embedding options, it may or may not have place sharing among the embedded and matrix heads to yield emergent stops.)

Note that in this configuration ABC, C is stronger than A. Specifically, C is a fricative in the comp of the matrix T, that is, an example of *identical iteration*, constrained by the homorganicity principle (13). Now let us look at another logical possibility for ABC, where A is stronger than C.

(15) Indirect domination in ABC, where A is a nasal and A is stronger than C
   a. r 0 f   b. n d r   c. m b r

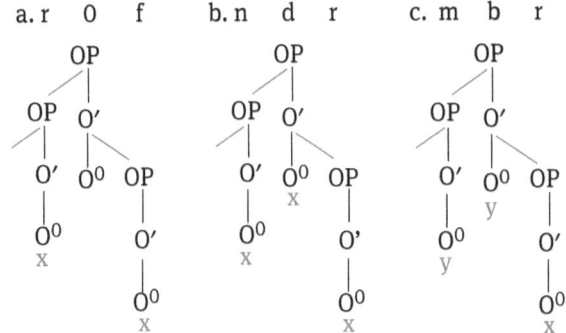

(15a) shows a silent matrix plosive with a nasal stop in the spec. This is an example of identical iteration as well, restricted by the homorganicity principle (13). If the nasal stop shares its head with the matrix, the matrix head is no longer empty so it is realised, yielding [ndr] (15b) and [mbr] (15c). Note that the laryngeal properties of the matrix plosive are not shown in (15).

Crucially, in both (14) and (15), the realisation of the matrix head (an *emergent stop*) is derived through the same mechanism of place-sharing with the matrix head. This is the only phonological (vs phonetically based) model that derives emergent stops in both *rising sonority* and *falling sonority* environments from the representation of the consonants themselves alone (cf. Recasens 2011, Ohala 2005).

The model also correctly predicts that nasal stops differ in their assimilation behaviour before plosives and fricatives. While nasals assimilate to plosives in place, Padgett (1991) lists the three most common types of behaviour with nasal stop+fricative pairs across languages as: (i) the nasal simply does not assimilate, receiving a default place; (ii) the nasal deletes; (iii) the nasal assimilates but simultaneously hardens the fricative to a stop or an affricate.

(16) Assimilation and fortition (x and y in the head stand for different place properties)

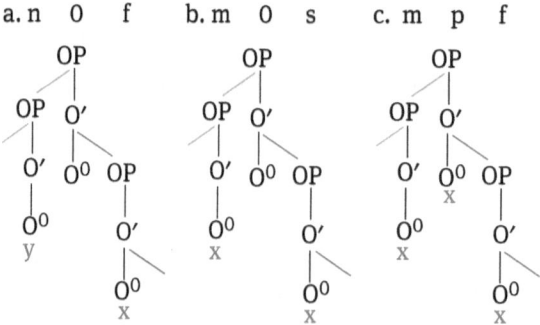

(16a) shows a non-homorganic pair such as [n, f] embedded in a silent matrix. (16b) shows a homorganic pair such as (m, f) in the same matrix. (16c) shows the matrix head sharing the place property x and therefore getting realised.

Nasal assimilation to a plosive is via immediate domination and it is an example of identical iteration, guaranteeing homorganicity (13). In contrast, assimilation to a fricative occurs across the matrix head (16b). This means that it is possible for the nasal stop not to assimilate to a fricative because the two are not in direct domination or identical iteration (16a).

If the nasal stop does assimilate (16b), the sharing of the head (place property) occurs over the empty matrix head. Once place-sharing is a property of the structure, all the available heads can potentially participate in it, therefore creating a chain of identical heads including the matrix one (16c). Place sharing with the matrix head, as well as over it, results in an affricate (16c). The system has a tendency towards recurring structures, of which identical iteration, as discussed in section 4.2, is one example and chain-sharing of heads (16c) is another. For now, let us observe this as an emergent property of the structures posited. The same tendency will come up in the discussion of place properties in upcoming work. The reason for this property is the subject of a separate paper.

The two common patterns, the lack of nasal place assimilation to fricatives or assimilation resulting in an affricate, directly follow from the structure of phonological primes themselves, viz. the spec and comp positions and embedding possibilities therein.

For reasons of space, I will not go into further types of indirect domination, or further predictions that follow from their structure. I will also not go into recursion at a depth of three, e.g. German *Punkt*.

5 A sketch of higher and lower structure

Embedding an OP in another OP is by no means the only type of recursion in the theory. Consonants (whether they have other consonants embedded in them or not) and vowels are embedded as arguments in a *domain phrase* DP. Furthermore, a DP can be embedded in another DP. The substance-free nature of the model makes it possible to build both lower and higher structure with the same tools, that is, asymmetrical dependency relations. Below I give the structure of the word, *grim*, to illustrate how larger and smaller domains look. The arguments for the internal structure of the head which yields dorsality (as in [g]), coronality (as in [r]) and palatality (as in [ɪ]) can be found in Mutlu (2017a, b).

(17) *grim*

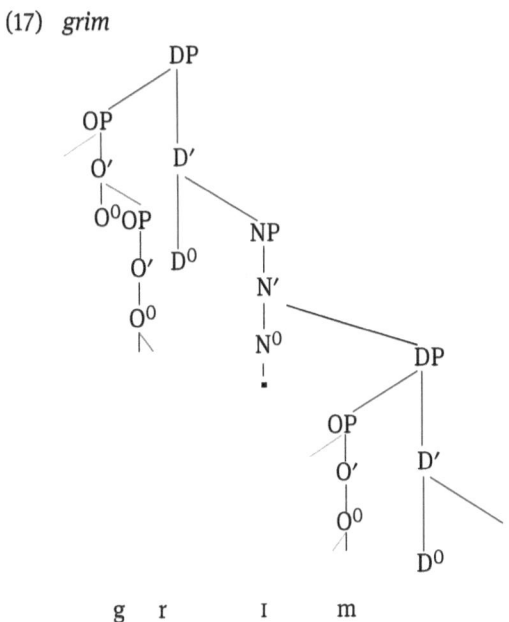

A *domain phrase* DP takes an onset phrase as an external argument, and a nuclear phrase NP as an internal argument. That is, the domain head D⁰ sits between a consonant (including any other consonants embedded in it) and a vowel. See Mutlu (2007ab) for the predictions that follow from the structure of the domain phrase. (17) illustrates a matrix DP, [grɪ]. D⁰ is empty, [gr] sits in its spec and [ɪ] sits in its comp. The nuclear phrase [ɪ] takes another DP as its complement. This embedded DP has an OP sitting in its spec, [m].

As for place properties, there are four possibilities for the internal structure of the phonological head: It can be empty, similar to the C_0 in *John knows that/ 0 I saw him*, it can be simplex as in *dragon*, or it can be a compound. If it is a compound, it can have two different kinds of dependencies in it. Consider *rabbit killer* vs. *killer rabbit*. In the former case, *rabbit* is the internal argument of *kill*, and in the latter case, it is the external argument of *kill*. A simplex head expresses palatality. Labials (and round vowels) have a compound head of the type *killer rabbit* and coronals (and non-high vowels) have a compound head of the type of *rabbit killer*. The mapping of these possibilities to place properties is based on the strength they add to a consonant, discussed in Mutlu (2017a, b) and to be discussed further in upcoming work. For vowels, these possibilities mean that there must be three basic vowels, apart from an empty one: [i, u, a]. Recursion within the phonological head itself yields complexity in vowels, as well as sibilancy and laterality in consonants (cf. Mutlu 2017b).

6 Conclusion

I have argued that consonant clusters and affricates are recursive structures on the basis that such modelling makes a number of accurate predictions on constituent structure, phonotactic strength and place assimilation/homorganicity. Existing models do not make these predictions from a single principle as the asymmetry principle does in this model. For space reasons I have provided only a partial sketch of the role of recursion in phonology; however, it is a promising line of research to pursue since it produces answers to long-standing questions of phonotactics.

References

Algeo, John. 1978. What consonant clusters are possible? *Word* 29(3), 206–224.
Backley, Phillip. 2011. *An Introduction to Element Theory*. Edinburgh: Edinburgh University Press.

Berrey, Lester V. 1940. Southern mountain dialect. *American Speech* 15(1),45–54.
Booij, Geert. 1999. *The phonology of Dutch*. Oxford: Oxford University Press.
Botma, Bert. 2004. *Phonological Aspects of Nasality: An Element-based Dependency Approach*. LOT Dissertation series 90. Utrecht: Holland Academic Graphics.
Carr, Philip. 2006. Universal grammar and syntax/phonology parallelisms. *Lingua* 116. 634–656.
Charette, Monik. 1990. Licence to govern. *Phonology* 7, 233–253.
Clements, George N. 1985. The geometry of phonological features. *Phonology Yearbook* 2, 225–252.
Clements, George N. 1987. Phonological feature representation and the description of intrusive stops. In Anna Bosch, Barbara Need and Eric Schiller (eds.), *Papers from the 23rd regional meeting of the Chicago Linguistic Society, part 2: Parasession on autosegmental and metrical phonology*, 29–50. Chicago, IL: Chicago Linguistic Society.
Cyran, Eugeniusz. 2001. Parameters and scales in syllable markedness: the right edge of the word in Malayalam. *Trends in Linguistics Studies and Monographs* 134, 1–42.
Demuth, Katherine and Margaret Kehoe. 2006. The acquisition of word-final clusters in French. *Catalan Journal of Linguistics* 5(1),59–81.
Di Sciullo, Anna M. 2005. Decomposing compounds. *SKASE Journal of Theoretical Linguistics* 2(3),14–33.
Dresher, B. Elan, and Harry G. van der Hulst. 1998. Head–dependent asymmetries in phonology: complexity and visibility. *Phonology* 15(3),317–352.
Fox, Anthony. 2005. *The Structure of German*. Oxford: Oxford University Press.
Fudge, Erik C. 1969. Syllables. *Journal of Linguistics* 5(1),253–286.
Harris, John. 1990. Segmental complexity and phonological government. *Phonology* 7(2), 255–300.
Harris, John. 1994. *English Sound Structure*. Oxford: Blackwell.
Harris, John. 1997. Licensing inheritance: an integrated theory of neutralisation. *Phonology* 14 (1),315–370.
Harris, John. 2006. The phonology of being understood: further arguments against sonority. *Lingua* 116(10),1483–1494.
Harris, John and Geoff Lindsey. 1995. The elements of phonological representation. In Jacques Durand and Francis Katamba (eds.), *Frontiers of Phonology: Atoms, Structures, Derivations*, 34–79. Harlow, Essex: Longman.
Holmes, Philip and Ian Hinchliffe. 2003. *Swedish: A Comprehensive Grammar*. London: Routledge.
Huber, Daniel. 2003. Velars and empty-headedness in Government Phonology. *Rivista di Grammatica Generativa* 28(1),45–56.
Hulst, Harry G. van der. 2015. The opponent principle in RcvP: binarity in a unary system. In Eric Raimy and Charles Cairns (eds.), *The segment in phonetics and phonology*, 149–179. Oxford: Wiley-Blackwell.
Jensen, Sean. 1994. Is ʔ an element?: towards a non-segmental phonology. *SOAS Working Papers in Linguistics and Phonetics* 4, 71–78.
Kaye, Jonathan, Jean Lowenstamm and Jean-Roger Vergnaud. 1985. The internal structure of phonological elements: a theory of charm and government. *Phonology Yearbook* 2, 305–328.
Kaye, Jonathan, Jean Lowenstamm and Jean-Roger Vergnaud. 1990. Constituent structure and government in phonology. *Phonology* 7, 193–231.

Kayne, Richard S. 1994. *The Antisymmetry of Syntax*. Cambridge, MA: MIT Press.
Kehrein, Wolfgang. 2002. *Phonological Representation and Phonetic Phasing: Affricates and Laryngeals*. Tübingen: Niemeyer.
Kenyon, John S. 1956. Syllabic consonants in dictionaries. *American Speech* XXXI, 245–251.
Kramer, Martin. 2009. *The Phonology of Italian*. Oxford: Oxford University Press.
Kristoffersen, Gjert. 2000. *The Phonology of Norwegian*. Oxford: Oxford University Press.
Morphy, Frances. 1983. Djapu, a Yolngu dialect. In Robert M. W. Dixon and Barry J. Blake (eds.), *Handbook of Australian Languages*, 1–188. Canberra: Australian National University Press.
Mutlu, Filiz. 2017a. Place asymmetries: Onset head vs domain head. Paper presented at Paper presented at the workshop The Interface Within. What relations hold between prosody and melody?, Meertens Institute, Amsterdam (13 March 2017).
Mutlu, Filiz. 2017b. Valence and saturation in phonology. MA thesis, Boğaziçi University.
Ohala, John J. 1997. Emergent stops: diachronic and phonetic data. *Proceedings of the 4th Seoul International Conference on Linguistics (SICOL) 11–15 August 1997*, 84–91. Seoul: Linguistic Society of Korea.
Ohala, John J. 2005. Phonetic explanations for sound patterns. In William J. Hardcastle and Janet Mackenzie Beck (eds.), *A Figure of Speech: A Festschrift for John Laver*, 23–38. London: Erlbaum.
Operstein, Natalie. 2010. *Consonant Structure and Prevocalization*. Amsterdam: John Benjamins.
Padgett, Jaye. E. 1991. Stricture in feature geometry. Ph.D. dissertation, University of Massachusetts, Amherst.
Picard, Marc. 1994. *Principles and Methods in Historical Phonology: From Proto-Algonkian to Arapaho*. Montreal: McGill-Queen's Press.
Pöchtrager, Markus A. 2006. The structure of length. PhD dissertation, University of Vienna.
Pöchtrager, Markus A. 2012, April. Till death do us part: What keeps clusters together?. Paper presented at the SOAS Linguistics Department Seminar, SOAS, University of London.
Prince, Alan S. 1984. Phonology with tiers. In Mark Aronoff and Richard T. Oehrle (eds.), *Language Sound Structure: Studies in Phonology Presented to Morris Halle by His Teacher and Students*, 234–244. Cambridge MA: MIT Press.
Recasens, Daniel. 2011. Articulatory constraints on stop insertion and elision in consonant clusters. *Linguistics* 49(5),1137–1162.
Reinhart, Tanya Miriam. 1976. The syntactic domain of anaphora. Ph.D. dissertation, Massachusetts Institute of Technology.
Rochemont, Michael and Peter W. Culicover. 1997. Deriving dependent right adjuncts in English. In Dorothee Beermann, David LeBlanc and Henk C. van Riemsdijk (eds.), *Rightward movement*, 279–300. Amsterdam: John Benjamins.
Schadler, Dagmar. 2006. Morphonotaktik im Schwedischen. *Wiener Linguistische Gazette*, 73, 1–19.
Schwartz, Geoffrey. 2016. On the evolution of prosodic boundaries–parameter settings for Polish and English. *Lingua* 171, 37–73.
Steriade, Donca. 1993. Closure, release, and nasal contours. In Marie K. Huffman and Rena A. Krakow (eds), *Nasals, Nasalization, and the Velum*, 401–470. San Diego, CA: Academic Press.
Szigetvári, Péter. 1997. On affricates. In Ágnes Bende-Farkas (ed.), *Proceedings of the First Symposium of Doctoral Students in Linguistics*. Budapest: Akadémiai Kiadó.

Weijer, Jeroen van de. 2014. Affricates in English as a natural class. In Johanneke Caspers, Yiya Chen, Willemijn Heeren, Jos Pacilly, Niels O. Schiller and Ellen van Zanten (eds.), *Above and beyond the segments: Experimental linguistics and phonetics*, 350–358. Amsterdam: John Benjamins.

Warner, Natasha. 2002. The phonology of epenthetic stops: Implications for the phonetics-phonology interface in optimality theory. *Linguistics* 40(377),1–28.

Yoshida, Shohei. 2001. An element-based analysis of affrication in Japanese. In Jeroen van de Weijer and Tetsuo Nishihara (eds.), *Issues in Japanese Phonology and Morphology*, 193–214. Berlin and New York: Mouton de Gruyter.

Hitomi Onuma and Kuniya Nasukawa
Velar softening without precedence relations

1 Introduction

This chapter presents an account of velar softening – the well-documented set of alternations between the velar stops /k g/ and the coronal consonants /s dʒ/ – using the Precedence-free Phonology approach (Nasukawa 2015, 2016; Nasukawa and Backley 2017; Backley and Nasukawa this volume). According to this approach, phonological representations refer only to elements, which are employed recursively throughout a structure in such a way that excludes all precedence relations between units. Velar softening takes place only when the target stops /k g/ are followed by a front vowel /ɪ, i, aɪ, e/ in one of the participating suffixes: e.g. /iˈlektrɪk/ 'electric' → /iˌlekˈtrɪsɪti/ 'electricity', /əˈnæləgəs/ 'analogous' → /əˈnælədʒi/ 'analogy' (Chomsky and Halle 1968: 219–223, Halle and Mohanan 1986: 79, Halle 1990: 62–64, Halle 2005). Since velar stops /k g/ do not alternate with /s dʒ/ when the stops are preceded by high front vowels (e.g. /pɪk/ 'pick' → */pɪs/, /pɪg/ 'pick' → */pɪdʒ/), any analysis must regard the precedence relation between /k g/ and front vowels as a key factor in triggering the process. Analysing velar softening is clearly a big challenge for Precedence-free Phonology, which excludes from phonological representation all properties associated with precedence relations.

This chapter is structured as follows. Section 2 reviews velar softening and considers new data which have not been included in previous studies. Then section 3 briefly describes the nature of phonological representations in Precedence-free Phonology. Section 4 follows the precedence-free analysis of Japanese palatalisation in Nasukawa (2016) by reanalysing velar softening as an agreement effect involving the |A|-headed |A I| set; this is done without referring to precedence relations between segments. Section 5 offers some concluding remarks.

2 Velar softening

2.1 Visibility of morphological structure in phonology

Before proceeding with our analysis of velar softening in English, we first establish what kind of morphological structure is involved in this process. In particular, we

https://doi.org/10.1515/9781501512582-008

focus on what kind of morphological structure is visible/invisible to phonology. Our discussion closely follows Harris (1994: 18–28), although there are also references to other sources and perspectives in the relevant literature (Kaye 1995: 301–318, Hayes 2009: Ch.10, cf. Lexical Phonology: Kiparsky 1985, Mohanan 1986).

It is obvious that words are divided into two morphological types: simplex and complex. The examples in (1) are all taken from English. Words which consist of a single morpheme (i.e. morphologically underived words) belong to the simplex type (1a), while those which comprise more than one morpheme (i.e. morphologically derived words) are categorised as complex, as in (1b). This distinction is illustrated in (1) with examples (Harris 1994: 18–20).

(1) Morphological structure
   a. Morphologically underived
      dog, strike, city, party, banana, put, write
   b. Morphologically derived
      i. Root-level
         Affixation: in-, -ity, -ic, -al, -ory, -ate, -ion, -ant, -th, ...
         'strong' verbs/nouns: blew, brought, sang, feet, mice, ...
      ii. Word-level
         Affixation: un-, -ed, -(e)s, -ing, -ness, -ly, -ful, -ship, -hood, -ment, ...
         Compounds: cart horse, seagull, blackboard, ...

Regarding the underived words in (1a), it is widely assumed that each item is stored in the lexicon as a form which conforms to both universal and language-specific static distributional patterns such as phonotactic constraints. One such pattern is the prohibition on strings of two identical consonants (anti-gemination, OCP: McCarthy 1986, Odden 1986, Yip 1988) in underived words in English, as in (2).

(2) Ban on a string of two identical consonants (C_iC_i) in English
   a. ha*pp*y /ˈhæpi/, pre*tt*y /ˈprɪti/, pu*ff*y /ˈpʌfi/, si*ss*y /ˈsɪsi/, spaghe*tt*i /spəˈgeti/
   b. su*cc*ess /səkˈses/; su*gg*est /səgˈdʒest/ (AmE) (su*gg*est /səˈdʒest/ (BrE))

The examples in (2a) show how two identical consonants (in the spelling) become a singleton in speech production because of the above anti-gemination *C_iC_i requirement. On the other hand, the examples in (2b) show that two identical consonants become heterogeneous as a result of velar softening in the second consonant of the two (e.g. su[kk]ess → su[ks]ess). In this way, these forms vacuously conform to the anti-gemination *C_iC_i requirement. (Note that, in addition to velar softening, British English also displays deletion of the first /g/ in the /gg/ sequence (e.g. su[gg]est → su[dʒ]est) (Halle 1990: 64). The same constraint *C_iC_i functions in morphologically complex words, as shown in (3), where a sequence of two identical Cs appearing across a morpheme boundary becomes a singleton C in order to conform to the constraint *C_iC_i.

(3) Ban on a string of C_iC_i in derived words in English
in-: in-nominate [ɪˈnɒmmət], in-nocuous [ɪˈnɒkjuəs], im-moral [ɪˈmɒrəl], im-mortal [ɪˈmɔːtəl], il-legal [ɪˈliːgəl], ir-regular [ɪˈregjʊlə]

In (4), on the other hand, a string of two identical Cs across a morphological boundary is permitted in English.

(4) No ban on a string of C_iC_i in derived words in English
un-: un-natural [ʌnˈnætʃərəl], un-necessary [ʌnˈnesəsəri], un-named [ˌʌnˈneɪmd]

According to Harris (1994) and Kaye (1995), the difference between (3) and (4) is attributed to the distinction between non-analytic and analytic morphology. Since the morphological boundary between the non-analytic prefix <in-> and a root/base is invisible to phonology, the resulting forms are seen as being no different from underived words, which must conform to the anti-gemination requirement. On the other hand, anti-gemination does not apply to the sequence of two ns in (4), since the nasal n of the prefix <un-> is structurally not adjacent to the root/base-initial n. In other words, anti-gemination fails to have any effect across the morphological boundary between the analytic prefix <un-> and the root/base, which is visible to phonology.

According to Harris (1994: 19), non-analytic morphological structure is constructed as *Root-level morphology*: that is, words with non-analytic morphology were constructed at an earlier point in the historical development of English word structure and are now regarded as being the same as underived lexical forms, even though they are morphologically and semantically complex. Therefore, all phonological regularities that operate in underived lexical items (e.g. anti-gemination, phonotactics and stress assignment rules) also apply to root-level derived forms. This view is evident from the fact that root-level (non-analytic) affixes are overwhelmingly of Greek or Latinate origin (except for a handful of unproductive Germanic suffixes such as <-th> ((Dressler 1985; cf. Kiparsky 1985, Mohanan 1986 in the context of Lexical Phonology).[1]

By contrast, the analytical complex structures in (4) are thought to be constructed as *Word-level morphology*: in other words, the relation between word-level affixes and a root/base is the same as the relation between the words which form a phrase; that is, adjacent segments, one belonging to a word-level affix and the other to a root/base, are considered to be accidentally adjacent. This is similar to the accidental adjacency found between neighbouring words (e.g. te*n* *n*ights, Dee*p* *P*urple).

2.2 Velar softening as a Root-level process

Since velar softening (in which /k g/ alternate with, respectively, /s ʤ/ before a front vowel such as /ɪ/ or /i/) is generally thought to result from the Root-level suffixation of morphemes such as *-ity*, *-ism* and *-ise/ize*, it is assumed to take place in the Root-level morphology in (1bi). In utterances, these suffixes are realised as -[ə]*ty*, -[ə]*zm* and -[aɪ]*se*/[aɪ]*ze*. However, as the spelling suggests, they were presumably pronounced -[ɪ]*ty*, -[ɪ]*zm* and -[ɪ]*se*/[ɪ]*ze* at some earlier stage in the history of English. Even if the pattern is viewed as a synchronic process, there seems to be a consensus that /ɪ/ is the lexical form of the initial segment of the suffixes. Thus, the /k/~/s/ alternation may be described by the rewrite rules exemplified in (5). Note that the data in (5) include a number of forms which have not been cited in previous studies (Halle and Mohanan 1985; Halle 1990, 2005).

(5) a. /k/ → /s/ / ___/ɪ/ -[ɪ]*ty*

atomic	/ətɒmɪk/	atomicity	/ætəmɪsɪti/
authentic	/ɔːθentɪk/	authenticity	/ɔːθentɪsɪti/
chronic	/krɒnɪk/	chronicity	/krɒnɪsɪti/
cyclic	/sɪklɪk/	cyclicity	/sɪklɪsɪti/
eccentric	/ɪksentrɪk/	eccentricity	/eksentrɪsɪti/
elastic	/ɪlæstɪk/	elasticity	/iːlæstɪsɪti/
electric	/ɪlektrɪk/	electricity	/ɪlektrɪsɪti/
ethnic	/eθnɪk/	ethnicity	/eθnɪsɪti/
metallic	/metælɪk/	metallicity	/metælɪsɪti/

---

[1] Root-level and word-level affixation are also referred to as level 1 and level 2 affixation, respectively, in frameworks such as Lexical Phonology (Kiparsky 1985, Mohanan 1986).

periodic	/pɪərɪɒdɪk/	periodicity	/pɪərɪədɪsɪti/
rhotic	/rəʊtɪk/	rhoticity	/rəʊtɪsɪti/
specific	/spəsɪfɪk/	specificity	/spesəfɪsɪti/
syllabic	/sɪlæbɪk/	syllabicity	/sɪləbɪsɪti/
tonic	/tɒnɪk/	tonicity	/təʊnɪsɪti/

b. /k/ → /s/ / ___/ɪ/ -[ɪ]zm

athletic	/æθletɪk/	athleticism	/æθletɪsɪzəm/
classic	/klæsɪk/	cllasicism	/klæsɪsɪzəm/
exotic	/ɪgzɒtɪk/	exoticism	/ɪgzɒtɪsɪzəm/
fanatic	/fənætɪk/	fanaticism	/fənætɪsɪzəm/
historic	/hɪstɒrɪk/	historicism	/hɪstɒrɪsɪzəm/
pedantic	/pɪdæntɪk/	pedanticism	/pɪdæntɪsɪzəm/
skeptic	/skeptɪk/	specticism	/skeptɪsɪzəm/

c. /k/ → /s/ / ___/ɪ/ -[ɪ]se/[ɪ]ze
(cf. /aɪ/ -ise/-ize in current surface pronunciaton)

critic	/krɪtk/	criticise	/krɪtɪsaɪz/
italic	/ɪtælɪk/	italicise	/ɪtælɪsaɪz/
metric	/metrɪk/	metricise	/metrɪsaɪz/
phonemic	/fəʊniːmɪk/	phonemicise	/fəʊniːmɪsaɪz/
politic	/pɒlətɪk/	politicise	/pəlɪtɪsaɪz/
public	/pʌblɪk/	publicise	/pʌblɪsaɪz/
romantic	/rəʊmæntɪk/	romanticise	/rəʊmæntɪsaɪz/

In all of these examples, the letters <c> at the end of the root/base and at the beginning of the suffixes are assumed to stand for /k/ and /ɪ/ respectively in underived forms. Then, /k/ alternates with /s/ when followed by /ɪ/ during Root-level suffixation. This may be described as a type of palatalisation: the palatality of /ɪ/ spreads to the position occupied by /k/ and the velarity of /k/ is replaced by palatality (cf. Halle 1990).

This analysis fails to describe the process in a satisfactory way, however, since the alternation between velarity and palatality accounts for the palatal /ʃ/ but not the coronal /s/. In order to derive the correct outcome /s/, a process which alternates velarity with coronality (rather than palatality) is needed: in other words, it is coronality rather than palatality which is assumed to be present in /ɪ/ and which spreads to the preceding /k/ position, and velarity is assumed to be replaced by coronality.

Halle (2005) offers one solution to this issue by proposing that palatalisation be expressed as the spreading of [DACor], one of the six monovalent (unary) Designated Articulater (DA) features. The [DACor] feature inheres in [-back] vowels such as /ɪ/. In (6) the X_2 position contains the structure for /ɪ/, from where [DACor] spreads to the preceding position X_1 containing velar /k/: this causes the DA feature [DADors] already present in X_1 to be deleted, allowing [DACor] to be shared by both positions.

(6) Palatality as [DACor] spreading (Halle 2005: 36)

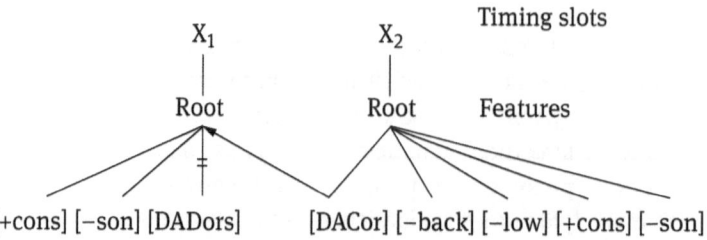

Since this rule alone cannot account for velar softening, Halle also posits the two rules in (7); (7a) concerns the /k/~/s/ alternation while (7b) concerns the voiced [g] in (9). The rule in (7a) changes the values of [continuant] and [anterior] in /k/ (in X_1) from minus to plus when X_1 shares [DACor] with X_2. As a result, the structure X_1 in (7a) is pronounced as the voiceless alveolar fricative [s].

(7) Palatality as [DACor] spreading (Halle 2005: 36)

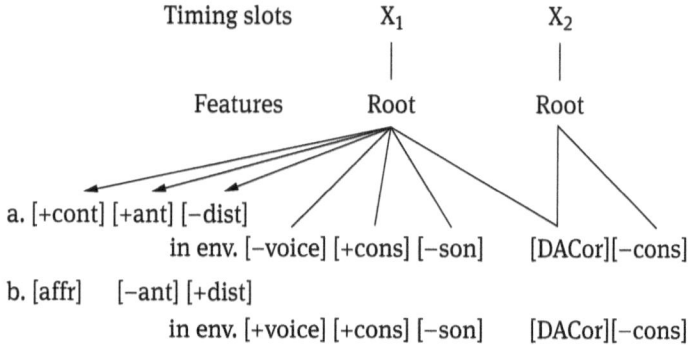

However, the analysis in Halle (2005) does not explain why it is only the values of [continuant] and [anterior] in X_1 which change when [DACor] is shared between X_1 and X_2. Ideally we would like an explanation for why the features [+continuant]/[+anterior] naturally or necessarily correlate with [DACor].

In addition, Halle (2005) raises another issue: the analysis cannot account for the palatalisation effect in (8), which occurs in the same context as the process in (5): the rule in (7a) brings about the /k/~/s/ alternation (velar softening) in (5) but not the /k/-/ʃ/ alternation (velar palatalisation) in (8).

(8) Velar palatalisation: /k/ → /ʃ/ / ___/ɪ/
    electric   /ilektrɪk/   electrician   /ilektrɪʃən/
    logic   /lɒdʒɪk/   logician   /ləʊdʒɪʃən/
    physic   /fɪzɪk/   physician   /fɪzɪʃən/
    magic   /mædʒɪk/   magician   /mədʒɪʃən/
    music   /mjuːzɪk/   musician   /mjuzɪʃən/
    tactic   /tæktɪk/   tactician   /tæktɪʃən/
    technique   /tekniːk/   tehnician   /teknɪʃən/

Even though the triggering environment in (8) is the same as in (5), to analyse the velar palatalisation in (8), there needs a rule which remains the value of [-anterior] but does change the values of [-distributed] and [-strident] in X_1 from minus to plus to have the segmental structure which is phonetically interpreted as [ʃ]. An explaination of why the feature-value changing rule applying to (5) is different from that applying to (8) must be provided.

To make matters worse, a further problem is found in analysing the other type of velar softening involving an alternation between /g/ and /dʒ/. Some examples are given in (9).

(9) /g/ → /dʒ/ / ___/ɪ, i/
    analogue   /ænəlɒg/   analogy   /ənælədʒi/
    pedagogue   /pedəgɒg/   pedagogy   /pedəgɒdʒi/
    rigor   /rɪgə/   rigid   /rɪdʒɪd/
    fungus   /fʌŋgəs/   fungi   /fʌndʒaɪ/
    esophagus   /iːsɒfəgəs/   esophagitis   /iːsɒfədʒaɪtɪs/

In (9), when plosive /g/ precedes /ɪ, i/ it alternates with the palato-alveolar affricate /dʒ/, rather than with coronal /z/ or palatal /ʒ/. That is, the voiced form of velar softening involves not only a change in the Designated Articulator but also affrication. Yet the analysis does not account for why /g/ is affricated whereas /k/ is not. To account for this, Halle (2005) proposes that /g/ undergoes the rule in (7b), which changes [-distributed] to [+distributed] and replaces [-continuant] with [affricate]. This rule requires the presence of [+voice], and results in a structure which is pronounced as [dʒ]. But again the analysis lacks a clear motivation, because in this case it does not explain why the sharing of [DACor] requires the presence of [+voice].

Like Halle's (2005) analysis, other accounts of velar softening (Halle and Mohanan 1985, Halle 1990) offer no real insights into the relation between cause and effect, although this is at least partly down to the representational models of prosody and melody that different authors have used. To address the issues raised above, we continue by analysing velar softening as a Root-level effect within an emerging model of phonological representation known as Precedence-free Phonology, which describes phonological structure by referring to head-dependency relations between monovalent melodic primes (elements) without specifying precedence relations between structural units. Such relations are taken to be redundant in representations, as they are merely a product of phonetic realisation (Nasukawa 2014, 2015, 2016; Nasukawa and Backley 2017).

3 Basic tenets of Precedence-free Phonology

3.1 Only elements and head-dependency relations

Precedence-free Phonology (PfP) is a model of representation in which the representations themselves contain 'elements' as the only units of phonological structure. There are six elements |A I U ʔ H N|, all of which are active in all languages. They are monovalent (single-valued, privative), and are to be understood as abstract units which exist only in mental representation. The set of elements divides into two groups, vocalic and consonantal. Their associated acoustic properties are described in (10).

(10) Typical acoustic exponence of elements (Harris and Lindsey 1995, 2000; Harris 2005; Backley 2011, Nasukawa 2014, 2015, 2016)
    a. Vocalic elements

	Label	Spectral shapes
|A|	'mass'	mass of energy located in the centre of the vowel spectrum, with troughs at top and bottom
|I|	'dip'	energy distributed to the top and bottom of the vowel spectrum, with a trough in between
|U|	'rump'	marked skewing of energy to the lower half of the vowel spectrum

    b. Consonant elements

	Label	Spectral shapes
|ʔ|	'edge'	abrupt and sustained drop in overall amplitude
|H|	'noise'	aperiodic energy
|N|	'murmur'	broad resonance peak at lower end of the frequency range

Element Theory does not maintain a strict distinction between (10a) and (10b), since all elements may appear in both vowel and consonant expressions. The phonetic categories (in consonants and vowels) associated with each element are listed below.

(11) Elements and phonetic categories (Nasukawa 2016: 3; Backley 2011)

	Realisation in C	Realisation in V
|A|	uvular, coronal PoA	non-high Vs
|I|	palatal, dental PoA	front Vs
|U|	labial, velar PoA	rounded Vs
|ʔ|	oral or glottal occlusion	creaky voice (laryngealised Vs)
|H|	aspiration, voicelessness	high tone
|N|	nasality, obstruent voicing	nasality, low tone

In the PfP approach, elements do not just represent melodic properties; they also project onto higher levels of structure and function as organizing units. There they concatenate to form prosodic constituents, replacing traditional prosodic units like nucleus, mora, rhyme, syllable and foot. More specifically, it is assumed that the constituent traditionally called 'nucleus' must be represented by one of the vocalic elements |A|, |I| or |U|, which serves as the head of a phonological structure. When |A|/|I|/|U| appears as a single element without dependent structure, as shown in (12), it is realised as a central vowel [ə]/[ɨ]/[ɯ]. This central vowel quality may be seen as a phonetic baseline on to which the acoustic patterns of dependent elements are superimposed.

(12) The head of a phonological structure
    a. |A| (= Nuc)   b. |I| (= Nuc)   c. |U| (= Nuc)
       [ə]   [ɨ]   [ɯ]
    e.g. English, Swedish e.g. Fijian, Cilungu e.g. Japanese, Northern Saraiki

PfP assumes that the choice of default vowel in a given language is determined by parameter: [ə] in English and Swedish, [ɨ] in Fijian and Cilungu and [ɯ] in Japanese and Northern Saraiki (Shackle 1976, Syed and Aldaihani 2014). In their minimal form, these three elements are defined acoustically as, respectively, the weak form of the 'mass', 'dip' and 'rump' acoustic patterns (for a detailed discussion, see Nasukawa 2014, cf. Harris 2005, Backley 2011).

In a departure from the standard model of Element Theory (Kaye, Lowenstamm and Vergnaud 1985, 1990; Harris 1994, 2005; Backley 2011), PfP assumes that the single-element structures in (12) are interpreted as baseline resonance ([ə], [ɨ] and [ɯ]) rather than as the full vowels [a], [i] and [u] because, as single-element expressions, they are structurally minimal; and as such they provide minimal (i.e. non-contrastive) phonological information. The vowels [ə], [ɨ] and [ɯ] have a special status in that they are often non-contrastive. Furthermore, they are often associated with weak prosodic positions, and are regarded as weak realisations of the peripheral vowels [a], [i] and [u] respectively.

By contrast, full vowels carry more lexical information and therefore contain more structure. A single-element structure can become lexically more informative through the introduction of Head-Dependency relations.

(13) The head of a phonological structure
  a. [_A A A]   b. [_A A I]   c. [_A A U]

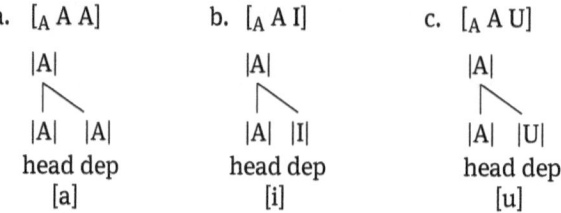

|A| |A| |A|
|A| |A| |A| |I| |A| |U|
head dep   head dep   head dep
 [a]   [i]   [u]

When the head element |A| takes another |A| as its dependent, as illustrated in (13a), the acoustically defined mass pattern of the dependent |A| (i.e. an exaggerated form of the baseline vowel [ə]) is superimposed onto the schwa-like baseline resonance (= the carrier signal). In effect, this superimposed mass pattern masks the baseline resonance, resulting in a structure that is phonetically realised as a low vowel [a]. In this configuration, an additional dependent unit functions as a lexically informative property and makes an active contribution to the phonetic salience of the structure as a whole. The same mechanism applies in (13b) and (13c) too. In the |A|-headed compound [|A||I|] in (13b), the baseline |A| resonance is also inaudible since the acoustic (dip) pattern of the dependent |I| element is superimposed onto it and the whole structure is phonetically realised as [i]. In the same way, the |A|-headed compound [|A||U|] in (13c) is realised as [u] since the acoustic pattern of the baseline |A| is masked by the acoustic (rump) pattern of the dependent |U| element.

All the structures in (13) employ the same mechanism of phonetic realisation in which the acoustic signature of the baseline (head element) is obscured by that of the dependent element. In other words, the head element makes a lesser contribution to the phonetic realisation of the whole structure while the dependent element makes a greater contribution (Nasukawa 2017). This mapping between structural roles and phonetic manifestation may be stated as follows (Nasukawa and Backley 2015).

(14) Roles of heads/dependents:
Heads are structurally important (obligatory) but recessive in contrastive terms; on the other hand, dependents are structurally recessive (optional) but rich in contrastive terms.

The theory assumes that the strength/weakness of a sound's contrastive role is expressible in acoustic terms by the degree of modulation of the carrier signal (acoustic baseline) (Ohala 1992; Ohala and Kawasaki-Fukumori 1997; Traunmüller 1994, 2005; Harris 2006, 2009, 2012).

(15) Roles of heads/dependents and their modulation
    HEADS   structure-building (can project to higher levels)
                  information-*poor*, *smaller* modulation
    DEPENDENTS non-structure-building (no projection)
                  information-*rich*, *bigger* modulation

In principle, this mapping between structural roles and phonetic interpretation applies to any phonological representation. As an illustration, consider the structure of the mid back vowels [o] and [ɒ], which require an additional level of element concatenation.

(16) Mid back vowels
    a. [$_A$ A[$_A$ AU]]   b. [$_A$ A[$_U$UA]]

[o] and [ɒ] in (16) both consist of three elements: the baseline element |A| and two dependents |A| and |U|. In the case of [o] in (16a), the highest element |A| takes the |A|-headed set [|A||U|] as its dependent. It is the most deeply embedded

part of the structure that is crucial to phonetic interpretation, so the lowest (dependent) |U| ensures that the whole expression is realised as the close mid back vowel [o]. In (16), the bigger the circle, the greater the acoustic contribution of the relevant element. Compare this with the structure for [ɒ] in (16b). The structure in (16b) has the same |A|-head, but in this case the head takes the |U|-headed compound [|U||A|] as its dependent. This time |A| is in the most embedded part of the structure, so the phonetic pattern of this lowest (dependent) |A| makes the greatest contribution to the whole expression (cf. Cinque 1993). The whole structure is realised as an open mid back vowel [ɒ]. The same asymmetric relation between elements is found in the spectral pattern of [ɒ], where the 'mass' pattern is stronger or more prominent than the 'rump' pattern, in comparison with [o].

Thus, phonetic realisation is determined not only by the kinds of elements which are present but also by the head-dependent relations between elements. Furthermore, all the required vowel categories are uniquely represented by recursive embedding.

3.2 Consonant structure in Precedence-free Phonology

To represent consonants, PfP incorporates similar structures and the same principle of phonetic realisation that was described above for vowels: as in (14), dependents are phonetically more prominent than heads in terms of the size of their modulated carrier signal (Nasukawa 2016, cf. Harris 2006). As a result, the most deeply embedded dependent in a domain is the most prominent (cf. Cinque 1993). Let us consider how the consonant portion of the CV structure [kʰi] is represented. (Note that the velar consonant in this example is relevant to the main topic of this paper, velar softening.) The structure in (17), taken from Nasukawa, et al. (2018), is that of CV-sized set in English which uses |A| (rather than |I| or |U|) as the parametrically determined baseline element. Unlike in (16) and the other structures described above, (17) shows a left-branching structure; this will facilitate our discussion (see below) of the linearisation of head-dependency structure. In principle, there is no difference between right- and left-branching structures in PfP, since there are no precedence relations between structural units.

(17) The phonological structure of [kʰi] in PfP

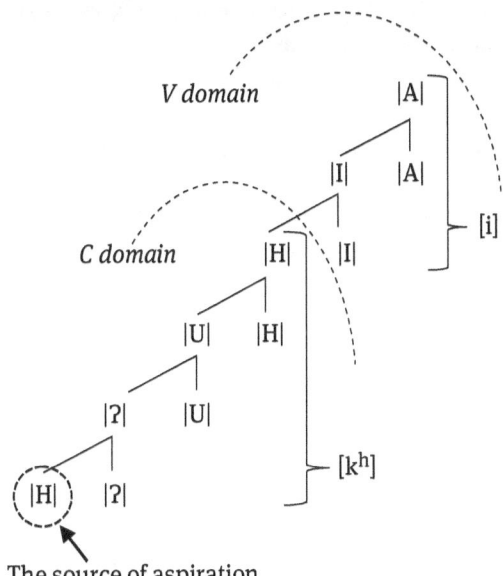

The source of aspiration

In (17), the baseline (head) of the whole structure is the highest |A|, which is phonetically realised as [ə]. When it appears in isolation, this head |A| is realised with the phonetic quality of the carrier signal. However, when a dependent element is present, the acoustic signature of this baseline resonance is masked by that of a dependent element. For example, in (17) the acoustic signature of |I|, the direct dependent of the highest head |A|, overrides that of |A|. Thus the |A|-headed expression |A I| is phonetically interpreted as [i].

Moving down one level in (17), this |I| (the dependent of the highest |A|) is now the head of the lower domain, where it takes the noise element |H| as a dependent. As described in the Element Theory and Government Phonology literature (Harris 1994, Nasukawa 2005, Backley 2011), |H| defines obstruency or voicelessness in element-based representations; its presence ensures that the structure from this point downwards has the characteristics of an obstruent.[2]

---

[2] This |H|-headed consonant domain cannot be pronounced simultaneously with the higher |A|-headed vowel domain because of a physiological incompatibility between the two domains. (The impossibility of pronouncing the C and V domains simultaneously has a parallel in syntax, i.e. multiple Spell-Out by phases (Hisao Tokizaki p.c.).) This is supported by a typological observation reported by Ladefoged and Maddieson (1996) that no languages have either vocalic obstruents or obstruent vowels.

The noise element which defines obstruency then takes the rump element |U| as its dependent, where a single token of |U| is interpreted as velar resonance (Nasukawa 2016, cf. Backley and Nasukawa 2009; note that two tokens of |U| define labiality). Then at the next level down, |U| takes the edge element |ʔ| as a dependent, which defines occlusion. The whole structure from the higher |H| downwards (i.e. [_H H[_U U ʔ]]]) is phonetically realised as a velar stop [k].

At the very bottom of the structure we find a second token of |H| which, as a dependent of |ʔ|, occupies the most deeply embedded part of (17). In this position the contrastive ability of |H| is highly salient. This follows the statements in (14) and (15), which describe how dependent elements are more prominent than heads in terms of the size of their modulated carrier signal (Nasukawa 2016, cf. Harris 2006). The most deeply embedded dependent in a domain is therefore the most prominent (cf. Cinque 1993). In the case of the lowest |H| in (17), it is phonetically realised in its exaggerated or prominent form – namely, aspiration. So, the C domain headed by the higher |H| is interpreted as an aspirated velar plosive [k^h]. Coupled with the V domain headed by |A|, the entire structure in (17) is phonetically interpreted as the CV-sized set [k^{h}i], which emerges as a result of a linearisation mechanism in which a domain located at a lower (phonetically more prominent) level (C domain) is phonetically realised before a domain located at a higher (phonetically recessive) level (V domain) (The principle of precedence: Nasukawa, et al. 2108).

We assume that in the consonantal part of the structure in (17), [k^h] is the unlenited representation of English /k/. This follows the phonotactic requirement in English which restricts [k^h] to strong (i.e. word-initial and stressed) positions (cf. other reflexes such as plain [k] and unreleased [k˺], which occupy weak (i.e. coda, word-final and inter-vocalic) positions). The form [k^h] associated with strong positions is assumed to be the unlenited or lexical form of /k/. Conversely, forms in weak positions are viewed as lenited/weak forms of their strong equivalents (Harris 1994, Nasukawa 2005, Backley 2011).

We now turn to the representation of /g/, the voiced counterpart of /k/. It is often said that the English 'voiced' velar stop is not really voiced: in precise terms, it is a voiceless unaspirated velar stop (except in intervocalic contexts). English and other languages of the same type (which have aspirated voiceless stops in the 'voiceless' series and unaspirated voiceless stops in the 'voiced' series) are called aspiration languages (cf. voicing languages such as Spanish and French) (Harris 1994, Honeybone 2008, Szigetvári 2008, Scheer and Ségétal 2008, Backley 2011). In addition, the laryngeal-source property of /g/ is phonologically inert while that of /k/ (voicelessness/aspiration) is phonologically active (e.g. progressive [–voice] assimilation in regular English plural suffixation and past tense suffixation). On this basis it may be assumed that the structure of /g/ lacks any element involved in expressing laryngeal contrasts, including the second token of the noise element |H| (for active voicelessness and aspiration), as shown in (18b). For comparison, the structure of /k/ is repeated in (18a).

(18) Representing the velar stops /k/ and /g/ in English

    a. /k/ [kʰ]   b. /g/ [k/g]

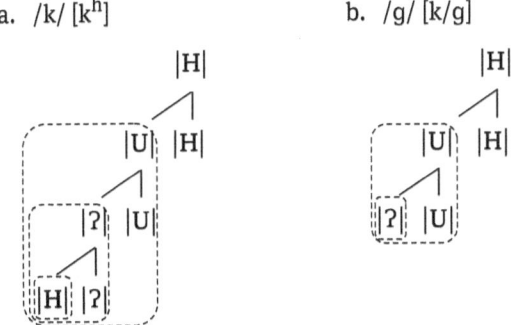

    3 domains under the head |H| 2 domains under the head |H|

It is apparent that there is a structural difference between (18a) and (18b): the structure of /k/ has three domains while that of /g/ has just two domains. In other words, /k/ is structurally more complex than /g/.[3] This complexity difference is also relevant to other types of obstruent. Since velar softening refers not only to /k g/ but also to /s z tʃ dʒ ʃ ʒ/ (see section 2.2), let us now discuss the representation of these coronals.

First, the voiceless coronal fricative /s/ – an alternant of /k/ as a result of velar softening – has the structure in (19a).

---

3 As in standard Element Theory (Harris 1994, 1997; Backley 2011, et passim), intervocalic voicing has two possible analyses. It may be treated as lenition (the result of element suppression: e.g. [kʰ] → [g] by suppressing the most deeply embedded |H|; [kʰ] → [ɣ] by suppressing the most deeply embedded |H| and |ʔ|), or it may be analysed as an instance of phonetic interpolation from the surrounding melodic context.

(19) Representing the coronal fricatives /s/ and /z/ in English

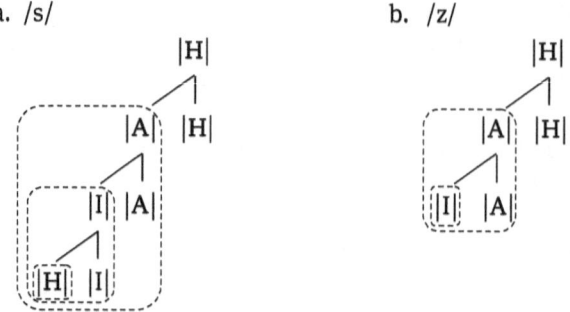

    3 domains under the head |H| 2 domains under the head |H|

In the structure of /s/, like that of /k/ ([kʰ]), the noise element |H| for obstruency occupies the highest position in (19a). This element |H| has a dependent |A|, which defines not only pharyngeality (flat/dark) in the consonant domain but also stridency when it appears with another place element (Scheer 2003, Nasukawa and Backley 2008). Since the dependent |A| of the first |H| has a further dependent |I| (palatality/frontness) (sharp/light) in (19a), |A| creates an effect of stridency. As a whole, the |A|-headed [|A||I|] set manifests itself as coronality (neutral). Moving one structural level down, |I| (now a domain head) takes the second token of |H| as a dependent. Like (17) and (18a), this |H| is the most deeply embedded dependent in the domain, so it contributes aspiration – a laryngeal-source characteristic of 'voiceless' obstruents in English. The structure of /z/, on the other hand, has no second token of |H| in the most deeply embedded part. In parallel with /k/ and /g/ in (18), /s/ is structurally more complex than /z/: /s/ has three domains while /z/ has only two.

Then, the affricate /ʤ/, which derives from /g/ as a result of velar softening, has the structure in (20b).

(20) Representing the palato-alveolar affricates /ʧ/ and /ʤ/ in English

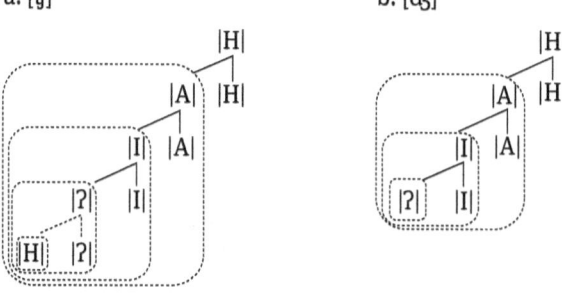

    4 domains under the head |H| 3 domains under the head |H|

We assume that the affricated version of English /z/ is /dʒ/, since /dz/ has no phonological status in English. Given this, the difference between /dʒ/ and /z/ comes down to the presence/absence of the edge element |ʔ|: the presence of |ʔ| makes the structure an affricate, as in (20b), while its absence makes the whole structure a fricative, as in (19b). As a result, /dʒ/ is structurally more complex than /z/: /dʒ/ has three domains while /z/ has two. What about /tʃ/, the 'voiceless' counterpart of /dʒ/? Since the voiceless series of English obstruents has a second token of |H| in the most deeply embedded part (see (18) and (19) above), /tʃ/ also has |H| in the lowest part of its structure; this gives it four domains and makes it structurally more complex than /dʒ/.

Finally, let us consider the structures of /ʃ/ and /ʒ/, where /ʃ/ is involved in velar palatalisation (/k/ → /ʃ/ / ___/ɪ/: e.g. electri[k] → electri[ʃ]ian), as noted in (8). The structure of /ʃ/ comprises the structure of /s/ ([H[A[I I H]A]H]) plus /j/ (consisting of a single |I|) as confirmed by assimilation effects (e.g. mi[s] + [j]ou → mi[ʃ]ou 'miss you'): [H[A[I[I I H]I]A]H] as in (21a). On the other hand, its 'voiced' counterpart /ʒ/ lacks a second token of |H| in the most deeply embedded part of the structure. As a result, /ʃ/ (with four domains) is structurally more complex than /ʒ/ (with three domains).

(21) Representing the palato-alveolar fricatives /ʃ/ and /ʒ/ in English
   a. [ʃ]   b. [ʒ]

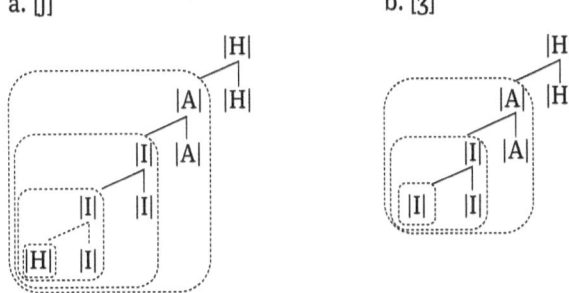

   4 domains under the head |H| 3 domains under the head |H|

In the following section we offer an analysis of velar softening which makes use of the precedence-free representations described above.

4 A Precedence-free Phonology approach to velar softening

4.1 Velar softening and morphological structure

Before discussing the segmental aspects of velar softening, this section considers the morphological properties of the relevant base forms (e.g. *electric*) and suffix forms (e.g. *–ity*). First, a word-final /k/ in English has the following structure, which is the same as the structure for /ki/ ([kʰi]) in (17) except that in word-final /k/ the highest |A| lacks a dependent |I|. Like Government Phonology, PfP assumes that all morphemes are represented in such a way that their structures are phonologically vowel-final, even if their phonetic realisation has a final consonant. Government Phonology represents this with an empty nucleus (i.e. a featureless vowel) in the final position of the morphological domain, while PfP uses a baseline element |A| without any dependent structure. As shown in (22), this bare |A| occupies the highest level in the whole 'CV' structure.

(22) a. Words ending with /k/ in English b. Suffixes starting with /ɪ/

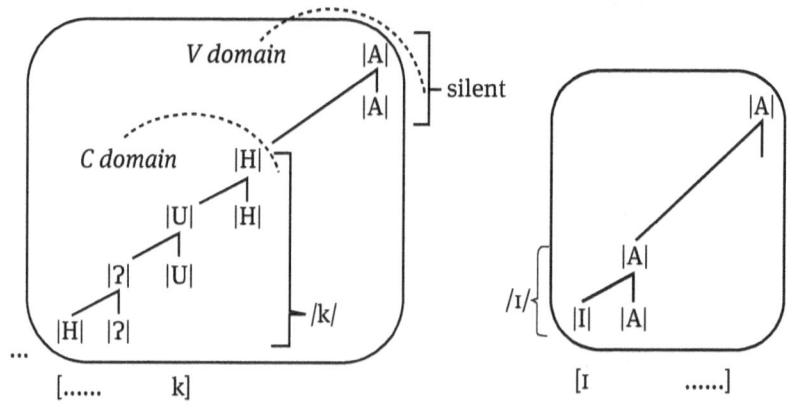

As depicted in (12a), |A| without a vocalic dependent structure is realised as a central vowel [ə]. In languages like English which allow words to end with a consonant, however, a vowel expression consisting only of the baseline |A| is phonetically silent by default, although it may be pronounced as [ə] under the appropriate conditions – for example, if Proper Government is not established (for a detailed discussion, see Harris 1994: 191–193). The equivalent to this mechanism of phonetic realisation in Government Phonology is called the Domain-Final-Empty-Nucleus parameter (Kaye, Lowenstamm and Vergnaud 1990, Harris 1994, Kaye 1995): an empty nucleus must be phonetically realised when the setting is OFF (default) in languages such as Japanese and Zulu, whereas it is silent when the setting is ON. The corresponding version of the Domain-Final-Empty-Nucleus Parameter is the Baseline-head Parameter in PfP (cf. Onuma (2015: 136), which employs the Ultimate-head Parameter (UHP) to account for this mechanism).

(23) The Baseline-head Parameter (BHP)
When the baseline head element of a given domain has no dependent in its vocalic portion, the baseline head element is p-licensed[4]
[OFF/ON]

In (22a) and also (22b) the highest-level |A| (for baseline resonance) cannot be perceived because it is phonetically silent; nevertheless, it must be present in the representation since the BHP parameter is set to ON in English. As a result, the structure in (22a) is phonetically realised as [... k]. In the case of languages such as Japanese and Zulu, however, where words always end phonetically in a vowel, the BHP parameter is set to OFF, so the highest-level element (e.g. |U| in Japanese) is phonetically realised (as a default vowel).

In the case of the suffix '-ity', the initial vowel /ɪ/ which triggers velar softening has the structure in (22b), where |I| – a dependent of the head element |A| in the V domain – is in the most deeply embedded part of the morpheme's structure and is therefore phonetically realised as the first segment of the suffix.

Based on the above structures, English suffixation may be described as follows.

---

[4] The term 'p-licensing' refers to 'prosodic-licensing' or 'proper-licensing' (Charette 1991, Harris 1994). If the baseline (i.e. the highest-level head) element is not p-licensed (OFF), then that element must be pronounced. On the other hand, if the baseline element is p-licensed (ON), then the element is suppressed (phonetically silent).

(24) Suffixation in English

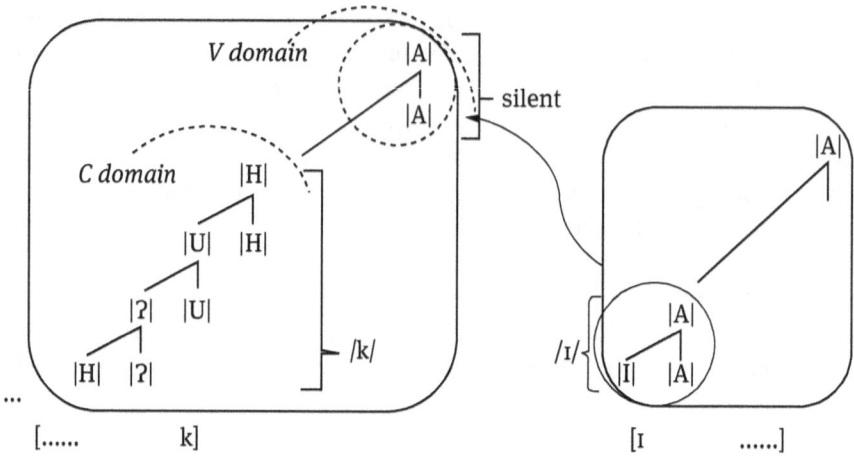

A suffix is morphologically more important and more fundamental than its base, since the morpho-syntactic category and the semantic properties of the whole concatenated word are often determined by the suffix (e.g. *electric* ADJECTIVE → *electric-ity* NOUN, where the suffix *–ity* determines the grammatical category of the whole word). For this reason, the representational structure of the suffix should ideally be attached to the highest part of the base, as shown in (24). When this happens, the lowest vocalic domain of the suffix is superimposed on to the highest vocalic domain of the base. So it is the entire structure of the suffix, and not just the circled portion, which dominates the structure of the base. We take this morphological operation to be typical of Root-level morphology, where two morphemes are tightly concatenated to give the effect of an underived lexical item (Nasukawa 2010: 2347–2350). The concatenated structure in (24) also conforms to the linearisation mechanism discussed in section 3.2: in linear terms, the base is followed by the suffix because a domain at a lower (i.e. phonetically more prominent) level is phonetically realised before a domain at a higher (i.e. phonetically recessive) level (Nasukawa, et al. 2018).

4.2 Velar softening: the /k/~/s/ alternation

We now describe how velar softening takes place during the morphological process just outlined. Let us first analyse the /k/~/s/ alternation. As already shown in (24), English Root-level morphology requires that the highest vocalic domain of the base is overridden by the lowest vocalic domain of the suffix, as illustrated below in (26a). In addition, we claim that there is a phonological operation which is driven by a specific morphological requirement, as defined in (25).

(25) ALT NonHi-NonLowV$_{SUFF}$ WITH HiV$_{BAS}$
Replace an expression which is neither highest nor lowest in the consonantal domain of the base with the copied lowest vocalic domain of the suffix.

Since the highest element in the C domain of the base in (26a) is the first token of |H| and the lowest element in the C domain is the second token of |H|, these must be preserved and parsed in accordance with (25). On the other hand, the elements in between (i.e. the |U|-headed [|?||U|] set) must be replaced by the structure of the suffix-lowest /ɪ/ (i.e. the |A|-headed [|I||A|] set). The motivation for this type of alternation is, we suggest, to produce a tighter concatenation akin to a non-analytic form; the effect is something similar to dovetailing. In addition, we assume that the motivation for leaving intact the highest and lowest elements of the C domain of the base may be attributed to their linguistically significant roles: as discussed in (14) and (15), the head (i.e. the first token of |H| in 26a) is structurally important (obligatory) while the dependent (i.e. the second token of |H| in 26a) is rich in terms of contrastive information. That is, the elements occupying the outermost (i.e. top and bottom) positions in a domain are resistant to phonological alternation.

(26) a. Velar softening: the /k/~/s/ alternation

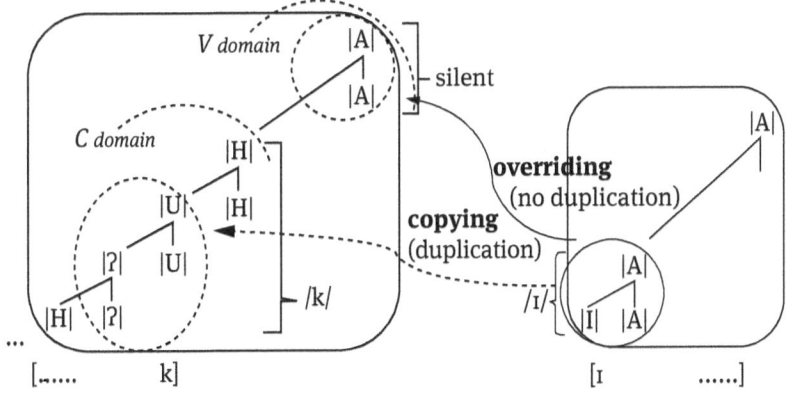

b. The structure of /sɪ/

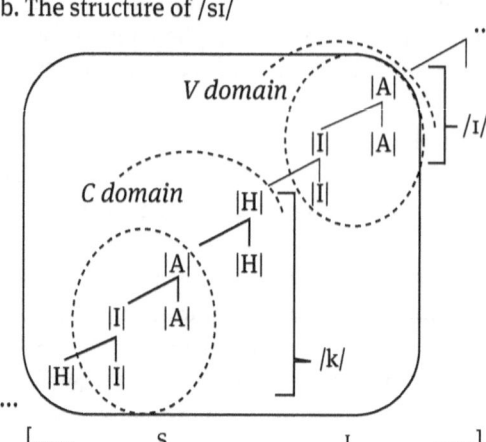

As a result of the operations shown in (26a), the expression in the C domain becomes [H [A [I I H] A]H] and is realised as [s].

Let us now consider why we do not observe alternations such as /k/~/tʃ/ and /k/~/ʃ/. First, the affricate /tʃ/ in (27a) (= 20a) has |?| in the central portion of its structure, flanked by the highest and lowest tokens of |H|. But in accordance with the morphological requirement in (25), a centrally located |?| (as well as |A| and |I|) in the structure for /k/ must be replaced by a copy of the lowest vocalic domain of the suffix. This is the reason why /tʃ/, which contains |?| in the centre of its structure in (27a), cannot be a derived form of /k/, which also contains |?| in the central position.

(27) a. The structure of /tʃ/   b. The structure of /ʃ/

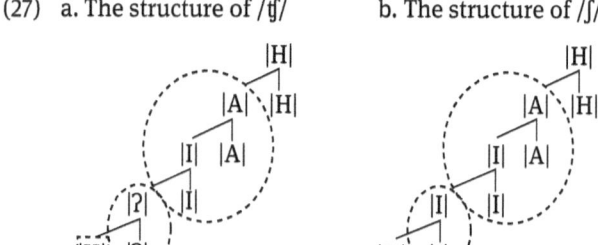

Next, the non-appearance of the alternation /k/~/ʃ/ is explained as follows. To arrive at the structure of /ʃ/ in (27b), |I| must occupy the position which is filled by |?| in /k/ (see (18a)). This would require a rule which replaces the centrally located |?| in /k/ with |I|. However, the suffix contains no source for the second token of |I| in /ʃ/, which means that /s/ is the only outcome of velar softening that is consistent with (25).

4.3 The /g/~/dʒ/ alternation

We now turn to the type of velar softening which involves the alternation /g/~/dʒ/. Here we also assume that the base-initial /g/ has the same structure as /k/ in (22a) in all but one respect: /k/ has a second token of |H| in the most deeply embedded portion of the C domain whereas /g/ contains no |H| in that position. In the case of the /g/~/dʒ/ alternation, we again assume that the elements positioned in between the highest and lowest elements (|H| and |ʔ| in 28a) must be replaced by a copied expression of [A I A] from the lowest part of the V domain in the suffix. As a result, we obtain the structure in (28b), which is phonetically interpreted as [dʒ] (see (20b) above).

(28) a. Words ending with /g/ in English

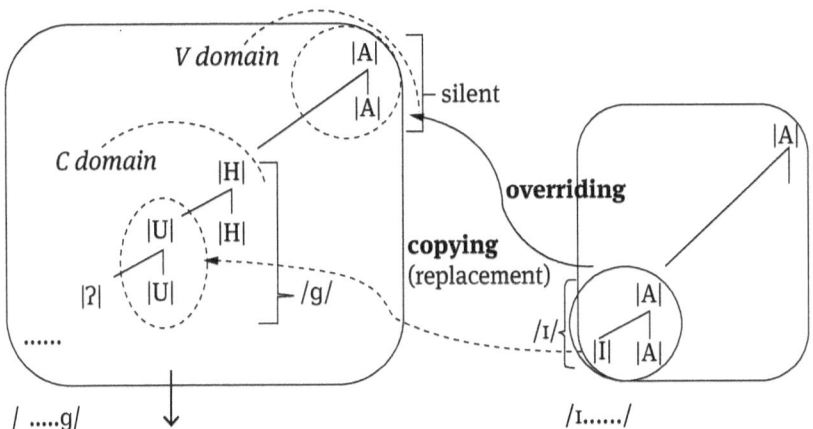

b. The structure of /dʒ/

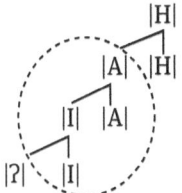

In (28) it is obvious that there is no violation of (25): the portion flanked by the highest |H| and the lowest |ʔ| is replaced by the structure of /ɪ/ from the lowest part of the suffix. But why does /g/ not alternate with other segments such as /z/ or /ʒ/? For convenience, the representations of /z/ and /ʒ/ are given below.

(29) a. The structure of /z/   b. The structure of /ʒ/

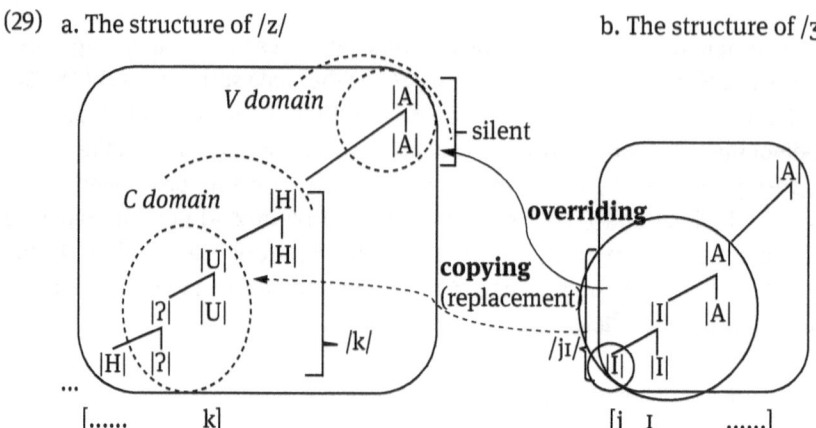

To derive the structure of /z/, the /ʔ/ element in the lowest position of the C domain must be deleted. Deleting |ʔ| violates the requirement in (25), however, which requires the lowest element of the C domain to remain intact. Meanwhile, obtaining the structure of /ʒ/ requires not only the deletion of |ʔ| but also the addition of a second token of |I|. Again, this would result in a violation of (25) (because the lowest element |ʔ| is deleted); moreover, there is no source for the second token of |I| in any part of the suffix. In view of these facts, we claim that /dʒ/ is the only possible outcome of velar softening which is consistent with (25).

4.4 Velar palatalisation

Finally, we consider the velar palatalisation effect /k/ → /ʃ/ / ___/ɪ/ (e.g. *electri* [k] → *electri*[ʃ]*ian*), which was discussed in (8). We assume that the initial part of the suffix *-ian* is /jɪən/ rather than /ɪən/; its phonological structure may be depicted as the right-hand structure in (30).

(30) The structure of –ian

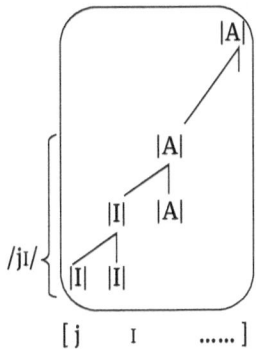

In comparison with the lowest vocalic part of the suffix involved in velar softening, an additional |I| is identified in the most deeply embedded portion of the structure. This |I| is assumed to be the source of the second token of |I| in the structure of /ʃ/ (cf. 21a). Taking the structure of -ian in (30) to be correct, the process in question may be captured as follows.

(31) a. The structure of /z/

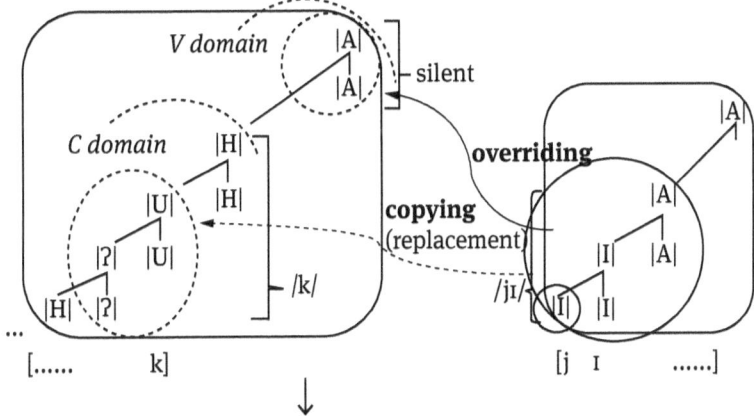

b. The structure of /ʃɪ/

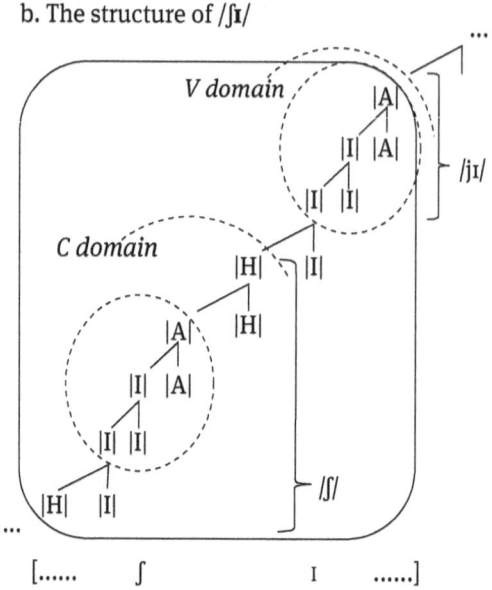

This process again adheres to the requirement in (25), which is also relevant to velar softening. The difference between the velar softening in (26) and (28) and the velar palatalisation in (31) may be attributed to a difference in the lexical structures of the two suffixes: the vowel of –*ian* has an additional token of |I| which is not present in –*ity*.

5 Concluding remarks

In this paper we have analysed English velar softening as a Root-level morphological operation without referring to precedence relations. Within the framework of Precedence-free Phonology we have proposed that the process in question may be viewed as an agreement effect involving the |A|-headed [A I] set: in velar softening, the elements which are flanked by the highest and lowest elements in the C domain of the base are overridden by the |A|-headed [A I] set in the lowest part of the suffix (ALT NONHI-NONLOWV$_{SUFF}$ WITH HIV$_{BAS}$). In addition, velar palatalisation proceeds along the same lines. The only difference between the two processes is that velar palatalisation shows an agreement effect involving the set of [$_A$ [$_A$ A I] I]: the elements that are sandwiched by the highest and lowest elements in the C domain of the base are replaced by the set of [_A_ [_A_ A I] I] from the lowest portion of the suffix. Again, there is no need to refer to precedence relations.

The analysis we have developed here shows that phonological phenomena such as velar softening are analysable without referring to precedence relations – which may be phonologically redundant (Nasukawa 2011). In order to challenge such a well-established tradition and to further validate the phonological representations proposed in Precedence-free Phonology, our future research will analyse other phonological phenomena which similarly show edge effects across boundaries and refer to the directionality of assimilation.

Acknowledgements: Earlier versions of this chapter were presented at the workshop 'Recursion in Phonology' held at Tohoku Gakuin University, Sendai, in September 2017; at the workshop 'Recursive Merge in Phonology', the 155th Meeting of the Japan Linguistic Society, held at Ritsumeikan University, Kyoto, in November 2017; at 'The 26th Manchester Phonology Meeting' held at the University of Manchester in May 2018; and at the conference 'Elements: State of the Art and Perspectives' held at the University of Nantes in June 2018. We thank the participants at these meetings for their constructive comments. Also, we are grateful to Phillip Backley and to two anonymous reviewers for comments and suggestions. This work was supported by MEXT/JSPS KAKENHI Grant-in-Aid for Scientific Research on Innovative Areas #4903 (Evolinguistics) Grant Number JP18H05081 and by Grant-in-Aid for Scientific Research (B) Grant Number JP26284067.

References

Backley, Phillip. 2011. *An Introduction to Element Theory*. Edinburgh: Edinburgh University Press.
Backley, Phillip and Kuniya Nasukawa. 2009. Representing labials and velars: a single 'dark' element. *Phonological Studies* 12, 3–10.
Backley, Phillip and Kuniya Nasukawa. This volume. *Recursion in melodic-prosodic structure*. In Kuniya Nasukawa (ed.), *Morpheme-Internal Recursion in Phonology*. Berlin and Boston: Mouton de Gruyter.
Charette, Monik. 1991. *Conditions on Phonological Government*. Cambridge: Cambridge University Press.
Chomsky, Noam and Morris Halle. 1968. *The Sound Patterns of English*. New York: Harper and Row.
Cinque, Guglielmo. 1993. A null theory of phrase and compound stress. *Linguistic Inquiry* 24, 239–297.
Dressler, Wolfgang U. 1985. On the predictiveness of natural morphology. *Journal of Linguistics* 21, 321–337.

Halle, Morris. 1990. Phonology. In Daniel N. Osherson and Howard Lasnik (eds.), *Language: An Introduction to Cognitive Science, Vol. 1*. Cambridge, MA: MIT Press, 43–68.
Halle, Morris. 2005. Palatalization/velar softening: what it is and what it tells us about the nature of language. *Linguistic Inquiry* 36, 23–41.
Halle, Morris and Karuvannur P. Mohanan. 1985. Segmental phonology of Modern English. *Linguistic Inquiry* 16, 57–116.
Harris, John. 1994. *English Sound Structure*. Oxford: Blackwell.
Harris, John. 2005. Vowel reduction as information loss. In Philip Carr, Jacques Durand and Colin J. Ewen (eds.), *Headhood, Elements, Specification and Contrastivity*. Amsterdam: John Benjamins, 119–132.
Harris, John. 2006. The phonology of being understood: further arguments against sonority. *Lingua* 116, 1483–1494.
Harris, John. 2009. Why final devoicing is weakening. In Kuniya Nasukawa and Phillip Backley (eds.), *Strength Relations in Phonology*. Berlin and New York: Mouton de Gruyter, 9–46.
Harris, John. 2012. Lenition. Intensive lecture series, The Graduate School of Tohoku Gakuin University.
Harris, John and Geoff Lindsey. 1995. The elements of phonological representation. In Jacques Durand and Francis Katamba (eds.), *Frontiers of Phonology: Atoms, Structures, Derivations*. Harlow, Essex: Longman, 34–79.
Harris, John and Geoff Lindsey. 2000. Vowel patterns in mind and sound. In Noel Burton-Roberts, Philip Carr and Gerry Docherty (eds.), *Phonological Knowledge: Conceptual and Empirical Issues*. Oxford: Oxford University Press, 185–205.
Hayes, Bruce. 2009. *Introductory phonology*. Malden, MA: Wiley-Blackwell.
Honeybone, Patrick. 2008. Lenition, weakening and consonantal strength: tracing concepts through the history of phonology. In Joaquim Brandão de Carvalho, Tobias Scheer, and Philippe Ségéral. (eds.), *Lenition and Fortition*. Berlin and New York: Mouton de Gruyter, 9–92.
Kaye, Jonathan D. 1995. Derivations and interfaces. In Jacques Durand and Francis Katamba (eds.), *Frontiers of Phonology: Atoms, Structures, Derivations*. Harlow, Essex: Longman, 289–332.
Kaye, Jonathan D., Jean Lowenstamm and Jean-Roger Vergnaud. 1985. The internal structure of phonological elements: a theory of charm and government. *Phonology Yearbook* 2, 305–328.
Kaye, Jonathan D., Jean Lowenstamm and Jean-Roger Vergnaud. 1990. Constituent structure and government in phonology. *Phonology* 7, 193–231.
Kiparsky, Paul. 1985. Some consequences of Lexical Phonology. *Phonology Yearbook* 2, 85–138.
Ladefoged, Peter and Ian Maddieson. 1996. *The Sounds of the World's Languages*. Oxford: Blackwell.
McCarthy, John J. 1986. OCP effects: Gemination and antigemination. *Linguistic Inquiry* 17, 207–263.
Mohanan, Karuvannur P. 1986. *The Theory of Lexical Phonology*. Dordrecht: Reidel.
Nasukawa, Kuniya. 2005. *A Unified Approach to Nasality and Voicing*. Berlin and New York: Mouton de Gruyter.
Nasukawa, Kuniya. 2010. No consonant-final stems in Japanese verb morphology. *Lingua* 120, 2336–2352.

Nasukawa, Kuniya. 2011. Representing phonology without precedence relations. *English Linguistics* 28, 278–300.

Nasukawa, Kuniya. 2014. Features and recursive structure. *Nordlyd* 41(1),1–19. *Special Issue on Features* edited by Martin Krämer, Sandra-Iulia Ronai and Peter Svenonius.

Nasukawa, Kuniya. 2015. Recursion in the lexical structure of morphemes. In Marc van Oostendorp and Henk van Riemsdijk (eds.), *Representing Structure in Phonology and Syntax*. Berlin and Boston: Mouton de Gruyter, 211–238.

Nasukawa, Kuniya. 2016. A precedence-free approach to (de-)palatalisation in Japanese. *Glossa: A Journal of General Linguistics* 1(1).9, 1–21, DOI: http://dx.doi.org/10.5334/gjgl.26

Nasukawa, Kuniya. 2017. The phonetic salience of phonological head-dependent structure in a modulated-carrier model of speech. In Bridget Samuels (ed.), *Beyond Markedness in Formal Phonology* (Linguistik Aktuell). Amsterdam: John Benjamins, 121–152.

Nasukawa, Kuniya and Phillip Backley. 2008. Affrication as a performance device. *Phonological Studies* 11, 35–46.

Nasukawa, Kuniya and Phillip Backley. 2015. Heads and complements in phonology: a case of role reversal? *Phonological Studies* 18, 67–74.

Nasukawa, Kuniya and Phillip Backley. 2017. Representing moraicity in Precedence-free Phonology. *Phonological Studies* 20, 55–62.

Nasukawa, Kuniya, Phillip Backley, Yoshiho Yasugi and Masatoshi Koizumi. 2018. Challenging cross-linguistic typology: right-edge consonantal prominence in Kaqchikel. *Journal of Linguistics* 56, 1–31.

Odden, David. 1986. On the role of the Obligatory Contour Principle in phonological theory. *Language* 62, 353–383.

Ohala, John J. 1992. Alternatives to the sonority hierarchy for explaining segmental sequential constraints. *CLS: Papers from the Parasession on the Syllable*, 319–338.

Ohala, John J. and Haruko Kawasaki-Fukumori. 1997. Alternatives to the sonority hierarchy for explaining segmental sequential constraints. In Stig Eliasson and Ernst Hakon Jahr (eds.), *Language and Its Ecology: Essays in Memory of Einar Haugen*. (Trends in Linguistics. Studies and Monographs, Vol. 100.) Berlin: Mouton de Gruyter, 343–365.

Onuma, Hitomi. 2015. On the status of empty nuclei in phonology. Ph.D. dissertation, Tohoku Gakuin University, Sendai, Japan.

Scheer, Tobias. 2003. On spirantisation and affricates. In Stefan Ploch (ed.), *Living on the Edge: 28 Papers in Honour of Jonathan Kaye*. Berlin and New York: Mouton de Gruyter, 283–301.

Scheer, Tobias and Philippe Ségétal. 2008. Positional factors in lenition and fortition. In Joaquim Brandão de Carvalho, Tobias Scheer, and Philippe Ségéral (eds.), *Lenition and Fortition*. Berlin and New York: Mouton de Gruyter, 131–172.

Shackle, Christopher. 1976. The Siraiki language of central Pakistan: a reference grammar. London: School of Oriental and African Studies, University of London.

Szigetvári, Peter. 2008. What and where? In Joaquim Brandão de Carvalho, Tobias Scheer, and Philippe Ségéral (eds.), *Lenition and Fortition*. Berlin and New York: Mouton de Gruyter, 93–129.

Syed, Nasir A. and Aldaihani, Sultan M. 2014. The emergence of the unmarked in loanword phonology: a harmonic serialism account. In Eugeniusz Cyran and Jolanta Szpyra-Kozłowska (eds.), *Crossing Phonetics-Phonology Lines*. Newcastle-upon-Tyne: Cambridge Scholars Publishing House, 219–234.

Traunmüller, Hartmut. 1994. Conventional, biological, and environmental factors in speech communication: a modulation theory. *Phonetica* 51, 170–183.
Traunmüller, Hartmut. 2005. Speech considered as modulated voice. Ms., Stockhlolms universitet.
Yip, Moira. 1988. The Obligatory Contour Principle and phonological rules: a loss of identity. *Linguistic Inquiry* 19, 65–100.

Markus Pöchtrager
Recursion and GP 2.0

1 Introduction

Recursion is one of the first concepts encountered in syntax, as the answer to how language makes "infinite use of finite means" in Wilhelm von Humboldt's characterisation. Not so in phonology, where common wisdom holds that there is no recursion, though opinions diverge to some extent.[1] The view that phonology lacks recursion is succinctly expressed in the following quote by Jackendoff (2007: 39): "[phonological] structures, though hierarchical, are not recursive, in that, unlike syntactic structures, they cannot be embedded indefinitely deeply in other structures of the same type. [Footnote not included/MAP.] For example, a rhyme cannot be subordinate to a syllable that is in turn subordinate to another rhyme." Such a difference makes phonology and syntax look very dissimilar.

At least two comments are in order here. Firstly, given mainstream assumptions about the organisation of the syllable and in fact the entire Prosodic Hierarchy (Nespor and Vogel 1986), the example given by Jackendoff would indeed be ruled out.[2] But it must be clear that this presupposes that mainstream assumptions are indeed correct. Notions such as rhyme and syllable, though commonplace in many if not most phonological theories, are theory-laden and by no means ubiquitous. Work in Government Phonology (Kaye, Lowenstamm and Vergnaud 1985, Kaye, Lowenstamm and Vergnaud 1990, Kaye 1990) has shown repeatedly that certain kinds of phonological constituents cannot and should not be maintained: Kaye, Lowenstamm and Vergnaud (1990) argued that the syllable as commonly understood was flawed and proceeded without it. Similar considerations held for the coda (Kaye 1990), which did not enjoy any status *qua* constituent in the theory and was considerably curtailed in its distribution. Yoshida (1990, 1996) argued that the mora becomes superfluous once Japanese constituent structure is properly understood, thus bridging the gap between languages that seemed to require the mora and those that did not, by giving up the mora altogether. The power of Jackendoff's quote rests on the reliability of the notions involved.

---

1 References will be given throughout the text.
2 In their foreword to the second edition, Nespor and Vogel (2007), the authors discuss and reject the possibility of recursion in certain areas of the Prosodic Hierarchy.

https://doi.org/10.1515/9781501512582-009

Secondly, there is the question of what exactly counts as an example for recursion. While the general definition of recursion (an operation that can apply to its own output) is clear, the devil is in the detail, and detail here is labelling. Minimalist syntax, as initiated by Chomsky (1995), limits itself to one structure building operation, merge. Merge takes two syntactic objects α and β, and builds a set {α, β} out of them. Merge is recursive, as it can take its own output and reapply to it to build e.g. {γ, {α, β}}; but crucially, merge as an operation is category-neutral. The output of merge should receive a label and the choice of label depends on the members of the set, with the details of the labelling procedure being debated, cf. Cecchetto and Donati (2005) for recent discussion of the issues involved. Given such category-neutrality, any kind of phrase (set of previously merged objects) contained in another phrase counts as an example of the application of merge. Under such a definition, a DP contained in a vP is created by a recursive operation, but that fact is easily concealed by the labels. The standard examples that come to mind when talking about recursion involve self-embedding, a particular kind of phrase contained in the same kind (CP in CP, DP in DP etc.). The point that this is a crucial difference has been made very forcefully by Nevins, Pesetsky and Rodrigues (2009), countering the claim that Pirahã lacks recursion in its syntax: the language seems to have restrictions on what type of constituent can be embedded in another type or itself, but it does not seem to lack recursion, understood as a property of a structure-building operation.

What does this mean for phonology? Jackendoff's quote, that there cannot be a syllable in a rhyme in a syllable, would certainly be accepted as correct by many. Yet in this article I am going to argue that it is incorrect. As already pointed out at the beginning of this section, much depends on the choice of model. Many properties of prosodic constituency as currently understood are indeed problematic from a syntactic point of view, but I submit that there are alternative ways of looking at phonology. Those alternatives are suggested by phonological evidence itself. Crucially, once they are accepted, commonalities between the two modules come out much more clearly. Indeed, I see this article as a contribution to the discussion of Structural Analogy (J. Anderson 1992), i.e. the idea that the different domains of grammar share a similar architecture, in particular syntax and phonology. In this article I will focus on the 'lower' levels of phonological constituency to show what kind of evidence we find for recursion there. By lower levels I am referring to the level of the prosodic word, the foot and the levels below.[3] I will look at recursion both in the general sense (as pure

---

[3] As will become clear, I am not wed to those notions. Also, I am staying away from higher layers of the Prosodic Hierarchy and the question to what extent they depend on and are

structure, without reference to node labels) and in the stricter sense of a constituent κ embedded inside κ.

At several points in the discussion I will make reference to Neeleman and van de Koot (2006), a relatively recent and detailed argument for fundamental differences between syntax and phonology. Their own view of a flat, string-based phonology is hardly compatible with the view presented here. As such, their article serves as an excellent comparison point. The reason I am singling out their work is for no other reason than that they provide a very detailed discussion of what they see as problematic in an attempt to make phonology more syntax-like.

2 Non-arbitrariness

Let us begin by clarifying one crucial notion which potentially clouds the comparison between syntax and phonology, viz. non-arbitrariness. Minimalist Syntax places great emphasis on the question of what drives a derivation. Uninterpretable features which have to be valued or checked are often presented as the answer to that question. As a result, movement happens for a reason, as a means to satisfy the needs of uninterpretable features. In this way, non-arbitrariness is established, i.e. a link between what happens and where/why it happens. (Though one might want to point out that the postulation of uninterpretable features for the sole reason of driving derivations has a certain aftertaste of circularity.)

A similar concern has been the central force behind one theory of phonology that has always seen itself as very close to syntactic theorising, i.e. Government Phonology (GP: Kaye, Lowenstamm and Vergnaud 1985, 1990, Harris 1994). One of its non-negotiable core assumptions is the Non-Arbitrariness Principle (NAP). The NAP demands that there be a connection between target and trigger,[4] a requirement which is not met in rewrite rules of the shape A → B / C __ D, since no connection is required between structural description and structural change. Autosegmental Phonology provided tools to remedy this, in that phonological events could be expressed as spreading, thus guaranteeing the required link:

---

isomorph with syntactic structures. Discussion of recursion at those levels inevitably leads to the question of which component of grammar is responsible for recursiveness there, phonology or syntax. For dicussion cf. Samuels (2009), Scheer (2008), Truckenbrodt (1995), Wagner (2005). I will remain agnostic whether there even is a reason to speak about the higher levels of the Prosodic Hierarchy, cf. Newell (2017) for discussion.

4 The Minimality Hypothesis (MH, Kaye 1992) complements the NAP. The MH excludes exceptions, extrinsic rule ordering and derived environment effects. The NAP and the MH are assumed to apply in tandem, cf. Pöchtrager and Kaye (2011), Pöchtrager (2014) for discussion.

spreading of a property P from α to β not only explains why β acquires P, but also why it acquires it in the context of α.[5]

This is a point which in my view has not been sufficiently clarified in the literature dealing with Structural Analogy. Neeleman and van de Koot's (2006) very detailed criticism does not address that issue, and their repeated reference to phonological rules suggests that their conception of phonology does not have to satisfy non-arbitrariness. Their proposal of a flat structure that integrates the Prosodic Hierarchy in the form of boundary symbols which can then be made reference to betrays their view of phonology as arbitrary, because what would the link be between any of those symbols and the phenomena they allegedly give rise to?[6] The emphasis that GP puts on the NAP is of course not an exercise in self-restriction, but is rooted in the desire to create a theory which is rich in empirical content. A model where anything can be caused by anything hardly makes predictions.

This is also relevant to the present article, which focuses on one particular offspring of GP, dubbed GP 2.0 (Pöchtrager 2006, 2009, 2010, 2015ab, Pöchtrager and Kaye 2013, 2014, Živanovič and Pöchtrager 2010). As we shall see in the following sections, the transition from earlier models of GP (which I will refer to as GP 1.x) to GP 2.0 was due to the existence of phenomena that eschewed a non-arbitrary account. But if the phenomena are real, the only conclusion can be that the theory must be (partially) wrong and/or incomplete. The shift from melody to hierarchical structure (sections 4–6) was motivated by such considerations, but this can only be appreciated if phonology is not simply seen as a system that allows random operations to take place. GP 2.0 shares with its predecessor GP 1.x the belief that phonology does conform to the NAP. Non-arbitrariness can be achieved by reference to melodic primes, but in GP 2.0 the notions of trade-off and asymmetric dependency play a central role, too.

3 When are trees needed?

Employing trees in phonology is certainly not a new idea, though in GP 2.0 they are put to use in areas where they had not been used before. I agree with García-Bellido (2005) that it is "the simplest possible hypothesis to approach

---

[5] See Kaye (1989), Kaye, Lowenstamm and Vergnaud (1990) and Pöchtrager (2014) for more detailed discussion.
[6] Here I concur with Scheer's (2008) assessment that the Prosodic Hierarchy does not fare any better in this regard.

variation" that "an organism might use the same operative mechanisms, at different levels of organization [...], unless it is proved that it does not." That is, given the ubiquity of hierarchy elsewhere in grammar, I would take it as the null-hypothesis that phonology is the same. Van der Hulst (2006, 2010) follows the same line of reasoning, pointing out that hierarchical structure is of course attested in other particulate systems outside of linguistics as well. In contrast to this, Neeleman and van de Koot (2006) remind us that hierarchical structure is a powerful tool and that theories should not be given more power than necessary. As they correctly point out, the fact that trees *can* be used in phonology does not imply that trees *must* be used. In order to settle the issue then, we have to ask what phenomena can *only* be explained by trees, instead of just *also* be explained. This raises the bar from just being satisfied with the null hypothesis to looking at why trees are actually necessary.

The central reason why syntax employs trees is that they allow for the expression of asymmetries, which could not be handled by flat structures. Those asymmetries permeate all of syntax, e.g. in binding phenomena or in structural ambiguities. A phrase like *a blue striped suit* (Everaert, Huybregts, Chomsky, Berwick and Bolhuis 2015) allows for two syntactic groupings and is thus ambiguous in interpretation:[7] either *blue* scopes over *striped suit*, or *blue striped* as a whole scopes over *suit*. Syntax cannot restrict itself to weak generative capacity, but must account for strong generative capacity as well. Hierarchical structure is essential in the expression of syntactic ambiguities.

Clear parallels to structural ambiguities are hard to come by in phonology, and they often allow for different interpretations. French [wa] can behave like a sequence of onset and nucleus (*la huaille* 'the mob') or like a complex nucleus without an onset (*l'oiseau* 'the bird'), as the behaviour of the definite article (and other determiners) shows when it changes according to whether the word counts as consonant- or vowel-initial. GP 1.x would have assumed the two structures in (1), as argued e.g. in Kaye (1989) and Kaye and Lowenstamm (1984):

(1) a. onset+nucleus   b. light diphthong

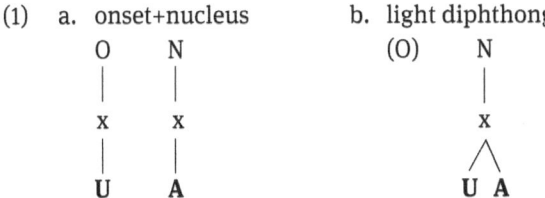

---

7 Di Sciullo (2005) argues that asymmetry is *the* central notion in grammar.

While this is an ambiguity, it is expressible without hierarchical structure. Other cases that come to mind are no different: the [je] of Spanish *llegar* 'to arrive' and *griego* 'Greek' can be dealt with in exactly the same way as French. The structural difference between the [pt] in English *kept* (with the two consonants strictly adjacent) and (identical) [pt] in *seeped* (with the two consonants separated by a morpheme boundary and thus an empty nucleus, cf. Kaye 1995 for arguments) is captured by the presence or absence of an empty nucleus and the syllabic affiliation of the first consonant. Those ambiguities could be expressed in hierarchical fashion, only so far we have not seen any compelling evidence for that. But those are exactly the kind of phenomena we will need to look for. We will return to this in section 6 where we shall see that the distribution of certain melodic primes furnishes the crucial piece of evidence that a 'flat' representation as in (1) is not sufficient. In order to show this, we will now need to start discussing the basic tenets of GP 2.0.

4 GP 2.0 and the internal structure of consonants

The central idea of GP 2.0 is this: many properties that have been assumed to be melodic are better understood by assuming that they are structural since they interact with structure. The first seedling can be traced back to Jensen (1994), who argued that the stop element **?**, responsible for the difference between stops and continuants, is better understood as a relation holding between two (consonantal) positions. Evidence for this came from languages like Pulaar where a consonant that is called upon to govern a preceding consonantal position automatically becomes a stop, be it in geminates or in certain cases of prefixation. Jensen argued that similar effects could be seen in other languages as well. A stop is not characterised by a certain melodic prime, then, but by the fact that it occurs in a certain configuration. While this held the promise of getting rid of the stop element, which was suspicious anyway because it seemed restricted to non-nuclear positions unlike the other elements, it was less clear what exactly the particular structure to replace it should look like, as Jensen's original proposal was fraught with difficulty.

The next step came with the analysis of length-related phenomena in Pöchtrager (2006). English vowels are systematically longer before lenis consonants than fortis ones.[8] In a pair like *bid* vs. *bit*, the vowel in *bid* (ending in a

---

[8] The term 'voicing' is avoided because it conflates several categories, cf. Harris (2009), Iverson and Salmons (2011) for recent discussion. English does not contrast voiced vs. voiceless,

lenis consonant) is nearly twice as long as that in *bit* (ending in a fortis consonant). Since all consonants are either fortis or lenis, this can be seen throughout the language (*leaf/leave, leak/league* etc.) This effect disappears dramatically in bisyllabic words (e.g. *tuba* vs. *super*).⁹ GP 1.x had no means to represent this additional length or to explain why it occurred. This is particularly damaging for a theory subscribing to the NAP, since the relation between vowel length and type of consonant remained unclear: fortis consonants were characterised by the element **H**, which lenis ones lacked, and there is no link between a lack of **H** (a melodic property) and extra length (a structural property expressed by amount of positions). As a way out, Pöchtrager (2006) proposed to reinterpret that melodic difference as one of structure, as follows: there is no melodic difference between the two series of consonant. Both of them have the same kind of structure, but while all of that structure is taken up in the case of fortis consonants, there is an unclaimed position within lenis consonants which can be taken up by a preceding vowel, thus leading to the extra length we observe. (2) illustrates this for *f* and *v*, taken from Pöchtrager (2006: 69).

(2) a. b.

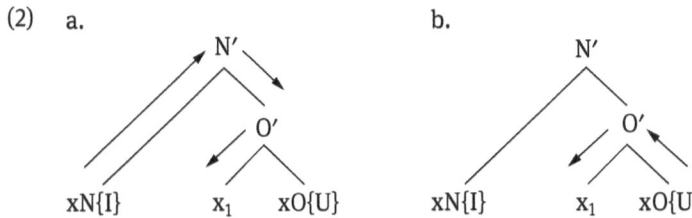

(2a) shows the nucleus and final consonant of the word *give*; xN stands for a nuclear head, it is annotated with the element **I** to give us the correct vowel, xO stands for an onset head (~consonant), annotated with **U**, encoding labiality. This xO projects up to O' which contains an unannotated point x1. The *v* is lenis, hence x1 is not claimed by xO but rather by xN, hence the lengthening of the vowel. In (2b), the nucleus and final consonant of the word *whiff*, x1 is taken up by xO to give us a fortis *f*. As a result, the preceding vowel does not lengthen.

This change in perspective allows for a non-arbitrary account of the English facts, in line with languages like Italian that show similar trade-off

---

but neutral (lenis) vs. voiceless (fortis), cf. also recent editions of Ladefoged's *Course in Phonetics* (Ladefoged and Johnson 2010).
9 Zue and Laferriere's (1979) argument that a difference remains is based on methodologically problematic data, cf. Kaye (2012) for discussion.

relations (*fāto* 'fate' vs. *fatto* 'fact').[10] Furthermore, it also made English practically identical to Estonian, whose length system is commonly seen as rather exotic. The reanalysis of English paved the way for making the two languages surprisingly similar. For example, in a word like *bead*, the vowel is already long and gets extra length due to the final consonant. This requires exactly the same kind of representation that is also necessary to understand Estonian overlength.[11]

The reinterpretation of lenis/fortis as a structural property had repercussions for the theory of constituent structure, which at the time simply was not fine-grained enough. Two elements, **?** and **H**, were eliminated and had to be replaced in some way. There is a sense in which (fortis) *f* is bigger than *v* (which is neither fortis nor a stop), but the (lenis stop) *b* is also bigger than *v*. Both times we are talking about bigger size, which raises the question of how the two differences in size are kept apart. The x-bar schema provides the means to express this difference while keeping both cases separate. A stop projects twice while a fricative projects only once. (3) illustrates the difference and also gives the representation of approximants, which are simple, non-projecting heads.

(3)   a.   stops   b.   fricatives   c.   approximants

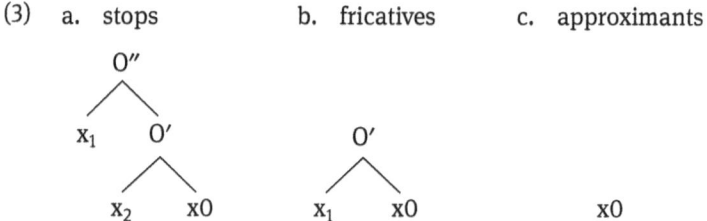

In both (3a–b) x_1 is involved in the expression of the fortis/lenis difference. The consonant is fortis if that position (x_1) is claimed by xO, otherwise lenis, cf. also (2). Approximants (3c) do not allow for a fortis counterpart. In (3a) we also see x_2; this position is usually claimed by xO to give stop interpretation. That is, in (3a) x_1 and x_2 fulfill different roles. But still, both layers count as the projection of an onset head. No matter if that head projects zero (3c), one (3b) or two (3c) times, we are always dealing with a consonant, in the same way that a syntactic head would determine class membership of the entire phrase, no matter if there

---

10 Similar but not identical: there are of course crucial differences between English and Italian. Italian has geminates (which involve three positions and have an effect on metrical structure), but English fortis consonants are not geminates (they only involve two positions and they never affect word stress). For detailed discussion of those differences cf. Pöchtrager (2006).
11 Similar disclaimers as in footnote 10 apply to Estonian overlong consonants.

is a complement, specifier, both or neither. Depending on where the non-head skeletal slots are integrated into the structure they take over different roles and contribute different properties to the projection of the onset head, in a similar way that complement and specifier play different roles with respect to the head in syntax. As a result of this reorientation, phonological structure at the level of the (traditional) segment got so fine-grained that it is unclear how the differences could be successfully expressed in a flat model.[12] It has led to a model that meets the category-free definition of recursion.

The discussion of English has shown that the upper layer of structure encodes the difference between fortis and lenis, but one might still have misgivings about replacing the stop element by structure. Is it really the case that both elements, **?** *and* **H**, display structural properties? The hierarchical structures in (3) were a means to make sure that both can be replaced by structure without the two types of structure getting into each other's way. The separation is only necessary if the stop element is indeed structural, and if such a separation is unnecessary, then also the case for the hierarchical structures in (3) is weakened.

In addition to the cases discussed in Jensen (1994), Québec French provides further evidence that stopness has a structural effect. In that variety of French, whether high vowels are tense or lax depends on the environment they occur in, cf. Bosworth (2017) for the most recent account. Before a word-final consonant we find the lax version, thus *vide* [vɪd] 'empty' but *vider* [vi'de] 'to empty'. This, however, is not the case if the final consonant is one of the set of lengthening consonants ('consonnes allongeantes'), {[r], [v], [z], [ʒ]}, in which it is still the tense (and lengthened) vowel that is found: *mur* [myːr] 'wall'. What is crucial is the set of lengthening consonants: They are exactly the ones that are lenis (which only take up little space) and *not* stops (thus take up even less space). In other words, they are extremely small consonants, and the lack of stopness is part of why they are so small. It is thus not surprising that they are the ones that allow lengthened tense vowels before them.[13]

---

[12] Superficially it seems that any claim to the extent that 'segments' have internal structure is hardly new. Feature geometry (Clements 1985) also assumes internal structure of individual segments, but of course of a very different kind: it is concerned with defining subsets of features that show common behaviour. This is very different from GP 2.0, where some successors of features, viz. elements, are *replaced* by structure in order to capture their behaviour in a non-arbitrary way. For example, the groupings of feature geometry have nothing to do with length-related phenomena, while the structures of GP 2.0 often (but not always) do.

[13] This also shows where the representations given in (3) are in need of improvement. In those structures, the lack of the layer that is responsible for stopness does not yet provide the

5 The element A as structure

Most versions of GP use the classic trinity of elements **A** ('non-high'), **I** ('front') and **U** ('round') for basic distinctions in vowel quality, similar to Dependency Phonology (Anderson and Ewen 1987) and Particle Phonology (Schane 1984). However, all three models have to countenance that **A** (or its respective congener) has properties different from the other two elements. Its special status is often (but not only) seen in the representation of vowel height, which seems more scalar in nature, rather than a privative or equipollent property. In Particle Phonology, the **a**-particle (the counterpart to the element **A**) is the only prime that can occur several times in an expression, thus capturing height degrees: a vowel with two **a**-particles is more open than one with only one, which in turn is more open than one without any. No such scale seems to be required for frontness or roundedness, and Schane (1984) stipulated that the **a**-particle had a unique status. Dependency Phonology simply stated that **A** enters into more combinatorial possibilities than other components, thus giving rise to more vowels along the height axis (Anderson and Ewen 1987). In GP 1.x, the weirdness of **A** had long been noted (Cobb 1997; Kaye 2000; Pöchtrager 2006), but hardly ever formalised. A first attempt was Kaye (2000), which dealt with **A** in consonants, where it represents coronality.

Following Kaye's lead, Pöchtrager (2009, 2010, 2012, 2013ab, 2015) tried to build the special status of **A** into the theory. Various phenomena suggest that **A** is involved with licensing (extra/bigger) structure. This is true both of (non-high) vowels and (coronal) consonants, both of which contain **A**. For example, English allows superheavy rhymes as in *count* if both consonants are coronal (contain **A**), but excludes **coump* and **counk* which do not meet that requirement. This also explains the difference between *east, boost, baste, boast*, all of them with a long vowel/diphthong, versus **easp, *boosk, *baspe, *boask*. We see an additional twist in Southern British English, where nuclei that contain **A** by itself can appear before any fricative+stop cluster: *clasp, task* and *draft*. This suggests that the **A** in the nucleus can 'make up' for the lack of **A** in *one* of the members of the cluster. Similar effects can be found in German, Finnish etc. (Pöchtrager 2010).

---

room necessary to guarantee the lengthening in Québec French. The representation of consonants in (3) goes back to Pöchtrager (2006) and is obviously still not fine-grained enough.

All of these phenomena suggest a structural reinterpretation of **A**. Again, while the verdict is clear, the precise implementation is difficult. Vowel reduction, another area where **A** plays a central role, provides valuable clues. The idea (proposed in Pöchtrager 2015b and expanded in Pöchtrager 2018) is as follows: vowel height has to do with size. The more open a vowel is, the bigger it is structurally. (More precisely: the greater the number of empty positions it has.) One very common pattern in vowel reduction is that unstressed positions prefer high(er) vowels: for example, languages with two series of mid vowels, open- and close-mid, ban the open-mid series from unstressed position (4). This is what we see in Italian, Slovenian, and (some varieties of) Brazilian Portuguese. Brazilian Portuguese (Cristófaro Alves da Silva 1992, Mateus and d'Andrade 2000, Wetzels 1995) is more complex than the others as it differentiates different types of unstressed position.

(4) Brazilian Portuguese

stressed	i	e	ɛ	a	ɔ	o	u
prestressed	i	e		a		o	u
unstressed final	i			ə			u

In GP 1.x, a reduction from [e] to [i] could be expressed as the loss of the element **A**, but the reduction from [ɛ] to [e] cannot be so expressed, since both vowels contain **A** and **I** and in GP 1.x they only differ in how the two elements are arranged with respect to each other (i.e. headedness). The same holds true for the back vowels. This bars a unified account of both cases of reduction.

If we follow the leads about **A** being structure, the picture changes. The idea is this: the more open a vowel, the greater the number of empty positions there are and, as a result, the bigger it is. This is depicted in (5), which requires some explanation: all structures represent vowels, and as has become clear in the analysis of vowel reduction, the simple structures that were used for vowels in (2), viz. a nuclear head xN that can project, will not do. Instead, (5) represents vowels as (potentially) two X-bar structures on top of each other. The heads (and their projections) are underlined. This allows for maximally four layers of structure; here we will only discuss cases of up to three. (The heads are simply noted down as x̲, since their status is still somewhat unclear.)

(5)

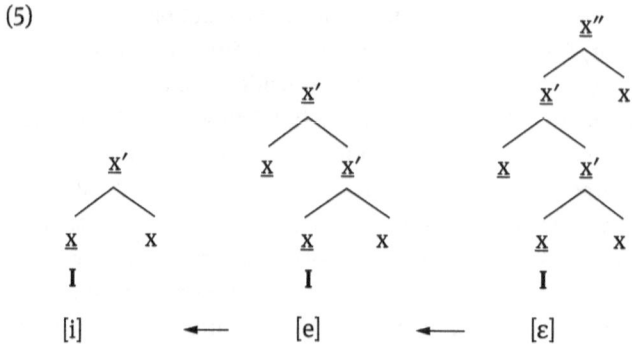

What this shows is that vowel height is a function of empty structure. The more open the vowel, the greater the amount of empty structure there is. With such a representation in place, vowel reduction can simply be expressed as a restriction on what is allowed to occur in unstressed position: stressed position allows for bigger structures, but only smaller structures can fit into an unstressed position. The reduction path [ɛ] → [e] → [i] consists in the removal of successive layers of structure. This captures the scalar nature of vowel height.

The reanalysis of **A** also makes predictions for consonants, as discussed in Pöchtrager (2013a, 2013b, 2016) as well as Kaye and Pöchtrager (2013). **A** was the element that defines coronals.[14] If **A** is replaced by structure in vowels, the same will have to be done in consonants. This makes coronals structurally bigger than other places of articulation. Taking into account what has been said about stops before, coronal stops will be particularly big as they combine the structure that is needed to express stopness and the structure that is needed to replace the old element **A**. It is then no surprise that in English it is exactly those consonants (*d/t*) that are lenited (by tapping and glottalisation), as in *city* ['sɪɾiː]/['sɪʔiː], rather than velars or labials. Furthermore, we already know from vowel reduction that unstressed position means less room for structure. This is typically seen in the vowels, but in English it can also affect the accompanying onset.

With three elements gone, structure has to shoulder a heavier burden than before. But this is more than a simple redistribution of work from one part of the theoretical calculus to another. The shift is motivated by the NAP. To the extent that **ʔ**, **H**, and **A** show interaction with structure they must be given structural interpretation themselves in order to even express that interaction.

---

14 I am aware that other proposals have been made for coronals, cf. the discussion in Backley (2011). I disagree with most of those arguments, though, as argued in Pöchtrager (2013b).

The resulting structures are much more complex than what is usually understood when talking about constituent structure in phonology. Only hierarchical structure seems to provide the means to capture such fine-grained distinctions.

6 Asymmetries

The ever-expanding structure also provides the backdrop for the expression of asymmetries between the remaining melodic primes. This point is crucial since it is a strong argument in favour of hierarchy instead of simply flat structure. Neeleman and van de Koot (2006: 1525) argue that syntax needs to capture (i) headedness and (ii) constituency. The relevance for constituency in both syntax and phonology is hardly denied these days; for phonology this marks a clear break from early Generative Phonology in the style of *Sound Pattern of English* (Chomsky and Halle 1968). As for headedness, in syntax it is connected to selectional requirements and asymmetry, and a strong argument for tree structures in syntax is that they allow the expression of asymmetric relations, as mediated by e.g. c-command. Asymmetries are central in both syntax and phonology (van der Hulst 2006: 674). Neeleman and van de Koot's (2006) position that such asymmetries are lacking from phonology is incorrect, in fact they are more common than usually assumed. This now takes us back to section 3, and to the question whether tree structures are simply convenient or also necessary. Contra Neeleman and van de Koot (2006) I hold that they are necessary, and the clearest evidence comes from what I refer to as Phonological Binding Theory, discussed on the basis of data from English, Putonghua and Japanese in Pöchtrager (2009, 2015), Živanovič and Pöchtrager (2010).

Binding theory is an attempt to understand the different behaviour of the remaining elements. Various phenomena suggest that at least the elements **I** (roughly: palatality) and **U** (roughly: labiality) are distributed in an asymmetric fashion in the tree. The distribution relies on notions like c-command, only expressible in hierarchical terms. English diphthongs provide a good example, since **I/U** are not evenly distributed across head and offglide. In *oi* (*boy*, *void*) the head contains **U** (as part of the mid rounded vowel), while the offglide is simply **I**. Exchanging **U** by **I** yields ungrammatical **eu*.[15] (6) gives the relevant structures as they would have looked like in GP 1.x (without melodic headedness indicated).

---

[15] Care has to be taken not to confuse diphthongs with any sequence of vowel and glide. Many English dialects have vocalised *l*, and the resulting sequence of vowel plus glide, unlike real diphthongs, does not show any phonotactic restrictions: any quality (*fill* [fɪw], *fell* [fɛw]

(6) a. licit *oi*   b. illicit **eu*

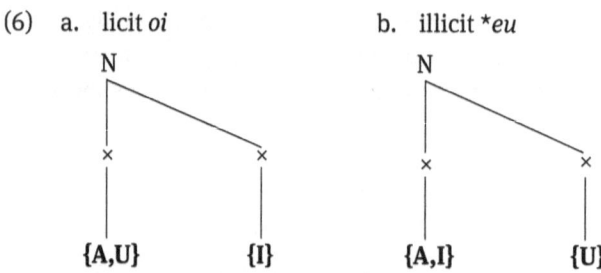

The ungrammaticality does not result from **I** or **U** alone; that is to say, **I** is fine in the head and offglide in English and so is **U**, each one without the other. Rather, it is the particular arrangement that is problematic. Flipping around the two elements leads to ungrammaticality. The question then is, why? Judging by (6), the best we can do is come up with a statement such as, if **I** is in the head, **U** cannot be in the offglide. A statement as stipulatory as this is hardly satisfactory.

In Pöchtrager (2009) it was proposed that the difference in grammaticality between (6a) and (6b) has nothing to do with linear order, but follows from conditions on which of the two elements can sit higher (and c-command) the other one. Even more importantly, the same conditions come back in Putonghua and Japanese. This is discussed in detail in Pöchtrager (2009, 2015) and Živanovič and Pöchtrager (2010). We will focus on the crucial data from English and Putonghua here that show that hierarchy is needed.

Consider first English. The head in both structures in (6) contained the element **A**, by now replaced by structure. The two structures in (6) must therefore be reanalysed as follows, in schematic fashion:

(7) a. licit *oi*   b. illicit **eu*

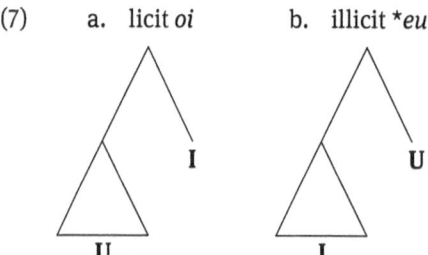

---

etc.) or quantity of vowel (*fill* [fɪw], *feel* [fiːw] etc.) is possible. There is a clear difference in constituency between diphthongs and vowel plus glide sequences.

The triangle represents the structure that replaces **A**, cf. the previous section. In (7a) that structure combines with **U** to yield a rounded vowel, and with **I** in (7b) to yield a front vowel. In both cases, the offglide (to the right) is simply one single element. That single element c-commands the element in the head of the diphthong (to its left). In Pöchtrager (2009, 2015) it was then proposed that the following binding restriction holds, which correctly excludes (7b).

(8) a. **I** can bind **U**, but **U** must not bind **I**.
     b. α binds β iff α c-commands β.

If excluding one structure in English was all the mileage we could get out of binding, then that would hardly be convincing. But as has been alluded to before, the same restrictions come back elsewhere. The charts in (9), taken from Pöchtrager (2015: 265), give 6 relevant cases of complex nuclei in Putonghua. They are all that is needed to understand the effects of binding. One word of warning, though: it is important to keep in mind that the chart represents complex *nuclei*: *waj* is marked as ungrammatical in (9c), but the *sequence* can in fact occur in the language as long as [w] is not part of the nucleus, but the onset. Constituency is crucial here.

(9) a.

onglide	head	offglide		onglide	head	offglide
j	e			w	o	
	ə				ə	
I→				U→		

b.

onglide	head	offglide		onglide	head	offglide
j	o	w		w	e	j
	ə				ə	
I		←U		U		←I

c.

onglide	head	offglide		onglide	head	offglide
j	a	w		*w	a	j
	a				a	
I		U		U		I

As (9a–b) show, a schwa in the nucleus can be coloured by an adjacent on- or offglide. Schwa plus **U** will give *o*, schwa plus **I** *e*. The offglide takes precedence over the onglide (9b): put differently, an onglide can only affect the schwa if there is no offglide (9a). This suggests that on- and offglide are not equal in status. The offglide is closer to the head. In other words, we are dealing with an X-bar structure as in (10): this captures the relative closeness to the head. We will not need to go into the internal structure of the head.

(10)

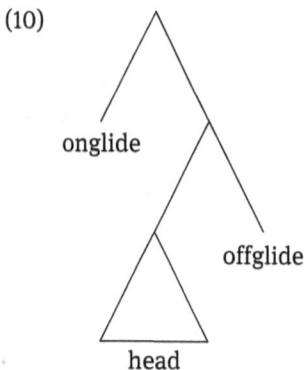

With this in mind, consider (9c). The head, *a*, is not affected by the on- or offglide. By (9a–b) we had to establish that the onglide sits higher than the offglide. In the first structure in (9c) **I** (in the onglide) c-commands and thus binds **U** (in the offglide). This is licit. As soon as we flip around the two elements, as in the second structure in (9c), ungrammaticality ensues. Note that this is the reverse (linear) order of what we saw in English. This demonstrates in a nutshell that it is not order that matters, but hierarchy.

This is a crucial result. To the extent that it seems rather difficult, if not impossible, to derive those effects in a flat model of phonological representation, the hierarchical structures employed in GP 2.0 seem vindicated.

It is even more promising that asymmetries between **I** and **U** are rather commonplace. As such, they provide rich material to test for constituency and serve as an argument for tree structures in parts of a phonological representation that are usually assumed to be free of them. Despite their prevalence, I/U asymmetries have received very little attention in the literature. In what follows I want to look at two more cases. While several details need to be worked out, the discussion shows us the general structure of the argument.

The first example comes from vowel harmony, where the asymmetry between **I** and **U** also shows its effect. Presence of **U**-harmony in a language typically implies I-harmony.[16] Furthermore, the former is always subject to more restrictions than the latter (Kaun 1995). Thus in Turkish **I** spreads to all other (short) nuclei, but **U** only to high targets (Charette and Göksel 1996, Polgárdi 1998, Pöchtrager 2010). In Yakut, **U** also spreads to non-high targets, but only if the trigger is non-high, too. The list could be continued. Some of those differences in behaviour follow as a corollary from Binding Theory. Consider high front rounded *ü* which contains **I** and **U**. In languages with harmony, such a combination could arise by **I** spreading onto *u* or **U** spreading onto *i*. While the former is attested (Finnish, Hungarian), the latter is not, bearing yet again testimony to the difference between the two elements. **U** spreading onto *i*, the unattested case, would require an **U** to make its way into an expression that already contains **I**. Under the assumption that the 'entry point' is on top of **I**, i.e. that an **U** would come to c-command an **I**, we immediately rule out the unattested case as it would lead to a binding violation with **U** binding **I**. This is schematically illustrated in (11).

(11) a. Grammatical 'creation' of *ü*   b. Ungrammatical 'creation' of *ü*

   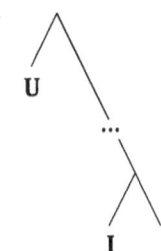

Consider next the lack of front rounded vowels in most of the Romance languages, Slavic, Japanese, English etc. In order to express this gap (like any other), GP 1.x employed licensing constraints which restricted, in a language-specific fashion, the combinatorial possibilities of elements. For English, Kaye (2001) simply postulated that **I** and **U** must not combine. This captures the facts but offers no deeper explanation, as such a ban was understood as an English idiosyncrasy and could not be derived from any more general principle. With Binding, such a general principle comes into reach: if **U** c-commands **I**, that

---

16 In her extensive survey, Kaun (1995) mentions only one case where this seems not to be true, viz. Khalkha Mongolian, cf. also Svantesson (1985). Another case is Yawelmani, but the GP 1.x analysis by Ploch (1998) makes clear that there are various problems that arise when attempting to deal with Yawelmani harmony as a *phonological* process, such as numerous absolute neutralisations.

combination will be excluded. There are two ways for that situation to arise. The two elements could mutually c-command each other (under sisterhood), or **U** could sit higher and therefore (asymmetrically) c-command **I**. If, for whatever reason, the two elements were forced into such an unfortunate configuration in English (unlike French, Finnish, Turkish etc.), front rounded vowels would be excluded. Instead of simply stating that those vowels are excluded, we now know where to look in order to understand why they are out.[17]

Co-occurrence restrictions like those in English could be restated in a flat model. Note, however, that the interpretation offered in the present article is simply a corollary of a more general theory on **I** and **U**. English diphthongs as well as Putonghua and Japanese glides (Pöchtrager 2015) make clear that a purely linear account will not do. Hierarchical structure is inevitable.

Other asymmetries can be derived from such a hierarchical account as well. Recall the discussion of vowel reduction in the previous section. The reduction path [ɛ] → [e] → [i] involves the loss of successive layers of structure. In Eastern Catalan, however, both [ɛ] and [e] reduce as [ə] (Wheeler 2005). Clearly, this involves the loss of structure *and* melody, since [ə] does not contain **I**. If we allow for some leeway in where **I** sits, that difference would follow automatically (Pöchtrager 2018): if reduction takes away the branch where **I** sits, melody and structure will be lost at the same time. The structures in (12), contrasting the two reduction patterns, illustrate this for [e].

(12) a.   b.

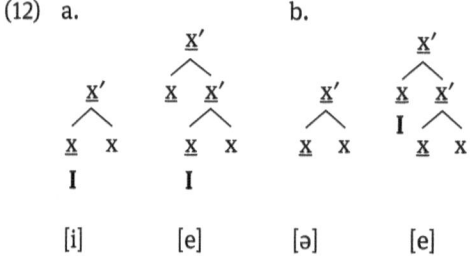

---

17 We already know from English diphthongs that **U** cannot bind **I**. Front rounded vowels are slightly different in that we are talking about what happens within one and the same vowel, not between the two vowels making up a diphthong.

One reviewer also points out the statements in (8) are assumptions, just like licensing constraints. In Živanovič and Pöchtrager (2010) we tried to reduce (8) to statements of an even more basic nature. This is not to deny that (8) or, in the case of successful reduction, the assumptions that (8) follows from are axioms. But while licensing constraints were (by definition) a language-specific means to explain variation, binding tries to capture recurring restrictions across languages by appealing to universal properties of elements.

All we are doing here is making use of a structure that is already set up. By exploiting the possibility that **I** can sit in different positions, we get further mileage out of the model. The reader is referred to Pöchtrager (2018) for further discussion and examples of similar cases involving **U**.

7 Foot as nucleus in nucleus

The quote by Jackendoff in section 1 excluded a rhyme inside a syllable inside a rhyme. This was an important example because it denied that a constituent of a certain type could be embedded within the same type. GP 2.0 employs structures that are very similar to the one Jackendoff deems impossible. There are differences simply because 'syllable' and 'rhyme' (in the mainstream understanding) have no status in the theory, in no version of GP. But still, and that is the crucial point, the structures that GP 2.0 uses do involve self-embedding. (13a) gives the structure of a bi-'syllabic' word with initial stress, i.e. a trochee, following Pöchtrager (2006). It consists of two onset-nucleus (ON) pairs where the second pair is embedded in the first.[18] Each onset-nucleus pair is contained in a box for the sake of clarity. (13b) gives the more mainstream, 'flat' representation where both syllables are sisters within the foot.

(13) a. b.

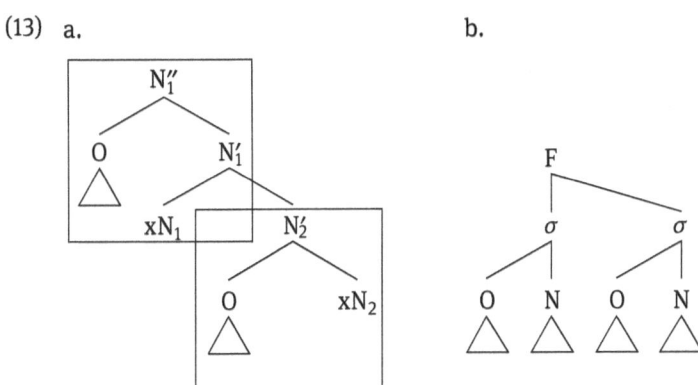

The two structures make different predictions for various phonological phenomena. Firstly, (13a) predicts that there is a constituent break between the initial onset and the rest of the foot. This defines the complementary environments

---

[18] Similar proposals can be found in van der Hulst (2010), Smith (1999), García-Bellido (2005) and Golston (2016).

where English allows [h] (in the initial onset) and [ŋ] (exactly not in the initial onset, but as part of its sister constituent.)[19] This also extends to other approximants ([w], [j]). They occur in initial onsets (*wonder, yonder*) but neither finally (*room,* *roo[w], *roo[j]) nor in word-medial onsets (*shower, dire* etc. involve diphthongs, not intervocalic approximants).[20] The same break is exploited in various rhyme schemes: alliteration pays attention to the initial onset (pre-stress), while end rhyme goes by the complement. If final nuclei are allowed to stay empty (as is commonly assumed in most versions of GP), then this covers both male and female rhyme.

Secondly, (13a) has implications for the analysis of metrical structure. In the representation of stress we find two basic proposals: either the use of metrical grids, where the number of grids represents different degrees of strength, or metrical trees, where the labelling of the branch designates its target as 'weak' or 'strong'. Neeleman and van de Koot (2006) argue against the latter option because such labelling violates fundamental principles which syntactic trees conform to, viz. Inclusiveness. Inclusiveness states that the properties of a dominating node must be derivable from the dominated nodes, but the labels 'weak'/'strong' do not follow from inherent properties of the dominated nodes themselves. Rather, they express relational properties where the label of a branch depends on the labels of other branches in the tree. Neeleman and van de Koot (2006) thus opt for metrical grids since those do not rely on trees and can easily be integrated into the authors' own, flat (string-based) model of phonological representations.

Note, however, that the representation in (13a) also encodes metrical prominence: the weaker nucleus (rather, a projection thereof) is embedded in the stronger one. Instead of relying on labelled branches, prosodic strength is encoded in the tree itself. Such a solution avoids one problem that labelled branches face. It is also very much in line with what Dependency Phonology assumes. As Anderson and Ewen (1987: 101) correctly point out in their discussion of labelled branches, there is no reason why there should be exactly one 'strong' branch (or exactly one 'weak' one, if strict binarity is enforced), except that we commonly interpret the dichotomy as such. On the other hand, in a structure like

---

[19] Most phonological models assume a break between onset and the nucleus, but here the onset is separated from the nucleus and the rest of the tree.

[20] Approximants can also occur in absolute initial position, even when an unstressed nucleus follows: *jojoba* [hə'hoʊbə]. Within the initial syllable, there is of course a constituent break between the [h] and the rest of that substructure, i.e. in this case only the schwa. As for the relation between the entire initial syllable [hə] and the foot ['hoʊbə], I will assume that the former is adjoined to the latter, which would leave the constituent break in (13a) unaffected.

the one in (13a), there will be one and only one nucleus that is not selected by another nucleus, and that will be the metrically strongest one. Hayes' (1995) property of culminativity comes for free and we get a simple definition of the head of the foot: the nucleus which is not itself selected by another nucleus.[21]

Thirdly, in GP 1.x it was assumed that nuclei have a strong relationship with each other, which shows itself not only in stress, but also in vowel harmony, proper government etc. It was assumed that they interact on a special level of (nuclear) projection. In the structure in (13a), that strong bond between nuclei is encoded as well: a nuclear head (or its projection) selects (the projection of) another nuclear head, and that one in turn can select the next etc. This is quite different from onset phrases, which are selected by the nucleus but do not select themselves.

Fourthly, conflating classical 'syllable' and foot structure leads us to expect that there should be interaction between the two, since they are in fact the same thing. All phonological phenomena will have to refer to one and the same tree forming the backbone. This kind of reasoning was the basis of Pöchtrager and Kaye (2014) which looked at metaphony vs. vowel harmony. Metaphony (or 'umlaut', as applied to Germanic, Italian, Korean etc.) typically goes from unstressed to stressed position and is riddled with lexical and morphological exceptions. As such, it does not qualify as a phonological process (cf. Pöchtrager 2014 for discussion of the relevant criteria). Vowel harmony often goes from stressed to unstressed position and, while not free from problems, is much more regular than metaphony and thus more likely to be phonological.[22] What both share is that melodic properties are passed along, even though in the case of umlaut not even that is particularly clear. (For example, when there is no overt trigger.) Part of the problem that Pöchtrager and Kaye (2014) were dealing with is the question: why are there no cases of umlaut (from weak to strong position) that are truly phonological? The representation in (13a) might hold the answer. If melodic properties are passed on along an asymmetric tree as the one in (13a), then it seems that going downhill (away from stress) is much easier than going uphill (towards stress), hence no umlaut *qua* phonological process.[23]

---

21 This is equivalent to Kaye's (1995: 303) Licensing Principle.
22 I am aware of Walker's (2005) article about harmony from unstressed to stressed position, but it is unclear to me to what extent the phenomenon she describes is truly phonological.
23 This is a dramatic simplification; the reader is referred to Pöchtrager and Kaye (2014) for details. Turkish immediately comes to mind as a potential problem. It is claimed to have final stress, yet vowel harmony goes from left to right, so towards stress. However, whether Turkish really has stress has been called into question, cf. Kamali (2011) and Özçelik (2014) who treat (final) stress as intonational prominence, i.e. as a higher level phenomenon.

In a way, this approach shares part of the objectives of Scheer and Szigetvari (2005) in that it attemps to integrate stress into the theory, something which only few studies in GP (or offsprings thereof) undertake.[24] They, too, merge constituent structure (at the level of the traditional syllable) with metrical structure. But their concern is the placement of stress, and not what it is as a formal object. The structure in (13a), on the other hand, has little to say about the placement of stress, but allows for the expression of the head of the domain.

The conflation of syllable and metrical structure as in (13a) also avoids another problem that Neeleman and van de Koot (2006) raise as an argument against tree-based phonological structures as employed in the Prosodic Hierarchy. The Prosodic Hierarchy consists of a fixed set of constituent types where any given constituent is properly included in one of the next-higher level (if there is one): syllable within foot, foot within clitic group etc. Inclusiveness, mentioned before, also militates against the labelling of nodes in such a tree, since the properties of a given node are not recoverable from the nodes it dominates. If, for example, a foot node dominates a syllable (or a nucleus, for that matter), the foot node is understood as different in kind from its dominee, thus violating Inclusiveness. The label F for foot is not the result of the projection of properties of σ for syllable. By merging both levels as in (13a), this obviously becomes a non-issue. The problem with Inclusiveness then stems from a particular choice of model, i.e. the Prosodic Hierarchy.

Such rethinking of the Prosodic Hierarchy as commonly understood makes clear that yet another issue, though related to the previous one, might actually be spurious or at least less problematic. Neeleman and van de Koot (2006) discuss whether vowel harmony could be understood as the percolation of a harmonic feature from the trigger of harmony up through the prosodic tree and then down again onto the target. Vowel harmony seems like an area where a case for trees can be made, because it is easy to interpret it as feature percolation traversing a tree-like structure. Yet, such an approach is deemed inadequate by the authors for two reasons: (i) what happens if the trigger is non-initial? How to avoid trickling down onto the initial position? (ii) Trickling down as such violates Inclusiveness, as information is passed down the tree, instead of projecting upwards. (14) illustrates both problems, building on Neeleman and van de Koot (2006: 1537), contrasting it to the alternative they prefer.

---

[24] Of course, one can find numerous references to stress and feet in the GP literature, but usually those notions were simply borrowed from other theories, under the potentially dangerous assumption that they can be grafted onto GP representations without modification.

(14) a. 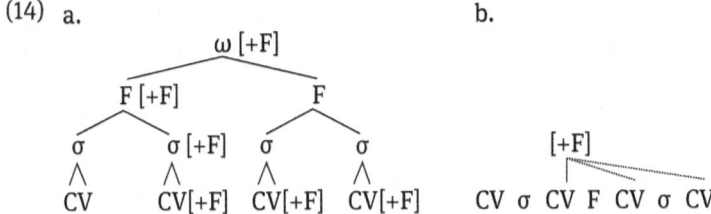 b.

It is somewhat difficult to assess Neeleman and van de Koot's claim as they only talk about the problem in the abstract. But there are at least three issues that deserve mention. Firstly, even if harmony is understood as the spreading of a feature along a linear string, as they prefer, they will have to deal with cases where spreading is blocked (even if we limit ourselves to spreading to the right). In Turkish, **I**-harmony is much freer than **U**-harmony, and in a word like *gör-dük-ler-i* 'what they have seen' **I** spreads all the way from the root to the end (all vowels are front). **U**, however, is stopped by the non-high vowel of the plural suffix *-ler* (only the vowels preceding it are round) and is then also unable to reach the possessive suffix *-i* at the very end, even though that is a high vowel and would thus qualify as a spreading target, had **U**-harmony not been cut off earlier. This is a general property of **U**-harmony in Turkish and must be taken into account by any theory. In a nutshell, there are cases of blocking that have (in all likelihood) nothing to do with any claims of constituent structure.

Secondly, the structure in (14a) is indeed problematic for a trickling-down approach, but of course the problem depends on a particular choice of constituency. If instead of (14a) we had a structure like in (15), things would look very different.

(15)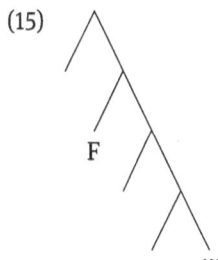

In such a structure harmony can start at any point (here designated by F for 'feature') and propagate downwards. In fact, such a structure would also take care of the directionality of harmony in that, ideally, the shape of the tree should make predictions about the propagation of vowel harmony.

Thirdly, and this relates to the previous point, there is the problem of information being passed downwards in the tree. Neeleman and van de Koot see this as a crucial difference between the two domains as information would have to be passed on in a direction that is generally disallowed in syntax. However, it remains to be seen to what extent anything is really 'passed on'. In the GP literature there is some discussion as to whether spreading is to be taken literally (copying of material) or simply seen as a matter of interpretation only: spreading from α to β would then only mean that β receives the same interpretation as α, without any claim that a particular melodic prime is present in both positions (Harris 1994: 164ff; Charette 2007; Denwood 2002 offers an account that bears similarity to syntactic checking). This is also the understanding of GP 2.0, for the simple reason that due to the shift from melody to structure, there are cases where there is simply no melody left to spread.[25] What this means is that harmony does not imply the transfer of properties, but rather that it determines the interpretation of a certain domain. That certain domain can be understood as delineated by c-command.[26] In (15), the feature F would harmonise everything that it c-commands. (What still needs to be accounted for, of course, is why certain vowels seem to act as 'islands', i.e. they are opaque, block harmony from applying to them and any vowel further down, as we saw in the Turkish example discussed before.)[27]

8 Limits of recursion

Any formal theory of an empirical domain will have to address the question of its predictive power. In a theory allowing for recursive structures it is incumbent on us to ask what the limits of recursion are, if any. Nasukawa (2015: 235–236), whose model of phonology allows for large-scale recursion, simply cites performance as the limiting factor. While performance will certainly exclude phonological objects that take two years to utter, just as it would exclude sentences of similar length, it does not immediately explain why *monomorphemic* phonological objects are not particularly long.[28] The problem

---

25 For details cf. Pöchtrager (2006: 80–84).
26 In Živanovič and Pöchtrager (2010) we argued that c-command is insufficient and that phonology must go one level higher, a relation dubbed c++command. It is my hope that eventually this looser definition will turn out to be unnecessary.
27 For some ideas on neutral (transparent and opaque) vowels cf. Pöchtrager (2017).
28 I exclude polymorphemic structures, in particular those of the so-called analytic type (Kaye 1995), since in those cases one cannot be certain that it is phonology which brings about those structures, rather than morphology. This harks back to fn. 3.

is twofold, involving both infinitely long phonological domains (weak generative capacity) and infinite depth and complexity of embedding (strong generative capacity).[29]

As for the first part, while there are numerous studies on the minimal size of phonological domains, there seems to be virtually no work on the maximal size, or on the question of whether there even is one. Given the extreme limitation of our knowledge in this area, it is difficult to draw conclusions.

As for the second part of the problem, van der Hulst (2010), whose system has parallels to the one explored here, does allow for infinitely deep embedding, but with a clean-up mechanism that then breaks the structures apart and flattens them out for rhythmic reasons. In this way he avoids the problem of infinite degrees of stress that would arise from indefinitely deep embedding. While such a clean-up mechanism is worth considering, it would be even more desirable to have a mechanism in place that does not lead to such a problem to begin with. Here, it might be worth considering interface conditions. Arsenijević and Hinzen (2010, 2012) argue that in syntax, there is *no* self-embedding within the same phase. For them, this has to do with conditions that must be met at the conceptual-intentional interface. If it could be shown that similar restrictions also hold at the sensory-motor interface, then that would be a way to curb overgeneration.[30] Now, opponents of the idea of structural analogy often stress that phonology, unlike syntax, lacks semantic interpretation, and thus, any comparison is futile.[31] Such criticism can be seen clearly in Carr (2006). Yet, what is seen as a problem could turn out to be an advantage: if recursion beyond a certain degree is dependent on semantic factors, as Arsenijević and Hinzen (2010, 2012) argue, and if phonology lacks semantics (in the sense of interfacing with the conceptual-intentional interface), then two birds can be killed with one stone. A recursive system can provide infinite recursion, but does not need to, cf. also Nevins, Pesetsky and Rodrigues (2009).[32]

---

29 The first problem poses itself for any phonological theory, including those with 'flat' representations.
30 For a recent attempt to put the sensory-motor interface in a more central place in phonology, cf. D'Alessandro and van Oostendorp (2016).
31 Though some see phonetics as that interpretation, cf. Blaho (2006), van der Hulst (2006).
32 However, it is difficult to apply Arsenijević and Hinzen's argument one-to-one in phonology. We want to understand why there are limits on recursion, without excluding recursion altogether. The representation of the foot in (13) is a case of self-embedding, yet it would be strange to argue that there is a phase boundary between the two nuclei, and even if that could be shown, it would only show why a nucleus can be embedded in another one, but say nothing on limits.

In a similar vein, the answer to both parts of the question might lie in one of the functions of phonology, i.e. as an addressing system for the mental lexicon (Kaye 1995; Jensen 2000; Ploch 1996, 1999). If one job of phonology is to provide a system for lexical look-up and if the lexicon needs to be populated with, say, 10,000 addresses/morphemes, then that will be possible to do without resorting to overly complex phonological structures. A system of 20 consonants, 5 vowels and a CVCV morpheme structure constraint would already reach that target (20×5×20×5 = 10,000), and many phonological systems are of course considerably more complex than that, despite the counterbalancing effect of various phonotactic restrictions.

Another avenue that seems worth exploring is the comparison to morphology. What is particularly interesting is that, despite the fact that morphology commonly relies on hierarchical structure,[33] recursion reaches its limits fairly soon outside of compounding. This is clear in the case of inflectional morphology, which often terminates a morphological construction, but it can also be seen in derivational morphology, where it is very unclear whether or to what extent recursion is allowed (Dressler 1989, Scalise 1994), especially of the self-embedding type: *great-great-great-great-grandfather* and *re-re-re-write* are possible, though their successful interpretation probably requires extralinguistic skills such as counting. Likewise, *nationalisation* is certainly fine, but ?*nationalisationalise* less so, with each cycle adding to the unacceptability (?*nationalisationalisationalise*). Clearly then, there are interesting parallels here.

9 Conclusion

In this article I have tried to argue that phonological structure is more fine-grained than commonly assumed, with structure taking over the role of many properties that used to be seen as melodic, as well as providing the scaffolding on which the remaining melodic primes have to interact. Such a shift in perspective makes phonology look much more syntax-like. Recursion, the hallmark of syntactic structure, can be found in phonology as well: in a limited fashion, but crucial nonetheless.

---

[33] With exceptions, cf. S. Anderson's (1992) a-morphous morphology.

References

Anderson, John. 1992. *Linguistic Representation: Structural Analogy and Stratification.* Berlin: Mouton de Gruyter.
Anderson, John M. and Colin J. Ewen. 1987. *Principles of Dependency Phonology.* Cambridge: Cambridge University Press.
Anderson, Stephen 1992. *A-Morphous Morphology.* Cambridge: Cambridge University Press.
Arsenijević, Boban and Wolfram Hinzen. 2010. Recursion as a human universal and as a primitive. *Biolinguistics* 4(2–3), 165–173.
Arsenijević, Boban and Wolfram Hinzen. 2012. On the absence of X-within-X recursion in human grammar. *Linguistic Inquiry* 43(3), 423–440.
Backley, Phillip. 2011. *An Introduction to Element Theory.* Edinburgh: Edinburgh University Press.
Blaho, Sylvia. 2006. The syntax of phonology: a radically substance-free approach. Ph.D. dissertation, University of Tromsø.
Bosworth, Yulia. 2017. High vowel distribution and trochaic markedness in Québécois. *Linguistic Review* 34(1), 39–82.
Carr, Philip. 2006. Universal grammar and syntax/phonology parallelisms. *Lingua* 116, 634–656.
Cecchetto, Carlo and Caterina Donati. 2005. *(Re)labeling.* Cambridge, MA: MIT Press.
Charette, Monik. 2007. Turkish Domains. In Meltem Kelepir and Balkız Oztürk (eds), *Proceedings of WAFL 2: Workshop on Altaic Formal Linguistics (MITWPL 54),* 1–20. Cambridge, MA: MIT Press.
Charette, Monik and Aslı Göksel. 1996. Licensing constraints and vowel harmony in Turkic languages. *SOAS Working Papers in Linguistics and Phonetics* 6, 1–25.
Chomsky, Noam. 1995. *The Minimalist Program.* Cambridge, MA: MIT Press.
Chomsky, Noam and Morris Halle. 1968. *The Sound Pattern of English.* New York: Harper and Row.
Clements, George N. 1985. The geometry of phonological features. *Phonology Yearbook* 2, 225–252.
Cobb, Margaret. 1997. Conditions on Nuclear Expressions in Phonology. Ph.D. dissertation, School of Oriental and African Studies, University of London.
Cristófaro Alves da Silva, Thaïs. 1992. Nuclear phenomena in Brazilian Portuguese. Ph.D. dissertation, School of Oriental and African Studies, University of London.
D'Alessandro, Roberta and Marc van Oostendorp. 2016. Gravitational Grammar. Paper presented at the CRISSP Anniversary, Brussels (15 December 2016).
Denwood, Ann. 2002. Vowel harmony in Government Phonology: Three for the price of one. *Altai Hakpo: Journal of the Altaic Society of Korea* 12, 155–182.
Di Sciullo, Anna Maria. 2005. *Asymmetry in Morphology.* Cambridge, MA: MIT Press.
Dressler, Wolfgang U. 1989. Prototypical differences between inflection and derivation. *Zeitschrift für Phonetik, Sprachwissenschaft und Kommunikations-forschung* 42(1), 3–10.
Everaert, Martin B. H., Marinus A. C. Huybregts, Noam Chomsky, Robert C. Berwick and Johan J. Bolhuis. 2015. Structures, not strings: linguistics as part of the cognitive sciences. *Trends in Cognitive Sciences* 19(12), 729–743.
García-Bellido, Paloma. 2005. The morphosyntax and syntax of Phonology: The svarabhakti construction in Spanish. *Estudios de Lingüística del Español* 22. http://elies.rediris.es/elies22/cap5.htm

Golston, Chris. 2016. The rhymes they are a changin': Bob Dylan and syllable structure. Paper presented at Phonology Colloquium, Stockholms Universitet.

Harris, John. 1994. *English Sound Structure*. Oxford: Blackwell.

Harris, John. 2009. Why final obstruent devoicing is weakening. In Kuniya Nasukawa and Phillip Backley (eds.), *Strength Relations in Phonology*, 9–45. Berlin and New York: Mouton de Gruyter.

Hayes, Bruce. 1995. *Metrical Stress Theory: Principles and Case Studies*. Chicago: The University of Chicago Press.

Hulst, Harry G. van der. 2006. On the parallel organization of linguistic components. *Lingua* 116. 657–688.

Hulst, Harry G. van der. 2010. A note on recursion in phonology. In Harry G. van der Hulst (ed.), *Recursion and Human Language*, 301–342. Berlin and New York: Mouton de Gruyter.

Iverson, Gregory K. and Joseph C. Salmons. 2009. Final Devoicing and Final Laryngeal Neutralization. In Marc van Oostendorp, Colin J. Ewen, Elizabeth Hume and Keren Rice (eds.), *The Blackwell Companion to Phonology*, 1622–1643. Hoboken, NJ: Wiley/Blackwell.

Jackendoff, Ray. 2007. *Language, Consciousness, Culture. Essays on Mental Structure*. Cambridge, MA: MIT Press.

Jensen, Sean. 1994. Is ʔ an element?: towards a non-segmental phonology. *SOAS Working Papers in Linguistics and Phonetics* 4, 71–78.

Jensen, Sean. 2000. A computational approach to the phonology of connected speech. Ph.D. dissertation, School of Oriental and African Studies, University of London.

Kamali, Beste. 2011. *Topics at the PF Interface of Turkish*. Cambridge, MA: Harvard University dissertation.

Kaun, Abigail Rhoades. 1995. The typology of rounding harmony: An optimality theoretic approach. Ph.D. dissertation, University of California, Los Angeles.

Kaye, Jonathan. 1989. *Phonology: A Cognitive View*. Hillsdale, NJ: Lawrence Erlbaum.

Kaye, Jonathan. 1990. 'Coda' Licensing. *Phonology* 7(2), 301–330.

Kaye, Jonathan. 1992. On the interaction of theories of Lexical Phonology and theories of phonological phenomena. In Wolfgang U. Dressler, Hans C. Luschützky, Oskar E. Pfeiffer and John R. Rennison (eds.), *Phonologica 1988. Proceedings of the 6th International Phonology Meeting*, 141–155. Cambridge: Cambridge University Press.

Kaye, Jonathan. 1995. Derivations and interfaces. In Jacques Durand and Francis Katamba (eds.), *Frontiers of Phonology: Atoms, Structures, Derivations*, 289–332. Harlow, Essex: Longman.

Kaye, Jonathan. 2000. A user's guide to Government Phonology (GP). Ms.

Kaye, Jonathan. 2001. Working with licensing constraints. In Katarzyna Dziubalska-Kołaczyk (ed.), *Constraints and Preferences*, 251–268. Berlin and New York: Mouton de Gruyter.

Kaye, Jonathan. 2012. Canadian Raising, eh? In Eugeniusz Cyran, Henryk Kardela and Bogdan Szymanek (eds.), *Sound, Structure and Sense. Studies in memory of Edmund Gussmann*, 321–352. Lublin: Wydawnictwo KUL.

Kaye, Jonathan and Jean Lowenstamm. 1984. De la syllabicité. In François Dell, Daniel Hirst, and Jean-Roger Vergnaud (eds.), *Forme sonore du langage*, 123–159. Paris: Hermann.

Kaye, Jonathan, Jean Lowenstamm and Jean-Roger Vergnaud. 1985. The internal structure of phonological elements: a theory of charm and government. *Phonology Yearbook* 2, 303–328.

Kaye, Jonathan, Jean Lowenstamm and Jean-Roger Vergnaud. 1990. Constituent structure and government in phonology. *Phonology* 7(2), 193–231.

Kaye, Jonathan and Markus A. Pöchtrager. 2013. GP 2.0. *SOAS Working Papers in Linguistics and Phonetics* 16, 51–64.

Ladefoged, Peter and Keith Johnson. 2010. *A Course In Phonetics*. 6th edition. Boston: Wadsworth.
Mateus, Maria Helena and Ernesto d'Andrade. 2000. *The Phonology of Portuguese*. Oxford: Oxford University Press.
Nasukawa, Kuniya. 2015. Recursion in the lexical structure of morphemes. In Henk van Riemsdijk and Marc van Oostendorp (eds.), *Representing Structure in Phonology and Syntax*, 211–238. Berlin: Mouton de Gruyter.
Neeleman, Ad and J. van de Koot. 2006. On syntactic and phonological representations. *Lingua* 116, 1524–1552.
Nespor, Marina and Irene Vogel. 1986. *Prosodic Phonology*. Dordrecht: Foris.
Nespor, Marina and Irene Vogel. 2007. *Prosodic Phonology*. 2nd edition. Berlin, New York: Mouton de Gruyter.
Newell, Heather. 2017. There is no word: implications for the phonology-syntax interface. Paper presented at the 40th GLOW Colloquium, Leiden (14 March 2017).
Nevins, Andrew, David Pesetsky and Cilene Rodrigues. 2009. Pirahã exceptionality: a reassessment. *Language* 85(2), 355–404.
Özçelik, Öner. 2014. Prosodic faithfulness to foot edges: the case of Turkish stress. *Phonology* 31, 229–269.
Ploch, Stefan. 1996. The role of parsing. *SOAS Working Papers in Linguistics and Phonetics* 6, 76–105.
Ploch, Stefan. 1998. Non-switch harmony in Yawelmani (and Turkish and Sakha). *SOAS Working Papers in Linguistics and Phonetics* 8, 209–238.
Ploch, Stefan. 1999. Nasals on my mind: the phonetic and the cognitive approach to the phonology of nasality, Ph.D. dissertation, School of Oriental and African Studies, University of London.
Pöchtrager, Markus A. 2006. The structure of length. Ph.D. dissertation. University of Vienna.
Pöchtrager, Markus A. 2009. Diphthongi, e$_i$ know thyselfi. Binding in Phonology. Paper presented at the 17th Manchester Phonology Meeting, University of Manchester (28–30 May 2009).
Pöchtrager, Markus A. 2010. The structure of A. Paper presented at the 33rd GLOW Colloquium, Wrocław (13–16 April 2010).
Pöchtrager, Markus A. 2012. Deconstructing **A**. Paper presented at MFM Fringe Meeting on Segmental Architecture (23 May 2012).
Pöchtrager, Markus A. 2013a. Alveolars, size and lenition. Paper presented at the 21st Manchester Phonology Meeting, University of Manchester (23–25 May 2013).
Pöchtrager, Markus A. 2013b. On A. Paper presented at the Workshop on Melodic Representation, University College London, University of London (12 March 2013).
Pöchtrager, Markus A. 2014. Alternations: the vipers in our bosom. *Dilbilim Araştırmaları* 2, 147–164.
Pöchtrager, Markus A. 2015a. Binding in Phonology. In Henk van Riemsdijk and Marc van Oostendorp (eds.), *Representing Structure in Phonology and Syntax*, 255–275. Berlin: Mouton de Gruyter.
Pöchtrager, Markus A. 2015b. Vowel reduction: sawing off the branch you're sitting on. Paper presented at the 23rd Manchester Phonology Meeting, University of Manchester (28–30 May 2015).
Pöchtrager, Markus A. 2016. It's all about size. In Péter Szigetvári (ed.), *70 snippets to mark Ádám Nádasdy's 70th birthday*. http://seas3.elte.hu/nadasdy70/pochtrager.html (accessed 14 March 2017).

Pöchtrager, Markus A. 2017. Transparent vowels: small cogs in large machines. Paper presented at the 25th Manchester Phonology Meeting, University of Manchester (25–27 May 2017).

Pöchtrager, Markus A. 2018. Sawing off the branch you are sitting on. *Acta Linguistica Academica* 65(1), 47–68.

Pöchtrager, Markus A. and Jonathan Kaye. 2011. What is this thing called Phonology? Paper presented at Leiden University Center for Linguistics (25 November 2011).

Pöchtrager, Markus A. and Jonathan Kaye. 2013. GP 2.0. *SOAS Working Papers in Linguistics and Phonetics* 16, 51–64.

Pöchtrager, Markus A. and Jonathan Kaye. 2014. Phony metaphony. Poster presented at the 22nd Manchester Phonology Meeting, University of Manchester (29–31 May 2014).

Polgárdi, Krisztina. 1998. *Vowel Harmony: An Account in Terms of Government and Optimality*. The Hague: Holland Academic Graphics.

Samuels, Bridget. 2009. The structure of phonological theory. Ph.D. dissertation, Harvard University.

Scalise, Sergio. 1994. *Generative Morphology*. Dordrecht: Foris.

Schane, Sanford A. 1984. The fundamentals of particle phonology. *Phonology Yearbook* 1, 129–155.

Scheer, Tobias. 2008. Why the prosodic hierarchy is a diacritic and why the interface must be direct. In Jutta Hartmann, Veronika Hegedűs and Henk van Riemsdijk (eds.), *Sounds of Silence: Empty Elements in Syntax and Phonology*, 145–192. Amsterdam: Elsevier.

Scheer, Tobias and Péter Szigetvári. 2005. Unified representations for stress and the syllable. *Phonology* 22(1), 37–75.

Smith, Norval. 1999. A preliminary account of some aspects of Leurbost Gaelic syllable structure. In Harry G. van der Hulst and Nancy Ritter (eds.), *The Syllable: Views and Facts*, 577–630. Berlin: De Gruyter.

Svantesson, Jan-Olof. 1985. Vowel harmony shift in Mongolian. *Lingua* 67, 283–327.

Truckenbrodt, Hubert. 1995. Phonological phrases: their relation to syntax, focus, and prominence. Ph.D. dissertation, Massachusetts Institute of Technology.

Wagner, Michael. 2005. *Prosody and recursion*. Ph.D. dissertation, Massachusetts Institute of Technology.

Walker, Rachel. 2005. Weak triggers in vowel harmony. *Natural Language and Linguistic Theory* 23, 917–989.

Watumull, Jeffrey, Marc D. Hauser, Ian G. Roberts and Norbert Hornstein. 2009. On recursion. *Frontiers in Psychology* 4, 1–7.

Wetzels, W. Leo. 1995. Mid-vowel alternations in the Brazilian Portuguese verb. *Phonology* 12(2), 281–304.

Wheeler, Max W. 2005. *The Phonology of Catalan*. Oxford: Oxford University Press.

Yoshida, Shohei. 1990. A government-based analysis of the 'mora' in Japanese. *Phonology* 7, 331–351.

Yoshida, Shohei. 1996. *Phonological Government in Japanese*. Canberra: The Australian National University.

Živanovič, Sašo and Markus A. Pöchtrager. 2010. GP 2, and Putonghua, too. *Acta Linguistica Hungarica* 57(4), 357–380.

Zue, Victor W. and Martha Laferriere. 1979. Acoustic study of medial /t,d/ in American English. *Journal of the Acoustical Society of America* 66(4), 1039–1050.

Clemens Poppe
Head, dependent, or both: Dependency relations in vowels

1 Introduction

In several related dependency-based approaches to segmental structure, segments are assumed to be made up of unary melodic primes that may enter into dependency relations. These primes are known as 'components' in Dependency Phonology (Anderson and Jones 1974; Anderson and Ewen 1987) and as 'elements' in Government Phonology (Kaye et al. 1985, 1990) and Element Theory (Harris and Lindsey 1995, Backley 2011). In this paper, I will adopt the term 'element' to refer to such unary melodic primes.

While dependency-based approaches all assume the same kind of basic building blocks, there is no consensus on how they may be combined and how they are phonetically interpreted (see Backley 2012 for an overview). For the purposes of this paper, we can distinguish between three types of element-based approaches. In one type of approach, elements are assumed to enter head-dependency relations. In the original version of Dependency Phonology (Anderson and Ewen 1987), in Government Phonology (Kaye et al. 1985, 1990), and in Element Theory (Harris and Lindsey 1995, Backley 2011), a distinction is made between 'head(ed)' or 'governing' elements and 'dependent' or 'governed' elements. In the second type of approach, which is known as Particle Phonology (Schane 1984), the relative strength of an element is determined not by its status as a head or a dependent, but by the number of times it occurs in the same representation. The third type of approach can be said to combine ideas from the first two approaches. For instance, in the different models proposed by van der Hulst (1988, 1989, 1995, 2005, 2012, 2015), as well as in the models proposed by Smith (2000) and Botma (2004), both head-dependency relations as well as the possibility of having identical elements within the same segment are available.

In this paper, evidence from English and Middle Korean will be presented in order to argue in favor of the third type of approach. Although allowing for both head-dependency relations as well as segment-internal recurring elements at first sight may appear to be unrestrictive, it turns out that such an approach is necessary to account for the vowel systems of English (RP) and two varieties of Korean (Middle Korean and Seoul Korean). It is shown that the vowel systems of these languages can be insightfully analyzed if we take what Ewen

(1995) calls a 'structural' approach to dependency. In the proposed model, which builds on proposals made by van der Hulst (1988), van de Weijer (1996), Smith (2000), and Botma (2004), the maximum number of identical elements per vowel is naturally limited to two. Moreover, it is argued that representations involving two identical elements need not be analyzed in terms of recursion.

The structure of this paper is as follows. In section 2, an overview of element-based approaches to vowel structure is given. Following this, in section 3 the vowel systems of RP English and Middle and Seoul Korean are discussed. I conclude that, besides the distinction between head and dependent elements in vowels, it is necessary to allow for vowels with two identical elements. Following this, in section 4 I show that in what Ewen (1995) calls a 'structural' rather than 'inherent' approach to dependency relations, the existence of these three types of vowels is only expected. Finally, I consider an alternative analysis based on recursion, concluding that the non-recursive analysis proposed in this paper should be preferred.

2 Element-based approaches to vowel structure

In this section I will give a brief introduction to vowel structure in element-based approaches to vowel structure based on the three elements |A I U|, with a focus on issues related to headedness and the question whether a single vowel may contain multiple instances of the same element.[1] For a more thorough introduction and for discussion of different types of element-based approaches, I refer to Backley (2011, 2012).

An important characteristic of elements is that they are unary primes: they are either present or absent in phonological representations. While elements are primarily thought of as abstract cognitive units rather than phonetic units, it has been shown that they can be defined in terms of acoustic patterns (Harris and Lindsey 1995). In recent years, there seems to be consensus on a basic set of six elements: the vocalic or resonance elements |A I U|, and the consonantal or non-resonance elements |ʔ H L| (Backley 2011, 2012). According to Backley (2012: 66–67), the vocalic elements can be defined acoustically and phonologically as in (1).

---

[1] For an alternative model that posits a fourth vocalic element, I refer to van der Hulst (1995, 2005, 2012, 2015). In his model, the four elements are derived from a more basic distinction between two basic building blocks, C ('consonantal') and V ('vocalic').

(1) Element   Acoustic   Phonological
    |A| high F1 (F1-F2 converge)   non-high vowels
    |I| high F2 (F2-F3 converge)   front vowels
    |U| lowering of all formants   rounded vowels

In analyses of vowel systems, the three vocalic elements |A I U| normally are used to represent the vowels [a i u], which from a cross-linguistic point of view are the three most basic vowels. However, many languages have more than three vowels. In order to account for the vowel systems of such languages, elements can be assumed to combine and form 'element compounds' (Backley 2011). For instance, the vowel system of a language with five vowels like (Tokyo) Japanese may be analysed as in (2).

(2) a |A|
     i |I|
     u |U|
     e |A I|
     o |A U|

There are also languages with vowel contrasts that cannot be captured by simply combining the three basic elements. For instance, it is possible for a language to distinguish between the two mid vowels [e] and [ɛ]. Both of these vowels can be represented by a combination of the elements |I| and |A|, as they are both front, non-high vowels. On the other hand, the two vowels differ in that [e] is realized higher and fronter than [ɛ]. Or, put differently, [ɛ] is realized lower and less front compared to [ɛ]. To express these differences in terms of element structure, different approaches have been taken.

In the approach known as Particle Phonology (Schane 1984), the same 'particle' is allowed to appear multiple times in the same segment. In this approach the difference between the two vowels [e] and [ɛ] (or [æ]) can be analysed as in (3), where the difference is whether the element |A| appears once or twice.

(3) [e] |A I|
    [ɛ] (or [æ]) |A A I|

While this is a possible way to distinguish between different mid vowels, a weakness of this type of analysis is that it is not clear how to limit the number of times an element may appear in the same expression. This issue is also relevant for more recent proposals that allow for recursion of elements, and will be discussed in more detail in section 4. As Particle Phonology does not distinguish between head and dependent elements, and therefore is of less relevance to the main issues discussed in this paper, I will not discuss this model in detail any further. However, its main insight that the same element may occur more than once in the same segment will be shown to be insightful.

A second, more popular approach has been to assume that elements may enter into head-dependency relations (Anderson and Ewen 1987, Kaye et al. 1985, 1990). Needless to say, in a dependency-based approach to phonological structure, such a move is only natural. The idea is that in a phonological expression that consists of two elements, one of the two elements functions as the head, and the other one will take the role of dependent. Because of the greater phonological strength of the head element, its contribution to the phonetic output is stronger than that of the dependent element. Based on these ideas, the vowels [e] and [ɛ] can both be analyzed as consisting of the elements |A I|; the difference between the two segments is which of the two elements functions as the head. Thus, if we indicate headedness by means of underlining, [e] has the structure |I̲ A|, while [ɛ] has the structure |I A̲|.

(4) [e] |I̲ A|
    [ɛ] |I A̲|

The head-dependent distinction and its relationship to phonological and phonetic salience has been applied to non-complex expressions as well. To give a concrete example, in Backley's (2011) approach, a vocalic slot that only contains the element |U| element is interpreted phonetically as the round back vowel [u] when this element functions as the head, but as the unrounded back vowel [ɯ] when it is the dependent element in an 'empty-headed' or 'headless' vowel, which can be defined as a vowel that does not contain a head element but does contain a dependent element.[2] Japanese is an example of a language with this unrounded back vowel, and the fact that it acts as the default epenthetic vowel may be seen as further evidence for analyzing this vowel as containing dependent |U|. From the viewpoint of contrastivity, however, it is arbitrary to distinguish between head and dependent elements in a language like Tokyo Japanese. As pointed out by van de Weijer (1996), in a language with a five-vowel system, dependency relations between the different elements are redundant. Furthermore, the default status of the vowel in [ɯ] can be captured by underspecification as well. This is

---

[2] Empty-headed vowels can be distinguished from what we may call 'empty vowels', i.e. vowels that do not contain any elements.

shown in (5), where a distinction is made between underspecified underlying representations and surface representations.

(5)   Underlying Surface
    a |A| |A|
    i |I| |I|
    u | | |U|
    e |A I| |A I|
    o |A U| |A U|

While there may be alternative analyses, the point is that from a phonological point of view there is no conclusive evidence for an analysis in which the element |U| has non-head status.³

Not all element-based approaches that are based on head-dependency relations allow empty-headed vowels. In Dependency Phonology (Anderson and Ewen 1987), dependent elements are only allowed in the presence of a head element. In other words, dependency relations are only relevant when more than one element is present. This type of approach will be discussed in some more detail in section 4.

A third type of approach combines the idea of dependency relations with the idea that the same segment may contain multiple instances of the same element (van der Hulst 1988; van de Weijer 1996; Smith 2000; Botma 2004).⁴ According to Smith (2000) and Botma (2004), the phonological function and phonetic interpretation of the vocalic elements |A I U| depends on whether they appear in a 'primary' node (i.e. a head position) or a 'secondary' node (i.e. a dependent position), as shown in (6).

(6) Element Primary (Head) Secondary (Dependent)
     |A| lowness   (more) constricted pharyngeal cavity
                              = retracted tongue root (RTR)

---

3 It should be pointed out that in consonants, headedness has been argued to play an important role in distinguishing between different feature classes. For instance, in Backley's (2011) approach, the element |U| may be interpreted phonetically as [labial] when it has head status, but as [velar] when it is dependent.
4 In this context the approach based on the complement tier proposed by Backley (1995) should also be mentioned. In this approach, head elements are analyzed as elements that occur on two different tiers, and dependent elements as elements that appear on a single tier.

|I| frontness (more) constricted palatal cavity
= advanced tongue root (ATR)
|U| backness (more) constricted labial cavity
= rounding

These interpretations are based on an earlier proposal by van der Hulst (1988) according to which elements have a 'dual interpretation' as in (7).

(7) Element Primary (Head)   Secondary (Dependent)
    |A| Pharyngeal constriction   Openness
    |I| Palatal constriction   Advanced tongue root (ATR)
    |U| Velar constriction   Rounding

In this approach, the vowel [u] can be represented as |U̲ U|, and the vowel [ɯ] as |U̲|. As mentioned above, in an element-based approach that does not allow for identical elements within the same expression, the difference between these two vowels can be expressed in terms of headedness: [u] will be represented as |U̲|, and [ɯ] b̲y̲ as |U|. In the same way, distinctions in RTR or ATR have also been analyzed in terms of a difference in headedness (see Backley 2012).

From the above discussion we may conclude that while the distinction between head and dependent elements is uncontroversial in element-based approaches, there is no consensus on whether a segment obligatorily contains a head element, and whether the same element may appear more than once within the same segment. While one may get the impression that the representations employed in the different approaches are notational variants, in this paper I will argue that both headedness and identical elements are necessary in a dependency-based approach. In other words, I will argue that the same element may appear as a head, as a dependent, or both, i.e. as a head and a dependent, in the same vowel.

3 Vowel structure in English and Korean

In this section, it will be argued that in order to account for the vowel systems of the RP variety of English and Middle Korean in an element-based approach that assumes the three vocalic elements |A I U|, it is necessary to posit vowels with identical elements. Furthermore, it is shown that while the existence of multiple 'weak' vowels in English does not provide us with evidence for empty-headed vowels, it seems necessary to analyze one of the two unmarked vowels of Middle Korean as an underlying empty-headed vowel. The implication of these findings is that it is necessary to allow for a three-way distinction based on head-dependent distinctions: in a vowel, the same element may appear as a head, as a dependent, or as both.

3.1 English

The purpose of this section is to show that existing element-based approaches to RP English vowel structure are problematic, and that by allowing for the same element to appear more than once within the same segment, the problems of these earlier analyses can be solved.

To start with, consider the RP English vowel system in (8) adapted from Backley (2011: 43), where I substituted [ɛ] for Backley's (2011) [e] to avoid confusion later on in the discussion. Although Backley (2011) simply calls the vowels in (8a) and (8b) 'short' and 'long', I have added the labels 'lax' and 'tense' to distinguish between the two types of vowels.

(8)   a. short/lax: [ɪ ʊ ʌ ɛ æ ɒ]
       b. long/tense: [iː uː ɑː ɔː ɜː]
       c. reduced: [ə ʊ ɪ ɨ]
       d. diphthongs: [aɪ eɪ ɔɪ aʊ əʊ ɪə eə (ʊə)]

The analysis of the short/lax and long/tense vowels proposed by Backley (2011) is given in (9). The examples added to the phonetic and phonological representations in (9) correspond to the 'standard lexical sets' proposed by Wells (1982). Because Backley (2011) treats [ɜː] as a weak vowel containing the non-head element |A|, it is not included in (9).

(9)   Phonetic   elements   example
      [iː] |I̲| FLEECE
      [ɪ] |I| KIT
      [uː] |U̲| GOOSE
      [ʊ] |U| FOOT
      [ɑː] |A̲| PALM
      [ʌ] |A| STRUT
      [ɔː] |A̲ U| THOUGHT
      [ɛ] |I̲ A| DRESS
      [æ] |I A̲| TRAP

As we can see in (9), Backley (2011) analyzes all non-reduced vowels as containing at least one head element. Unstressed 'weak' vowels, on the other hand, are analyzed as containing only a non-head element (or no element at all), as we will see below when we discuss the evidence for distinguishing between the four reduced vowels in (8). For now, what matters is that what can be called pairs of short/lax and a long/tense pairs are identical in terms of element structure. For instance, both [ɪ] and [iː] contain the single head element |I|. This reflects that not the tense-lax distinction, but the long-short distinction is taken as basic in Backley's (2011) analysis. Thus, the difference between the two types of vowels is analyzed in terms of the number of 'x-slots', as in (10), where the short/lax vowel [ɪ] has a single x-slot (10a), and the long/tense vowel [iː] has two x-slots (10b).

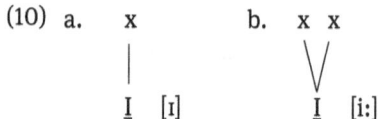

Note that headedness must be used to distinguish between different short/lax vowels. Both [ɛ] and [æ] are analyzed as containing the elements |A| and |I|, the difference lying in which of the two is the head. The fact that two lax vowels must be analyzed as contrasting in terms of headedness shows that the tense-lax distinction cannot be captured in terms of headedness in the first place.[5] This also holds for the slightly different analyses proposed by Harris (1994) and Durand (2005), who also need to use headedness to distinguish between certain lax vowels.[6] Thus, despite the fact that the difference between tense and lax

---

[5] In the analysis proposed by Harris (1994) and Durand (2005), lax vowels contain the phonologically empty element |@|. According to Harris (1994), the default element |@| acts like a canvas to which phonological elements with actual content are added. In this sense, it cannot be treated as a real element on a par with the vowel elements |A I U|. This means that, as pointed out by Backley (1995), in a representation like |A, @|, there actually is no dependent element. Similarly, in a representation like |A, @|, there is no head element. Because of these problems, I do not adopt the element |@| proposed by Harris (1994). A different approach that makes use of a fourth element is proposed by van der Hulst (1995, 2005, 2012, 2015), who posits a counterpart to |A| that corresponds to [high] or [tense]. While it may be possible to analyze the tense-lax distinction in English by introducing this fourth element, in this paper I will try to develop an analysis based on the three vocalic elements |A I U|, which are better motivated than the fourth element.

[6] Note that even though Harris (1994) distinguishes between tense and lax vowels in terms of element structure, he also posits an extra weight unit for tense vowels.

vowels often serves as an example of how headedness may be relevant in distinctions between segments (Harris 1994), it is not possible to analyze the tense-lax distinction in (RP) English in terms of this property.

Not only Backley (2011), but also Harris (1994) and Durand (2005) analyze the distinction between short/lax vowels and long/tense vowels in terms of length: the former have a single x-slot, whereas the latter have two x-slots. While this type of analysis has been popular for a variety of reasons, most of which are in some way related to syllable structure (see Durand 2005), there is an important reason why an analysis based on skeletal slots should be rejected: the tense vs. lax distinction cannot be reduced to one of length in certain varieties of English. As pointed out by Giegerich (1992), who takes the tense-lax distinction to be basic, in Standard Scottish English vowel length cannot be posited as a distinctive feature because it is context-dependent. What is more, in many varieties of Dutch it is also impossible to derive the tense-lax distinction from an underlying distinction in terms of length (see van Oostendorp 2000).

If the distinction between short/lax vowels and long/tense vowels cannot be distinguished either in terms of length, or in terms of headedness, we need another solution. Here I propose to borrow from Particle Phonology (Schane 1984) the idea that it is possible for an element to appear more than once in the same vowel. More concretely, I propose an architecture for vowels consisting of an obligatory head place node and an optional dependent place node which both branch from the vocalic root node (V), as in (11). For the sake of clarity, underlining is redundantly used to indicate headedness of the place node and elements that may associate to this node.

(11)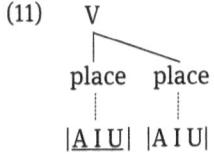

The proposed architecture is similar to that proposed in Smith (2000) and Botma (2004), but differs from it in that no manner node is posited for vowels. The reason for this is that such a manner node would be redundant in vowels (see van de Weijer 1996). Thus, vowels differ from consonants in that they lack a manner node.

In (12), it is shown what the underlying representations of the tense and lax high front vowels of English look like in the proposed model. Although association lines and the place nodes to which the elements associate are omitted from the representations in (12), the representation in (12b) is meant to express that both elements are properly associated to a place node. We will come back to the importance of the concept of association in section 4.

(12)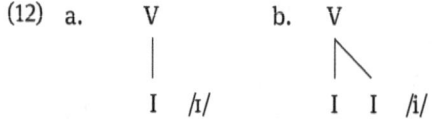

The idea behind the analysis is that in tense vowels a head element is 'enhanced' by the presence of another instance of the same element (see van der Hulst 2015).[7]

The difference in length between tense and lax vowels that exists in most varieties of English (and other Germanic languages) can be derived by means of constraints on surface representations. For instance, we could assume that in the default case, a vowel is linked to a single weight unit (here represented as a V-slot), but that there is a preference for vocalic nodes to dominate only a single instance of the same element, the result of which is that a second weight unit is projected, as in (13), where the inserted V-node is marked by '< >', and the line ending in an arrow indicates the secondary association to the inserted V-node.

(13)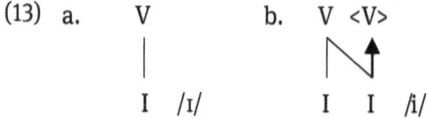

The analysis resembles Anderson's (1993, 1994) analysis of tense vowels in which an element links to two categorical features |V|,[8] both of which are associated to a timing slot above the level of the segment.[9] In section 4 we will

---

[7] Note that van der Hulst (2015) proposes that the feature [tense] is the same as the feature [ATR], represented by dependent | |, an extra element which functions as the counterpart to |A|. The analysis of tense vowels proposed in this paper is similar in spirit to that proposed by Smith and van der Hulst (1990) for tense vowels in Zürich German.

[8] Note that in the vocalic root nodes indicated by V in the present analysis correspond to Anderson's (1993, 1994) suprasegmental 'timing nodes' (which correspond to the skeletal slots in Backley (2011) and Durand (2005)) rather than to his feature |V|, which is part of the 'categorial gesture'.

[9] Anderson (1993, 1994) assumes that every instance of the feature |V| associates to its own timing slot as a 'universal default', which may of course be overridden (as in Standard Scottish English) . Here I assume that the preference of tense vowels to be long in languages

consider the similarities and differences between these two approaches in more detail.[10]

Next, I will sketch two possible analyses of the English vowel system based on the architecture of vowels in (11). The first one is a revision of the analysis in Backley (2011) in which the four pairs [i:]~[ɪ], [u:]~[ʊ], [ɑ:]~[ʌ], and [ɔ:]~[ɒ] are analyzed as differing in terms of the number of x-slots, and the pair [ɛ]~[æ] in terms of headedness. In (14), the element presentations of the short/lax vowels and the long/tense vowels in the revised analysis are given.[11] An assumption underlying the representations in (14) is that in the absence of evidence for dependent status of an element, it will become a head element by default. This assumption will be motivated in section 4.

(14) | Phonetic | elements | example |
|---|---|---|
| [ɪ] | |I̲| | KIT |
| [i:] | |I̲ I| | FLEECE |
| [ʊ] | |U̲| | FOOT |
| [u:] | |U̲ U| | GOOSE |
| [ʌ] | |A̲| | STRUT |
| [ɑ:] | |A̲ A| | PALM |
| [ɒ] | |A̲ U| | CLOTH |
| [ɔ:] | |A̲ A U̲ U| | THOUGHT |
| [ɛ] | |A̲ I| | DRESS |
| [æ] | |A I̲| | TRAP |

In the analysis in (14), the underlying x-slots proposed by Backley (2011) for long/tense vowels are simply replaced by extra dependent elements that are identical to the head elements of the relevant vowels. The choice for |A̲ A U̲ U| as the representation of [ɔ:] rather than |A̲ A U| or |A̲ U U| explains the absence of diphthongization in this vowel. Also, in this way we can say that the

---

like English is regulated by a language-specific constraint (which could be phonetically motivated).

10 Although a review of Anderson's (1994) analysis of the RP vowel system lies beyond the scope of this paper, it should be pointed out that his analysis differs in several important ways from the proposals to be made below in this paper. In section 4, only the formal differences between his model and the model defended in this paper are discussed.

11 The long vowel [ɜ:] can be analyzed in at least two ways, namely as a vowel consisting of two empty V-slots (i.e a long 'empty vowel'), or as a vowel containing two V-slots with a single head element |A̲| in both V-slots.

distinction between tense and lax is that in the former all head elements are enhanced by an identical dependent element. Importantly, apart from the number of instances of an element within a vowel, headedness is used in order to distinguish between the two lax vowels [ɛ] and [æ].

While an analysis along the lines of (14) is possible, a possible objection would be that it results in an asymmetrical vowel system in the sense that not all lax vowels have tense counterparts. A symmetrical analysis is possible if we base our analysis on that of Honeybone (2010). Honeybone's (2010: 54) phonemic analysis, which is largely based on proposals made by Giegerich (1992), is given in (15). Because Honeybone's (2010) analysis is an attempt at a partly polylectal analysis that holds for dialects of English that have the maximum number of contrasts, I have added the RP phonetic realizations to the symbols he uses to represent phonemes.

(15) long/tense   short/lax   (adapted from Honeybone 2010: 54)
      /i/→[iː]   /u/→[uː]   /ɪ/→[ɪ]   /ʊ/→[ʊ]
      /e/→[eɪ]   /o/→[əʊ]   /ɛ/→[ɛ]   /ʌ/→[ʌ]
      /a/→[ɑː]   /ɔ/→[ɔː]   /æ/→[æ]   /ɒ/→[ɒ]

Honeybone (2010), who uses the empty element |@| to represent laxness in lax vowels, proposes the following representations to translate the symmetry at the phonemic level to the level of element structure.

(16) long/tense   short/lax   (adapted from Honeybone 2010: 56)
      |I| |U| |I @| |U @|
      |I A| |U A| |I A @| |U A @|
      |A I| |A U| |A I @| |A U @|

While Honeybone's (2010) analysis is insightful, the use of the empty element |@| is problematic (see footnote 5). Another possible weakness, pointed out by Honeybone (2010) himself, is that the vowel /a/, which in RP is realized as [ɑː], contains the element |I|. Still, the |I| in his representation is redundant, and could be said to be inserted as a default element in non-back vowels. Alternatively, it can be left out altogether, although as a result of this the system would not be completely symmetrical from the viewpoint of element structure anymore.

The analysis can be improved by replacing the element |@| used by Honeybone (2010) by a second instance of the head element in the long/tense vowels. By doing so, we arrive at the representations in (17), where the vowels [ɑː] and [æ] are given with an |I| between parentheses to indicate its status as a possible default element.

(17) long/tense   short/lax   (new 'symmetrical' analysis)
      |I̲ I| |U̲ U| |I̲| |U̲|
      |I̲ I A| |U̲ U A| |I̲ A| |U̲ A|
      |A̲ A (I)| |A̲ A U| |A̲ (I)| |A̲ U|

First of all, observe that as in the 'asymmetrical' analysis in (14), the 'symmetrical' analysis in (17) also makes contrastive use of both identical elements and headedness, although not for the same vowel pairs. Whereas in the asymmetrical analysis headedness is used to distinguish between the lax vowels [ɛ] and [æ], in the symmetrical analysis it is used to distinguish between [ʌ] and [ɒ]. Also note that the distinction is made in different ways: where in the asymmetrical analysis [ɛ] has two head elements (|A̲ I̲|) and [æ] only one (|A̲ I|), in the symmetrical analysis both [ʌ] and [ɒ] have one head and one dependent element (|U̲ A| vs. |A̲ U|). In the latter representations, |U̲| can be thought to be interpreted as [back], |U| as [round], |A̲| as [low], and |A| as [non-high]. Importantly, the proposed representations allow us to analyze underlying tenseness as the recurrence of the head element that is shared with the lax counterpart of a tense vowel in a reasonably straightforward way.

Apart from the symmetry that can be obtained in the analysis based on (17), the underlying representations in (17) can also be used to motivate the diphthongized realizations in RP. In a diphthong like [eɪ], one of the two elements (in this case the coronal element |I|) appears twice, which triggers the insertion of an extra V-slot to which the originally non-head |I| element is associated (18a). The extra |I| is what underlyingly distinguishes this vowel from [ɛ], which contains only one instance of |I| (18b). As mentioned above, in section 4 it will be proposed that in the default case an element will have head rather than dependent status, which means that the structures in (18a) and (18b) can both be analyzed as containing two head elements, |A| and |I|. The difference between [eɪ] and [ɛ] thus solely lies in the extra |I| element in the underlying representation of the diphthong. In the same way, the second part of the diphthong [əʊ] can be motivated by the recurrence of the element |U| in the underlying representation of /o/, which triggers the insertion of an extra V-slot to which the originally non-head instance of this element links (18c). Because its lax counterpart /ʌ/ only contains a single instance of |U|, no extra V-slot is inserted (18d).

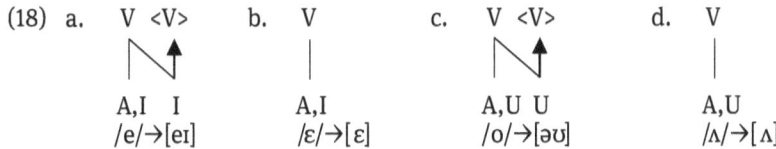

(18) a.   V <V>   b. V   c.   V <V>   d.   V
           ⟋⤴ | ⟋⤴ |
           A,I I   A,I   A,U U   A,U
           /e/→[eɪ]   /ɛ/→[ɛ]   /o/→[əʊ]   /ʌ/→[ʌ]

A possible objection against the analysis proposed for [əʊ] in (18c) is that the phonetic interpretation of the first part of this diphthong does not reflect its element structure. Note, however, that this is no problem if we allow for a certain amount of 'slack' (Scheer 2010) between phonological representations and phonetic interpretation. In the case at hand, the important thing is that there is no contrast with a diphthong pronounced [oʊ]. Furthermore, even so-called long monophthongs can be realized with diphthongization, i.e. [ɪi] and [ʊu] rather than [i:] and [u:] (Wells 1982). The question thus is how much slack we want to allow between phonology and phonetics. An alternative solution to this problem would be to say that the head element |U| is deleted from the first part of the diphthong but that its presence in the input still triggers the underlyingly dependent |U| to be linked to an inserted V-slot. The first part of the diphthong will then be represented by |A|. A related issue is that in the case of [ɔ:], which has the underlying representation |A̲ A U|, there is no diphthongization. Again, we may either say that this is due to slack between the phonological representations and phonetic realization, or we may assume that |U| is inserted in the surface phonological form of [ɔ:], yielding |A̲ A U̲ U|, as in the asymmetrical analysis in (14) above.

Importantly, nothing hinges on the decision to distinguish between the two types of diphthongs discussed here. If we do not want to allow this amount of slack between phonological representations and phonetic interpretation, an issue which we will come back to below, it is easy to adjust the symmetrical analysis and simply say that there is no tense-lax distinction in mid vowels. In that case, the diphthongs [eɪ] and [əʊ] can be treated like what Giegerich (1992) refers to as 'true diphthongs' like [aɪ] and [aʊ], which must be assumed to have two underlying V-slots (or, if we analyze these diphthongs as closed syllables with a coda, as a V-slot followed by a C-slot; see Szigetvári 2016).

For diphthongs ending in [ə], there are again at least two types of analysis available. First, we may posit an underlying empty V-slot, as in (19a). Alternatively, we may posit an underlying |A|, as in (19b), where it has head status, or as in (19c), where it has dependent status. Note that as there is no contrast between diphthongs ending in [ə] and diphthongs ending in [ʌ], it does not matter whether we posit a head or a dependent |A|. A potential problem for the structure in (19c) though is that there turns out to be no convincing evidence for empty-headed vowels in English, as we will see shortly. In any case, the structure of these diphthongs is not predictable from their element structure, and must be assumed to have two lexically specified vocalic slots.

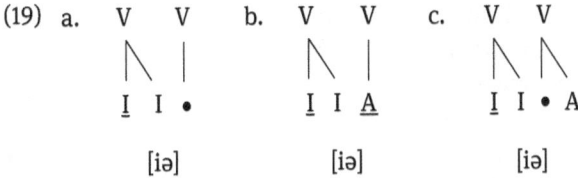

As an interim summary, we may conclude that by allowing identical elements in the same vowel, the tense-lax distinction in English can be insightfully accounted for. Of the two different analyses that were sketched, the symmetrical analysis is more elegant. Which of the two analyses does a better job in explaining alternations, dialectal variation, and historical change is a topic that requires further research. However, regardless of the analysis we adopt, the surface length distinction between tense and lax vowels can be derived from an underlying distinction in element structure without making reference to an arbitrary [tense] feature (see Lass 1976, Durand 2005). In the proposed analyses, the only thing that the different tense vowels have in common is that it contains two instances of one and the same element, resulting in enhancement of certain properties of this element. As we have seen, the phonetic details of this enhancement may differ per vowel.

In the model proposed in this section, both the number of instances of an element within a segment as well as headedness are distinctive properties. As such, the approach may seem less restrictive than an approach that uses only one of these properties. We will come back to this issue in section 4. For now, what matters is that by allowing for both a distinction between head and dependent elements, as well as the possibility to have multiple (nodes linked to) instances of the same element in one vowel, we can account for the tense-lax contrast and distinctions between different lax vowels.

Let us now move on to another interesting question on which opinions vary in the literature, namely the question of whether empty-headed expressions should be allowed or not. In the approach taken in this paper, such vowels would have the structure in (20a), where an empty-headed vowel containing |I| is contrasted with the lax (20b) and tense (20c) vowels of English.

(20) a.   V   b.   V   c.   V
         /\ | /\
        • I   I   I I

         [?]   [ɪ]   [i(ː)]

As a structure like that in (20a) is at least theoretically possible, let us consider whether there is evidence for it in English. Before we do so, it may be pointed out that the idea of 'weak' vowels that contain no head element (or no element at all) is attractive from the viewpoint of relations between prosody and melody. In stress-accent languages like English, prosodically strong positions like the head syllable of a foot show the full range of vowel distinctions, whereas prosodically weak positions like the dependent syllable of a foot prefer reduced vowels. If 'weak' or reduced vowels in unstressed syllables like [ə] have an empty-headed vowel containing only |A|, and non-reduced vowels like [a] in stressed syllables have headed |A|, the weakness in melodic structure can be said to be reflected in the melodic structure (see Backley and Nasukawa 2009). With this relationship between prosody and melody in mind, Backley (2011) actually uses headedness to distinguish between full vowels (vowels in stressed syllables) and weak vowels (vowels in unstressed syllables). The empirical evidence he gives for this approach are stress-related vowel alternations like those in (21), where the relevant vowels are underlined as in Backley (2011: 52), with bold type added to indicate the vowels that appear in stressed syllables.

(21) Vowel reduction in English simplex vowels (adapted from Backley 2011: 52)

Stressed				Unstressed		
Vowel	Structure	Example		Vowel	Structure	Example
[iː]	|I|	d**e**fect (n.)		[ɪ]	|I|	def**e**ctive
[ɪ]		h**i**story				hist**o**rical
[uː]	|U|	b**eau**ty	→	[ʊ]	|U|	bea**u**tician
[ʊ]		w**oo**d				Holl**y**wood
[ɑː]	|A|	dr**a**ma		[ə]	|A|	dr**a**matic
[ʌ]		s**u**lphur				s**u**lphuric

Let us start with the representation of [ə], which according to Backley (2011) contains dependent |A|. Backley (2011) interprets alternations such as *dr[ɑː]ma~dr[ə]matic* as evidence for the existence of two different processes that may apply to vowels in weak positions: vowel shortening and loss of headedness. The evidence for a process of loss of headedness comes from the alternation between [ɑː] and [ə]; if only length were involved, we would have expected the reduced vowel to be [ʌ], which is not the case.

One of the reasons why Backley (2011) does not analyze [ə] as an empty nucleus (see Kaye 1990, among others) is that he uses this representation for a vowel that he transcribes as [ɨ]. According to Backley (2011), [ɨ] appears in a word like *badges* [ˈbædʒɨz], which minimally contrasts with the word *badgers* [ˈbædʒəz]. While such minimal pairs exist, it seems arbitrary to transcribe the second vowel in badges as [ɨ] rather than [ɪ]. Even if the pronunciation [ˈbædʒɨz] exists, this can be seen as a variant of the form [ˈbædʒɪz]. Indeed, [ɪ] is how the vowel in contexts like this is transcribed in Wells (1990). In the absence of a phonological vowel [ɨ], which Backley (2011) represents as containing no element at all, an empty nucleus can be assumed to be the representation of [ə]. The analysis of [ə] as an empty vowel is also motivated by variation in reduction. For instance, the second syllable in a word like *stimulus* may be pronounced either [ˈstɪmjʊləs] or [ˈstɪmjələs]. This makes sense if the latter form is a fully reduced form in which the element |U| is simply suppressed. If [ə] is analyzed as |A|, however, we need to assume that |U| is replaced by |A|, which is an unattractive idea.

Backley (2011) seems to assume that by analogy to alternations such as *dr[a:]ma~dr[ə]matic*, in other vowels in unstressed position headedness is removed as well. This implies that the non-weak lax vowels [ɪ ʊ] and the weak vowels [ɪ ʊ] have similar phonetic qualities, yet different phonological representations. The non-weak lax vowels contain a head element |I̲| or |U̲|, whereas their weak counterparts contain a dependent element |I| or |U|. The idea thus is that two phonetically similar or identical vowels may have different representations depending on whether they appear in a prosodically strong or weak position (i.e. the head or dependent syllable of a foot). While it may be true that [ɪ ʊ] have different phonetic realizations depending on where in a foot they appear, it is not necessary for such phonetic details to be reflected in their phonological representations. First of all, there is no phonological evidence to treat the vowels [ɪ] and [ʊ] on a par with [ə]. That is, under the analysis proposed by Backley (2011), the reduction can be explained in terms of vowel shortening only. This means that there is no clear evidence that the unstressed vowels [ɪ] and [ʊ] must be analyzed as containing only a dependent element. A related problem is that apart from [ə] and the lax vowels [ɪ] and [ʊ], long/tense vowels and diphthongs may also appear in unstressed syllables. An example taken from Wells (1990) is *acorn*, which is realized as [ˈeɪkɔːn]. One way out of this problem would be to say that what seem to be unstressed syllables with tense vowels actually have stress. It may be clear, however, that such reasoning would be circular.

Summarizing, it seems better to analyze [ə] as an empty nucleus, and unstressed [ɪ] and [ʊ] as simply |I̲| and |U̲| in all cases. Reduction in pairs like *defect~defective* can then be captured in terms of the suppression of one of two identical elements. Thus, |I̲ I|, which is realized as [iː], becomes |I̲|, which is realized as [ɪ].

From the above we may conclude that there is no evidence for empty-headed vowels in English. Consequently, English cannot provide us with evidence for the existence of a three-way contrast in which three vowels are distinguished by whether the same element appears functions as a head, a dependent, or both. In the next section, however, a case will be made for the existence of such a three-way contrast in Middle Korean.

3.2 Middle Korean

Middle Korean was a language with seven distinct simple vowels: [i ɨ u ʌ o ə a] (K-M Lee 1972, Lee and Ramsey 2011, Ko 2012). The language is well-known for its vowel harmony system: it had a group of 'bright' vowels [a ʌ o], a group of 'dark' vowels [ɨ u ə], and a 'neutral' vowel [i]. The 'bright' vowels and 'dark' vowels could not appear in the same (morpho-)phonological domain, although both of them could appear together with the neutral vowel.

The phonological specification of the vowels and the type of harmony has been subject of a lot of controversy. Work by Park (1983), Kim (1988, 1993) and Ko (2012), among others, has made clear that Middle Korean vowel harmony involved retracted tongue root (RTR) harmony. According to Kim (1993) and Ko (2012), the vowel triangle in (22) reflects the phonetic properties of the different vowels. The diagonal lines indicate the non-RTR (upper) and RTR (lower) members of pairs of alternating vowels.

(22) Middle Korean vowels (Ko 2012: 174, following Kim 1993: 81)

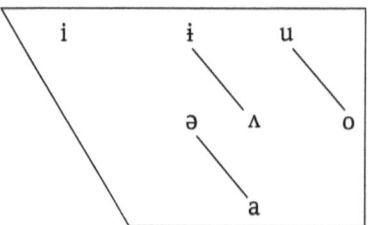

According to Ko (2012), who adopts the contrastive hierarchy framework proposed by Dresher (2009), the Middle Korean vowel system can be analyzed as in (23).

(23) Middle Korean vowels (contrastive features, Ko 2012)
    i [cor] ɨ [ ]   u [lab]
          ʌ [RTR] o [lab][RTR]
          ə [low]
          a [low] [RTR]

The analysis in (23) is based on the contrastive hierarchy in (24).

(24)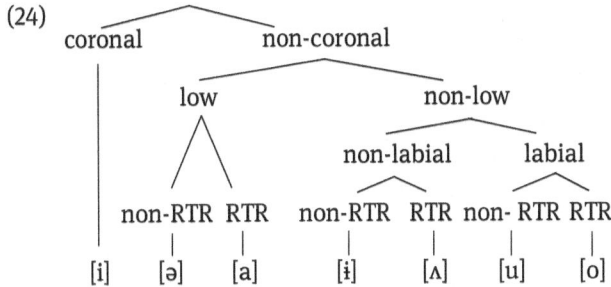

Let us assume that the analysis by Ko (2012) is descriptively adequate, and consider how this system can be interpreted in terms of elements. We will start with reviewing an existing element-based analysis by van der Hulst (1988).

Middle Korean is one of the languages that van der Hulst (1988) analyzes to introduce his model based on the 'dual interpretation' of elements, which was already mentioned in section 2. In this model, the vowels |A I U| have dual interpretations depending on whether they appear as a head or a dependent. The element |U| is interpreted as [velar] when it is a head element, but as [round] when it is a dependent element. In the same way, when |A| appears as a head element, it is interpreted as [pharyngeal], but when it appears as a dependent element, it is interpreted as [open]. Based on this dual interpretation of elements, van der Hulst (1988) proposes the following vowel structures for Middle Korean.

(25) Middle Korean vowels (elements, adapted from van der Hulst 1988)
 i |I| ɨ |U| u |U U|
          ʌ |U A| o |U U A|
          ə |A|
          a |A A|

If we follow Smith (2000) and Botma (2004) and interpret head |A| as [low] and dependent |A| as [RTR] rather than as [pharyngeal] and [open] as in van der Hulst (1988), the analyses by van der Hulst (1988) and Ko (2012) turn out to be quite similar. This becomes even clearer if we present van der Hulst's (1988) analysis in terms of a contrastive hierarchy.[12]

---

[12] For discussions of the use of contrastive hierarchies in element-based approaches, see Scheer (2010) and Dresher (2014).

(26)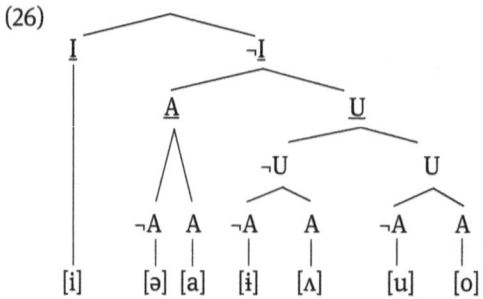

The main difference is that the second split in the hierarchy in (26) involves the opposition between |A| and |U|, whereas in Ko's (2012) analysis the opposition is between the presence vs. the absence of the element [low]. This shows that the representations proposed by van der Hulst (1988) are partly redundant. The reason for this redundancy is that his model does not allow empty-headed expressions. If we do allow such structures, however, his analysis can be simplified as follows.

(27) Middle Korean vowels (elements, simplified)
    i |I| ɨ |A| u |U|A|
             ʌ |A| o |U A|
             ə |A|
             a |A A|

The vowel system in (27) is identical to that proposed by Ko (2012), the only difference being the nature of the melodic primes. This becomes even clearer if we express the analysis in terms of a contrastive hierarchy, as in (28).

(28)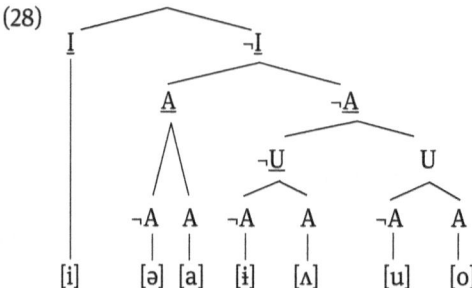

In both the original and simplified element-based analyses, the possibility for a segment to contain two identical elements plays an important role. The main difference between the two analyses is that in van der Hulst's (1988) analysis there are no empty-headed vowels, whereas such vowels do exist in the revised analysis. Let us see whether there are empirical reasons to adopt the revised analysis rather than van der Hulst's (1988) original analysis.

As pointed out by Ko (2012), the vowel /ɨ/ and its RTR counterpart /ʌ/ behave as unmarked vowels in Middle Korean, and are involved in several (morpho-)phonologi-cal alternations. For instance, the grammatical morphemes discussed in Lee and Ramsey (2011) include many suffixes and some particles that start with either [ɨ] or [ʌ] (depending on vowel harmony) when the base of attachment ends in a consonant, but without a vowel when the base ends in a vowel. In (29), examples of the ending -(ʌ/ɨ)myə 'and also' (adapted from Lee and Ramsey 2011: 216) are given.

(29) a. mol-[ʌ]myə   'to not know-and also'
     b. mit-[ɨ]myə   'believe-and also'
     c. hʌli-myə   'break through-and also'

No matter whether one treats these forms as involving insertion, deletion, or morphological selection, the fact that the same two vowels show up in one of the allomorphs of many different morphemes suggests that [ɨ] and [ʌ] are both some kind of default vowel. The two vowels have also been claimed to be phonologically weak from a historical point of view (Whitman 1985, 1994), and are often referred to as 'minimal vowels' in diachronic studies of Korean (Ito 2013, Lee and Ramsey 2011, Martin 1992). The 'minimal' or 'weak' character of /ɨ/ can still be observed in modern varieties of the language, where the suffixes in (29) now only have an allomorph starting with [ɨ], as the vowel /ʌ/ has disappeared from all but one of the modern dialects, Cheju Korean (Lee and Ramsey 2000: 118), where it is realized as [ʌ] or [ɔ] (Ramsey and Lee 2011: 156).

The 'minimal' or 'weak' character of the two vowels is reflected in the revised element-based analysis: /ɨ/ is not specified for any element, and /ʌ/ is only specified with dependent |A|. The analysis proposed by van der Hulst (1988), on the other hand, does not reflect well the idea that [ɨ] and [ʌ] are unmarked and weak vowels in the phonology of Middle Korean and other stages of the language. In the analysis by van der Hulst (1988), the only thing that the minimal vowels have in common is that they are headed by |U|. However, this also holds for the vowels /u/ and /o/. In other words, it is not possible to account for the status of [ɨ] and [ʌ] as weak vowels based on the surface forms.

Still, it would be premature to conclude that it is impossible to account for the weakness of the two vowels in an analysis that adopts the surface representations proposed by van der Hulst (1988). We could make use of underspecification and say that empty-headed vowels are allowed at the underlying level, but not at the surface level. The most straightforward way to keep his surface representations and remove the redundancy from the underlying representations is to assume that the head element |U̲| is inserted to avoid empty-headed vowels, and possibly also completely empty nuclei. This analysis can be represented as in (30), where elements between parentheses are those that appear in surface forms only.[13]

(30) Middle Korean vowels (elements, insertion of default |U̲|)
    i |I̲| ɨ |(U̲)| u |(U̲) U|
            ʌ |(U̲) A| o |(U̲) U A|
            ə |A̲|
            a |A̲ A|

Admittedly, in this analysis we cannot account for the fact why [u] does not show the same weak behavior as [ʌ] even though it contains only a single dependent element in the underlying form. Still, this is not a major problem, and could be due to a constraint against the deletion of |U|. What matters is that, like in the case of English, if we distinguish between underlying and surface representations, the analysis in which empty-headed surface vowels are not allowed cannot be called inferior to the analysis in which such vowels are allowed. Moreover, the fact that in Cheju Korean the reflex of Middle Korean [ʌ] is either [ʌ] or more back and rounded [ɔ] (Lee and Ramsey 2011: 156) may actually be interpreted as evidence in favor of positing the surface specification |U̲ A| for Middle Korean [ʌ].

In summary, while Middle Korean had two weak vowels, [ɨ] and [ʌ], if we distinguish between underlying and surface representations, it is not necessary to analyze one of these vowels as a surface empty-headed vowel in an approach in which a vowel may contain two identical elements.

Now that we have seen that an element-based analysis based on recurring elements is able to account for the Middle Korean data, I would now like to show that the analysis is also well-motivated from a diachronic point of view. In the feature-based analysis in Ko (2012), the weak character of the two minimal vowels can be accounted for by the lack of a place feature. In this sense, the element-based analysis cannot be said to have an advantage over the feature-based analysis. However, when it comes to the relation between Middle

---

[13] At the underlying level, the only difference with the analysis in (27) is that |U| is replaced by |U̲|. Therefore, the only change that needs to be made in the contrastive hierarchy in (28) is to change the split between |¬U̲| and |U̲| into a split between |¬U| and |U|.

Korean and modern (Seoul) Korean, the analysis of RTR harmony as dependent |A| harmony does seem to have an advantage over the feature-based analysis.

In Seoul Korean, it is possible to distinguish between the 'bright' vowels [a ɛ o] and the 'dark' vowels [ə e u i ɨ].[14] Although vowel harmony in modern Korean is not as productive as it was in Middle Korean, vowel harmony can still be observed in the mimetic stratum, and partly in morpho-phonological alternations in verbs and adjectives. Examples of mimetic forms taken from Lee and Yoshida (1998) are given in (31). According to these authors, the forms with bright vowels, which they call 'light' vowels, have 'lighter' meanings than those with dark vowels.

(31) a. bright-bright dark-dark
      kaŋcʰoŋ   kəŋcʰuŋ   'skipping'
      cʰals'ak   cʰəls'ək   'lapping'
      p'ɛcok   p'icuk   'protruding'
      c'ɛlkaŋ   c'ilkəŋ   'chewing'
  b. bright-dark dark-dark
      kaŋcʰuŋ   kəŋcʰuŋ   'skipping'
      omcuk   umcuk   'shivering'
      p'ɛtul   p'itul   'zigzag'
  c. dark-dark dark-bright
      p'icuk   *picok   'protruding'
      c'ilkəŋ   *c'ilkaŋ   'chewing'

As can be seen in (31a), mimetic forms may take on different shapes, where [a] alternates with [ə], [o] with [u], and [ɛ] with [i]. As shown in (31b), however, high vowels (all of which are dark) may appear freely after any vowel. When the first syllable contains a high vowel, on the other hand, it may not be followed by a bright vowel, as shown in (31c). The generalization that can be made is that any dark vowel in non-initial position must be preceded by another dark vowel. This suggests that regardless of the element or feature that is used to describe dark vowels, the feature 'dark' in non-initial position is only allowed if the initial syllable contains the same feature.

In (32), examples taken from Lee (2004) and Lee and Yoshida (1998) show how the infinitive suffix [-a/ə] alternates based on the final vowel of the stem.

---

14 There is evidence that the vowels [e] and [ɛ] (or [æ]) have merged in the speech of most speakers of Seoul Korean (see Shin et al. 2013: 99–101). A discussion of the consequences of this merger for the analysis of the Seoul Korean vowel system lies beyond the scope of this paper.

(32) a cap-a   'take-INF'
     nok-a   'melt-INF'
   b mɛc-ə   'tie-INF'
   c cuk-ə   'die-INF'
     me-ə   'carry-INF'
     ki-ə   'crawl-INF'
     nɨc-ə   'be late-INF'

As can be seen in (32a) and (32c), verbs whose final syllable (in this case only syllable) contains [a] or [o] take the allomorph with the bright vowel [a], whereas verbs with a dark vowel in the final syllable ([u], [e], [i], or [ɨ]) take the allomorph with the dark vowel [ə]. However, the verb in (32b) shows that 'vowel harmony' in the verbal paradigm is better analyzed as a morphophonological alternation rather than the application of a phonological rule: although the stem contains the vowel [ɛ], the allomorph [-ə] rather than [-a] is selected. This can be thought to be related to the merger of [ɛ] and [e] mentioned in footnote 14. Moreover, as pointed out by Lee (1994), even verbs whose final syllable contains [a] or [o] in colloquial speech may take the allomorph [-ə]. Therefore, vowel harmony in Korean verbs (and adjectives) cannot be said to be fully regular anymore. Still, even if the rules of vowel harmony are morphophonological rather than phonological, these rules need representations to refer to. Let us see whether we can come up with an element-based analysis in which we can account for the partially continuing relevance of vowel harmony in Seoul Korean.

Lee and Yoshida (1998) propose the element specifications for Seoul Korean in (33).

(33) Seoul Korean vowels (Lee and Yoshida 1998)
     i |I| ɨ | | u |U A|
     e |A I| ə |A| o |A̲ U|
     ɛ |A̲ I| a |A̲|

Based on these element specifications, they analyze Seoul Korean vowel harmony as 'A-head alignment': an element unspecified for headedness only becomes headed when licensed by a lexical instance of |A̲|.[15]

---

[15] Lee (2004) analyzes Korean vowel harmony in Korean as ATR-harmony in which the feature [ATR] is expressed by the additional element |Ɨ| (see Kaye et al. 1985).

In an approach that allows identical elements in the same vowel, we may posit the representations for the vowels of Seoul Korean in (34) instead.

(34) Seoul Korean vowels (new analysis)
 i |I| ɨ |(U)| u |(U) U A|
 e |I̲ A| ə |A| o |(U) U A|
 ɛ |I̲ A A| a |A̲ A|

As can be observed in (35), the revised element-based analysis of Seoul Korean is nearly identical to that of Middle Korean. The main difference is that the vowel [ʌ] was lost. Note that the newly created vowels [e] and [ɛ] have exactly the same structure as the vowels of which they are historically combinations. This means that in the newly proposed element-based approach, dependent |A| harmony can still be observed in Seoul Korean, but simply is becoming less active and not fully regular.

(35) Seoul Korean   Middle Korean
 I |I| i |I|
 ɨ |(U)| ɨ |(U)|
 (-) (-)   ʌ |(U) A|
 u |(U) U| u |(U) U|
 o |(U) U A| o |(U) U A|
 ə |A| ə |A|
 a |A A| a |A A|
 e |A̲ I| (ə + i) (|A| + |I|)
 ɛ |A̲ A I| (a + i) (|A̲ A| + |I|)

While the representations are highly similar to those of Middle Korean, their phonetic interpretations are not the same: whereas dependent |A| was interpreted as [RTR] in Middle Korean, it seems to have been reinterpreted as [non-high] in Seoul Korean. Depending on whether the element |A| occurs once or twice in the vowel, its phonetic interpretation differs: one instance of |A| yields a mid vowel, regardless of headedness. Two instances of |A|, on the other hand, yield a low vowel. We may thus conclude that Seoul Korean vowel harmony involves dependent |A|, which is interpreted as [non-high] or [low] depending on whether it appears once or twice (cf. Particle Phonology; Schane 1984).

In the analysis based on contrastive features proposed by Ko (2012), the feature systems of Middle Korean and Seoul Korean are quite different. As a result, the same generalizations about changes in vowel harmony cannot be made.

This becomes clear when we compare the element-based analysis with the analysis proposed by Ko (2012).

(36) | Vowel | Elements | Contrastive features |
|---|---|---|
| /i/ | |I̲| | [high] [cor] |
| /ɨ/ | |U| | [high] |
| /u/ | |U̲| | [high] [lab] |
| /o/ | |U̲ A| | [lab] |
| /ə/ | |A̲| | [ ] |
| /a/ | |A̲ A| | [low] |
| /e/ | |A̲ I| | [cor] |
| /ɛ/ | |A̲ A I̲| | [low] [cor] |

As can be seen in (36), there is no feature that either all the 'bright' vowels /a ɛ o/ or all the 'dark' vowels /ə e u i ɨ/ have in common. Therefore, it is not clear how (the remnants of) vowel harmony in Seoul Korean could be accounted for in the contrastive feature approach.[16]

Another problem for the analysis in Ko (2012) is that the weak vowel [ɨ] has a feature specification, whereas the vowel [ə], which does not behave as an unmarked vowel in Seoul Korean, is not specified for any feature. In the newly proposed element-based analysis, on the other hand, the unmarked character of [ɨ] is properly reflected in its representation.[17]

The fact that the representations of vowels in Seoul Korean are nearly identical to those of Middle Korean can be taken as support for the element-based analysis, and thereby as additional evidence for the approach in which the same element may appear twice in the same segment.

The conclusions we can draw on the basis of the discussion of Middle Korean are similar to those drawn in the section on English above. In both languages, it seems necessary to allow for vowels that contain two instances of the same vowel. At the same time, in both languages there is no strong evidence for empty-headed vowels (other than totally empty nuclei) in surface forms. Still, there is one important difference between the languages: in English, it only seems necessary to posit a single 'weak' vowel, the empty nucleus [ə], whereas in Middle Korean it seems necessary to posit an empty-headed vowel

---

16 Ko (2012) does not discuss (the remnants of) vowel harmony in modern varieties of Korean.
17 See Rhee (2002) for different types of arguments for treating Seoul Korean [ɨ] as an underlying empty nucleus. Note though that Rhee (2002) assumes [ɨ] remains empty at the surface. Whether analyzing [ɨ] as a surface empty vowel is to be preferred to analyzing it as a vowel with inserted |U| is a question that is not relevant for the points made here.

that contrasts with a completely empty vowel at the underlying level. Moreover, this empty-headed vowel also contrasts with two other vowels that contain the same element. As a result, there is a three-way distinction between |A| ([ʌ]), |A̲| ([ə]), and |A̲ A| ([a]).

Before we move on to a discussion of how the proposed model compares to related dependency-based models, some comments on the cross-linguistic interpretation of elements are in order. In earlier approaches that allow the same element to appear twice in the same vowel (van der Hulst 1988, Smith 2000, Botma 2004) that the interpretation of elements is cross-linguistically universal. Evidently, the above analyses proposed for English and Korean are only possible if we depart from this assumption. In the analysis proposed for Middle Korean, dependent |A| was argued to be interpreted as [RTR]. For Seoul Korean, on the other hand, it was proposed that dependent |A| functions as the feature [non-high]. It thus seems that the same dependent element may be interpreted differently in different stages of the same language. What is more, in the analysis proposed for English, the interpretation of the expression |A̲ A| is [tense], even though tenseness has been claimed to be related to [ATR] rather than [RTR].[18] From this we may conclude that that both within and across languages, the same element may be interpreted in quite different ways, depending on the vowel system. Considering the existence of 'slack' between phonological representations and the phonetic output, it seems better to assume that elements "provide some gross indication" (Scheer 2010: 2531) rather than very specific phonetic features. In the context of this paper, giving up the universal interpretation of dependent elements allows us to analyse the feature [tense] as 'enhancement' of some of the basic properties of the element by using it twice, which seems a good characterization of tenseness. Thus, element-based representations should be phonologically motivated and roughly match the acoustic properties that have been proposed to define the elements in question, without insisting on fixed cross-linguistic phonetic realizations for head and dependent instances of elements in different contexts.

4 Identical elements in vowels and infra-segmental structure

In the previous section, evidence was presented for vowels with identical elements, one head and one dependent. Furthermore, evidence was presented for

---

[18] See Harris (1994) for some discussion of the relation between [ATR] and [tense].

the existence of empty-headed vowels at the underlying level. It was also shown how such vowels can be represented in a model in which a vowel branches into a head and a dependent place node. In this section, it will be discussed how the proposed model differs from related dependency-based approaches.

4.1 Inherent dependency versus structural dependency

As discussed above, element headedness can be defined in terms of dependency relations between different elements within the same segment (Anderson and Ewen 1987). Van der Hulst (1989) points out that under the original relational definition of melodic dependency, which Ewen (1995) calls 'inherent dependency', the concept of headedness can be formally expressed as in (37), where the head element 'governs' the dependent element.

(37)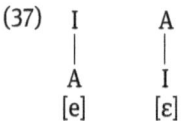

A consequence of this formalism is that a dependent element may only be present in the presence of a head element that governs it (Ewen 1995). However, as discussed by Ewen (1995), dependency can also be defined in 'structural' terms, as in feature geometry models (Clements 1985, McCarthy 1988). In such an approach, the vertical lines in (37) can be said to express 'geometrical anchorage' (Durand 1990) rather than dependency in terms of 'relative contributions' of the different elements to the segment (Ewen 1995). Van der Hulst (1989) points out that if we assume headedness to involve domination, it can also be expressed structurally as in (38), where there is a head-dependency relation between two sisters (adapted from van der Hulst 1989: 260).

(38)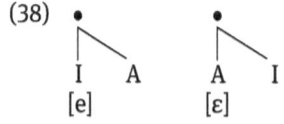

The representations in (38) at first sight appear to be identical to those adopted in this paper. Concerning representations like this, van der Hulst (1989) remarks that a common assumption about constituent-based headedness is that the head of the two sisters is of the same type as the mother node. If so, one may wonder whether the representations in (38) are simply notational variants of those in (39), which involve recursion of elements in a way similar to that in the fully recursive model proposed by Nasukawa (2014), which will be discussed below.

(39) a.   I   b.   I   vocalic node

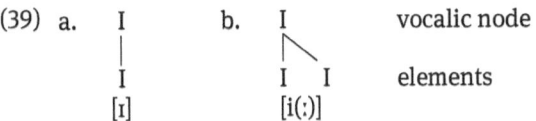

         I   I I   elements
        [ɪ]   [i(ː)]

In this paper, I do not adopt the view that elements themselves project to higher level structure. One reason for this is that it is not clear how we could represent an empty-headed segment if the projecting head node is absent.[19] Rather, as pointed out in the previous section, I assume that the place nodes are terminal nodes to which elements may be associated, as in (40), where dependency relations are indicated by solid lines, and association is indicated by dotted lines. These representations do more justice to the idea that elements are melodic primes as opposed to structural units.

(40) a.   V   b.   V   vocalic node

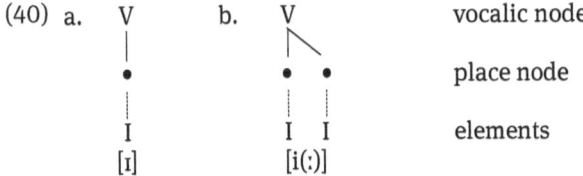

         •   • •   place node

         I   I I   elements
        [ɪ]   [i(ː)]

The structural view of headedness adopted in this paper is crucial for the proposed analyses, because it enables us to posit empty-headed vowels. I will now illustrate the difference between the structural and inherent interpretations of headedness more concretely by taking another look at the analyses proposed for English and Korean.

In the analysis of English proposed in the previous section, the difference between lax and tense vowels was argued to lie in the number of underlying elements. If we represent two identical elements as elements that are linked to separate place nodes, the two vowels [ɪ] and [iː] can be represented as in (41), where the second root node ('<V>') is assumed to be inserted to satisfy a constraint that forces segments with two identical elements to have two root

---

[19] In section 4.3 below, it will be shown how this can be done in the model proposed by Nasukawa (2014) in which head-dependency relations are reversed.

nodes. The arrow on the line pointed at the inserted V-node in (41b) again indicates that the link between the place node and the root node is inserted as well.

(41) a. V   b. V <V>   root node

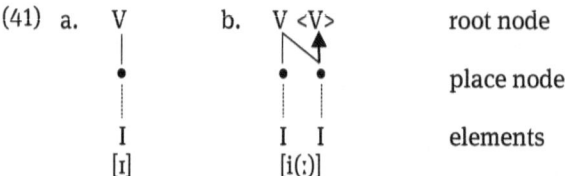

                                place node

         I   I I   elements
         [ɪ]   [i(ː)]

In the approach based on inherent dependency, the difference between these two vowels can be expressed as in (42) (see Anderson 1993, 1994). Note that in this approach neither of the timing slots is assumed to be underlying.

(42) a. •   b. •   timing slot

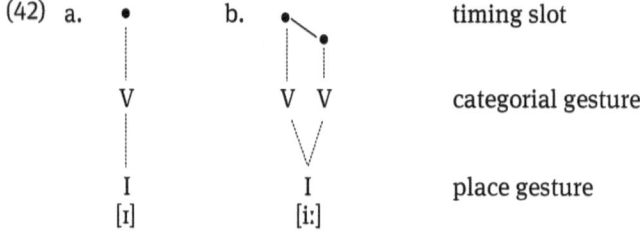

         V   V V   categorial gesture

         I   I   place gesture
         [ɪ]   [iː]

While the structures in (41) and (42) have a number of important similarities, there are also some important differences. One obvious difference is that the representation in (41) contains two identical elements, whereas its counterpart in (42) contains a single element that is associated to two |V| elements in the so-called categorial gesture. While it may be possible to represent vowels with the same element in both the head and the dependent node in the structural approach to headedness as well, it is not immediately clear what the consequence of this would be for processes like delinking and spreading. While lack of space prevents me from considering this issue in detail, I would like to point out that we should either rule out elements that are linked to both the head and dependent node at the same time, or rule out identical elements within the same vowel, because otherwise we would expect both types of vowels to be able to contrast with each other.

A more crucial difference between the structures in (41) and (42) lies in the interpretation of the relations between the different nodes. The difference between these relations is expressed by distinguishing between solid lines, which indicate relations of dependency, and association lines, which do not. To understand the importance of this difference, let us consider the representation in (43), which contains two |V| elements, the first of which does not have a place element associated to it.[20] In the inherent approach, the absence of a place element does not prevent the left-hand |V| element from being phonetically interpreted. Furthermore, it is not the case that the place element |A|, which is associated to the right-hand |V|, is dependent by virtue of being associated to the right-hand |V| rather than the left-hand |V| in the categorial gesture. Rather, in the absence of another place element, there is no dependency relation. The whole structure thus would be phonetically interpreted as something like a short diphthong [əa].

(43)

If we distinguish between underlying and surface representations as in Anderson (1994), however, empty-headed vowels in the approach based on inherent dependency may be represented as in (44b), which contrasts both with the structure in (44a) which contains a single element, and the one in (44c) which contains two identical elements. The representations in (44) correspond to the three vowels which only contain |A| in Middle Korean discussed in section 3.2.

(44)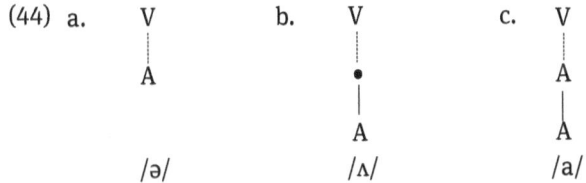

In the structural approach, on the other hand, the representations in (44) would be as in (45).

---

20 Note in passing that the representation in (43) is not in line with the idea that "[a]s a universal default, each instance of V is associated with a 'timing slot' in the suprasegmental structure" (Anderson 1993: 423). See Anderson and Ewen (1987) for discussion of the representation of short diphthongs in Dependency Phonology.

(45) a.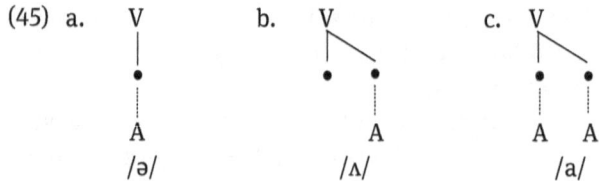

Although the representations in (44) and (45) may look like representational variants, there are two differences. For one, the representation in (44c), but not the one in (45c), involves an element directly dominating another instance of the same element. For another, in the structural approach, the number of identical elements is naturally constrained to two, whereas this is not the case in the inherent approach in (44).

It remains an open question whether surface empty-headed vowels are allowed. All we can say for now is that we were not able to find clear evidence for such vowels in English and Middle Korean. In section 3, it was argued that underlyingly empty-headed vowels may still be argued to contain the element |U| in the surface form, as in (46b).

(46) a.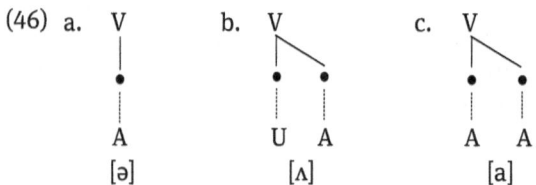

In the absence of evidence to the contrary, we may assume that surface empty-headed vowels are not allowed due to a simple principle which says that every segment must contain a head element.

Summarizing, although no good arguments can be found in English for the need for empty-headed vowels (section 3.1), an underlying empty-headed vowel was argued to be necessary in the analysis of Middle Korean, which had a vowel system with multiple weak vowels (section 3.2). While such underlying empty-headed vowels are possible in both the inherent and the structural approach to headedness, an advantage of the structural approach is that the number of identical elements per segment is naturally limited to two.

4.2 Head-dependent asymmetries and segmental complexity

In the model proposed in this paper, a vowel may contrast with another vowel not only in terms of the presence vs. the absence of a melodic prime, but also in terms of whether there is an element linked to the head node, to the dependent node, or to both the head and the dependent nodes. While these distinctions should be sufficient to account for any vowel system – an assumption that will obviously need further research – the question arises what happens with elements in languages with relatively simple vowel systems in which it is not necessary to use the head-dependent distinction and the option of identical elements, let alone both.

Starting with a three-vowel system consisting of [i a u], we may simply assume that on the surface these vowels will contain the elements |I|, |A|, and |U|, respectively. The fact that headedness is redundant in a vowel system like this can be accounted for by simply assuming that the V-slot will only dominate a single node, which by default is the head. This idea can be expressed by means of the Head-by-Default principle in (47).

(47) Head-by-Default: An element is linked to the head node by default.

The Head-By-Default principle contrasts with the more generally accepted idea that an expression may have only a single head (Kaye et al. 1985, 1990; Harris 1994). Clearly, the Head-By-Default principle is better compatible with the idea that, all else being equal, heads allow for more complexity than dependents than a principle that limits the number of head elements to one.[21] The principle can be seen as related to the head-dependent asymmetries discussed in van de Weijer (1996) and Dresher and van der Hulst (1998): heads are structurally strong, and as such may contain a rich amount of structure, whereas dependents are structurally weak, and therefore may contain only a limited amount of structure. More concretely, vowels without a place-specified head may be avoided because the dependent node may not be more complex than the head node. It should be clear that because the Head-By-Default principle is a default mechanism, it will only apply in the absence of evidence for dependent status of an element. In other words, the principle interacts with other principles or constraints, such as language-specific licensing constraints (see Charette and Göksel 1994, 1996; Kaye 2001), which specify the possible element combinations and head-dependent combinations in a language. To give a concrete

---

[21] See also Anderson and Ewen (1987), who allow a dependency relation called 'mutual dependency'.

example, in a fully worked out analysis of English vowels based on the 'symmetrical' representations in (17) in section 3, we would need to explain why it is possible for the mid tense vowels to have more dependent elements than head elements.

While in a three-vowel system consisting of the vowels [i a u] all elements can be thought to be specified at the surface, at least at the underlying level, one of them may be left underspecified (Dresher 2014). Evidence for underspecification may come from phonological processes like default vowel epenthesis. Whether it is always necessary to assume underlying underspecification is a question that cannot be answered in the present paper (see Anderson 1994, Scheer 2010 and Dresher 2014 for discussion).

A five-vowel system consisting of the vowels [i e a o u] can be assumed to have two additional representations for [e] and [o], namely |A I| and |A U|. As in a system like this headedness is again redundant, all elements can be assumed to have head status.

Next, let us consider a system with the seven full vowels [i e ɛ a ɔ o u]. In the case of seven vowels, only combining the different elements does not suffice. Therefore, we need to introduce either distinctions in headedness, or vowels with two identical elements. The representations of these two options are given in (48) and (49).

(48) a. V　　　　 b. V
　　　　 ⋀　　　　　　 ⋀
　　　　I　A　　　　　A　I
　　　　[e]　　　　　　[ɛ]

(49) a. V　　　　 b. V
　　　　 ⋀　　　　　　 ⋀
　　　　I,A　I　　　　A,I　A
　　　　[e]　　　　　　[ɛ]

It may be clear that the representations in (48) are simpler than those in (49). What is more, even if our theory allows for identical elements within the same segment, this may still be seen as a marked case. Based on these two arguments, we may assume that vowels in which the same element acts as both a head and a dependent will only be posited if there is clear evidence for this. Such clear evidence can be thought to be available in a vowel system with the ten full vowels [i ɪ e ɛ a ɑ ɔ o ʊ u]. In a system like this, the vowel pairs [i]~[ɪ], [e]~[ɛ], and [a]~[ɑ] can only be analysed by allowing the same element in both the head and the dependent.

Based on the above line of reasoning we may conclude that contrasts in vowel systems will typically be based on the distinctive properties in (50), in that order.

(50) a. presence vs. absence of elements
 b. presence vs. absence of elements;
 head vs. dependent
 c. presence vs. absence of elements;
 head vs. dependent;
 head vs. dependent vs. head and dependent

Summarizing, the segmental architecture proposed in this paper accommodates the analysis of vowels with identical elements and vowels that lack a head place element. The former type of vowel was argued to be necessary in the analysis of English vowels, and both types of vowels in the analysis of vowels in Middle Korean. Furthermore, the proposed segmental architecture also obviates issues related to headedness in simple vowel systems in which there is no evidence on the basis of which it can be determined which of two (or more) elements is the head and which the dependent.

4.3 A recursion-based alternative approach

In the final part of this section, let us briefly consider the implications of the data and analyses discussed in this paper for the fully recursive model developed by Nasukawa (2014) which is adopted in some of the papers in this volume (Lin, this volume, Backley and Nasukawa this volume, Onuma and Nasukawa this volume). In section 4.1, I argued against an approach in which elements themselves are taken to be structural nodes. In 'Precedence-free Phonology' (Nasukawa 2014), however, this idea is adopted. Nasukawa (2014) takes the idea of element recursion to its logical extreme and proposes that the nucleus itself is one of the three vocalic elements |A I U|, the choice among which is made on a language-particular basis. Examples of representations of vowels are given in (51). The nucleus and its projections form the structure of syllables (A″) in which the onset, which is left empty, occupies the specifier position.

(51)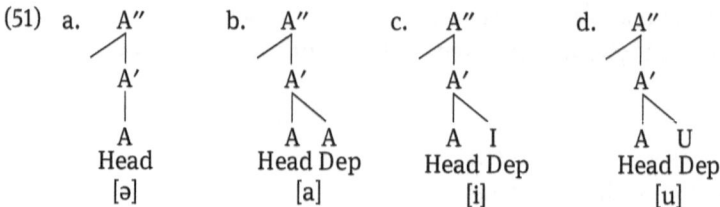

In the fully recursive model, the roles of heads and dependents are reversed. This is a crucial move, as this is what makes it possible to analyze weak vowels as lacking structure while at the same time assuming that elements are structural units themselves. This means that a weak vowel like [ə] can be analyzed in terms of a structure in which a head element lacks a complement (51a). Non-weak vowels, on the other hand, are analyzed as a structure in which a dependent element is the complement to a projection of the head (51b, c, d). The weakness of head elements is also reflected by their failure to make any contribution to the phonetic interpretation of the whole expression in the presence of dependent elements. This becomes clear from the forms in (51c) and (51d), where |A| is not phonetically interpreted. In other words, the phonetic content of a head element is suppressed if it has a complement.

As in the fully recursive analysis recursion is potentially unlimited, the model is prone to the same criticism as Particle Phonology (Schane 1984). Still, as it is possible to argue that recursion will be limited by performance-related factors such as memory (Nasukawa 2014), let us focus on some empirical issues. More concretely, I would like to discuss some implications of the analysis proposed for Middle Korean in this paper for the precedence-free model (for a discussion of English vowel structure in Precedence-free Phonology, see Onuma and Nasukawa, this volume).

In the analysis proposed in the present paper, RTR vowels have a dependent |A|, whereas non-RTR vowels lack this element. Interestingly, because of the reversal of the roles of head and dependents in Precedence-free Phonology, a direct 'translation' of the analysis of the underlying forms proposed in section 3 would imply that RTR vowels contain |A| as a head, as in (52a) and (52c), whereas non-RTR vowels do not, which are headed by |U|, as in (52b) and (52d). The representation of the neutral vowel [i], which is omitted from (52), can be assumed to involve a structure headed by the element |I|.

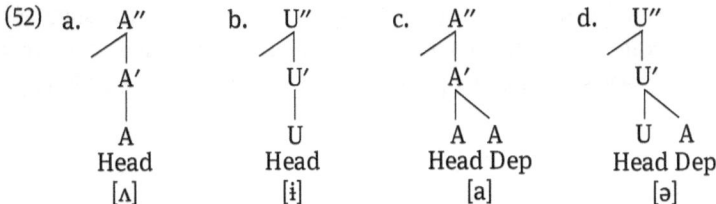

In an analysis based on the structures in (52), the generalization will be that vowels with headed by |U| may not appear in the same domain as vowels headed by |A|. While an analysis along these lines may be possible in theory, it can only be adopted if we give up the assumption that languages choose a single 'baseline' element for the head position. Furthermore, it is necessary to allow for a head element that dominates a dependent element to have an influence on the phonetic interpretation, because otherwise [a] and [ə] would be interpreted in the same way. In any case, any other analysis in which |A| has a dual interpretation seems unavailable. Thus, if an analysis based on representations like those in (52) is rejected, it would seem to be necessary to use a different element to represent [RTR]. However, it is not clear how in such an approach it would be possible to analyze the diachronic change in vowel harmony in Korean in an insightful way. For these reasons, I conclude that the non-recursive approach proposed in this paper is to be preferred to a recursive approach based on the model proposed by Nasukawa (2014) and Backley and Nasukawa (this volume).

5 Conclusion

In element-based approaches to melodic structure, there is no agreement on questions like whether head elements are obligatory, whether the same segment may contain identical elements, and whether a segment may contain multiple head elements. Based on a discussion of vowel structure in English and Middle Korean, I have shown that apart from headed vowels, we need to allow for both empty-headed vowels (although in underlying forms only), as well as vowels in which the same element appears both as a head and as a dependent. I have also shown that in a structural approach to segment-internal dependency relations, the existence of all these types of vowels follow from the proposed architecture of vowels: the root node dominates a head node and an optional dependent node, and an element may be linked to the head, the dependent, or both. In this model, the number of nodes with an identical element is naturally constrained to a maximum of two.

Acknowledgements: I would like to thank Jeroen van de Weijer, an anonymous reviewer, and the editor for comments on earlier versions of this paper. All errors are mine. This work was supported by JSPS KAKENHI Grant Number 15F15005.

References

Anderson, John M. 1993. Morphology, phonology and the Scottish vowel-length rule. *Journal of Linguistics* 29, 419–430.

Anderson, John M. 1994. Contrastivity and non-specification in a dependency phonology of English. *Studia Anglica Posnaniensia* XXVIII, 3–35.

Anderson, John and Colin J. Ewen. 1987. *Principles of Dependency Phonology*. Cambridge: Cambridge University Press.

Anderson, John and Charles Jones. 1974. Three theses concerning phonological representations. *Journal of Linguistics* 10, 1–26.

Backley, Phillip. 1995. A tier geometry for vowel systems. *UCL Working Papers in Linguistics* 7, 399–436.

Backley, Phillip. 2011. *An Introduction to Element Theory*. Edinburgh: Edinburgh University Press.

Backley, Phillip. 2012. Variation in Element Theory. *Linguistic Variation* 12(1), 57–102.

Backley, Phillip and Kuniya Nasukawa. 2009. Headship as melodic strength. In Kuniya Nasukawa and Phillip Backey (eds.), *Strength Relations in Phonology*, 47–77. Berlin and New York: Mouton de Gruyter.

Botma, Bert. 2004. Phonological Aspects of Nasality: An Element-based Dependency Approach. LOT Dissertation series 90. Utrecht: Holland Academic Graphics.

Carr, Philip. 1992. Strict cyclicity, structure preservation and the Scottish vowel-length rule. *Journal of Linguistics* 28, 91–114.

Charette, Monik and Asli Göksel. 1994. Vowel harmony and switching in Turkic languages. *SOAS Working Papers in Linguistics and Phonetics* 4, 31–52.

Charette, Monik and Asli Göksel. 1996. Licensing constraints and vowel harmony in Turkic languages. *SOAS Working Papers in Linguistics and Phonetics* 6, 1–25.

Clements, George N. 1985. The geometry of phonological features. *Phonology Yearbook* 2, 225–252.

Dresher, B. Elan. 2009. *The Contrastive Hierarchy in Phonology*. Cambridge: Cambridge University Press.

Dresher, B. Elan. 2014. Contrastive hierarchies in Element Theory. Paper presented at the conference 'Theoretical Issues in Contemporary Phonology: Reading Tobias Scheer, École des Hautes Études en Sciences Sociales (EHESS), Paris (6–8 February 2014).

Dresher, B. Elan and Harry van der Hulst. 1998. Head-dependent asymmetries in phonology: complexity and visibility. *Phonology* 15, 317–352.

Durand, Jacques. 1990. *Generative and Non-linear Phonology*. London: Longman.

Durand, Jacques. 2005. Tense/Lax, the vowel system of English and phonological theory. In Phillip Carr, Jacques Durand and Colin J. Ewen (eds.), *Headhood, Elements, Specification and Contrastivity: Phonological Papers in Honour of John Anderson*, 77–97. Amsterdam: John Benjamins.

Ewen, Colin J. 1995. Dependency relations in phonology. In John A. Goldsmith (ed.), *The Handbook of Phonological Theory*, 570–585. Oxford: Basil Blackwell.
Giegerich, Heinz J. 1992. *English Phonology: An Introduction*. Cambridge: Cambridge University Press.
Harris, John. 1994. *English Sound Structure*. Oxford: Blackwell.
Harris, John and Geoff Lindsey. 1995. The elements of phonological representation. In Jacques Durand and Francis Katamba (eds.), *Frontiers of Phonology: Atoms, Structures, Derivations*, 34–79. Harlow, Essex: Longman.
Hayata, Teruhiro. 1975. A note on vowel harmony in Middle Korean. *Gengo Kenkyu* 68, 104–118.
Honeybone, Patrick. 2010. How symmetrical are English vowels? *Language and Language Behavior* 9 (The Linguistic Society of St. Petersburg), 33–63.
Hulst, Harry van der. 1988. The dual interpretation of |I|, |A|, and |U|. *NELS* 18, 208–222.
Hulst, Harry van der. 1989. Atoms of segmental structure: components, gestures, and dependency. *Phonology* 6, 253–284.
Hulst, Harry van der. 1995. Radical CV Phonology: the categorial gesture. In Jacques Durand and Francis Katamba (eds.), *Frontiers of Phonology: Atoms, Structures, and Derivations*, 80–116. Harlow, Essex: Longman.
Hulst, Harry van der. 2005. The molecular structure of phonological segments. In Philip Carr, Jacques Durand and Colin J. Ewen (eds.), *Headhood, Elements, Specification and Contrastivity: Phonological Papers in Honour of John Anderson*, 193–234. Amsterdam: John Benjamins.
Hulst, Harry van der. 2012. A minimal framework for vowel harmony. In Bert Botma and Roland Noske (eds.), *Phonological Explorations: Empirical, Theoretical and Diachronic Issues*, 155–190. Berlin: Mouton de Gruyter.
Hulst, Harry van der. 2015. The opponent principle in RcvP: binarity in a unary system. In Eric Raimy and Charles Cairns (eds.), *The Segment in Phonetics and Phonology*, 149–179. Malden, MA: Wiley-Blackwell.
Ito, Chiyuki. 2013. Korean accent: Internal reconstruction and historical development. *Korean Linguistics* 15(2), 129–198.
Kaye, Jonathan D. 1990. Coda licensing. *Phonology* 7, 301–330.
Kaye, Jonathan D. 2001. Working with licensing constraints. In Katarzyna Dziubalska-Kołaczyk (ed.), *Constraints and Preferences*, 251–268. Berlin and New York: Mouton de Gruyter.
Kaye, Jonathan D., Jean Lowenstamm and Jean-Roger Vergnaud. 1985. The internal structure of phonological elements: a theory of charm and government. *Phonology Yearbook* 2, 305–328.
Kaye, Jonathan D., Jean Lowenstamm and Jean-Roger Vergnaud. 1990. Constituent structure and government in phonology. *Phonology* 7, 193–232.
Kim, Juwon. 1988. Moumcohwa.wa selchwuk–Hwunminjengum haylyey.uy selchwuk.ey tayhaye [Vowel harmony and 'selchwuk'–on the tongue retraction in Hwunminjengum]. *Eoneohak* 9/10.
Kim, Juwon. 1993. *Moumcohwa.uy yenku* [A study on vowel harmony in Korean]. Kyeungsan: Yeungnam University Press.
Ko, Seongyoon. 2012. Tongue root harmony and vowel contrast in Northeast Asian languages. Ph.D. dissertation, Cornell University.
Lass, Roger. 1976. *English Phonology and Phonological Theory*. Cambridge: Cambridge University Press.

Lee, Duck-Young and Shohei Yoshida. 1998. In Eugeniusz Cyran (ed.), *Structure and Interpretation: Studies in Phonology*, 195–204. Lublin: Wydawnictwo.
Lee, Duck-Young. 2004. Korean vowel harmony: ATR Harmony. *Hangeul* 223: 157–199.
Lee, Iksop and S. Robert Ramsey. 2000. *The Korean language*. Albany, NY: State University of New York Press.
Lee, Ki-Moon. 1972. *Kwukesa Kaysel* [Outline of the History of the Korean Language], 2nd Edition. Seoul: Tower Press.
Lee, Ki-Moon and S. Robert Ramsey. 2011. *A History of the Korean Language*. Cambridge: Cambridge University Press.
Martin, Samuel E. 1992. *A Reference Grammar of Korean: A Complete Guide to The Grammar and History of the Korean Language*. Rutland, VT: Charles E. Tuttle.
McCarthy, John J. 1988. Feature geometry and dependency: a review. *Phonetica* 43, 84–108.
Nasukawa, Kuniya. 2014. Features and recursive structure. *Nordlyd* 41(1),1–19. Special issue on Features edited by Martin Krämer, Sandra-Iulia Ronai and Peter Svenonius.
Oostendorp, Marc van. 2000. *Phonological Projection: A Theory of Feature Content and Prosodic Structure*. Berlin and New York: Mouton de Gruyter.
Park, Jong-Hee. 1983. *Kwuke Umwunlon Yenkwu* [A study on Korean phonology]. Chonbuk: Wonkwang University Press.
Rhee, Sang-Jik. 2002. Empty nuclei in Korean. Utrecht: LOT Dissertation series 61. Utrecht: Holland Academic Graphics.
Schane, Sanford A. 1984. The fundamentals of particle phonology. *Phonology Yearbook* 1, 129–155.
Scheer, Tobias. 2010. How to marry (structuralist) contrast and (generative) processing: review of B. Elan Dresher 2009, *The Contrastive Hierarchy in Phonology. Lingua* 120, 2522–2534.
Shin, Jiyoung, Jieun Kiaer and Jaeeun Chan. 2013. *The Sounds of Korean*. Cambridge: Cambridge University Press.
Smith, Norval. 2000. Dependency phonology meets OT: a proposal for a new approach to segmental structure. In Joost Dekkers, Frank van der Leeuw and Jeroen van de Weijer (eds.), *Optimality Theory: Phonology, Syntax, and Acquisition*, 234–276. Oxford: Oxford University Press.
Smith, Norval and Harry van der Hulst. 1990. Züritüütsch umlaut and the non-existence of the feature [tense]. In Joan Mascaró and Marina Nespor (eds.), Grammar in progress: a festschrift for Henk van Riemsdijk, 397–409. Dordrecht: Foris.
Szigetvári, Péter. 2016. No diphthong, no problem. In Jolanta Szpyra-Kozłowska and Eugeniusz Cyran (eds.), *Phonology, Its Faces and Interfaces*, 123–141. Frankfurt am Main: Peter Lang.
Weijer, Jeroen van de. 1996. *Segmental Structure and Complex Segments*. Tübingen: Niemeyer.
Wells, John C. 1982. *Accents of English* (Three volumes). Cambridge: Cambridge University Press.
Wells, John C. 1990. *Longman Pronunciation Dictionary*. Harlow, Essex: Longman.
Whitman, John. 1985. The phonological basis for the comparison of Japanese and Korean. Ph.D. dissertation, Harvard University.
Whitman, John. 1994. The accentuation of nominal stems in Proto-Korean. In Young-Key Kim-Renaud (ed.), *Theoretical Issues in Korean Linguistics*, 425–439. Stanford: CSLI Publications.

Geoffrey Schwartz
Defining recursive entities in phonology: The Onset Prominence framework

1 Introduction

The concept of recursion is an important one in theoretical linguistics. Most notably, the apparently recursive properties that may be observed in syntactic structures have been invoked to defend Chomsky's claims about the human language faculty. The ability to create an infinite number of sentences by embedding additional phrases within a phrase (*the cat that ate the rat that ate the spider that ate the fly* etc.) is suggested to be unique to humans (see e.g. Lasnik 2000), and a property of all human languages. Although this claim has been the subject of a fair amount of scholarly debate, what has been questioned in this debate is not the fact of recursion itself, but rather its universality (Everett 2005) or whether it may be taken as evidence for generative grammar (Pullum and Scholz 2010) as envisioned by Chomsky.

One area of linguistic structure in which scholars have made strong claims against the possibility of recursion is phonology. For example, Pinker and Jackendoff (2005) state that unlike relative clauses in syntax, which may be embedded inside other relative clauses, this possibility does not exist in phonology. This basic assumption is accepted among most phonologists, in large part because Prosodic Phonology (Nespor and Vogel 1986), the most widely adopted model of phonological structure, contains an explicit ban on recursive structures. This ban, known as the Strict Layer Hypothesis (Selkirk 1984) requires prosodic categories to be parsed units of the next level down in the Prosodic Hierarchy (see discussion in van der Hulst 2010). Thus, a 'foot' is claimed to be made up of syllables, and you cannot embed one syllable inside another. Likewise, a Prosodic Word is made up of Feet, and it is widely assumed that you cannot embed one Foot inside another.

In order to evaluate claims of recursion in human language, it is necessary to have agreed-upon definitions of the units that are supposed to recur. For the most part, this has not been a problem for syntax – the constituent status of the relative clauses that recur in the example given above is not controversial, even if labels and particular structural details have changed over the years. In the case of phonology, however, this is a more serious problem. While a majority of authors employ traditional units such as the phoneme and the syllable in their analyses, in many cases this is done simply for descriptive convenience. There is in fact little consensus as to what the units of phonological analysis actually are, and whether they are universal or language-specific. For example, Schiering, Bickel and Hildebrandt (2010) discuss evidence suggesting that there is no Prosodic Word in Vietnamese, and that Limbu must contain two distinct types of Prosodic Word constituent between the level of the Foot and the Prosodic Phrase. With regard to smaller phonological entities, some have argued that distinctive features are emergent rather than universal (e.g. Mielke 2008), and numerous authors have questioned the phoneme and the syllable, suggesting they are epiphenomenal. Particularly lively has been the debate about the prosodic properties of post-vocalic 'final' consonants – for some scholars they are 'codas' while for others they are 'onsets' preceding an empty 'nucleus' (e.g. Harris and Gussmann 1998, Scheer 2004). In sum, although the different types of phonological units that have been proposed are useful for analyzing selected phenomena in individual languages, arriving at a universal set of phonological entities has proved quite challenging. Yet until this challenge is met, there is no real way of evaluating claims that phonology does or does not have recursion.

This chapter will provide a summary overview of the representations and mechanisms of the Onset Prominence framework (OP: Schwartz 2010, 2013, 2016), which attempts to meet this challenge by showing how traditional units such as the segment and the syllable may evolve in different ways in different languages from a single restricted set of universal entities. With a trimmed inventory of phonological structures based on a universal CV (stop-vowel) hierarchy, it becomes apparent that phonology is indeed recursive. In essence, each 'segment' is a sort of recursion of the CV unit, but contains ambiguities that govern how individual segments are extracted from the hierarchy. With regard to larger entities, OP hierarchical units can combine into larger prosodic constituents in two different ways: by means of a recursive 'submersion' process that builds downwards, or through a non-recursive 'adjunction' process that builds upwards.

The rest of this chapter will proceed as follows. Section 2 will discuss the problem of units in phonology, with particular attention to how various types of phonological entities have been labelled. Section 3 introduces the OP representational primitives and phonotactic mechanisms, with particular attention to the recursive submersion parameter. Section 4 offers some final remarks to conclude the chapter.

2 The units of phonology and their labels

As mentioned earlier, in order to describe recursion in language it is necessary to have explicit definitions of the units that are supposed to recur. Unfortunately, defining the appropriate units for phonological analysis has been anything but a straightforward endeavor. This section will focus on the origins of two types of units that are frequently assumed to play a role in phonological grammars, the syllable and the segment. It will be argued that these units should be thought of as derivative rather than primitive entities.

2.1 The segment and its origins

The role of the segment in phonological analysis is inevitably connected with the widespread use of alphabetic orthographic systems in which each grapheme is intended to correspond to a presumed single unit of speech. In this connection, it has long been assumed that "it is possible to describe speech as a sequence of segments" (International Phonetic Association 1999: 5). Ladd (2011), in tracing the history of the International Phonetic Alphabet, notes that the beginnings of segmental transcription reach back to the late 19th century, and were originally motivated by irregularities in the English spelling system. The system that was established was later extended to descriptions of other languages, accompanied by the assumption that 'similar' sounds across languages should be transcribed with the same symbol.

This assumption has persisted among phonologists and many phoneticians, for whom the 'segment' is a key descriptive element of speech, despite what is referred to in speech perception research as the 'linearity problem' (see e.g. Wright, Frisch, and Pisoni 1999). It has been known, at least since the advent of spectrographic analysis in the second half of the 20th century, that there is no one-to-one correspondence between the acoustic signal and any perceived string of phonological 'segments'. In many cases, a single portion of speech may contain acoustic information about multiple segments. Thus, the initial portion of a 'vowel' in a CV sequence typically contains formant transitions that enable listeners to identify the preceding consonant. In other cases, the acoustic consequences of the articulation of a single segment may extend over distinct and multiple acoustic events. For example, the articulation of a stop consonant is associated with (a) a silent closure period, (b) a burst of noise whose spectral properties encode place of articulation, and (c) formant movement that is realized over the initial portion of the vowel. In a stop-vowel sequence, the initial portion of the 'vowel' is clearly ambiguous with regard to its 'segmental' affiliation. Inasmuch as it is a robust periodic signal with identifiable formant structure, it has to be referred to as a 'vowel' from the point of view of speech production. However, it appears that the primary function of vowel onset in communication is as acoustic background for the perception of the preceding consonant.

Although the linearity problem clearly represents a challenge to the status of the segment for any phonological analysis that purports to encode the sound structure of spoken language,[1] Ohala (1992) makes an evolutionary case for the segment as a unit that evolves in different languages, but is not primitive. For Ohala, the segment should be seen as a derivative unit that creates a perceptual advantage for speech transmission, and may therefore be expected to evolve in a large number of languages. These perceptual advantages stem from the following factors. First, the coordination of multiple articulatory gestures associated with segmental organization results in acoustically robust modulations that are more easily recoverable by listeners than single gestures. Second, the quantal nature of the articulatory-acoustic relationship (Stevens 1989) results in a certain degree of acoustic stability in the speech signal, even in the face of articulatory variability.

Perhaps it is these very advantages that have led to the segment's ubiquity in phonological theory, a notion Ladd (2011) refers to as *phone idealization*, the assumption that segmental transcription may form a descriptively adequate representation of speech. When combined with the influence of generative linguistics, most evident for phonology in Chomsky and Halle's (1968) *Sound Pattern of English* (SPE), phone idealization shaped the theoretical landscape in a way that promoted a more abstract unit, the phoneme, as the fundamental building block for phonological analysis. As a result, most subsequent research seeking to describe the relationship between phonology and phonetics operated on the assumption that the physical details of speech are governed by 'phonetic implementation rules', which assign numerical values to the phonological features that are assumed to be the building blocks of phonemes. Little or no attempt was made to model Ohala's segmental 'evolution' (but see Blevins 2004), or incorporate the linearity problem into a phonological framework. The Onset Prominence framework represents an attempt to alter this trend by proposing a theory of the mechanisms by which segments derive from a single hierarchy of phonetic events.

2.2 Parsing syllable positions

The syllable is another unit that creates challenges for phonological theory. Unlike the aforementioned issues with the segment, however, the problems

---

[1] At least two additional challenges may be identified that will not be discussed here due to space restrictions. The first is the problem of speaker normalization, since the acoustic properties of the same sound produced by two different speakers may differ substantially. The second problem concerns what many phonologists might refer to as levels of representation and the question of how much physical detail to encode in transcription.

related to the syllable have received a great deal of attention from phonological theorists. In fact, the literature on the syllable is huge, so for the purposes of this discussion we will focus on one relatively small-scale issue related to syllable structure: the status of post-vocalic 'coda' consonants. In this area, phonetic considerations suggest the existence of structural ambiguities that may be seen to create parameters that are truly phonological in nature. In short, it will be shown that there are phonetic reasons to posit two types of 'coda', and that an adequate theory of phonological representation needs to explain the origins of both.

The ambiguous nature of 'coda' consonants becomes evident when we look at data from loanword adaptation, in which we often come across a process referred to as perceptual epenthesis. Perceptual epenthesis is in essence an illusion on the part of listeners, who hear a vowel when none has been produced. The phenomenon occurs when listeners whose L1 is a language with simple phonotactics, are exposed to consonants in positions where they are absent in L1. Polivanov (1931, cited in Boersma 2009) was among the earliest scholars to describe the phenomenon, observing that Japanese learners of Russian apparently hear the word *tak* 'so' as /takɯ/, as suggested by their L2 production. In more recent years, experimental methods have clearly established that the effect is perceptual (see e.g. de Jong and Park 2012), and that speech production constraints have little to do with it. There is of course nothing difficult in producing a final stop – the difficulty lies in parsing its position.

The ambiguities associated with parsing final stop consonants may be gleaned from a simple acoustic display. 'Coda' stops are made up of two phases, a silent or near-silent closure period, followed by a release burst that produces aperiodic noise. The silent closure may serve as an acoustic 'landmark' (cf. Stevens 2002) which serves as a reset for listeners. That is, what follows the closure, which creates a natural acoustic boundary, may be reinterpreted as 'initial'. In this connection, it may be noted that this perspective on perceptual epenthesis would have us expect that stops should be more likely than other 'coda' consonants to induce epenthesis on account of their silent closure period, which is of course absent from fricatives and sonorant consonants. This effect has indeed been observed experimentally (see De Jong and Park 2012). At the same time, however, the stops must be released to induce this effect, and epenthesis data from English loanwords into Korean is sensitive to this very question (Kang 2003). In addition, the release of all consonant constrictions, not only those of stops, has a tendency to be perceptually reinterpreted as schwa, leading to countless cases of vowel epenthesis diachronically (Silverman 2011). In sum, the auditory properties of post-vocalic consonants predict two possible phonological parses, one in which the consonant is indeed a 'coda' and another in which it is interpreted as an 'onset'.

The ambiguity of final consonants is in many respects evident in the differing views of their status with regard to prosodic structure. Traditional syllabic theory uses the label 'coda', a sub-component in the larger constituent referred to as the 'rhyme' (or 'rime'). Another theory equates the second part of the 'rhyme' with a single unit of prosodic weight known as the 'mora' with the goal of unifying cases in which long vowels and VC sequences behave similarly for processes such as stress assignment. In yet another view, final consonants are seen simply as 'onsets', but as onsets to defective syllables with a silent or empty nucleus.

It is the 'onset'-based view of 'coda' consonants that has the most significant implications for the question of recursion. If a word is 'monosyllabic' according to standard descriptions, yet the final consonant is an 'onset', then clearly what we are witnessing is indeed a syllable, or at least a portion thereof, inside another syllable. Most theorists, however, would not see it this way, having accepted to mainstream claims that a 'syllable' must contain a 'nucleus', and that phonology is not recursive. Van der Hulst (2010: 309–310) has an interesting perspective on this question, suggesting that theoretical bias against recursion is simply a question of labels.

> This analogy indeed invites the question why 'complements' within the syllable are not syllables, just like the complements in syntactic phrases? It would seem that the apparent lack of recursion within the syllable is an artifact of using the labels that we traditionally use. If the right labels are used we see that .... 'codas' are 'syllables inside syllables'.
> (van der Hulst 2010: 309–310)

In what follows, we shall provide an overview of the Onset Prominence framework, in which both segments and syllabic structures derive from a single hierarchy of phonetic events derived from a stop-vowel sequence. In this way, it is possible to offer a principled explanation of the origins of both segments and syllables, and how they may differ in their prosodic behavior in different languages. We shall see that it is indeed necessary to alter the traditional labels associated with these entities, as suggested by van der Hulst, and that phonology is indeed recursive.

3 Recursive mechanisms in the Onset Prominence framework

This section will illustrate the perspective of the Onset Prominence framework (Schwartz 2010, 2013, 2016) on the question of phonological recursion. Along the way, we shall see recursion in three different forms (3.1). Segments themselves represent a recursion of a CV representational primitive. In the realization of segments, melodic specifications may recur at lower hierarchical levels due to a trickling process. Finally, a structural recursion mechanisms referred to as submersion allows for iterations of the OP hierarchy within a single prosodic constituent. This final type of recursion, referred to as submersion, provides a unified perspective on a range of diverse phonological issues, which will be illustrated in 3.2. The discussion of OP representations in this section will be brief, focusing on principles necessary for describing recursion. The most complete published presentation of the framework may be found in Schwartz (2016).

3.1 OP representational primitives and parameters

The Onset Prominence representational environment is based on a hypothesis that manner of articulation is a structural property (Steriade 1993, Golston and van der Hulst 1999, Pöchtrager 2006). Manner categories are extracted from a hierarchical structure derived from the phonetic events associated with a CV sequence in which the consonant is a stop. The top node (Closure) is derived from stop closure, the Noise node from aperiodic noise associated with frication and release bursts, the Vocalic Onset (VO) node captures periodicity with formant structure associated with CV transitions as well as sonorant consonants. The Vocalic Target (VT) node houses (more or less) stable formant frequencies that define vowel quality. The hierarchy is presented in (1), while examples of different categories of manner of articulation extracted from it are shown in (2).

(1) The Onset Prominence representational hierarchy

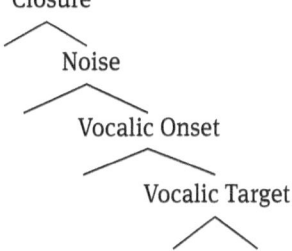

(2) Manner categories in OP segmental representations

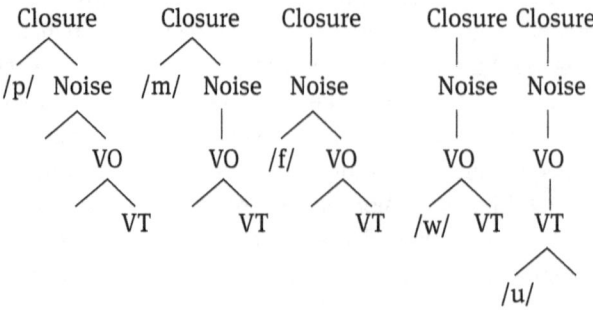

If we consider the relationship between the structure in (1) and the structures in (2), we see that each individual 'segment' in (2) represents a recursion of the CV unit in (1).[2] At the same time, however, these units may differ in their structural properties in accordance to which phonetic events of the hierarchy are missing. Missing elements are encoded as unary nodes, which act as placeholders to define hierarchical levels. For example, the approximant /w/ in the 4th tree from the left in (2) has unary Closure and Noise nodes, since approximant articulations lack complete both complete vocal tract closure as well as aperiodic noise bursts.

The name *Onset Prominence* is a reflection of the fact that since the OP hierarchy is built from a stop-vowel sequence, each consonant type is 'initial' in its canonical realization. Thus, the prominence of a given 'onset' derives from the hierarchical level of a given segment's highest binary node. In this way, the term Onset Prominence may be seen as a measure of consonantal strength, the inverse of sonority. In what follows, we shall see how the default initial position of OP segmental representations opens the door for recursive mechanisms in the formation of larger prosodic constituents.

In the trees in (2), the segmental symbols are simply shorthand for place and laryngeal specifications. The main mechanisms for the realization of these features may also be described as recursive. The structures in (3) show a /ba/ sequence, containing a labial specification (shown here as an element {U}) and

---

2 This is a different conception of recursion from what is usually described for syntax. In syntax, embedding one phrase inside another produces a larger phrase, but each embedded unit is identifiable as a separate entity. OP segmental structures may not be separated from the CV unit from which they are formed. Nevertheless, they are recursive in that the OP hierarchy must recur for segmental representations to emerge. One might consider an analogy from biology, in which an organism's genetic code recurs in each new cell that is produced.

a vocalic element {A}.[3] Laryngeal specifications are not shown here. The labial specification is assigned at the Closure level, a natural expression of the fact that the stop's place of articulation is defined by its closure location. However, the labial constriction has acoustic effects that go beyond the closure level, affecting the acoustic quality of both the noise burst (the Noise node) and the CV transition (the VO node). Thus, we posit that this specification recurs on lower level nodes by means of a 'trickling' mechanism, which is blocked by the assignment of the vowel's melody. Thus, the tree on the right in (3) is simply a more detailed view of the tree on the left, showing the phonetic effects of the Closure-level {U} assignment.

(3) The realization of melody in OP structures

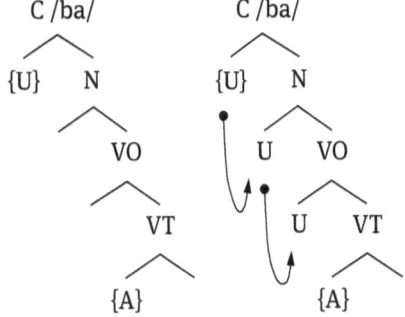

One additional aspect of OP representations that needs to be mentioned at this time is the status of the Vocalic Onset node. In the trees in (2), VO is shown as part of consonant representations, encoding CV transitions following obstruents, and approximants on their own. However, VO is derived from a portion of the signal that is, strictly speaking, vocalic, and may be parametrically included in vowel representations or excluded from consonant representations. This is shown below in (4), in which the manner distinctions from (2) are converted to a vowel-based VO system. Parameter settings associated with VO affiliation have far-reaching consequences for explaining cross-linguistic differences in phonological systems. For discussion, see Schwartz (2016).

---

[3] Pöchtrager has argued against the element {A}, which is used here mainly for illustrative purposes and is not explicitly adopted in the theory. For further discussion of the origins and behavior of melodic elements in the OP environment, see Schwartz (2017).

(4) Manner distinctions with vocalic VO affiliation[4]

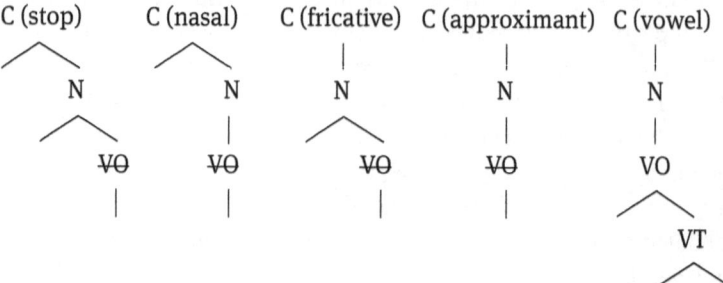

The fundamental constituent-forming mechanism in the OP environment is called *absorption*, by which a lower-level vowel structure is joined with a higher-level consonant into a CV. This is shown in (5).

(5) Formation of /ta/ constituent via absorption

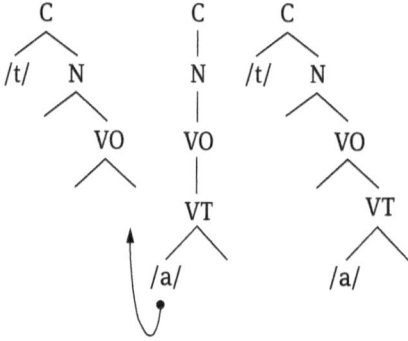

Absorption is motivated by a requirement of prosodic minimality, Minimal Constituent (MC), by which any structure without active binary nodes both above and below the VT level may not stand alone as a prosodic constituent. Absorption, then, is a repair mechanism that allows OP structures to satisfy the MC constraint.

One question that should come to mind at this point is what happens when the final tree in a string violates MC, but cannot be absorbed into the structure to its left because it is not lower in the OP hierarchy. In other words, what happens when a consonant is not 'initial'. In such cases, there are two logical possibilities. In the first, the tree is adjoined to the preceding constituent at a

---

[4] Note that approximants in this system lack any active structure whatsoever, as a consequence of which such systems maybe associated with a process of 'promotion' (Schwartz 2016).

higher level of structure. This is shown in the structures in (6), in which we see a representation of the Polish word *kosz* /koṣ/ 'basket'. On the left we the constituent structures of the individual segments in the word (the /ko/ sequence has already undergone absorption). The final fricative may not be absorbed into the preceding constituent. As a result, a higher level of structure is activated (labeled PW here for Prosodic Word), and the prosodic structure of the word is shown on the right, with two constituents built down from the Closure level.

(6) Adjunction of a final consonant

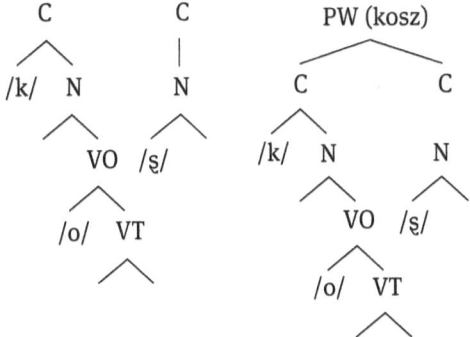

The second possible fate for final 'segments' is that the tree is attached to the bottom of the preceding constituent through a mechanism called *submersion*. This is shown in (7), a representation of the English word *quick*.

(7) Submersion of a final consonant

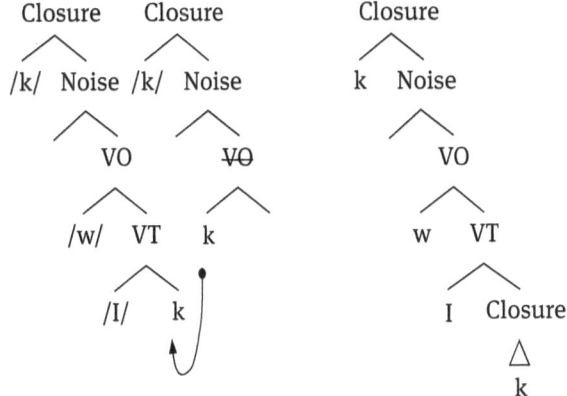

On the left, the melody associated with the final /k/, which is 'stranded' under the VO node that is absent in final position, is realized under the /kwɪ/

sequence. One the right, the entire structure of the /k/ has been submerged. It is suggested that the submersion of melody depicted on the left is a precursor to the structural mechanism shown on the right. In other words, the submersion mechanism originates with minimal melodic entities, and may later be extended to encompass entire prosodic constituents.[5] The final product of the structural submersion mechanism is a single recursive prosodic unit that contains two iterations of the OP hierarchy built down from a single Closure node. In English, submerged structures are a requirement of minimal prosodic words, encoding the familiar prohibition of monosyllabic words ending in a short or lax vowel (see Schwartz 2016).

3.2 The unifying power of submersion

Of the OP mechanisms described so far, it is submersion that most resembles the type of recursion that is observed in syntactic structures, and thus warrants the most attention. Significantly, submersion offers a unifying perspective on a range of diverse phonological issues, from the weakness of 'codas' and intervocalic consonants, to word-boundary effects, as well as rhythmic organization and stress assignment systems. As illustrations of these effects, our examples will refer to two languages: English, in which we find submersion, and Polish, in which it is absent.

3.2.1 The structure of prosodic words in English

Comparing the structures in (6) and (7), we see that there are two different configurations that produce what in traditional descriptions are called 'codas'. Submerged 'codas' such as those we see in English are lower in the OP hierarchy than 'onset' consonants, while adjoined consonants occur at the same level. The variable levels at which the two types of 'codas' appear is a natural expression of what is often referred to as 'coda' weakness. Submerged codas are weaker and more susceptible to weakening processes, including stop release suppression that is common in English, and approximant vocalization of post-vocalic /l/ in /r/ in various dialects of English.

---

[5] One motivation for the submersion mechanism is the status of the VO node in the representation of consonants in a given language. When VO is part of consonant representations, final position creates a mismatch by which the VO level melody of the consonant is 'stranded', and uses the preceding vowel for its realization. For details, see Schwartz (2016).

The submersion mechanism may also result in CVCV trochees, which has a similar effect of weakening consonants by placing them lower in the OP hierarchy. Thus, submersion gives us the context where intervocalic lenition is to be expected. This is shown below in a representation of the English word *pity*, which contains the intervocalic lenition context.

(8) Submersion in English *pity*

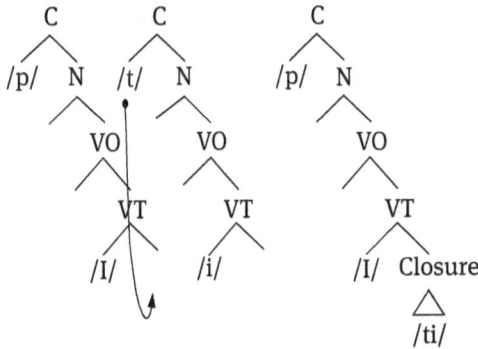

Long vowels may also be a reflection of submerged structures, arising from sequences of two individual vowel structures. This is shown in (9).

(9) Long vowels formed from submersion

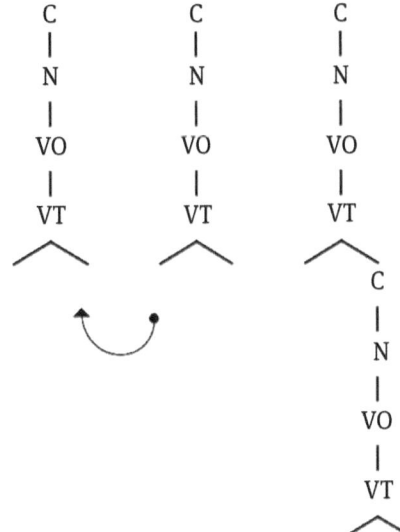

In the trees in (7), (8), and (9), we see that the submersion parameter gives us a unified way of representing CVCV sequences, codas and long vowels, which comprise the three possibilities for minimal prosodic words in English.

A clarification is necessary at this point. The recursive structures posited here for English are not the only mechanism for the representation of CVCV sequences, codas, and long vowels. As shown above such entities may be due to adjunction rather than submersion. The difference is in the predictions for the behavior of such configurations, which will become clearer as we look at larger prosodic structures.

3.2.2 Larger prosodic structures

In English, submersion produces not only recursive prosodic words, but also phrases. This is shown in (10), in which we see a template for a prosodic word on the left and a phrase on the right. Note that in each case, a single tree encompasses both word and phrase-level units.[6]

(10) Prosodic word and phrase templates via submersion in English

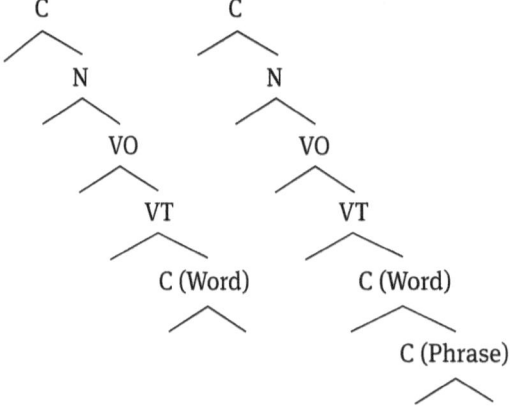

By contrast, adjunction builds flatter words and phrases, as shown below in (11).

---

[6] For a more detailed illustration of submersion in English phrases, see Schwartz (2016).

(11) Word and phrase structure resulting from adjunction

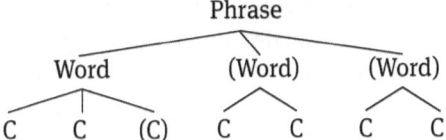

Stress patterns in submerged vs. adjoined structures are very different. Submersion results in individual 'syllables' being housed at different levels of a single prosodic constituent. As a consequence, there is no string of syllables that could be used as a base for an algorithm responsible for stress assignment. This leads to unpredictable lexical stress, which is phonetically quite robust, and significant reduction of unstressed syllables. In this way, submerged prosodic structures predict rhythmic organization that is compatible with what is often referred to as 'stress-timing'. In adjunctive prosodic structures, by contrast, we observe a truly flat string of constituents built down from the Closure level. As a result, the differences in prominence between stressed and unstressed units are less robust – there is less reduction. In addition, syllable-based stress-assignment algorithms may operate in adjoined structures, resulting in fixed stress systems, most commonly assigning stress to the initial or the penult. In sum, the submerged structure in (10) predicts the co-occurrence of vowel reduction with mobile stress that is phonetically strong, while adjunction in (11) results in fixed stress that is predicted be relatively weak, and to co-occur with minimal vowel reduction.

The present discussion also raises the question about how stress placement may or may not fall out from the proposed structures. In this regard there are a number of considerations. First, considering the fact that it is vowels that typically bear stress, one function of stress may be thought of as a phonetic boost for an entity that is at the bottom of the hierarchy. In other words, vowels, despite the fact that they are the most 'sonorous' segments that are phonetically best-equipped to bear stress, are of lesser prominence than consonants in the representational hierarchy. The more prominent position of consonants in the OP hierarchy is a reflection of the fact that consonants bear a much greater functional load in the formation of lexical contrasts in a language. In other words, stress may be inherently attracted to units that are at a phonological disadvantage.

Another issue concerns what might be referred to as default stress. Independent of stress 'assignment', certain phonological units are going to be more perceptually prominent than others. In particular, domain-initial syllables which are subject to primacy effects, and domain-final syllables which are subject to recency effects, may be perceived has having greater prominence. These effects may be expected even when speakers do not actively produce such prominence. Thus, in adjunctive systems described as having 'fixed' initial or final stress, prominence originates as a default phonetic effect rather than an active mechanism in the phonological grammar. Such effects may be enhanced by processes of initial strengthening (Fougeron and Keating 1997) and final lengthening (Wightman et al. 1992), which can in turn contribute to the further entrenchment of initial or final stress patterns. Among fixed stress systems, penultimate stress is one of the most common. From the perspective of the OP environment, penultimate stress is motivated by the need to give a phonetic boost to a perceptually disadvantaged syllable. Since penultimate position is separated from strong initials (in words with 3 or more syllables), and directly preceding a final which has a tendency to undergo lengthening, this position is clearly at a perceptual disadvantage. Thus, penultimate algorithms assign prominence to the second to last VT node. This is shown below in (12) in a representation of Polish *podstawówka* /pod.sta.ˈvuv.ka/ 'primary school'. Stress is assigned to the second to last active VT node, which is highlighted.

(12) Polish *podstawówka* 'primary school'

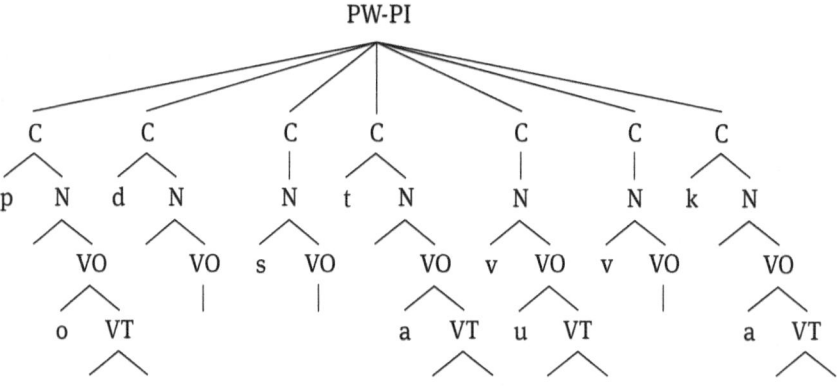

In English, a language with larger submerged prosodic constituents, stress is somewhat more complex. Although in many respects it is unpredictable, there are several patterns. OP representations offer a useful perspective on these patterns. Two generalizations are given below, after which we will show how they may be brought together using OP structures
- Stress placement in English appears to be based on the 'foot' rather than the 'syllable'
- There are many effects in English of what might be called prosodic weight

The first of these generalizations is evident in words with two trochaic feet, such as *Cinderella* or *origami*, both of which show primary stress on the third syllable. Both words are constructed of two trochaic 'feet',[7] the second of which is stressed. Notably, the structure of English feet in the OP environment may be reconstructed from their segmental makeup. Consider the word Cinderella as a string of individual segmental trees as shown below in (13).

(13) Segmental string in *Cinderella*, upward arrows represent absorption, downward arrows submersion

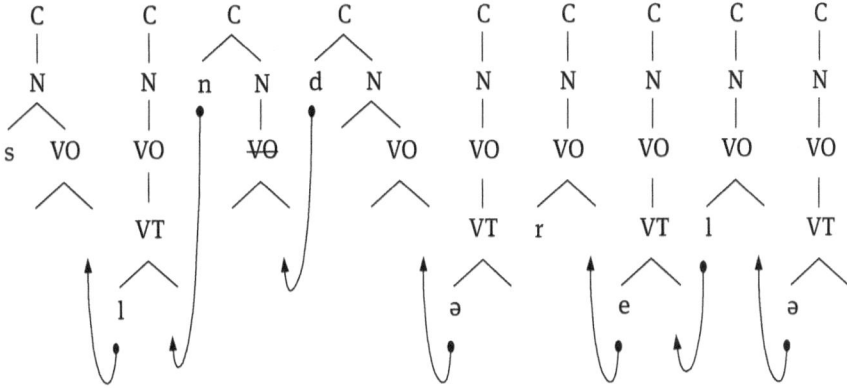

Through the mechanisms of absorption (the upward arrows) and submersion (the downward arrows), the constituent structure of the word, normally thought of as its 'foot' structure, may be read directly from the segmental string. Crucially, constituent formation proceeds from right to left, until each tree is prosodically viable according to the MC requirement, as well an English requirement for submerged structure.[8] This leaves us with two constituents shown in (14). The final tree is assigned primary stress.

---

[7] The term 'foot' is used here for descriptive convenience, analogously with 'segment' and 'syllable'. The Foot has no formal universal status in the OP framework, but constituents with 'foot'-like behavior may emerge from submersion.
[8] This is the MINIMALPRODICWORD-ENGLISH (MPW-ENG) constraint. For details, see Schwartz (2016).

(14) Foot structure in *Cinderella* derived from (13)

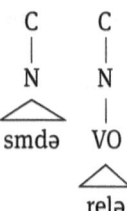

With regard to the second generalization, the term prosodic weight is used instead of 'syllable' weight. In essence, the claim is that in languages like English that allow submerged trochees, both 'syllables' and 'feet' are contained in single constituents. Thus, weight is a property of entire prosodic constituents, not just syllables. Consider the word *holiday*. In (15) below we see the segmental string, to which a run-through of absorption and submersion mechanisms reveal the foot structure in (16). Note that in this word, primary stress lands on the first of these feet rather than the second, presumably because the *holi-* constituent is heavier than the *-day* constituent. This weight stems from the fact that an entire CV sequence is submerged in *holi-*, while *-day* only contains a single submerged VT node.

(15) Segmental string of English *holiday*

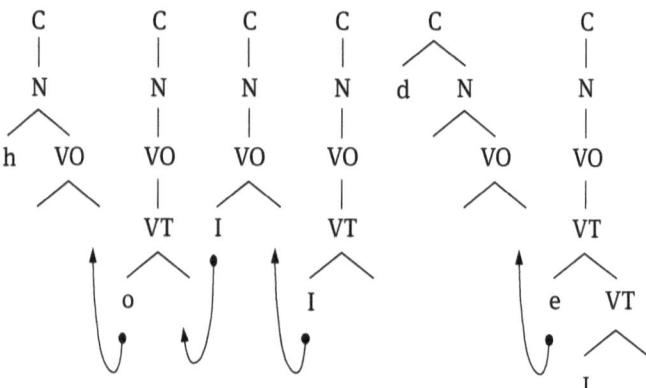

(16) Derived foot structure of *holiday*

```
C    C
|    △
N   day
△
holi
```

To conclude this section, it is worthwhile at this time to recap the main effects associated with submersion in OP structures. These effects range from motivating segmental lenition processes including flapping/glottaling of /t/ and the suppression of coda stop release, to the organization of larger prosodic constituents relevant for determining stress patterns.

4 Final remarks

In this chapter we have seen illustrations of the recursive mechanisms in the Onset Prominence representational framework. The crucial aspect of the framework is that it offers explicit definitions of its representational primitives and the mechanisms from which phonological entities with traditional labels such as the segment, syllable, and foot are derived. With these definitions in place, it is then possible to address the question of recursion in phonology. As we have seen, the primitives of phonological representation clearly may be arranged in a recursive manner.

From the perspective of OP representations, it may be suggested that the general resistance to the notion of recursion in phonology is on one level, as suggested by van der Hulst (2010), an 'artefact of the labels that are used', while on another level it is the result of restrictions imposed upon phonology by phonetics. That is, the type of unlimited recursion found in syntactic structures is not formally prohibited from phonological grammars. Rather, its absence is simply a reflection of limitations imposed by the speech perception and production systems. One primary appeal of the Onset Prominence framework is that it offers an environment in which certain aspects of speech, in particular the 'overlap' between sounds and the linearity problem, are formally encoded in the phonological grammar. As a result, it offers a more insightful view of the relationship between speech and phonology than any theory based on a linear segmental string.

The phonological literature is characterized by a deep divide between generative phonology and exemplar-based models, which in their strongest formulation deny the primitive status of any phonological unit, and question the utility of phonology as an academic field. It may be suggested that the impetus behind the exemplar approach is the failure of units like the segment to capture the gradient and dynamic properties of speech. In other words, phoneticians have identified the problems with the segment, but phonological theory has been unable to provide a viable alternative. One of the motivations behind the development of OP representations is to fill this gap, and offer a model in which certain ambiguities in speech are represented phonologically. It is my hope that this perspective can help to bridge the divides between different theoretical backgrounds.

References

Blevins, Juliette. 2004. *Evolutionary Phonology: The Emergence of Sound Patterns*. Cambridge: Cambridge University Press.
Boersma, Paul. 2009. Cue constraints and their interactions in phonological perception and production. In Paul Boersma and Silke Hamann (eds.), *Phonology in Perception*, 1–24. Berlin: Mouton de Gruyter.
Chomsky, Noam and Morris Halle. 1968. *The Sound Pattern of English*. New York: Harper and Row.
Everett, Daniel. 2005. Cultural constraints on grammar and cognition in Pirahã: another look at the design features of human language. *Current Anthropology* 46, 621–646.
Fougeron, Cécile and Patricia Keating. 1997. Articulatory strengthening at edges of prosodic domains. *Journal of the Acoustical Society of America* 101(6),3728–3740.
Golston, Chris and Harry G. van der Hulst. 1999. Stricture is structure. In Ben Hermans and Marc van Oostendorp (eds.), *The Derivational Residue in Phonological Optimality Theory*, 153–174. Amsterdam: John Benjamins.
Harris, John and Edmund Gussmann. 1998. Final codas: why the west was wrong. In Eugeniusz Cyran (ed.), *Structure and Interpretation: Studies in Phonology*, 139–162. Lublin: Folium.
International Phonetic Association. 1999. *Handbook of the International Phonetic Association*. Cambridge: Cambridge University Press.
de Jong, Kenneth and Hanyong Park. 2012. Vowel epenthesis and segment identity in Korean learners of English. *Studies in Second Language Acquisition* 34, 125–155.
Kang, Yoonjung. 2003. Perceptual similarity in loanword adaptation: English post-vocalic word-final stops to Korean. *Phonology* 20(2),219–273.
Ladd, D. Robert. 2011. Phonetics in phonology. In John A. Goldsmith, Jason Riggle, and Alan C. Yu (eds.), *Handbook of Phonological Theory*, 2nd edition, 348–373. Oxford: Blackwell.
Lasnik, Howard. 2000. *Syntactic Structures Revisited: Contemporary Lectures on Classic Transformational Theory*. Cambridge, MA: MIT Press.
Mielke, Jeff. 2008. *The Emergence of Distinctive Features*. Oxford: Oxford University Press.
Nespor, Marina and Irene Vogel. 1986. *Prosodic Phonology*. Dordrecht: Foris.
Ohala, John. 1992. The segment: primitive or derived? In Gerard J. Docherty and D. Robert Ladd (eds.), *Papers in Laboratory Phonoloy II: Gesture, Segment, Prosody*, 166–183. Cambridge: Cambridge University Press.
Pinker, Steven and Ray S. Jackendoff. 2005. What's special about the human language faculty? *Cognition* 95(2),201–236.
Polivanov, Evgenij D. 1931. La perception des sons d'une langue étrangère. *Travaux du Cercle Linguistique de Prague* 4, 79–96. [The subjective nature of the perceptions of language sounds. In Evgenij D. Polivanov. 1974. *Selected Works: Articles on General Linguistics*, 223–237. The Hague: Mouton.]
Pöchtrager, Markus A. 2006. The structure of length. Ph.D. dissertation, University of Vienna.

Pullum, Geoffrey and Barbara Scholz. 2010. Recursion and the infinitude claim. In Harry G. van der Hulst (ed.). *Recursion and Human Language*, 113–138. Berlin and New York: Mouton de Gruyter.
Hulst, Harry G. van der. 2010. A note on recursion in phonology. In Harry G. van der Hulst (ed.), *Recursion and Human Language*, 301–342. Berlin and New York: Mouton de Gruyter.
Scheer, Tobias. 2004. *A Lateral Theory of Phonology: What Is CVCV, and Why Should It Be?* Berlin and New York: Mouton de Gruyter.
Schiering, René, Balthasar Bickel and Kristine Hildebrandt. 2010. The prosodic word is not universal, but emergent. *Journal of Linguistics* 46(3),657–709.
Schwartz Geoffrey. 2010. Auditory representations and the structures of GP 2.0. *Acta Linguistica Hungarica* 57(4),381–397.
Schwartz, Geoffrey. 2013. A representational parameter for onsetless syllables. *Journal of Linguistics* 49(3),613–636.
Schwartz, Geoffrey. 2016. On the evolution of prosodic boundaries: Parameter settings for Polish and English. *Lingua* 171, 37–73.
Schwartz, Geoffrey. 2017. Formalizing modulation and the emergence of phonological heads. *Glossa: a journal of general linguistics* 2(1), 81.
Selkirk, Elisabeth. 1984. *Phonology and Syntax: The Relation between Sound and Structure*. Cambridge, MA: MIT Press.
Silverman, Daniel. 2011. Schwa. In Marc van Oostendorp, Colin J. Ewen, Elizabeth Hume and Keren Rice, (eds.), *Companion to Phonology*, 628–642. Hoboken, NJ: Wiley-Blackwell.
Steriade, Donca. 1993. Closure, release, and nasal contour. In Marie K. Huffman and Rena Krakow (eds), *Nasals, Nasalization, and the Velum*, 401–470. San Diego: Academic Press.
Stevens, Kenneth. 1989. On the quantal nature of speech. *Journal of Phonetics* 17, 3–45.
Stevens, Kenneth. 2002. Toward a model of lexical access based on acoustic landmarks and distinctive features. *Journal of the Acoustical Society of America* 111(4),1872–1891.
Wightman, Colin W., Stefanie Shattuck-Hufnagel, Mari Ostendorf and Patti J. Price. 1992. Segmental durations in the vicinity of prosodic phrase boundaries. *Journal of the Acoustical Society of America* 91, 1707–1717.
Wright, Richard, Stephen Frisch and David Pisoni. 1999. Speech perception. In J. G. Webster (ed.), *Wiley Encyclopedia of Electrical and Electronics Engineering*. New York: Wiley.

Ali Tifrit
Obstruent liquid clusters: Locality, projections and percolation

1 Introduction

Rhotics and laterals (Rice and Avery 1991, Rice 1992, Backley 2011) act as targets for the same processes and share distributional properties, one of which is the possibility to form an onset cluster with an obstruent. This is one of the main arguments to group rhotics and laterals together as a natural class (Wiese 2011). In this paper, I investigate the behavior of liquids and the case of /Obstruent+Liquid/ (OL) clusters in a modified Government Phonology 2.0 framework (GP2.0: Pöchtrager 2006, Pöchtrager and Zivanovic 2010).

Most of the recent work on OL clusters have been conducted in a CV framework (Lowenstamm 1996, Scheer 2004). I first illustrate the questions arising in this perspective and, in particular, the cases where OL clusters act sometimes as a single element and sometimes as two distinct objects. I then underline the theoretical issues that are related to the *flatness* of the CV model (*Locality* and *Infrasegmental Government*). I propose that the way out is to consider that the representations contain much more structure than what is generally assumed. After discussing the internal content of liquids, I put forward that contrary to other classes of consonants, what characterizes liquids is their inability to project and their search for a hosting structure. I then reconsider classical cases of lenition, surface changes, compensatory lengthening by loss of an onset and metatheses by formalizing them in GP2.0.

2 Unexpected properties of OL clusters

An interesting part of the activity of the liquids is their ability to contract a relationship with obstruents. There is a debate concerning this affinity: should we consider Obstruent+Liquid as 'clusters', i.e. as two independent consonants (potentially separated by an empty nucleus: √OvL)? Or should we analyse OL as a single object: an 'affricate' linked to one consonantal position (√OL)? In this part, I review evidence of the peculiar behaviour of OL clusters, mainly in a CV framework (Lowenstamm 1996, Scheer 2004). The question relies primarily on the monopositionality or the bipositionality of these clusters. I discuss the treatment given to these groups in this framework and underline the problems they cause.

https://doi.org/10.1515/9781501512582-012

Next, I examine data from French with the case of the reduction of OL+schwa#, and the cases of intervocalic lenition of OL clusters from Latin to French and in Gorgia Toscana. I conclude this section with the problem of locality.

2.1 Mono or bipositionality

Lowenstamm (2003), Scheer and Ségéral (2007), Scheer (2014) point out, in a CV framework, that OL clusters can be analysed as occupying one or two positions. Both types may coexist in the same language as is the case in Czech, for example. Lowenstamm (2003: 12–15) argues that the two representations can explain epenthesis targeting some prefixes in Czech: the following examples (1a) and (1b) show a contrastive behaviour related to the structure of the OL cluster.

(1) Czech (Lowenstamm 2003:15)

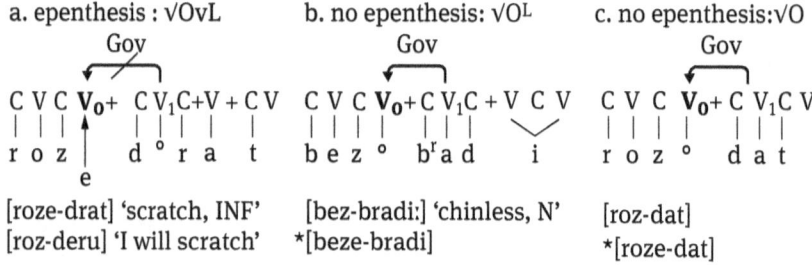

[roze-drat] 'scratch, INF'   [bez-bradi:] 'chinless, N'   [roz-dat]
[roz-deru] 'I will scratch'   *[beze-bradi]   *[roze-dat]

In (1a), epenthesis occcurs at the end of the inchoative prefix [roz] because of the presence of an unexpressed vowel between the obstruent /d/ and the liquid /r/ in [drat]. This empty nucleus is unable to properly govern the preceding vowel V_0. Hence, the ungoverned V_0 surfaces and we obtain [roz**e**-drat].

However, if the nucleus V_1 is filled with segmental material, as in [deru], it is able to properly govern the preceding nucleus and V_0 remains empty: no epenthesis happens and for example, [roz-deru] surfaces. These examples clearly show the alternation between a full vowel and an empty vowel inside the OL cluster. We can hypothesize that the underlying representation of [drat] is /d v_1 rat/ where the intervening vowel can be either filled or left empty: √OvL.

In (1b), epenthesis is systematically blocked. The OL 'cluster' in [brad] acts as a single consonant. Located in the V_1 position, [a] has the ability to govern the preceding nucleus V_0. The same happens in (1c), with an initial simplex consonant that does not provoke epenthesis: [a] can properly govern V_0 and this vowel can remain silent. In other words, [**br**ad] acts as if there were no vowel intervening between the two members of the cluster and we can consider that its underlying representation is /bʳad/ with no alternating vowel between the obstuent and the liquid. These segments behave as contour segments interpreted as a single consonant, hence the 'affricate': √O^L.

Lowenstamm's conclusion is that there is no cluster at all: so-called 'branching onsets' are either two consecutive consonants separated by one nucleus or a single contour segment.

In order to keep the same representation for the two types, √OvL and √O^L, one has to postulate an unexpressed vowel, embedded in OL, that may have the ability to govern but will never surface. I will discuss how GP2.0 and the use of structured representations can get rid of this issue in section 3. For now, I turn to an example showing one problem with this analysis.

2.2 OL+schwa#

In this section, I discuss an example of the special behaviour of OL clusters, namely when they are followed by a schwa in French. While some authors posit two possible realizations for this sequence, others consider that there are more variants.

Dell (1966) and Scheer (2000) consider that there are two ways to pronounce these groups in final position when they precede a consonant or a pause. Either the whole cluster is kept as it is (2a), or the liquid is lost, as a consequence of the loss of the final schwa (2b):

(2) French OLə# conservation and suppression
   a. Conservation b. Suppression
      ɛ̃kχwajablə   ɛ̃kχwajab   incroyable   *unbelievable*
      aʁtiklə   aʁtik   article   *article*
      katχə   kat   quatre   *four*
      kadʁə   kad   cadre   *frame*
      gofχə   gof   gaufre   *waffle*
      povʁə   pov   pauvre   *poor*

In a rule-based analysis, Dell (1966: 9–11) proposes two ordered rules. The first one is an optional rule, EFFIN(2),[1] that erases the final schwa when preceded by two consonants:
   EFFIN(2) (FAC): ə → Ø / CC_#

---

[1] EFFIN stands for *effacement final*, i.e. *final deletion* while LIQUEF stands for *effacement des liquides*, i.e. *liquids deletion*.

The second rule, LIQUEF (Dell 1966: 10), is an obligatory rule that applies after EFFIN(2) and erases the liquid (L) when preceded by an obstruent and followed by a consonant or a pause:

LIQUEF (OBL): L → Ø / [-son] _ # C^2

In (3), for example, *incroyable* 'incredible' can be pronounced [ɛ̃kʁwajablə] or [ɛ̃kʁwajab]: if the two rules apply sequentially, they derive the correct output first by erasing schwa and then by erasing the liquid. If EFFIN(2) does not apply, neither does LIQUEF and the full form is generated.

(3) French OLə#: rule-based analysis

                 ɛ̃kʁwajablə#C   ɛ̃kʁwajablə#C

EFFIN(2):	ɛ̃kχwajabl#C	erase final schwa *OPTIONAL*
LIQUEF:	ɛ̃kχwajab#C	erase the liquid *OBLIGATORY*
output	[ɛ̃kχwajab]	[ɛ̃kχwajablə]

Scheer (2000) shares the same analysis in that the trigger of liquid deletion is the loss of schwa. In (4a), the final schwa licenses[3] (Lic, '⇐') the relation contracted between the liquid, the licensee, and the obstruent. This relationship, Infrasegmental Government (IG, '←'), is established from right to left and the liquid infrasegmentally governs the obstruent. In order to do so, the liquid must be licensed by the following final schwa. Thus, whenever schwa disappears, as in (4b), the licensing condition is not fulfilled and IG is lost. By consequence, the whole final CV-unit, C_1V_1 in (4b), is elided.

(4) French OLə#: CV-based (only relevant information)

    a. <u>Conservation</u>: ə licences /l/   b. <u>Suppression</u>: ə-loss: the whole [C_1V_1] is lost.
       – Licensing   – no Licensing
       – IG   – no IG

C_0	V_0	C_1	V_1 #	C_0	V_0	C_1	V_1 #
b	←	1	⇐ ə	b	⤫	1	⤫
	IG		Lic		IG		Lic

---

2 Notice that for Dell (1966: 10) '#' stands for the boundary and 'C' for any consonant. Dell (1966: note7, 47) underlines that for some speakers, the rule applies to whatever follows the frontier. He illustrates this point with French *l'autre ami*, 'the other friend', pronounced [lotami] instead of [lotχami].

3 Charette (1990).

If we consider that French has only two options exemplified in (2a) and (2b), then both the rule-based and the representational proposals explain what happens to the final OLə# groups. Schwa seems to drag off the liquid: whenever schwa falls the liquid will follow.

However, there are intermediate options between the preservation of the whole group and the loss of the liquid. Actually, following Laks (1977), one can show that there are four possibilities forming a gradual process from Conservation to Suppression.[4] The extra-configurations were first discussed in Grammont (1914:114–115) where all the examples involve OLə# segments. Grammont (1914: 114) observed that, even if it is more frequent to delete the liquid, whenever final schwa is preceded by a cluster of consonants and if the last consonant is a liquid, "on se borne à la chuchoter ou à la souffler; elle est par conséquent dépourvue de vibrations glottales et de voix".[5] These two extra steps are illustrated in (5b) and (5c):

- Devoicing: as its name implies, the liquid, if voiced, loses its voicing as in the examples in (5b);
- Aspiration: which Laks (1977: 116) defines as "un bruit résiduel proche de l'aspiration" 'a residual noise close to aspiration' that I transcribe as a superscript h[6] and that is illustrated in the examples in (5c).

(5) French OLə#: CV-based (only relevant information)

a. Conservation	b. Devoicing	c. Aspiration	d. Suppresion	
ɛ̃kχwajablə	ɛ̃kχwajabl̥	ɛ̃kχwajab^h	ɛ̃kχwajab	unbelievable
aʁtiklə	aʁtikl̥	aʁtik^h	aʁtik	article
katχə	katχ̥	kat^h	kat	four
kadʁə	kadχ̥	kad^h	kad	frame
gofχə	gofχ̥	gof^h	gof	waffle
povʁə	povʁ̥	pov^h	pov	poor

Considering this continuum Conservation > Devoicing > Aspiration > Suppression, it becomes difficult to represent these variants. As we noted for the case in (4b), when schwa is unpronounced, nothing can license the liquid, or the aspiration noise, and by consequence they should not surface. Nevertheless, let us imagine that schwa disappears and that the liquid is still able to appear in this position. This situation is represented in (6a).

---

4 See also Brand and Ernestus (2015).
5 Which can be translated as follows: *one only whispers it or breathes it, [the liquid] is by consequence devoid of glottal vibrations and voicing.*
6 This diacritic does not entail that I consider the resulting group as an aspirated obstruent.

(6) Devoicing and Aspiration (only relevant information)
   a. Devoicing: *maintained/l/*
      – no Licensing
      – no IG
      – FEN: ON
   b. Aspiration: *noise*
      – no Licensing
      – no IG
      – FEN: ON

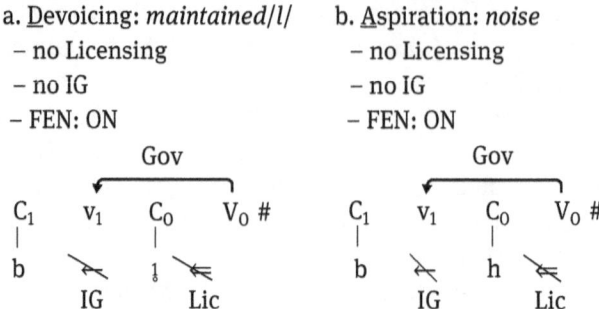

In (6a), devoicing of the liquid is due to the absence of a supporting vowel. The two consonants cannot contract IG because the liquid is unlicensed. The representation in (6b) illustrates the loss of content affecting the liquid and leading to the perceived aspiration noise. The first problem we encounter is that all conditions are the same as in (6a), and it becomes difficult to explain the difference on the surface.

For both (6a) and (6b), one major consequence is that the obstruent, in C_1, must be considered as a coda and the consonant in C_0, [l̥] or [h], as an onset.

Another problem of this approach is that, if V_0 is lost, v_1 is ungoverned but must remain silent. In all the cases of the continuum, from the maintaining of the whole group to the suppression of the liquid, there are no traces of a vowel or a transitional schwa between the obstruent and the following liquid/noise.

One can still argue that the parameter on Final Empty Nucleus (FEN) is ON[7] and silences v_1. But why is the empty nucleus unable to license the preceding liquid? Why would some segmental material (devoiced liquid, noise) be left in this position, as it is totally unlicensed by the lost final schwa?

Before giving an answer to these questions, I turn to another peculiarity of these OL clusters, namely the behaviour of these clusters in intervocalic position where the obstruent weakens whereas the liquid is unattained. I will first discuss the diachronic case (illustrated with Gallo-Romance) and then turn to the synchronic case (illustrated with Gorgia Toscana).

2.3 Lenition of OL clusters

Intervocalic obstruents are regularly weakened from Latin to French: in this lenition environment, stops get voiced, spirantized and sometimes erased. For

---

[7] This parameter gives an empty final nucleus the ability to govern when ON.

instance, the Latin labial stop [p], after a phase of voicing [b], turned to a fricative [β] or [v] in Gallo-romance: as in Latin [ripa] *shore* > Gallo-Romance [riβa] > Modern French [ʁiv] *rive*. This lenition path is expected whenever a consonant is surrounded by vowels. As Lass (1984: 181) underlines "V_V is a prime weakening environment: all things being equal we expect lenition here". The table in (7) gives examples of this regular pattern for labial, coronal and dorsal obstruents in Gallo-Romance.

(7) Lenition of intervocalic labials, coronals and dorsals in Gallo-Romance

	Latin	Gallo-Romance			Modern French
		IIIrd c.	IVrth c.	Vth c.	VIth c. – VIIIth c.	
[labial]	debe:re	devere	riba	riva	devoir	to have
	ripa		tiebedu	tievdo	rive	to bank
	tepidum				tiéde	lukewarm
[coronal]	mutare		mudare		muðare	muer	to moult
	videre		nadivu		viðere	voir	to see
	nativu				naðivu	naïf	naive
[dorsal]	lokare	logare	loyare		louer	to rent
	seku:	seguru	seyuru		sûr	safe
	rum negare		neyare		nier	to deny

This type of weakening was typical of Western Romance dialects (Brandao de Carvalho 2008, 207–233). For example, *Gorgia Toscana*, the lenition taking place in Tuscan dialects described by Marotta (2008), seems to follow the same path synchronically: this lenition process targets stops in intervocalic position even across word-boundaries. For example, Standard Italian *a'pɛrto* 'open', *'laːto* 'side', *la 'paːga* 'the salary', *la 'dotʃːa* 'the shower' are realized in Gorgia Toscana as *a'ɸɛrto, 'laːðo, la 'ɸaːɣa, la 'ðotʃːa*, respectively (Marotta 2008: 242–243).

What is interesting and, in a way, unexpected here is that OL clusters in the same intervocalic position are targeted by the same weakening process. From Latin to French as in the examples in (8), we can observe the lenition of labials, coronals and dorsals when they are part of an intervocalic OL cluster.[8]

---

[8] See also Loporcaro (2005) for a discussion on the status of OL in a diachronic perspective.

(8) OL Lenition from Latin to French (Bourciez 1958: §§132, 144, 168)

	Latin		French	
labial+L	ca̲p(u)lu	kablə	chable/câble	cable
	le̲p(o)re	ljɛʁə	lièvre	hare
	ca̲pra	ʃɛʁə	chèvre	goat
	la̲bra	lɛʁə	lèvre	lip
coronal+L	pe̲tra	pjɛʁ	pierre	stone
	nu̲trire	niʁiʁ	nourrir	feed
	*bu̲t(i)ru	bœʁ	beurre	butter
	*ri̲d(e)re	ʁiʁ	rire	laugh
dorsal+L	la̲crima	laʁm	larme	tear
	sa̲cramentu	sɛrmã	serment	oath
	fla̲grare	flɛʁe	flairer	sniff
	ma̲c(u)la	maj	maille	mesh
	ori̲c(u)la	oʁej	oreille	ear

Again, *Gorgia Toscana* applies weakening of the obstruent in OL groups word internally as shown in the examples in (9) from Marotta (2008):

(9) Gorgia Toscana: Word internally (Marotta 2008: 242)

Standard Italian	Tuscan		
ka:pra	'ka:ɸra	capra	*goat*
ri'bret:so	ri'βret:so	ribrezzo	*disgust*
'li:tro	'li:θro	litro	*liter*
'la:dro	'la:ðro	ladron	*thief*

We have seen that in Gorgia Toscana lenition of single stops applies internally and across word boundaries. One can see, in the following examples in (10), that OL clusters undergo the same lenition path across boundaries:

(10) Gorgia Toscana: Across boundaries (Marotta 2008: 243)

Standard Italian	Tuscan		
lo 'bru:tʃi	lo 'βru:ʃi	lo bruci	*(you) burn it*
lo 'trɔ:vi	lo 'θrɔ:vi	lo trovi	*(you) find it*
la 'drɔ:ga	la 'ðrɔ:ɣa*	la droga	*the drug*
la 'krɛma	la 'xrɛ:ma	la crema	*the cream*
la 'grɔt:a	la 'ɣrot:a	la grotta	*the cave*

Why is this unexpected? Bafile (1997) and Marotta (2008) noticed that, for Florentine, and more generally Tuscan, the environment cannot be defined as strictly intervocalic. The following rule of lenition from Bafile (1997: 29)[9] shows the distance from the first vowel, V_1, to the second V_2: the obstruent is not adjacent to V_2 in the OL groups: **[-snr, -cnt] → [+cnt] / $V_{1\_}$ (#) {(Liquida), (semiconsonante)}V_2**

Marotta (2008: 243) underlines that, "[s]ince all these segments do not block *gorgia*, the process appears to be constrained only by the left side of the string; therefore, the triggering context of *gorgia* may simply be defined as postvocalic."

In other words, the V_V environment may only trigger lenition if the obstruent is alone. In the case of OL group lenition in Gorgia Toscana, the only relevant context is the preceding vowel V_. Brun-Trigaud and Scheer (2012: 184), discussing the case of lenition in Gallo-Romance, take an opposite position: they argue that both members of the cluster "act with respect to lenition as if they were alone". They suggest that the obstruent is lenited as if the liquid was not there, as if the obstruent were in direct contact with the following expressed vowel.

2.4 Locality

The monopositionality vs. bipositionality problem also arises in cases of OL lenition. For Brun-Trigaud and Scheer (2012), an empty nucleus is present between the obstruent and the liquid. This empty nucleus is muted as it is enclosed in an IG domain[10] and it does not need to receive any interpretation. Moreover, it never surfaces, hence it should not be able to modify the structure of the obstruent by governing it. Brun-Trigaud and Scheer (2012) and Scheer (2014) suggest that, even though OL clusters are linked by IG, the embedded empty nucleus is still able to license or govern the preceding vowel or consonant.

The reason relates to a more general theoretical claim about *locality*.[11] The following figures in (11) sum up the two options.

---

9 In a more standard fashion: [-son, -cont] → [+cont] / $V_{1\_}$ {(#) {([+son, +voi, +cons]), ([+son, -voi, -cons])}V_2.
10 Notice that IG has no effect on the surface. If IG were responsible for the lenition of the obstruent, we would expect that OL clusters lenite in initial or in post-consonant position, which is not the case.
11 Brun-Trigaud and Scheer (2012: 187–189) and Scheer (2014: 4–5), see also Piggott and van der Hulst (1997) for a detailed formulation and its implication for nasal harmony.

Imagine that we have an empty nucleus v_2 preceding the OL cluster. In (11a), since v_1 is enclosed in an IG domain, it has no power: neither government, nor licensing ability. The only nucleus able to mute v_2 is V_0. To govern the empty nucleus, V_0 has to pass over v_1 which is a member of the same category: V. By doing so, it violates the locality condition: V_0 cannot ignore the presence of v_1 because both stay at the same level and, moreover, v_2 should be invisible to V_0 because it is masked by v_1.

(11) v_1 and the locality condition
    a. v1: locality violation   b. v1: no locality violation
    – no Government ability   – Government ability
    – no Licensing power   – Licensing power
    – IG   – IG

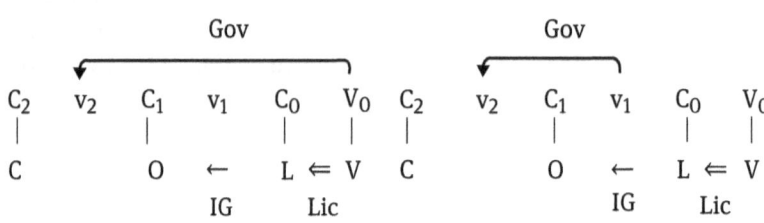

Now, if we give v_1 the ability to govern and license v_2, as in (11b), the problem of locality vanishes. The following example in (12) from Scheer (2014: 11) illustrates the change from Latin *pa̱atre* to French [pɛʁ] *père* (father) where the empty nucleus v_1 in the IG domain is licensing V_2 and allowing V_3 lengthening. When the obstruent is lost, both C_1 and v_1 are erased and V0 inherits the licensing of V_2.

(12) Lat. *paatre* > Fr. *père* (**pèrre*, parre) (*father*, Scheer 2014: 11)

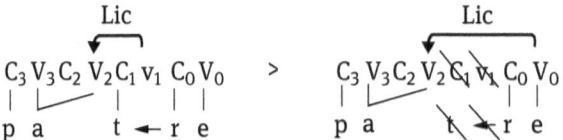

On the other hand in (13), Latin *petra* > French [pjɛʁ] *pierre* (stone) seems to behave differently: it exhibits compensatory lengthening of the liquid. This time, the vowel in V_2, [ie], is short and does not need extra space. v_1 must be governed by V_0 in order to obey the locality condition. When the obstruent is erased, there is no loss of C_1v_1: V_0 still governs v_1 and C_0, the liquid /r/, spreads on C_1.

(13) Lat. *petra* > **pietra* > Fr. *pierre* (*stone*, Scheer 2014: 11)

Scheer's conclusion is that we need to give more power to this enclosed nucleus. Even if it is totally invisible on the surface. We will see in the following sections that we can, and need to, dispense with this extra nucleus.

2.5 Summary

We are left with the following three configurations for OL clusters.

(14) Three configurations for OL clusters

a. noIG	b. IG	c. contour
C_1 v_1 C_0 V_0	C_1 v_1 C_0 V_0	C V
| | |	| | |	| |
O L V	O ← L V	OL V

In (14a), v1 should appear on the surface whenever it is ungoverned (as in the Czech case). In the case of OL+schwa# in French, as long as V_0 is expressed and has the ability to govern v_1, the configuration seems licit. However, there is no way to explain why the liquid should fall when schwa is lost. In the case of lenition, one should explain why the obstruent weakens while it is not in contact with a full vowel, apart from considering that it happens because it is in coda position.

In (14b), IG can elegantly explain why the liquid disappears in the case of OL+schwa# in French. The main problem is that v_1 never appears in all these cases, which seems highly arbitrary. This arbitrariness gets worse if we give v_1 the power to govern or license the preceding vowel or consonant while the main purpose of IG is to get rid of v_1. Another objection is the total lack of power of IG: it never affects the nature of the consonants embedded in this domain.

In (14c), the obstruent and the liquid form a contour segment and there is no need to invoke a v_1 vowel between the two consonants.[12] As Lowenstamm

---

[12] However, against 'parcimony', this solution runs the risk of multiplying the number of segments in a system: the phonology would have to encode liquids, obstruents and these contour segments.

(2003: 3) remarks, with this representation "there is no need for a third type, the popular branching onset." Here, schwa can disappear without impacting the contour. O^L and schwa can be manipulated independently. One option would be to consider that schwa licenses this contour and, if it disappears, the unlicensed liquid exponent may be lost. In the case of lenition, one will still have to explain why the liquid exponent would survive at the expense of the obstruent.

In the case of OL+schwa# reduction, the three types in (14) may explain the presence vs. absence of the liquid but fail to represent the intermediary stages (e.g. Devoicing and Aspiration). The same applies to OL lenition.

I argue, in the following sections, that the problem lies in the lack of structural relationships between the members of the OL clusters. Moreover, the misperception of these 'clusters' is a consequence of giving the same status to obstruents and liquids. v_1 is a mere artefact of the model. The only way to explain these behaviours is to (re)introduce structured representations.

3 Structured representations

In this section, I show how Government Phonology 2.0 (GP2.0) is able to overcome the difficulties underlined in the previous section. I begin by briefly presenting the GP2.0 framework and the recursive representations I will exploit for vowels and obstruents. I then turn to the question of the internal content and of the structure of the liquids. I propose a representation devoid of projection that constitutes an answer to the misperception of the categories of obstruent and liquids. I also reconsider their content and propose to adopt ® as the representative element of this class.

3.1 GP2.0

One major assumption of Element Theory (ET: Backley 2011; Harris 1990, 1994; Kaye, Lowenstamm and Vergnaud 1985; Scheer 1996) is that every prime should be directly phonetically interpretable. For example in (15), |I| can be interpreted on the surface as [i] when attached to a nuclear position, N, and as [j] when linked to an onset or a coda (Kaye and Lowenstamm 1984: 133, Backley 2011: 65):

(15) |I|: [i] and [j]

N	O	syllable level
|	|	
x	x	skeletal level
|	|	
I	I	element level
[i]	[j]	interpretation

Jensen (1994) and Brandão de Carvalho (2002) pointed out some inconsistencies with Element Theory. As Brandão de Carvalho (2002) underlines, the 'voicing' element, |L|, has no direct interpretation: there is no segment that is only 'voiced', |L| must always be used in conjunction with other elements and it can never appears alone. Its status as a prime is questionable. The answer provided by Brandão de Carvalho is that *voice* is not an element and corresponds to a contour: a relationship between skeletal positions.

Another assumption is that elements are independent from the syllable-tier: as we have seen in the preceding example, |I|[13] can attach to an onset or a nucleus and the resulting segment will differ: a glide [j] in the first case, a vowel [i] in the latter case. However some elements, like |h| 'noise', or |ʔ| 'occlusion', are only used with a 'consonantal' position.[14] We are left with a set of elements that are active only for consonants and that means that there is some sort of redundancy between the syllable positions and the segmental content.

It appears that aspiration or voicing, i.e. laryngeal contrasts, relies on the relations contracted between segments rather than on their elementary content. In the same way, 'manner' contrasts seem to relate to the space allocated to segments rather than to the presence or absence of noise or occlusion elements. For example, in Element Theory, as in a classical theory of features, the opposition /t/~/d/ would generally rely on the absence vs. the presence of the element |H| as in (16a).

---

13 Similar considerations apply to |U|.
14 But see Backley (2011: 122–124), where the occlusion element |ʔ| is used to describe laryngealized vowels (creaky voice).

(16) Lenis ~ Fortis: content vs. structure

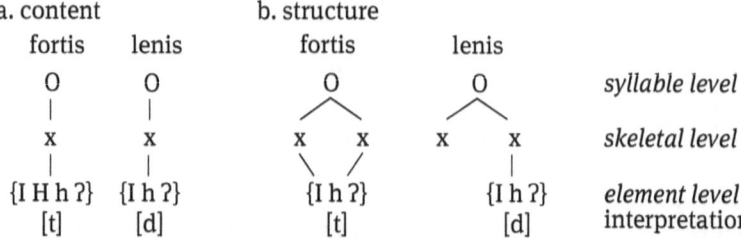

One reason to adopt GP2.0 is the willingness to reduce the number of primes manipulated in the representations. In this perspective, there is no difference in content between /t/ and /d/. The opposition is of the 'fortis'~'lenis' type: /t/ and /d/ share the same structure but differ in the number of positions they occupy, as in (16b).[15] The fortis uses its two positions and is longer than the lenis, which uses only one position. The unused x in the structure of the latter can remain free or be used, for example, to lengthen a preceding vowel.

The structure representation do not make use of |H| and we can go a step further. Let us consider that the stop/fricative contrast is also structural: we can get rid of noise |h| and occlusion |ʔ| elements. To represent the difference between stops and fricatives, we use recursive structures.

(17) Stops and fricatives in GP2.0

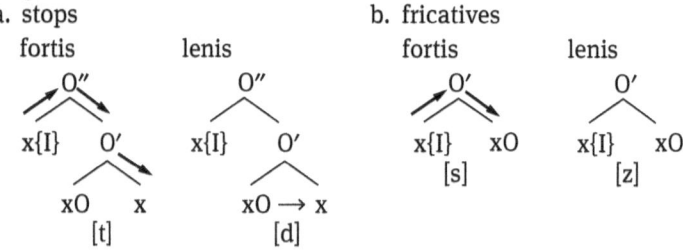

The structures are built with two types of objects: x, corresponding to the skeletal units in the preceding figures in (17), and xO which is the head of the Onset. These objects merge to project another level: stops in (17a) project two levels, O' and O", while fricatives, in (17b) only project once (O').

In these representations of stops and fricatives, which are different from Pöchtrager (2006) but can be considered as an extension of Živanovič and

---

[15] See Pöchtrager (2006: 34) for examples of the structures of [f] and [v]. I use here a different set of elements for coronals (|I|) and dorsals (|IU|). Labials are still defined by the |U| element.

Pöchtrager (2010), only x-positions can be annotated. It means that these positions can bear elementary material, for example x{I}. The arrows, bolded in (17a) and (17b), represent *melodic-command*, which is a relationship from an annotated x to an unannotated x or a head. It expresses the same relation as in figure (16b) and it means, for the fortes, that the content located in the upper x in the structure, {I} in this case, is also interpreted in the lower x position of the structure. *Control*, symbolized by "→", is a licensing relation between a head and an unannotated complement which silences an x.[16]

Vowels respond to the same principles. [i] and [u], in the following examples in (18) project one level N' from the association of a head of a Nucleus, xN, and a complement, x, annotated with an |I| and an |U| element respectively. On the other hand, [a] and [ə] are totally empty: they do not bear elementary content.

(18) Cardinal vowels and *ə*

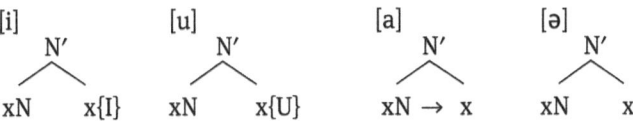

Mid vowels, like [e] and [o] in (19), are composed of the structure of [i] and [u] respectively and the structure corresponding to [a]. This representation is equivalent to the fusion of |A| with |I| and |U| in the classical ET framework, i.e. |A.I| and |A.U|.

(19) Mid-vowels *e* and *o*

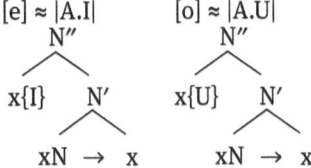

This set of structures constitutes our building blocks for vowels and consonants. The main property of these segments is their ability to project another level: N', O' or O". I now turn to the representation of liquids.

---

16 "An unannotated x in a non-maximal onset projection must be controlled by its xO" (Pöchtrager, 2006: 77).

3.2 Liquids: rhotics and laterals

Liquids share distributional properties with nasals as part of the sonorant set of segments. Another main attribute of this class is their assimilatory power. Following Rice and Avery (1991) and Rice (1992), this class is characterized by the presence of the Spontaneous Voice or Sonorant Voice (SV) node. For example, in order to treat assimilations in Toba Batak, Rice and Avery (1991: 109) propose that the nasal /n/, which, in this language, assimilates to the following liquid (e.g. *nr > rr, nl > ll* but *rn > rn, ln > ln*), is represented as a bare SV node which is later filled at the phonetic level with nasal by a default rule. /l/ and /r/ are not targeted by the assimilation rule due to the presence of the 'continuant' node, as we can see in (20):

(20) Coronal sonorants (Rice and Avery 1991: 109)

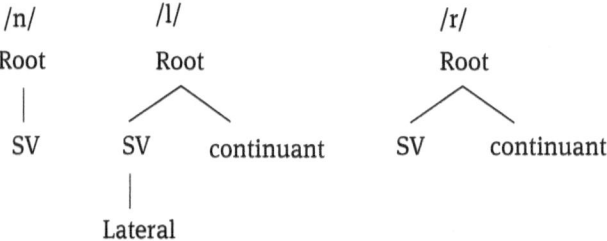

The liquid assimilation in Toba Batak also shows an asymmetry between the lateral and the rhotic where *rl > ll* but *lr > lr*. For Rice (2005: 40), "Based on the asymmetries, and taking assimilation asymmetries as a markedness diagnostic, one can claim that /r/ patterns as if it were less marked than /l/." However, as she remarks,[17] Hungarian exhibits the opposite behaviour: *rl > rl* but *lr > rr*, where the unmarked segment seems to be the lateral.

There are two questions here: what is the internal content of these segments and what is their structure? In a geometrical feature framework, the answer to the first question is that this set contains an SV node. The answer to the second question is that the structure of the liquids may vary cross-linguistically. In a GP2.0 framework, these questions translate in terms of the nature of the elementary content and of the structure of these segments.

As underlined by Rice (1992: 91), the definition of the rhotics, laterals and coronal nasals in Harris (1990, 1994) is the mirror image of her proposal[18]

---

17 Rice (2005: 41).
18 Rice (1992) treats the Toba Batak liquid assimilation as a case of feature spreading whereas Harris (1990) would treat them as decomposition (|?|-loss).

where nasals are the more complex and rhotics are simpler as shown in the following representations in (21):

(21) Coronal sonorants (Harris 1994)

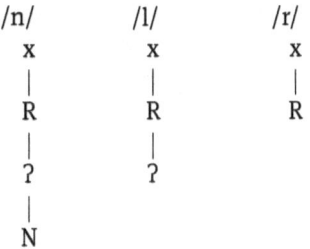

The defining element of this category is |R| which corresponds to the coronal gesture and one may find this |R| associated with other elements in /t/ or /s/, as shown in the lenition trajectory in (22).

(22) Coronals lenition trajectory (Harris 1990: 269)

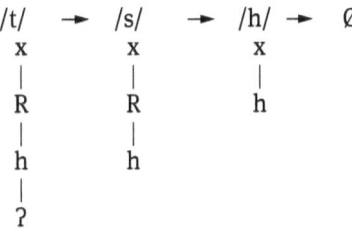

These representations are mainly proposed in order to explain processes like lenition trajectories. As seen on the preceding figure in (22), spirantisation /t/ → /s/, debuccalisation /s/ → /h/ and loss /h/ → Ø are seen as decomposition, or loss of |ʔ|, |R|, |h| respectively. In the same vein, glottaling,[19] where plosives turn to glottal stops /t/ → [ʔ] (e.g. *city* > *ci*[ʔ]*y*), and tapping, where /t/ → [ɾ] (e.g. *city* > *ci*[ɾ]*y*), can also be seen as decomposition processes. Moreover, the preceding representations constitute a direct translation of the government abilities of these segments through the *Complexity Condition*:

Complexity Condition (Harris 1990: 274)
Let α and β be segments occupying the positions A and B respectively. Then, if A governs B, β must be no more complex than α.

---

19 Harris (1990: 285).

In order to rule out, for example, /r+Obstruent/ sequences as licit onsets, the idea is that the relation between these two segments is due to their internal makeup. The obstruent containing more elements must govern /r/, which contains only one element (|R|). This ensues that /r+Obstruent/ clusters are heterosyllabic and can never be considered as complex onsets, but only as a coda+onset. If we consider the reverse order, /Obstruent+r/, the obstruent can govern the liquid and both segments will form a licit complex onset.[20]

3.3 The '|A|' analysis and the non-projecting structures of liquids

In this section, I adress an alternative proposal concerning the internal content and the structure of the liquids. I present the hypothesis whereby liquids do not contain |R| but the element |A|.

Backley (1993) discusses the effects of the *Complexity Condition* on forms like *swim* or *swine*, where /s/, composed of |R| and |h| elements, is considered as an initial coda.[21] Recall that [w] is the actualisation of |U| in an onset postion. In order for /#sw/ to be interpreted as a coda followed by an onset, [s] and [w] must be at least equal in complexity, and this is not the case here: [s] is more complex than [w], and /#sw/ is seen as illicit. The only way to get rid of this problem is to lessen the weight of [s] by reducing the number of elements it is made of.

This leads Backley to reconsider the internal content of coronals, and to question the status of |R| as a primitive. If for Harris (1994: 123) "the independent interpretation of |R| is a coronal tap", it is the only visible effect of this element. The consequence is that we should dismiss with |R| as a primitive. The

---

[20] Rice (1992: 69) takes the same approach concerning government/licensing, except that her definition focuses on the presence/absence of an SV node: "An additional consonant can be licensed in an onset position only if (i) branching onsets are allowed in the language (ii) the consonant has less SV structure than the following syllabified consonant [...] i.e. it governs the following syllabified consonant. [...] A consonant A governs an adjacent consonant B if A has less SV structure than B". Like Harris (1990), Rice (1992: 70) proposes that there should be a minimal sonority distance between the governor and the governee. Notice that this goverment relationship is reversed with respect to Infrasegmental Government where sonorants govern obstruents (in the CV-Strict framework, relationships are always regressive).
[21] Kaye (1992).

fricative is thus represented as |h|[22] alone corresponding to 'unmarked oral friction'[23] which is, by default, interpreted as coronal.

If |R| is not part of the set of elements anymore, what are rhotics made of? Backley's (1993) answer is that /r/ corresponds to a non-nuclear |v|.[24] Flapping of /t/ corresponds to the loss of all the elements of this segment: all that remains is an empty slot which is interpreted as [ɾ]. The same principle rules the production of schwas/default vowels. Whenever a nuclear position is properly governed, it does not surface, but if it is left ungoverned, |v| is expressed and can vary across languages[25] and it can also vary depending on the elementary environment.

For example, discussing the cases of intrusive and linking-r in English, Broadbent (1991) proposes that, just like [j] and [w] are the correspondents of [i] and [u] respectively, the approximant [ɹ] is the glide counterpart of schwa.[26] For Backley (2011: 169), linking-r is the product of the spreading of the |A| element contained in the preceding vowel. If the latter contains an |I| or an |U|, a glide, [j] or [w], appears as exemplified in (23) from Backley (2011: 172).

(23) Linking (Backley 2011: 172)

	Linking |I|	Linking |U|	Linking |A|
preceding vowel	{iː ɪ eɪ aɪ ɔɪ}	{uː ʊ əʊ aʊ}	{ɛː ɑː ɔː ə ɪə eə ʊə}
resulting glide	[j]	[w]	[ɹ]
example	fly [j]away	go [w]away	far [ɹ]away

---

22 In order to keep the contrast between the coronal fricative and the glottal fricative, Backley (1993) exploits the properties of the cold vowel |v| and considers that [s] is the result of the fusion of |v| as operator and |h| as head (i.e. |v.h|) whereas the latter, [h], results form the fusion of |h| as operator and |v| as head (i.e. |h.v|). In contemporary words, [s] corresponds to headed |h| while [h] corresponds to unheaded |h|. Hence, the lenition process from /s/ → /h/ corresponds to a headedness reversal.
23 While the glottal fricative is |h|: a "basic fricative without any oral resonance" (Backley, 1993: 322).
24 This is congruent with the analysis proposed by Rice (1992: 76), who argues for the lack of Place node for /r/ when discussing the imbalance between /r/ and /l/ with respect to their ability to form a cluster with the coronal obstruents (e.g.*tl, *dl vs. tr, dr).
25 See Onuma (2015) for an in-depth view concerning empty nuclei and Nasukawa (2014) for a (recursive) use of |I|, |A|, |U| as [ɨ], [ə], [ɯ] respectively.
26 An alternative analysis is proposed by Harris (1994: 248), where the intrusive/linking-r is a floating /r/ part of the lexical representation but unassociated with a syllabic position. This floating segment, as in *liaison* in French, anchors whenever an empty onset is available at the beginning of the next word.

Whenever an empty onset follows a 'non-high' lax vowel, like [ɛː ɑː ɔː ə], an /r/ is inserted. Broadbent (1991: 300) concluded that, because (i) all low vowels contain |A|, (ii) an empty onset contains the cold vowel |v|, the result of the *Glide Formation* is the fusion of both elements, |A.v| ≈ [ə], and that this resulting 'schwa in an onset is realized as r'. As an example, the linking-r in *Lisa* [ɹ] is explained by the propagation of |A| in the following empty Onset slot which is thus interpreted as [ɹ], as shown in (24):

(24) Propagation of |A| (Backley 2011: 173)

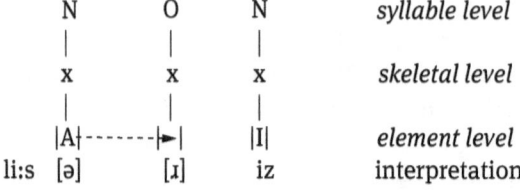

This case has led Element Theory to the hypothesis that the main element in rhotics is the 'mAss' element: |A|.²⁷ This claim is supported by their influence on neighbouring vowels where rhotics tend to provoke lowering (Wiese 2011: 6, Backley 2011: 89). It has also been noted (Hall 1993: 87–88, Scheer 1996: 163) that historical /r/, in final and preconsonantal positions, regularly vocalized to an |A| segment in standard German (noted as [ä], [ʌ̯]). The same approach is taken in GP2.0 where, as in (25), /r/ is considered as the equivalent of the semi-vowels [w, j] and where the rhotic contains an |A| element.

(25) Semi-vowels and r as non-projecting structures (Pöchtrager 2006: §2.3.4 p.91)
    [w]   [j]   [r]
    xO{U} xO{I} xO{A}

Structure aside, laterals and coronal nasals, in (26), are also defined by the use of |A| in Pöchtrager (2006: 86–87).

---

27 Notice that Harris (1994: 259) differentiates the tap /ɾ/ (which is only made of the element |R|) from a dark /r/ (|@R|, dorsal) and a clear /r/ (|IR|, apical/laminal) approximant.

(26) *l* and nasals (Pöchtrager 2006: 86–87)

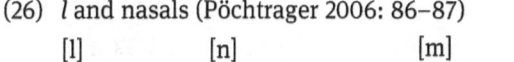
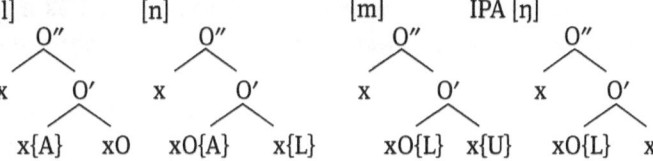

As we can see, the previous representations are, modulo the structure, a direct borrowing of the Element Theory hypothesis.

3.4 SV, |R|, |v| or |A| or structure?

However, using the 'mAss' element is not without problems. Recall the structure for [a] and [ə], given in (18), and repeated for convenience in (27) below:

(27) The emptiness of [a] and [ə]

	[a]	[ə]
ET:	|A̲|	|A|
GP2.0:	N′ ⟋⟍ xN → x	N′ ⟋⟍ xN x

In the ET framework, [a] and [ə] correspond to headed |A| and non-headed |A| respectively. In the GP2.0 framework, as proposed in Pöchtrager and Zivanovic (2010), there is no use of the |A| element. This element is replaced by structure.[28] Exploring Putonghua rimes, authors show that all the vowels, except /ɨ, ə, a/, result form glide-colouring. Simply put, the only lexical vowels in Putonghua are /ɨ, ə, a/: [e, ɛ] and [o, ɔ] appear in the vicinity of an *i*-glide and *u*-glide, respectively. Spreading of I and U melodies is constrained by m-command and by the space provided by lexical vowels which do not bear any element. If these structures are empty, it seems paradoxical to (re)introduce the |A| element in the formalism.

We have seen that there are several options concerning the internal content of the sonorant class. Whether SV, |R|, |v| or |A|, each approach is able to isolate

---

[28] Notice that Živanovič and Pöchtrager (2010) use adjunction structures for /a/ and /ə/ while the present proposal uses regular projecting structures for these vowels. This difference is not crucial for the rest of the analysis.

this specific category from the rest of the segments on the basis of a shared intrinsic feature. I take the view that what has been interpreted as a feature shared by rhotics, laterals and the nasal liquid (sonorancy) is a structural matter that I shall now discuss.

Before this, I will say a word concerning the symbol ® I will use for liquids. As we have seen, the set of elements proposed in the literature is quite diverse: |R|, |A|, SV, or |v|. Each element of this set says something necessary in order to define this class of sonorants. They are coronals (|R| or |A|[29]), spontaneously voiced (SV) and in a way 'unmarked' (|v|). My proposal is that even if their structure informs us much more than their internal content, we still need to distinguish, for instance, rhotics from semi-vowels and, more importantly, from completely empty onsets. I therefore propose to use ® as a shortcut and as a reminder of these specific properties. I will use it as a dummy-element: I will not consider that ® is part of the set of elements.

The idea is to generalize the 'non-projecting structures', as proposed by Pöchtrager (2006) for the rhotics and the semi-vowels, to the whole class of sonorant, i.e. liquids and, for now, the coronal nasal.[30] The following figures in (28) illustrate the structures I propose.

(28) *r* as projectionless, *l* and *n* as adjunction structures

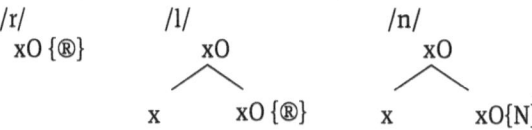

What unifies the members of this class is their structural abilities: in this view, coronal sonorants cannot be seen as full-fledge segments but rather as deficients and in need of a host.[31]

---

[29] Concerning coronality, one can add the hypothesis that |I| is the element defining coronal sonorants. For example, Backley and Nasukawa (2011) suggest that the tap /r/ of Japanese non-past marker *-ru* results from the same process as linking-*r* in English except that it is made of the element |I| in a non-nuclear position, as it appears in the vicinity of /i,e/.

[30] I am not certain that using projection structures for the labial and the dorsal nasals is mandatory, as there is a set of evidence that they sometimes behave as the coronal nasals and sometimes as regular stops. For further arguments on this distinction refer to Voeltzel (2016). Notice that in the representation of nasals, following Nasukawa (1997), I will use |N| instead of |L|.

[31] In a Declarative Phonology perspective, Angoujard (2012: 5–6) proposes that liquids do not occupy a position *per se*, rather they stay in an intermediary position in between the initial position (i) and the peak (sommet) of the curve (la plage) which is associated with a rythmic template.

The structure of /r/ is unchanged[32]: it is a non-projecting head containing ®. On the other hand, /l/[33] and /n/ are 'adjunction structures': even though both the head xO and the complement x associate, they do not project an O' level. I fully adopt the definition of adjunctions except for f which needs to be modified to take into account the preceding discussion about the internal content of sonorants:

Adjunction (Pöchtrager 2006: 166)

Adjunction is defined as a structure where
    a. a node α is split in two parts, α1 and α2, and
    b. α2 dominates both α1 and an unannotated x, yielding the following structure:
    c.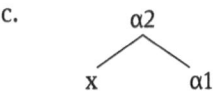
    d. The nodes α1 and α2 are identical with respect to their level of projection.
    e. Only α1 is annotated with melody.

Adjunction is possible iff
    f. α1 is annotated for the element A *for the elements |L| or |®|*.
    g. α2 does not project.

Modifying (f) by replacing element |A| by elements |L| or |®| predicts that units bearing |L| or |®| may exhibit a uniform behaviour which relies on their ability to form an adjunction.

Because they do not project, liquids will need a hosting projection. The only available hosts are onset or nucleus projections, namely only obstruents and vowels, since they can recursively project different levels of structure and are able to support a projectionless structure.

---

[32] Pöchtrager's (2006: 168) idea was that the structure without adjunction may be the tap, [ɾ]. The adjunction structure I use for /l/ corresponds to the trill [r]. I will show that the difference between these two types of /r/ is mainly due to the nature of their host.
[33] One advantage of this representation is that adding an {I} element to the complement position x would define a palatal /ʎ/, while adding {U} will end up in a dark lateral /ɫ/. Clear /l/ has no element associated with the complement.

The following example illustrates the case of a stop (see (29a)) and a vowel (see (29b)) hosting /r/ where {E} stands for any elementary content. As we can see, the /stop+r/ structure results from merging the structure of an obstruent, which has two levels of projections (O″), with the projectionless structure of /r/. Merging results in an additional projection O‴. This third level is a projection of the head of the obstruent structure xO (bold indicates the path from the head to the third level of projection). The same merging mechanism is responsible for the N″ projection derived from the head (xN) of the vowel structure.[34]

(29) Hosting structures and /r/
 a. /stop+r/   b. /r+vowel/

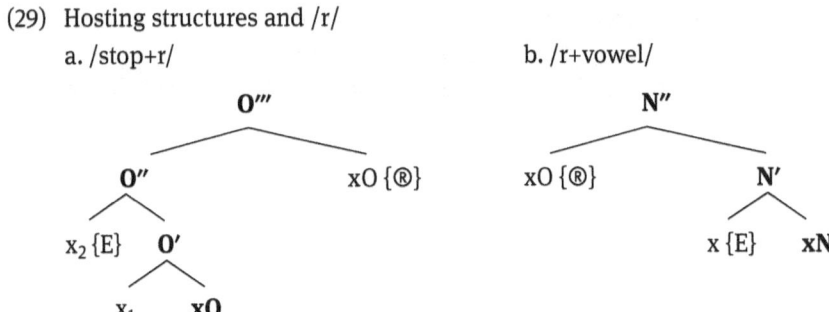

Both structures in (29) predict that xO{®} is in a way 'unseen' by the neighbouring segments: what is visible is the extra-projection of an Onset or a Nucleus. Hence, processes can either directly target this extra-projection or the unit bearing the extra-projection. In the first case, we expect the loss:
- of the content of xO{®} leaving only an xO,
- of the head and the content, which can either leave remnants in the form of an x-position or a total loss Ø.

In the second case, focusing on the OL groups, we expect that the unit bearing the extra-position undergoes the standard lenition path in intervocalic position. Its behaviour should not be different than that of an obstruent 'alone'. We thus expect the following path: voicing > spirantisation > place loss/debuccalisation > deletion. Each step of this path is respectively reinterpreted as: loss of the m-command > pruning of the structure > elementary loss > deletion.

---

[34] The proposal in (28) and the structures in (29) bear resemblance with the Onset Proeminence model developed by Schwartz (2016: 54–59). In this model, liquids and glides lack a Noise node and are hosted under the Vocalic Onset (VO) node. They can merge with the preceding consonant and be hosted in the VO node of the consonant (absorption, Schwartz 2016: 57, fig. 23). They can also merge with the following vowel and in this case, they are hosted at the Closure level, hence acting as obstruents but still lacking a Noise node (promotion, Schwartz 2016: 58, fig. 25).

In the next sections, I will show how this works on the various cases of lenition and on the final OLə groups. I will then explore its consequences.

4 Back to OL clusters

My proposal is that so-called OL clusters constitute a particular structure built of two radically different objects: projecting vs. projectionless. Adopting the structures in (29), I will reinterpret the cases of lenition of OL clusters and reconsider the case of OLə# in French. I will then explore the cases of liquids in Faroese and in Samothraki Greek, as both give crucial information and support for this hypothesis. I will end by discussing the case of metathesis in Sardinian, reinterpreted as percolation of the liquid.

4.1 Lenition and schwa-loss

Recall that we left the problem of lenition and schwa-loss with three unsatisfactory options: using Infrasegmental Government, no Infrasegmental Government and a contour solution. I propose here to reanalyze both cases using the recursive structures provided by GP2.0.

4.1.1 Lenition of OL

The examples given in (12) p̲atre 'father' and (13) pe̲tra 'stone' were extremely simplified. The table in (30) describes these cases in more detail, as well as an additional form Latin mu̲tare > French muer 'moult'. This last form mu̲tare, from Zink (1986: 64–65), shows the regular pattern of lenition where intervocalic [t] from Latin evolved to the voiced coronal [d], then spirantized to [ð] in Gallo-Romance and was eventually deleted. The same path was followed by OL clusters, namely (30a) *voicing*, (30b) *spirantisation*, (30c) *loss* and in (30d) *the ultimate loss of the final schwa*.

(30) Lat. p̲atre, pe̲tra, mu̲tare > Fr. père 'father', pierre 'stone', muer 'moult'

change	datation	process	petra	patre	mutare
dipthongization	IIIrd	ɛː > ɛɛ > iɛ	piɛtra		
a. coronal voicing	IVth	t > d	piɛdra	padre	mudare

Gallo-Romance dipthongization	VIth	a: > aa > aɛ		paɛtre	mudaɛre
b. coronal spirantization		d > ð	piɛðrə	paɛðre	muðaɛre
diphthong closing	VIIth	iɛ > ie	pieðrə		muðɛr
monophthongization		aɛ > ɛ		pɛðrə	
u-palatalization	VIIIth				myðɛr
c. coronal loss VCrV>VrV	(IXth)- XIth	VŏrV > VrV	pierə	pɛrə	**myɛr**
r-(compensatory) lenghtening		r > rr	pierrə	pɛrə	–
semi-vocalization Loi de position	XIIIth XVIIth	ie > je jeC > jɛC	pjerrə pjɛrrə	pɛrə	mɥe (mfr)
r-degemination		rr > r		pjɛrə	
d. schwa#-loss		ə# > Ø	**pjɛr**	**pɛr**	

Notice that I integrated *r*-compensatory lengthening in the table in (30). I subscribe to Pope's (1934: 149) remark that "ð appears to have been sometimes assimilated to *r*, sometimes simply effaced, and the conditions under which these processes take place have not yet been determined". This is especially true for the two cases under scrutiny, *patre* and *petra*. From the XIIth to the XIIIth c., *pet̲ra* was written as <piere, perre, pere> and one has to wait until circa the XVth c. for a generalisation of the use of <pierre> as the standard form. The same hesitation is observed for *pat̲re* between two written forms <perre, pere> except that the stabilisation is around the XIIth c., when the use of <pere> was generalized. One can only speculate by looking at the "minimal pair" *pat̲re* <pedre>, at the beginning of XIth c., *pet̲ra* <peddre> and at the end of Xth c.: did spirantisation occur at the same time for both forms? Is <r> vs. <rr> due to true compensatory lengthening, opposing simple and geminated rhotics, or does the difference lie in the internal content, opposing a tap and a trill? This issue is still open to debate.

I now turn to the interpretation of the lenition process in GP2.0. I begin with the form [patre] in (31). The bisyllabicity of *patre* is rendered by the two nuclear projections N1''' of [a] and N2''' [e]. For readability reasons, I noted the phonetic realization of each part of the representation. The structure of the OL cluster I propose is given in bold: O''' is the extra-level projected by the obstruent [t] to host the projectionless liquid [r]. This onset is embedded under N2‴, which is under the dominance of N1″: this is the structure of an intervocalic obstruent or OL *group*, as is the case here.

(31) [patre]

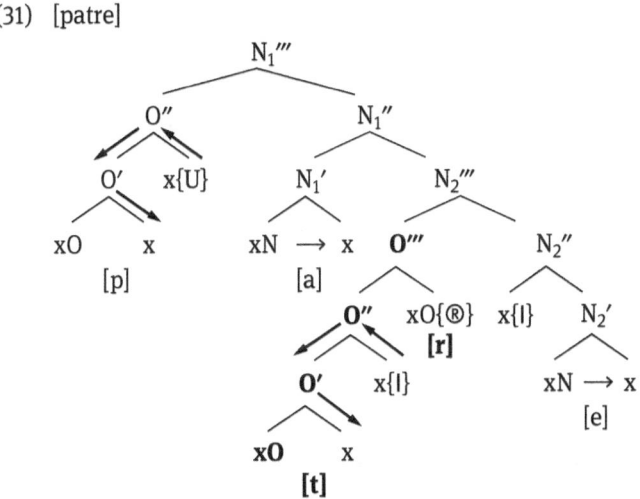

The V_V environment provokes the lenition of the obstruent and the first step is voicing which is now expected because O‴, the maximal projection of xO, is the target of the lenition. This translates, in (32), by the loss of the m-command. The result on the surface is [d]. [r] does not block this process: as if it were not there.

(32) [padre] >> voicing as m-command loss

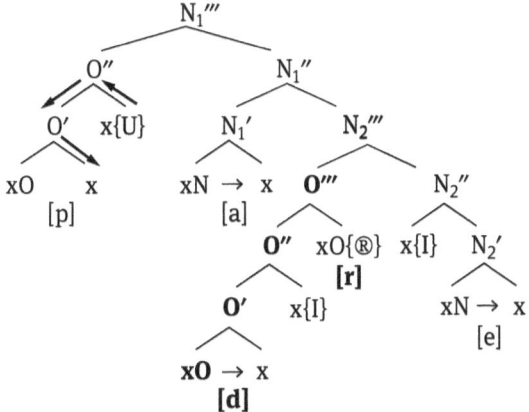

Once voicing occurred, the next step is the spirantisation, illustrated in (33). Recall that the difference between a stop and a fricative in this framework is the number of projections. What we observe here is the pruning of the structure of the stop which now projects only once and is interpreted as the coronal fricative [ð]. [r] is still protected under the extra-projection.

(33) [paɛðre] >> spirantisation as projection loss

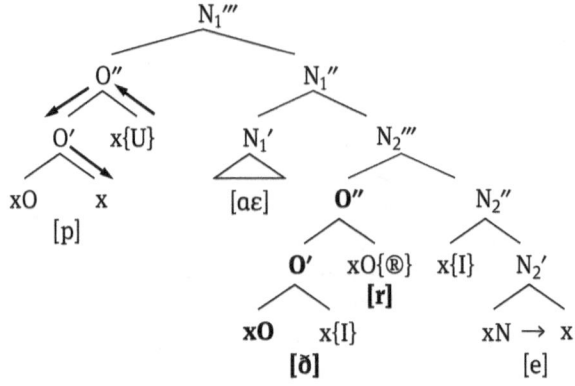

The difference between diachronic lenition and Gorgia Toscana is based on the fact that only step b of (30) – *spirantisation* – applies: there is no change in voicing. Recall the example in (9) *liter* and *thief* which are pronounced as ['liːtro], ['laːdro] in standard Italian and ['liːθro], ['laːðro] in Gorgia Toscana. The following figures (34a) and (34b), which show only the relevant information, illustrate both cases of voiced and unvoiced stops followed by a liquid and undergoing intervocalic spirantisation. The circled part is the one subject to pruning. As one can notice, in (34a), the m-command coming from x_2 and responsible for the unvoiced nature of the obstruent is still there and is still active: the resulting fricative is thus unvoiced. On the other hand, the voiced obstruent, in (34b), lacks m-command and, after pruning, the resulting fricative is voiced.

(34) Gorgia Toscana lenition
    a. /unvoiced stop+r/   b. /voiced stop+r/

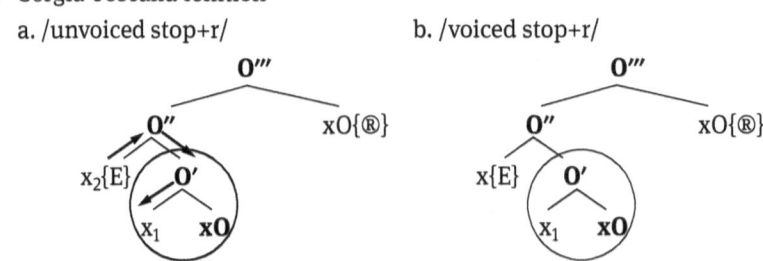

The last two steps of the diachronic lenition, in (35) and (36), are cases of reconfiguration. The loss of the coronal entails the loss of the extra-projection O''' because [r] is unable to project. For this reason, we would expect the liquid to disappear, contrary to fact. I argue that this is because N_2' (at this stage the following vowel is a schwa) is able to keep [r] under this extra-projection in [pɛrə] so that [r] is directly dominated by a nucleus (bolded in 35).

(35) [pɛrə] >> obstruent loss

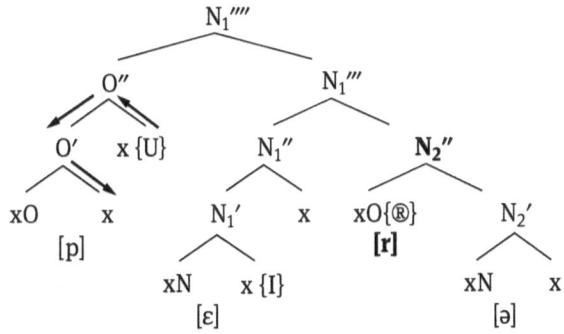

The last stage, illustrated in (36), is the loss of schwa in final position: the final empty nucleus is still there as xN_2 (bolded in (36)), but is no longer pronounced. [r] is again saved by a nucleus and docks under N_1'''.

(36) [pɛr] >> schwa loss

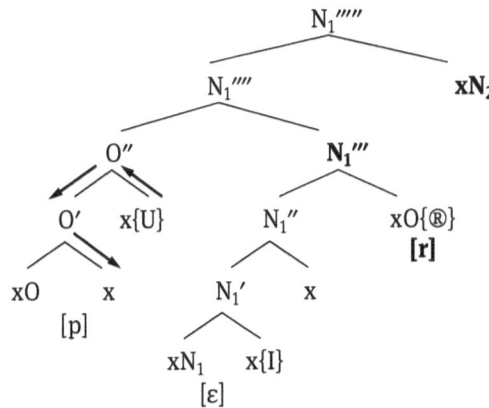

These last two examples (35) and (36) are actually revealing of the opportunism of [r], which seems to be able to travel from onsets to nuclei provided an extra-projection is made available.

4.1.2 Schwa loss

The cases of OL+ə# in French are somewhat different from the preceding lenition case: while in the latter, the obstruent was lost, the former, as a consequence to the loss of schwa, affects the liquid. As I mentioned before, there are four variants for this loss:
- Conservation: where the whole cluster and schwa are realized >> [dʁə],
- Devoicing: which happens when schwa is lost and where devoicing touches the liquid whenever it is already voiced >> [dχ],
- Aspiration: in this case, we find traces of noise or friction >> [dʰ] (recall that this transcription does not mean that it is an aspirated consonant).
- Suppression: where the liquid totally disappears >> [d].

These possibilities can now be represented using recursive structures and the projectionless status of /r/.

The figure in (37) gives the 'standard configuration' C for the French *cadre* [kadʁə] 'frame'. In this representation, only the relevant parts are given, namely the OL+ə# cluster [dʁə] and its reflexes.

(37) ca[dʁə] >> Conservation

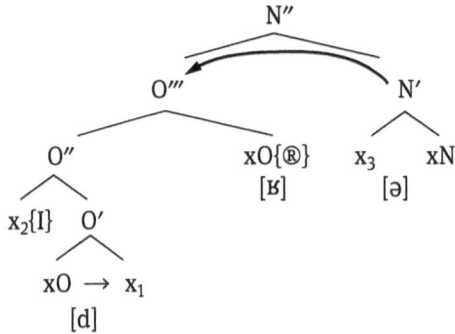

The liquid is hosted by the obstruent which, as we have already seen in the case of lenition, projects an extra level O‴. Both consonants are dominated by the nuclear projection N″ and there is no intervening empty nucleus between the structure of the obstruent and the liquid. The nucleus licenses the whole onset structure and also the interpretation of the liquid as a voiced segment.

In French, the rhotic has two variants: a voiced variant ([ʁ]), when preceded by a voiced obstruent and an unvoiced one ([χ]), when preceded by an unvoiced obstruent. The schwa-loss entails devoicing of the liquid. In (38), the final empty nucleus (xN) does not license the liquid or any structure, hence it is devoiced and we obtain [dχ].

(38) ca[dχ] >> Devoicing

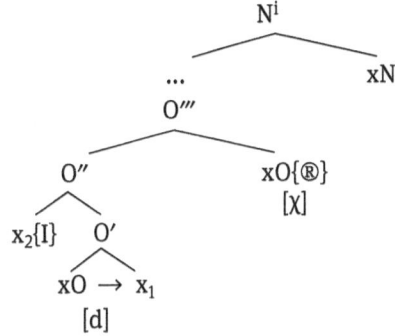

The structure in (39) accounts for the aspiration of the obstruent: it is the result of the loss of the elementary content (|®|). The consequence of the debuccalisation is that the whole structure is interpreted as a *pseudo-aspirated* segment.

(39) ca[dʰ] >> Aspiration

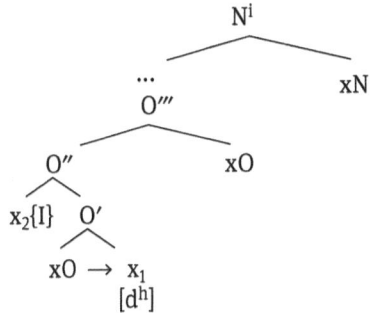

The total loss of the liquid – *Suppression* – is represented in (40) and corresponds to the structure of a final consonant followed by an empty nucleus. The deletion of a projection does not entail any change in the structure of the obstruent, which still surfaces as [d].

(40) ca[d] >> Suppression

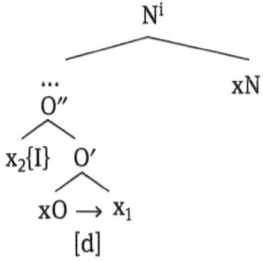

The configurations depicted in (38) and (39) are both answers to a unique condition: the loss of the nuclear licenser. The difference lies in the behaviour of the onset head which licenses either the content of the liquid or only the head of the liquid.

4.2 Consequences on the representations: no IG and no v_1

In the preceding sections, I have shown that it is possible to treat the cases of intervocalic OL clusters if we enrich the structures of the representations. Furthermore, there are two unsubstantiated objects that are no longer needed: Infrasegmental Government (IG) and v_1.

The alleged empty nucleus enclosed between the obstruent and the liquid is no longer necessary.[35] In fact, because of the absence of an intervening nucleus, there is no *locality violation*: the two expressed nuclei, surrounding the OL cluster in the case of lenition, are visible to each other.

On the account defended here, IG is not necessary either: the only motivation for this kind of government was to quiet v_1; it had no effect on the consonants that contracted this relationship. Nevertheless, we cannot discard IG on the basis of this sole argument. The fact that liquids do not project and can be hosted by nuclei, [xO{®}]$_N$, and onsets, [xO{®}]$_O$, must have visible consequences. The cases of rhotics in Faroese and compensatory lengthening in Samothraki Greek, to which I now turn, illustrate the contrast between the structures I propose.

---

[35] One needs to keep in mind that, as for Czech, there are empty nuclei which can be subject to Proper Government and which can surface whenever the licensing conditions are met. This never occurs in the cases of OL+ə# and VOLV under scrutiny.

4.2.1 [xO{®}]_N vs. [xO{®}]_O Faroese

Faroese (Thráinsson et al. 2012, Adams and Petersen 2014, Voeltzel 2016) has one rhotic /r/ which has two allophonic[36] realizations: an approximant [ɹ] and a trill [r]. The approximant has a wider distribution than the trill. The table in (41)[37] recaps the environment for each variant and clearly shows that one can only find the trill after a stop [p, t, k, b, d, g]. In initial and final position, only the approximant is attested.

(41) The distribution of rhotics in Faroese (Voeltzel 2016)

#_V	['ɹɛnːa]	renna	'run'	Adam and Peterson (2014:642)
	['ɹɔːa]	Ráða	'advice'	Adam and Peterson (2014:641)
	['ɹad͡ʒːa]	reiggja	'swing'	Adam and Peterson (2014:648)
Vː_V	['dʊiːɹʊɹ]	dýrur	'expensive'	Adam and Peterson (2014:647)
	['nʊiːɹa]	nýra	'kidney'	Adam and Peterson (2014:647)
	['vœuːɹʊ]	vóru	'were'	Adam and Peterson (2014:654)
_C	['t͡ʃʰɪ̥rt͡ʃa]	kirkja	'church'	Adam and Peterson (2014:658)
	['skɔrpa]	skorpa	'crust'	Adam and Peterson (2014:662)
	['mɔrkna]	moyrkna	'rot'	Adam and Peterson (2014:649)
V_#	['dœʰtːɪɹ]	dóttir	'daughter'	Adam and Peterson (2014:644)
	['kʰlœuːkʊɹ]	klókur	'clever'	Adam and Peterson (2014:645)
	['ʃɛgvʊɹ]	sjógvur	'sea, ocean'	Adam and Peterson (2014:645)
C_V	['pʰɛgv]	prógv	'examination'	Adam and Peterson (2014:645)

---

[36] For Thráinsson et al. (2012: 45f), /r/ has a "retroflexed variant [which] occurs (somewhat sporadically) in connection with /t, d, s, n, l/, which are then retroflexed also". Adams and Petersen (2014: 663) underline that the retroflexion is heard only before the fortis coronal stop /t/ and, moreover, they mention that a "lightly rolled [r] is heard after *b, d, g, p, t* and *k*".

[37] The data are from Voeltzel (2016). She presents two types of corpora: one based on first hand data and another based on second hand data. The latter is formed of harmonized data found in the literature on Faoese. In this table, I use the harmonized forms found in Adams and Petersen (2014) which are closest to the harmonization and differ, here, on the transcription of lenis stops and affricates.

[ˈdreɛːʰpa]	drepa	'kill'	Adam and Peterson (2014:642)
[ˈɛaːʰkraɹ]	akrar	'field'	Adam and Peterson (2014:639)
[grœːn]	Grøn	'green'	Adam and Peterson (2014:648)

What is of importance here is that a model which ignores the structural difference between an obstruent and a liquid would only be able to take note of the realization of /r/ as [ɹ] in the initial position, and as [r] after a consonant. It would not be able to make any reference to syllable constituents, since both are in onset position. Moreover, it would need to consider that the environments {#_V, V_V}, classically a fortition and lenition position, share something.

However, on my proposal, the explanation for the attested distribution is rather straightforward. Whenever the liquid is hosted by the onset, as in (42a), it is realized as [r],[38] whenever it is hosted by a nuclear (extra)projection it is realized as [ɹ], as in (42b).

(42) Hosting structures and /r/ in Faroese
 a. /stop+r/ >> [r]   b. /r+vowel/ >> [ɹ]

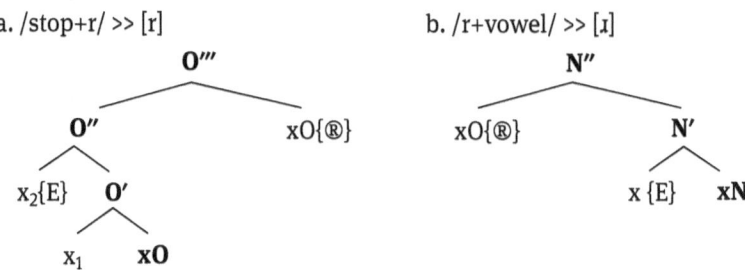

The case of /r/ in Faroese thus constitutes the kind of evidence we need to assess the distinction between [xO{®}]_N and [xO{®}]_O. The surface interpretation is only due to this difference in the localisation of the projectionless structure.

4.2.2 Samothraki Greek

Another interesting example is the case of compensatory lengthening in Samothraki Greek described by Topintzi (2006ab), Kiparsky (2011), Katsika and

---

[38] Notice that this is true for stops. In the cases of /labial fricative+liquid/ clusters as in frá [frɔaː] 'from', frægur [ˈfɹɛaːvʊɹ] 'good', frysta [ˈfɹɪsta] 'freeze', the liquid behaves as if it were located under a nucleus. It is related to the unclear status of the labial fricatives sometimes described as a fricative, an approximant or a glide (Thráinsson et al. 2012: 46).

Kavitskaya (2015). Basically, when a coda is lost we expect lengthening of a preceding vowel: /ONC/ → /ON:/. The unexpected case, as it is typologically rarer,[39] is when the onset is deleted and the nucleus lengthens: /ONC/ → /N:C/.

The following data in (43) are from Katsanis (1996), cited in Topintzi (2006b: 74–75), and compare the forms in Standard Greek (StG) and Samothraki Greek (SmG):

(43) Compensatory lengthening in Samothraki Greek (Topintzi 2006: 74 –75)

	StG	SmG		Data from
#_V	rafts	á:fts	'tailor.MASC'	Katsanis (1996:50–51)
	ríyaɲ	í:yaɲ	'oregano'	
	rúxa	ú:xa	'clothes'	
	róya	ó:ya	'nipple, berry (of a grape)'	
C_V	prótos	pó:tus	'first'	Katsanis (1996:54–56)
	vrisi	ví:s'	'tap'	
	fréna	fé:na	'brakes'	
	xróma	xó:ma	'colour'	
	krató	ka:tó	'I hold'	
	ɣráfo	ɣá:fu	'I write'	
	θrónos	θó:nus	'throne'	
	ðrákos	ðá:kus	'dragon'	
V_V	θaró	θaó	'I reckon'	Katsanis (1996:52)
	léftirus	léftius	'free'	
	varéλ	vaéλ	'barrel'	
	θiríða	θiíða	'ticket window'	
	kséru	kséu	'I know'	
	lurí	luí	'strap, strip'	

---

39 Topintzi (2006b: 106–109). Beltzung (2008) and Topintzi (2011: 1297), who establish a typology of compensatory lengthening, show that other languages may also be subject to the nucleus lengthening following an onset loss. One such language is Onondaga (Iroquaian), which also targets /r/.

{_C, V_#}	arpázu	'I grab'	Katsanis (1996:48)
	karpós	'seed'	
	fanár	'lantern'	
	figár	'moon'	Katsanis (1996:58)

Samothraki Greek diverges from *standard* Greek in that /r/ can erase in initial position or when it is part of an OL cluster provoking compensatory lengthening. This /r/ does *survive* in final and in preconsonantal positions. When it is intervocalic, it erases but we do not observe compensatory lengthening.

When compensatory lengthening occurs, again, the explanation is obvious. In the case of the standard Greek, the liquid is located under a nucleus: [xO{®}]ₙ. Kiparsky (2011: 57) proposes that [r+vowel]ₙ forms a *rising diphthong* in Samothraki where the liquid is "incorporated into the syllabic nucleus as [a] moraic element". The following examples (44a) for the OLV group and (44b) for the initial /r/ (showing only relevant information) show how the /obstruent+ r+vowel/ group rather than being interpreted as [[obstruent+r]ₒ[vowel]ₙ] has been interpreted as [[obstruent]ₒ[r+vowel]ₙ] by speakers of Samothraki Greek.

(44) /r/ under nucleus in Samothraki Greek

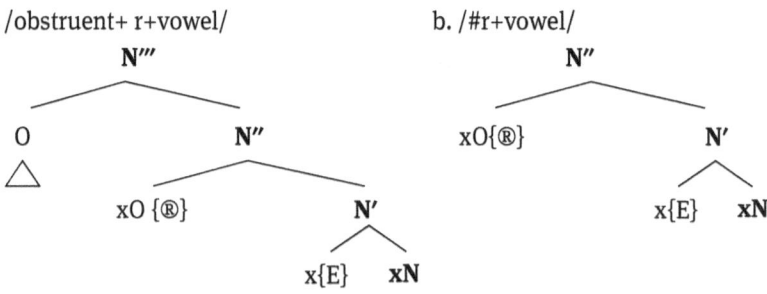

The evolution in Samothraki Greek does not only consist in losing the internal content of the liquid, the head is also lost: xO{®} → x. This position is then used as an extra position allowing m-command by the annotated x{E} of the vowel. This is illustrated in the following figures in (45) (the arrows indicate m-command):

(45) /r/ compensatory lengthening in Samothraki Greek
   a. /obstruent+ r+vowel/   b. /#r+vowel/

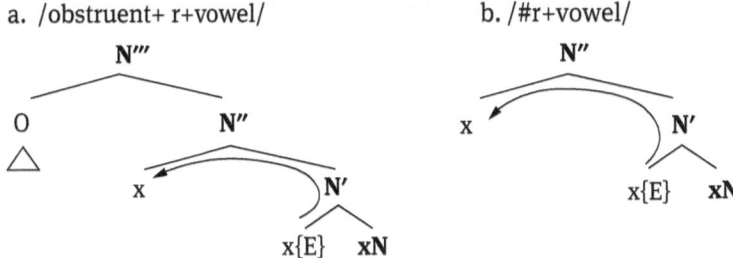

Now imagine that the liquid would have left its head in Samothraki Greek. M-command would ask xO{ } to interpret the elementary content of the following vowel, for example |I| or |U|, and we would obtain [j] or [w]. Imagine also that |A| were still an element under the hypothesis that the liquid is made-up of |A|, then a [r] would surface. However, this is never the case, which means that what is left from Standard Greek is a non-headed extra position: an unannotated x, corresponding to extra-space and in need of licensing. This provokes compensatory lengthening.

In the {_C, V_#} environments, /r/ seems to be protected in coda position, under the nucleus. The absence of compensatory lengthening in V_V has no explanation yet, except maybe for Topintzi (2006b: 91), who invokes a constraint which prohibits a long vowel followed by another vowel: *Super-Long Vocalic Hiatus (*S-L VH) / *V:V

The absence of compensatory lengthening means that the coda position is totally lost and there are no remains of the xO{®} structure at all. Katsika and Kavitskaya (2015) show that, phonetically, the durations of resulting vowels are the same in *Vowel Coalescence* and *Compensatory Lengthening*. Unfortunately, they do not test cases of intervocalic r-deletion where surrounding vowels differ. Topintzi (2006b: 91) takes note that *luri* 'strap' is interpreted as *luí* but not *lu:í or *luí:. Beltzung (2008) brings forward cases of compensatory lengthening in intervocalic position where the first nucleus lengthens, so we cannot exclude this possibility. In this environment, we would expect semivocalisation of the first vowel, *lwi:, or glide insertion, *luwi[40] or *luji.[41] In order to come up with a

---

40 Though Topintzi (2006a: 199) insists on the absence of a dorso-velar glide /w/ in standard Greek, one can imagine that the hiatus is solved on the surface by [w].
41 Both forms can be observed in Faroese glide insertion described in Anderson (1972) and treated in a GP2.0 framework by Voeltzel (2016). In this case, the intervocalic fricative <ð>, which is lost in modern Faroese, is reinterpreted as [w] or [j] depending on the nature of the flanking vowels. Voeltzel's (2016: 346–372) hypothesis is that what is left of this segment is an xO which is m-commanded by the preceding or the following vowel.

sound explanation for this case, one would need more data. Tracking these possibilities in the Northern varieties of Greek would tell us more about the status of the projectionless liquid and its remnants in Samothraki Greek.

We have seen with the Faroese example that the localisation of projectionless structure has consequences on the phonetic interpretation. We have also seen with the Samothraki Greek example that the lack of projection explains the lengthening of the vowel: the liquid is an onset on the surface, but because it is hosted by a nucleus, this latter can lengthen and this is not an exceptional behaviour. I now turn to a last case, Sardinian metathesis, where we observe the peculiar behaviour of /r/ in OL groups.

4.3 Percolation and Sardinian 'metathesis'

I have already discussed the *opportunism* of /r/. So far, we have only seen cases where the liquid docks on the 'nearer' landing site (onset when the nucleus is lost, nucleus when the onset is lost). The aim here is to show that the claim that liquids are projectionless is compatible with the so-called cases of metathesis. Ultan (1978: 374) insists that the "disproportionately high and widespread frequency of occurrence of liquids in metathesis is proverbial". Grammont (1933: 339–348) analyses the metatheses in Bagnères-de-Luchon as an anticipatory phenomenon affecting liquids when they are initially combined with a consonant in a non-initial syllable. The liquid 'moves' to the initial syllable. For example,[42] Latin *capra* 'goat', *uesperas* 'vespers', *pauperu* 'poor' are respectively realized as *crabo*, *brespes*, *prawbe* in Bagnères-de-Luchon. This process informs us on another property of the projectionless structures. In what follows, I will show that the lack of projection enables the liquids to *percolate* to another site. I will take Sardinian as an example of this treatment. All the data are from Molinu (1999), Lai (2014, 2015a) and include three major varieties:
- at the north: the Logudorese (L);
- at the south: the Campidanese (C)
- in the center: the Nuorese and Barbagia (N)

According to Molinu (1999: 164), 'metathesis' is an active process in certain regions of Sardinia (for example Genoni and Senorbi: G&S, in the center/center-south, part of Campidanese). In other regions, it is quite rare and lexicalized.

---

[42] Grammont (1933: 339).

Tertenian (T), which is part of the Campidanese area, underwent metathesis and the forms analysed by Lai (2014) are completely lexicalized.

Lai (2014) groups metatheses in two types: *Long Distance Metathesis* and *Local Metathesis*.[43] I will use the terms coined by Lai, although we will see that my definition will slightly differ from her, and is closer to Molinu (1999).

4.3.1 Long Distance Metathesis: *templa > trempa*

The following table in (46) gives examples of the *Long Distance Metathesis*. According to Lai (2015a), this type of metathesis targets the liquid /r/ which migrates to the initial syllable of the word to form an OL cluster even if the liquid was part of well-formed OL cluster:

(46) Sardinian Long Distance Metathesis

Sardinian	Latin, Italian		Variety	Data from
kraβa	capra$_{Latin}$	'goat'	L&T	Molinu(1999:161)
krɔnta	contra$_{Latin}$	'against'	N	Molinu(1999:161)
kran'nuɣa̯	conuc(u)la$_{Latin}$	'distaff'	T	Lai(2014:152)
kro'βai	Cop(u)lare$_{Latin}$	'combine'	T	Lai(2014:152)
kro'βekku	cooperc(u)lu$_{Latin}$	'lid'	T	Lai(2014:152)
'brɔstu	vostru$_{Latin}$	'yours'	N	Molinu(1999:160)
brɛntɛ	ventre$_{Latin}$	'belly'	N	Molinu(1999:162)
prɛta	petra$_{Latin}$	'stone'	N	Molinu(1999:161)
pre'issa	pigritia$_{Latin}$	'laziness'	T	Lai(2014:152)
pre'uɣu	peduc(u)lu$_{Latin}$	'louse'	T	Lai(2014:152)
tre'aːtu	teatro$_{Italian}$	'theatre'	L&N	Molinu(1999:161)
trɛmpa	templa$_{Latin}$	'cheek'	T	Lai(2014:152)

---

[43] The two metatheses took place (in Tertenian)/ began (for the varieties where it is still active) at different times: the first type occured/began around the XIth–XIIIth c. while the second type took place/began during the XVIIth c. Lai (2015a: 273–276) and Molinu (1999: 161) proposes the same chronology.

frabːika	fabbrica_{Italian}	'plant'	L&N	Molinu(1999:161)
frɛ'aldzu	februariu_{Latin}	'february'	L&N	Molinu(1999:161)
fri'ardʒu	februariu_{Latin}	'february'	T	Lai(2014:152)
fre'nuku	fenuc(u)lu_{Latin}	'fennel'	N	Molinu(1999:161)
fre'nuɣu	fenuc(u)lu_{Latin}	'fennel'	T	Lai(2014:152)
vritiku	vitricu_{Latin}	'stepfather'	N	Molinu(1999:161)
in'treu	integru_{Latin}	'honest'	L&N	Molinu(1999:161)
Is'priku	speculu_{Latin}	'mirror'	N	Molinu(1999:161)

The last two examples [in'treu] and [is'priku] from Lat. *integru* and *speculu*, respectively, shows that if the word begins with a vowel, the liquid docks on the first stop in onset position it meets on its way up. One can say that the attractor is an obstruent at the left, since nothing prohibits a liquid in initial position in Sardinian.

4.3.2 Local Metathesis: *korbu* > *kroβu*

Local Metathesis describes the cases which more closely resemble the classical metathesis. For Lai (2015a: 277), in *Local Metathesis*, "liquids from a stop-plus-liquid have moved to a coda position". Table (47) illustrates this apparent permutation.

(47) Local Metathesis in Tertenian Lai (2014: 152)

Sardinian	Latin	Variety
ar'βili	aprile_{Latin}	T
marði	matricer_{Latin}	T
tʃe'narβa	cenapura_{Latin}	T
sorɣu	socru_{Latin}	T
sir'βɔni	subulone_{Latin}	T
birðiu	vitricu_{Latin}	T
pɛrða	petra_{Latin}	T

Recall that Tertenian metathesis is not active anymore, but data from other varieties show a different behaviour of the liquid. As Molinu (1999: 162) points out, metathesis can occur if /r/ can dock on a phonetically realized onset. Moreover, she stresses the fact that, in northern varieties metathesis is incompatible with sonorants /m, n, l, j/, /s/ and affricates[44] which is not the case in southern varieties. This can explain the examples *marði* and *soryu* in (47).[45] They are special instances of Long Distance Metathesis where the initial consonant does not constitute a licit landing site.

Here, I will consider that *Local Metathesis* is targeting /r/ in coda position. Molinu explains that because /r/ is unlicensed in coda position, it has to move and to find another site.

The metathesis is, here, 'local' for two reasons: (i) first, the liquid can move from the coda to the expressed onset as in the following examples in (48) of its own syllable.

(48) Local Metathesis: Up movement (Data from Molinu 1999)

Sardinian	Latin,Italin,Central Sardinian		Variety	Page
a'dron:u	adorno_{Italin}	'ornated'	L&N	160
a'ʒrɔβa	a'rjɔla / ar'dʒɔla_{Central Sardinian}	'area'	G&S	165
'mratsu	'marθu_{Central Sardinian}	'march'	G&S	164
'tsrup:u	'θurpu_{Central Sardinian}	'blind'	G&S	164
tʃro'βeɟ,:u	ker'βeɟ,:u_{Central Sardinian}	'brain'	G&S	164
sre'βiri	ser'βirε_{Central Sardinian}	'to serve'	G&S	164
drɔ'm:irε	dormire_{Latin}	'to sleep'	L&N	160
frɔm:a	'forma	'form'	L&N	160
fro'm:iʒa	formicular_{Latin}	'ant'	L&N	160
frai'ɣarε	fabricare_{Latin}	'to make'	L&N	161
gri'l:anda	ghirlanda_{Italin}	'garland'	L&N	160
'kroβu	'korβu_{Central Sardinian}	'raven'	G&S	164
'drutʃ:i	'durkε_{Central Sardinian}	'sweet'	G&S	164

---

44 Molinu (199: 162–163).
45 However, forms like *birðiu* 'stepfather', *perða* 'stone' in Tertenian are still unexplainable but correspond to Nuorese *vritiku* and *preta* from Latin *vitricu* and *petra* respectively.

tru'mːentu	turmentu_{Latin}	'torment'	L&N	160
'braβa	'barβa_{Central Sardinian}	'beard'	G&S	164
'prokːu	'porku_{Central Sardinian}	'pork'	G&S	164
prɛta	petra_{Latin}	'stone'	N	161

(ii) Second, the liquid can move from a coda to the next onset on the right to form a licit OL cluster as in (49)[46] where for example the form for grass, which is realized as *'ɛrβa* in the Center part of Sardinia, is spelled as *'ɛbra* in G&S and shows the *downward* movement of the liquid.

(49) Local Metathesis: Down movement (Data from Molinu 1999: 165)

Genoni and Senorbi	Central Sardinian	
'ɛbra	'ɛrβa	'grass'
'oʒru	'orju / 'ordʒu	'barley'
'aβru	'arβu	'white'
a'ʒrɔβa	a'rjɔla / ar'dʒɔla	'area'
'neβrju	'nɛrβju	'nerve'
'laðru	larðu'	'lard'
'saðru	'sarðu	'sardinian'
'suðru	'surðu	'deaf'
	'burðu	'bastard'
	'karðu	'pot'

The next examples in (50), from Genoni and Senorbi (Molinu 1999: 165), show the behaviour of /'ɛrba/ 'grass' which is realized as *'ɛβra* in isolation (see (50a)). Whenever the preceding word ends with a consonant, the upward movement applies, as shown in (50b).

---

[46] *'buðru* 'bastard' < *burdu* and *'kaðru* 'pot' < *kardu* are still difficult to explain as we would expect *brudu and *kradu. Molinu (1999: 167f.) argues that these cases are not part of the metathesis scheme but rather a reorganization of the internal structure of the two segments: the laryngeal node of /d/ ([_{LAR}[voiced]]) has been delinked and attached to the liquid. A similar approach is taken by Frigeni (2005).

(50) *grass*: Up and Down movement
   a. down
      /ˈɛrba/ → ˈɛβra 'grass'
   b. up
      /ˈkusta ˈɛrba/ → ˈkusˈtrɛβa 'this grass'
      /ˈnun tʃi at ˈɛrba/ → ˈnun tʃa ˈdrɛβa 'there is no grass'
      /ˈpap:at ˈɛrba/ → ˈpap:a ˈdrɛβa 'it is eating grass'
      /sa ˈɛrba/ → ˈsrɛβa 'the grass'
      /is ˈɛrbas ˈmalas/ → iˈsrɛβa ˈmaʀaza 'the weeds
      /unu kundʒaˈtu dɛ ˈɛrba/ → u- ɣundʒaˈðudriˈɛβa 'a grass field'
      (Molinu 1999: 165)

The next case in (51), from Molinu (1999: 166), illustrates the influence of lenition on the metathesis. In isolation, the *Central Sardinian* form *ˈbɛrβɛɛ* 'ewe' is realized as (51a) *brɛˈβɛi* in Genoni and Senorbi. Adding the article *ũ* 'an' in (51b) provokes the loss of the initial voiced consonant [b]. The consequence is that the liquid moves downward to form an OL cluster.

(51) *ewe*: Up and Down movement
   down
   /ˈbɛrβɛɛ/ → a. brɛˈβɛi *ewe*
              → b. ũ ɛˈβrɛi *an ewe*
   (Molinu 1999: 166)

To sum up, bidirectionality, up and down movement, is triggered by the presence of a licit onset: some varieties of Sardinian accept, for example, affricates as hosting consonants (Molinu 1999: 164), while other do not.

In the case of Long Distance Metathesis, [tem]σ_1[pla]σ_2 > [trem]σ_1[pa]σ_2, the liquid, coming form an OL cluster, docks on the left edge provided there is a licit consonant to harbor it.[47]

In the case of Local Metathesis, the liquid is already in a coda position and docks either on the onset of the same syllable, [kor]σ_1[bu]σ_2 > [kro]σ_1[βu]σ_2 *kroβu*, or on the onset of the following syllable [bɛr]σ_1[βɛɛ]σ_2 > [brɛ]σ_1[βɛi]σ_2 / [ɛ]σ_1[βrɛi]σ_2, if the onset of the first syllable is empty.

Lastly, it must be noted that intervocalic liquids do not change position: for instance, in *fraiˈɣarɛ* 'to make', from Latin *fabricare*, the second /r/ does not

---

[47] In the case of Tertenian, if no consonant is available in the first syllable, it docks on the coda of this initial syllable.

move. The conditions are different and we are thus left with three environments, $\{V_1\_CV_2, V_1C\_V_2\}$ and $\{V_1\_V_2\}$, which are summed-up in the following table:

(52) Conditions on metathesis

Environment	$V_1\_CV_2$	$V_1C\_V_2$	$V_1\_V_2$
Position	Coda	OL	0
Metathesis	Yes	Yes	No
Conditions	C Government-Licensed	C Government-Licensed	V Licensed

When in intervocalic position, the liquid is directly licensed by a vowel, V_2 in table (52). On the other hand, metathesis is triggered by specific conditions on government: when in coda position or part of an OL group, the liquid is, respectively, governed by the preceding or the following consonant. This latter, in order to govern its complement, must be government-licensed by the following nucleus[48]: it is this indirect mode of government that is responsible for the metathesis.

Recall that the liquid is projectionless and its fate is to find a hosting site. In the case of Sardinian, the host is always a projecting onset: either an O' or an O''. The liquid has to transfer its content from the initial extra level to a hosting onset: to do so, it *percolates*. There are mainly two reasons to use percolation over the analysis in terms of *floating consonant* or *movement*.

First, treating the liquid as a *floating consonant* is problematic. The floating liquid could dock anywhere in the structure and, both the data I presented and the conditions on government I described seem to show that this is not the case.

Second, I argue that percolation should be preferable over *movement*. Movement generally entails a trace. This analysis is appealing because the 'trace' could be used by the neighbouring consonants. For instance, Molinu (1999: 169–170) notices that the metathesis of a /r/ formerly in coda position (Local Metathesis) involves compensatory lengthening. This compensatory lengthening could be the result of the availability of a remnant x-position. However, the fact that compensatory lengthening concerns only unvoiced obstruents is problematic. If a position is left empty after metathesis, any type of consonant should be able to lengthen. I thus consider that the *movement and trace* analysis is not necessary. Moreover, if compensatory lengthening

---

[48] Charette (1990: 244).

appeared mandatory,[49] one could reasonably consider that the preceding nucleus is m-commanded by the following onset. This configuration can be interpreted as compensatory legthening.

In morphology, percolation has been mainly used to describe feature 'transfer' to demonstrate the procedure of categorial changes in affixation (Lieber 1980). In phonology, it has been used in order to explain the syllabicity of a segment (Kaye and Lowenstamm 1984), or to discuss the question of the association between categorial positions and featural content (Hayes 1990).

Most of these definitions of percolation consider feature transmission and in the case of /r/, one can hesitate between |®|, an element alone, and xO{®}, i.e. Head and Content. Regarding this point, the Feature Percolation Convention II of Lieber (1980: 88) is the most interesting because it entails that percolation of an affix morpheme will transmit all the features associated to this affix:

Feature Percolation Convention II (Lieber 1980: 88):
All features of an affix morpheme, including category features, percolate to the first branching node dominating that morpheme.

Lieber (1980: 85) treats the example of the adjective *breakable* which derives from a Verb [break]$_V$ by affixation: [[break]$_V$able]$_A$. The idea is that [able] bears the feature Adjective and transmits it to the resulting adjective. But, it also transmits all its other features and, in the example discussed by Lieber, the feature [+latinate] percolates too. We can then explain why the Noun *breakableness* [[[break]$_V$able]$_A$ness]$_N$ is a licit word: this is because *-ness*, bearing the feature [-latinate], can combine with an adjective bearing the feature [+latinate].

Of interest to us here is that Lieber's Percolation Conventions deal with *all* the features: they retrieve any information and transmit them to an upper node. The following convention from Hayes (1990: 41) does the same, but this time, in the case of the association of an autosegmental node and the features of a segment. It adds the case of deletion of all the features by losing an association line:

Percolation convention (Hayes 1990: 41):
When linkages are assigned or removed from a node N, the assignments and deletions are automatically carried over to all nodes dominated by N.

---

[49] Lai (2015b: 46–48) discusses the case of initial geminates in Sardinian. She underlines that gemination is not distinctive in Sardinian: "For example, a word such as *maccu* 'fool' (from Latin MACCU(M)) can be pronounced either [makku] and [maku]" (Lai 2015: 47). In the GP2.0 perspective, although it must be defined more precisely, this lengthening can be analysed as m-command of a nuclear unannotated position.

Hayes (1990: 41) exemplifies the case of /p/ associated with a C position by projection. All the (geometrical) features of [p], $_{Root}$[[$_{Lar}$[spread glottis, -voice]] [$_{SupLar}$[-nasal] [$_{PM}$[$_{Manner}$[-sonorant, -continuous]] $_{Place}$[labial]]]], are associated with C. Delinking of [p] entails delinking of all these features.

4.3.3 Analysis

I propose that in the case of Sardinian no metathesis occurs. The liquid *simply* percolates to the highest available onset projection. I give here the definition of Percolation I use for Sardinian[50] which targets xO{®} when subject to government by a government-licensed consonant:

xO{®} Percolation Sardinian:
i. All features of a projectionless xO{®} subject to indirect government percolate to the highest projecting Onset of the structure.
ii. If failing, probe down the structure, and percolate to the nearest projecting Onset.

Following (i), all the features of the liquid (head: xO, and content: {®}) transfer to the highest realized onset: the liquid follows the path of nucleus projections until it finds an available onset. By (ii), if there is no onset available, the liquid goes down the structure and docks on the first available realized onset.

In the previous sections, I mentioned three types of 'metathesis': *Long distance*, *Local* and *Up and Down*. The definition of percolation proposed here allows us to speak of all these metatheses as one single phenomenon resulting from the same (percolation) mechanism.

A. Long Distance Methatesis *(53) tempra > (54) trempa*

The following representations illustrate the case of long distance metathesis. The example of *tempra > trempa*. In (53), I give the representation of *tempra*. As we can see, the obstruent /p/ projects an extra level, O''', in order to host the liquid xO{®}. (I give the path followed in bold in the figure).

---

[50] As we have seen, in Tertenian, only stops can host an xO{®} while in Genoni and Senorbi, xO{®} can be hosted by stops and fricatives. In order to encode the difference between varieties, the percolation convention can be parametrized (e.g. Parameter Tertenian: Percolate only to an O'' structure).

(53) *tempra*

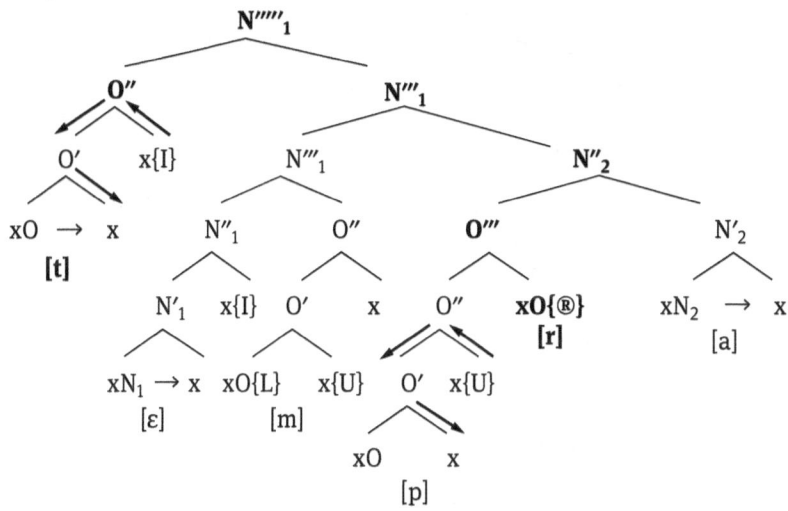

When percolation applies, it targets the highest onset of the structure: this is the coronal obstruent /t/ hosted by the maximal projection of N_1. xO{®} percolates to this onset which, in turn, projects the extra-level needed. It results in the metathesized *trempa* illustrated in (54).

(54) *trempa*

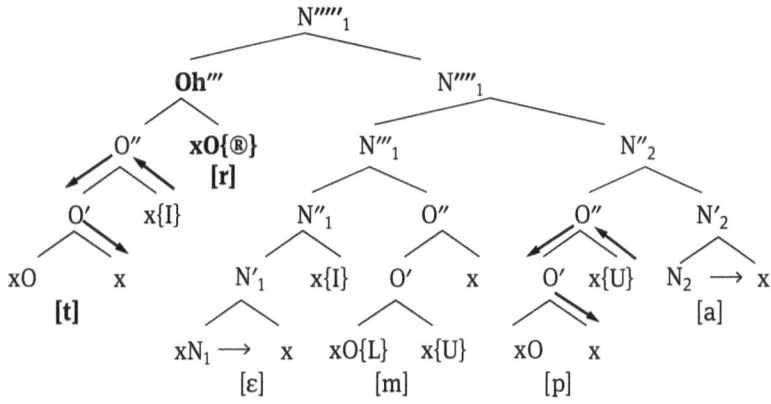

B. Local Metathesis *(55) korbu > (56) kroβu*

Local Metathesis follows exactly the same principle. Our example is (55) *korbu* > (56) *kroβu* where /r/ begins in a coda position, hosted by a nuclear projection.

(55) *korbu*

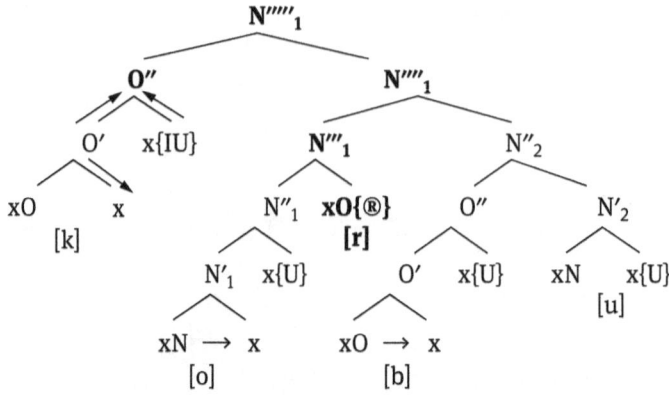

The same principle of percolation applies and targets the liquid which transfers all its content to the highest onset of the structure: /k/. It results in an OL cluster at the beginning of the word illustrated in (56) *kroβu*.

(56) *kroβu*

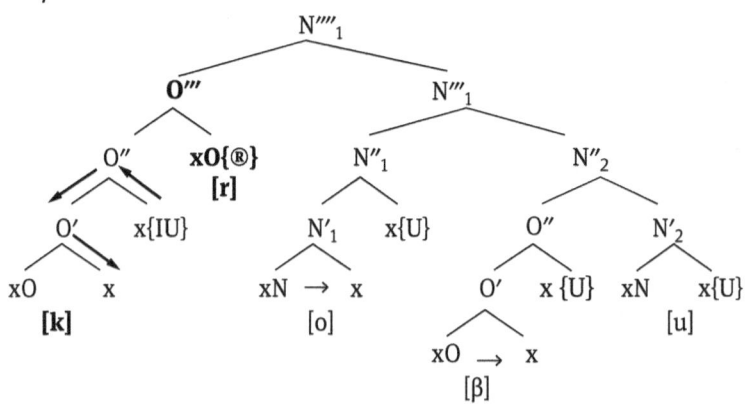

In the Local and Long Distance Metatheses examples, the liquid percolates up the structure because it finds a licit landing site: the highest obstruent of the structure.

I now turn to the case of *Up and Down* metathesis where the conditions differ in that, in some cases, the liquid is unable to dock on this highest position.

C. Up and Down (57) *berbei* > (58) *breβei*, (59) *eβrei*

In order to illustrate the *Up and Down* metathesis, I use the case of (57) *berbei* which can either result in (58) *breβei* or (59) *eβrei*. The following representation in (57) gives the structure of *berbei*. Notice that /r/ is located under a nucleus in a coda.

(57) *berbei*

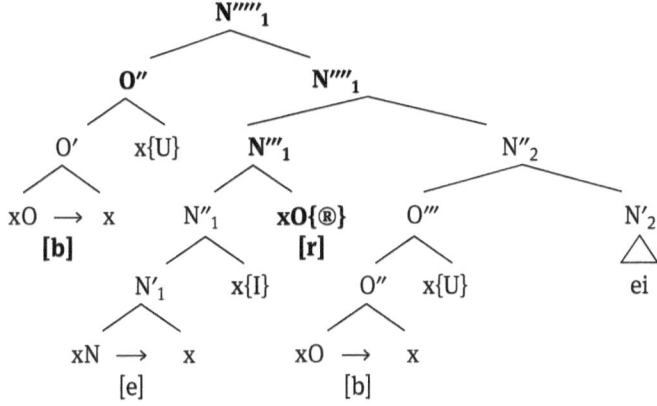

As in the case of *korbu* > *kroβu*, the liquid targets the highest projecting onset and percolation applies: all the material is transferred to the initial /b/ and we obtain an initial OL cluster as in (58) for *breβei*.

(58) **breβei**

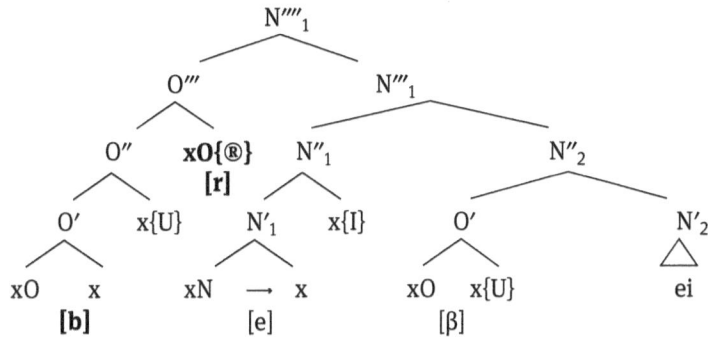

If preceded by a vowel, the initial consonant /#b/ is lost and the liquid goes down the structure. This is illustrated in (59), which gives the representation of *eβrei*, that is, *breβei* preceded by the definite determiner *sa* 'the ewe'. In this case, the second condition of the xO{®} Percolation Sardinian comes into effect: xO{®} probes the structures and encounters an empty xO at the beginning of the word. This xO is unprojecting: it is an empty initial onset and it does not form a licit site for the liquid, as it is unable to project. The consequence is that, by probing the rest of the structure, the liquid percolates down – in this case, on the nearest projecting onset under N'''₂. The result is the form *eβrei*.

(59) *eβrei*

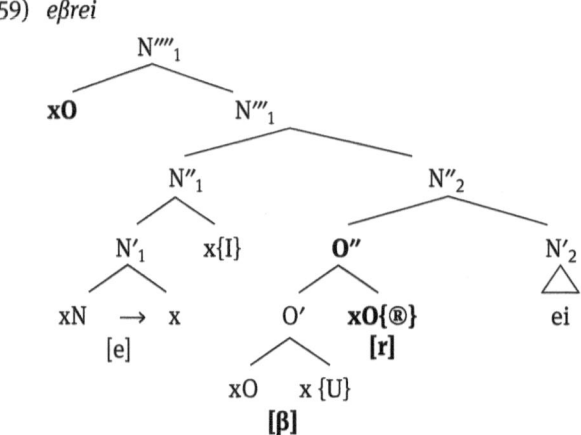

Summing up the discussion on Sardinian, we cannot consider that the behaviour of the liquid in Sardinian relates to metathesis: there is no swapping of consonant or positions. Indeed, it is a property of liquids to percolate, and my hypothesis is that this characteristic is a consequence of their structure.

5 Conclusion

In this paper, I have explored several cases of OL clusters. I defended the idea that these groups suffered misconception: the obstruent and the liquid are clearly unequal. The former can project another level, while the latter cannot and must find a host.

Given the formalisation in GP2.0, most of the properties and behaviour of OL clusters are now expected. Voicing of obstruent in intervocalic position is due to the transparency of the liquid under the additional onset projection. The obstruent is reachable by the nucleus "as if" the liquid was not there. The *intermediate* stages in the case of schwa loss in French are now explained not solely on the presence of an expressed schwa but also on the power given to the obstruent part of the cluster: the host, the onset, can still protect its guest, the liquid, even if the final schwa is erased.

On another level, we have seen that differences in quality, for example in Faroese, can be explained by the position occupied by the liquid: the surface realization of /r/ depends on its location in the structure. Hence, compensatory lengthening in Samothraki Greek is explained by the fact that, the liquid is hosted under a nucleus projection. The loss of the liquid can thus trigger the lengthening of the nucleus.

The last phenomenon we explored, Sardinian 'metathesis', exploits a salient property of non-projecting structures: their ability to find a proper host via the mechanism of percolation.

One important consequence of the analysis defended here is that the problem of locality for OL groups does not arise anymore (the current analysis does not require the presence of an empty vowel between the two segments in all the cases we discussed). This is due to the use of structured representations. As a consequence, *Infrasegmental Government* is no longer necessary. This treatment of OL groups has theoretical consequences and some of them need to be further explored. For instance, future work should show that other non-projecting structures (sonorants and semi-vowels[51]) can undergo percolation. In order to refine the principle I just sketched, we should also identify the conditions inhibiting this process.

Acknowledgements: I would like to thank Sabrina Bendjaballah, Rosangela Lai, Oana Lungu, Lucia Molinu and Laurence Voeltzel for their useful comments and suggestions on improving previous drafts of this work. I thank two anonymous reviewers for their comments. I am especially grateful to Kuniya Nasukawa, the editor of this volume, for his encouragement and patience all over the process. Remaining errors are my own.

References

Adams, Jonathan and Hjalmar P. Petersen. 2014. *Faroese: A Language Course for Beginners.* Tórshavn: Stiðin.
Angoujard, Jean-Pierre. 2012. L'Attrait de la plage. Ms.
Anderson, Stephen R. 1972. The Faroese vowel system. In Michael Brame (ed.), *Contributions to Generative Phonology*, 1–21. Austin, TX: University of Texas Press.
Backley, Phillip. 1993. Coronal: The undesirable element. *UCL Working Papers in Linguistics* 5, 301–323.

---

51 Ultan (1978: 374) observes that "the more resonant a sound, the more susceptible it is to metathesis". My claim is quite different because the cases under consideration here are treated as percolation, not as metathesis. Nevertheless, I do expect the non-projecting structure, in particular glides, to act the same. This is partly discussed, for example, in Ultan (1978: 377), with W+C > CW, i.e. glide+obstruent → obstruent+glide.

Backley, Phillip. 2011. *An Introduction to Element Theory*. Edinburgh: Edinburgh University Press.
Bafile, Laura. 1997. La spirantizzazione toscana nell'ambito della teoria degli elementi. *Studi linguistici Offerti E G. Giacomelli Dagli Amici E Dagli Allievi*, 27–38. Firenze: Unipress.
Beltzung, Jean-Marc. 2008. L'allongement compensatoire dans les représentations phonologiques: nature, contraintes et typologie. Ph.D. dissertation, Université Paris III, Paris.
Bourciez, Jean. 1958. *Précis De Phonétique Française*. Paris: Klincksieck.
Bourciez, Edouard and Jean Bourciez. 1967. *Phonétique Française: Etude Historique*. Paris: Klincksieck.
Brand, Sophie and Mirjam Ernestus. 2015. Reduction of obstruent-liquid-schwa clusters in casual french. Paper presented at the 18th International Congress of Phonetic Sciences (ICPhS 2015). University of Glasgow, Glasgow, Scotland (10–14 August 2015).
Brandão de Carvalho, Joaquim. 2002. De la syllabation en termes de contour CV. EHESS Habilitation Thesis, Paris.
Carvalho, Brandao de. 2008. Western Romance. In Joaquim Brandão de Carvalho, Tobias Scheer and Philippe Ségéral (eds.), *Lenition and Fortition*, 207–233. Berlin: Mouton de Gruyter.
Broadbent, Judith. 1991. Linking and intrusive *r* in English. *UCL Working Papers in Linguistics* 3, 281–302.
Brun-Trigaud, Guylaine and Tobias Scheer. 2010. Lenition in branching onsets in French and in ALF dialects. In Petr Karlík (ed.), *Development of Language through the Lens of Formal Linguistics*, 15–28. Munich: Lincom Europa.
Brun-Trigaud, Guylaine, and Tobias Scheer. 2012. La lénition des attaques branchantes en français et dans les dialectes de l'ALF. In Mario Barra-Jover, Guylaine Brun-Trigaud, Jean-Philippe Dalbera, Patrick Sauzet and Tobias Scheer (eds.), *Études de Linguistique Gallo-romane*, 183–198. Saint-Denis, Ile-De-France: Presses Universitaires de Vincennes.
Charette, Monik. 1990. Licence to govern. *Phonology* 7, 233–253.
Dell, François C. 1966. Les règles phonologiques tardives et la morphologie dérivationnelle du français. (Topics in French phonology and derivational morphology). Ph.D. dissertation. Massachussetts Institute of Technology.
Frigeni, Chiara. 2005. The development of liquids from Latin to Campidanian Sardinian: the role of contrast and structural similarity. *Toronto Working Papers in Linguistics* 24, 15–30.
Grammont, Maurice. 1914. *Traité Pratique de Prononciation Française*. Paris: Delagrave.
Grammont, Maurice. 1933. *Traité de Phonétique*. Paris: Delagrave.
Hall, Tracy Alan. 1993. The phonology of German /R/. *Phonology* 10, 83–105.
Harris, John. 1990. Segmental complexity and phonological government. *Phonology* 7, 255–300.
Harris, John. 1994. *English Sound Structure*. Oxford: Blackwell.
Hayes, Bruce. 1990. Diphthongisation and coindexing. *Phonology* 7, 31–71.
Jensen, Sean. 1994. Is ʔ an element?: Towards a non-segmental phonology. *SOAS Working Papers in Linguistics and Phonetics* 4, 71–78.
Katsanis, Nikolaos. 1996. *Το γλωσσικό; ιδίωμα τησ Σαμοθράκης*. [The Dialect of Samothraki Greek]. Δήμος Σαμοθράκης [Municipality of Samothraki].
Katsika, Argyro and Darya Kavitskaya. 2015. The phonetics of *r*-deletion in Samothraki Greek. *Journal of Greek Linguistics* 15, 34–65.
Kaye, Jonathan and Jean Lowenstamm. 1984. De la syllabicité. In François Dell, Daniel Hirst and Jean-Roger Vergnaud (eds.), *Forme Sonore du Langage*, 123–159. Paris: Hermann.

Kaye, Jonathan, Jean Lowenstamm and Jean-Roger Vergnaud. 1985. The Internal structure of phonological elements: A theory of charm and government. *Phonology Yearbook* 2, 305–328.

Kaye, Jonathan. 1992. Do you believe in magic?: The story of s+ C sequences. *SOAS Working Papers in Linguistics and Phonetics* 2, 293–313.

Kiparksy, Paul. 2011. Compensatory lengthening. In Charles E. Cairns and Eric Raimy (eds.), *Handbook on the Syllable*, 33–70. Leiden: Brill.

Lowenstamm, Jean. 1996. CV as the only syllable type. In Jacques Durand and Bernard Laks (eds.), *Current Trends in Phonology: Models and Methods*, 419–44. CNRS, Université Paris X and University of Salford: University of Salford Publications1.

Lai, Rosangela. 2014. Positional factors in the evolution of Sardinian Muta cum Liquida: A case study. *L'ittalia Dialettale* 75, 149–160.

Lai, Rosangela. 2015a. Lateral relations in Sardinian Metathesis: A unified account. In Domenico Russo (ed.), *The Notion of Syllable across History: Theories and Analysis*. Newcastle upon Tyne: Cambridge Scholars Publishing.

Lai, Rosangela. 2015b. *Word-initial geminates in Sardinian*, Quaderni di Linguistica e Studi orientali. Firenze: Firenze University Press.

Laks, Bernard. 1977. Contribution empirique à l'analyse socio-différentielle de la chute de /r/ dans les groupes consonantiques finals. *Langue Française* 39, 101–125.

Lass, Roger. 1984. *Phonology: An Introduction to Basic Concepts*. Cambridge: Cambridge University Press.

Lieber, Rochelle. 1980. On the organization of the lexicon. Ph.D. dissertation, Massachussetts Institute of Technology.

Loporcaro, Michele. 2005. La sillabazione di «muta cum liquida» dal latino al romanzo. In Sandor Kiss, Luca Mondin and Giampaolo Salvi (eds.), *Latin et Langues Romanes: Études de Linguistique Offertes à József Herman à L'occasion de Son 80ème Anniversaire*, 419–430. Tübingen: Walter de Gruyter.

Lowenstamm, Jean. 2003. Remarks on mutae cum liquida and branching onsets. In Stefan Ploch (ed.), *Living on the Edge: 28 papers in honour of Jonathan Kaye*, 339–363. Berlin and New York: Mouton de Gruyter.

Marotta, Giovanna. 2008. Lenition in Tuscan Italian (gorgia toscana). In Joaquim Brandão de Carvalho, Tobias Scheer and Philippe Ségéral (eds.), *Lenition and Fortition*, 235–271. Berlin and New York: Mouton de Gruyter.

Molinu, Lucia. 1999. Métathèse et variation en sarde. In Jacques Durand and Chantai Lyche (eds.), *Phonologie: Théorie et Variation*, Cahiers de Grammaire 24, 153–181. Toulouse: Université de Toulouse-Le-Mirail.

Nasukawa, Kuniya and Phillip Backley. 2011. The internal structure of 'r' in Japanese. *Phonological Studies* 14, 27–34.

Nasukawa, Kuniya. 1997. Melodic structure in a nasal-voice paradox. *UCL Working Papers in Linguistics* 9, 403–423.

Nasukawa, Kuniya. 2014. Features and recursive structure. *Nordlyd* 41(1),1–19. *Special issue on Features* edited by Martin Krämer, Sandra-Iulia Ronai and Peter Svenonius.

Onuma, Hitomi. 2015. On the status of empty nuclei in phonology. Ph.D. dissertation, Tohoku Gakuin University, Sendai.

Paradis, Carole and Jean-François Prunet (eds.). 1991. *The Special Status of Coronals: Internal and External Evidence*. San Diego: Academic Press.

Piggott, Glyne and Harry van der Hulst. 1997. Locality and the nature of nasal harmony. *Lingua* 103, 85–112.

Pöchtrager, Markus A. 2006. The Structure of length. Ph.D. dissertation, University of Vienna.
Pope, Mildred Katharine. 1934. *From Latin to Modern French with especial consideration of Anglo-Norman: Phonology and Morphology*. Manchester: Manchester University Press.
Rice, Keren D. and Peter Avery. 1991. On the relationship between laterality and coronality. In Carole Paradis and Jean-François Prunet (eds.), *The Special Status of Coronals: Internal and External Evidence*, 101–123. San Diego: Academic Press.
Rice, Keren D. 1992. On deriving sonority: a structural account of sonority relationships. *Phonology* 9(1),61–99.
Rice, Keren D. 2005. Liquid relationships. *Toronto Working Papers in Linguistics* 24, 29–42.
Scheer, Tobias. 1996. Une théorie de l'interaction directe entre consonnes: contribution au modèle syllabique CVCV. Ph.D. dissertation, Université Paris VII.
Scheer, Tobias. 2000. L'immunité de schwa en début de mot. *Langue Française* 126, 113–126.
Scheer, Tobias. 2004. *What Is CVCV and Why Should It Be?* Berlin and New York: Mouton de Gruyter.
Scheer, Tobias. 2014. Muta cum liquida in the light of Tertenia Sardinian metathesis and compensatory lengthening Lat. V_ tr > Old French Vrr. In Marie-Hélène Côté and Eric Mathieu (eds.), *Variation within and across Romance Languages: Selected Papers from the 41st Linguistic Symposium on Romance Languages*, 77–99. Amsterdam: Benjamins.
Scheer, Tobias and Philippe Ségéral. 2007. Le statut syllabique multiple des séquences muta cum liquida: l'exemple du gallo-roman. In Bernard Combettes, Christiane Marchello-Nizia and Sophie Prévost (eds), *Etudes Sur le Changement Linguistique en Français*, 261–282. Nancy: Presses Universitaires de Nancy.
Schwartz, Geoffrey. 2016. On the evolution of prosodic boundaries: Parameter settings for Polish and English. *Lingua* 171, 37–73.
Thráinsson, Höskuldur, Hjalmar P. Petersen and Jógvan í Lon Jacobsen. 2012. *Faroese: An Overview and Reference Grammar*. Tórshavn: Føroya Fróðskaparfelag.
Topintzi, Nina. 2006a. Moraic onsets. Ph.D. dissertation, University College London, University of London.
Topintzi, Nina. 2006b. A (not so) paradoxical instance of compensatory lengthening: Samothraki Greek and theoretical implications. *Journal of Greek Linguistics* 7(1), 71–119.
Topintzi, Nina. 2010. *Onsets: Supra Segmental and Prosodic Behaviour*. Cambridge: Cambridge University Press.
Topintzi, Nina. 2011. Onsets. In Marc van Oostendorp, Colin J. Ewen, Elizabeth V. Hume and Keren Rice (eds.), *The Blackwell Companion to Phonology*, 1285–1308. Malden, MA: Wiley-Blackwell.
Ultan, Russell. 1978. A typological view of metathesis. In Joseph Greenberg (ed.), *Universals of Human Language 2*, 367–402. Stanford, CA: Stanford University Press.
Voeltzel, Laurence. 2016. Morphophonologie des langues scandinaves. Hiérarchie segmentale et complexité syllabique. Ph.D. dissertation, University of Nantes.
Wiese, Richard. 2011. The representation of rhotics. In Marc van Oostendorp, Colin J. Ewen, Elizabeth V. Hume and Keren Rice (eds.), *The Blackwell Companion to Phonology 1*, 711–729. Malden, MA: Wiley-Blackwell.
Zink, Gaston. 1986. *Phonétique Historique du Français*. Paris: Presses Universitaires de France.
Živanovič, Sašo and Markus Pöchtrager A. 2010. GP 2, and Putonghua too. *Acta Linguistica Hungarica* 57, 357–380.

Hisao Tokizaki
Recursive strong assignment from phonology to syntax

1 Introduction

In this paper, I argue that stress assignment is structure-dependent from the morpheme-internal level to the syntactic level. I propose a rule called Set Strong, which assigns a Strong label to a set of elements when it is merged with a terminal. This study gives support to the view that languages can have recursive structures, starting from morpheme-internal phonology.

Cinque (1993) generalizes Chomsky and Halle's (1968) Nuclear Stress Rule and Compound Stress Rule, and argues that stress is assigned to the most deeply embedded element both in phrases and in compounds. However, Cinque's rule is based on X-bar theory, which was replaced with bare phrase structure and abandoned in the minimalist framework (cf. Chomsky 1995). We need to reformulate Cinque's rule in terms of Merge. We also need to investigate the possibility that the same stress assignment rule applies below the compound level (cf. Giegerich 2004: 6).

In section 2, I discuss the mechanism of stress assignment in a phrase and a compound. I review Cinque's (1993) stress assignment rule and Reinhart's (2006) metrical rule, and point out their problems in the current syntactic theory. As an alternative rule for stress assignment, I propose Set Strong, which applies at every Merge operation. Section 3 has a discussion of stress in words, including affix and bound morphemes. In section 4, I discuss stress in morphemes. I will review the mechanism of Dependent Stress (Nasukawa and Backley 2015) and argue that Set Strong explains the weight-sensitive stress and the fixed stress in languages of the world. Section 5 concludes the discussion.

2 Stress in phrases and compounds

2.1 The depth of embedding: Cinque (1993)

Let us start with stress location in phrases and compounds. There have been proposed a number of approaches to stress location in phrases and compounds, which can be grouped into a syntactic approach (Chomsky and Halle 1968, Cinque 1993, Reinhart 2006, Kahnemuyipour 2009 and Sato 2012), a semantic approach (Bolinger 1972, Schmerling 1976 and Okazaki 1998) and a hybrid approach (Zubizarreta 1998) (for more relevant works, see Ladd 2008). In this paper, I will pursue the syntactic approach.

First, I will review the stress assignment rule by Cinque (1993), which can be formulated as in (1).

(1) Assign stress to the most deeply embedded constituent in a structure.

This rule applies both to phrases and compounds as shown in (2) and (3) (Cinque 1993: 250, 275).

(2)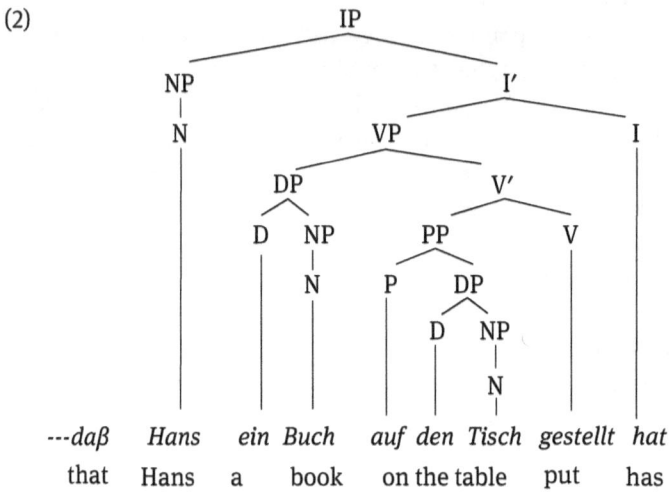
---daß Hans ein Buch auf den Tisch gestellt hat
that Hans a book on the table put has

(3) a.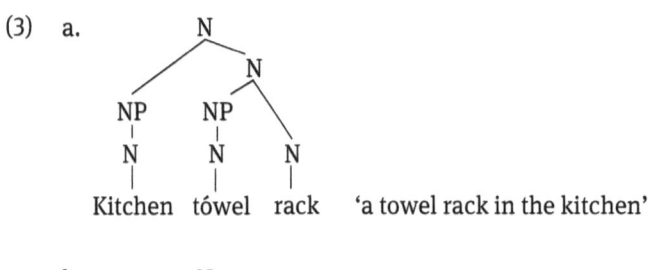
Kitchen tówel rack 'a towel rack in the kitchen'

b.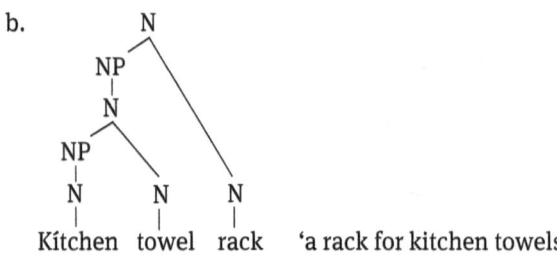
Kítchen towel rack 'a rack for kitchen towels'

In the IP in (2), the phrasal stress is assigned to *Tisch*, which is the most deeply embedded element in the phrase structure. Similarly, the compound stress is assigned to *towel* in (3a) and to *kitchen* in (3b), which are the most deeply embedded element in each structure.

Cinque's rule nicely explains the position of main stress both in phrases and in compounds. However, it has two problems in the current framework of generative syntax. First, Cinque's rule crucially relies on X-bar theory, which has been replaced with bare phrase structure in the minimalist syntax (Chomsky 1995). Namely, Cinque's rule can assign stress to the bottom of the X-bar theoretic structure in (4), which assumes non-branching NPs. However, it cannot determine stress location at the first merge in the bare phrase structure without non-branching projection, as shown in (5).

(4) a. 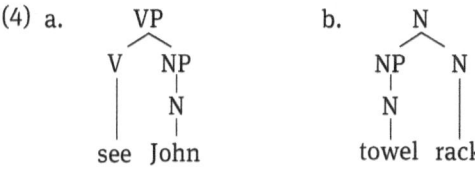   b.

(5) a. 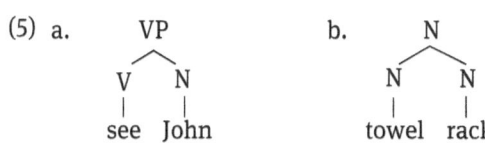   b.

In the bare phrase structure (5a), *see* and *John* are embedded at the same level. Similarly, in the compound (5b), the two nouns *towel* and *rack* are embedded at the same level. Cinque's rule cannot assign the main stress to the complement *John* and the modifier *towel* in (5a) and (5b).

Second, Cinque's rule has a conceptual problem. The rule is global in the sense that it needs to look through the whole structure and to compare the depth of embedding for all the terminals. For example, consider Cinque's example (2) above, which is repeated here as (6).

(6)
.. daß [IP [NP Hans] [I′ [VP [DP ein [N Buch]] [V′ [PP auf [DP den [NP [N Tísch]]]] gestellt]] hat]]
    that   Hans   a   book   on   the   table   put   has

In order to decide which terminal is the most deeply embedded in the structure (6), it is necessary to compare the depth of *Tisch* with *Buch* embedded in the DP *ein Buch*, which is merged with V' *auf den Tisch gestellt*. Counting and comparing the numbers of nodes dominating *Tisch* and *Buch* until reaching the IP at the top would not be a local computation. In terms of economy of computation, therefore, Cinque's rule is not plausible.

Thus, Cinque's stress assignment rule cannot be tenable in the minimalist program of linguistic theory. In section 2.3, I will propose an alternative rule for stress assignment that assumes bare phrase structure and does not need global computation. Before moving to the proposal, in the next section let us review another rule based on metrical trees.

2.2 Metrical Rule: Reinhart (2006)

Following Cinque's insight about the depth of embedding, Reinhart (2006: 133) proposed the Generalized Stress Rule, as formulated in (7) (cf. Szendrői 2001).

(7) Generalized Stress Rule (metrical-tree version)
     Assign a Strong label to the node that is syntactically more embedded at every level of the metrical tree. Assign Weak to its sister node.

Reinhart illustrates the application of this rule with the example sentence *Max read the books* in (8).

(8)
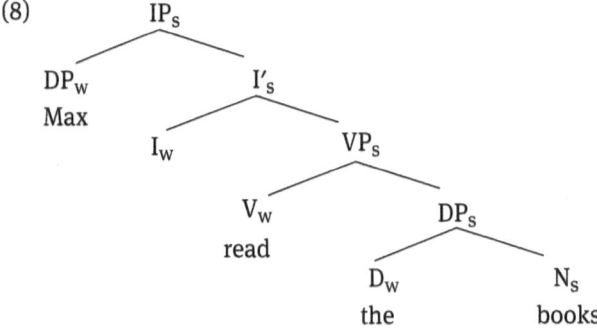

It is not clear what Reinhart means by "the node that is syntactically more embedded at every level of the metrical tree" because the sisters of every node are at the same level of embedding. For example, V and its sister DP are at the same level of embedding. Rather, (7) seems to intend that at every level of a metrical tree, Strong is assigned to the node that dominates more deeply embedded nodes. Then, at every branching node (except the DP at the bottom) in (8), the right-hand node dominates more deeply embedded nodes and is assigned a Strong label. For example, the bottom DP *the books* dominates more deeply embedded nodes D *the* and N *books*, and is assigned S; V *read* is assigned a Weak label as the sister of the DP$_S$.

Since Reinhart's stress rule (7) is based on Cinque's (1993) idea of embedding depth, it suffers from the same problems as Cinque's rule does. First, Reinhart argues that *books* is dominated only by S and is assigned the primary stress in the sentence. However, the problem of the first merge arises here as well as in Cinque's (1993) rule. It is not clear why the N node dominating *books* is assigned S in Reinhart's example (8), because the N is at the same level of embedding as D. In other words, the N *books* does not dominate more deeply embedded nodes.

Second, the label assignment in the rule (7) needs global computation. It must compare the depth of the nodes dominated by the sister nodes at every metrical level of the metrical tree. Let us take for example the structure in (2), which is repeated here as (9), where the S/W labels are shown only for the nodes under discussion, namely the DP dominating *ein Buch* and the V' dominating *auf den Tisch gestellt*.

(9)

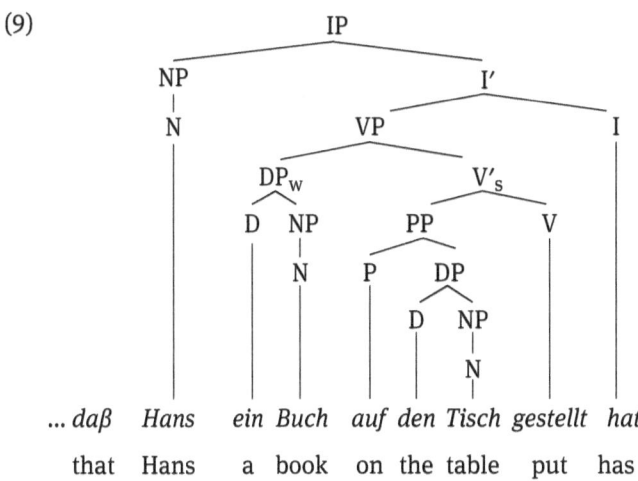

The rule (7) must look through the DP *ein Buch* and the V' *auf den Tisch gestellt* to find the most deeply embedded nodes *Buch* and *Tisch* in them, in order to compare their depths of embedding. Thus, Reinhart's rule (7) has a conceptual problem as well as an empirical problem in the minimalist program of linguistic theory.

2.3 Set Strong

The problems with the rules proposed in Cinque (1993) and Reinhart (2006) stem from the fact that the rules count and compare the depths of embedding between the nodes dominated by the sisters of a node. In this section, I explore an alternative analysis that does not refer to the depth of embedding. In Tokizaki (2015), I proposed the rule Set Strong (10), which assigns a Strong or Weak label to nodes in a morphosyntactic structure.

(10) Set Strong: Assign S(trong) to a set and W(eak) to a terminal when they are merged.

This rule assigns S/W labels to phrases and compounds as shown in (11).

(11) a. [[$_W$ eat] [$_S$ good fóod]]
b. [[$_S$ kítchen towel] [$_W$ rack]]

In the verb phrase (11a), a terminal (verb) *eat* is merged with a set (noun phrase) *good food*; *eat* is assigned W and *good food* S. Similarly, in a recursive compound (11b), the contained compound noun *kitchen towel* is a set and is assigned S and the noun head *rack* is a terminal and is assigned W. The labels S/W in (11a) and (11b) match the main stress locations in the verb phrase and the recursive compound.

However, here again we encounter a problem with the first Merge. At the very first derivation of (11a) and (11b), both of the syntactic objects to be merged (*good* and *food*; *kitchen* and *towel*) seem to be terminals. How can we determine the stress location in *good food* and *kitchen towel* in (11a) and (11b)? Since Set Strong assigns W to terminals, *food* and *kitchen* cannot receive S.

A possible solution to this problem is to use the idea of the single-membered set {α} proposed by Kayne (2009). I assume that *food* and *kitchen* are single-membered sets when they are merged with *good* and *towel*, respectively. Then, we can assign S to *food* and *kitchen*, as shown in (12).

(12) a. [[$_W$ good] {$_S$ food}]
b. [{$_S$ kitchen} [$_W$ towel]]

There remains the problem of how to decide which word is a single-membered set and which is a terminal. I will not discuss this matter here for reasons of space (but see Tokizaki 2018b).

We need to consider the case where both of the merged nodes are sets, such as the DP *ein Buch* and the V' *auf den Tisch gestellt* in (2) and (9). In Tokizaki (2018b), I proposed that Transfer to PF (Spell-Out) is triggered by the Obligatory Counter Principle (OCP) in phonology. When two sets are merged, both of them are assigned S by Set Strong. Since the pair S-S is a violation of OCP, one of the merged sets must be sent to PF in order to make a set-terminal (S-W) pair. In the case of (2) (= (9)), either *ein Buch* in DP or *auf den Tisch gestellt* in V' must be Transferred to PF as shown in (13a) and (13b).[1]

(13) a. [$_{VP}$ [$_{DP}$ *ein* {$_N$ *Buch*}] [$_{V'}$ [$_{PP}$ *auf den* {*Tisch*}] *gestellt*]]
 b. [$_{VP}$ [$_{DP}$ *ein* {$_N$ *Buch*}] [$_{V'}$ [$_{PP}$ *auf den* {*Tisch*}] *gestellt*]]

Set Strong can apply to (13a) and (13b) to give the representations in (14a) and (14b).

(14) a. [$_{VP}$ [$_{DP(S)}$ *ein* {$_N$ *Buch*}] [$_{V'(W)}$]]
 b. [$_{VP}$ [$_{DP(W)}$] [$_{V'(S)}$ [$_{PP}$ *auf den* {*Tisch*}] *gestellt*]]

Since both of the results (14a) and (14b) are fine for Set Strong, we expect both options are available for PF interface. Transferring the second set as in (13a) is similar to the standard assumption that the complement of a phase head is sent to PF (Chomsky 2000). On the other hand, Transferring the first set as in (13b) conforms to the idea that the order of Transfer matches the linear order of Transferred constituents (cf. Uriagereka's (1999) idea of 'giant compound'). I will leave this matter open. The point here is that we do not face a problem of global computation because of phases by multiple Spell-Out (cf. Uriagereka 1999 and Chomsky 2001). We do not need to compare the depth of the words embedded in the two sets, i.e. *Buch* and *Tisch*, both of which receive a phrasal stress as the deepest word in each Transferred domain.

The remaining issue is how we can explain the intuition that the stress on *Tisch* is stronger than the stress on *Buch* in (2). I argue that among the stressed words, the last one (i.e. *Buch*) receives intonational prominence as well as stress, which makes

---

[1] Alternatively, *the complement* in one of the merged sets can be sent to PF in order to make a set-terminal (S-W) pair, as shown in (i).

(i) a. [$_{VP}$ [$_{DP}$ *ein* {$_N$ *Buch*}] [$_{V'}$ [$_{PP}$ *auf den Tisch*] *gestellt*]]
 b. [$_{VP}$ [$_{DP}$ *ein* {$_N$ *Buch*}] [$_{V'}$ [$_{PP}$ *auf den Tisch*] *gestellt*]]

This idea conforms to the general view of Transfer, which sends the complement of a phase head to LF and PF (cf. Chomsky 2000). However, the Transferred PP *auf den Tisch* and N *Buch* do not seem to match a phonological phrase ($_{PhonP}$ *auf den Tisch gestellt*) and ($_{PhonP}$ *ein Buch*). If we take the view that a Spell-Out domain is a prosodic domain (cf. Dobashi 2003, among others), we should assume that the whole constituent rather than the complement of a merged constituent is Transferred to PF as a prosodic phrase, as shown in (13) (cf. Ott 2011 for the view that a phase head is sent to Transferred to PF with its complement).

the word most prominent in all the whole constituents (cf. Bing 1979). This idea also explains the fact that a long constituent in a specifier position does not have main stress in the whole constituent, as shown in (15) (cf. Cinque 1993: 268).

(15) a. [$_{DP1}$ [$_{DP2}$ The [man [from {Philadelphia}]]] [$_{D'1}$'s {$_N$ hát}]
 b. [$_{TP}$ [$_{DP}$ The [man [from {Philadelphia}]]] [$_{T'}$ will [$_{VP}$ meet {Máry}]]

Just before the DP *the man from Philadelphia* merges with D' *'s hat* or T' *will meet Mary* to become the specifier of DP$_1$ or TP, D'$_1$ *'s hat* or VP *meet Mary* is Transferred to PF so that Set Strong successfully assigns S to the DP and W to D'$_1$ or T'. The rightmost stressed word *hat* and *Mary* receive intonational prominence in addition to stress and become more prominent than *Philadelphia*, which receives stress as the deepest element in the Transferred unit DP$_2$ in (15a) and the DP in (15b).

In sum, Set Strong has advantages over Cinque's (1993) and Reinhart's (2006) stress rules. First, Set Strong applies to bare phrase structure without non-branching nodes (Chomsky 1995) and not to X-bar theoretic structure. Second, Set Strong does not have a problem in the first Merge, which I argue combines a terminal with a single-membered set. Third, Set Strong is local (not global) in the sense that it applies at every Merge without comparing the depth of the nodes dominated by the merged nodes. Unlike Cinque's and Reinhart's rules, Set Strong does not count the number of branching nodes at the end of the derivation.

In the following sections, I argue that Set Strong recursively assigns metrical labels in constituents from within a morpheme to a sentence (or a discourse if we assume hierarchical structure between sentences (cf. Tokizaki 2008).

2.4 Comparison with other minimalist theories of stress assignment

2.4.1 Kahnemuyipour (2009)

Before turning to the analysis of stress in terms of Set Strong, I will briefly discuss the differences of our rule and other minimalist theories of stress assignment. Here I will briefly discuss Kahnemuyipour (2009) and Sato (2012), both of whom also argue that phase is a key to stress assignment.[2]

Kahnemuyipour (2009) argues that sentential stress is assigned at the phase to the highest phonologically non-null element (i.e. the phonological border) of

---

[2] For a detailed review of Kahnemuyipour (2009), see Ortega-Santos (2010) and Tokizaki (2011).

the spelled-out constituent or the SPELLEE (YP in a phase [$_{HP}$ XP [$_{H'}$ H YP]]). This is the contrary view to the standard analyses (including ours) that put stress on the lowest element (Chomsky and Halle 1968, Cinque 1993). In order to derive sentence stress on the direct object rather than on the verb, Kahnemuyipour assumes that the verb always moves out of the VP (a spell-out domain) to v. However, this assumption has not been well supported, especially in SVO languages, as pointed out by Kratzer and Selkirk (2007) and Ortega-Santos (2010). In our theory, we do not need to assume the V-to-v movement.

The second point of difference between Kahnemuyipour (2009) and the analysis presented here is that Kahnemuyipour's theory only deals with sentence stress and not with the other phrasal stress, compound stress and word stress. This is because his theory crucially depends on the multiple Spell-Out, which applies at a phase (vP or CP) but not at the other phrases (NP, PP, VP and IP), compounds and words. His stress assignment rule cannot be generalized to apply to these categories unless we assume that all these categories are also phases. This assumption seems implausible. The analysis presented here naturally captures the generalization that the same rule Set Strong applies to all the morphosyntactic categories including phrases, compounds and words.

2.4.2 Sato (2012)

Another theory about phrasal stress is proposed by Sato (2012). Assuming Multiple Spell-Out at phases, he argues that the head of the rightmost or leftmost Major Phrase in phonological representation receives maximal prominence. He argues that languages choose a phonological edge for stress assignment within each Spell-Out domain (rightmost: English, Spanish, Italian, French and Japanese; leftmost: Persian and German).

One of the disadvantages of his analysis in terms of the phonological directionality parameter is that it misses the generalization that languages with object-verb order (OV languages: Persian and German) choose leftmost for the parameter while languages with verb-object order (VO languages: English, Spanish, Italian and French) choose rightmost for the parameter.[3] Assuming a phonological parameter in addition to the syntactic head directionality parameter would be redundant and would represent a problem in language acquisition.

---

3 Although Sato (2012) argues that Japanese (an OV language) has rightmost stress, it has been generally claimed that Japanese has prominence at the left edge of a prosodic phrase (cf. Selkirk and Tateishi 1988, 1991).

The second problem with Kahnemuyipour's (2009) analysis also applies to Sato's (2012) analysis. Sato's analysis does not explain (compound) word stress and phrasal stress other than sentential stress because these categories are not phases in the standard assumption. His analysis, similarly to Kahnemuyipour (2009), misses a generalization that our analysis can explain in terms of Set Strong, which applies to all the categories including clauses, phrases and (compound) words.

In sum, our analysis in terms of Set Strong has some advantages over Kahnemuyipour's (2009) and Sato's (2012) analyses. Below, I will discuss the stress location in a word and a morpheme, which is outside of the scope of their analyses.

3 Stress in a word

3.1 Stem and affix

First, let us consider the stress location in words consisting of stems and affixes. Kager (2000: 123) observes that Germanic languages such as Dutch, English and German have a word-based stress system that places the stress peak on a syllable in the stem rather than in a suffix (Stem Stress). His example of *onveránderlijkheid* 'unalterability' illustrates Stem Stress, as shown in (16).

(16) a.   [ánder]   'other'
    b.   [ver- [ánder]]   'alter'
    c.   [[ver- [ánder]] -lijk]   'alterable'
    d.   [on- [[ver- [ánder]] -lijk]]   'unalterable'
    e.   [[on- [[ver- [ánder]] -lijk]] -heid]   'unalterability'
            un-   en-   other   -able -ity

Here I assume that the stem is a (single-membered) set {*ánder*} while the affixes are terminals. One reason for this assumption is that the stem needs no complement, as in (16a). On the other hand, affixes need a complement, as shown in (16b) to (16e): they cannot appear by themselves (*ver/*lijk/*on/*heid*). Set Strong assigns S to a stem (St) and W to an affix (Af) as shown in (17).

(17)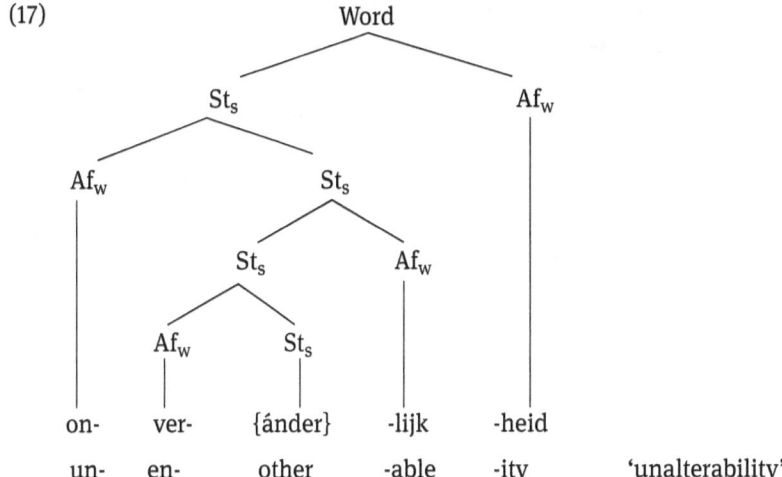

Thus, Set Strong recursively applies to a pair made up of a set and a terminal in a word, and correctly explains the fact that the stem receives the primary stress in Germanic languages.[4]

A problem with this analysis is the fact that there are some stress-bearing suffixes in Germanic languages. For example, English has a number of suffixes bearing word-stress as shown in (18).

(18) a. Japán > Japan-ése
b. emplóy > employ-ée

Yavaş (2011: 165) lists stress-bearing suffixes in English including *lemon-áde, million-áire, realiz-átion, absent-ée* (exception: *commíttee*), *mountain-éer, Japan-ése, pictur-ésque, kitchen-étte, laryng-ítis* and *honor-ífic*. Note that these stress-bearing affixes always constitute heavy syllables, as pointed out by

---

[4] This theory predicts that complex (longer) words are more likely to get phrasal stress than simplex (shorter) words. This seems to be generally the case, as shown by the example phrases in (i).

(i) a. define words
b. redefine words

The verb *redefine* in (ib) is more complex and more likely to receive the phrasal stress than the simplex verb *define* in (ia). The morphosyntactic complexity is also related to the richness of information from the semantic point of view.

Yavaş. Then, we can ascribe the stress on affixes to the heaviness of syllables, which I will discuss in section 4.2.[5]

As for Dutch, Booij (1999: 113) lists four native stress-bearing suffixes (*-erij, -es, -in, -ij*) (cf. van Oostendorp 2002). However, as Booij (1999: 111) points out, most native suffixes of Dutch are stress-neutral (e.g. *-e, -el, -en, -er, -erd, -erig, -ing, -nis, -s, -sel, -st, -ster, -t, -te, -tje, -achtig, -baar, -dom, -heid, -ling, -loos, -schap*). Although we still need to explain why the four affixes are stress-bearing, we can say that a stem generally receives the primary stress in Dutch words.

Note that a stem is also more likely to receive the primary stress than affixes in languages other than Germanic. McCarthy and Prince (1995: 116) propose Root-Affix Faithfulness Metaconstraint (Root-Faith >> Affix-Faith). Smith (1998) proposes a constraint STEMSTRESS to account for the fact that, all else being equal, stems have priority over suffixes for stress in Tuyuca, a Tucanoan language spoken in Colombia and Brazil. Alderete (2001) argues that root-controlled accent is seen in Cupeño (Uto-Aztecan), Russian and Japanese. Caballero (2011) also discusses Choguita Rarámuri (Tarahumara) (Uto-Aztecan) in terms of STEMSTRESS. All these works support the idea that a stem is more likely to receive the primary stress than affixes. The analysis in terms of Set Strong presented here gives a principled explanation to the question why a stem (or root) has privileged status over affix in word stress.

3.2 Bound morphemes

We can extend our analysis to words consisting of bound morphemes only (e.g. *re-ply, re-port, sub-mit*) if we take etymology into consideration. A number of bound morphemes in English were originally stems, which I argue are sets. Then, Set Strong assigns S to a morpheme that was once a stem and W to a morpheme that has been an affix. For example, in some English words consisting of bound morphemes, there is a bound morpheme that was a stem borrowed from other languages, as shown in (19).

---

[5] Trevian (2015: 75) notes that stress-bearing suffixes in English are generally Latinate loans (mainly French) or Neo-Greek combining forms.

(19) a. [re- {plý}] (again-fold (Latin)) (verb/noun)
　　b. [re- {pórt}] (back-carry (Latin)) (verb/noun)
　　c. [sub {mít}] (under-send (French)) (verb, cf. noun: *submíssion*)

Here, the bound morphemes *ply, port* and *mit* are etymological stems and receive stress. I assume that these morphemes are single-membered sets although they are bound morphemes, which cannot appear by themselves in English.

One might argue that in some English nouns, the primary stress falls on the affix rather than on the etymological stem, as shown in (20).

(20) a. [$_N$ ré- {cord}] ← [$_V$ re- {córd}] (back- heart (Latin))
　　b. [$_N$ ím- {port}] ← [$_V$ im- {pórt}] (in- carry (Latin))

It is conceivable that some kind of historical restructuring occurred in these words. The stem in the original language lost its stem status somewhere in the history of the English language. The whole word was reanalyzed as a combination of bound morphemes. Then, the Germanic word-initial stress system in English assigned the primary stress to the affix on the left (cf. Halle and Keyser 1971, Lahiri, Riad and Jacobs 1999: 375). The change is illustrated in (21).

(21) a. [$_V$ re- {córd}] (back- heart (L)) → [$_N$ re-cord] → [$_N$ ré-cord]
　　b. [$_V$ im- {pórt}] (in- carry (Lt)) → [$_N$ im-port]] → [$_N$ ím-port]

We still need to explain why this change occurred in nouns and not in verbs. A possible explanation is given by Bolinger (1965), who argues that nouns tend to occur in sentence initial position (cf. Jespersen 1954: section 5.7, Campbell 1959: 30). Although this is an interesting topic, I will not discuss this matter here.

As an alternative to the diachronic explanation presented above, we can explore a synchronic explanation of the relation between stress in nouns and verbs. Words consisting of bound morphemes such as (21) consist of a prefix and a stem, both of which are a single morpheme. Then, nothing prevents us from assuming that either a prefix or a stem can be a single-membered set (e.g. {ré}-*cord* or *re*-{córd}). Then, Set Strong assigns stress either on a prefix or on a stem. The word-initial stress corresponds to nouns while the word-final stress corresponds to verbs according to the general stress patterns of English. This synchronic explanation might be preferred to the diachronic explanation due to its simplicity. However, we must explain why nouns have word-initial stress while verbs have word-final stress. Then, we need to refer to the history of English stress system (for a stress retraction rule in Old English which retracted the stress from stems to noun- and adjective-forming prefixes, see Halle and Keyser 1971, Lahiri, Riad and Jacobs 1999: 375).

4 Stress in a morpheme

4.1 Dependent Stress (Nasukawa and Backley 2015)

Nasukawa and Backley (2015) argue that stress falls on the dependent rather than on the head in a head-dependent pair. They point out the similarity between syntactic phrases such as (22) and word-internal structure such as (23), where H stands for head and D dependent.

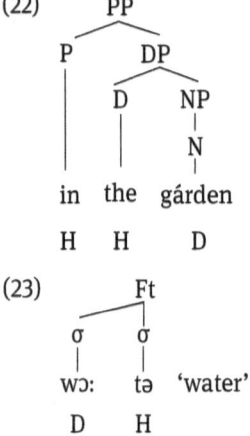

(22)
```
        PP
       /  \
      P    DP
      |   /  \
      |  D    NP
      |  |    |
      |  |    N
      |  |    |
      in the gárden
      H   H   D
```

(23)
```
        Ft
       /  \
      σ    σ
      |    |
      wɔː  tə   'water'
      D    H
```

Their idea, which can be called Dependent Stress, is also based on Cinque's (1993) idea that the main stress falls on the most deeply embedded element in a hierarchical structure. Although their idea is interesting, we need to know how we can define the head and the dependent of a foot in a structure like (23), where both syllables are at the same level of embedding. We could argue that in (23) the first syllable wɔː is a set while the last syllable tə is a terminal, as shown in (24a), but we still need to explain why this is the case and not the other way around, as in (24b).

(24) a. [{σS wɔː} [σW tə]]
     b. [[σW wɔː] {σS tə}]

In the next section, I argue that a heavy syllable is a set while a light syllable is a terminal, in order to derive weight-sensitive stress from Set Strong.[6]

4.2 A heavy syllable is a set: Weight-factors and the structure of syllables

In order to apply Set Strong to a word-internal structure, we need to show that a heavy syllable is a set of some entities while a light syllable consists of a single entity. First, let us consider the types of heaviness in the world's languages. Goedemans and van der Hulst (2005) classify the languages with a weight-sensitive stress system into subgroups in terms of the weight factors shown in (25), where the number in square brackets shows the number of languages in the world.

(25) a. Long vowels or closed syllables make heavy [35]
Hopi (Uto-Aztecan; Arizona): If the first syllable is light, stress falls on the second: *ho'nani* 'badger', but if the first is heavy, it is stressed: *'sipmasmi* 'silver bracelet', *'naatıhota* 'to hurt oneself'.
b. Long vowels make heavy [65]
Iraqw (Southern Cushitic, Tanzania): *ba'ʔeeso* 'bushbucks' vs. *'wawitmo* 'king' (the closed syllable does not draw stress onto itself)
c. Coda consonants make heavy (mostly languages that have no long vowels) [18]
Amele (Madang, Papua New Guinea): stress falls on the first heavy syllable *iti'tom* 'righteous' or the first syllable *'nifula* 'kind of beetle'
d. prominence (other factors are heavy for stress) [41]
e. lexical (lexical stress, diacritic weight) [38]
f. Combined (two of the above factors determine weight) [42]
g. No weight (fixed stress), or weight factor unknown [261]
Initial, second, third, antepenultimate, penultimate, ultimate

---

6 Another interesting question is what decides the linear order between head and dependent/complement in a foot. Considering the fact that most languages have suffixes rather than prefixes (cf. the Righthand Head Rule (Tokizaki 2017)), it seems that the head of a foot, which is smaller than a word, should also be linearized at the right of its dependent/complement as in (23) and (24) (cf. Tokizaki and Kuwana 2013).

Let us consider how we can account for these stress patterns with Set Strong. The basic idea of weight-sensitive stress systems in (25a-f) is that stress falls on a heavy syllable rather than on light syllables. As can be seen in (25), there are two basic elements that make a syllable heavy: long vowel and coda consonant. We can distinguish a heavy syllable (represented here as Σ) from a light syllable (σ) in terms of empty segments (ø), as shown in (26) and (27).

(26) light syllable (σ)

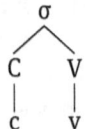

(27) a. heavy syllable with long vowel (Σ)

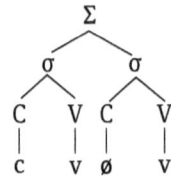

b. heavy syllable with coda consonant (Σ)

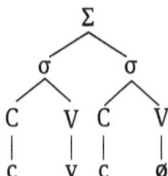

A light syllable (σ) is a simplex unit dominating a consonant and a vowel as in (26); a heavy syllable (Σ) consists of two σs, one of which has an empty segment (ø): an empty consonant as in (27a) or an empty vowel as in (27b). Then we can give a principled answer to the question why stress falls on a heavy syllable rather than on light syllables. A heavy syllable is a set while a light syllable is a terminal at the syllable level (σ or Σ). For example, let us consider the structure of *arena* and *veranda* in English.

(28) a.

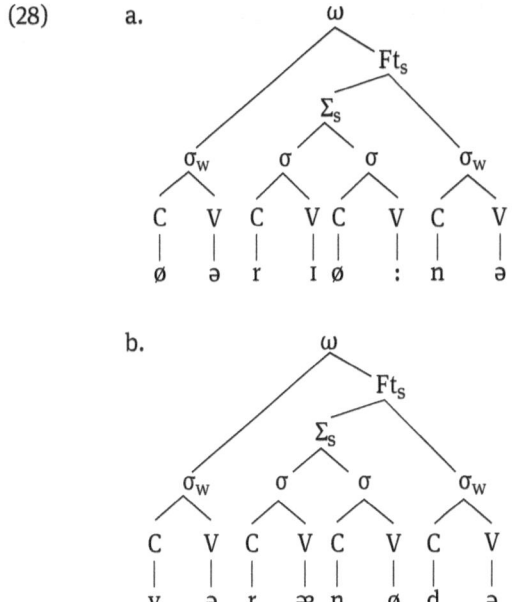

In (28a) and (28b), Set Strong assigns S to the branching syllable (Σ), a set consisting of two σs, rather than to its sister syllable (σ), which is a terminal syllable. Thus, we can correctly predict the weight-sensitive stress in languages where long vowels or closed syllables make heavy as in (25a).[7]

What can we say about the types of weight listed in (25b) to (25g)? If our analysis is on the right track, languages that do not count vowel length and coda consonant for heaviness are expected to have a simple syllable (σ) rather than a complex syllable (Σ) for a syllable with a long vowel or a coda consonant, as shown in (29).

(29) a. "heavy" syllable with a long vowel not counted as heavy

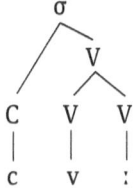

---

[7] We can argue that in a heavy syllable Σ, S is assigned to the first σ (rɪ in (28a) and ræ in (28b)), which consists of two substantives C and V. The second σ in a heavy syllable Σ, which receives W, is more of a terminal than a set because it contains only one substantive V in (28a) or C in (28b).

b. "heavy" syllable with a coda consonant not counted as heavy

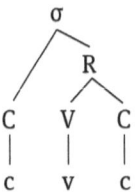

In these languages, a vowel (the bottom V on the left in (29a)) merges with the following segment (the last V in (29a) or C in (29b)) to make a long vowel (the top V in (29a) or a rhyme (R in (29b))) rather than a syllable (σ). Then, the weight-factor typology in (25) can be recaptured in terms of branching syllables (Σ) in (27) and non-branching syllables (σ) in (29), as shown in (30).

(30) a. Long vowels or closed syllables make heavy [35]: (27a), (27b)
  b. Long vowels make heavy [65]: (27a), (29b)
  c. Coda consonants make heavy (no long V) [18]: (27b), (29a)
  d. Prominence (other factors are heavy for stress) [41]
  e. Lexical (lexical stress, diacritic weight) [38]
  f. Combined (two of the above factors determine weight) [42]
  g. No weight (fixed stress), or weight factor unknown [261]: (29a), (29b)

I will discuss how stress is assigned to a fixed position in a word in languages with no weight-sensitivity (30g) in the next section. Of course, we need independent support for these structural differences in syllable structure between languages. I will leave this for future research (cf. Gordon 2006, 2016 for the typology of syllable weight).

Finally, I would like to point out a merit of our analysis. Set Strong makes a prediction that there is no language that assigns stress to a light syllable rather than heavy syllables if the language has heavy syllables as well as light syllables. As far as I know, this is the case in the world's languages. Set Strong gives us a principled answer to the question why this is a universal property of languages.

4.3 Fixed stress and recursion

Finally, let us consider the fixed-stress system. If the idea of Set Strong is on the right track, we expect the structure of words with word-initial stress and with word-final stress to be left-branching and right-branching as shown in (31).

(31) a.
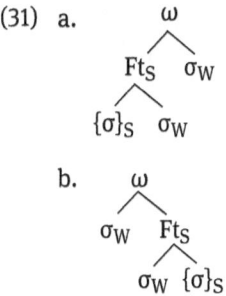

b.

In (31a), the initial syllable is assumed to be a single-membered set and is assigned S by Set Strong. Similarly, in (31b) the final syllable is assigned S. A question is what kind of languages choose (31a) or (31b).

In the holistic typology of languages, it has been argued that the word-stress location matches the compound stress and the phrasal stress location (cf. Plank 1998 for an overview). For example, Bally (1944) argues that "progressive" languages such as French have accent on the final position of words, compounds and phrases while "anticipating" languages such as German have accent on the initial position of words, compounds and phrases. Similarly, discussing the typology of Austroasiatic languages, Donegan and Stampe (1983) argue that Munda languages have initial accent on words and phrases while Mon-Khmer languages have final accent on words and phrases. If the rhythmic holism of stress location in words and phrases generally holds in the world's languages, we predict that Set Strong recursively applies to a unidirectional (left/right-branching) tree, ranging from a syllable to phrases, as shown in (32).

(32)
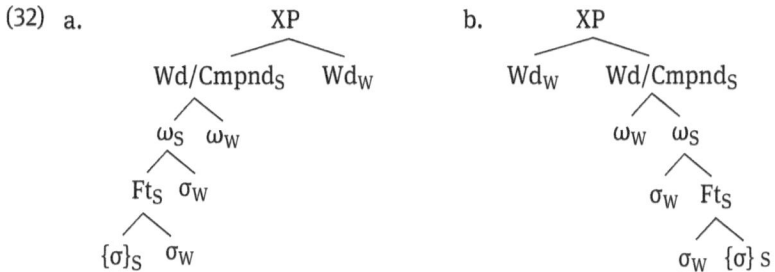

Assuming that the structure from syllable to phrase is unidirectional, we can explain the rhythmic holism argued by Bally (1944) and Donegan and Stampe (1983) in terms of Set Strong.

We still need to derive the fixed stress locations other than initial and ultimate stress in words. Goedemans and van der Hulst (2005) list the locations of fixed stress as in (33), where the numbers of languages are shown in square brackets.

(33) a. Initial [92]
    b. Second [16]
    c. Third [1]
    d. Antepenultimate [12]
    e. Penultimate [110]
    f. Ultimate [51]

We propose a mechanism Flip, which applies freely to a hierarchical structure to change the linear order of sisters in Externalization (for Externalization, see Chomsky 2012). In order to derive penultimate stress (33e), which is the largest group in the world's languages with fixed stress (110 languages), we can Flip the ultimate syllable and the penultimate syllable in right-branching structure (31b), as shown in (34).[8]

(34)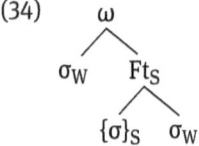

Another Flip between the top syllable and the foot in (34) gives word-initial (or antepenult) stress as shown in (32a) ([ω [Fts {σ}s σw] σw]). We should note that this explanation holds if the number of syllables in a word is three. For languages with more than three syllables in a simplex word, we may need another mechanism to derive their stress location. This is also an interesting topic, but is far beyond the scope of this paper.[9]

---

8 We assume that Flip is free of cost. Thus, the fact that penultimate stress (33e) is the most popular stress pattern in the world does not conflict with the idea that the penultimate stress is the result of Flip applied to the ultimate stress.

9 I assume that Flip freely applies to every level of sisters in (32a) or (32b) to change the linear order of constituents, and gives the variation of stress location in the world's languages. This amounts to saying that a hierarchical structure created by Merge has no left to right order in morphosyntax, like a Calder's mobile in the air, which is linearized when it is laid on the ground (i.e. linearized at the morphosyntax-PF interface) (Uriagereka 1999: 251). See the discussion in the Conclusion and Tokizaki (2018a).

4.4 Word stress, compound stress and phrasal stress

Before concluding the discussion, let us consider the relation between word stress, compound stress and phrasal stress. I have argued that the same mechanism of stress assignment Set Strong applies to both phrases and (compound) words. It is clear that we need both (compound) word stress (shown with ´) and phrasal stress (shown with underscore here), as exemplified in (35).

(35)
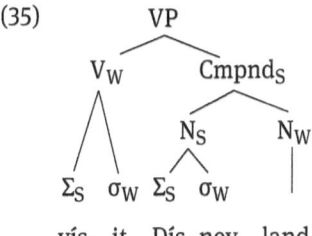

Here, the first syllable of *visit* and *Disney* receives word stress because of the S assigned to them. The word *Disney* receives compound stress when merged with *land* and assigned S. The compound *Disneyland* receives a phrasal stress when merged with the verb *visit*. In other words, the first syllable of *Disney* receives the primary stress in the whole phrase because it is dominated only by S. Thus, metrical trees with labels S and W correctly represent word stress, compound stress and phrasal stress.

4.5 Secondary stress

Another point of discussion is the secondary stress in words and phrases. As Set Strong applies to both words and phrases and determines the primary stress in them, the same mechanism should determine the secondary stress. Following the original insight of Chomsky and Halle (1968), I argue that secondary stress is assigned to the element dominated by only S under the top W assigned by the last Merge (for the same idea, see Reinhart (2006: 136)). For example, in the example (35) above, the secondary phrasal stress is assigned to the syllable *vis*, which is dominated by S (assigned when merged with *–it*) and W (assigned when visit is lastly merged with *Disneyland*). As for compound word stress, *land* receives the secondary stress in *Disneyland* because *land* is dominated by the W, which is assigned when it is lastly merged with *Disney*. As for word stress, let us consider the example in (36).

(36)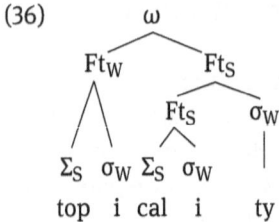

Here, *top* receives the secondary word stress because it is immediately dominated by S (Σ_S) and dominated by W (Ft_W) which is assigned at the last Merge in (35). Thus, we can formalize the secondary stress in words, compounds and phrases with the same rule Set Strong.

We could go on to argue that the tertiary stress is assigned to the element dominated by only S under the top and the second highest Ws assigned by the last and the second last Merge in words and phrases. However, the stress levels below the secondary stress are not substantial. It seems that we do not need to discuss them here.

5 Conclusion

So far, I have proposed and illustrated a rule Set Strong, which assigns a metrical label Strong (S) to a set, which may be a single-membered set or a branching node. It is argued that Set Strong does not have the problems of Cinque's (1993) stress rule and Reinhart's (2006) metrical rule, namely the problems of first Merge and globality of computation. I have shown that Set Strong recursively applies at every level of constituent structure, ranging from syllable structure to phrase structure. The resulting structure with metrical labels is interpreted at the syntax-phonology interface and is assigned the main stress in the location that is dominated only by Strong. The analysis presented here shows that recursion of structure and rule application is present in morpheme-internal phonology as well as in phrasal phonology.

Finally, let us consider the relation between structure and linear order in the whole grammar. In the above argument, I assume that Flip changes the basic order of constituents at Externalization of constituent structure. However, we can also argue that syllables, words and phrases have hierarchical structure but do not have linear order in the morphosyntactic component, like an Alexander Calder mobile hanging in the air (cf. Uriagereka 1999: 251). Their order is determined only at Externalization (in the mobile simile, only when it is laid on a desk) according to the phonological conditions or preferences of the language (which we can think of as variously shaped desks). Then, we do not need to assume Flip to derive the various stress locations. If this is the case, exploring the output conditions and preferences in the world's languages should be our next challenge.

Acknowledgements: I would like to thank Kuniya Nasukawa for a general discussion of the topic. Thanks also go to two anonymous reviewers for their valuable comments and suggestions. This work was supported by JSPS Grant-in-Aid for Scientific Research (KAKENHI) (B) Grant Numbers 26284067 and 15H03213.

References

Anderson, John and Colin J. Ewen. 1987. *Principles of Dependency Phonology*. Cambridge: Cambridge University Press.
Anderson, John and Charles Jones. 1974. Three theses concerning phonological representations. *Journal of Linguistics* 10, 1–26.
Backley, Phillip. 2011. *An Introduction to Element Theory*. Edinburgh: Edinburgh University Press.
Alderete, John. 2001. *Morphologically Governed Accent in Optimality Theory*. New York: Routledge.
Bally, Charles. 1944. *Linguistique Générale et Linguistique Française*. 2nd edition. Berne: Francke.
Bing, Janet Mueller 1979. Aspects of English prosody. Doctoral dissertation, University of Massachusetts, Amherst. [Distributed by GLSA, University of Massachusetts, Amherst. Published by Garland, New York, 1985.]
Bolinger, Dwight L. 1965. Pitch Accent and Sentence Rhythm. In Isamu Abe and Tetsuya Kanekiyo (eds.), *Forms of English: Accent, Morpheme, Order*, 139–180. Tokyo: Hakuou.
Bolinger, Dwight L. 1972. Accent is predictable (if you're a mind-reader). *Language* 48, 633–644.
Booij, Geert. 1999. *The phonology of Dutch*. Oxford: Clarendon Press.
Caballero, Gabriela. 2011. Morphologically conditioned stress assignment in Choguita Rarámuri (Tarahumara). *Linguistics* 49 (4), 749–790.
Campbell, Alistair. 1959. *Old English Grammar*. Oxford: Oxford University Press.
Chomsky, Noam. 1995. *The Minimalist Program*. Cambridge, MA: MIT Press.
Chomsky, Noam. 2000. Minimalist inquiries: the framework. In Roger Martin, David Michaels and Juan Uriagereka (eds.), *Step by Step: Essays on Minimalist Syntax in Honor of Howard Lasnik*, 89–155. Cambridge, MA: MIT Press.
Chomsky, Noam. 2001. Derivation by phase. In Michael Kenstowicz (ed.), *Ken Hale: A Life in Language*, 1–52. Cambridge, MA: MIT Press.
Chomsky, Noam. 2012. *The Science of Language: Interviews with James McGilvray*. Cambridge: Cambridge University Press.
Cinque, Guglielmo. 1993. A null theory of phrase and compound stress. *Linguistic Inquiry* 24, 239–298.

Chomsky, Noam and Morris Halle. 1968. *The Sound Pattern of English*. New York: Harper and Row.
Cinque, Guglielmo. 1993. A null theory of phrase and compound stress. *Linguistic Inquiry* 24, 239–297.
Dobashi, Yoshihito. 2003. Phonological phrasing and syntactic derivation. Cornell University dissertation.
Donegan, Patricia Jane and David Stampe. 1983. Rhythm and the holistic organization of language structure, *Papers from the Parasession on the Interplay of Phonology, Morphology and Syntax*, 337–353. Chicago: Chicago Linguistic Society.
Giegerich, Heinz J. 2004. Compound or phrase?: English nounplusnoun constructions and the stress criterion. *English Language and Linguistics* 8, 1–24.
Goedemans, Rob and Harry van der Hulst. 2005a. Fixed stress locations. In Haspelmath, Martin, Matthew S. Dryer, David Gil and Bernard Comrie (eds.), *The World Atlas of Language Structures*, 62–65. Oxford: Oxford University Press.
Goedemans, Rob and Harry van der Hulst. 2005b. Weight-sensitive stress. In Haspelmath, Martin, Matthew S. Dryer, David Gil and Bernard Comrie (eds.), *The World Atlas of Language Structures*, 66–69. Oxford: Oxford University Press.
Goedemans, Rob and Harry van der Hulst. 2005c. Weight factors in weight-sensitive stress systems. In Haspelmath, Martin, Matthew S. Dryer, David Gil and Bernard Comrie (eds.), *The World Atlas of Language Structures*, 70–73. Oxford: Oxford University Press.
Gordon, Matthew Kelly. 2006. *Syllable Weight: Phonetics, Phonology, Typology*. New York: Routledge.
Gordon, Matthew Kelly. 2016. *Phonological Typology*. Oxford: Oxford University Press.
Halle, Morris and Samuel Jay Keyser. 1971. *English Stress: Its Form, Its Growth, and Its Role in Verse*. New York: Harper and Row.
Haspelmath, Martin, Matthew S. Dryer, David Gil and Bernard Comrie. 2005. *The World Atlas of Language Structures*. Oxford: Oxford University Press.
Jespersen, Otto. 1954. *Sounds and Spellings: A Modern English Grammar on Historical Principles, Volume 1*. London: Routledge.
Kager, René. 2000. Stem stress and peak correspondence in Dutch. In Joost Dekkers, Frank van der Leeuw and Jeroen van de Weijer (eds.), *Optimality Theory: Phonology, Syntax, and Acquisition*, 121–150. Oxford: Oxford University Press.
Kahnemuyipour, Arsalan. 2009. *The Syntax of Sentential Stress*. Oxford: Oxford University Press.
Kayne, Richard S. 2009. Antisymmetry and the lexicon. *Linguistic Variation Yearbook* 8, 1–31.
Kratzer, Angelika and Elisabeth Selkirk. 2007. Phase theory and prosodic spellout: the case of verbs, *The Linguistic Review* 24, 93–135.
Ladd, Robert D. 2008. *Intonational Phonology*, 2nd editionn. Cambridge: Cambridge University Press.
Lahiri, Aditi, Thomas Riad and Haike Jacobs. 1999. Diachronic prosody. In Harry van der Hulst (ed.), *Word Prosodic Systems in the Languages of Europe*, 335–422. Berlin: Walter de Gruyter.
McCarthy, John and Alan Prince. 1995. Faithfulness and reduplicative identity. In Jill N. Beckman, Laura Walsh Dickey and Suzanne Urbanczyk (eds.), *Papers in Optimality Theory, University of Massachusetts Occasional Papers* 18, 249–384. Amherst: GLSA, University of Massachusetts.

Nasukawa, Kuniya and Phillip Backley. 2015. Heads and complements in phonology: a case of role reversal? *Phonological Studies* 18, 67–74.
Okazaki, Masao. 1998. *English Sentence Prosody: The Interface between Sound and Meaning*. Tokyo: Kaitakusha.
Oostendorp, Marc van. 2002. The phonological and morphological status of the prosodic word adjunct. *Linguistische Berichte Sonderheft* 11, 209–235.
Ortega-Santos, Ivan 2010. Review of *The syntax of Sentential Stress* by Arsalan Kahnemuyipour. *Journal of Linguistics* 46, 523–528.
Ott, Denis. 2011. A note on free relative clauses in the theory of phases. *Linguistic Inquiry* 42, 183–192.
Plank, Frans. 1998. The co-variation of phonology with morphology and syntax: a hopeful history. *Linguistic Typology* 2, 195–230.
Reinhart, Tanya. 2006. *Interface Strategies: Optimal and Costly Computations*. Cambridge, Mass: MIT Press.
Sato, Yosuke. 2012. Phonological interpretation by phase: nuclear stress, domain encapsulation, and edge sensitivity. In Ángel J. Gallego (ed.), *Phases: Developing the Framework*, 283–307. Berlin: Mouton de Gruyter.
Schmerling, Susan F. 1976. *Aspects of English Sentence Stress*. Austin: University of Texas Press.
Selkirk, Elizabeth and Koichi Tateishi. 1988. Constraints on minor phrase formation in Japanese. *Proceedings of the 24th Annual Meeting of the Chicago Linguistic Society: Part One: The General Session*, 316–336. Chicago, IL: Chicago Linguistic Society.
Selkirk, Elisabeth and Koichi Tateishi. 1991. Syntax and downstep in Japanese. In Carol Georgopoulos and Roberta Ishihara (eds.), *Inter Disciplinary Approaches to Language: Essays in Honor of S.-Y. Kuroda*, 519–543. Dordrecht: Kluwer Academic Publishers.
Smith, Jennifer. 1998. Noun faithfulness and word stress in Tuyuca. In Jennifer Austin and Aaron Lawson (eds.), *Proceedings of ESCOL 97*, 180–191. Ithaca: CLC Publications.
Szendrői, Kriszta. 2001. Focus and the syntax-phonology interface. Doctoral dissertation, University College London, University of London.
Tokizaki, Hisao. 2008. *Syntactic Structure and Silence: A Minimalist Theory of Syntax-Phonology Interface*. Tokyo: Hituji Syobo.
Tokizaki, Hisao. 2011. Review of *The syntax of Sentential Stress* by Arsalan Kahnemuyipour. *Studies in English Literature*, English Number 52, 222–231.
Tokizaki, Hisao. 2017. Righthand Head Rule and the typology of word stress. *KLS* 37, 253–264. Kansai Linguistic Society.
Tokizaki, Hisao. 2018a. Externalization, stress and word order. *Proceedings of Sophia University Linguistic Society* 32, 18–34.
Tokizaki, Hisao. 2018b. Obligatory Contour Principle and minimalist syntax. In Hisao Tokizaki (ed.), *Phonological Externalization vol. 3*, 73–83. Sapporo University. http://id.nii.ac.jp/1067/00007527/
Tokizaki, Hisao and Yasutomo Kuwana. 2013. Unattested word orders and left-branching structure. In Theresa Biberauer and Ian Roberts (eds.), *Challenges to Linearization*, 211–234. Berlin: Mouton de Gruyter.
Trevian, Ives. 2015. *English Suffixes: Stress-assignment Properties, Productivity, Selection and Combinatorial Processes*. Bern: Peter Lang.

Uriagereka, Juan. 1999. Multiple spell-out. In Samuel D. Epstein and Norbert Hornstein (eds.), *Working Minimalism*, 251–282. Cambridge, MA: MIT Press.
Yavaş, Mehmet. 2011. *Applied English Phonology*, 2nd edition. Malden, MA: Wiley-Blackwell.
Zubizarreta, Maria Luisa. 1998. *Prosody, Focus, and Word Order*. Cambridge, MA: MIT Press.

Language Index

Basaa 148n4
Botswana
– Eastern Botswana 148
– Northern Botswana 147
Brazilian Portuguese 247
Bulgarian 27, 27n2

Catalan 254
Chinese 72–74n18, 76, 123, 123n10, 125, 126, 151
– Wu (Shanghainese) 151
Cilungu 21, 215
Czech 330, 360n35

Djapu 188
Dutch 61, 62, 66, 67n9, 76, 76n19, 77n21, 78, 80, 81, 81n24, 82, 84, 84n28, 85, 88, 91, 94, 100, 100n44, 101, 106, 108n51, 188, 275, 392, 394

English 6, 12, 18, 20, 21, 32, 63, 64, 66, 75, 85n31, 91, 92, 99, 99n40, 101, 103, 104, 106, 108, 134, 186, 188, 193, 194, 196, 198, 207, 208, 209, 210, 215, 218, 220, 221, 222, 223, 224, 225, 226, 232, 242, 242n8, 244, 244n10, 245, 246, 248, 249, 250, 251, 252, 253, 255, 267, 272, 273–274n5, 276n9, 284, 288, 292, 293, 295, 298, 299, 301, 303, 309, 311, 317, 318, 319, 320, 322, 323, 324, 347, 392, 394, 394n5, 395, 398
– Middle English 120
– RP (Received Pronunciation) 6, 267, 273, 275, 277n10, 278, 279
– Standard Scottish English 275, 276n9
Estonian 244, 244n11

Faroese 353, 360, 361–362, 365n41, 366, 378
Fijian 215
Finnish 246
French 183, 188, 242, 245, 329, 331, 332, 332n2, 334, 335, 338, 339, 347n26, 353, 358, 378, 401
– Quebec French 6, 245, 245n13

German 106, 184, 189, 194, 195, 198, 246, 348, 392, 401
Germanic 99n40, 209, 392, 393, 394, 395
Gorgia Toscana 330, 335, 336, 337, 356
Greek 209, 242, 366
– Samothraki Greek 353, 360, 362–366, 378

Hungarian 344

Ikalanga 144, 145, 147, 148, 150
Italian 27, 28, 29, 188, 243, 244n10, 247

Japanese 20, 73n16, 103, 117, 120, 121, 121n6, 122, 123, 123n10, 123n12, 124, 125, 133, 135, 136n32, 139, 188, 207, 215, 225, 237, 249, 250, 253, 269, 270, 311, 391n3

Kammu 99
Kaqchikel 32
Korean 117, 121, 122, 122n7, 125, 126, 128n24, 132, 137, 137n34, 139, 287, 290, 290n15, 292n16, 293, 295, 311
– Cheju Korean 287, 288
– Middle Korean 6, 267, 272, 284–293, 297, 298, 301, 302, 303
– Seoul Korean 268, 289, 289n14, 290, 291, 292, 292n17, 293

Latin 330, 334, 335, 338, 353, 366, 369n45, 371

Maga Rukai (Formosan language) 118, 120

Nambya 149
Northern Saraiki 215
Nyamwezi/Kinyamwezi 171, 172

Polish 171, 173, 317, 318, 322
Putonghua 6, 249, 250, 251, 254, 349
Puyo-pongo Quechua 174, 175

Russian 27, 27n2, 311, 394

https://doi.org/10.1515/9781501512582-014

Sardinian 353, 366, 368, 371, 372, 373n49, 374, 378, 379
Sino-Japanese 4, 117, 118, 119, 120, 121, 122–123n9, 125n15, 127n22, 132, 139, 140
Sino-Korean 3, 117, 118, 119, 121, 122–124n14, 132, 139, 140
Slovene 27, 28, 29
Slovenian 247
Spanish 220, 242
Swati/SiSwati 144, 149
Swedish 12, 84n28, 184, 188, 189, 193, 215

Tsonga 144, 145, 146, 147, 148, 150

Tsou (Formosan language) 3, 117, 117n1, 118, 119, 121, 122–124n14, 129n27, 132, 136n33, 139, 140
Tsua 144, 148, 151
Turkish 25, 52n12, 193, 194, 197, 253, 257n23, 259, 260
Tuscan 335, 337

Xhosa 144, 145, 149
Xiang 151

Zulu 144, 145, 149, 225

Subject Index

'light v' 60, 61, 67–72, 73, 112

absorption 316, 323, 324
adjunct 96, 107, 133
– adjunction 3, 50, 58n1, 70, 70n13, 94, 96, 98, 98n39, 99, 99n42, 100, 101, 101n47, 103n49, 107, 109, 112, 308, 320, 321, 349n28, 351, 351n32
agreement 5, 207, 232, 303
ambiguity 66n8, 242, 312
argument structure 67
asymmetry 4, 24, 52, 53, 121, 153, 164, 169, 182, 187, 188, 190, 193, 241n7, 249, 252, 344
– asymmetry principle 202
autonomous interpretation 17
autonomous phonetic signature 17

balance 38, 41–42, 48, 49n4
bare phrase structure 58n1, 383, 385, 386, 390
baseline 21, 22, 23, 25, 26, 27, 138n34, 215, 216, 217, 218, 219, 224, 225, 225n4, 303
bidirectional 118, 139, 371
binding 52n11, 100, 241, 251, 253, 254n17

c-command 51, 52, 52n11, 85n30, 100, 105, 198, 249, 251, 252, 253, 254, 260, 260n26
C-domain 30
Closure node 318
Comp (complement) 132, 133, 134, 190, 191, 192, 193, 195, 196, 198, 199
complementation 3, 70n13, 96, 100, 100n44, 101, 103
complex expression 17, 26, 140, 270
Complexity Condition 51, 345, 346
compound 24, 118, 120, 121, 128, 131, 136, 187, 202, 383–392, 401, 403, 404
concatenation 2, 25, 29, 217, 227
Contrastive Hierarchy 284, 285, 286, 288n13
coordination 94, 100–101n45, 102, 310

decomposition 4, 117–140, 344n18, 345
DEE 170–176
dependency 6, 27n2, 45, 60, 121, 156, 157, 157n8, 159, 160, 201, 240, 267–299n21, 303
– dependent 2, 6, 14, 18, 19, 21, 23, 24, 26, 29, 30, 31, 32, 88, 96, 101, 121, 133, 134, 135, 136, 136n31, 137, 138, 156, 157n9, 167, 181, 187, 190, 215, 216, 217, 218, 219, 220, 222, 225, 227, 261, 267–271n3, 274n5, 276n7, 303, 396, 397n6
– dominance 176, 355
– indirect domination 198–201
– inherent dependency 294–298
Dependency Phonology 19, 24, 45, 119n3, 121, 160, 246, 256, 267, 271, 297n20
Depressors/depressor effect 4, 143–152, 154, 160, 161, 164, 165, 167–170, 176
diachronic change 117, 303

elements 2, 6, 13, 14, 15–17, 19, 21, 23, 24, 29, 33, 37–44, 48, 49n4, 49n8, 52, 53, 109, 119, 119n4, 131, 152, 163, 167, 183, 214–218, 227, 245n12, 267, 268
– element A (as structure) 246–249
– element geometry 4, 143, 154, 160, 161–164, 167, 171, 172, 176
– Element Theory 15, 17, 24, 26, 29, 37, 39, 40, 44, 53, 118, 119–119n3, 122, 136n32, 143, 152, 152n6, 176, 182, 215, 219, 221n3, 267, 341, 348, 349
– identical (recurring) elements 6, 156, 268, 272, 279, 281, 283, 286, 288, 291, 293–303
– resonance elements 14, 15, 16, 21, 29, 49, 268
elements
– **element A (as structure)** 250
emergent stops 5, 181, 184, 192, 198, 200
enhancement 26, 281, 293

Feature Geometry 45, 46, 47, 143, 153, 154–155, 156, 157, 176

features 12, 13, 14, 15, 17, 22, 37–40, 45, 46, 47, 53, 71, 79, 104, 105, 106, 109, 151, 152–154, 156, 158, 182, 183, 185, 211, 212, 213, 239, 259, 276, 288, 289, 291, 292, 293, 294, 310, 314, 341, 344, 350, 373, 374
Flip 402
formant transitions 309
fortis/lenis 158, 243, 244, 245, 342

geminate 80, 82, 84, 242
generative capacity 241
Government Phonology (GP) 13, 19, 46, 48–50, 61, 85, 181, 185, 224, 237, 239, 267
Government Phonology 2.0 (GP 2.0) 48–50, 181, 185, 186, 187, 237–262, 340

headedness 24, 40, 53, 121, 122, 153, 247, 249, 268, 270, 272, 274, 275, 277, 278, 279, 281, 282, 283, 290, 291, 294, 295, 296, 298, 299, 300, 301
– head-dependency 14, 18, 19, 20, 23, 25, 33, 121, 214–218, 267, 270, 271, 294
highest vocalic domain 226
homorganicity 196, 197, 199, 200, 202

identical iteration 197, 199, 200
Infrasegmental Government (IG) 332, 334, 337, 338, 339, 353, 360, 379
intervocalic 82, 124, 129, 130, 172, 220, 256, 318, 319, 330, 334, 335, 337, 352, 353, 355, 356, 360, 364, 365, 371, 372
intonational prominence 389, 390

labelling 19, 23, 238, 256, 258
laryngeal contrasts 221, 341
laryngeals/laryngeal specification 104, 105, 106, 143, 159, 314
licensing 20, 86, 164, 246, 253, 299, 332, 338, 343, 365
linearity 309, 310, 325
locality 338, 379
– locality violation 360
lowest vocalic domain 226, 227, 228

manner of articulation 109, 313
– affricate 145, 165, 181, 182, 184, 185, 188, 189, 194, 195, 196, 197, 200, 202, 213, 222, 228, 329, 331, 369, 371
– glide 11, 72–76, 92, 117–140, 172, 185, 341, 347, 349, 365
– lateral 61, 163, 185, 344, 350
– liquid 64, 65, 90, 92, 103, 106, 108, 109, 189, 197, 329–379
– obstruent 31, 32, 72, 83, 87, 145, 160, 182, 188, 195, 219, 221, 222, 223, 315, 329, 330, 332, 334, 335, 337, 338, 339, 340, 346, 351, 352, 355, 356, 358, 359, 360, 362, 364, 368, 374, 376, 378
– offglide 139, 249, 250, 251, 252
– onglide 252
– rhotic 193, 344, 347, 348, 350, 354, 358, 360, 361
– sibilant 189, 193, 197
– sonorant 47, 72, 74, 77, 78, 80, 81, 82, 83, 84, 87, 88, 91, 92, 93, 103, 106, 107, 108, 151, 165, 193, 313, 344, 345, 349, 350, 369
merge 67, 68, 72, 82, 83, 88, 120, 238, 342, 385, 387, 388, 400, 403
– external Merge 80, 83, 84, 88
– first Merge 385, 387, 388, 390, 404
– submersion 187, 308, 313, 317, 318–325
metathesis 353, 366–378
metrical 62, 85, 95, 97, 110, 256, 258, 383, 386, 387, 390, 403, 404
– metrical label 404
– metrical structure 256, 258
Minimal Constituent (MC) 316, 323
Minimality Hypothesis 152, 181, 383, 390–392
minimum strength difference 192, 193, 195, 196
modulation of the carrier signal 25, 32
morphology 209, 210, 226, 262, 373
– analytic/non-analytic morphology 209
– bound morpheme 383, 394, 395
– root-level morphology 209
– underived words 208, 209, 211, 226
– word-level morphology 210
multiple Spell-Out 389, 391

Subject Index — 413

Noise node 313, 314, 315
non-arbitrariness 239–240
- Non-Arbitrariness Principle 239, 240, 243, 248

Onset Prominence (OP) 181, 186, 187, 307–326

Particle Phonology 24, 40, 246, 267, 269, 275, 302
percolation 258, 329–379
phonotactics 187, 189, 194, 197, 202, 209, 311
- consonant cluster 91, 92, 105, 107, 181, 182, 183, 191, 202
place of articulation 106, 107–109, 168, 182, 309, 315
- coronality 193, 201, 211, 222, 246
- palatality 189, 201, 202, 211
- velarity 198, 211
positional difference 139
precedence 32, 252
- precedence relation 33, 207–233
- Type A (CV) precedence 32
- Type B (VC) precedence 32
Precedence-free Phonology (PfP) 13, 17, 19, 20, 26, 30, 207, 214–233
Prince languages 197
processes 11, 29, 44, 117, 118, 122–140, 188, 232, 282, 296, 300, 312, 318, 322, 325, 345, 352, 354
- affrication 188, 213
- aspiration 12, 31, 32, 104, 106, 144, 151, 153, 160, 168, 190, 219, 220, 221, 222, 333, 341, 359
- compensatory lengthening 125, 338, 354, 360, 362, 364, 365, 372
- devoicing 103, 106, 334, 358
- glide formation 117–140
- glottalisation 160, 248
- hardening 200
- lenition 11, 124, 189, 220, 248, 319, 325, 335, 354
- nasalisation 160, 188
- place assimilation 201
- spirantisation 173, 345, 352, 354, 356

- spreading 80, 84, 107, 211, 212, 239, 253, 259, 260, 296, 347
- tapping 248, 345
- velar palatalisation 173, 174, 212, 223, 230, 232
- velar softening 207, 208, 210, 212, 213, 218, 221, 222, 223, 224–233
- weakening 130, 318, 335
projection 19, 58, 62, 64, 69, 70, 71, 73, 83, 96, 102, 190, 197, 244, 247, 257, 258, 302, 329–379
Prosodic Phonology 307
prosody 11, 12–15, 17, 19, 20, 33, 164, 165, 214, 282
- foot 11, 13, 14, 17, 18, 20, 23, 33, 61, 62, 63, 79, 85, 93, 94, 95, 96, 97, 98, 99, 100, 101, 111, 112, 215, 238, 255, 257, 258, 282, 283, 307, 322, 323, 324, 325, 396, 402
- melody-prosody 12, 13, 17, 20
- minimal prosodic word 318, 320
- prosodic hierarchy 14, 15, 17, 19, 33
- Prosodic Phrase 308
- prosodic structure 11–33, 59, 164, 312, 317, 320–325

Radical CV Phonology 37, 46, 60, 143, 156–159, 160, 166, 187
representations 11, 12, 13, 14, 15–33, 37, 39, 40, 41, 42, 44, 45, 52, 53
- amount of complexity 18
- embedding 18, 24, 25, 29, 30, 31, 41, 42, 43, 44, 57, 59, 63, 77, 93, 94, 95, 96, 110, 111, 112, 181, 383–386, 387, 396
- hierarchy 154
- Multi-layered representations 143–176
- surface form 129, 287, 288, 292, 298
- tiers/levels of representation 13, 60, 139
- underlying form 129, 288, 292, 302
Root node 154, 296, 303

saturation 191–201
set 40, 42–44, 52, 53, 397–400, 401
- Set Strong 383, 387–390, 391, 392, 393, 394, 395, 397, 398, 400, 401, 403, 404
- set theory 44–53
- single-membered set 388, 390, 395, 401, 404

Subject Index

slack in phonetic interpretation 280, 293
sonority slope 11, 104, 105, 183, 185
Sound Pattern of English (SPE) 109
Sound Pattern of English (SPE) 249, 310
Spec (specifier) 58, 61, 65, 66, 73, 74, 77, 78, 79, 80, 83, 84, 86, 88, 91, 92, 94, 133, 134, 135
Spontaneous Voice/Sonorant Voice (SV) 344, 349–353
Stress 321, 322, 383–405
– Compound Stress Rule 383
– Dependent Stress 383, 396–397
– fixed stress 321, 322, 383, 402
– phrasal stress 389, 391, 392, 401, 403–404
– secondary stress 403, 404
– Stem Stress 392
– stress assignment 209, 312, 318, 321, 383, 384, 386, 390–392
– stress-bearing suffix 393
– weight-sensitive stress 383, 397, 398, 399
– word stress 391, 392, 403, 404
Strict Layer Hypothesis 307
structure 11, 12, 13, 14, 15, 17, 18, 19, 20, 23, 24, 25, 26, 27, 29–33, 37, 42, 44, 47, 48, 51, 52, 53, 57, 58, 59, 60, 61, 62, 63, 64, 66, 70, 72, 73, 75, 76–88, 91, 93–102, 121, 132, 134, 135, 136, 137, 138, 140, 154, 159, 160, 161, 163, 166, 167, 168, 170, 171, 174, 176, 182, 183, 186, 187, 189, 191, 192, 196, 197, 201, 202, 207, 209, 211, 213, 215, 216, 217, 218–223, 224–232, 237, 240, 241, 242, 245, 248, 249, 251, 252, 254, 255, 256, 257, 258, 259, 262, 268, 270, 272–293, 297, 301, 302, 303, 307, 313, 314, 316, 317, 318–325, 330, 337, 340, 342, 343, 344, 346, 349, 350, 351, 353, 354, 356, 358, 359, 365, 366, 372, 374, 376, 377, 385, 387, 390, 396, 397–400, 404
– recursive structure 12, 31, 57, 59, 96, 110, 117–140, 163, 164, 174, 176, 182, 184, 202, 260, 307, 320, 342, 353, 383
– structural analogy 45, 60, 112, 238, 240, 261
– structural dependency 294–298

syllable 11, 12, 14, 17, 18, 19, 21, 23, 27, 29, 30, 33, 57, 58, 59, 60, 61, 62, 63, 64, 65, 66, 67, 71, 72–88, 89, 90, 91, 93, 94, 95, 96, 97, 98, 99, 100, 101, 103, 104, 105, 106, 107, 110, 111, 112, 125, 143, 146, 148, 181, 188, 196, 215, 237, 238, 255, 257, 258, 275, 280, 282, 283, 289, 290, 301, 307, 308, 309, 310–312, 321, 323, 324, 325, 341, 362, 366, 367, 369, 371, 392, 393, 396, 397–400, 401, 402, 403, 404
– branching syllable 399, 400
– closed syllable 62, 64, 106, 397, 399
– coda consonant 78, 106, 397, 398, 399, 400
– light syllable 62, 397, 398, 400
– nucleus 11, 12, 13, 14, 17, 18, 20, 21, 22, 23, 33, 57, 58, 64, 74, 75, 77, 78, 79, 81, 82, 84, 85, 86, 91, 94, 103, 104, 106, 107, 108, 131, 132, 164, 169, 170, 215, 224, 225, 241, 242, 243, 246, 252, 255, 257, 282, 283, 301, 308, 312, 330, 331, 334, 337, 338, 339, 341, 343, 351, 352, 357, 358, 359, 360, 364, 365, 366, 373, 374, 377, 378, 379
– (super)heavy syllable 85, 87, 89, 91, 100, 196, 393, 397–405
– syllable head 64, 103
– syllable structure 29
– syllable-sized domain 18

tone 16, 44, 46, 107, 143, 146, 148, 151, 152, 153, 154, 156, 160, 161, 165, 169, 176
tone-consonant interaction 143, 176
Transfer 388, 389, 390

unidirectional 118, 190, 401

valence 189–191
V-domain 30
Vocalic Onset (VO) node 313, 315, 316, 317, 391
Vocalic Target (VT) node 313, 316, 322, 324
voicelessness 31, 144, 166, 167, 219, 221
voicing 103, 105, 106, 144, 145, 151, 152, 153, 160, 164, 165, 167, 168, 169, 174, 175, 176, 182, 190, 335, 341, 352, 353, 355, 356

vowels 15, 16, 18, 20–29, 31, 32, 37–53, 65, 72, 75, 76, 77, 78, 79, 86, 87, 92, 93, 103, 117, 118, 119, 120, 121, 122, 123, 125, 126–128, 129, 130, 131, 132, 133, 137, 138, 139, 148, 160, 165, 181, 182, 188, 201, 202, 207, 211, 215, 216, 217, 218, 242, 245, 246, 247, 248, 253, 254, 259, 260, 262, 267–303, 312, 319, 320, 321, 335, 340, 343, 347, 348, 349, 350, 351, 365, 397, 399, 400
– default vowel 12, 13, 18, 20–23, 27, 215, 287, 300, 347
– diphthong 51, 52, 64, 76, 92, 93, 108, 109, 120, 196, 246, 249, 254, 256, 277, 279, 280, 283, 297
– empty vowel 283, 293, 330, 379, 398
– empty-headed vowel 191, 198, 271, 272, 280, 281, 282, 283, 287, 288, 292, 293, 294, 295, 297, 298, 303
– high vowel 18, 117, 118, 125, 126, 127, 129, 130, 131, 132, 137, 138, 139, 245

– long vowel 93, 108, 109, 196, 365, 398, 399, 400
– mid vowel 17, 18, 24, 27, 28, 117, 118, 119, 120, 121, 122, 123, 124, 125, 126–128, 132, 133, 134, 135, 136, 137, 138, 139, 247, 269, 280, 291, 343
– tense/lax 28, 64, 65, 76–88, 245, 273, 274, 275, 277, 278, 279, 280, 281, 283, 295
– vowel harmony 252, 257, 258, 259, 284, 287, 289, 290, 291, 292, 303
– vowel lowering 117–140
– vowel reduction 11, 20, 21, 27, 28, 29, 247, 248, 254, 282, 321
– vowel weakening 26–29
– vowel-glide alternations 11
– weak vowel 18, 22, 23, 273, 282, 283, 287, 288, 292, 298, 302

X-bar 58, 59, 60, 61, 64, 70, 72, 73, 75, 93–94, 102, 103, 105, 112, 132, 247, 252, 383, 385, 390

www.ingramcontent.com/pod-product-compliance
Lightning Source LLC
Chambersburg PA
CBHW031411230426
43668CB00007B/270